Exam 70-215

MCSE
Windows® 2000
Server
TRAINING GUIDE

New
Riders

Dennis Maione, MCT

MCSE TRAINING GUIDE (70-215):
ICA WINDOWS® 2000 SERVER

International Standard Book Number: 0-7357-0968-8

Library of Congress Catalog Card Number: 00-100409

Printed in the United States of America

First Printing: August, 2000

04 03 02 01 00   7 6 5 4 3

Interpretation of the printing code: The rightmost double-digit number is the year of the book's printing; the rightmost single-digit number is the number of the book's printing. For example, the printing code 00-1 shows that the first printing of the book occurred in 2000.

Trademarks

Warning and Disclaimer

PUBLISHER
David Dwyer

EXECUTIVE EDITOR
Al Valvano

ACQUISITIONS EDITORS
Nancy Maragioglio
Ann Quinn

MANAGING EDITORS
Gina Brown
Sarah Kearns

PRODUCT MARKETING MANAGER
Stephanie Layton

PUBLICITY MANAGER
Susan Petro

DEVELOPMENT EDITORS
Chris Zahn
Susan Brown Zahn

PROJECT EDITOR
Caroline Wise

COPY EDITOR
Audra McFarland

TECHNICAL REVIEWERS
Brian Komar
David Neilan
Robert L. Bogue
Ed Tetz

SOFTWARE DEVELOPER
Lloyd Work

MEDIA SPECIALIST
Michael Hunter

INDEXER
Brad Herriman

PROOFREADER
Debra Neel

COMPOSITOR
Ron Wise

MANUFACTURING MANAGER
Chris Moos

MANUFACTURING COORDINATOR
Jim Conway

COVER DESIGNER
Aren Howell

Contents at a Glance

Table of Contents

3 Configuring and Troubleshooting Hardware Devices and Drivers 221

4 Managing, Monitoring, and Optimizing System Performance, Reliability, and Availability   257

6 Configuring and Troubleshooting Windows 2000 Network Connections   437

Part II: Final Review

Part III: Appendixes

About the Authors

Lead Author

Dennis Maione is a Microsoft Certified Trainer and consultant, a Lotus Business Partner specializing in Lotus Notes solutions (development and infrastructure), and a software developer (VB, Java, and JavaScript). In addition to writing books, he spends his time helping people and companies make smart choices about network infrastructure, security, and software. He has been working with Windows NT since version 3.51 and has played with Windows 2000 since it was NT 5.0, pre-beta.

Not to have his real life crowded out by business interests, he spends the remainder of his free time with his wife and three children reading, scuba diving, and troubleshooting his home LAN ("Daddy, how come *Reader Rabbit* won't run?").

Dennis is the owner of IKTHUSE Consulting Inc., based in Winnipeg, Manitoba, Canada. If you want to contact him about his books, you can email books@ikthuse.com. If you want to know more about IKTHUSE Consulting, check out http://www.ikthuse.com.

Oh yeah, *Jars of Clay* has not responded to his last pitiful cry to be their lead singer so he is giving up on them. Does anyone know if *Creed* has any openings?

Contributing Authors

Rory McCaw is currently a Microsoft Certified Trainer for a Canadian Certified Technical Education Centre. Rory holds numerous Microsoft certifications and has developed and delivered presentations for Microsoft at Comdex on Windows 2000. Prior to training, Rory worked for an Internet solution provider where he was responsible for the implementation and administration of Microsoft LANs, WANs, and network security.

David Gore, MCSE + I, has been working in the Information Technology field since 1977 and has been involved with the engineering/architecture and administration of a wide range of medium- and large-scale systems. For the last six years, he has been working extensively with a wide range of Microsoft products, such as Windows NT 4.0 and 2000, Exchange, SMS, SQL, Proxy Server, IIS, and VB. He currently resides in Naperville, IL with his wife and son.

About the Technical Reviewers

Brian Komar, MCSE+I, MCT, is an Independent Consultant currently doing lots of work with Microsoft Corporation. Tasks include acting as the Technical Lead for the Windows 2000 security course, reviewing published materials, delivering Windows 2000 MOC courses, and consulting and speaking at several conferences on Windows 2000 Active Directory and Security design topics.

In his spare time, Brian enjoys travelling with his wife, Krista.

David Neilan has been working in the computer/network industry for more than eight years, the last five dealing primarily with network/Internet connectivity and security. From 1991 to 1995, he worked for Intergraph, dealing with graphics systems and networking. From 1995 to 1998, he worked for Digital Equipment, working with DEC firewalls and network security. From 1998 to present, he has worked for Online Business Systems, dealing with LAN/WAN and Internet security. He is also designing network infrastructures to support secure LAN/WAN connectivity for various companies utilizing Microsoft 2000 products, Cisco products, and the Internet to create secure virtual private networks.

Robert L. Bogue is the Chief Operating Officer of AvailTek, Inc. AvailTek is a software development and systems integration company headquartered in Carmel, IN. Robert has contributed to over 100 book projects and numerous magazine articles and reviews. Robert is MCSE, CNA, A+, Network+, and I-Net+ certified. When he's not busy killing trees or getting certified he enjoys pushing the envelope with new technology. Robert can be reached at Rob.Bogue@AvailTek.com.

Edward Tetz graduated from Saint Lawrence College in Cornwall, Ontario with a diploma in Business Administration in 1990. He spent a short time in computer sales, which turned into a computer support position. He has spent the last eight years providing system and LAN suport for small and large organizations. In 1994 he added training to his repertoire. He is both a Microsoft Certified Trainer and a Microsoft Certified Systems Engineer. He has experience with Apple Macintosh, IBM OS/2, and all Microsoft operating systems. He is currently an Information Technology Coordinator and an instructor for PBSC Computer Training, delivering certified training in most Microsoft products. He would like to thank his wife, Sharon, and their children, Emily and Mackenzie. If not for their love, support, and understanding, he would not be able to find the time or will to write and edit.

Dedication

This book is dedicated to my family, both immediate and extended, and the people who make up the community that is my support; these people help me to make smart choices about life. Specifically, to the woman I love, Debra, you cannot imagine how much I rely on you to help me through these projects. To Emma, Alexander, and Noah, thank you for being you. Always remember that, despite the bad choices I sometimes make, I will always love you and am proud of all you do. Finally, to anyone else I know and love (fill in your name here), thank you for your patience with me as I grow up into the image of Jesus.

Dennis Maione

Acknowledgments

In addition to acknowledging the existence of the six billion plus people on this planet, I must point out some people who have been significant in the production of this work (and it has been a lot of work). First, thanks to Nancy Maragioglio for choosing me again. I really do appreciate your continued faith in me, and I know that everything we work on together will be a success. Thanks to Chris Zahn and Susan Brown Zahn for doing a bang-up job with the editing and keeping me true to the intent of the book (I know it was hard sometimes). Thanks to David Gore and Rory McCaw

for acting as contributing authors. Thanks to Brian Komar, David Neilan, and Rob Bogue for technical editing and comments; although I won't share my royalties with you, without you, this book would not have even approached the quality that it has. Finally, thanks to the team of developers at Microsoft for building such a great product; the DOJ might think you are bad, but I think you are doing a pretty good job. (Maybe you can move to Canada!)

—Dennis Maione

Tell Us What You Think!

As the reader of this book, *you* are our most important critic and commentator. We value your opinion and want to know what we're doing right, what we could do better, what areas you'd like to see us publish in, and any other words of wisdom you're willing to pass our way.

As the Executive Editor for the Certification team at New Riders Publishing, I welcome your comments. You can fax, email, or write me directly to let me know what you did or didn't like about this book—as well as what we can do to make our books stronger.

Please note that I cannot help you with technical problems related to the topic of this book, and that due to the high volume of mail I receive, I might not be able to reply to every message.

When you write, please be sure to include this book's title, author, and ISBN number (found on the back cover of the book above the bar code), as well as your name and phone or fax number. I will carefully review your comments and share them with the author and editors who worked on the book.

Fax: 317-581-4663

Email: nrfeedback@newriders.com

Mail: Al Valvano
                Executive Editor
                Certification
                New Riders Publishing
                201 West 103rd Street
                Indianapolis, IN 46290

How to Use This Book

New Riders Publishing has made an effort in its *Training Guide* series to make the information as accessible as possible for the purpose of learning the certification material. Here, you have an opportunity to view the many instructional features that have been incorporated into the books to achieve that goal.

CHAPTER OPENER

Each chapter begins with a set of features designed to allow you to maximize study time for that material.

List of Objectives: Each chapter begins with a list of the objectives as stated by Microsoft.

Objective Explanations: Immediately following each objective is an explanation of it, providing context that defines it more meaningfully in relation to the exam. Because Microsoft can sometimes be vague in its objectives list, the objective explanations are designed to clarify any vagueness by relying on the authors' test-taking experience.

OBJECTIVES

This chapter will help you prepare for the "Installing Windows 2000 Server" section of the exam by giving you information necessary to make intelligent choices regarding the method of installation and the preparations required for such an installation.

Microsoft provides the following objectives for "Installing Windows 2000 Server":

Perform an attended installation of Windows 2000 Server.

▶ This objective is necessary because someone certified in the use of Windows 2000 Server technology must be able to install a Windows 2000 server as a member server in a Windows 2000 domain. This will include installations from a bootable CD-ROM and from the four-disk set.

Perform an unattended installation of Windows 2000 Server.

• Create unattended answer files by using Setup Manager to automate the installation of Windows 2000 Server.

• Create and configure automated methods for installation of Windows 2000.

▶ This objective is necessary because someone certified in the Windows 2000 Server technology should understand how to automate the installation of member servers in a Windows 2000 domain over a network. This will include creating answer files, as well as deploying installation using these answer files. In addition, it will involve familiarity with the new disk duplication and Remote Installation features of Windows 2000.

CHAPTER 1

Installing Windows 2000 Server

Chapter Outline: Learning always gets a boost when you can see both the forest and the trees. To give you a visual image of how the topics in a chapter fit together, you will find a chapter outline at the beginning of each chapter. You will also be able to use this for easy reference when looking for a particular topic.

STUDY STRATEGIES

▶ There are many testable items in this long chapter. Remember that Microsoft will incorporate multiple items together into single questions, so make sure you know how these topics are interrelated.

▶ Of course, you should read and understand the concepts in this chapter and go through the review and exam questions at the end.

▶ In order to really understand the topics, you should implement the strategies in the Step by Step examples, and you need to do the exercises. Because of the nature of some of the interoperability sections, you might find it difficult to actually implement the solutions unless you have a number of test machines and access to other operating systems (like NetWare and Macintosh computers). However, you will still find that "going through the motions" will help to make the concepts in this chapter concrete. I suggest that you install the services and go through the configurations until a lack of equipment forces you to stop. Of course, if you can get hold of NetWare servers (regardless of the version) or a Macintosh system or two, you will be able to more fully implement the solutions presented.

▶ Interoperability has always been a big point on the exams—and this is still the case. Make sure you are familiar with the services required to interoperate with NetWare, Macintosh, and UNIX. Specifically for NetWare, be sure that you have an outline in your mind of what steps need to be taken to set up the GateWay for NetWare Service and get it to provide NetWare access to clients. Be sure that you understand

(the software interface) and the print device (the hardware component), you do not even have to have a print device to do the printer module. For the network portions, you will benefit from having a second machine to use as a client with network hub to allow you to connect them (or at the very least a null network cable to directly connect them). You will not be able to implement the encrypted Web connections (using server and client certificates) unless you obtain or create certificates. If you already have certificates then use them; if not, you could use the Windows 2000 Certificate Authority to create them. However, that procedure is not outlined in this chapter.

▶ For the previous points mentioned, make sure that you go through all the configuration properties and that you understand how the configuration is done. Open the Security tab for an NTFS file resource or a printer and fix them, and what their settings do, in your mind.

▶ In the Dfs section, you will be able to implement standalone regardless of your setup. However, domain-based Dfs will require that you have a Windows 2000 domain controller running in Native mode. If you do not have such a machine, then you will be able to implement only part of the Dfs solutions.

▶ Nothing can replace experience. Working through all the modules, understanding their content, and implementing the Step by Steps is a beginning. However, you will greatly benefit from having to work out some of these solutions in an environment where the result is defined but the path to it is not; this will

Study Strategies: Each topic presents its own learning challenge. To support you through this, New Riders has included strategies for how to best approach studying in order to retain the material in the chapter, particularly as it is addressed on the exam.

INSTRUCTIONAL FEATURES WITHIN THE CHAPTER

These books include a large amount and different kinds of information. The many different elements are designed to help you identify information by its purpose and importance to the exam and also to provide you with varied ways to learn the material. You will be able to determine how much attention to devote to certain elements, depending on what your goals are. By becoming familiar with the different presentations of information, you will know what information will be important to you as a test-taker and which information will be important to you as a practitioner.

Note: Notes appear in the margins and contain various kinds of useful information, such as tips on the technology or administrative practices, historical background on terms and technologies, or side commentary on industry issues.

Objective Coverage Text: In the text before an exam objective is specifically addressed, you will notice the objective is listed to help call your attention to that particular material.

EXAM TIP

Printer Terminology Terminology is very important, especially for the exam. Keep in mind that when the exam makes reference to a printer, it is talking about a software interface, not a physical device. The device is called a "print device"; all the software that you install and the icon you see in the Printers window is referred to as a printer. In order to make this clearer, I will often refer to this as the "virtual printer." The term "virtual printer" has been known to show up in Microsoft documentation, but I don't envision it making its way to the exam.

Exam Tip: Exam Tips appear in the margins to provide specific exam-related advice. Such tips may address what material is covered (or not covered) on the exam, how it is covered, mnemonic devices, or particular quirks of that exam.

Warning: In using sophisticated information technology, there is always potential for mistakes or even catastrophes that can occur through improper application of the technology. Warnings appear in the margins to alert you to such potential problems.

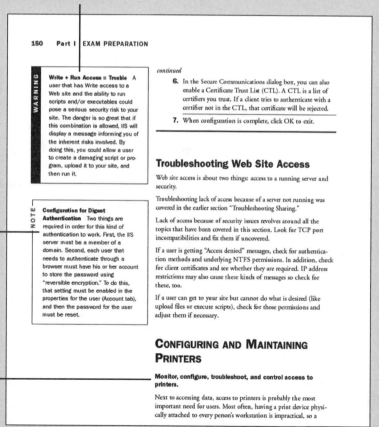

150   Part I   EXAM PREPARATION

WARNING

Write + Run Access = Trouble A user that has Write access to a Web site and the ability to run scripts and/or executables could pose a serious security risk to your site. The danger is so great that if this combination is allowed, IIS will display a message informing you of the inherent risks involved. By doing this, you could allow a user to create a damaging script or program, upload it to your site, and then run it.

NOTE

Configuration for Digest Authentication Two things are required in order for this kind of authentication to work. First, the IIS server must be a member of a domain. Second, each user that needs to authenticate through a browser must have his or her account to store the password using "reversible encryption." To do this, that setting must be enabled in the properties for the user (Account tab), and then the password for the user must be reset.

continued

6. In the Secure Communications dialog box, you can also enable a Certificate Trust List (CTL). A CTL is a list of certifiers you trust. If a client tries to authenticate with a certifier not in the CTL, that certificate will be rejected.

7. When configuration is complete, click OK to exit.

Troubleshooting Web Site Access

Web site access is about two things: access to a running server and security.

Troubleshooting lack of access because of a server not running was covered in the earlier section "Troubleshooting Sharing."

Lack of access because of security issues revolves around all the topics that have been covered in this section. Look for TCP port incompatibilities and fix them if uncovered.

If a user is getting "Access denied" messages, check for authentication methods and underlying NTFS permissions. In addition, check for client certificates and see whether they are required. IP address restrictions may also cause these kinds of messages so check for these, too.

If a user can get to your site but cannot do what is desired (like upload files or execute scripts), check for those permissions and adjust them if necessary.

CONFIGURING AND MAINTAINING PRINTERS

Monitor, configure, troubleshoot, and control access to printers.

Next to accessing data, access to printers is probably the most important need for users. Most often, having a print device physically attached to every person's workstation is impractical, so a

STEP BY STEP

6.12 Configuring a Server as a First Network DNS on a Windows 2000 Server

1. From the Start menu, choose Programs, Administrative Tools, DNS.

2. In the DNS console, select your server name, open the Action menu, and choose Configure the Server.

3. At the Welcome to the Configure the DNS Server Wizard, click Next.

4. At the Root Server dialog box, choose This Is the First DNS Server on This Network and click Next (see Figure 6.32).

5. At the Forward Lookup Zone dialog box, choose Yes, Create a Forward Lookup Zone and click Next (see Figure 6.33).

continues

FIGURE 6.32
Create a new zone.

Figure: To improve readability, the figures have been placed in the margins wherever possible so they do not interrupt the main flow of text.

Step by Step: Step by Steps are hands-on tutorial instructions that walk you through a particular task or function relevant to the exam objectives.

volume from five 1GB segments of free space, the usable area is (5–1)/5 or 80% of the total hard drive space. That would leave you with 4GB of the original 5GB because 1GB would be used to maintain the fault tolerance.

RAID-5 volumes have moderate write performance (reduced because the parity information must be calculated as the data changes) but excellent read performance because the data is stored on many hard drives, all of which can be accessed independently of one another.

Like striped volumes, RAID-5 volumes cannot be used to hold the System or Boot partition of a Windows 2000 installation.

IN THE FIELD

FAULT TOLERANCE PUTS STRAIN ON YOUR SERVER

All fault-tolerant disk volumes (mirrors and RAID-5) require additional overhead (processor and memory). This is a result of maintenance of the fault-tolerant data as it is being written to the volume. The performance change in your Windows 2000 server may or may not be significant to you or your user community. In a system dedicated to storage of data or retrieval of data, you may see noticeable increases or decreases in system performance when using this fault tolerance method.

In a system in which the primary operation a user performs is queries on a database, the increase in read performance may be significant in terms of throughput. If the system is designed to store data, mirroring may produce disk bottlenecks. You may only know whether these are significant by setting up two identical computers, implementing mirroring on one and not on the other, and then running Performance Monitor on both under simulated load to see the performance differences. For more information on monitoring, see Chapter 4, "Managing, Monitoring, and Optimizing System Performance, Reliability, and Availability."

REVIEW BREAK

The Disk Manager

Partitions and volumes are more than theory. Of course, you need a tool to be able to create and manage partitions and volumes. That tool is the Disk Manager, and it is a sub-component of the Computer Management console.

The next Step by Step shows how to start the Disk Manager.

In the Field Sidebar: These more extensive discussions cover material that perhaps is not directly relevant to the exam, but which is useful as reference material or in everyday practice. In the Field may also provide useful background or contextual information necessary for understanding the larger topic under consideration.

Review Break: Crucial information is summarized at various points in the book in lists or tables. At the end of a particularly long section, you might come across a Review Break that is there just to wrap up one long objective and reinforce the key points before you shift your focus to the next section.

CASE STUDIES

Case Studies are presented throughout the book to provide you with another, more conceptual opportunity to apply the knowledge you are developing. They also reflect the "real-world" experiences of the authors in ways that prepare you not only for the exam but for actual network administration as well. In each Case Study, you will find similar elements: a description of a Scenario, the Essence of the Case, and an extended Analysis section.

CASE STUDY: IN YOUR TOWN INC.

THE ESSENCE OF THE CASE
This case requires that the following results be satisfied:

▶ Allow Isaiah to connect to head office servers to do administration when he is on the road.

▶ Secure the communications between his laptop and servers while administration is going on.

SCENARIO
Isaiah is the network administrator for In Your Town Inc. (IYT), a national company with 30 regional offices in the United States and Canada. Although IYT has a number of national locations, it has very few employees and a small IT staff (Isaiah and two technical assistants), which works out of the head office in New Orleans, Louisiana. As a result, Isaiah finds himself traveling a great deal to service servers in different locations (there is at least one Windows 2000 server in each regional office). When he is on the road, Isaiah would like to be able to administer the Windows 2000 servers at the head office from his laptop.

Not only does Isaiah want to be able to do simple administration (like creating new users and checking printer queues), he also wants to be able to start and stop services, start performance monitors, observe running tasks, and restart servers that may have problems.

Essence of the Case: A bulleted list of the key problems or issues that need to be addressed in the Scenario.

Scenario: A few paragraphs describing a situation that professional practitioners in the field might face. A Scenario deals with an issue relating to the objectives covered in the chapter, and it includes the kinds of details that make a difference.

Analysis: This is a lengthy description of the best way to handle the problems listed in the Essence of the Case. In this section, you might find a table summarizing the solutions, a worded example, or both.

CASE STUDY: IN YOUR TOWN INC.
continued

ANALYSIS
Windows 2000 Server has features that will allow Isaiah to satisfy both his accessibility and his security issues. First, he can install the Terminal Services component of Windows 2000 Server and configure it to operate in Administration mode. This, coupled with the installation of the Terminal Services client on his laptop, will enable him to connect remotely to a local session on each server. This feature will work as long as he is inside the firewall. However, on the road, the firewall will prevent direct access to his servers from his laptop. That can be overcome by installing the RRAS services on a server inside the firewall (or by configuring a new server to be an RRAS server). Finally, in order for Isaiah to connect

to the RRAS server, he will need to do three things: configure the RRAS server to accept VPN connections (PPTP), configure his laptop to connect to the RRAS server to establish VPN sessions, and open port 1723 in the firewall to allow the VPN traffic to pass through.

Using this configuration, Isaiah will be able to use any Internet connection to establish a VPN connection, through his firewall to his RRAS server at his head office. Having established that connection, he can then use the Terminal Services client to establish a session with any of his servers, and he will be able to perform secure administration of his servers.

The following table summarizes the solution.

OVERVIEW OF THE REQUIREMENTS AND SOLUTIONS IN THIS CASE STUDY

Requirement	Solution Provided By
Access to server sessions	Installing Terminal Services on servers in Administration mode; installing Terminal Services client on roaming laptop

CHAPTER SUMMARY

Summarized briefly, this chapter covered the following main points.

◆ **Installing, configuring, and updating devices.** This includes the recognition of Plug and Play for most new devices, the presence of the Device Manager, and the ability to manually install and configure non-Plug and Play devices.

◆ **Configuring driver signing options.** This allows you, the administrator, to create a policy on the need for drivers to be signed to ensure validity and to enforce such a policy to keep corrupt or non-verified drivers from being installed.

◆ **Troubleshooting hardware problems.** This is required whenever you encounter problems with drivers. This may be the

KEY TERMS

• user mode
• kernel mode
• driver
• Device Manager
• driver signing
• system log

EXTENSIVE REVIEW AND SELF-TEST OPTIONS

At the end of each chapter, along with some summary elements, you will find a section called "Apply Your Knowledge" that gives you several different methods with which to test your understanding of the material and review what you have learned.

Chapter Summary: Before the Apply Your Knowledge section, you will find a chapter summary that wraps up the chapter and reviews what you should have learned.

Key Terms: A list of key terms appears at the end of each chapter. These are terms that you should be sure you know and are comfortable defining and understanding when you go in to take the exam.

Chapter 4   MANAGING, MONITORING, AND OPTIMIZING SYSTEM   **339**
PERFORMANCE, RELIABILITY, AND AVAILABILITY

APPLY YOUR KNOWLEDGE

Exercises

4.1   Set Application Priority

In this exercise, you learn how to set application priority at time of invocation and how to reset while it is running. You will also learn how to stop a process using the Task Manager. Note that this exercise will cause your server to stop responding, forcing you to power it off suddenly. Make sure you do not have any critical applications running when you do this exercise.

Estimated Time: 15 minutes

1. The CD-ROM that comes with this book contains a folder called Application Demo. Copy that folder to the hard drive on your Windows 2000 server.

2. From the Start menu, choose Programs, Accessories, Command Prompt.

3. From the Command Prompt, navigate to the location where you copied the Application Demo folder.

4. At the cursor, type **Start /Low Counter**. When it starts running, move the counter dialog box to the bottom of your screen. Note how quickly this program counts, even at low priority.

5. At the cursor, type **Start /Normal Counter**. When it starts running, move the second counter to the bottom of your screen. Note that this counter is counting quickly, but the low priority counter is no longer counting quickly.

6. Right-click the taskbar and choose Task Manager. Make sure that when it comes up, you can still see both counters (see Figure 4.60). Click the Processes tab on the Task Manager.

FIGURE 4.60
You can modify the data shown in the Task Manager by using the View menu.

Review Questions

1. What are the four application execution priorities, and what numeric ranges does each fall into?

2. Name three ways to change the execution priority of an application (whether it's running or not).

3. What are the two types of logs available in Performance Monitor, and how can you distinguish them from one another?

4. What is the purpose of an alert, and what are three of the actions that can be taken when one happens?

5. What limitation of Windows 2000 Backup should lead you to schedule backups for times when as few people are accessing the server as possible?

6. What are three ways to invoke the Windows

Exercises: These activities provide an opportunity for you to master specific hands-on tasks. Our goal is to increase your proficiency with the product or technology. You must be able to conduct these tasks in order to pass the exam.

Review Questions: These open-ended, short-answer questions allow you to quickly assess your comprehension of what you just read in the chapter. Instead of asking you to choose from a list of options, these questions require you to state the correct answers in your own words. Although you will not experience these kinds of questions on the exam, these questions will indeed test your level of comprehension of key concepts.

Exam Questions: These questions reflect the kinds of multiple-choice questions that appear on the Microsoft exams. Use them to become familiar with the exam question formats and to help you determine what you know and what you need to review or study more.

APPLY YOUR KNOWLEDGE

Exam Questions

1. Jim is the network administrator for two identical Windows 2000 servers in a high school. They both have SCSI CD-ROM drives, and all data is on NTFS partitions. He has just found one of his servers turned off. When he turns it back on, Jim gets an error that NTOSKRNL.EXE cannot be found and it will not boot. He suspects that a vandal in the school has deleted the file. He does not have the Windows 2000 Server CD-ROM, but he has disks and a CD-ROM writer. How can Jim recover his server?

   A. Boot his server to Safe Mode and then copy the NTOSKRNL.EXE file from the other server using a disk.

   B. Boot his server to the Recovery console using the setup disk set and copy NTOSKRNL.EXE using a disk.

   C. Boot his server to DOS and copy the NTOSKRNL.EXE from the other server using a CD-ROM with the file copied from the other server.

   D. Boot his server to the Recovery console using a secondary boot on the server and copy the NTOSKRNL.EXE using a CD-ROM with the file copied from the other server.

2. Pavel wants to determine whether or not his server is short of memory. Under light load, users get good response. However, as load increases, so does the lack of responsiveness. Which of the following counters will aid him in determining whether memory is the bottleneck in his system? (Choose two.)

   A. Memory\pages/sec

   B. Paging File\% Usage

   C. Processor\Interrupts/sec

   D. Network Segment\% Net Utilization

Answers to Review Questions

1. The four priorities are Idle—sometimes called Low (0–6), Normal (6–11), High (11–15), and Realtime (16–31). For more information, see the section "Maintaining Windows 32-Bit Applications."

2. There are three ways to change the priority of an application. The first way is to start it at a command line (or from a shortcut) using the syntax **Start /priority applicationname**. The second way is to change its priority in the Task Manager while it is running. The third way is to set the foreground boost for all normal applications in the advanced page of the System Properties. For more information, see the section "Maintaining Windows 32-Bit Applications."

3. The two kinds of logs available in Performance Monitor are counter logs and trace logs. They are distinguished by their collection trigger and how much control you have over the information you collect. The collection of data in a counter log is controlled by time interval passing, and you can finely control the kind of data you collect through the application of object counters. The collection of data in a trace log is controlled by events that happen (like user logon), and you have little control over the specific information collected outside of a general category of data. For more information, see the section "Collecting Data Using Performance Monitor."

Answers and Explanations: For each of the Review and Exam questions, you will find thorough explanations located at the end of the section.

Suggested Readings and Resources

1. Microsoft Windows 2000 Server Resource Kit: *Microsoft Windows 2000 Server Internetworking Guide* (Microsoft Press)

   • Chapter 2: Routing and Remote Access Service

   • Chapter 3: Unicast IP Routing

   • Chapter 7: Remote Access Server

   • Chapter 8: Internet Authentication Service

   • Chapter 9: Virtual Private Networking

   • Chapter 16: NetBEUI

2. Microsoft Windows 2000 Server Resource Kit: *Microsoft Windows 2000 Server Deployment Planning* Guide (Microsoft Press)

   • Chapter 7: Determining Network Connectivity Strategies

   • Chapter 11: Planning Distributed Security

   • Chapter 7: Windows Internet Name Service

   • Chapter 8: Internet Protocol Security

4. *Microsoft Windows 2000 Professional Resource Kit* (Microsoft Press)

   • Chapter 13: Security

   • Chapter 21: Local and Remote Network Connections

   • Chapter 22: TCP/IP in Windows 2000 Professional

   • Chapter 23: Windows 2000 Professional on Microsoft Networks

   • Chapter 24: Interoperability with NetWare

5. Microsoft Official Curriculum course 1557: *Installing and Configuring Microsoft Windows 2000*

Suggested Readings and Resources: The very last element in every chapter is a list of additional resources you can use if you want to go above and beyond certification-level material or if you need to spend more time on a particular subject that you are having trouble understanding.

Introduction

MCSE Training Guide: Windows 2000 Server is designed for advanced users, technicians, or system administrators with the goal of certification as a Microsoft Certified Systems Engineer (MCSE). It covers the Installing, Configuring, and Administering Microsoft® Windows® 2000 Server exam (70-215). This exam measures your ability to implement, administer, and troubleshoot Windows 2000 Server as a member server of a domain in an Active Directory environment.

This book is your one-stop shop. Everything you need to know to pass the exam is in here, and Microsoft has approved it as study material. You do not have to take a class in addition to buying this book to pass the exam. However, depending on your personal study habits or learning style, you may benefit from buying this book *and* taking a class.

Microsoft assumes that the typical candidate for this exam will have a minimum of one year's experience implementing and administering network operating systems in medium to very large network environments.

HOW THIS BOOK HELPS YOU

This book takes you on a self-guided tour of all the areas covered by the Installing, Configuring, and Administering Microsoft® Windows® 2000 Server exam and teaches you the specific skills you will need in order to achieve your MCSE certification. You will also find helpful hints, tips, real-world examples, and exercises, as well as references to additional study materials. Specifically, this book is set up to help you in the following ways:

- ◆ **Organization.** The book is organized by individual exam objectives. Every objective you need to know for the Installing, Configuring, and Administering Microsoft® Windows® 2000 Server exam is covered in this book. We have attempted to present the objectives in an order that is as close as possible to that listed by Microsoft. However, we have not hesitated to reorganize them where needed to make the material as easy as possible for you to learn. We have also attempted to make the information accessible in the following ways:

  - The full list of exam topics and objectives is included in this introduction.

  - Each chapter begins with a list of the objectives to be covered.

  - Each chapter also begins with an outline that provides you with an overview of the material and the page numbers where particular topics can be found.

  - The objectives are repeated where the material most directly relevant to it is covered (unless the whole chapter addresses a single objective).

  - The CD-ROM included with this book contains, in PDF format, a complete listing of the test objectives and where they are covered within the book.

◆ **Instructional Features.** This book has been designed to provide you with multiple ways to learn and reinforce the exam material. Some of those helpful methods are described here.

- *Objective Explanations.* As mentioned previously, each chapter begins with a list of the objectives covered in the chapter. In addition, immediately following each objective is an explanation in a context that defines it more meaningfully.

- *Study Strategies.* The beginning of the chapter also includes strategies for how to approach studying and retaining the material in the chapter, particularly as it is addressed on the exam.

- *Exam Tips.* Exam tips appear in the margin to provide specific exam-related advice. Such tips may address what material is covered (or not covered) on the exam, how it is covered, mnemonic devices, or particular quirks of the exam.

- *Review Breaks and Summaries.* Crucial information is summarized at various points in the book in lists or tables. Each chapter ends with a summary as well.

- *Key Terms.* A list of key terms appears at the end of each chapter.

- *Notes.* These appear in the margin and contain various kinds of useful information such as tips on technology or administrative practices, historical background on terms and technologies, or side commentary on industry issues.

- *Warnings.* When using sophisticated information technology, there is always the potential for mistakes or even catastrophes that occur because of improper application of the technology. Warnings appear in the margin to alert you to such potential problems.

- *In the Field.* These more extensive discussions cover material that may not be directly relevant to the exam but that is useful as reference material or in everyday practice. In the Field may also provide useful background or contextual information necessary for understanding the larger topic under consideration.

- *Step by Steps.* These are hands-on tutorial instructions that walk you through a particular task or function relevant to the exam objectives.

- *Case Studies.* Each chapter concludes with a Case Study. The cases are meant to help you understand the practical applications of the information covered in the chapter.

- *Exercises.* Found at the end of the chapters in the "Apply Your Knowledge" section, exercises are performance-based opportunities for you to learn and assess your knowledge.

◆ **Extensive practice test options.** The book provides numerous opportunities for you to assess your knowledge and practice for the exam. The practice options include the following:

- *Review Questions.* These open-ended questions appear in the "Apply Your Knowledge" section at the end of each chapter. They allow you to quickly assess your comprehension of what you just read. Answers to the questions are provided later in a separate section titled "Answers to Review Questions."

- *Exam Questions.* These questions also appear in the "Apply Your Knowledge" section. Use them to help you determine what you know and what you need to review or study further. Answers and explanations for them are provided in a separate section titled "Answers to Exam Questions."

- *Practice Exam.* A Practice Exam is included in the "Final Review" section. The Final Review section and the Practice Exam are discussed later in this chapter.

- *ExamGear.* The special Training Guide version of the *ExamGear* software included on the CD-ROM provides further practice questions.

NOTE For a description of the New Riders *ExamGear, Training Guide Edition* software, please see Appendix C, "Using the *ExamGear, Training Guide Edition* Software."

◆ **Final Review.** This part of the book provides you with three valuable tools for preparing for the exam.

- *Fast Facts.* This condensed version of the information contained in the book will prove extremely useful for last-minute review.

- *Study and Exam Prep Tips.* Read this section early on to help you develop study strategies. It also provides you with valuable exam-day tips and information on exam/question formats such as adaptive tests and case study-based questions.

- *Practice Exam.* A practice test is included. Questions are written in styles similar to those used on the actual exam. Use it to assess your readiness for the real thing.

The book includes several other features, such as a section titled "Suggested Readings and Resources" at the end of each chapter that directs you toward further information that could aid you in your exam preparation or your actual work. There are valuable appendices as well, including an overview of the Microsoft certification program (Appendix A), a description of what is on the CD-ROM (Appendix B), and what is essentially a manual for the Exam Gear, Training Guide Edition test simulation software (Appendix C).

For more information about the exam or the certification process, contact Microsoft:

Microsoft Education: 800-636-7544

Internet: `ftp://ftp.microsoft.com/Services/MSEdCert`

World Wide Web: `http://www.microsoft.com/train_cert`

CompuServe Forum: `GO MSEDCERT`

WHAT THE INSTALLING, CONFIGURING, AND ADMINISTERING MICROSOFT® WINDOWS® 2000 SERVER EXAM (70-215) COVERS

The Installing, Configuring, and Administering Microsoft® Windows® 2000 Server Exam (70-215) covers the Windows 2000 Server topics represented by the conceptual groupings or units of the test objectives. The objectives reflect job skills in the following areas:

◆ Installing Windows 2000 Server

◆ Installing, Configuring, and Troubleshooting Access to Resources

◆ Configuring and Troubleshooting Hardware Devices and Drivers

◆ Managing, Monitoring, and Optimizing System Performance, Reliability, and Availability

◆ Managing, Configuring, and Troubleshooting Storage Use

◆ Configuring and Troubleshooting Windows 2000 Network Connections

◆ Implementing, Monitoring, and Troubleshooting Security

Before taking the exam, you should be proficient in the job skills represented by the following units, objectives, and sub-objectives.

Installing Windows 2000 Server

Perform an attended installation of Windows 2000 Server.

Perform an unattended installation of Windows 2000 Server.

◆ Create unattended answer files by using Setup Manager to automate the installation of Windows 2000 Server.

◆ Create and configure automated methods for installation of Windows 2000.

Upgrade a server from Microsoft Windows NT 4.0.

Deploy service packs.

Troubleshoot failed installations.

Installing, Configuring, and Troubleshooting Access to Resources

Install and configure network services for interoperability.

Monitor, configure, troubleshoot, and control access to printers.

Monitor, configure, troubleshoot, and control access to files, folders, and shared folders.

◆ Configure, manage, and troubleshoot a stand-alone Distributed File System (Dfs).

◆ Configure, manage, and troubleshoot a domain-based Distributed File System (Dfs).

◆ Monitor, configure, troubleshoot, and control local security on files and folders.

◆ Monitor, configure, troubleshoot, and control access to files and folders in a shared folder.

◆ Monitor, configure, troubleshoot, and control access to files and folders via Web services.

Monitor, configure, troubleshoot, and control access to Web sites.

Configuring and Troubleshooting Hardware Devices and Drivers

Configure hardware devices.

Configure driver signing options.

Update device drivers.

Troubleshoot problems with hardware.

Managing, Monitoring, and Optimizing System Performance, Reliability, and Availability

Monitor and optimize usage of system resources.

Manage processes.

◆ Set priorities and start and stop processes.

Optimize disk performance.

Manage and optimize availability of system state data and user data.

Recover systems and user data.

◆ Recover systems and user data by using Windows Backup.

◆ Troubleshoot system restoration by using Safe Mode.

◆ Recover systems and user data by using the Recovery Console.

Managing, Configuring, and Troubleshooting Storage Use

Configure and manage user profiles.

Monitor, configure, and troubleshoot disks and volumes.

Configure data compression.

Monitor and configure disk quotas.

Recover from disk failures.

Configuring and Troubleshooting Windows 2000 Network Connections

Install, configure, and troubleshoot shared access.

Install, configure, and troubleshoot a virtual private network (VPN).

Install, configure, and troubleshoot network protocols.

Install and configure network services.

Configure, monitor, and troubleshoot remote access.

◆ Configure inbound connections.

◆ Create a remote access policy.

◆ Configure a remote access profile.

Install, configure, monitor, and troubleshoot Terminal Services.

◆ Remotely administer servers by using Terminal Services.

◆ Configure Terminal Services for application sharing.

◆ Configure applications for use with Terminal Services.

Configure the properties of a connection.

Install, configure, and troubleshoot network adapters and drivers.

Implementing, Monitoring, and Troubleshooting Security

Encrypt data on a hard disk by using the Encrypting File System (EFS).

Implement, configure, manage, and troubleshoot policies in a Windows 2000 environment.

◆ Implement, configure, manage, and troubleshoot Local Policy in a Windows 2000 environment.

◆ Implement, configure, manage, and troubleshoot System Policy in a Windows 2000 environment.

Implement, configure, manage, and troubleshoot auditing.

Implement, configure, manage, and troubleshoot local accounts.

Implement, configure, manage, and troubleshoot Account Policy.

Implement, configure, manage, and troubleshoot security by using the Security Configuration Tool Set.

HARDWARE AND SOFTWARE YOU'LL NEED

As a self-paced study guide, *MCSE Training Guide: Windows 2000 Server* is meant to help you understand concepts that must be refined through hands-on experience. To make the most of your studying, you need to have as much background on (and experience with) Windows 2000 Server as possible. The best way to do this is to combine studying with work on Windows 2000 Server. This section gives you a description of the minimum computer requirements you need to enjoy a solid practice environment.

◆ Windows 2000 Server software

◆ Windows 2000 Professional software

◆ A server and a workstation computer on the Microsoft Hardware Compatibility List (the upcoming hardware requirements apply to both)

◆ Administrator access to a Windows 2000 Domain Controller (recommended)

◆ Pentium 133MHz (or better) processor

◆ 2GB (or larger) hard disk

◆ VGA (or Super VGA) video adapter and monitor

◆ Mouse or equivalent pointing device

◆ CD-ROM drive

◆ Network Interface Card (NIC)

◆ Presence on an existing network, or use of a 3-port (or more) hub to create a test network

◆ Internet access with functional browser

◆ 64MB of RAM (128MB recommended)

It is fairly easy to obtain access to the necessary computer hardware and software in a corporate business environment. It can be difficult, however, to allocate enough time within the busy workday to complete a self-study program. Most of your study time will occur after normal working hours, away from the everyday interruptions and pressures of your regular job.

ADVICE ON TAKING THE EXAM

More extensive tips are found in the Final Review section titled "Study and Exam Prep Tips," but keep this advice in mind as you study:

◆ **Read all the material.** Microsoft has been known to include material not expressly specified in the objectives. This book has included additional information not reflected in the objectives in an effort to give you the best possible preparation for the examination—and for the real-world experiences to come.

◆ **Do the Step by Steps and complete the Exercises in each chapter.** They will help you gain experience using the specified methodology or approach. All Microsoft exams are task- and experienced-based and require you to have experience actually performing the tasks upon which you will be tested.

◆ **Use the questions to assess your knowledge.** Don't just read the chapter content; use the questions to find out what you know and what you don't. If you are struggling at all, study some more, review, and then assess your knowledge again.

◆ **Review the exam objectives.** Develop your own questions and examples for each topic listed. If you can develop and answer several questions for each topic, you should not have any difficulty passing the exam.

NOTE **Exam-taking Advice** Although this book is designed to prepare you to take and pass the Installing, Configuring, and Administering Microsoft® Windows® 2000 Server certification exam, there are no guarantees. Read this book, work through the questions and exercises, and when you feel confident, take the Practice Exam and additional exams using the *ExamGear, Training Guide Edition* test software. This should tell you whether or not you are ready for the real thing.

When taking the actual certification exam, make sure you answer all the questions before your time expires. Do not spend too much time on any one question. If you are unsure, answer it as best you can; then mark it for review when you have finished the rest of the questions. However, this advice will not apply if you are taking an adaptive exam. In that case, take your time on each question. There is no opportunity to go back to a question.

Remember, the primary object is not to pass the exam—it is to understand the material. If you understand the material, passing the exam should be simple. Knowledge is a pyramid: To build upward, you need a solid foundation. This book and the Microsoft Certified Professional programs are designed to ensure that you have that solid foundation.

Good luck!

NEW RIDERS PUBLISHING

The staff of New Riders Publishing is committed to bringing you the very best in computer reference material. Each New Riders book is the result of months of work by authors and staff who research and refine the information contained within its covers.

As part of this commitment to you, the NRP reader, New Riders invites your input. Please let us know if you enjoy this book, if you have trouble with the information or examples presented, or if you have a suggestion for the next edition.

Please note, however, that New Riders staff cannot serve as a technical resource during your preparation for the Microsoft certification exams or for questions about software- or hardware-related problems. Please refer instead to the documentation that accompanies the Microsoft products or to the applications' Help systems.

If you have a question or comment about any New Riders book, there are several ways to contact New Riders Publishing. We will respond to as many readers as we can. Your name, address, or phone number will never become part of a mailing list or be used for any purpose other than to help us continue to bring you the best books possible. You can write to us at the following address:

New Riders Publishing
Attn: Al Valvano
201 W. 103rd Street
Indianapolis, IN 46290

If you prefer, you can fax New Riders Publishing at 317-817-7448.

You also can send email to New Riders at the following Internet address:

nrfeedback@newriders.com

NRP is an imprint of Pearson Education. To obtain a catalog or information, contact us at nrmedia@newriders.com. To purchase a New Riders book, call 800-428-5331.

Thank you for selecting *MCSE Training Guide: Windows 2000 Server.*

Exam Preparation

This chapter will help you prepare for the "Installing Windows 2000 Server" section of the exam by giving you information necessary to make intelligent choices regarding the method of installation and the preparations required for such an installation.

Microsoft provides the following objectives for "Installing Windows 2000 Server":

Perform an attended installation of Windows 2000 Server.

▶ This objective is necessary because someone certified in the use of Windows 2000 Server technology must be able to install a Windows 2000 server as a member server in a Windows 2000 domain. This will include installations from a bootable CD-ROM and from the four-disk set.

Perform an unattended installation of Windows 2000 Server.

- **Create unattended answer files by using Setup Manager to automate the installation of Windows 2000 Server.**

- **Create and configure automated methods for installation of Windows 2000.**

▶ This objective is necessary because someone certified in the Windows 2000 Server technology should understand how to automate the installation of member servers in a Windows 2000 domain over a network. This will include creating answer files, as well as deploying installation using these answer files. In addition, it will involve familiarity with the new disk duplication and Remote Installation features of Windows 2000.

CHAPTER 1

Installing Windows 2000 Server

Upgrade a server from Microsoft Windows NT 4.0.

▶ This objective is necessary because someone certified in the Windows 2000 Server technology should understand how to upgrade a current Windows NT 4.0 machine (Server or Workstation) to a Windows 2000 member server. This will include both the preparation and the implementation of an upgrade.

Deploy service packs.

▶ This objective is necessary because someone certified in the Windows 2000 Server technology should understand how to apply incremental upgrades and software fixes through the use of service packs periodically released by Microsoft.

Troubleshoot failed installations.

▶ This objective is necessary because someone certified in Windows 2000 Server technology should understand how to diagnose installation problems and how to recover from installation failures.

STUDY STRATEGIES

▶ In past Server exams, installation has had its fair share of the focus. This exam will be no different. In addition to being able to answer the standard questions about manual installation, be prepared to be questioned on the new features that Windows 2000 Server has that previous versions of Windows NT did not have. That means you should be prepared for questions on Setup Manager, Sysprep, and RIS. In addition, you should know the pitfalls of upgrading a Windows NT 4.0 server to Windows 2000 so that if scenario questions come up about it, you are prepared. In addition, you also need to be aware of the new service pack technology so that you can correctly answer questions about slip-streaming and its benefits.

▶ Preparation for this section requires hands-on experience. You should try as many installation options as you have time and equipment for. Start by reading and understanding the content of this chapter. Then do the exercises and questions in the Apply Your Knowledge section. Finally, go back through the Step by Steps and work through them, especially those that cover material for which there were no exercises. Only through practice and repetition you will be able to answer the myriad of question forms (from straight informational to scenario-based) that you will see on this exam.

INTRODUCTION

It is probably redundant or obvious to say that a good installation is essential to the proper operation of your Windows 2000 member server. If you do not install properly, you will spend a lot of time subsequent to installation fixing your configuration. Moreover, the more installations you do, the more efficient you will want the process to be. To build your knowledge base, this chapter will deal with a wide variety of attended and unattended installation methods. It addresses the pros and cons of the methods to ensure that you are doing the right thing at the right time.

WINDOWS 2000 SERVER AND THE 70-215 EXAM

The prelude to the published exam objectives states that the 70-215 exam covers areas of Windows 2000 Server functionality as it relates to your ability to "...implement, administer, and troubleshoot Windows 2000 Server as a member server of a domain in an Active Directory environment." As a result, this text presupposes that you are operating in an environment in which you have already set up (or have available) a Windows 2000 domain controller. In addition, no attempt will be made to explain Active Directory, except where it is imperative to the understanding of a member server concept (that is for another text and other exams).

A *member server* is a Windows 2000 server that functions in a domain but does not hold a copy of the Active Directory. As a result, it does not validate domain logon, but it might validate logon into the local machine. Member servers require the presence of a domain controller in order to create a computer account to enable them to join a domain. Member servers generally perform functions such as file and print services, application services (like running an email server) and Web services (like being a Web server). All of these will be discussed in other chapters.

The exam focuses on five main areas of installation: attended installations, unattended installations, upgrades from NT 4.0, incremental installations of services packs, and troubleshooting installation. Each of these topics will be covered in detail in the following sections.

PREPARING FOR INSTALLATION

You need to take a number of factors into consideration when installing Windows 2000 Server (either as a fresh installation or as an upgrade). Those factors include hardware compatibility, software compatibility, disk and partition sizing, and current operating system upgradability. You must consider and deal with each of these factors before you attempt to install Windows 2000 Server.

Hardware Compatibility

Windows 2000 has very strict hardware requirements. If you do not meet them, at best, some of your components will not function properly and, at worst, the operating system will not install at all. Two criteria are required in order to install and operate Windows 2000 Server:

◆ The components must meet the minimum requirements for installation (see Table 1.1).

◆ The components must be on the Hardware Compatibility List.

Minimum Hardware Requirements

The minimum hardware requirements refer to the processor type and speed, the amount of disk space, and the amount of memory available. In the past, Microsoft published minimum installation requirements (for example, the minimum hardware required to install the operating systems). However, the published minimums now reflect the minimum hardware required to run servers in specific configurations. As a result, you may be able to install Windows 2000 Server with less than the minimum requirements, but the servers you install will not function effectively in a production environment. Table 1.1 outlines the minimum requirements.

TABLE 1.1

MINIMUM REQUIREMENTS FOR WINDOWS 2000 SERVER OPERATING SYSTEM INSTALLATION

Component	Published Minimums
Processor	Pentium 133 (also see Note)
RAM	256MB
Free disk space	1GB on a single partition*

* This disk space must be contiguous on a single partition. Please see the updated minimum requirements as posted at `http://www.microsoft.com/windows2000/guide/platform/overview/default.asp`.

NOTE

Alpha chips Support for the Compaq Alpha chip has been discontinued because Compaq is no longer supporting Windows 2000 on the Alpha chip.

It should be noted that the minimum hardware requirements have increased considerably since NT 4.0, and if you were running your NT 4.0 machine at or near the minimum hardware requirements, you will need to upgrade your hardware before upgrading to Windows 2000 Server.

The Hardware Compatibility List (HCL)

The Hardware Compatibility List (HCL) is Microsoft's published list of hardware components that have been fully tested with Windows 2000. Items that are listed in the HCL are guaranteed to function (at least to a bare minimum) with Windows 2000. If you want to ensure that all your hardware will function properly under Windows 2000, you should consult the current version of the HCL, which can be found on the Internet at `http://www.microsoft.com/hcl`.

Note that although many products will be on the HCL (which means they have been tested and found to function with Windows 2000), not everything is. If the manufacturer has a driver available for the device that has been created for Windows 2000, the device should function. However, any problems with the driver should be addressed to the manufacturer, not Microsoft.

Software Compatibility

In addition to confirming that your hardware is Windows 2000 compatible, you should also make sure your software is Windows 2000 compatible. This software compatibility extends not only to the installation and operation of the Windows 2000 operating system, but also to applications that formerly operated under DOS, Windows 9x, or Windows NT 4.0. The fact is, some software will no longer function (or function properly) under Windows 2000.

In the era of Windows NT 4.0 and Windows 9x, Microsoft published guidelines for the creation of software for these platforms. Although the guidelines were clear in terms of what the operating systems would allow developers to do, they often left loopholes that developers took advantage of to improve performance of their applications. Microsoft has not changed their guidelines so much as they have closed up the non-compliance holes. This means that software written to the old guidelines will still work. However, software written to take advantage of loopholes prohibited in the guidelines may not work.

In order to check your software, you can do two things. First, you can consult the software compatibility Web site at `http://www.microsoft.com/Windows2000/upgrade/compat/default.asp`. This Web site allows you to search for your software products online to check for compatibility or allows you to download a "Readiness Analyser" that will check for hardware and software issues offline. After the search, a list will be returned indicating the status of that software. The possible statuses are Certified (tested by the vendor and by an independent firm to ensure that it functions correctly under Windows 2000), Ready (tested by the vendor only), and Planned (a Windows 2000 compatible version is in the works). Any software that is not listed has not been verified through the Microsoft-sanctioned channels.

If you do not find your software product on the above Web site, do not be dismayed (at least not yet), because the second step is to contact the software vendor or to test it yourself. In many cases, I have found that software that is not on the Web site works just fine. Also, there are vendors who have released Windows 2000-ready versions of their software but who have not bothered to register it on Microsoft's Web site. Of course, if you are using software that was developed in-house, you will have to get your developers to test it thoroughly on Windows 2000 before you release it to your users.

Disk Size and Partitions

In order to install Windows 2000 Server on your computer, you have to have disk space—and a reasonable amount of it. Table 1.1 showed you what you need: 685MB of free space is required, and 1GB is recommended. That free space must be on a single partition, so two 500MB partitions will not do. If this is a typical Windows 2000 installation, you will want to install the operating system on your active partition (usually the C: drive), but you do not have to. If you plan to dual-boot your Windows 2000 Server with another operating system, you will want to install Windows 2000 onto another partition. If you do this, Microsoft is going to use different terms to describe the partition from which your computer starts up and the one on which the Windows 2000 operating system files are stored.

Microsoft uses the term "System partition" to describe the active partition, that is, the one your computer's BIOS wants to begin the boot process from. This partition is usually, but not always, the C: drive. This partition contains the Master Boot Record and system files that allow Windows 2000 to take control of the boot process.

Microsoft uses the term "Boot partition" to describe the partition where the Windows 2000 operating system files are stored. These files are commonly found in a folder called WINNT. They are files that Windows 2000 uses to complete the startup process and to run Windows 2000 after it is started.

In most cases, it is recommended that you install Windows 2000 on the same partition as you are booting from (the active partition). This would mean that the Boot and System partitions would be in the same location, which is often called the System/Boot partition (although this in not actually a term defined in the official documentation). The only case where this would not be done is when you are going to dual-boot (or multiple boot) Windows 2000 with one or more other operating systems—a practice that is recommended only for test systems.

When you have found a partition to install on, you may want to format it. You don't have to format it in advance because the installation process has a utility to create new partitions as well as to format them. If you do choose to pre-format the partition, you have the following format choices: NTFS, FAT16, and FAT32. These format types will be discussed in detail in Chapter 2, "Installing, Configuring, and Troubleshooting Access to Resources." To summarize,

NTFS is a proprietary file format used only by Windows NT and Windows 2000; FAT16 is a universal file format that is used in most operating systems; and FAT32 is an enhanced version of FAT16 that is supported by Windows 95 (OSR2) and Windows 98 in addition to all versions of Windows 2000.

Current Operating System Upgradability

In the event that you want to upgrade a machine running another operating system to Windows 2000, you have a number of paths. The working definition this book uses for *upgrade* is "the ability to install a new operating system without having to completely re-configure the resulting system and without having to reinstall the software." Upgrades to Windows 2000 Server can be done directly from Windows NT 4.0 Server and from Windows 3.51 Server. Because of the new fluidity of domain controller roles, the current role of the server is not significant.

In the case of other operating systems (like DOS, for example), you will have to choose whether to remove (or install over) the existing operating system or to dual-boot with it. Dual-boot means that you will choose which of the operating systems you will boot from at system startup and that all software will have to be installed once for each operating system.

After taking the preceding steps, you are ready to install Windows 2000 Server on your computer.

ATTENDED INSTALLATIONS OF WINDOWS 2000 SERVER

Perform an attended installation of Windows 2000 Server.

Attended installations of Windows 2000 Server are very common, and therefore, are the first installation topic covered in the objectives.

When Microsoft says "attended," they are pointing to any installation where all the questions of configuration are answered by the person doing the installation at the time the installation is being performed. This is as opposed to an *unattended installation*, during which the answers are provided by a script that has been created beforehand. There are four ways to perform an attended installation:

◆ Boot to a CD-ROM, thereby invoking the setup routine.

◆ Boot to a current operating system with CD-ROM support and manually invoke the setup routine.

◆ Boot to a set of four setup disks and then provide the CD-ROM when prompted.

◆ Boot to a network-aware operating system and invoke setup over the network.

In the final analysis, all the above methods end up the same; only the ways they start are different.

Install by Booting to a CD-ROM

If you have a computer whose BIOS supports booting from a CD-ROM, you can set up Windows 2000 Server without installing an operating system on your hard drive and without requiring network support. To do so, configure your computer to boot to the CD-ROM in the BIOS and then follow the instructions in Step by Step 1.1.

STEP BY STEP

1.1 Installing Windows 2000 from a Bootable CD-ROM

1. Insert the Windows 2000 CD-ROM into the drive and boot your computer. After you have confirmed that you want to boot to your CD-ROM, Setup will automatically begin and start copying files. The initial prompts will appear, as shown in Figure 1.1:

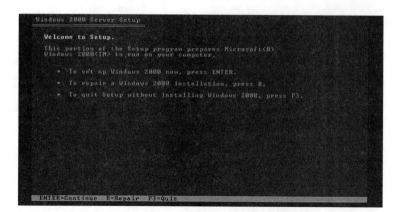

FIGURE 1.1
Choose to install, repair, or exit.

2. When prompted, press Enter to set up Windows 2000.

3. When the licensing agreement is displayed, press F8 to continue.

4. When prompted, either choose the partition to install Windows 2000 on or create a new partition in unpartitioned space (see Figure 1.2). If you choose to create a new partition, you will be prompted for the size, in megabytes, that you want the partition to be. This partition can be any size up to and including the size of the hard drive, regardless of the size. This is a change from NT 4.0, in which you were limited to 4GB as an initial partition size. If you do create a new partition, you will be returned to the above screen, and you can select the new partition and press Enter to continue.

continues

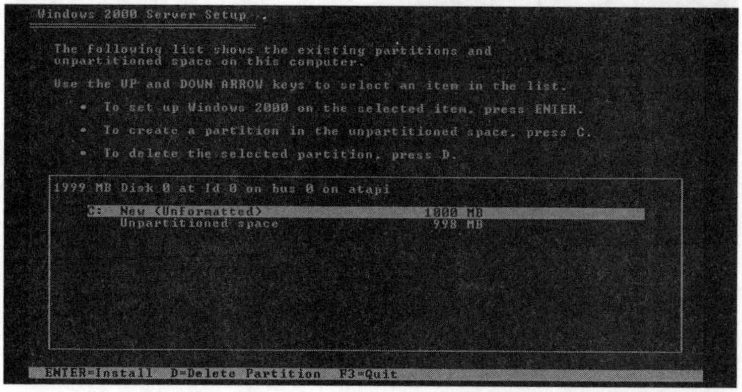

FIGURE 1.2
Select a partition to install on or create a new one.

continued

5. If the partition you chose was not already formatted, you will be prompted to format with either NTFS or FAT file system. If you format with the FAT file system and the partition is larger than 2GB, Setup will format it with FAT32; otherwise, it will be formatted with FAT16. If the partition was already formatted, you can choose to leave the partition formatted as is, you can format it using either NTFS or FAT, or you can convert it from its existing format to NTFS (this preserves any data already on the partition).

At this point, after the new partition is formatted (if you chose to do so), Setup will copy files onto your hard drive (see Figure 1.3) and reboot your system in preparation for the GUI part of the setup. Once the setup has started, you will be presented with a screen prompting you to click Next to continue with system information gathering. You can click the Next button if you want; however, if you do not, after about 30 seconds, the device installation will begin anyway.

The next screen is the Installing Devices screen, where Setup detects and installs devices such as your keyboard and mouse (see Figure 1.4).

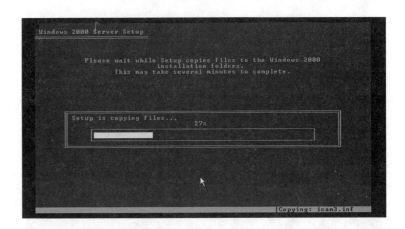

FIGURE 1.3
Setup copies files onto your hard drive before rebooting your server to the GUI portion of Setup.

6. When the Regional Settings screen appears (see Figure 1.5), you have the option of changing the system and user locales (the locations that indicate how currency, numbers, and dates appear), and the keyboard layout. If you want, you can change either of these by clicking the Customize button for either (or both) and choosing a different country location. If you do not customize these settings, the locales will be set to English (United States), and the keyboard will be configured as US. Click Next to progress to the next screen.

7. On the Personalize Your Software screen, type your name and the name of your company. You cannot continue until you have typed something into the Name field. Click Next to continue.

8. On the Your Product Key screen (see Figure 1.6), type the product key found on the jewel case (or stamped onto your certificate of authenticity) for your Windows 2000 Server CD. Click Next to continue.

continues

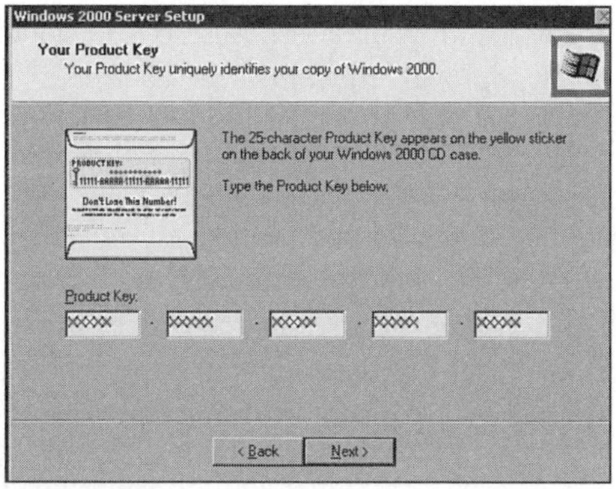

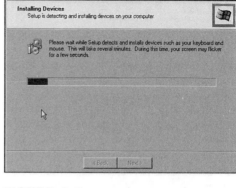

FIGURE 1.4
It may take a considerable amount of time for Setup to detect all your devices.

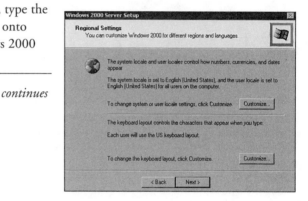

FIGURE 1.5
Modify regional settings and keyboard layout here.

FIGURE 1.6
Enter the product key (found on the back of your CD-ROM) to continue.

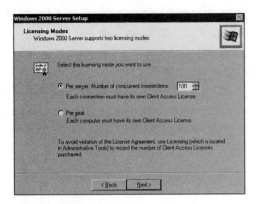

FIGURE 1.7
Select either Per Server (and the number of concurrent connections) or Per Seat licensing.

continued

9. The Licensing Modes screen allows you to indicate what type of licenses you have for this server (see Figure 1.7). Your choices are Per Server and Per Seat. By default, Per Server is chosen with 5 Client Access Licenses (CALs) selected; however, you can change either of those settings.

To know what choice to make, you must first understand the licensing modes available. Per server is a connection-based license model. In it, you purchase one license for every connection made to a specific machine. If you have one server and 10 users will connect to it at any one time, you would purchase 10 CALs. If a single user makes a connection to two different servers at the same time, that user will be using a CAL on each of the servers. That scenario is where per seat comes in. Per seat licensing effectively licenses a user to make connections to servers. Instead of monitoring the total number of connections made, all that really matters is the number of users making those connections. If you have five servers and 25 users and each user makes a simultaneous connection to each of the servers, you would need only 25 CALs with per seat licensing. With per server licensing, you would need 125 licenses to provide the same licensed access.

The rule of thumb on licensing is that if the number of simultaneous connections made by your users is larger than the number of users you have, you should be looking at per seat licensing. Most organizations start out with per server licensing and then switch over to per seat at some point. A Microsoft sales representative can help you more with pricing options for different licensing schemes.

10. The next screen is the Computer Name and Administrator Password dialog box (see Figure 1.8). In it you configure a name for your computer and then type in the password for the Administrator account (which is created automatically when the Server software is installed). The default computer name is generated automatically and is a combination of the first word in the company name you entered in step 7 above and a set of seven randomly generated letters. You can keep the default name or type in your own.

Having done that, type in (and confirm) the password for the local administrator account. Ensure that your password conforms to good security standards; in other words, it should contain seven or more characters, include upper and lowercase characters, should be a combination of letters and numbers, and should not be any readily anticipated word or name from your personal or business life (like the name of your children, pets, or business). Having completed these fields, click Next to continue.

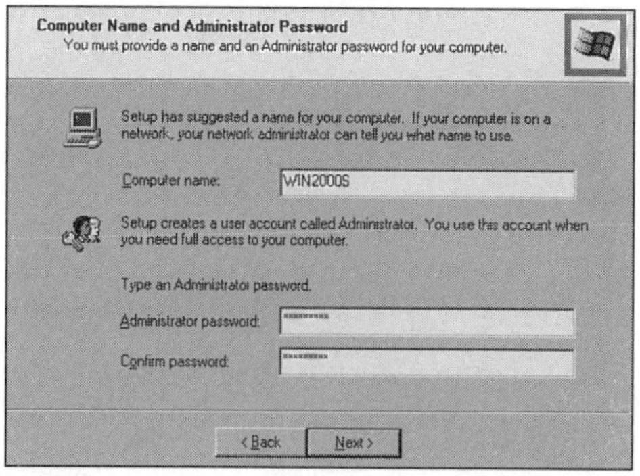

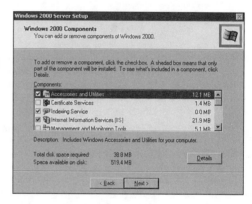

FIGURE 1.8
Enter a computer name and a password for the local Administrator account.

11. The next screen is the Windows 2000 Components screen (see Figure 1.9). In this dialog box, you can choose the optional components you want to install at this time.

The configuration screens that follow are largely based on the choices you make here. The following bulleted list outlines the categories of components you can install at this point.

FIGURE 1.9
Select the optional Windows 2000 components that you want to install at this time (these components can be added later if desired).

- *Accessories and Utilities.* This includes programs like Calculator, games, and multimedia utilities. By default, all these options are selected.

- *Certificate Services.* This is the utility for providing Web-based digital certificates to your company. Under NT 4.0, this component was used to replace services like those provided by companies such as Verisign for in-house applications. Under Windows 2000, digital certificates are used for a variety of enhanced security transmissions, including IPSec, EFS, and L2TP. (These will all be discussed in later chapters.) By default, none of these components are selected. Installing these services at this time will affect their functionality, for example the type of Certificate Authority and type of certificates available.

- *Indexing Service.* Used to index the contents of a server's hard drive to allow quick searching. This component is selected by default.

continues

continued

- *Internet Information Services (IIS).* This is the Web server services for Windows 2000 and allows for the publishing of HTTP- and FTP-based content in either an intranet or Internet context. By default, all components of IIS are selected except FTP, the News Server, and Visual Interdev Remote Deployment Support. Windows 2000 includes version 5.0 of IIS.

- *Management and Monitoring Tools.* This includes tools for monitoring network traffic and content, tools for implementing the administration of Connection Manager, and SNMP traps. By default, none of these tools are selected.

- *Message Queuing Services.* Used in *n*-tier applications, this service provides for stateless communication between a user and a back-end database or other input gathering system. Queues act like caches, controlling the flow of data to destinations and ensuring that messages reach their destinations. By default, none of these services are selected.

- *Networking Services.* This groups the major networking support services including DNS, DHCP, and WINS (among others). By default, none of these services are installed.

- *Other Network File and Print Services.* This category includes file and print services for Macintosh and UNIX. By default, none of these services are installed.

- *Remote Installation Services.* This provides the capability to remotely install Windows 2000 Professional on remote boot-enabled client computers. By default, this service is not installed.

- *Remote Storage.* This allows for the use of magnetic tape as a dynamic storage medium for infrequently used files. By default, this service is not installed.

- *Script Debugger.* A tool for the debugging of scripts running on your server. By default, this tool is installed.

- *Terminal Services.* Services that allow your computer to act as a host to PC Thin clients running Terminal Server Client software. This allows for all processes at a client's station to be hosted directly on the server with little or no processing at the client's side. By default, these services are not installed.

- *Terminal Services Licensing.* Configures your server as a license issuer to terminal service clients. This is required only if your Terminal Server is running in Application Mode. By default, this tool is not installed.

- *Windows Media Services.* Allow your server to provide streaming media support to clients. By default, these services are not installed.

12. If you have a modem installed in your server, the Modem Dialing Information dialog box will appear. You must provide at least a country of origin and an area code in order to proceed to the next screen. Click Next to continue.

13. In the Date and Time Settings dialog box, you are prompted for the current date and time as well as the time zone you are currently in (and whether you observe Daylight Savings Time in your location). Click Next to complete the configuration of your server.

    At this point, networking settings are detected, and networking components are installed.

14. In the Networking Settings dialog box, you are prompted for the kind of networking settings you want configured (see Figure 1.10). If you choose Typical (the default), the Client for Microsoft Networks will be installed, as will File and Print Sharing and TCP/IP with the DHCP (automatic address configuration) client. If you choose Custom, you can manually add new clients (such as a NetWare

NOTE

Other Options In order to simplify the step-by-step procedure, I have not provided detail on the installation of anything but the default choices. Other options will be discussed in detail in other chapters as they are applicable to the Windows 2000 Server exam. At that point, details on the installation of other services will be given, which could, for an experienced administrator, be applied at this point in the installation process.

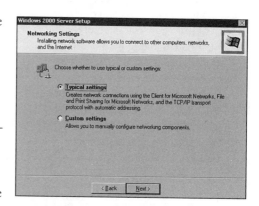

FIGURE 1.10
Choose Typical network settings or Custom settings.

continues

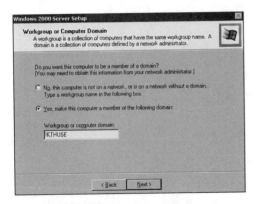

FIGURE 1.11
Choose the kind of network membership this server will have (Domain or Workgroup).

NOTE

Computer Account Required for Domain Membership When a computer joins a domain it means that it becomes part of the domain structure; it also means that users logging in at the server's console will have the option of providing domain login credentials or local computer login credentials. To be able to join a domain, either a computer account must exist in Active Directory or it must be created at the time the server is installed. This computer account is independent of any user and simply indicates that a specific (Windows 2000) computer will allow users to log in to the domain from it. This computer account provides authentication of the computer in the Active Directory. To create such an account, a user must have that right granted in the security model of the domain.

---

continued

client), services, or protocols (like NWLink or NetBEUI). In addition, you can also manually configure TCP/IP to use static addressing. These options will differ depending on the options you chose during the network components section (for example, NetWare protocols are automatically added if Novell Services is selected).

---

15. In the Workgroup or Computer Domain screen, you can configure what kind of a network group this computer belongs to (see Figure 1.11). If you choose No, This Computer is Not on a Network..., you need to type the name of the workgroup that this server belongs to in the text box provided. If this server is part of a domain (as this book will assume), you need to provide the name of the domain this server is to be made part of. When you click Next, if you have decided to join a domain, you will be prompted for the name and password of a user in the domain who has sufficient rights to create computer accounts (see note at the left). If you do not have this information, you will have to make the computer a member of a workgroup in order to continue, and then you can join the domain later.

    After the domain membership has been established (which may take a couple of minutes), the Installing Components dialog box will appear, and Setup will install all the components that have been requested thus far in the process.

    Finally, the Performing Final Tasks dialog box appears, and the final configuration of your server is completed. These two steps may take a long time to complete, so be prepared.

---

16. When the Completing the Windows 2000 Setup Wizard dialog box appears, remove the CD-ROM from your drive and click Finish to restart your server.

Install by Manually Invoking Setup from a CD-ROM or a Network Share

If you have a 32-bit Microsoft operating system installed on the target computer that will read from the CD-ROM, you can run SETUP.EXE. If CD-ROM Autorun is turned on on your system, inserting the Windows 2000 Server CD-ROM into the drive will also invoke SETUP.EXE. Alternatively, you can also invoke the program WINNT32.EXE, which is found on the CD-ROM in the I386 folder. In addition, if you have network connectivity, you can connect to a share point on another computer that has the Windows 2000 Server files on it and run SETUP.EXE or WINNT32.EXE from there. After you begin the Setup process, it will progress exactly as described in Step by Step 1.1.

Install by Manually Invoking WINNT from a CD-ROM or a Network Share

If you have MS-DOS or Windows 3.x installed on the target computer, you have two choices. If you have a CD-ROM drive in that machine and the appropriate drivers to access it from DOS, you can use a program called WINNT to begin the installation. If you do not have access to a local CD-ROM but you have a networking client installed on the target machine, you can connect to a network share to which the Windows 2000 Server CD has been copied and use the WINNT program to begin the installation. This procedure is outlined in Step by Step 1.2.

STEP BY STEP

1.2 Installing Windows 2000 from DOS Using a CD-ROM

  1. At a DOS prompt, type **SMARTDRV** and press Enter. This will load the SmartDrive program, which will greatly reduce the time it takes to copy files from the CD-ROM.

---

  2. Insert your Windows 2000 CD into the CD-ROM drive and change to that drive letter.

---

continues

continued

3. Navigate to the I386 folder on the CD and type **WINNT**. This will start the Setup program.

4. At the screen shown in Figure 1.12, type in the location of the I386 directory you just navigated to. In the example shown, the CD-ROM is designated as the D-drive, so the setup routine defaulted to that location. When the path is correct, press Enter to continue, and the file copying process will commence.

5. When the screen shown in Figure 1.13 appears, press Enter to reboot and continue. From this point, the installation will progress as outlined in steps 2 through 15 of Step by Step 1.1.

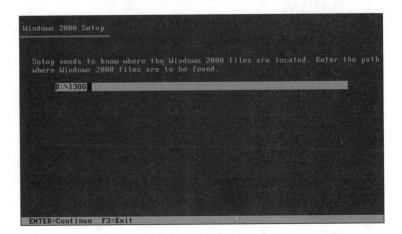

FIGURE 1.12
Enter the location of the Windows 2000 files (or accept the default).

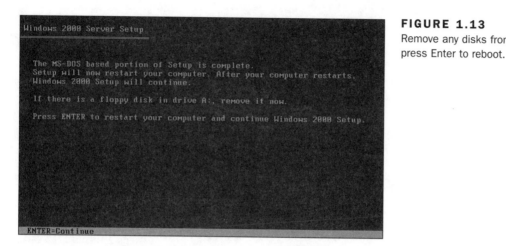

Install by Using Setup Diskettes and a CD-ROM

If you have a machine with no current operating system on it that will not boot from a CD-ROM, you must use this method. Setup disks are a set of four disks that form a minimal installation of Windows 2000 (the closest thing you have to booting Windows 2000 from disk). Having made the disks, you boot from the first one and progress through all four, at which point you will be prompted to insert the CD-ROM in the CD-ROM drive, and the installation will continue using that medium.

The disks are created using either MAKEBOOT.EXE or MAKEBT32.EXE, both of which are found in the BOOTDISK folder on your Windows 2000 Server CD-ROM. Both programs do the same thing; however, the "32" version is designed to be run under 32-bit operating systems, whereas the other is designed to be run under 16-bit operating systems, like DOS and Windows 3.1.

Step by Step 1.3 walks you through the process of creating the setup disks.

N O T E **For NT 4.0 Users** Under NT 4.0, you created a three-disk set by using the command WINNT /ox (or WINNT32 /ox if you were doing it from an existing NT machine). This switch no longer exists under Windows 2000, and you must create the set (which is now four disks) using one of the executables mentioned above.

STEP BY STEP

1.3 Creating the Setup Disk Set

1. From any operating system from which you can access a CD-ROM, navigate to the BOOTDISK folder.

2. If you are using a 16-bit operating system, run MAKEBOOT.EXE; if you are using a 32-bit operating system, run MAKEBT32.EXE. See Figure 1.14 for an example of this screen.

3. When prompted, type the letter of your floppy drive.

4. Insert a blank disk (labeled *Windows 2000 Setup Boot Disk)* into the floppy drive and press Enter.

5. When prompted, insert another blank disk (labeled *Windows 2000 Setup Disk #2*) into the floppy drive and press Enter.

6. When prompted, insert a third blank disk (labeled *Windows 2000 Setup Disk #3*) into the floppy drive and press Enter.

7. When prompted, insert a fourth blank disk (labeled *Windows 2000 Setup Disk #4*) into the floppy drive and press Enter.

8. Remove the final disk and place them in a safe place for use later.

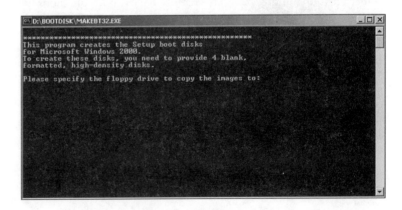

FIGURE 1.14
You can create a Setup disk set using the MAKEBOOT or MAKEBT32 utility.

After you create a set of Setup disks, you can begin the process of installing Windows 2000 Server. Step by Step 1.4 outlines the process up to the final GUI setup.

STEP BY STEP

1.4 Installing Windows 2000 with Setup Disks

1. Insert the disk labeled *Windows 2000 Setup Boot Disk* into your floppy drive and boot your computer.

2. When prompted, insert the disk labeled *Windows 2000 Server Setup Disk #2* and press Enter.

3. When prompted, insert the disk labeled *Windows 2000 Server Setup Disk #3* and press Enter.

4. When prompted, insert the disk labeled *Windows 2000 Server Setup Disk #4* and press Enter. Eventually you will see the screen shown in Figure 1.15.

5. When prompted (as in Figure 1.15), press Enter to set up Windows 2000.

continues

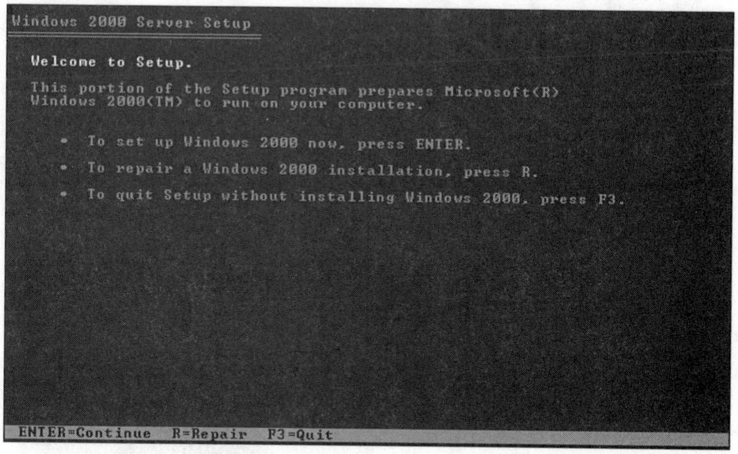

FIGURE 1.15
Choose to install, repair, or exit Setup.

continued

6. When the licensing agreement appears, press F8 to continue. Eventually, the screen shown in Figure 1.16 will appear.

7. When prompted, either choose the partition on which you want to install Windows 2000 or create a new partition in unpartitioned space. If you choose to create a new partition, you will be prompted for the size, in megabytes, that you want the partition to be. This partition can be any size up to and including the size of the hard drive, regardless of the size. This is a change from NT 4.0, in which you were limited to 4GB as an initial partition size. If you do create a new partition, you will be returned to the above screen. Select the new partition and press Enter to continue.

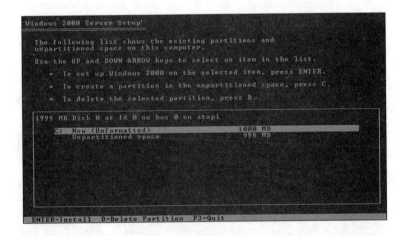

FIGURE 1.16
Choose a partition to install on or create a new one.

8. If the partition you chose was not already formatted, you
   will be prompted to format it as NTFS or FAT. If you format with the FAT file system and the partition is larger
   than 2GB, Setup will format it with FAT32; otherwise, it
   will be formatted with FAT16. If the partition was already
   formatted, you can choose to leave the partition formatted
   as is, or you can format it using either NTFS or FAT. If
   the partition is formatted with FAT or FAT32, you also
   have the choice of converting it to NTFS. This will
   change the format type without destroying the data currently on the partition.

9. At this point, after the new partition is formatted (if you
   chose to do so), you will be prompted to insert the
   Windows 2000 Server CD-ROM. You should remove
   Windows 2000 Server Setup Disk #4 from your floppy
   drive. Setup will copy installation files to your hard drive
   in preparation for the GUI setup, and then it will reboot
   your system.

   From this point, the installation will progress as outlined
   in steps 6 through 16 of Step by Step 1.1.

Although attended installations are common, there may be times
when a number of similar servers need to be installed. To do that, an
unattended installation is preferable. The next section deals with that
method of installation.

UNATTENDED INSTALLATIONS OF WINDOWS 2000 SERVER

Perform an unattended installation of Windows 2000 Server.

Unattended installation methods allow for installation of Windows
2000 Server to be done with little or no user intervention. They are
beneficial when a number of similar servers need to be installed.
When configured properly, unattended installations can be completely hands-off once the installation has begun.

There are three main methods of unattended installation: installation from scripts, installation using disk images and third-party distribution software, and installation using Remote Installation Services. All three will be covered on the exam, but only script installation will be covered in detail. Therefore, this chapter provides in-depth coverage of the configuration and deployment of script-based installation. It includes an overview and some basic configuration tips in the other two installation methods, but will not cover them in detail because the exam does not do so.

Script-Based Unattended Installation

The premise of the script-based installation is that you create a scenario where the installation progresses like a normal attended installation except that where a user would normally answer questions, you have a text file that provides the answers. Once the installation has begun, if you have configured the answers properly, no intervention is required.

This list outlines the basic components of a script-based installation:

◆ *The I386 directory from the Windows 2000 CD-ROM.* This is copied into a server-based folder and shared (unattended installations are almost exclusively network-based).

◆ *The WINNT.EXE or WINNT32.EXE programs.* WINNT is for DOS-based installations; WINNT32 is used for upgrades from 32-bit Windows operating systems.

◆ *An answer file providing the generic answers to setup questions.* This is typically a file with a .txt extension (although the extension does not matter).

◆ *A uniqueness database file.* This file, which has a .udf extension, provides the answers to computer specific questions that will change from machine to machine (for example, the computer name).

◆ *A batch file or command line that invokes the unattended installation.*

Although you can create the answer file using any text editor, in order to make it simple to create and to ensure that you do not leave out crucial information, a wizard is available to aid you.

Using the Setup Manager to Create Unattended Answer Files

The Setup Manager is part of the Windows 2000 Support Tools located in the \Support\Tools folder on the Windows 2000 CD-ROM. It is stored in a file called Deploy.cab and must be extracted from that .cab file before it will operate. Step by Step 1.5 runs you through the process of extracting the Setup Manager.

STEP BY STEP

1.5 Extracting the Setup Manager

1. From the Windows 2000 Server CD-ROM, navigate to the \Support\Tools folder and double-click the Deploy.cab file.

2. Select the files SETUPMGR.EXE and SETUPMGX.DLL, right-click either of them, and choose Extract from the menu that appears.

3. When the Browse for Folder dialog box appears, browse to the location to which you want to extract the Setup Manager files (it is recommended that you use *systemroot*\system32, but that is not required).

4. Create a shortcut to the SETUPMGR.EXE file on the desktop and/or in the Start menu so that you can easily invoke it when required.

When the Setup Manager is extracted and accessible, you can use it to create an answer file. Step by Step 1.6 outlines creating an answer file.

STEP BY STEP

1.6 Creating an Answer File to Install Windows 2000 Server with the Setup Manager

1. Using the shortcut you created in Step by Step 1.5, start the Setup Manager Wizard.

continues

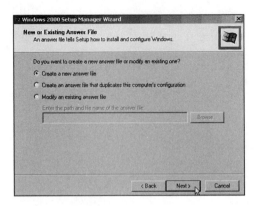

FIGURE 1.17
The New or Existing Answer Files screen.

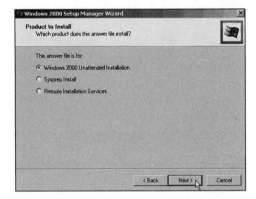

FIGURE 1.18
The Product to Install screen.

continued

2. At the Welcome to the Windows 2000 Setup Manager Wizard screen, click Next to continue.

3. At the New or Existing Answer File screen (see Figure 1.17), choose whether you want to create a new answer file, have the current computer's settings be the defaults for the wizard, or modify an existing answer file. Then click Next.

4. At the Product to Install screen (see Figure 1.18), choose the product that this answer file is designed to install. Your choices are Windows 2000 Unattended Install, Sysprep Install, and Remote Installation Services. Choose Windows 2000 Unattended Install and click Next.

5. At the Platform screen (see Figure 1.19), choose the product (Server or Professional) for which you want to create an answer file.

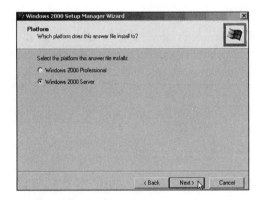

FIGURE 1.19
Indicate which platform you want to create an answer file for.

6. At the User Interaction Level screen (see Figure 1.20), specify how much control the user will have over the installation process and how much interaction he or she will have. Your choices are fully described here:

- *Provide Defaults.* The user will be prompted to review (and perhaps change) the information you provide. This gives the user a guide to follow but allows for deviation in any area.

- *Fully Automated.* The user will see (perhaps only briefly) all the processes as they happen, but he or she will not be able to make any manual changes to the settings.

- *Hide Pages.* The user may be prompted for information, but only where you do not provide answers to questions. This is useful where you want some of the answers to be predefined but not all of them. This choice provides standardization in some areas and flexibility in others. In instances where all the information on a setup page has been provided, the user does not see the page.

- *Read Only.* You provide the answers to the questions, and the user will be prompted for information that you do not provide (just like the previous choice). However, pages that have been filled in will be displayed. Also, when pages are displayed, the user will be unable to modify those questions for which you provided answers.

- *GUI Attended.* The text-based setup is completely automated, but the GUI setup must be attended by a user who can answer the questions.

Assuming you want to create a fully automated setup, choose Fully Automated and click Next to continue.

7. At the License Agreement screen (see Figure 1.21), accept the licensing agreement by clicking the check box. Then click Next to continue.

continues

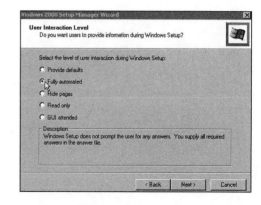

FIGURE 1.20
The User Interaction Level screen.

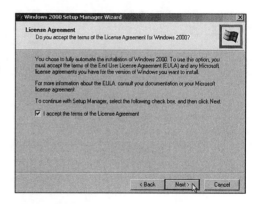

FIGURE 1.21
The License Agreement screen.

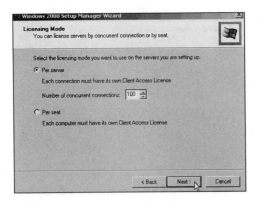

FIGURE 1.22
The Licensing Mode screen.

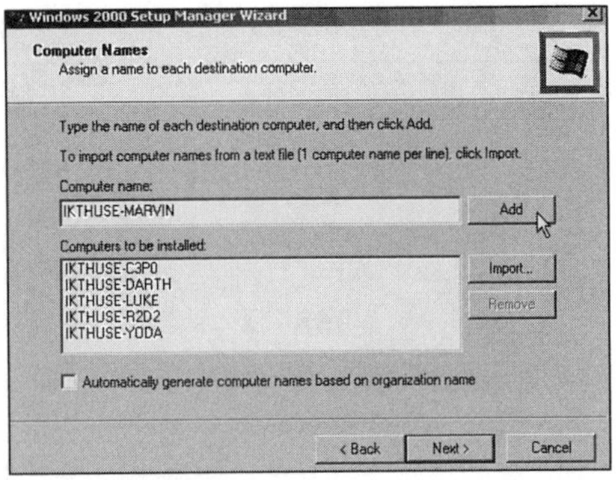

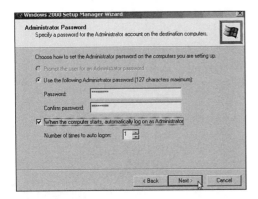

FIGURE 1.23
The Computer Names screen.

FIGURE 1.24
The Administrator Password screen.

continued

8. At the Customize the Software screen, fill in your name and organization and click Next.

9. If you chose Windows 2000 Server in step 5, the Licensing Mode screen will appear next (see Figure 1.22). Choose the licensing type (either Per Server or Per Seat), fill in the number of concurrent connections (if you chose Per Server), and click Next to continue.

10. At the Computer Names screen (see Figure 1.23), type in the names of each of the computers you will be installing using this automated file. After you type each computer name, click the Add button. You can continue to do this until all your computer names have been added. You also have the option of importing the names from a text file (using the Import button) or simply having Windows 2000 generate unique names for each machine (select the Automatically Generate Computer Names Based on Organization Name check box). Click Next to continue.

11. At the Administrator Password screen (see Figure 1.24), provide an administrator password for the computers you are installing. This password will be the same for each of the machines, so you might want to change them manually after the installation is complete. In addition to setting the password, you can also set the computer to automatically log on as the administrator. This option can be set to auto logon as many as 99 times before a user will be prompted for a password. This feature not only allows for multiple automated logons as software is installed and the machine is restarted by the installation process, but also allows for the security of passwords and manual logon once the allotted number of automatic occurrences is exceeded. Click the Next button when you are finished with this screen.

12. At the Display Settings screen (see Figure 1.25), choose the Colors, Screen Area, and Refresh Frequency that is appropriate for the computers you will install with this script. If they are all the same and you want to choose specific settings, do so. If they are not all the same, you will want to leave the settings at default to ensure that you do not try to set any machines to values they cannot handle. When you are done, click Next to continue.

13. At the Network Settings screen (see Figure 1.26), choose the type of network settings you want for each machine. If you choose Typical, each computer installed with this script will have the Microsoft Networking Client and TCP/IP with DHCP enabled. If you choose Custom, you will be prompted for the number of network adapters in each machine and you will be able to manually set networking properties (such as TCP/IP properties, additional clients, and so on).

14. At the Workgroup or Domain screen (see Figure 1.27), you can choose how these machines will participate in your network structure—whether in a workgroup or a domain. If you choose a domain, you will enter the domain name and whether you need to create a computer account at installation time. If you do, you will need to provide the credentials of a user who is allowed to add computer accounts to Active Directory.

15. At the Time Zone screen, choose the time zone that the machines will be in and click Next.

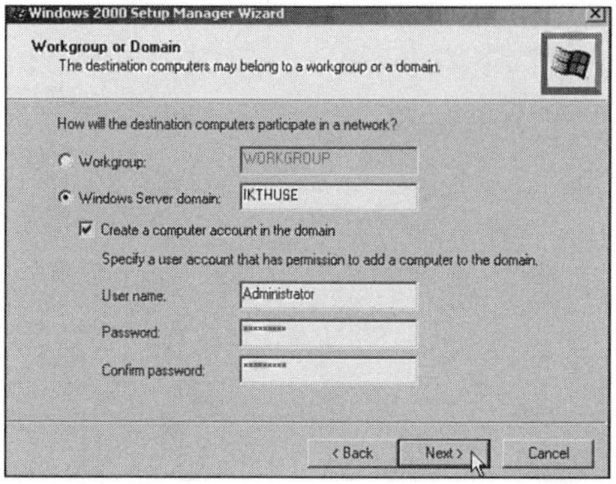

continues

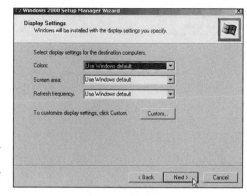

FIGURE 1.25
The Display Settings screen.

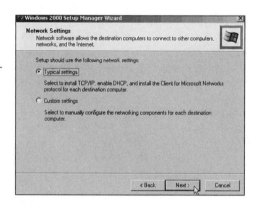

FIGURE 1.26
The Network Settings screen.

FIGURE 1.27
The Workgroup or Domain screen.

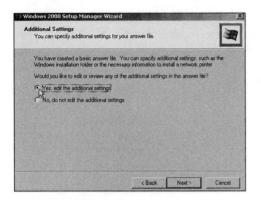

FIGURE 1.28
The Additional Settings screen.

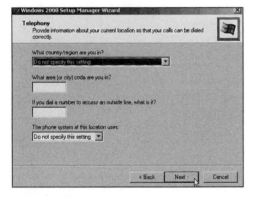

FIGURE 1.29
The Telephony screen.

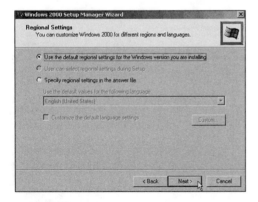

FIGURE 1.30
The Regional Settings screen.

continued

16. At the Additional Settings screen (see Figure 1.28), you can choose to add additional setup parameters to the basic answer file you are creating. If you choose Yes, you will proceed through the next five steps; otherwise, you will skip directly to step 22. Click the Next button to continue.

17. The first additional setting is the Telephony screen (see Figure 1.29). In it, you can choose location information for telephony configuration on the target machines. If you leave the settings at Do Not Specify This Setting, they will not be put into the answer file.

18. The second additional setting is the Regional Settings screen (see Figure 1.30). Regional settings include such options as language settings, time locales, currency, numbers, and dates. Click Next to continue.

19. The third additional setting is the Languages screen (see Figure 1.31). Windows 2000 allows for the installation of support for more than just the primary language. You can choose which of the available languages you want to install automatically. Select as many languages as you require, and then click Next.

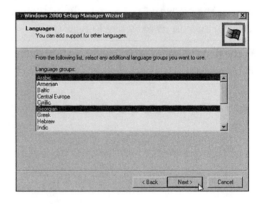

FIGURE 1.31
The Languages screen.

20. The fourth additional setting is the Browser and Shell Settings screen (see Figure 1.32). You can use the default settings, use an autoconfiguration script (created by the IE Administration Kit), or specify proxy and default home page settings. Specify the settings appropriate to your environment by selecting a radio button. If you do not choose to use the default settings, you can customize the choice you made using the Settings buttons. When you finish, click Next to continue.

21. The fifth additional setting is the Installation Folder screen (see Figure 1.33). In it, you can specify the location for the installation folder. You can install into the WINNT folder (the default), have the system create a unique name, or specify the folder name yourself.

22. The sixth additional setting is the Install Printers screen (see Figure 1.34). Here you can configure to which printers the destination machines should be connected. The first time a user logs onto one of these computers, the network printers you configure here will also be attached (provided that the user login has access to the printers). Click Next to continue.

continues

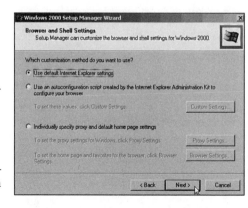

FIGURE 1.32
The Browser and Shell Settings screen.

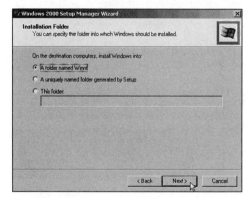

FIGURE 1.33
The Installation Folder screen.

FIGURE 1.34
The Install Printers screen.

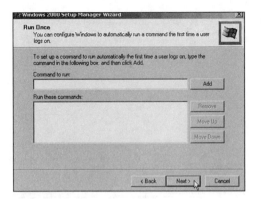

FIGURE 1.35
The Run Once screen.

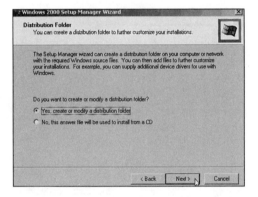

FIGURE 1.36
The Distribution Folder screen.

continued

23. The final additional setting is the Run Once screen (see Figure 1.35). On this screen, you can specify any commands you want to run after the installation has completed. These are most often setup files for installing software. You can use the Move Up and Move Down buttons to change the order in which these commands are executed. When you finish, click the Next button to continue.

24. On the Distribution Folder screen (see Figure 1.36), you choose whether to create a distribution folder. A distribution folder is a network share that contains the files you need for the automated installation. If you do not choose to create a distribution folder, you will have to provide the CD-ROM at each installation point. You will follow steps 25–30 only if you choose to create or modify a distribution folder by choosing Yes. Make your choice and click Next. (If you chose No, skip to step 31.)

25. If you choose to use a distribution folder, the Distribution Folder Name screen appears (see Figure 1.37), prompting you for the path and share name of the folder you want to create or modify. Whether you choose to create or modify a distribution folder, you will have to provide the path and the share name for it.

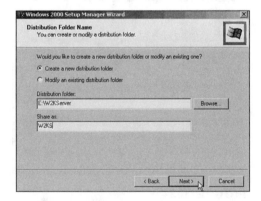

FIGURE 1.37
The Distribution Folder Name screen.

26. On the Additional Mass Storage Drivers screen (see Figure 1.38), you can provide the locations for drivers that need to be installed but are not part of the Windows 2000 Server driver set. This setting is used to install drivers for devices such as hardware RAID controllers. By specifying these drivers, you will not only modify the script to install them, but you will also modify the distribution folder to include these drivers.

27. On the Hardware Abstraction Layer screen (see Figure 1.39), you can specify a new HAL to replace the default one. This is typically used if you are an OEM retailer who provides Windows 2000 Server with your hardware. By using this setting, you can substitute your custom HAL when installing Windows 2000 Server on client machines.

28. On the Additional Commands screen (see Figure 1.40), you can specify the execution of additional setup or configuration routines. Because no user will be logged on when they run, these must be routines that can run in that state.

29. On the OEM Branding screen (see Figure 1.41), you can specify logos and backgrounds for the installation process. These will be displayed while the automated installation is taking place.

continues

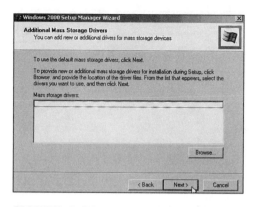

FIGURE 1.38
The Additional Mass Storage Drivers screen.

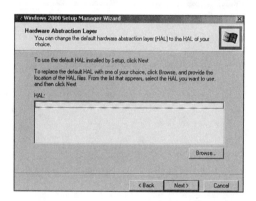

FIGURE 1.39
The Hardware Abstraction Layer screen.

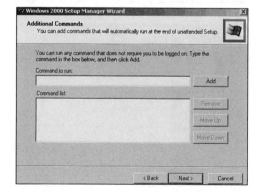

FIGURE 1.40
The Additional Commands screen.

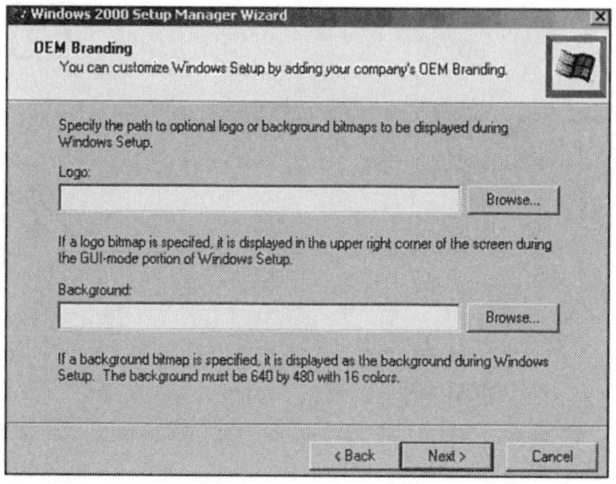

FIGURE 1.41
The OEM Branding screen.

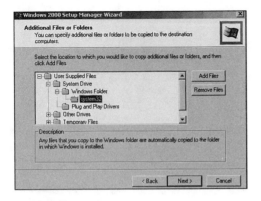

FIGURE 1.42
The Additional Files or Folders screen.

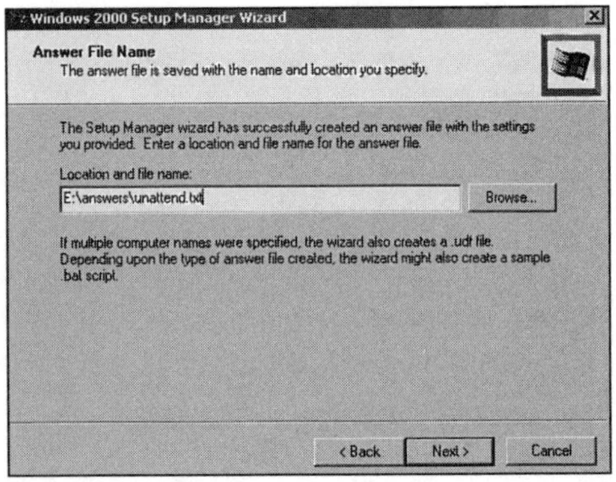

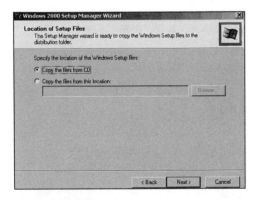

FIGURE 1.43
The Answer File Name screen.

30. On the Additional Files or Folders screen (see Figure 1.42), you can indicate additional files or folders that are to be placed onto the target computers at installation time. This may be data, programs, or other special files that are required on the target computers. You can indicate where these files are to be placed by selecting a particular folder in the provided tree and then clicking the Add Files button.

31. On the Answer File Name screen (see Figure 1.43), you can indicate the name and path of the answer file to be created from the responses you gave. This screen also indicates that if you specified more than one computer name (in step 10), a .udf file would be created. This .udf file (uniqueness database file) will contain the computer-specific information for each machine you specified. The path you indicate must exist at this point; the wizard will not create it. When you are done, click Next to continue.

32. On the Location of Setup Files screen (see Figure 1.44), you indicate the location where the setup files are stored. This is used to create your distribution folder. You can specify the CD or a local or network location.

33. When the Setup Manager Wizard finishes copying files, click Next to continue.

34. When the Completing the Windows 2000 Setup Manager Wizard screen appears (see Figure 1.45), note the files it has created. Then click Finish to exit.

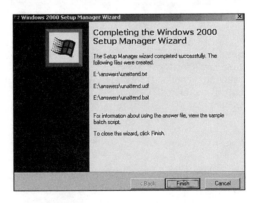

FIGURE 1.45
The Completing the Windows 2000 Setup Manager Wizard screen.

FIGURE 1.44
The Location of Setup Files screen.

The following is a sample of an answer file (answer.txt), which could
have been created using a text editor:

```
;SetupMgrTag
[Unattended]
    UnattendMode=FullUnattended
    OemPreinstall=Yes

[GuiUnattended]
    AdminPassword=PASSWORD
    TimeZone=20

[UserData]
    ProductID=111111-111111-111111-111111-111111
    FullName="Dennis T. Maione"
    OrgName="IKTHUSE Consulting Inc."

[Display]
[LicenseFilePrintData]
    AutoMode=PerServer
    AutoUsers=100

[TapiLocation]

[RegionalSettings]

[MassStorageDrivers]

[OEMBootFiles]

[OEM_Ads]

[SetupMgr]
    ComputerName0=IKTHUSE-YODA
    ComputerName1=IKTHUSE-R2D2
    ComputerName2=IKTHUSE-C3P0
    ComputerName3=IKTHUSE-DARTH
    ComputerName4=IKTHUSE-LUKE
    DistFolder=E:\W2Kserver
DistShare=W2KS

[Identification]
    JoinDomain=IKTHUSE
    CreateComputerAccountInDomain=Yes
    DomainAdmin=ADMINISTRATOR
    DomainAdminPassword=password

[Networking]
    InstallDefaultComponents=Yes
```

If you study the preceding file, you will notice that the sections
(headed by titles in square brackets) roughly correspond to the
screens where you filled in answers in the wizard.

The .udf file was created because a number of computer names were entered in the wizard. The .udf file will look something like this:

```
;SetupMgrTag
[UniqueIds]
    IKTHUSE-YODA=UserData
    IKTHUSE-R2D2=UserData
    IKTHUSE-C3P0=UserData
    IKTHUSE-DARTH=UserData
    IKTHUSE-LUKE=UserData

[IKTHUSE-YODA:UserData]
    ComputerName=IKTHUSE-YODA

[IKTHUSE-R2D2:UserData]
    ComputerName=IKTHUSE-R2D2

[IKTHUSE-C3P0:UserData]
    ComputerName=IKTHUSE-C3P0

[IKTHUSE-DARTH:UserData]
    ComputerName=IKTHUSE-DARTH

[IKTHUSE-LUKE:UserData]
    ComputerName=IKTHUSE-LUKE
```

The structure of a .udf file is like that shown above. It begins with a set of computer names under the heading [Uniqueids]. What follows is a section for each computer, with the heading [computername:UserData], and under that is the unique variable name (such as ComputerName) and the value associated with that. By using a combination of a single answer file and a single .udf file, you can avoid having to create an answer file for every machine you are going to install.

With the answer files created, your task is simply to invoke the Setup routine and indicate the answer files to use. That is the first topic in the next section.

Installing Windows 2000 Server Using Answer and Uniqueness Files

Unlike the attended forms of installation, unattended installations do not use the SETUP.EXE program. Instead they use a program called WINNT.EXE. Actually, there are two forms of that program: WINNT.EXE (which installs from DOS-based operating systems such as MS-DOS and Windows 3.x) and WINNT32.EXE (which installs from 32-bit operating systems such as Windows 9x and Windows NT).

Although WINNT/WINNT32 can be used for attended installations, its strength is in providing command-line syntax for unattended installations. It does this by providing a number of switches that control how the installation is to progress, and it allows you, among other things, to dictate the name and location of the answer and .udf files. Table 1.2 outlines the switches for WINNT and WINNT32 and their functions.

> **N O T E**
>
> **WINNT32 Is Used for All 32-bit OSs**
> It is important to note that whereas under NT 4.0, WINNT32 could only be used for installations onto other NT systems, now the functionality has been extended to all 32-bit operating systems. Therefore, although you previously had to use WINNT for Windows 95 installations, now you use WINNT32.

TABLE 1.2

SWITCHES FOR WINNT AND WINNT32

WINNT	WINNT32	Function
/a	N/A	Enables accessibility options.
/e:*command*	/cmd:*command*	Executes a command before the final phase of Setup.
/i:*inf_file*	N/A	Specifies the name of the setup information file.
/r:*folder*	/copydir:*folder*	Specifies an optional folder to be installed in the system root directory.
/rx:*folder*	/copysource:*folder*	Specifies an optional folder to be used for installations and then deleted when the installation is done.
/s:*path*	/s:*path*	Specifies the location of the installation files for Windows 2000 Server.
/t:*drive*	/tempdrive:*drive*	Specifies the location that the temporary installation files can be copied to and the location where Windows 2000 will be installed (this becomes the Boot partition).
/u:*file*	/unattend:[*num*]:[*file*]	Specifies the location of the answer file for unattended installations and the number of seconds to wait between copying the files and restarting the computer.
/udf:*file*	/udf:*id,file*	Specifies the location of the uniqueness database file for unattended installations. ID is the identifier within the UDF that defines the unique installation options for this computer.
N/A	/cmdcons	Specifies that files required for command-line repair console be installed.
N/A	/debug level:*file*	Creates a log file when conditions of certain severity occur during installation. By default level, this is 2 (warning).
N/A	/syspart:*drive*	Copies files to a hard drive and marks it as active. Used to begin installation to a hard drive, which will then be relocated to another machine (its permanent home).
N/A	/checkupgradeonly	Checks your computer to see if it can be upgraded to Windows 2000. This option does not actually perform an installation; instead, it creates a log file (winnt32.log for NT or upgrade.txt for Windows 9x), indicating the results of an upgrade.

/OX No Longer Valid   You can no longer use the /ox switch for WINNT or WINNT32 to create a Setup disk set. As outlined in Step by Step 1.3, you must use the MAKEBOOT.EXE utility for that task.

Having seen that table and the process for creating answer and .udf files, you're ready for an example. Suppose you wanted to create a batch file for the installation of a server called IKTHUSE-R2D2 from the sample answer file and .udf file shown earlier. Your batch file would look like this:

```
net use q: \\ikthuse-yoda\w2ks
net use r: \\ikthuse-yoda\answers

q:\winnt /s:q: /u:r:\answer.txt /
udf:ikthuse-r2d2,r:\answer.udf
```

This code supposes that the installation is being done from a machine that is running MS-DOS and that has network connectivity.

Although creating unattended installations using scripts is a very popular method, many people have found that other methods can be quicker and more efficient. The next section deals with disk duplication as an installation technique.

Unattended Installations Using Disk Duplication

Disk duplication, the process by which the entire hard drive of one machine is duplicated to the hard drive of another, is not a new concept. People have been doing it in one form or another for years, using third-party products like Ghost (now owned by Symantec Corporation). The idea that I can configure a machine completely (right down to all the application software I want), copy the disk, and then transfer it down to a target machine is very appealing.

The disk duplication process formalizes the steps for creating a duplicate of a hard drive and allows for automated setup using the SYSPREP.EXE program. Sysprep, like the Setup Manager, is a tool stored in the deploy.cab file (located in the \Support\Tools folder on the CD-ROM). It is recommended that you extract the Sysprep files from this .cab file into a folder called Sysprep, as outlined in Step by Step 1.7.

STEP BY STEP

1.7 Extracting and Making the Sysprep Utility Available

1. From the Windows 2000 Server CD-ROM, navigate to the \Support\Tools folder and double-click the Deploy.cab file.

2. Select the files SYSPREP.EXE, SETUPCL.EXE, and deptool.chm (the help file). Right-click any of them and choose Extract from the menu that appears.

3. When the Browse for Folder dialog box appears, browse to the location to which you want to extract the Setup Manager files (it is recommended that you use *bootpartition*\sysprep, but that is not required).

4. Create a shortcut to the SYSPREP.EXE file on the desktop and/or in the Start menu so that you can easily invoke it when required.

After you extract the Sysprep tool, you can use it to duplicate a disk. In Step by Step 1.8, which describes this process, the "master computer" is the machine you are using as a model for your disk duplicates.

STEP BY STEP

1.8 Duplicating a Disk with SYSPREP.EXE

1. Install and configure Windows 2000 on the master computer.

2. Log onto the computer as Administrator.

3. Install and configure all applications on the master computer.

4. Run SYSPREP.EXE on the master computer.

continues

continued

5. Use a disk imaging tool on it to create an image of the master computer's hard drive. A third-party tool like Norton's Ghost will have to be used for this step.

6. Copy the image onto a CD-ROM, into a network share location, or onto a hard drive to be placed into the target computer.

7. Copy the image to one or more target computers.

When the image has been transferred to a target machine, that machine is restarted and is configured through a minimum of questions to the user. One of the problems in disk duplication in the past has occurred when the information on the target machine needed to be different from that on the source machine (for example, Security Identifiers—SIDS—and computer names). Sysprep takes care of that and they are modified when the target machine is restarted.

If you want to completely automate the process, you can have Sysprep create a SYSPREP.INF file that provides answers to the setup routine that runs when the target machine is started after the disk image has been placed on it. This .INF file can make the installation completely automated (which is why this discussion falls under the topic of unattended installations).

Using SYSPREP.EXE

The role of SYSPREP.EXE is to prepare a disk for duplication. When the disk is prepared, a third-party tool can be used to copy the duplicated drive onto other machines. SYSPREP.EXE, which is run from the Tools Management console or from a command line, configures the disk image so that SIDS and other unique information are removed and ready to be re-created on the target machine. This ensures that no conflicts arise in interaction with other machines that have the same SID.

Table 1.3 outlines some additional parameters for SYSPREP.EXE that will allow you to control how it operates from a command line.

TABLE 1.3

SWITCHES FOR **SYSPREP.EXE**

Switch	*Function*
-quiet	Runs the target computer's setup with no user interaction.
-pnp	Forces the detection of Plug and Play resources on the destination computer. This ensures that any Plug and Play devices on the target computer are detected rather than simply configuring for the devices on the source computer.
-reboot	Restarts the configuration computer when Sysprep is complete rather than simply shutting it down. This will invoke the Setup program on the configuration computer and is used only when you want to verify that the setup program is going to function properly.
-nosidgen	Prevents the regeneration of SIDs on the target computer. This is useful when you are transferring the contents of one machine to another for the purposes of decommissioning the original. The new machine then becomes an exact duplicate of the first.

If you want to completely automate the installation, you will create a SYSPREP.INF file (which takes the same form as a script-based answer file) and place it into a SYSPREP folder on the C drive of your configuration computer. When the setup program runs on the target computer, it will check for this file and will use it if it's present.

Unattended Installations Using Remote Installation Services

Given the proper network configuration, remote installation of Windows 2000 is possible. Although this is an interesting topic, it must be stated at the outset that this feature will not install Windows 2000 Server, only Windows 2000 Professional. As such, it is not strictly an unattended Windows 2000 method. However, using the Remote Installation Services still falls under the category of automated Windows 2000 installations and, therefore, might find its way onto the exam.

Remote Installation Services provides a way to take control of another machine for the purpose of installing Windows 2000 Professional on it. It has advantages over other methods because you can oversee the installation, but you don't have to be at the site of the target computer. To use this service, you will run the Remote Installation Services Setup Wizard. But first you will have to verify that your network is capable of doing remote installation.

Preparing for Remote Installation

To use the Remote Installation Services, your clients must be able to support remote installation. In addition to the standard requirements for the installation of Windows 2000 Professional (Pentium 166, 32MB of RAM, and 800MB of free disk space), they also must have certain networking capabilities. One of the following three criteria must be met:

◆ The system must meet the current Network PC (Net PC) specification. This specification is the definition for what is commonly termed a "thin client." Machines of this sort generally are without floppy or CD-ROM drives and must be managed from an external source. A machine such as this must have the network adapter set as its primary boot device in the system BIOS. In addition, in order for the installation to progress properly, the user account that is used to perform the installation must be granted the "Log On As a Batch Job" right in the domain policies. Finally, users must have the ability to create computer accounts in the domain that the Windows 2000 Professional installation is joining.

◆ The system must have a network card with a Pre-Boot Execution Environment (PXE) boot ROM and a BIOS set to allow starting from the PXE boot ROM. PXE is a network card technology that allows the card to interact with the network before an actual operating system boot has been accomplished. This allows the card to obtain a TCP/IP address and be communicated to from the outside, in the example case, for the purpose of having Windows 2000 Professional installed on it. The requirements for this are that the card has a PXE boot ROM integrated into it, that the computer's BIOS be set to start from the network card, and that the user permissions be set as for the Net PC described in the previous bullet.

◆ The client must have a Remote Boot Disk available for the target machine. If the target machine is not Net PC compliant and it does not have a PXE boot ROM on its network card, you can create a remote installation boot disk. This will allow you to take control of the machine for the purpose of installing Windows 2000 Professional. You can create such a disk by running the RBFG.EXE program (found in the \RemoteInstall\Admin folder) on the RIS server. The user permissions for the target machine must be the same as for a Net PC machine.

As long as the client system meets one of the above network criteria, you can create an RIS server by running the RIS Setup Wizard as described in Step by Step 1.9.

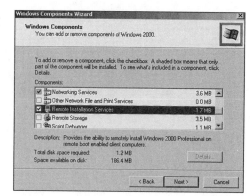

FIGURE 1.46
Select the Remote Installation Services check box.

STEP BY STEP

1.9 Creating an RIS Server

1. From the Control Panel, start the Add/Remove Programs application.

2. Click the Add/Remove Windows Components button to bring up the Windows Components Wizard.

3. Select the Remote Installation Services check box (see Figure 1.46), and then click Next to continue.

4. Click Finish to exit the Wizard.

5. When prompted, restart your server.

6. After the reboot, the Windows 2000 Configure Your Server window should appear. If it does, click the Finish Setup link to configure RIS (see Figure 1.47). If it does not, click the Start button, choose Run, and then type **risetup** to enter the Configuration Wizard (skip to step 8).

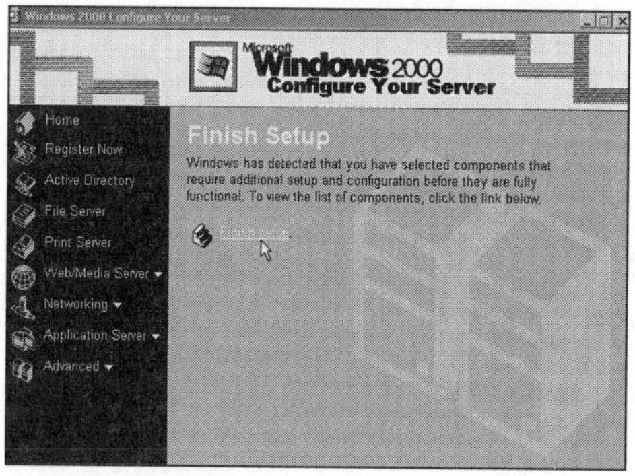

FIGURE 1.47
Click the Finish Setup link to complete the RIS setup.

continues

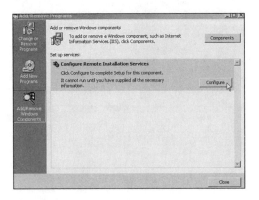

FIGURE 1.48
Clicking the Configure button will bring up the
Configuration dialog box for RIS.

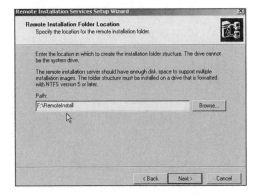

FIGURE 1.49
Specify the location for the installation folder.

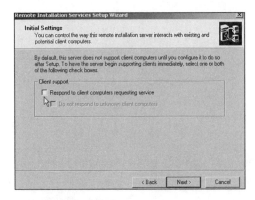

FIGURE 1.50
It is recommended that you do not activate
RIS at this point.

continued

7. When the Add/Remove Programs window appears,
click the Configure button next to the RIS entry (see
Figure 1.48).

8. At the Remote Installation Services Setup Wizard screen,
click the Next button to continue.

9. In the Remote Installation Folder Location screen, enter
the path for the Remote Install folder (see Figure 1.49).
This location must be on an NTFS partition, and it cannot be the system (active) partition.

10. From the Initial Settings screen, you can choose to activate
RIS immediately (see Figure 1.50). Although it is possible
to do so, it is recommended that you wait until configuration is complete before you activate it. Click Next to
continue.

11. At the Installation Source Files Location screen (see
Figure 1.51), enter the path to the Windows 2000
Professional source files. Click Next to continue.

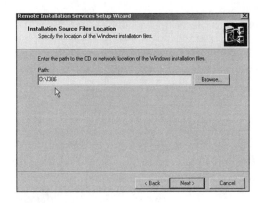

FIGURE 1.51
Specify the location of the source files for
installation.

12. On the Windows Installation Image Folder Name screen (see Figure 1.52), enter the name for the folder you want Setup to create to hold the Windows 2000 Professional source files. Click Next to continue.

13. At the Friendly Description and Help Text screen (see Figure 1.53), enter a description for the end user to allow him or her to correctly identify the installation desired. You can also add help text if desired. Then click Next.

14. At the Review Settings screen, click Finish to complete the setup. The setup program displays the dialog box shown in Figure 1.54 as it finishes the configuration.

Configuration for many machines will be done via BIOS settings. However, if your computer does not conform to the Net PC or the PXE standards, you will have to create a Remote Boot Disk. The following Step by Step outlines that procedure.

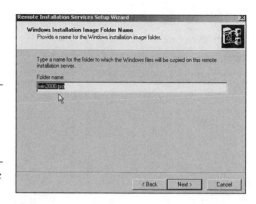

FIGURE 1.52

Provide a name for the folder where you want to place the installation files.

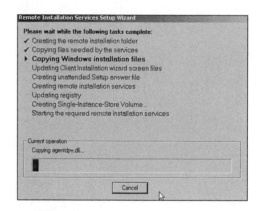

FIGURE 1.54

Setup completes the configuration process, indicating the progress as it goes.

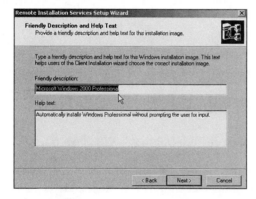

FIGURE 1.53

Type in a description for the installation created with this process.

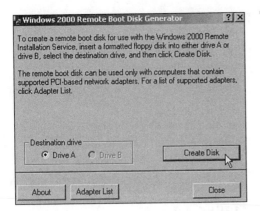

FIGURE 1.55
Click Create Disk to begin the process.

STEP BY STEP

1.10 Creating a Remote Boot Disk

1. From your RIS server, run RBFG.EXE which is found in the \RemoteInstall\admin\i386 folder. (The actual path will depend on how you filled in the field in step 9 of Step by Step 1.9).

2. Insert a formatted disk into the floppy drive.

3. At the Windows 2000 Remote Boot Disk Generator screen, click the Create Disk button to begin disk generation (see Figure 1.55).

4. When the process is complete, remove the disk and label it "Remote Boot Disk."

From the client side, the machine will then boot, and it will seek out the RIS server and download the list of images to choose from. Then installation begins.

UPGRADING AN NT 4.0 MEMBER SERVER TO WINDOWS 2000

Upgrade a server from Microsoft Windows NT 4.0.

In the early stages of the deployment of Windows 2000 worldwide, the scenario of upgrade from NT 4.0 to Windows 2000 will arise frequently. Fortunately, the upgrade of an NT 4.0 member server to a Windows 2000 member server is very straightforward. Moreover, unlike the upgrade of domain controllers, you do not have to worry about when in the total domain upgrade you change over your member servers. A Windows 2000 member server can reside comfortably in a workgroup, an NT 4.0 domain, or a Windows 2000 domain.

There are two main ways of upgrading an NT 4.0 Server to Windows 2000. You can use the setup program from a network share or from a local CD-ROM (attended), or you can use the WINNT32 program from a network share (unattended).

STEP BY STEP

1.11 Performing an Attended Upgrade of an NT 4.0 Member Server to Windows 2000

1. From the Windows 2000 CD-ROM, run SETUP.EXE.

2. When asked if you want to upgrade to Windows 2000, click Yes to continue (see Figure 1.56).

3. In the Welcome to the Windows 2000 Setup Wizard screen, choose Upgrade to Windows 2000 (Recommended) and click Next (see Figure 1.57).

4. In the License Agreement screen (see Figure 1.58), choose I Accept This Agreement and click Next.

5. In the Report System Compatibility screen (see Figure 1.59), you will be informed about any services that might not function properly when the upgrade is complete. Those services that might be problematic are disabled by the Setup program. On this screen, you can see more details about the problems that might occur (click Details), or you can export the report to a text file for detailed investigation later (click Save As). Click the Next button when you are satisfied that the areas identified will not pose any major problems.

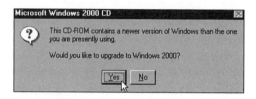

FIGURE 1.56
Confirm that you want to upgrade your machine to Windows 2000.

FIGURE 1.57
Confirm that you want to upgrade rather than install a fresh copy of Windows 2000.

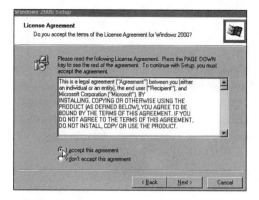

FIGURE 1.58
You have to accept the license agreement to continue.

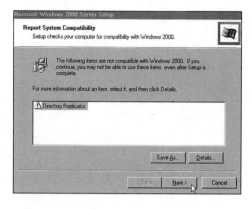

FIGURE 1.59
A report is generated to warn you of possible system problems that might occur when the upgrade is complete.

The setup program will copy files onto your hard drive and then restart your computer. A text mode will take care of copying files and preparing for the GUI setup. When this phase is complete, the computer will restart.

After restarting, the server will enter text mode where it will copy files. When that is complete, the server will again reboot and enter GUI mode. If you requested for your Boot partition to be converted to NTFS, after the first reboot, the conversion will take place and Windows 2000 will reboot again.

After restarting, your server will again enter GUI mode, where it will perform hardware detection and network configuration. After a brief pause (which you can avoid by clicking Next), Windows 2000 Components will be installed. When that is complete, final tasks (like configuring the Start menu and removing temporary files) are taken care of and, when the upgrade is complete, the server reboots.

Unattended upgrades can be performed using WINNT32.EXE from a network share. You have two primary options when installing. First, you can use an answer file and a .udf just like you would with a regular unattended installation. In this case, you can use the same wizard to help you create these files (see Step by Step 1.6). Second, you could use WINNT32.EXE with the /unattend switch. This switch indicates that the installation is to progress without user input and that the answers to the setup questions are to be provided by looking at (and duplicating) the current NT 4.0 configuration. For simple upgrades, this is the easiest method.

DEPLOYING SERVICE PACKS

Deploy service packs.

Microsoft's vision of the future of software upgrades revolves around service packs. A service pack is an executable that provides for the replacement of one set of files with another. In the case of an operating system (like NT 4.0), service packs have been a way to distribute bug fixes and fixes to security holes. However, beginning with NT 4.0's Service Pack 4, Microsoft began to release upgrades and additions to operating system functionality. For example, Service Pack 4 introduced the Microsoft Management Console for the purposes of providing an integrated security interface.

With Windows 2000, Microsoft's plan is to release services packs on a regular schedule to fix bugs or security flaws. This plan is designed to keep the size of service packs to a manageable level.

In many regards, Windows 2000 service packs are not very different from Windows NT 4.0 service packs. When they are released, the intent is for you to install the service pack on all your Windows 2000 computers in order to implement any fixes included in them. However, one significant improvement has been made in the application of services packs: That is the concept of *slipstreaming*.

Before you can understand slipstreaming, a digression into service packs on NT 4.0 is necessary. Under NT, if you installed a service pack, you had to ensure that if you made modifications to the operating system that involved reading files from the CD or a network share, you subsequently reinstalled the service pack. This was because the files found on the CD or in the network share were pre-service pack versions, and re-application was necessary to ensure that all components of the operating system were up to the current service pack.

Slipstreaming makes this unnecessary. With slipstreaming, changes from the service pack can be applied to the source files found on a local folder or network share (by using the /slip switch when running UPDATE.EXE for the service pack). This means that when you subsequently access those files, you will obtain the fixed versions of those files, not the old ones. This saves time because it means that the service packs will have to be applied to any machine only once (provided that it uses a network share as its installation source) and not multiple times as services (and other operating system components) are installed. In addition, this also means that new installations over the network will also automatically be up-to-date with the current service pack.

It must be noted that slipstreaming does not remove the need to install the service pack on each machine. What it does remove is the need to install the service pack on fresh Windows 2000 installations and the need to install the service pack after making operating system changes.

As of this writing, there were no service packs to install, so the only things you can use for concrete demonstration are the services packs for NT 4.0. However, that knowledge can be applied to service packs under Windows 2000.

In the standard service pack installation, two major things happen. First, the files that are going to be replaced are copied into a backup directory so that the installation can be reversed if necessary. Although this is an optional process prompted for by the service pack installation routine, it is always recommended that you use it. Second, the service pack replaces the operating system files that it finds installed on the target system with the new versions of those files.

Step by Step 1.12 covers the recommended procedure for installing a service pack.

STEP BY STEP

1.12 Installing a Service Pack

1. Install the service pack using the setup program.

2. Back up the existing files by choosing that option in the Service Pack installation setup program.

3. Reboot your computer to allow the changes to take effect.

If you update the network share holding your Windows 2000 files, the above procedure is all that is necessary. However, if you do not install from a network share, you will also need to reapply the service pack to individual machines after every modification of the operating system (this includes the installation of drivers and services).

TROUBLESHOOTING FAILED INSTALLATIONS

Troubleshoot failed installations.

Unfortunately, installations of Windows 2000 Server sometimes fail. A variety of factors might cause such a thing to happen. As a system administrator, you need to know as much about the causes for failure as you can to ensure that you can quickly recover from such a failure.

Most problems with installation are caused by an installer not following the correct procedures. Granted, some failures are caused by faulty media. However, those are the exception, not the rule. In general, if you follow the procedures outlined to this point in the chapter, you will have successful installations.

If there is any question about any of your hardware or software being Windows 2000 compatible, it is recommended that you run the upgrade check tool, which is part of the WINNT32 program. Executing `WINNT32 /checkupgradeonly` from the Windows 2000 Server CD-ROM will generate a report telling you about possible issues. This report details hardware that may not work without new drivers and software that is not Windows 2000 compatible, that might not be Windows 2000 compatible, or that needs to be reinstalled after the upgrade. It also will identify system settings that will not function the way they used to or that will be disabled by the setup routine. If you have many servers, you are advised to run the upgrade check on a representative sample of your servers so you can anticipate problems and, using hardware and/or software upgrades, pre-empt them.

The most frequent reasons for failure are listed here:

◆ *Minimum hardware requirements are not met.* Windows 2000 Server has minimum hardware requirements that must be met in order for installation to be complete. If the processor is too slow, there is not sufficient RAM, or the amount of free disk space is insufficient, you will have to upgrade your server before installation can continue. This may be the case even when you are upgrading from NT 4.0 because of the increased minimums in these areas.

◆ *Hardware is not on the HCL.* If hardware is not on the HCL, it may not be detected and installed properly. If the hardware is a network card, you might not be able to contact a domain controller or a network server, and the installation may fail. Check the Microsoft HCL Web site and run the upgrade check to see if there are going to be any HCL problems.

◆ *Media errors.* If there seems to be a problem with the Windows 2000 Server Installation CD-ROM, contact your software vendor to request a replacement.

◆ *Failure of dependency service to start.* At installation, this error is most often caused by an improperly configured network adapter. Make sure that the hardware is detected properly, and then manually change properties if required.

◆ *Inability to connect to the domain controller.* If you are joining a domain, you will have to contact a domain controller to create or check for a computer account. Ensure that the correct name has been given for the domain and that a domain controller can be contacted from your location.

◆ *Automated installation fails.* Check the parameters you specified for the installation. If you got information incorrect or if you manually created or modified the answer file or .udf file, you might have introduced errors.

◆ *RIS installation fails.* Verify that you have correctly configured the RIS server and that its services have started. Make sure the client meets the client criteria, and confirm that the network is functioning properly.

CASE STUDY: WHIPPETS AND WIDGETS

ESSENCE OF THE CASE

This case requires that the following end results be satisfied:

▶ Configure 15 identical Windows 2000 servers

▶ Make the configuration of the above servers as simple as possible and as quick as possible

▶ Find a way to save the configuration to allow for similar installations to be performed in the future

SCENARIO

Whippets and Widgets is a dog breeding and metal fabrication company (built from the dreams of the founders, Edna and Rodger Coombs). In business for 30 years, they have created 15 small offices in the towns surrounding Kalamazoo, Michigan, where they have their Head Office location. Edna hired Arnold last year to take over their network, which had grown too complex for Rodger (a career dog breeder and computer hacker) to manage on his own. The current network infrastructure comprises a domain controller at the Head Office that is used to authenticate login for all the Windows 95 and 98 users in the branch offices.

Arnold realizes that the idea of logging in over a WAN is not very good, but he has been given another job: to install file and print servers at each of the 15 branch locations. Because he will have free reign to purchase the new equipment, he has decided to purchase identical machines for all locations. His problem is that he needs an effective way of installing software on each machine without the tedium of manually configuring each one. He would also like to be able to configure any number of additional machines with the same configuration should the need arise.

CASE STUDY: WHIPPETS AND WIDGETS

ANALYSIS

Given Arnold's problem, it is obvious that he needs some kind of automated installation solution. The tedium of installing 15 machines manually would probably bore him to death, not to mention take up a lot of his time. In addition, a manual installation would have to be well-documented to be repeated in the future. If he could create an unattended installation, he could ensure that the servers are installed while he performs some other task. In addition, if he configures an unattended installation, he can use that configuration in the future on any new machines the company purchases.

Because he wants to set up an unattended installation, Arnold must look at the different methods available. Although an RIS solution is possible, it typically needs specialized configuration and perhaps specialized hardware that will not have any lasting benefit. Therefore, his best bet is either a scripted installation from a network share (using unattended answer files

and a uniqueness database file) or a solution that uses Disk Duplication (through the Sysprep program and a third-party imaging program like Norton's Ghost) to distribute disk images to the destination machines.

Both of these solutions are acceptable; actually, a combination of the two is probably the best way to go. Because the machines are all identical, they are perfect candidates for the use of Sysprep and disk duplication. However, if Arnold purchases new equipment in the future that is not identical, the master disk created here will probably not work. If, however, he creates a scripted installation (which makes use of Plug and Play to detect hardware), he can be sure that the master computer used to create the disk for duplication is identical to the current master. Therefore, every time he purchases new hardware (which is different from the current standard), he can simply use the script to install and then create a new master for that series of machines.

The following table summarizes the solution.

OVERVIEW OF THE REQUIREMENTS AND SOLUTIONS IN THIS CASE STUDY

Requirement	Solution Provided By
Configure 15 identical servers.	Unattended installation using answer files to configure the master and using disk duplication to configure the additional machines.
Make the configuration simple and quick.	Disk duplication to configure multiple identical machines.
Save the configuration for future use.	Unattended installation using answer files to configure a new master, and then using disk duplication to configure additional machines matching the hardware profile.

CHAPTER SUMMARY

This chapter discussed the main installation topics you will encounter on the Windows 2000 Server exam. These included attended and unattended installations, upgrades from NT 4.0, service pack deployment, and installation troubleshooting.

Each of these is important not only from an exam perspective (you must know them to pass), but also from the perspective of System Administrators or Technicians who are going to install Windows 2000.

For one-time (or unique) installations, knowledge of attended installations is required. You have to be able to start the installation given a number of machine-specific circumstances, and you have to be able to answer the questions asked by the setup program.

For multiple installations on similar platforms, unattended installations will make your life much easier. By setting up and deploying unattended installations, you can save time, make yourself more productive, and avoid repetitive work.

If you are migrating from an existing NT 4.0 implementation, you need to understand the implications of upgrading and the mechanics of the upgrade process. This will help you avoid some painful mistakes in the process.

As Windows 2000 matures, you will also need to be able to install service packs. In the future, this procedure will become part of regular server maintenance.

Finally, you have to be able to troubleshoot if your installation fails. Mostly, this means understanding how things should function when everything is okay. However, you will also need to be able to adapt to things going wrong and quickly diagnose and repair problems.

KEY TERMS

Before taking the exam, make sure you are comfortable with the definitions and concepts for each of the following key terms.

- member server
- HCL
- System partition
- Boot partition
- attended installation
- unattended installation
- computer account
- WINNT
- WINNT32
- MAKEBOOT
- MAKEBT32
- setup disks
- unattended answer file
- Uniqueness Database File (UDF)
- Setup Manager
- Sysprep
- Remote Installation Services (RIS)
- Remote Boot Disk
- service pack
- slipstreaming

APPLY YOUR KNOWLEDGE

Exercises

1.1   Creating an NT Setup Disk Set

In this exercise, you learn how to create the four-disk set required for installing Windows 2000 Server and required for repairing your server using the Emergency Repair Disk (discussed in Chapter 4, "Managing, Monitoring, and Optimizing System Performance, Reliability, and Availability"). This will introduce you to one of the fundamental installation and repair tools that you will always need to keep on hand. To complete this exercise you will need the following items:

- The Windows 2000 Server CD-ROM or the files on an accessible local or shared location

- Four floppy disks

Estimated Time: 10 minutes

1. Insert the Windows 2000 Server CD-ROM into the CD-ROM drive of a Windows machine.

2. From the Start menu, choose Run. In the dialog box that appears, type the following:

    <CD-DRIVE>:\BOOTDISK\MAKEBT32

    where *<CD-DRIVE>* is the letter of your CD-ROM drive.

3. When prompted, type the letter of your floppy drive.

4. Label a disk *Windows 2000 Setup Boot Disk*. When prompted, insert it into the floppy drive and press Enter. The disk's contents will be overwritten.

5. Label a disk *Windows 2000 Setup Disk #2*. When prompted, insert it into the floppy drive and press Enter.

6. Label a disk *Windows 2000 Setup Disk #3*. When prompted, insert it into the floppy drive and press Enter.

7. Label a disk *Windows 2000 Setup Disk #4*. When prompted, insert it into the floppy drive and press Enter.

8. When the process is complete, remove the final disk in preparation for Exercise 1.2.

1.2   Installing a Windows 2000 Member Server in a Windows 2000 Domain

This exercise shows you how to install Windows 2000 Server in the role of a member server. Be aware that because hardware configuration varies from system to system, you will need to know how Windows 2000 references network adapter drivers and video drivers on your particular system. To complete this exercise, you will need the following items:

- A computer capable of supporting Windows 2000 Server (with a CD-ROM drive)

- The four setup disks you created in Exercise 1.1

- The Windows 2000 Server CD-ROM

Estimated Time: 45 minutes

This exercise assumes that the machine you are installing on has a hard drive (of 3GB or larger) that has no partitions on it. As a result, the process will create partitions and format them. If that is not the case, you will have to adapt some of the steps and skip others.

1. Power off your machine, insert Disk 1 of the four-disk set, and turn the machine back on.

2. When prompted, insert Disk #2 and press Enter to continue.

3. When prompted, insert Disk #3 and press Enter to continue.

4. When prompted, insert Disk #4 and press Enter to continue.

5. When presented with the Welcome to Setup screen, press Enter to begin the installation.

6. When presented with the License Agreement, press F8 to agree and continue.

7. When presented with the partition screen, press C to create a new partition and enter a size of 2000MB. When the partition has been created, press Enter to install Windows 2000 on it.

8. When prompted for the file system, select NTFS and press Enter to continue.

9. When prompted, remove the final setup disk to prepare for system restart and GUI mode.

10. When prompted, click Next to continue (if you do not respond, Setup will continue anyway).

11. When prompted for Regional Settings, leave them at default and click Next to continue.

12. When prompted for your name and company, fill those fields in and click Next.

13. When prompted for the product key, locate that key on your Windows 2000 Server CD-ROM case and type it into the fields. Click Next to continue.

14. When prompted for licensing information, leave the mode at Per Server and enter the number of licenses you have (default of 5 is sufficient for our purposes). Click Next to continue.

15. When prompted for a computer name, type **WIN2000S**. Type the password **password** into the two password fields. Click Next to continue.

16. When prompted for components to install, deselect everything except Accessories and Utilities. Click Next to continue.

17. If you're prompted for modem information, select your country, type in your area code, and then click Next.

18. When you're prompted for date and time, fill in the fields and click Next to continue.

19. When you're prompted for network settings, *if you have a DHCP server on your network,* select Typical Settings, click Next to continue, and move to step 24. Otherwise, follow steps 20 through 23.

20. Choose Custom Settings and click Next.

21. Double-click Internet Protocol (TCP/IP).

22. In the Internet Protocol (TCP/IP) Properties dialog box, select Use the Following IP Address and use the following values: IP Address = 10.10.10.1; Subnet mask = 255.255.255.0; Default gateway = leave blank.

23. Click OK to complete the TCP/IP configuration.

24. When you're prompted for workgroup or domain membership, select Yes, Make This Computer a Member of the Following Domain and type in the name of the domain that is set up on your LAN. If you do not have a domain at your location, you will have to choose a workgroup. Click Next to continue.

APPLY YOUR KNOWLEDGE

25. When you're prompted to complete installation, click Finish.

26. When prompted, log in as Administrator.

27. When the Configure Your Server dialog box appears, close it.

1.3 Using Setup Manager to Create an Installation Script

This exercise shows you how to install the Setup Manager and how to create an installation script for installing Windows 2000 Server in an unattended setup. To complete this exercise you will need the following:

- A Windows 2000 server
- The Windows 2000 Server CD-ROM

Estimated Time: 45 minutes

1. On the Windows 2000 Server CD-ROM, navigate to the \SUPPORT\TOOLS\ folder and double-click the DEPLOY.CAB file.

2. Select the files SETUPMGR.EXE and SETUP-MGX.DLL, right-click either of them, and choose Extract from the menu that appears.

3. In the Browse for Folder dialog box, browse to *systemroot*\system32 and click OK to extract to that location.

4. Navigate to the *systemroot*\system32 folder and, having selected SETUPMGR.EXE, copy it to the Clipboard.

5. Right-click the Start menu button and select Open All Users from the popup menu. In the window that appears, navigate to

\Programs\Administrative Tools, right-click in the window, and choose Paste Shortcut from the popup menu.

6. Rename the shortcut you just created to Setup Manager, and then close the windows you have opened during this process.

7. Create a shortcut to the SETUPMGR.EXE file on the desktop and/or in the Start menu so that you can easily invoke it when required.

8. From the Start menu, choose Programs, Administrative Tools, Setup Manager.

9. At the Welcome to the Windows 2000 Setup Manager Wizard screen, click Next.

10. At the New or Existing Answer File screen, accept the default of Create a New Answer File and click Next.

11. At the Product to Install screen, choose Windows 2000 Unattended Installation and click Next.

12. At the Platform screen, choose Windows 2000 Server and click Next.

13. At the User Interaction Level screen, choose Fully Automated and click Next.

14. At the License Agreement screen, click the check box and click Next.

15. At the Customize the Software screen, fill in your name and organization and click Next.

16. At the Licensing Mode screen, choose Per Server and enter **5** as the number of concurrent connections. Then click Next.

17. At the Computer Names screen, type **AutoServer** and click Add. Then click Next.

18. At the Administrator Password screen, type **password** into both fields and click Next.

19. At the Display Settings screen, leave the defaults and click Next.

20. At the Network Settings screen, leave the default of Typical Settings and click Next.

21. At the Workgroup or Domain screen, select Windows Server Domain and type in a Domain name (any one will do for this exercise). Click Next to continue.

22. At the Time Zone screen, select your time zone and click Next to continue.

23. At the Additional Settings screen, select No, Do Not Edit the Additional Settings and click Next.

24. At the Distribution Folder screen, choose Yes, Create or Modify a Distribution Folder and click Next.

25. At the Distribution Folder Name screen, type in the path to a location where you can create a new folder (for example, c:\win2000dist) and type **Win2000** as the share name. Click Next to continue.

26. On the Additional Mass Storage Drivers screen, click Next.

27. On the Hardware Abstraction Layer screen, click Next.

28. On the Additional Commands screen, click Next.

29. On the OEM Branding screen, click Next.

30. On the Additional Files or Folders screen, click Next.

31. On the Answer File Name screen, leave the location and filename set to the default and click Next.

32. On the Location of Setup Files screen, leave the selection at Copy the Files from CD and click Next.

33. When the Setup Manager Wizard finishes copying the files, click Next.

34. When the Completing the Windows 2000 Setup Manager Wizard screen appears, note the files it has created, and then click Finish to exit.

1.4 Upgrading a Windows NT 4.0 Member Server to Windows 2000

This exercise shows you an upgrade from Windows NT 4.0 Server. It is assumed that you have a server to upgrade, so the procedure begins from that point. To complete this exercise, you will need the following items:

- A Windows NT 4.0 member server with a CD-ROM drive
- The Windows 2000 Server CD-ROM

Estimated Time: 45 minutes

1. From the Windows 2000 CD-ROM, run SETUP.EXE (this may happen automatically if your CD-ROM is set to Autorun).

2. When you're asked to upgrade to Windows 2000, click Yes.

3. In the Welcome to Windows 2000 Setup Wizard screen, choose Upgrade to Windows 2000 and click Next.

APPLY YOUR KNOWLEDGE

4. In the License Agreement screen, choose I Accept This Agreement and click Next.

5. In the Your Product Key screen, type in the 25-character product key from the jewel case of your Windows 2000 Server CD-ROM, and then click Next.

6. If the Report System Compatibility screen appears, click Next to continue.

7. Allow the upgrade to continue on its own.

The setup program will copy files onto your hard drive and restart your computer. A text mode will take care of copying files and preparing for the GUI setup. When this phase is complete, the computer will restart.

After restart, the server will enter text mode, where it will copy files. When that process is complete, the server will again reboot and will enter GUI mode. If your Boot partition was not originally NTFS and you requested that it be converted, after the first reboot the conversion will take place, and Windows 2000 will reboot again.

Your server will again enter GUI mode, where it will perform hardware detection and network configuration. After a brief pause (which you can avoid by clicking Next), Windows 2000 components will be installed. When that process is complete, final tasks (like configuring the Start menu and removing temporary files) are handled. The server then reboots.

Review Questions

1. What three methods can be used to begin Windows 2000 Server setup, and under what circumstances is each one used?

2. What program is used to aid you in creating automated setup scripts, and where is it found?

3. What is the purpose of a service pack, and where can you get the latest one?

4. What are the minimum hardware requirements (processor, RAM, and free disk space) for installing Windows 2000 Server?

5. What are the three unattended installation methods discussed in this chapter, and how do they work (provide a general overview)?

6. What does the term "member server" mean, and what are the network requirements for configuring one?

Exam Questions

1. You are a technician in a large IT department. You have a Windows NT 4.0 member server with the following hardware specifications: RAM=256MB; Processor=Compaq Alpha; Hard Drive=20GB; Free Space=1GB. You are trying to upgrade to Windows 2000 member server, but the installation fails every time.

Which of the following is a reason your upgrade will fail?

APPLY YOUR KNOWLEDGE

A. Windows 2000 requires 256MB of RAM to install on an Alpha processor.

B. Windows 2000 cannot be upgraded from Windows NT 4.0, it must be reinstalled.

C. Windows 2000 requires 1.5GB of free disk space for installation.

D. Windows 2000 is not supported on the Alpha platform.

2. You are the system administrator of a large Windows 2000 network. The current installation base includes 500 clients running Windows 2000 Professional, 3 domain controllers running Windows 2000 Advanced Server, and 5 member servers providing Application, Print, File, and Web services. You need to install Windows 2000 Professional on 500 more client machines in the next month.

What should you do in order to be able to deploy these clients without using any additional non-Microsoft software? (Choose two.)

A. Use Setup Manager to create scripted installations and deploy them with batch files on the local machines.

B. Create and deploy disk images using the Sysprep utility.

C. Use the Setup Manager to create scripted installations and deploy them using the RIS service.

D. Use the WinDiff utility to create scripted installations and deploy them with batch files on the local machines.

3. You are a hardware vendor who sells Windows operating systems with your products. You are creating scripted installations for your technicians

to run on the machines they are configuring. You want to ensure that the text-based setup is completely automated but that the graphical portion prompts the owners of the machines for all their specific information. The dialog box shown in Figure 1.60 appears when you are using the Setup Manager to create your scripts.

How will you change this screen to ensure that the scripts meet your specifications?

A. Change to Provide Defaults.

B. Change to Hide Pages.

C. Change to Read Only.

D. Change to GUI Attended.

4. Emma is a system administrator for a company that is currently implementing a Windows 2000 infrastructure. The company has 5 regional offices across North America (2 in Canada and 3 in the United States), and they are all interconnected with T1 lines. Having set up a domain controller, Emma is about to configure 10 servers with identical hardware including 256MB RAM, two 18GB IDE hard drives, and dual Pentium III 600Mhz processors. These servers, which will all end up in one of the five regional offices, are intended to perform a variety of functions, including Web Service, File and Print Service, and Application Service.

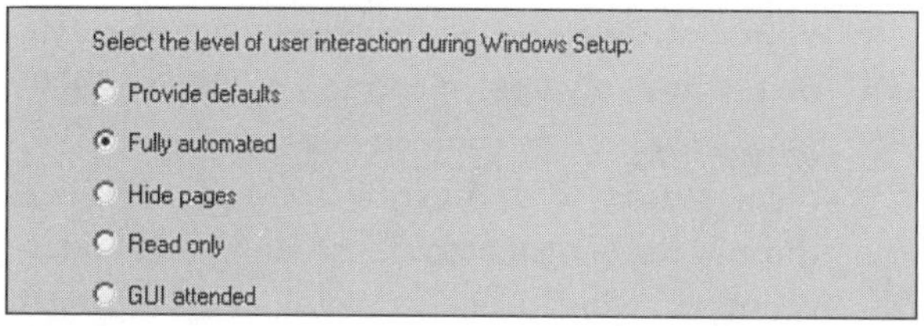

FIGURE 1.60
Use this figure with question 3.

APPLY YOUR KNOWLEDGE

Required Result:

Servers are all to be installed with Windows 2000 Server.

Optional Desired Results:

Servers are installed with a minimum amount of effort at their destination sites.

Servers should be able to be configured by summer interns with a minimum of training or experience with Windows 2000 Server.

Servers end up as members of the domain.

Proposed Solution:

Emma will install and configure each of the servers by connecting them to the LAN at the Head Office where she works. She will set them up as member servers by configuring each with a computer account in the domain.

Which results will the proposed solution produce?

A. The proposed solution produces the required result and all the optional results.

B. The proposed solution produces the required result but only one of the optional results.

C. The proposed solution produces the required result but only two of the optional results.

D. The proposed solution does not produce the required result.

5. Emma is a system administrator for a company that is currently implementing a Windows 2000 infrastructure. The company has five regional offices across North America (two in Canada and three in the United States), and they are all interconnected with T1 lines. Having set up a domain controller, she is about to configure 10 servers with identical hardware including 256MB RAM, two 18GB IDE hard drives, and dual PIII 600Mhz processors. These servers, which will all end up in one of the five regional offices, are intended to perform a variety of functions including Web Service, File and Print Service, and Application Service.

Required Result:

Servers are all installed with Windows 2000 Server.

Optional Desired Results:

Servers are all to be installed with a minimum amount of effort at their destination sites.

Servers should be able to be configured by summer interns with a minimum of training or experience with Windows 2000 Server.

Servers end up as members of the domain.

Proposed Solution:

Emma will use Setup Manager to create unattended text files and uniqueness database files for each of the computers. These files will include configuration settings for completely setting up the machines, including adding them to the domain. The servers will be shipped to their permanent sites, and then a student working at each site will run a batch file that will begin the automated setup routine.

Which results will the proposed solution produce?

A. The proposed solution produces the required result and all the optional results.

B. The proposed solution produces the required result but only one of the optional results.

APPLY YOUR KNOWLEDGE

C. The proposed solution produces the required result but only two of the optional results.

D. The proposed solution does not produce the required result.

6. Gary is the system administrator in a Microsoft Certified Technical Education Center. He manages the hardware and software on 90 Intel-based PCs that students use for both application and technical training. Gary has a dedicated file server to which all the machines in his center can connect. In the course of his job, Gary has a need to install Windows 2000 Server on one or more computers. The configuration of these machines is rarely the same, but he sometimes installs ten or more computers at once. He is looking for the most effective way of making the Windows 2000 installation files available for installation to any of these 90 machines.

What should Gary do to implement the best solution?

A. Gary should create a share on a file server and copy the contents of the CD-ROM to that share.

B. Gary should purchase a CD-ROM writer and create 10 copies of the Windows 2000 CD.

C. Gary should put the content of the Windows 2000 CD-ROM onto 10 floppy disk sets.

D. Gary should keep one copy of the CD-ROM and install his servers one at a time with that copy.

7. You are an administrator for a company with a 20-computer LAN. Currently, your network has one Windows NT 4.0 domain controller, one Windows NT 4.0 member server, and 18 Windows 98 client computers. You want to upgrade your NT 4.0 servers to Windows 2000 Server, but you do not know whether your hardware and software will be compatible with Windows 2000.

Which course of action is best?

A. Back up both servers, run the upgrade, and if it fails, restore from backup.

B. Check the hardware in the machines against the HCL on the Microsoft Web site; check the hardware resources (RAM, processor, disk space) against the minimum requirements published in this book; run WINNT32 with the /checkupgradeonly switch; back up the servers and, if all goes okay, run the upgrade.

C. Run the upgrade process. If it fails, Setup will inform you and abort without causing any damage.

D. Check the hardware in the machines against the HCL on the Microsoft Web site; check the hardware resources (RAM, processor, disk space) against the minimum requirements published in this book; run WINNT32 with the /verifyupgradability switch; back up the servers and, if all goes okay, run the upgrade.

APPLY YOUR KNOWLEDGE

8. Pauline is the administrator of a large Windows 2000-based network. She oversees the maintenance of 20 Windows 2000 servers. All her servers were installed from network shares. Which of the following are benefits of the new service pack slipstreaming functionality if it is used properly?

   A. It will ensure that she will not have to install service packs on her currently existing servers.

   B. It will ensure that she will not have to reinstall service packs on her servers after service installation.

   C. It will ensure that she will not have to install service packs on new servers after initial installation.

   D. It will ensure that new versions of Windows will be incrementally available; she will not ever have to upgrade her servers to a new version of Windows.

9. Alexander is a computer technician in a small company. He is responsible for the installation and maintenance of hardware and software. He has just received a new server on which he wants to install Windows 2000 Server, but it has no partitions or operating systems installed on it.

   Of the following, which techniques will he be able to use to install Windows 2000 Server on this computer? (Choose two.)

   A. Configure the BIOS to boot from a CD-ROM, insert the Windows 2000 CD in the drive, and restart.

   B. Create a RIS disk and install over the network.

   C. Use a set of four Setup disks and the CD-ROM.

   D. Use the WINNT program over the network.

   E. Perform a push install using SMS.

10. Noah is a system administrator in an international company. He has a Windows 98 computer with 256MB of RAM, a 4GB hard drive, and a Pentium II processor. He has a need for a Web server and wants to install Windows 2000 Server on his computer. The hard drive on his computer currently has two partitions, both of which are formatted with FAT32.

    What does Noah need to do to install Windows 2000 Server on this computer?

    A. He needs to format the partitions with FAT16.

    B. He needs to format the partitions with NTFS.

    C. He needs to upgrade the RAM to 128MB and the hard drive to at least 8GB.

    D. Nothing; he can install Windows 2000 Server on this machine just the way it is.

11. Debra is a salesperson in a small car dealership. The network security structure was just upgraded from a Windows 2000 Professional Workgroup to a Windows 2000 Server domain. Despite the addition of a domain controller to the network, she can only log in to her local machine.

    Of the following, what needs to be configured to allow Debra to log onto the domain?

    A. A computer account needs to be created for her machine in the domain.

    B. She needs to log on using an Administrative password.

C. She needs to add a second network card connected directly to the domain controller.

D. A Windows 2000 Professional machine cannot be configured to log into a Windows 2000 Server domain.

12. Bubba is the only IT professional in his company. He works in a small department that has a Windows 98 workgroup. He has just received a new computer with nothing on the hard drives. He wants to install Windows 2000 Server to make it a file and print server, and he has the Windows 2000 Server CD-ROM. Due to miscommunication, the BIOS has been configured with a password, and he cannot set up the machine to boot from the CD-ROM. He needs to create a set of setup disks to begin the installation of Windows 2000.

How can he accomplish this?

A. Bubba needs to find another Windows 2000 server on which to run the MAKEBT32 program from his Windows 2000 CD.

B. Bubba needs to find another Windows 2000 computer (Server or Professional) on which to run WINNT32 with the /ox switch from his Windows 2000 CD.

C. Bubba can use any of his Windows 98 computers and run the MAKEBOOT program from his Windows 2000 CD.

D. Bubba can use any of his Windows 98 computers and run the MAKEBT32 program from his Windows 2000 CD.

13. Angela is the Windows 2000 network administrator in a school. She had been running Windows 2000 for six months when the first service pack came out. At that time, she installed the service pack on all her Windows 2000 servers, allowing the install process to back up the old configuration before proceeding with the installation. In addition, she also used slipstreaming on her network share as was recommended by Microsoft. Now she wants to install a new service on one of the machines. What steps reflect the best way to ensure that the service is covered by the service pack?

A. She should install the service using the CD-ROM as the source and then reapply the service pack.

B. She should install the service using the network share as the source and then reapply the service pack.

C. She should install the service using the network share as the source (there is no need to reapply the service pack).

D. She should uninstall the service pack, install the service using the CD-ROM as the source, and then reapply the service pack.

14. Albert is a system administrator tasked with implementing a RIS installation procedure. Of the following hardware, which is most critical in his client computer to deploy installation using RIS?

A. The network card must be RIS compliant.

B. The video card must be SVGA.

C. The hard drive must be IDE.

D. There must be 128MB or more of memory.

APPLY YOUR KNOWLEDGE

15. Lori needs to use the Sysprep tool to prepare for Windows 2000 Professional deployment. Where will she find this tool?

    A. In the Windows 2000 Professional Resource Kit.

    B. In the Windows 2000 Server Resource Kit.

    C. On the Windows 2000 Server CD in the deploy.cab file

    D. On the Windows 2000 Server CD in the sysprep.cab file.

Answers to Review Questions

1. The three programs used to start a Server setup are Setup, WINNT, and WINNT32. Setup is used for an attended installation on a Windows 32-bit platform; it can be invoked manually or by the AUTORUN.INF file when the CD is inserted into the drive. WINNT is used for an attended or unattended installation from a 16-bit platform (like Windows 3.1 or DOS). WINNT32 is used for an unattended install from a Windows 32-bit platform. For more information, see the sections "Attended Installations of Windows 2000 Server" and "Script-Based Unattended Installation."

2. The program for aiding in the creation of installation scripts is called the Setup Manager, and it is found on the Windows 2000 Server CD-ROM in the path \Support\Tools\deploy.cab. To use it, you must extract the .EXE file and the associated .DLL to a folder on your hard drive. It will create both answer files and UDF files for you using a wizard. For more information, see the section "Using the Setup Manager to Create Unattended Answer Files."

3. Service packs are designed to allow incremental upgrades to a piece of software—in this case, to the Windows 2000 operating system. Service packs distribute bug fixes and security patches. Service packs can be obtained from the Microsoft Web site or from other distribution media, such as TechNet and MSDN. For more information, see the section "Deploying Service Packs."

4. The minimum hardware requirements for the installation of Windows 2000 Server are RAM=256MB; Processor=166Mhz Pentium; and Free Disk Space=1GB. These are only minimums, so they require upgrading as the number of clients and the complexity of processing on a server increases. For more information, see the section "Minimum Hardware Requirements."

5. The three unattended installation methods described are scripted installations using answer files and uniqueness database files, disk duplication using Sysprep and disk imaging software, and remote installation by booting to a network location. Scripted installations use answer files and uniqueness database files to define responses to the installation prompts. In essence, this is a regular installation in which the answers are provided by a file instead of by a user. Disk duplication relies on the Sysprep program to prepare a machine to have its disk duplicated by a third-party program (like Norton's Ghost), and that disk image is then placed into a network share or onto a CD-ROM. After the image has been created, it is copied onto a destination machine as an image that requires only that a mini-setup wizard be run to complete configuration. Finally, remote installation requires a RIS server and client machines that are capable of

booting to a network location. Often these are thin clients without floppy drives or CD-ROMs. The client connects to a network location, and the installation progresses from there instead of from a local machine. For more information, see the section "Unattended Installations of Windows 2000 Server."

6. A member server is a Windows 2000 Server machine that is configured to participate as part of a domain but lacks Active Directory and, therefore, does not validate domain logon. Member servers typically provide one or more of the following services on a network: print services, file services, application services, or Web services. To configure a member server, you must have a domain defined and that requires a machine configured as a domain controller (running Active Directory). For more information, see the section "Windows 2000 Server and the 70-215 Exam."

Answers to Exam Questions

1. **D.** All of the hardware in the server makes it a candidate for successful upgrade from Windows NT 4.0 except its processor. Support for the Compaq Alpha (formerly the Digital Alpha) processor was discontinued in 1999 when Compaq ceased to exist. As a result, Windows 2000 does not have a version for the Alpha chip, and the upgrade will fail. None of the other choices are true. For more information, see the section "Hardware Compatibility."

2. **A, C.** Although Sysprep will help create disk images, it requires third-party software to deploy those images. WinDiff is used to compare two machines; it is not used to create unattended installations. Both batch files and RIS can take advantage of the scripts the Setup Manager creates to perform unattended installations, and both use only software provided by Microsoft (the Windows 2000 Server CD-ROM and the Support Tools included on the Windows 2000 CD-ROM). For more information, see the section "Unattended Installations of Windows 2000 Server."

3. **D.** The GUI Attended mode will provide answers for the text-based part of the installation but will prompt for all the GUI answers. For more information, see the section "Using the Setup Manager to Create Unattended Answer Files."

4. **C.** By doing the work herself, Emma can ensure that the required result (having the servers installed) is completed. In addition, she can ensure that the amount of effort required at their destinations is kept to a minimum by installing everything at her site and then shipping the computers out. Finally, by configuring them manually, she can also ensure that they end up as member servers in the domain. However, she has done nothing to ensure that people with a minimum of training and experience will be able to configure the machines. Even if they could, she has given them no opportunity because she is doing all the work herself. For more information, see the section "Attended Installations of Windows 2000 Server."

APPLY YOUR KNOWLEDGE

5. **A.** By configuring unattended installations using Setup Manager, Emma ensures that the software will be installed and that the machines will end up as domain members. In addition, because the unattended installation is invoked by a batch file, the summer student starting it does not need to know much about the installation process. Furthermore, because the configuration is simply running a batch file, it can be done with a minimum of effort at the destination site. For more information, see the section "Script-Based Unattended Installation."

6. **A.** The most flexible and accessible solution is to copy the files from the CD-ROM onto a network share and access it from there. Creating multiple copies not only has questionable ethical implications, it also means a finite number of connections (the number of CDs created). In addition, it also means local installation from a CD-ROM, which is typically slower than a network installation and requires a CD-ROM drive in every machine. It is not possible to install from floppy disks (if it were, the set would be hundreds of disks in size). Finally, it is impractical to install sequentially from a single CD-ROM. For more information, see the section "Attended Installations of Windows 2000 Server."

7. **B.** A thorough check must be performed before you try to upgrade a machine. You can do this by following the procedure in choice B. It is foolhardy to believe that a backup entitles you to play hit-and-miss with server upgrades. If you plan, you can avoid mistakes rather than having to correct them (which causes servers to be down much longer). In addition, although some problems might not cause Setup to fail, they will prevent your newly upgraded server from functioning.

Choice D is incorrect because the switch `/verifyupgradability` does not exist. For more information, see the section "Upgrading an NT 4.0 Member Server to Windows 2000."

8. **B, C.** Slipstreaming ensures that the network share containing the Windows 2000 Server installation files is updated with the fixes that a service pack provides. This ensures that changes made to a Windows 2000 server that require the installation files will automatically install the updated versions of files, provided that they are from an updated network share. In addition, this ensures that new installations will automatically end up with the fixed files installed without having to manually install the service pack prior to operating system installation.

Slipstreaming updates do not remove the requirement for installation of service packs on existing machines, and it is Microsoft's stated goal to provide fixes only via service packs, not operating system upgrades. For more information see the section "Deploying Service Packs."

9. **A, C.** RIS will not work because it does not currently support the installation of anything but Windows 2000 Professional. WINNT will not work because it requires network connectivity, which implies an operating system, installed on the machine (which is not possible if no partitions exist). A push install using SMS also requires an operating system on the client machine. For more information, see the section "Attended Installations of Windows 2000 Server."

APPLY YOUR KNOWLEDGE

10. **D.** Because Windows 2000 now supports the FAT32 file format, Noah does not have to do anything to prepare the machine. The current hardware configuration meets the minimum specifications; therefore, he does not need to upgrade. He might want to convert his hard drive to NTFS, but that is not required for installation. For more information, see the section "Preparing for Installation."

11. **A.** To log into a domain from a Windows 2000 machine, a computer account must exist in Active Directory for that computer. This allows the computer to "join the domain," thereby allowing users to log into the domain from that machine. For more information, see the section "Attended Installations of Windows 2000 Server."

12. **D.** You can create setup disks from any machine running a Microsoft operating system if it has CD-ROM support and a floppy disk. As a result, Bubba does not need to go to a Windows 2000 machine; he can use his Windows 98 machines. C is not correct because Windows 98 is a 32-bit operating system; therefore, he cannot use the MAKEBOOT program. Instead, he needs to use MAKEBT32. For more information, see the section "Install by Using Setup Diskettes and a CD-ROM."

13. **C.** Because slipstreaming can be used to update the files on a network share, there is no requirement for reinstalling the service pack after installing a service. Slipstreaming ensures that the installation files have already had the service pack installed before they are used to install a new service. It is true that if she uses the Windows 2000 Server CD-ROM as the source for her service installation, she will have to reapply the service pack. However, the question focused on the "best way," and updating using slipstreaming is the best way. For more information, see the section "Deploying Service Packs."

14. **A.** Of the hardware mentioned, the only one that is required is the RIS-compliant network card. This card must conform to one of three criteria. It must be installed in a Net PC compliant machine, or it must contain a PXE boot ROM, or it must have a driver available in the Remote Boot Disk configuration utility. For more information, see the section "Unattended Installations Using Remote Installation Services."

15. **C.** Like the Setup Manager, the Sysprep tool is available on the Windows 2000 CD-ROM and is compressed in the deploy.cab file. You do not have to purchase additional tools to obtain it. For more information, see the section "Unattended Installations Using Disk Duplication."

APPLY YOUR KNOWLEDGE

Suggested Readings and Resources

The following are some recommended readings in the area of installation:

Windows 2000 Deployment Guide is available on the Internet at http://www.microsoft.com/windows2000/library/resources/reskit/dpg/default.asp. Reference any installation and deployment chapters. This is probably the best source anywhere on Windows 2000 topics.

1. Windows 2000 Server Resource Kit: *Microsoft Windows 2000 Server Deployment Planning Guide* (Microsoft Press).

    • Part 4: Windows 2000 Upgrade and Installation

2. *Microsoft Windows 2000 Professional Resource Kit* (Microsoft Press).

    • Chapter 5: Customizing and Automating Installations

3. Microsoft Official Curriculum course 1557: *Installing and Configuring Microsoft Windows 2000*

    • Module 2: Installing Microsoft Windows 2000

    • Module 16: Upgrading a Network to Windows 2000

4. Microsoft Official Curriculum course 1567: *Preinstalling and Deploying Microsoft Windows 2000 Professional*

    • Module 2: Automating an Installation of Windows 2000 Professional

    • Module 4: Creating and Deploying an Image of Windows 2000 Professional

5. Microsoft Official Curriculum course 2152: *Supporting Microsoft Windows 2000 Professional and Server*

    • Module 1: Installing or Upgrading to Windows 2000

    • Module 11: Maintaining the Windows 2000 Environment

    • Module 16: Implementing Windows 2000 Servers and Clients

Microsoft provides the following objectives for "Installing, Configuring, and Troubleshooting Access to Resources":

Install and configure network services for interoperability.

▶ This objective is necessary because someone certified in the use of Windows 2000 Server technology must be able to configure such a server to operate in an environment where Windows 2000 is not the only network operating system. Access to printers and data must be configured so that all clients can access those resources (if security considerations do not make that inappropriate). Primary interoperation is with Novell NetWare clients and servers but also extended to UNIX and Macintosh clients.

Monitor, configure, troubleshoot, and control access to printers.

▶ This objective is necessary because someone certified in the use of Windows 2000 Server technology must understand how to grant and deny access to printers. In addition, such a person needs to be able to monitor and perform routine maintenance on the printer. Finally, such a person needs to be able to troubleshoot problems with access and performance relating to printers.

CHAPTER 2

Installing, Configuring, and Troubleshooting Access to Resources

Monitor, configure, troubleshoot, and control access to files, folders, and shared folders.

- **Configure, manage, and troubleshoot a standalone Distributed file system (Dfs).**

- **Configure, manage, and troubleshoot a domain-based Distributed file system (Dfs).**

- **Monitor, configure, troubleshoot, and control local security on files and folders.**

- **Monitor, configure, troubleshoot, and control access to files and folders in a shared folder.**

- **Monitor, configure, troubleshoot, and control access to files and folders via Web services.**

▶ This objective is necessary because someone certified in the use of Windows 2000 Server technology must understand the methods for providing access to data resources. In addition, such a person must be able to control access to those resources and to troubleshoot problems that might prevent access to resources.

Monitor, configure, troubleshoot, and control access to Web sites.

▶ This objective is necessary because someone certified in the use of Window 2000 Server technology must be able to configure a Web server using IIS and to control access to it. In addition, such a person must be able to prevent unauthorized users from accessing the server and must be able to troubleshoot problems relating to too much or too little access.

- ▶ There are many testable items in this long chapter. Remember that Microsoft will incorporate multiple items together into single questions, so make sure you know how these topics are interrelated.

- ▶ Of course, you should read and understand the concepts in this chapter and go through the review and exam questions at the end.

- ▶ In order to really understand the topics, you should implement the strategies in the Step by Step examples, and you need to do the exercises. Because of the nature of some of the interoperability sections, you might find it difficult to actually implement the solutions unless you have a number of test machines and access to other operating systems (like NetWare and Macintosh computers). However, you will still find that "going through the motions" will help to make the concepts in this chapter concrete. I suggest that you install the services and go through the configurations until a lack of equipment forces you to stop. Of course, if you can get hold of NetWare servers (regardless of the version) or a Macintosh system or two, you will be able to more fully implement the solutions presented.

- ▶ Interoperability has always been a big point on the exams—and this is still the case. Make sure you are familiar with the services required to interoperate with NetWare, Macintosh, and UNIX. Specifically for NetWare, be sure that you have an outline in your mind of what steps need to be taken to set up the GateWay for NetWare Service and get it to provide NetWare access to clients. Be sure that you understand what protocols are required and where they are required.

- ▶ Sharing, NTFS security, printing, and Web implementation and security can all be configured even if you only have one machine. Because there is a logical distinction between the printer (the software interface) and the print device (the hardware component), you do not even have to have a print device to do the printer module. For the network portions, you will benefit from having a second machine to use as a client with network hub to allow you to connect them (or at the very least a null network cable to directly connect them). You will not be able to implement the encrypted Web connections (using server and client certificates) unless you obtain or create certificates. If you already have certificates then use them; if not, you could use the Windows 2000 Certificate Authority to create them. However, that procedure is not outlined in this chapter.

- ▶ For the previous points mentioned, make sure that you go through all the configuration properties and that you understand how the configuration is done. Open the Security tab for an NTFS file resource or a printer and fix them, and what their settings do, in your mind.

- ▶ In the Dfs section, you will be able to implement a standalone Dfs on a Windows 2000 Server regardless of whether you have access to a Windows 2000 domain controller. However, domain-based Dfs will require that you have a Windows 2000 domain controller running in Native mode. If you do not have such a machine, then you will be able to implement only part of the Dfs solutions.

- ▶ Nothing can replace experience. Working through all the modules, understanding their content, and implementing the Step by Steps is a beginning. However, you will greatly benefit from having to work out some of these solutions in an environment where the result is defined but the path to it is not; this will develop critical thinking skills and will make concrete the concepts here. As you read these chapters, think to yourself, "How would I implement these solutions," and you will be on your way to forming the integration skills required not only to pass the exam, but also to use this information in the world beyond this book.

INTRODUCTION

This chapter will help you prepare for the "Installing, Configuring, and Troubleshooting Access to Resources" section of the exam. Because many Windows 2000 member servers will be used for file and print servers, it is essential that you thoroughly understand the many ways to provide access to resources and the ways to secure those resources. In this case, the resources are data and printers. As is indicated in the exam objectives, your understanding of a wide variety of access methods is expected.

This chapter provides an overview of the access methods available and how to implement them. It will also provide you with strategies and techniques for securing your data and printers against those people who are not authorized to use them.

LOCAL GROUPS AND USERS

Any discussion of access to resources presupposes an understanding of groups. Part of making a resource available on the network is controlling access to it. This is done through a Discretionary Access Control List (DACL) that is part of the sharing properties.

Although all the access could be granted based on specific user names, that is not very efficient. For example, let us assume that a system has 20 folders with data in them, and all of the folders need to be accessed by the 20 members of the accounting department, but no one else. As we will see in the next section, we could share the folders and then place each of the 20 users in each of the 20 DACLs. But that requires making 400 individual entries. And that is only the beginning. If a person leaves the accounting department or someone joins the department, all 20 folders would have to be modified. Instead of working with the 20 individuals, a single group could (dare I say, should?) be used.

You could create a single group and call it by some meaningful name—like *Accounting*. The membership of this group is then populated with the people in the accounting department. Then the group is placed in the DACL of each of the shared folders. Access for each individual user is then granted based on the group's access level. Not only is this an easier method for populating the DACL of each folder (one entry instead of 20), but it is also easier to change access. A change in the accounting department means only one change to the group. That change then will be reflected in all the DACLs the group is a member of.

Local groups are used to control access to resources on specific machines, whether those resources are data folders or printers. On a server or a Windows 2000 Professional workstation, the local groups are part of the local security model for the machine.

Three other group types will be part of this discussion, although all are found exclusively on domain controllers. Those three are universal groups, global groups, and domain local groups. Universal groups can consist of members (people or computers) or other groups from any domain in an Active Directory forest. They can be used to grant access to any resources in the forest. Global groups can contain global groups or users from the domain in which they are created and can be added to any universal groups or domain local groups in the forest. Finally, domain local groups can contain global groups from the domain in which they exist, universal groups from the forest, or members from the forest. Domain local groups are used to grant access only to domain resources in the domain in which they exist.

The purpose of all these group types is to provide convenient mechanisms for applying permissions to access resources. The use of groups is always recommended over the use of individual user or computer accounts.

This discussion of local users, groups, and (later on) security, is important because when it comes to security, local means everything. If a server is a member of a workgroup, it is an authority unto itself. Users log on locally to the machine, and it validates those logons locally in its own security database. These are called *local users*. If you want to group together users for administrative ease, you can create groups that are local to the machine. These are called *local groups*. Finally, you give access permission to a resource at the local machine level. In the end, the local machine controls all access to the resources it holds.

Even when a Windows 2000 server joins a domain, it is still king of all it holds. But, in joining a domain, it gives some of its control away because the administrators for the domain (called *Domain Admins* in the Active Directory) are added to its local Administrators group. The administrators of the domain are able to administer each server in the domain. However, it is to be noted that this ability is not inherent in the fact that they are domain administrators; it is dependant on some person (in this case, a process) giving them administrative access on the local machine. If a local member server administrator were to remove the Domain Admins group from the local Administrators group, the domain administrators would no longer have administrative rights on that server.

Typically, when it comes to giving access to resources on a server (for example, one that has joined a domain and has access to groups and users in the Active Directory), the following pattern is followed:

1. Domain users can be added to universal, global, or domain local groups in the Active Directory. These groups are much like the local groups created on a server; however, unlike local groups, these groups can become members of other groups. Therefore, the domain administrators have the ability to group domain users together for domain-wide purposes.

2. Local groups are created on each server with the purpose of grouping users who need the same rights to perform functions or the same permissions to access resources on the server. In addition, if a server is a member of the domain (even if it is not a domain controller), the Domain Local groups created in its domain can also be used to control access to resources on the server. This means that local groups that have a consistent membership across many servers no longer have to be created on each server (as they were in versions of NT).

3. Local users, global groups, and universal groups can then be used to populate the local groups on the server (the population of domain local groups is similar except that you cannot use local users from a specific server to populate these groups). Local users are created only when there is no good reason to create a user who has access to resources across the whole domain but who only needs access to resources on a local machine. These cases are rare, but they do exist.

4. Permissions are then granted to access resources by adding local groups to the DACLs of the local resources.

In general the pattern of group memberships and permissions is as follows:

domain accounts → universal groups → global groups → domain local groups → permission to access resources

Alternatively, if you are using local accounts, these accounts would be added to local groups on the server and would be used to grant access to resources.

To put this methodology to use, you need to know how to manage local groups and users.

Managing Local Groups

Managing local groups consists of the following activities: creating local groups, modifying group memberships, renaming groups, and deleting local groups. You can see and manage groups from the Computer Management window.

Creating and maintaining local groups is done in the Computer Management console on a server (on a domain controller, it is done in the Active Directory). The following steps lead you through the process of creating a local group.

STEP BY STEP

2.1 Creating a Local Group on a Server

1. From the Start menu, select Programs, Administrative Tools, Computer Management. The Computer Management window shown in Figure 2.1 appears.

2. Under System Tools, expand the Local Users and Groups folder and click on the Groups folder. This will expose the local groups (shown on the right side).

3. Right-click the Groups folder and choose New Group from the menu that appears.

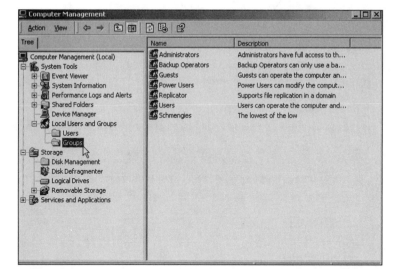

FIGURE 2.1
You can see and manage groups from the Computer Management window.

4. In the GroupName dialog box (see Figure 2.2), enter a group name and description, and then click the Add button to add members to the group.

5. When the Select Users or Groups dialog box appears (see Figure 2.3), you can choose the location where users or groups you want to add to the new group are stored. In the figure, the server IKTHUSE-MATRIX has its own accounts list. However, because it is also part of an Active Directory domain called ikthuse.com, it has access to accounts and groups from that domain (as well as other domains that might be in the forest). A server can draw from any or all of the larger directories it is a part of to select members for its groups.

6. Choose any of the users or groups listed and click the Add button to add to the new group. To remove an entry that you have added in error, select the entry and press the Delete key on your keyboard. When you are finished, click OK to save the group membership.

7. You're returned to the GroupName dialog box. To save the group, click the Create button.

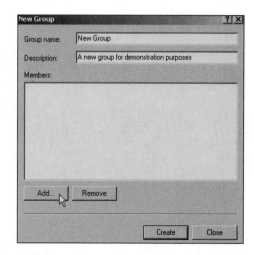

FIGURE 2.2
Adding a new group begins with naming it.

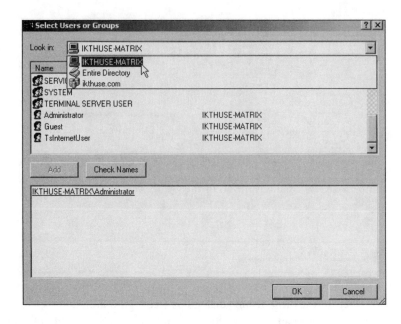

You might want to modify the members of a group after it has been
created. To do so, follow Step by Step 2.2.

STEP BY STEP

2.2 Modifying the Membership of a Local Group on a Member Server

1. From the Start menu, select Programs, Administrative
   Tools, Computer Management.

2. Under System Tools, expand the Local Users and Groups
   folder and click on the Groups folder. This will expose the
   local groups (shown on the right side).

3. Double-click the name of the group you want to modify.

4. In the GroupName Properties dialog box, click the Add
   button.

5. From the Look In pull-down menu, choose the location
   where the users or groups you wish to add as members to
   this new group are stored.

6. Choose any of the users or groups listed and click the Add button to add to the new group. To remove an entry you have added in error, select the entry and press the Delete key on your keyboard. When you are finished, click OK to save the group membership.

7. You are returned to the GroupName Properties dialog box. To save the group, click the OK button.

You can also rename any group in the group listing. When you do that, the group name will be changed everywhere that it appears (for example, in a DACL). Step by Step 2.3 addresses renaming.

STEP BY STEP

2.3 Changing the Name of a Local Group on a Member Server

1. From the Start menu, select Programs, Administrative Tools, Computer Management.

2. Under System Tools, expand the Local Users and Groups folder and click on the Groups folder. This will expose the local groups (shown on the right side).

3. Right-click the name of the group you want to rename and choose Rename from the menu that appears.

4. Type in the new group name and press Enter to make it permanent.

NOTE

Windows 2000 Allows Group Renaming The renaming of groups is new for Windows 2000. Under NT, it was not possible to rename a group. Instead, you had to create a new group, make its membership the same as the old one, and then add it to all the DACLs that the old group was a member of. Then you would delete the original group.

The final act of group maintenance is to delete a group. You should be very careful when deciding whether to delete a group. If you delete a group, it will be removed from the DACLs of all the resources it was added to. This means that deletion can cause widespread irreversible changes. Remember that you can rename groups, and that might be all you really need to do. If you do need to remove a group, it is an easy thing to do, as shown in Step by Step 2.4.

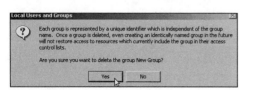

FIGURE 2.4
Deleting a group can have serious implications.

STEP BY STEP

2.4 Deleting a Local Group on a Member Server

1. From the Start menu, select Programs, Administrative Tools, Computer Management.

2. Under System Tools, expand the Local Users and Groups folder and click on the Groups folder. This will expose the local groups (shown on the right side).

3. Right-click the name of the group you want to delete and choose Delete from the menu that appears.

4. The Local Users and Groups dialog box appears, warning you of the consequences of deleting a group (see Figure 2.4). Click the Yes button.

Managing Local Users

As has been mentioned already, a local user on a Windows 2000 member server is one who exists only on that machine and does not exist in the domain's Active Directory. Local users are generally created only when you need to give access to resources to someone who does not log into your domain. This could be to give access to a workgroup user who logs on locally to another machine on your network or to give access to a Web user who needs to be authenticated but whose account you do not want cluttering up your Active Directory. That said, there is one local account that is always available—that is the Administrator for the computer. This account is created when the operating system is installed, and it cannot be removed. This account may be used when you need to log into the local machine to do maintenance and, for whatever reason, a domain logon is not possible.

Local users can be given any rights that domain users can be given. The real difference is that they exist only within the context of the local server. As with group maintenance, local account maintenance consists of the following tasks: creating a new account, renaming an account, and deleting an account.

Like local group maintenance, local account maintenance is done in
the Computer Management console. Follow these steps to create a
local account on a server.

STEP BY STEP

2.5 Creating a Local Account on a Member Server

1. From the Start menu, select Programs, Administrative
Tools, Computer Management.

---

2. Under System Tools, expand the Local Users and Groups
folder and click on the Users folder (see Figure 2.5). This
will expose the local accounts (shown on the right side).

---

3. Right-click the Users folder and choose New User from
the menu that appears.

continues

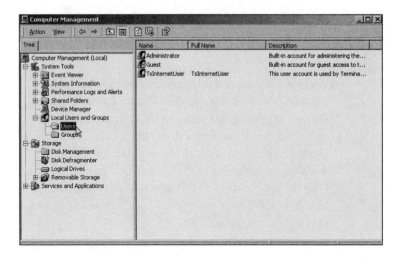

FIGURE 2.5
You can see and manage users from the
Computer Management window.

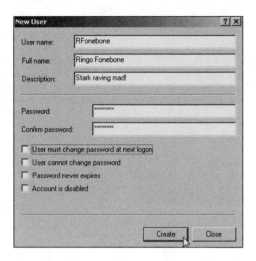

FIGURE 2.6
Set the initial account properties when creating a user.

continued

4. In the New User dialog box (see Figure 2.6), fill in the User Name (the short name the user logs in with), the Full Name (a descriptive name for the user), a Description for the user (if appropriate), and a Password. Repeat the password in the Confirm Password box. The dialog box also contains four check boxes for you to select from.

If you select User Must Change Password at Next Logon, the user is forced to change his password the next time he logs in. You might use this option if you've given out a generic password to start with but you want each individual user to change to a new non-generic one. If you select this check box, the next two are unavailable.

If you do not select the User Must Change Password at Next Logon check box, you can choose User Cannot Change Password. If you do, the user will be unable to change his or her password; it can be modified only from this dialog box. This is useful for guest accounts where more than one person knows the password and logs in with the account. If you select this check box, the first one becomes unavailable.

If you do not select the User Must Change Password at Next Logon check box, you can choose Password Never Expires. Normally, the account policy defined for the server indicates how long a password remains good before it must be changed. This check box overrides any password expiration policy and ensures that a password can be kept the same indefinitely. However, if the computer is a member of a domain, this policy may be overridden by the domain's group policy.

The final check box is Account Is Disabled. Selecting this check box makes the user account unusable. This feature is often used when a user leaves the company but you want to hold onto the account in case someone else ends up with the same job and, therefore, the need for the same data access. If an account is deleted, the access that user had is removed from all DACLs. This is not reasonable in the instance where one person is replaced with another.

Instead of deleting the account, it is better to disable the account and then rename the account with the new user's name when a replacement is hired.

5. When all the information in the New User dialog box is filled in, click the Create button to create the account.

In addition to creating a local account, renaming such an account is a task that you might have to perform. Step by Step 2.6 walks you through this process.

STEP BY STEP

2.6 Renaming a Local Account

1. From the Start menu, select Programs, Administrative Tools, Computer Management.

2. Under System Tools, expand the Local Users and Groups folder and click on the Users folder. This will expose the local accounts (shown on the right side).

3. Right-click the name of the user you want to change and choose Rename from the menu that appears.

4. Type the new user name and press Enter.

Deleting users is a task you should undertake only with much forethought. When a user account is created, it is assigned a Security Identifier (SID). This SID is unique, and it is what identifies a specific user account (thus allowing you to change a user name without it affecting the permissions the user has). If you delete an account, all traces of that user are erased. Even if you create a new user with the same user name, the SID is different, and the new user will have to be added to groups and DACLs all over again. It is recommended that if a user account is no longer needed because the owner has left the company, you should disable it for a time. This keeps the account available in case a new user who needs the same rights and permissions is hired by the company. Then you can simply rename the account and change its properties to reflect the new user.

The following Step by Step outlines how to delete a user account.

STEP BY STEP

2.7 Deleting a Local User Account

1. From the Start menu, select Programs, Administrative Tools, Computer Management.

2. Under System Tools, expand the Local Users and Groups folder and click on the Users folder. This will expose the local accounts (shown on the right side).

3. Right-click the name of the user you want to change and choose Delete from the menu that appears.

4. When the warning dialog box appears, click Yes to complete the deletion.

Now that you've been introduced to local user and group accounts, it is time to look at data access using these accounts.

GIVING AND CONTROLLING DATA ACCESS

Monitor, configure, troubleshoot, and control access to files, folders, and shared folders.

The roles of a server can be categorized into three main areas: file server, print server, and applications server. This first section deals with the first role—the file server. The primary function of a file server is to provide centralized access to data over the network. As such, it is potentially accessible to anyone who has physical access to your network. Moreover, as if the risks from internal people getting access to data (sometimes sensitive data) were not enough, the idea of the Web server providing access to the entire computerized population of the world simply adds to the security risks. This section starts from the simplest scenario (that of sharing data) and then moves to more complex scenarios to configure and administer (like Dfs and Web services).

You'll begin with the start of most network access: sharing folders from the server.

Configuring and Controlling Shared Access

The genesis of the network was the desire to allow a number of people to exchange information by way of computer. Because physically exchanging data on some sort of removable mass media is not generally very efficient, the network allows for the rapid exchange of data electronically through its infrastructure. The file server provides a centralized (and readily accessible) storage location for that information. Data is stored in folders, and in order to provide network access to those folders, they need to be shared.

Preparing to Share

On a Windows 2000 server, sharing information requires that a number of things are in place:

- ◆ The Server service must be running (this activates the ability for a user to share information).

- ◆ The data must be present on the server.

- ◆ The container in which the data is held must be shared (that container could be a hard drive, a floppy drive, a CD-ROM, or a folder).

The first criteria should be in place already. Unless the Server service has been shut down, it should be running by default. If it did not start, you have a problem, because that generally means your network did not start. You should check your network cards and drivers to make sure that everything is functioning normally.

The Server service is the software component that allows the server computer to be contacted from other network machines and allows the server computer to respond to requests. It is important that you do not confuse the service name (Server service) with the operating system (Windows 2000 Server). Windows 2000 Professional has a Server service, which must be running in order to share data. Windows 9x (98 and 95) has a Server service; it is called File and Print Sharing and is enabled through the Network properties.

To check the condition of the Server service and to stop and start it, if necessary, follow Step by Step 2.8.

STEP BY STEP

2.8 Starting and Stopping the Server Service

1. From the Start menu, choose Programs, Administrative Tools, Services. This will bring up the Services console.

2. Navigate down the list of services until you find the one called Server. To its right, the Status column should say Started and Startup Type should be Automatic (that means that it starts when the operating system is started). Figure 2.7 shows an example of this.

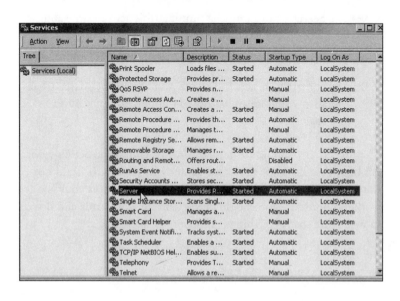

FIGURE 2.7
In the Services console, you can start, stop, and pause services.

3. Start the service by right-clicking the word Server and choosing Start from the menu that appears. Stop the service by right-clicking the word Server and choosing Stop. The option called Pause is used to prevent more people from connecting to the Server service without disconnecting the people who are currently using it. Finally, the Restart option will stop and then start a service (a new feature that has been very well received by Administrators!).

When you have verified that the Server service is running and you have copied the data you want to share onto your computer (or had someone create it there), you're ready to share the server.

Setting Up and Maintaining Sharing

Not just anyone can share folders on a Windows 2000 server. In order to do so, you must be in either the Administrators or the Power Users group on the local machine. Both are built-in groups— that is, they are created when the operating system is installed. Because they are built-in groups, the members of those groups have certain rights on the machine. One of the rights given to these groups is the ability to share files.

It is important to note that whether in or out of a domain context, access to resources on a server is completely controlled by the local security model. When a server joins a domain, its local Administrators group gets a new member, the Domain Admins group from the domain it just joined. However, it is only at the discretion of the local machine that this group is added (permission to do so is given when a local administrator adds a computer to the domain). This means that regardless of the authority a user enjoys in the domain, any of the servers can be made off-limits by a restrictive access policy on that machine.

When a folder is shared, access to it over the network is controlled by a DACL. This DACL contains a list of users or groups and the permission they have to access the data over the network. It should be noted that share-level
permissions control only access over the network. If a user is able to

log locally onto a server, by default, that user is able to access all data and can do anything with it he or she desires; this is called Full Control access.

Three levels of access can be given to a DACL entry (person or group): Full Control, Change, and Read. Full Control means a user can do anything to the files in the folder, including looking at the content, changing the content, and deleting the files. It also means that on drives formatted with NTFS, the NTFS permissions can be changed over the network. Change allows for modification of all files but does not allow permissions to be modified over the network. Read allows for the contents of a folder to be viewed and each file to be opened in Read-Only mode. It also allows for files to be copied from the shared folder to another location but does not allow files to be copied into the folder nor removed from it.

When managing the DACL, the administrator can give each user or group different permissions, depending on the need for security and the user's need for data access. By default, the system group Everyone is given Full Control. This group is maintained by Windows 2000, and its membership cannot be modified. It means what its name implies: Everyone has full access to the files in the folder.

In Step by Step 2.9, you will see that permissions allow you to explicitly give or explicitly take away a specific access level. So you can give a group explicit Read access, and if no one else is listed in the DACL, everyone else is implicitly denied access. You can also explicitly add a group or, by denying access, explicitly remove all their access.

Permissions granted in the DACL are cumulative (with one exception, which is discussed shortly). If you are explicitly listed and implicitly listed as a member of one or more groups, you will get the combination of all the permissions given to you. So, if you are listed as having Read access and you are in a group that is given Change access, you will get Change access. The exception to this rule occurs when either your explicit listing or your group memberships prevent access; then you will have access taken away. Because permissions always err on the side of caution, deny always takes precedence over allow.

In addition, DACLs enable you to both allow and deny permissions. This means that, rather than simply not giving someone permission to access a resource, you can explicitly deny access to that resource. Explicit denial always takes precedence over any permissions allowed. This comes in handy when the person is a member of a group that is allowed access to some resource. In general, that person needs membership in that group with the associated resource access. However, as it pertains to one specific file, that person should not be given access. In this case, you can give the group access but explicitly deny the person access. With the exception of the person explicitly denied access, all members of the group will have access to the file.

STEP BY STEP

2.9 Sharing a folder From a Member Server

1. Using Windows Explorer or My Computer, navigate to the folder you want to share.

2. Right-click and choose Sharing from the menu that appears.

3. In the *FolderName* Properties dialog box (see Figure 2.8), choose the Share This Folder option button and enter a share name (this is the name that users will use to connect to the shared folder). The share name may or may not be the same as the name of the folder. Also, choose a user limit for simultaneous connections to this folder. The default for this property is Maximum Allowed, but you can restrict the number of simultaneous users by choosing a maximum. You might want to do this if the amount of processor power or server memory warrants a restriction on the demands you want users to be able to put on the server. Click the Permissions button to set security on this folder.

4. In the Permissions for *FolderName* dialog box, you can set permissions for the people or groups that are allowed to access this data over the network. By clicking the Add button, you can choose from any available directory the names of people and/or groups who are allowed to access the data (see Figure 2.9).

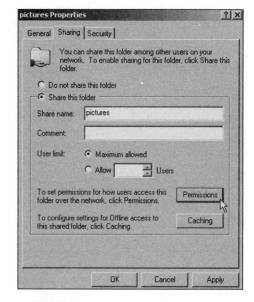

FIGURE 2.8
Choose a share name that users will find intuitively useful.

continues

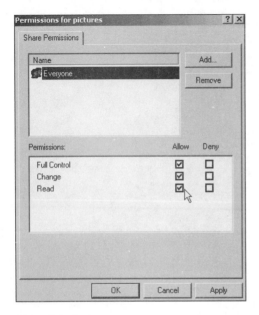

FIGURE 2.9
Share permissions can be set to any (or all) of
Full Control, Change, and Read.

continued

   5. Click the OK button until you have exited the sharing
   properties. The folder will then be displayed with a sharing hand holding it.

To modify the share permissions for a folder, you can follow Step by
Step 2.9 and change the permissions selected in the Permissions for
FolderName dialog box.

To remove sharing from a folder, open the sharing properties and
click the Do Not Share This Folder option button.

Troubleshooting Sharing

Suppose you receive a phone call from a user saying, "I can't get my
data." This can happen for a number of reasons. The potential problems can be divided into three major categories: problems with the
user, problems with permissions, and problems with the network.

Although they seem trivial to an administrator, problems with the
user are not trivial to the user. A user might have chosen to look on
the wrong server, or he might be typing the name of the network
share incorrectly. Stepping the user through the process and checking
spelling and syntax are the best remedies for these kinds of problems.

Problems with permissions are a little more difficult to diagnose.
First of all, you need to see whether a user is supposed to be able to
do what he or she is attempting. Then you need to verify that the
combined permissions do not prevent some action. For example, if a
group is given Change permission but a user has had Change permission explicitly denied, the user will not be able to change data.

Finally, network problems are the most difficult to diagnose because
they can be so varied. The network itself may be problematic (did
you wiggle the cable?). If that is the case, an icon will show up in the
system tray (near the clock in the lower-right corner of the screen)
showing a network connection with a red X through it to indicate a
loss of network connectivity. The drivers for the network cards at the
server or client end may be the issue (did you try to access the share
from another client?). The Server service might be stopped (or might
never have started). The folder might not be shared at all.

Although it is tempting to believe that the major problems with sharing are an inability to access data, more problematic is when users have too much access to data. It is easy to rectify a problem of insufficient access by giving an apology and fixing the access issue. However, when someone gets too much access, the data might be deleted, or sensitive information might fall into the wrong hands. In those cases, being sorry is not going to be enough.

One of the really mind-bending "features" of sharing is the ability to share folders in a directory tree at different levels. The problem with this is that, whereas the structure of data folders is apparent when you look at your disk locally, they are not apparent when you look at a browse list of the folders available. Because you can share a folder at one level and then share folders inside it at another, it's possible that you might have left open a back door into your data that a shrewd user might take advantage of. The following example will make this clear.

In the directory structure shown in Figure 2.10, you can see that the folder called Pictures is shared, as are the folders called Public Pictures and Secret Pictures, which are subfolders of the Pictures folder. It is apparent to you what the structure looks like because you can see the view of it on the disk. If I were to tell you that Pictures is shared with Read access to the Everyone group, you could look at the structure and know that access to the Just Pictures folder would be Read when someone accessed it over the network. However, if I also told you that access to the Secret Pictures folder was Full Access, how would that be affected by the access level of Read given to the parent folder? Well, the answer to that depends on how a user accesses the data.

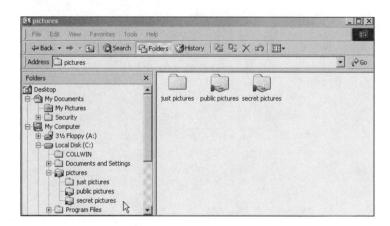

FIGURE 2.10
Knowledge of the file structure does not always help you know what access users have to the data.

As you can see in Figure 2.11, when a user looks through a browser list for the folders shared from a specific server, the list is flat; there is no notion or representation of the on-disk hierarchy. If a user happens to access the data through the Pictures share, that user will get only Read access to any folder inside it. However, if a user accesses the Secret Pictures share, that user will get Full Control, despite the fact that if he or she accessed the same data though the Pictures share he or she would have only Read access.

This example is akin to locking the doors in your house but leaving a bedroom window open. A thief trying to get into the bedroom by entering the front door would be stymied. However, a simple walk around the house would reveal the open window and allow access to the room in question.

An administrator must take special care to ensure that access at one level does not counteract the access given at another.

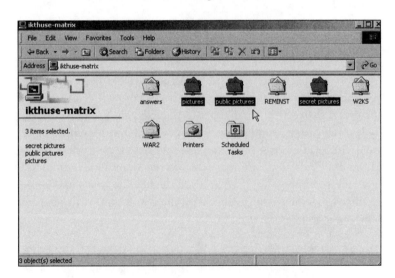

FIGURE 2.11
To a user browsing the shares, the on-disk tree structure is not apparent; everything looks flat.

Configuring and Controlling Local Access

In the previous section, you learned about your ability to control access to data via the network; unfortunately, some problems need to be overcome. First, in share-level access, there is no way to secure the files inside of a folder without sharing it first, and, moreover, there is no way to apply one level of security on one file and apply another level of security on another file in the same shared folder.

Second, there is still the issue of local access to files. Can you secure files when the person trying to access them has local access to the computer hosting them?

The NTFS File System

The answer to these problems is found in the NTFS file structure and the properties inherent in it. NTFS is a proprietary file structure available only to Windows NT and Windows 2000 computers. Windows NT supports NTFS version 4, and Windows 2000 supports version 5 (version 5 has been enhanced to provide file encryption, among other things, and is not 100 percent compatible with version 4). One of the features of the NTFS file system (to be talked about in greater depth in Chapter 5, "Managing, Configuring, and Troubleshooting Storage Use") is the ability to locally secure files and folders.

For security reasons, it is recommended that you format all drives on your Windows 2000 server with NTFS. The only reason not to is if you are dual-booting your server with another operating system that does not support NTFS, but that should happen only in test environments, so it is not a consideration at this point. However, for a variety of reasons, partitions might not be formatted that way. They may be formatted FAT or FAT32 instead. This will make it impossible to locally secure files and folders. It is not advised that you simply reformat all your drives because your data will be lost (or at best you will have to recover from a backup). Moreover, if you are talking about your System partition or Boot partition, reformatting will mean reinstalling your operating system. However, there is a way to change your file system from FAT/FAT32 to NTFS: through the CONVERT function.

> **NOTE**
>
> **NT 4.0 SP4 Provides Limited Interoperability with NTFS v. 5**
> Service Pack 4 of NT 4.0 introduced an NTFS driver that allows Read and limited interoperability with NTFS v5. If a machine is configured to dual boot between NT 4.0 and Windows 2000, it is imperative that the NT 4.0 machine be at SP4 or higher in order to access any of the data on an NTFS v5 partition.

CONVERT.EXE is a non-destructive conversion routine that will do a one-time one-way conversion from FAT or FAT32 to NTFS. It should be stressed that at this time, this is one-way; you cannot convert back after your file system has been converted. On a more positive note, the only changes made to your server after the file system has been converted will be good. There are no adverse effects from converting, and your users will see absolutely no change to the way things work (except for those who fall victim to your enhanced security).

The conversion routine is said to be "non-destructive" because it will do the conversion without causing data loss. Having said that, though, I would always do a full backup of my server before a conversion because nothing (except the usual metaphysical and social things) is guaranteed in life, and you are better to be safe than really, really sorry.

The following steps outline the conversion process.

STEP BY STEP

2.10 Converting a Partition from FAT/FAT32 to NTFS

1. From the Start menu, choose Run. In the Run dialog box, type **convert *driveletter:* /fs:ntfs**, where *driveletter:* is the letter of the partition you want to convert.

2. If the partition is currently in use—which is always the case if you are converting the Boot or System partition—you will be informed that the conversion will happen the next time you restart your machine. The best practice is to boot immediately to allow the conversion to happen without delay.

Setting Up and Maintaining Local File and Folder Security

You set up and maintain local file and folder security in much the same way you do shared security. Other than the fact that one is for network access and the other is for local access, there are few other noticeable differences in the two security models. First, whereas share-level security is able to control access to a folder only, local security can control security down to the file level. Second, with sharing, subfolders under a shared root are not automatically shared, they are available only because of their presence under the shared folder. However, local security is automatically inherited by any container built inside the local root. This means that if you secure a folder locally and then create a new folder inside it, that new folder will inherit the local security properties of its parent folder. Third, although there are only three levels of share security (Full Control, Change, and Read), there are many more granular settings with local security.

Table 2.1 presents a list of the most granular NTFS permissions.

TABLE 2.1

SPECIAL LOCAL (NTFS) SECURITY PERMISSIONS

Permission	Function
Traverse Folder/Execute File	This permission allows or denies users the ability to pass through (traverse) a folder they do not have access to in order to get to a folder or file they do have access to. This property is applicable only if the user privilege *Bypass Traverse Checking* is not turned on in the system policy. By default, *ByPass Traverse Checking* is turned on for all users. Therefore, setting this permission has no effect.
List Folder/Read Data	This permission allows a user to list the contents of a folder that it is applied to. When applied to files, it allows or denies the ability to open a file for reading.
Read Attributes	Allows or denies the ability to look at file or folder attributes (like System, Archive, or Read Only). These attributes are defined by the file system.
Read Extended Attributes	Allows or denies the ability to look at special file or folder attributes. These are created by special software applications and will vary from application to application.
Create Files/Write Data	Allows or denies the ability to create new files (when applied to a folder) or to edit files to make changes anywhere in that file (when applied to a file).
Create Folders/Append Data	Allows or denies the ability to create new folders in a folder (when applied to a folder) or to append data to a file without changing existing data in that file (when applied to a file).
Write Attributes	Allows or denies the ability to modify file or folder attributes (like System, Archive, or Read Only). These attributes are defined by the file system.
Write Extended Attributes	Allows or denies the ability to modify special file or folder attributes. These are created by special software applications and will vary from application to application.
Delete Subfolders and Files	Allows or denies the ability to delete subfolders and files from a folder (functions only when applied to a folder). This will apply even if explicit delete permission is denied to the child folders or files.

continues

| TABLE 2.1 | *continued* |

SPECIAL LOCAL (NTFS) SECURITY PERMISSIONS

Permission	*Function*
Delete	Allows or denies the ability to delete the folder or file to which it is applied. This can be overridden if the Delete Subfolders and Files permission has been granted to its parent.
Read Permissions	Allows or denies the ability to look at the permissions applied to a file or a folder.
Change Permissions	Allows or denies the ability to modify the permissions applied to a file or a folder.
Take Ownership	Allows or denies the ability to become the owner of a file or a folder. If you have ownership of a file or a folder, you can always change permissions, regardless of any other permissions on a file or folder.

Next you will look at the default groupings used to separate these permissions into more manageable units. The basic folder permissions are Full Control, Modify, Read & Execute, List Folder Contents, Read, and Write. The basic file permissions are Full Control, Modify, Read & Execute, Read, and Write. Tables 2.2 and 2.3 list the basic local permissions that can be granted and which of the special permissions they encompass.

| TABLE 2.2 |

BASIC LOCAL (NTFS) SECURITY PERMISSIONS FOR FOLDERS

Special Permission	*Full Control*	*Modify*	*Read & Execute*	*List Folder Contents*	*Read*	*Write*
Traverse Folder/ Execute File	X	X	X	X		
List Folder/ Read Data	X	X	X	X	X	
Read Attributes	X	X	X	X	X	
Read Extended Attributes	X	X	X	X	X	
Create Files/ Write Data	X	X				X
Create Folders/ Append Data	X	X				X
Write Attributes	X	X				X

Special Permission	Full Control	Modify	Read & Execute	List Folder Contents	Read	Write
Write Extended Attributes	X	X				X
Delete Subfolders and Files	X					
Delete	X	X				
Read Permissions	X	X	X	X	X	X
Change Permissions	X					
Take Ownership	X					
Synchronize	X	X	X	X	X	X

TABLE 2.3

BASIC LOCAL (NTFS) SECURITY PERMISSIONS FOR FILES

Special Permission	Full Control	Modify	Read & Execute	Read	Write
Traverse Folder/ Execute File	X	X	X		
List Folder/Read Data	X	X	X		
Read Attributes	X	X	X	X	
Read Extended Attributes	X	X	X	X	
Create Files/ Write Data	X	X			X
Create Folders/ Append Data	X	X			X
Write Attributes	X	X			X
Write Extended Attributes	X	X			X
Delete Subfolders and Files	X				
Delete	X	X			
Read Permissions	X	X	X	X	X
Change Permissions	X				
Take Ownership	X				
Synchronize	X	X	X	X	X

Now that you know the local file and folder permissions, the next topics are how to actually apply and maintain these permissions.

Applying file or folder permissions is much the same as applying permissions to a network share. The major difference is that, by default, when you apply a certain permission, it is cascaded down to all the files and folders in the hierarchy beginning with the folder you are applying to. In addition, by default, when you create a new file or folder in an already existing folder, this new object will also inherit the security properties of its parent container. Unless you explicitly break the connection between the parent container and a child object, you will not be allowed to modify the permissions on the child; the permissions will remain grayed out. If you remove the ability for a child object to inherit permissions from the parent, you will be presented with a few options that let you specify the initial permissions for the child object (remembering that the child was, until that point, receiving all its permissions from its parent). You can choose either copy or remove. If you choose to copy the permissions from the parent, those permissions will be present in the child, but you will be able to modify them to suit the current object. If you choose to remove the permissions of the parent from the child, all that will remain are permissions that were added to the child when the parent permissions were still being inherited. If no permissions were added, the Names list will be empty.

It should also be noted that every file and folder on an NTFS partition has local security applied to it. By default, the Everyone group has Full Control locally. The following steps walk you through modifying permissions.

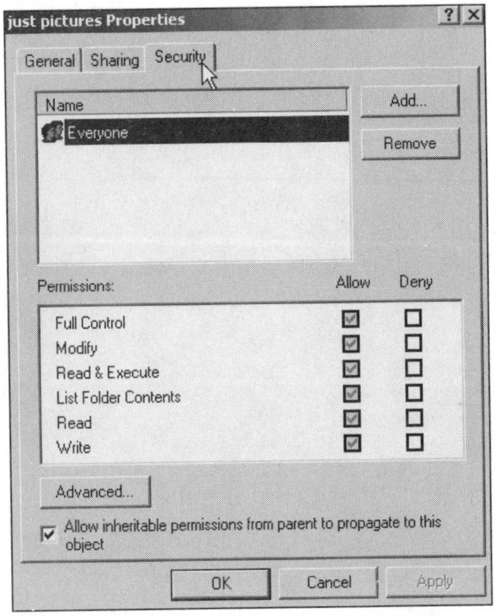

FIGURE 2.12
Several security permissions can be applied locally.

STEP BY STEP

2.11 Modifying File or Folder Local Permissions

1. Navigate to the object for which you want to change permissions.

2. Right-click the object and select Properties from the menu that appears.

3. In the Properties dialog box, click the Security tab at the top to see the local permissions that are applied (see Figure 2.12).

4. Click the Add button to get a list of users and groups that you can add to this local ACL. After you make those choices, you're returned to this dialog box, where you can then apply the permissions desired for the specific people or groups.

5. To remove a user or group from the DACL, select the user or group in the Name list and click the Remove button.

Permissions that show up as check marks in gray boxes are being inherited from the parent container. If you want to override these settings, remove the current check box by selecting the other permission (if it is currently Allow, select Deny), and then change it to how you would like it. If you do not want future changes in the parent to affect this object, deselect the check box labeled Allow Inheritable Permissions from Parent to Propagate to This Object.

6. To set more granular permissions for a user or group, click the Advanced button. In the Access Control Settings dialog box (shown in Figure 2.13), click the Add button.

7. Having selected a user or group from the directory of your choice, you can set specific special permissions for that user or group (see Figure 2.14).

Although local security solves a number of security issues, it does introduce a problem that only it can resolve. That is the problem of a file or folder being secured by its owner for only that person's access and then that person leaving the company. Because the file or folder is secured, it can be accessed only by the person who secured it, and therefore, that data is lost. One way to access the data is to change the user's password and then log on as that user. The problem is that further maintenance of that resource will have to be done by that user account.

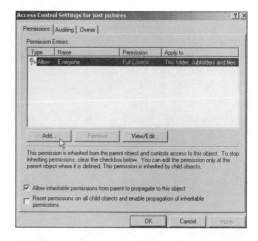

FIGURE 2.13
NTFS permissions can be assigned even more granularly than the standard permissions.

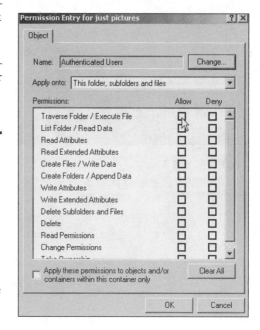

FIGURE 2.14
Any of the permissions can be granted or denied to a user.

Taking ownership is one way to take back the control of locally secured files. By default, an administrator has the ability to take ownership of any file or folder on his or her server. An administrator can choose whether to have their individual account or the Administrators group as the owner of a file or folder. However, all other users must be assigned the Take Ownership permission to take ownership of a file or folder (just as it was in NT 4). Step by Step 2.12 shows you how to take ownership of a file or folder.

STEP BY STEP

2.12 Taking Ownership of a File or Folder

1. Log on as someone with the ability to take ownership of the file or folder in question.

2. Right-click the object to take ownership of and choose Properties from the menu that appears.

3. Click on the Security tab in the Properties dialog box and then click the Advanced button.

4. In the Access Control Settings dialog box, click the Owner tab.

5. On the Owner tab, choose the user you want listed as the new owner, and then click OK (see Figure 2.15). If you also want to take ownership of all the folders and files inside this object, you can click the Replace Owner on Subcontainers and Objects check box.

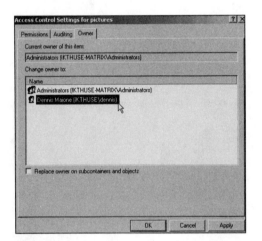

FIGURE 2.15
The ability to take ownership of a resource can be given to anyone.

Troubleshooting Local File Security

Troubleshooting local file security is a fairly simple matter. Because what you are dealing with is individual users accessing local objects, if the file exists, lack of access or too much access is going to be caused by permission problems. To rectify such problems, log on as an administrator, check to see what the current permissions on the object are, and repair them if necessary.

When Local File Security Interacts with Shared Folder Security

Local security applies across the board to all accesses to a file, whether over the network or local. If I have Read access locally, by default I will have Read access if I try to access the same file through a share. However, because permissions can be applied at a share level, some interesting scenarios can arise. The question is, how do local (NTFS) permissions interact with share (network) permissions? The answer is that the most restrictive of the permissions will always apply. Think of local permissions and share permissions as exterior and interior doors to a building, and think of the permissions as being the size. If you must pass through both doors to get to the inside (file or folder access), you will be limited by the most restrictive of the two doors. If the exterior door (let's call that share security) is very large but the interior door (local security) is very small, you must deal with the small door to gain access. If the situation is reversed, you must still deal with the small door to get in. Therefore, if your share security permissions are Full Control but your local permissions are Read, you cannot get more than Read access to the data.

Although this sounds confusing, it really makes things simpler. If you want to ensure that permissions act the same for a user whether he or she is accessing data locally or over the network, you should do the following:

◆ Set all the share permissions to Authenticated Users with Full Control.

◆ Ensure that the host partition is formatted (or converted to) NTFS.

◆ Apply local permissions restricting users to appropriate levels.

This will ensure that share permissions do not interfere with users being able to access data, and it makes your job as an administrator that much easier because you do not have to deal with two sets of permissions and circumstances.

The Distributed File System (Dfs)

If you have many file servers in your organization and many shares on each one, you may run up against the problem of users being confused about where to go to get what. (As an administrator, I am often confused about such things, and I am supposed to know what I am doing!) As soon as you distribute the location of your shares, you invite problems with users locating them.

The Distributed file system (Dfs) started as an add-on to Windows NT 4.0 and is now an integrated part of the Windows 2000 Server operating system. Dfs allows you to collect a number of share points in a virtual tree. This collection makes it appear to a user browsing a server that all data is located under a certain tree structure when, in fact, the data remains scattered all over your network on different file servers. As indicated in Figure 2.16, although the shared folders are on servers 2 and 3, it will appear as though they are on server 1, thanks to Dfs.

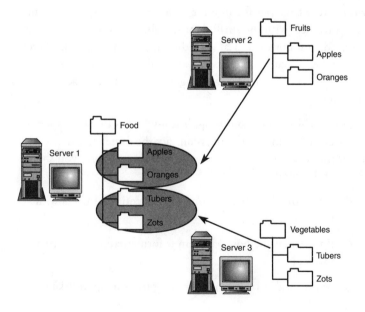

FIGURE 2.16
Dfs creates a virtual tree structure.

All characteristics of the local and share security that apply to the Dfs links will apply. The Dfs root cannot give out more access to a share than the local host of the share is willing to give. (In fact, there is no security configuration available within Dfs; it is all controlled from the remote location.) As with any other network access point, it is recommended that you use NTFS security to provide the best, most consistent access control to your shared data.

All Dfs requires is the Dfs service installed on one or more servers, a configured Dfs root, and access to remote shares on non-Dfs servers. The following steps outline the basic procedure for setting up Dfs:

1. Share folders on one or more servers.

2. Create a Dfs root.

3. Add Dfs child nodes (links) to the Dfs root.

In this section, you will be introduced to two methods of administering a Dfs: locally on a server and in a domain-wide structure in the Active Directory.

> **NOTE**
>
> **Dfs-Aware Clients Are Required** A Dfs root can be accessed only by a client operating system that understands Dfs. Such operating systems include Windows 2000 (all versions), Windows NT 4.0 (all versions), and Windows 98. Windows 95 can be Dfs enabled by downloading the Dfs client and installing it at each client station. This client software is available on the Windows 2000 Server CD-ROM in the path Clients\Win9x.

Standalone Dfs

In a standalone Dfs structure, the administration of the Dfs is controlled by a server, and no redundancy is built into it; in other words, if the main Dfs machine goes down, there is no way to get to the data that has been collected under its Dfs root.

The first step in the configuration process is to install the Dfs root on a server. For a standalone Dfs, this is done as outlined in Step by Step 2.13.

STEP BY STEP

2.13 Installing a Standalone Dfs Root.

1. From the Start menu, choose Programs, Administrative Tools, Distributed File System. You should see a window like the one shown in Figure 2.17.

continues

continued

FIGURE 2.17
A Dfs server is configured in the Dfs
Management console.

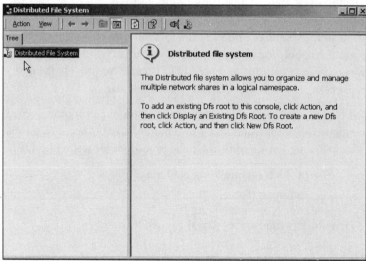

FIGURE 2.18
The Dfs Wizard allows you to create a new
Dfs root.

2. At the main Dfs screen, create a Dfs root by selecting New Dfs Root from the Action menu. This will invoke the New Dfs Root Wizard (see Figure 2.18).

3. At the Welcome to the New Dfs Root Wizard screen, click Next to continue.

4. At the Select the Dfs Root Type screen, choose Create a Standalone Dfs Root (see Figure 2.19). Click Next to continue.

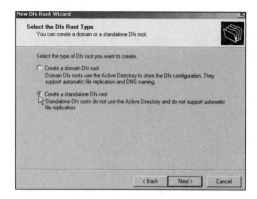

FIGURE 2.19
With the wizard, you can create a domain or
standalone Dfs root.

5. In the Specify the Host Server for the Dfs Root screen (see Figure 2.20), type the name of the Dfs server. (If you're configuring it on the machine that will be the root, the name of the current machine will be the default.) Click Next to continue.

6. At the Specify the Dfs Root Share screen (shown in Figure 2.21), you can either choose a share that has already been established to be the Dfs root or you can create a new share. If you create a new share, the folder that you are going to share must already exist. Click Next to continue.

7. In the Name the Dfs Root screen (see Figure 2.22), type a comment that describes the purpose of this Dfs tree. Then, click Next.

continues

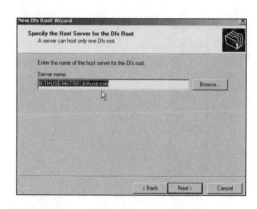

FIGURE 2.20
A Dfs root must be hosted on a machine on your LAN.

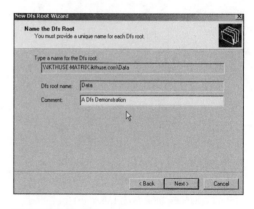

FIGURE 2.22
For administrative purposes, every Dfs root must have a unique name.

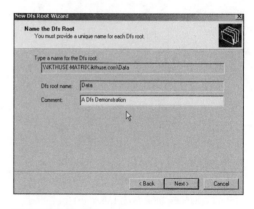

FIGURE 2.21
You can host your Dfs root from an existing share or create a new one.

FIGURE 2.23
The final page displays your settings and allows you to complete the task.

FIGURE 2.24
Select New Dfs Link from the shortcut menu to start the wizard that allows you to create a link to a virtual share.

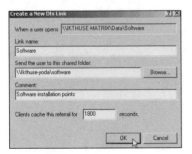

FIGURE 2.25
A Dfs link must have a name accessible by the user and a configured folder that the name connects to.

continued

> **8.** At the Completing the New Dfs Root Wizard screen (see Figure 2.23), click Finish.

Now that your Dfs root has been established, you will want to maintain it. Maintenance of a standalone Dfs root consists of three tasks: adding Dfs links, removing Dfs links, and disabling Dfs links. You will add a new Dfs link when the Dfs tree needs to be expanded through the addition of a new link. Removing a node is necessary when you no longer need a node and that need is deemed to be permanent. You will disable a Dfs link when you want to temporarily prevent a certain node from being accessed from within the Dfs tree. By disabling a node, you can prevent users from accessing it but ensure that it can easily be reactivated. Step by Step 2.14 walks you through adding a Dfs link to a Dfs root.

STEP BY STEP

2.14 Adding Dfs Links to a Dfs Root

1. From the Dfs console, right-click on the Dfs root under which you want to add a new link and select New Dfs Link from the menu that appears (see Figure 2.24).

2. In the Create a new Dfs Link dialog box (see Figure 2.25), fill in the name of the link (that is what the user will see under the Dfs root), the share that this link connects to, a comment describing the content of the share, and a referral cache time. The cache referral time is the length of time a Dfs client will store the location of the link to the remote machine. When this cache time expires, the client will have to consult with the Dfs server to reload the location. The default for this is 1800 seconds (30 minutes).

3. Repeat steps 1 and 2 until the Dfs tree is complete. When you finish, exit the Dfs Manager.

The second task you might need to perform is removing a Dfs link from the Dfs root. Step by Step 2.15 outlines that process.

STEP BY STEP

2.15 Removing a Dfs Link from an Existing Dfs Root

1. Open the Dfs Manager.

2. Right-click the Dfs child node you want to remove and select Remove Dfs Link from the menu that appears.

3. A message appears, informing you that deleting the link will not delete any of the files in the link. Click Yes to remove the link from your Dfs tree.

4. Close the Dfs Manager.

The final task outlined here is disabling and enabling a Dfs link. Step by Step 2.16 shows you that procedure.

STEP BY STEP

2.16 Disabling and Enabling a Dfs Link in a Dfs Root

1. Open the Dfs Manager and expand the root you want to maintain.

2. In the left panel, click the Dfs link you want to enable or disable.

3. In the right panel, right-click the path to the Dfs link and choose Take Replica Offline/Online from the menu that appears. If the link is currently enabled, it will be disabled, and a warning icon (a yield sign with an exclamation point in it) will be displayed on it. If the link is currently disabled, it will be enabled, and an information icon (a white circle with a green check mark) will be displayed on it.

> **NOTE**
>
> **Disabled Links Are Still Visible to Clients** Even if a Dfs link is disabled, it will still appear to the user when the Dfs root is opened. However, when the user tries to access it, an error message will appear, informing the user that the network location is inaccessible.

Troubleshooting access problems with standalone Dfs has to do primarily with configuring the Dfs properly. You have to ensure that the computers and shares you are linking to are set up and are accessible to the Dfs root. In addition, the share security needs to be set up so that users can access the right information. Because a standalone Dfs is not fault tolerant, ensuring that the Dfs root is always up is a major consideration in troubleshooting resource access. A more insidious problem occurs with clients that do not support Dfs. If a Windows 95 client tries to connect but does not have the proper software loaded, it will be unable to connect. If only some clients connect and others do not, the client software is probably to blame.

Domain-Based Dfs (Fault-Tolerant Dfs)

Although standalone Dfs works well in a small environment, when the number of clients you are serving increases, the need to have the Dfs root available on a consistent basis increases. Standalone Dfs has a weakness: If the Dfs root server goes down, the entire tree becomes inaccessible (unless you know what servers the child nodes are hosted on). By using the domain Active Directory to store the Dfs structure and by providing redundant locations to child nodes, you can ensure that your Dfs tree is available if your Dfs server goes down and that there is fault tolerance in the child nodes as well.

As its name implies, domain-based Dfs requires that the server hosting the Dfs root be part of a Windows 2000 domain. This is required because the Dfs information is stored in the Active Directory, and only a domain controller has a copy of the Active Directory.

The steps for creating a domain-based (fault-tolerant) Dfs root are listed here:

1. Share folders on one or more servers.

2. Create a fault-tolerant Dfs root using the Dfs Manager on a member server.

3. Add links to remote child nodes.

4. Add a second (or more) Dfs root server as a replica of the first.

5. Add replicas of the shared folders (if desired).

Creating a domain-based Dfs root is almost the same as creating a standalone version, as illustrated by Step by Step 2.17.

STEP BY STEP

2.17 Creating a Domain-Based Dfs Root

1. From the Start menu, choose Programs, Administrative Tools, Distributed File System.

2. At the main Dfs screen, create a Dfs root by selecting New Dfs Root from the Action menu (this will invoke the New Dfs Root Wizard).

3. At the Welcome to the New Dfs Root Wizard screen, click Next.

4. At the Select the Dfs Root Type screen (shown in Figure 2.26), choose Create a Domain Dfs Root and click Next.

5. At the Select the Host Domain for the Dfs Root screen (shown in Figure 2.27), choose the domain in which this Dfs will be defined. This defines which Active Directory domain will store the Dfs information. Click Next to continue.

6. In the Select the Host Server for the Dfs Root screen, type the name of the Dfs server. (If you're configuring it on the machine that will be the root, the name of the current machine will be the default.) Click Next to continue.

7. From the Specify the Dfs Root Share screen, either you can choose a share that has already been established to be the Dfs root, or you can create a new share. If you create a new share, the folder that you are going to share must already exist. Click Next to continue.

8. In the Name the Dfs Root screen, type a comment that describes the purpose of this Dfs tree. Click Next to continue.

9. At the Completing the New Dfs Root Wizard screen, click Finish.

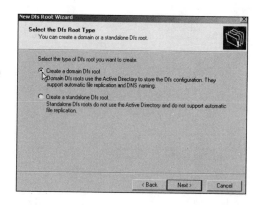

FIGURE 2.26
Begin by indicating that you want to create a domain-based Dfs root.

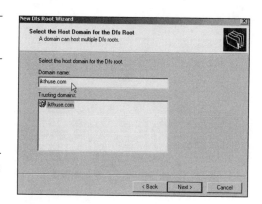

FIGURE 2.27
A domain-based Dfs must be configured to be hosted by a specific Windows 2000 Active Directory domain.

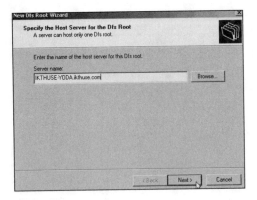

FIGURE 2.28
When you create a Dfs root replica, you must choose a machine to host it.

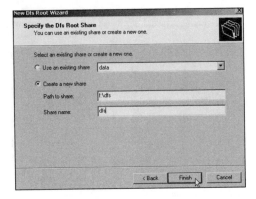

FIGURE 2.29
Like the original, a Dfs root replica must have a shared root.

To add, remove, or disable child nodes in the domain-based Dfs structure, refer to Step by Steps 2.14, 2.15, and 2.16. Those procedures are the same whether the Dfs is domain-based or standalone.

Simply storing the Dfs root information in the Active Directory does not make it fault tolerant. You must also set up replicas of the Dfs structure on one or more servers to enable fail over. By setting up root replicas, you can ensure that a user trying to access the Dfs root when the Dfs root server is down will be automatically (and transparently) redirected to another location for the tree information. Step by Step 2.18 walks you through the process of setting up root replicas.

STEP BY STEP

2.18 Creating and Enabling a Dfs Root Replica

1. From the Dfs Manager, right-click the root you want to replicate and select New Root Replica from the menu that appears.

2. At the Specify the Host Server for the Dfs Root screen (see Figure 2.28), enter the name of an additional Dfs root server for this Dfs root. Click Next to continue.

3. At the Specify the Dfs Root Share screen, either choose an existing (empty) share on the new Dfs root server or create a new share by specifying the local path to a folder and a share name (see Figure 2.29). Then click Finish.

At this point, fault tolerance has been set up, but it is not enabled. To enable it, you must configure a replication policy to define how the fault-tolerant roots get information about the main root. This is outlined in Step by Step 2.19. Note that for automatic replication to work properly, the file system on the Dfs roots must be NTFS.

STEP BY STEP

2.19 Enabling Dfs Root Replication

1. From the Dfs Manager, right-click the Dfs root you want to manage and select Replication Policy from the menu that appears.

2. In the Replication Policy dialog box (see Figure 2.30), enable the folders for automatic replication by clicking on the folder in the window and then clicking the Enable button. Then you must define the master—that is, the primary source for Dfs root information (the first folder enabled becomes the default master). To define the master, click the folder you want to be the master and then click the Set Master button.

3. Click OK to continue.

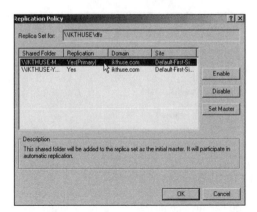

FIGURE 2.30
The replication policy governs the synchronization of Dfs information from server to server.

The Dfs Manager also allows you to configure replication of shared folders. This ensures that if a host server is not available, another replica of the same data will be provided automatically to the user. Therefore, if a user clicks on a folder inside the Dfs tree and the server hosting that folder is not available, the Active Directory is searched, and if a replica of that folder has been configured, it will be presented to the user automatically. Step by Step 2.20 walks you through configuring folder replication in a domain-based Dfs.

STEP BY STEP

2.20 Configuring Folder Replication in a Domain-Based Dfs

1. On the left side of the Dfs Manager, locate and right-click the folder you want to create a replica of. Choose New Replica from the menu that appears.

continues

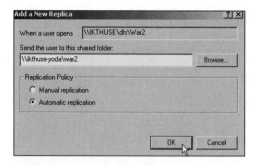

FIGURE 2.31
In addition to replicating the Dfs root structure,
you can also configure replication of folder
information.

continued

2. In the Add a New Replica dialog box, enter the path to a shared folder that you want to maintain as an exact duplicate of the source folder (see Figure 2.31). Choose a replication type of either manual or automatic. Automatic is preferred because replication happens without your intervention. The underlying file systems must be NTFS in order for automatic replication to function.

3. When you finish, click OK.

With the addition of replication, a Dfs can be made completely redundant, and therefore, data will be accessible to users on a continuous basis.

Troubleshooting domain-based Dfs is much like troubleshooting standalone Dfs. You have to ensure that the links you have established are accessible by the root Dfs server. However, you must also ensure that Active Directory is accessible (that a domain controller is up and running) so that Dfs information can be obtained. Some troubleshooting problems incurred with standalone Dfs can be avoided in domain-based Dfs simply by ensuring that redundancy has been configured (replication of root and folder information).

Configuring and Controlling File Access via Web Services

In addition to sharing files over the network using regular share-level security, if you choose to install Internet Information Services (IIS) on your server, you can also share folders to Web browser clients. Like sharing over the network, Web sharing is very straightforward; however, the steps are different. Web sharing provides access to browser users (should you desire it), but it does not share the folder over your internal network. Therefore, if you want a folder to be shared over the network as well as being Web-shared, you will have to share it twice.

Preparing for Web Sharing

Web sharing requires two things. First, you must be running IIS, specifically the WWW service on your server. Second, you must have Administrator or Power User access to your server. The default installation of Windows 2000 Server actually includes IIS, so it might already be configured on your server. If it is not, you will have to install it. Step by Step 2.21 outlines the installation process for IIS.

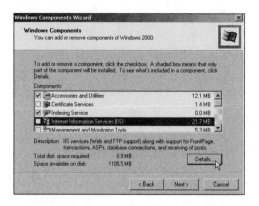

FIGURE 2.32
IIS is installed in the Windows Components Wizard.

STEP BY STEP

2.21 Installing IIS on a Windows 2000 Member Server

1. From the Control Panel, double-click the Add/Remove Programs icon.

2. In the Add/Remove Programs dialog box, click Add/Remove Windows Components.

3. In the Windows Components Wizard dialog box (see Figure 2.32), click on Internet Information Services (IIS) and then click the Details button.

4. From the Internet Information Services (IIS) dialog box (see Figure 2.33), select the following components: Common Files, File Transfer Protocol (FTP) Server; Internet Information Services Snap-In; and World Wide Web Server. Optionally, you can also select Documentation and Internet Services Manager (HTML). The Internet Services Manager (HTML) allows you to administrate most aspects of your IIS server from a browser. When you finish, click OK. Then click Next in the Windows Components dialog box.

5. At this point, configuration will begin. When you're asked for the CD-ROM, insert it into the drive to complete the installation. When installation is complete, exit the components wizard and the Add/Remove Programs dialog box.

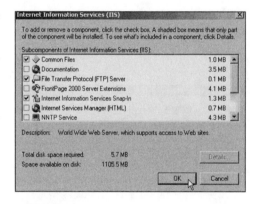

FIGURE 2.33
Certain IIS files are required for Web sharing to work properly.

This installation process modifies your server in two ways. First, it creates a folder called Inetpub on your hard drive (generally on the Boot partition). Second, it creates two local user accounts, one called IUSR_*servername* (for granting anonymous access to browser clients) and another called IWAM_*servername* (the account that IIS uses internally to start out-of-process applications). The anonymous user account (IUSR_*servername*) is especially useful because when you need to control anonymous access to published resources, you will need to refer to this account. Any user that connects to your Web server who is not authenticated will use the name IUSR_*servername* and will have whatever access has been given to that account (this account is a member of the local group Guests to restrict access even further).

After IIS has been installed, an additional tab appears in the Properties dialog box for your folders; it's called Web Sharing.

Setting Up and Maintaining Web Sharing

Web folders can be made accessible to any or all the Web sites you have configured on your server; you are not restricted to only the default site. These folders will appear as virtual folders on your Web site and will be accessible when a user types in addresses similar in format to the following:

```
http://servername/webfolderalias
```

Of course, you (or your Web developers) will be able to create HTML links to the folders as well.

The following Step by Step describes the mechanics of sharing a folder via IIS.

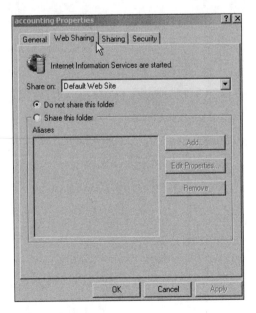

FIGURE 2.34
Web Sharing is separated from other network folder sharing.

STEP BY STEP

2.22 Sharing a Folder via Web Services (IIS)

   1. Right-click the folder you want to share and choose Sharing from the menu that appears.

   2. In the Folder Properties dialog box, select the Web Sharing tab (see Figure 2.34) .

3. In the Share On field, choose the site you want to share this folder on. All the virtual sites you have configured on your Web server will appear in the pull-down list.

4. Select the radio button labeled Share This Folder.

5. When the Edit Alias dialog box appears (see Figure 2.35), fill in an alias name (the name that a Web user will be able to reference this Web share by; it does not have to be the same as the folder's real name). Then choose one or more access permissions from the four security levels. Read means that users will be able to look at content. Write means that users will be able to upload into the folder. Script source access means that users will be able to view the source of script files in the folder. Directory browsing means that users will be able to browse the folder's contents and its subfolders. Generally, only Read access is given to publicly accessed folders.

Finally, choose an application permission. None means that no scripts or applications present in the folder can be run by a browser client. Scripts means that script files can be executed. Execute means that all programs in the folder can be run by browser clients. If you select Write access and Scripts application permissions, a dialog box will appear, indicating that you are allowing users to upload scripts they can then run (a potentially dangerous situation). You will be asked to confirm that you really intended to allow that. When you finish configuring these settings, click OK.

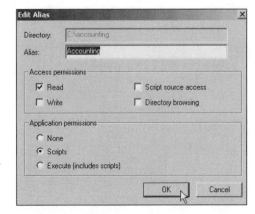

6. If the folder you are sharing resides on a FAT partition, you are done; you can click OK to complete Web sharing. If the folder is on an NTFS partition, you need to set NTFS permissions. Click the Security tab at the top of the Properties dialog box.

FIGURE 2.35
The Alias is the name a Web user will use to access the data.

continues

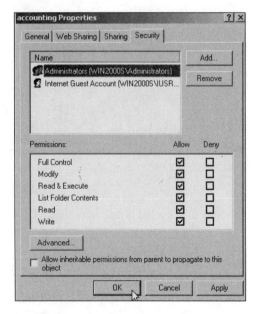

FIGURE 2.36
NTFS permissions are usually used to restrict access to a Web-shared folder.

continued

7. From the Security tab (see Figure 2.36), add local permissions for all the users you want to allow to access this folder over the Web by clicking the Add button and adding them from the directory of your choice. You can add users and groups as you normally would. However, to allow anonymous users to access the data, either you must explicitly add the IIS anonymous users, or you must implicitly add these users by adding the local group Guests. You will need to set as much NTFS permissions for any user as you have given out access in step 4. If you gave out Read and Write access, you must also give out Read and Write NTFS permission, otherwise the lesser of the access levels will prevail for your Web users. Click OK when you are done.

To modify or to stop Web sharing, you can return to the properties for the folder and add a new alias, remove an existing alias, or stop sharing altogether. If you stop sharing, all the aliases for the folder will be removed, and you will have to re-create them if you change your mind.

Web Sharing in Its Context

Web sharing does not happen in a vacuum. You have to realize that the shared permissions you assign are going to interact with both the local NTFS security that you have applied to the shared data as well as the security you have set up for the Web site the folder is shared under.

Like shared folder permissions, Web sharing interacts with local security. If Web sharing is configured for a folder that is on an NTFS partition, the more restrictive of the two permissions will be effective for a Web browser client connecting to the folder. For example, if the anonymous Web user account (IUSR_*servername*) has been given Read access through NTFS permissions and the folder has been given Web Sharing permissions of Read and Write, a Web Browser client connecting to the share will get only Read access (the more restrictive of the two permissions). Conversely, if the

Guests group is given Full Control through NTFS permissions (thus giving the anonymous Web account Full Control) but you have given out only Read access to the Web share, browser clients will get only Read access to the data.

In addition to NTFS security, you also need to know what the security is on the whole Web site that you are sharing under. Any browser client trying to get to a Web share must pass through the Web site security before it gets to that share. If the site is secured so that only Read access is allowed, even if Write access is given to the Web share, that access will not be effective for the browser client trying to access the data.

Troubleshooting Web Sharing

A number of things can go wrong with Web sharing. The first major problem is a lack of an IIS server. Without a local IIS server, you will not be able to find the Web Sharing tab on the Properties dialog box for your folder. To solve this, install IIS on your Windows 2000 server.

After an IIS server has been configured, the next problem may be your permissions to share a folder. You must have Power User or Administrator access to be able to Web share a folder. If your user account is not a member of one of those two groups, you need to gain membership or have one of the members create Web shares for you.

If the folders have been shared, the next problems might be those of access. The major problems are going to be with server access (is the server up and is the Web service running?) and permissions.

Lack of server access can result from a number of things. The server itself may not be running. If it is, the Web service may not be running. If it is, the Web site in which the folder is being shared may not be enabled. If it is, the TCP port it is running on might not be the default (port 80). Any or all of these things can prevent users from accessing the Web folder you have configured.

Problems related to the server being down (that is, the operating system is not running) are beyond the scope of this particular discussion. The bottom line is that the server must be running in order to provide access to your Web folders.

If the Web service itself is not running, you can start it by following Step by Step 2.23.

STEP BY STEP

2.23 Starting the World Wide Web Publishing Service

1. From the Start menu, choose Programs, Administrative Tools, Services.

2. Scroll down the Services list until you find World Wide Web Publishing Services. Right-click it and choose Start from the menu that appears.

3. Exit the Services console.

If the Web service is running, the problem might be that the Web site is not running. To start it, you need to open the IIS Services Manager console. Step by Step 2.24 leads you through the process of starting a Web site.

STEP BY STEP

2.24 Starting a Web Site

1. From the Start menu, choose Programs, Administrative Tools, Internet Services Manager.

2. In the IIS Console window, you can locate your Web sites by expanding the Console Root, Internet Information Services, and Your Server. When you see your Web site in the tree under the name of your server, right-click it and choose Start from the menu presented.

3. Exit the IIS console.

Finally, even if the Web site is up, if the administrator of the site has configured access on a TCP port other than the default (80), Web users will not be able to get to the Web site without specifying the new port in the URL. For the purposes of this discussion, a TCP port can be thought of like a TV channel. You may have your TV on, but if it is not tuned to the right station you will not be able to get to the program you want. All browsers are configured to access Web sites on port 80. If the Web server is not "listening" on port 80, either the server needs to be changed or the Browser has to be told which port to connect on. If the port is not 80 and you want Web users to connect, you can give them the port number. Then they will be able to connect using the following syntax:

```
http://servername:portnumber/foldername
```

For example, to connect to the folder Accounting on a server called Win2000S using the port 8080, you would use the following syntax:

```
http://Win2000S:8080/Accounting
```

To find out what the port is or change it, follow Step by Step 2.25.

STEP BY STEP

2.25 Discovering and Changing a Web Server's TCP Port

1. From the Start menu, choose Programs, Administrative Tools, Internet Services Manager.

2. In the IIS Console window, you can locate your Web site by expanding the Console Root, Internet Information Services, and your server. When you see your Web site in the tree under the name of your server, right-click it and choose Properties.

3. In the Web Site Properties dialog box, the Web Site tab contains a field called TCP Port (see Figure 2.37). That number is your TCP port number. If you change that, all browsers (and HTML links coded into pages) will have to explicitly use that TCP port number. Therefore, it is not a good idea to change it without first consulting your Web master to discuss the implications.

4. Click OK to update the Web site's properties.

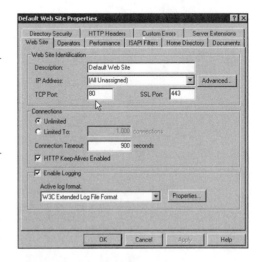

FIGURE 2.37
The TCP port number can be used to effectively hide a Web site from those who do not know the number.

When a user is able to connect to your Web site, the issue of permissions might come up. Remember from the discussion in the last section that all the levels of permissions interact to form an effective permission. As a result, you must check permission levels at the NTFS level, the Web folder level, and at the Web site level. Thus far, the only one of these three that has not been discussed is the Web site level. That's covered in the next section.

CONTROLLING ACCESS TO WEB SITES

Web sites are made available through the Web service component of Internet Information Services. Because these Web sites contain data, they need to be secured at one level or another (even if that security is to leave everything unsecured).

To publish any material to either an intranet or the Internet, you must first install IIS. You can look back to Step by Step 2.21 for instructions on how to do that. From that point, any security you want to place on your Web site(s) can be done through the Internet Services Manager (which you bring up by choosing Start, Programs, Administrative Tools, Internet Services Manager).

The following list outlines ways in which you can control access to your Web site:

- ◆ Changing the TCP port
- ◆ Changing access permissions
- ◆ Changing execute permissions for scripts and programs
- ◆ Changing authentication methods (including enabling and disabling anonymous access)
- ◆ Adding IP address and domain name restrictions
- ◆ Adding server certificates for Secure Socket Layer (SSL) transmissions
- ◆ Authenticating users with client certificates

These topics will be discussed in the following sections.

Controlling Web Site Access Through TCP Port Number

Most common TCP/IP utilities have specific TCP ports associated with them, and the software that allows you to use these expect the ports to conform to the standard defaults. However, like a TV channel, these ports can be changed. If a certain set of data is being broadcast on a certain port, and that port is not the default port for that utility (like port 80 for HTTP traffic), the port must be determined in order to access the data. This may sound trivial, but because there are more than 65,000 TCP ports to choose from, you can hide your site from most casual users by choosing any TCP port other than 80.

Of course, this is not very robust security because if someone knows what port you are running on, that person will be able to return to your site. In addition, if you have a port sniffer or a security scanner, you would be able to easily determine the port that a particular Web server is running on. However, it is a good way to hide information from people who do not know what they are looking for.

If you change the TCP port for your Web site (to 8080, for example), any browser client who wants to access your site will have to manually type in the TCP port number along with the address of your site. For example, if your site was www.mydata.com and you were using TCP port 8080, a browser client would access your site with the URL http://www.mydata.com:8080.

Step by Step 2.25 showed you how to determine and change a Web site's TCP port.

Controlling Web Site Access Through Access Permissions

One of the most common ways to secure a Web site is to change the global settings for what all users can do. By making a Web site Read-Only, for example, you ensure that no one will be able to accidentally or purposefully make changes to the content of your site.

WARNING

Change the Port Right Away   If you want to change the TCP port number, you should do it before any Web developers begin developing content for it because any links to your site need to be hard-coded with the TCP port number. If you change the TCP port number after the page development has been done, extensive re-coding will have to be done (something your Web developers will not appreciate).

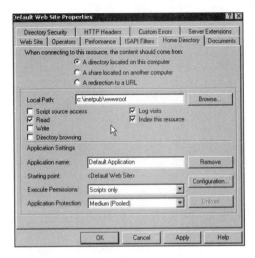

FIGURE 2.38
Web access rights can be used to restrict the file-level permissions of the files on a site.

As you can see in Figure 2.38, there are four access rights that you can control for the entire site: Script Source Access, Read access, Write access, and Directory Browsing access.

Enabling Script Source Access allows users to see the source code behind the HTML page they are currently viewing. This would allow users to access not only HTML but also JavaScript, VBScript, and ASP source code.

Read access allows users to look at the content of the Web page and download files. If Read access is not enabled, no users will be able to access the content on the site.

Write access enables users to upload content to the site. This includes being able to modify the HTML or script content as well as placing new files into the site folder on your server.

Directory Browsing allows users to see a file listing in your Web site's main folder. This would allow a user to know what the names of your files are and to navigate through your file path to subfolders in your Web site. If this is not enabled, users must connect through the HTML pages you have set up on your Web site. If no default HTML page has been configured, browser clients will not be able to navigate your Web site at all.

You will need to make choices about which of these rights you want to enable for your user community. Remember that these rights are global across all users of your Web site; they will not discriminate. If you want to allow some users to upload files while denying other users, you will have to give Web site rights to Write and then control access using NTFS permissions on the local files or folders themselves.

You will also notice in Figure 2.38 that there is a logging setting. This setting, which is usually enabled, allows you to log all user interaction with this site. This log will allow you to monitor who is connecting to your site and what he or she is doing. The logging options (including the location of the log file) can be configured on the Web Site tab of the Web site's Properties dialog box.

Step by Step 2.26 shows you how to adjust the site access permissions.

STEP BY STEP

2.26 Changing Site Access Permissions

1. From the Start menu, choose Programs, Administrative Tools, Internet Services Manager.

2. In the IIS Console window, you can locate your Web site by expanding the Console Root, Internet Information Services, and Your Server. When you see your Web site in the tree under the name of your server, right-click it and choose Properties from the menu that appears.

3. In the Web Site Properties window, click the Home Directory tab. There you see check boxes under the Local Path field that you can use to set site access permissions. Select or deselect the appropriate rights.

4. Click OK to update the Web site's properties.

Controlling Web Site Access Through Execute Permissions

Another way to control site access is through execute permissions. Execute permissions (shown at the bottom of Figure 2.38) define what kind of scripts or executables a browser client can invoke on your site. The Execute Permissions include None, Scripts Only, and Scripts and Executables.

If you select None, no scripts will run on this Web site. This is obviously problematic because it means that Active Server Page scripts, JavaScript, and VBScript will not function. However, this is the most secure route to take because scripts can damage data and the underlying file system.

If you select Scripts Only, scripts (such as ASP, JavaScript, and VBScript) will run on this Web site. However, executables cannot be invoked.

Write + Run Access = Trouble   A user that has Write access to a Web site and the ability to run scripts and/or executables could pose a serious security risk to your site. The danger is so great that if this combination is allowed, IIS will display a message informing you of the inherent risks involved. By doing this, you could allow a user to create a damaging script or program, upload it to your site, and then run it.

If you select Scripts and Executables, a user will be able to invoke any script or executable the user can get at. Although this provides a lot of functionality to the user, it is the most dangerous option in terms of security.

Step by Step 2.27 demonstrates how to change a site's execute permissions.

STEP BY STEP

2.27 Changing Site Execute Permissions

1. From the Start menu, choose Programs, Administrative Tools, Internet Services Manager.

2. In the IIS Console window, you can locate your Web site by expanding the Console Root, Internet Information Services, and Your Server. When you see your Web site in the tree under the name of your server, right-click it and choose Properties from the menu that appears.

3. In the Web Site Properties window, click the Home Directory tab. Click the Execute Permissions drop-down arrow to see the list of permissions (see Figure 2.39). Choose the level of script execute privileges you want to give out for your site.

4. Click OK to update the Web site's properties.

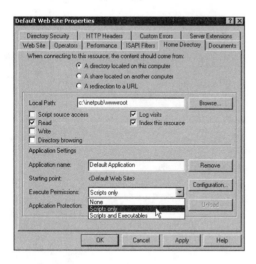

FIGURE 2.39
Execute permissions control the execution of programs and scripts on your Web server.

Controlling Web Site Access Through Authentication Methods

One of the strengths of using IIS as a Web server on a Windows 2000 server is the ability to integrate Windows 2000 computer or domain security into Web access. Essentially, you have the ability to force users to provide names and passwords from the local machine accounts or from the Active Directory to access Web sites. This eliminates the need to create your own security model.

Web authentication happens at two levels: anonymous and authenticated. Anonymous access is the first method attempted when a user tries to connect to any Web site. If anonymous access is disabled, or if a Web user tries to access a function that cannot be performed by an anonymous user, authenticated access is attempted. Anonymous access does not require a password. However, authenticated access always requires confirmation of identity, which might be in the form of a password challenge. But security information may be passed transparently (such as Integrated Windows access or with Client certificates, both of which will be covered later).

Under IIS, anonymous access is mapped to a user account. Therefore, any attempt to access a Web site anonymously will treat the user as though he or she were logged in as the anonymous IIS account. By default, the name of this account is IUSR_*servername*. That means that if your server were called "Green," the anonymous user account would be called "IUSR_Green" unless you change it to something else.

One way of securing your Web site is to disable anonymous access to the whole site. Then for any attempted access, the browser client will be prompted for a name and password to access the site. Another way to secure your site is to put NTFS security locally on some or all of your Web site. If you do this, for any attempted access of files or folders that do not allow anonymous access, a name and password will be required (whether the user is prompted for it depends on the type of authentication you require).

If you do require that a user log on to your site (or some portion thereof), you can set the type of authenticated access you want to require. There are three levels: basic authentication, digest authentication for Windows domain servers, and Integrated Windows authentication.

Basic authentication is the least secure but most accessible across a variety of browsers. This kind of authentication sends all login information in clear text. Unfortunately, if someone is "watching" your logon using a "packet sniffer" or other network analysis tool (Windows 2000 or NT Network Monitor, for example), he or she might be able to capture your user name and password as you log on. Basic authentication needs to be used for all browsers that do not support Integrated Windows authentication (non-Microsoft).

Although sending passwords in clear text is a security risk, this can be overcome by using server certificates and SSL (covered later).

When a user logs in using basic authentication, the user's combined name and password are checked against the directory that IIS has been told to use (either local or an Active Directory for the domain). If the name and password pass authentication, local security is checked on the files the user is trying to access, and if the user name has appropriate access in the ACL, access continues. If the name and password do not pass authentication, the user is prompted repeatedly until the user cancels the login operation. If the user name is not authorized to access the resource it is trying to access, it will pass authentication but be given an "Access denied" message.

A second—and more secure—type of authentication is digest authentication. It is similar to basic authentication. However, it uses a hashing algorithm to encrypt data sent between the browser and the server. This hashing algorithm is classed as one-way in that it can be used to encrypt but not decrypt the data. This type of authentication works only on browsers that support the HTTP 1.1 standard and can respond to the requests the IIS server is making. At this point, only IE4.x and IE5.x support this authentication method. Although this method has some advantages over basic authentication, it has a major security flaw in that the password must be stored in clear text on the domain controller in order for the reverse encryption to be processed and compared. As a result, it is rarely used.

If digest authentication is configured and either the user's browser is not capable of using this type of authentication or the user's account has not been configured properly (as described in the Note titled "Configuration for Digest Authentication"), the authentication will fail.

The final authentication method is Integrated Windows authentication (formerly called NTLM or Windows NT Challenge/Response authentication). This method uses special encryption protocols to secure the authentication process. Unlike the other two authentication methods, IWA does not initially prompt for a user name and password. Instead, it checks the Windows logon currently in force on the client's machine. If this can be determined and authenticated, the user might never know that any restrictions are in place on the site. If the user does not authenticate or a Windows logon name cannot be determined, the browser will display a logon dialog box.

NOTE

Configuration for Digest Authentication Two things are required in order for this kind of authentication to work. First, the IIS server must be a member of a domain. Second, each user that needs to authenticate through a browser must have his or her account to store the password using "reversible encryption." To do this, that setting must be enabled in the properties for the user (Account tab), and then the password for the user must be reset.

The benefit of this authentication method is its security. The disadvantages are that it does not work through a proxy server and that it works only on Internet Explorer 2.x or later (no Netscape support). This type of authentication is best used in an intranet environment where the browser type is known.

Step by Step 2.28 demonstrates changing the kind of user authentication required by your Web server.

STEP BY STEP

2.28 Changing Site Authentication Methods

1. From the Start menu, choose Programs, Administrative Tools, Internet Services Manager.

2. In the IIS Console window, you can locate your Web site by expanding the Console Root, Internet Information Services, and Your Server. When you see your Web site in the tree under the name of your server, right-click it and choose Properties from the menu that appears.

3. In the Web Site Properties window, on the Directory Security tab, click the Edit button in the section labeled Anonymous Access and Authentication Control (see Figure 2.40).

4. From the Authentication Methods dialog box, choose whether or not you want anonymous access to be configured (see Figure 2.41). If you do, you can choose to modify the account used for anonymous access or its password. To do that, click the Edit button and type in a new account name and password.

5. If you want to enable basic authentication, select the appropriate check box. When the Internet Service Manager warning comes up about the nature of basic authentication, click Yes to continue. Click Edit to define the location of the accounts used to authenticate Web users. If you leave it at default, the local accounts for the server will be used. You can also enter a domain name to access an Active Directory to use for authentication; however, both cannot be used.

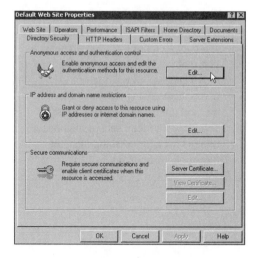

FIGURE 2.40
You can configure access authentication from the Directory Security tab of the Properties dialog box.

FIGURE 2.41
You can configure anonymous access and/or any of three authentication methods.

continues

continued

6. If you want to enable digest authentication or Integrated Windows authentication, select the appropriate check boxes.

7. Click OK to update the Web site's properties.

> **N O T E**
>
> **Multiple Authentication Methods** If you choose more than one authentication method, after attempting anonymous access, IIS will attempt to authenticate using the most secure method (Integrated Windows) first. Then it will try less secure methods until all avenues of authentication have been exhausted.

Controlling Web Site Access Through IP Address and Domain Name Restrictions

You can control the access that people have to your Web site to include only people with certain IP addresses (from within your company, for example) or to exclude people with certain addresses. By using IP address and domain name restrictions, you can ensure that even if someone obtains a user name and password that is valid, that person could still be prevented from accessing data. This could allow company employees to access the intranet when they are at their desks (with known TCP/IP addresses) but prevent them from accessing the intranet from home (where they have unknown or unauthorized TCP/IP addresses). In that scenario, you, as administrator, could configure your home IP address to be accessible but exclude all others.

When you restrict based on IP addresses or domain names, you can configure single IP addresses, multiple addresses based on a network ID and a subnet mask, or addresses falling into a certain domain. If you choose to restrict based on domain (for example, to exclude all users whose IP addresses are registered to BADGUYS.com), your IIS server will have to do a reverse lookup on each IP address that traffic comes from. This is always very time and resource intensive and might not yield accurate results. Caution should be exercised when choosing this method.

Disallowing accesses using this method has precedence over all other access a user might have been given to the Web site.

This method for changing site address and name restrictions is covered in Step by Step 2.29.

STEP BY STEP

2.29 Changing Site IP Address and Domain Name Restrictions

1. From the Start menu, choose Programs, Administrative Tools, Internet Services Manager.

2. In the IIS Console window, you can locate your Web site by expanding the Console Root, Internet Information Services, and Your Server. When you see your Web site in the tree under the name of your server, right-click it and choose Properties from the menu that appears.

3. In the Web Site Properties window, on the Directory Security tab, click the Edit button in the section labeled IP Address and Domain Name Restrictions (see Figure 2.42).

4. In the IP Address and Domain Name Restrictions dialog box, choose whether you want to implicitly grant access except to listed addresses or to implicitly deny access except to listed addresses (see Figure 2.43). Then click the Add button.

5. From the Deny Access On or Allow Access On dialog box (see Figure 2.44), choose Single Computer and enter the IP address, or choose Group of Computers and enter the network address and subnet mask, or choose Domain Name and enter the domain name. Then click OK to exit.

6. Click OK until you exit back to the IIS console.

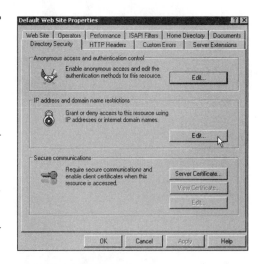

FIGURE 2.42
You can configure IP address and domain name restrictions from the Directory Services tab of the web site's Properties dialog box page.

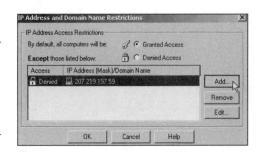

FIGURE 2.43
You can explicitly grant or explicitly deny access by IP address or domain name.

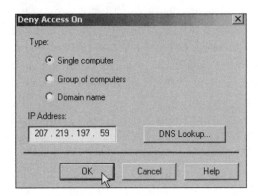

FIGURE 2.44
You can deny access by specific IP address.

Securing Web Access Using Certificates

Certificates are a final way of securing Web access and authenticating users. In Windows 2000, the use of certificates is pervasive, as much of the security uses certificates in one way or another. As a result, the discussion of certificates here will be restricted to their use in Web transactions.

The idea of the certificate as it applies to Web transactions is that an entity (server or client) proves its identity to another using a piece of identification—the certificate. The passport will provide an excellent example of how certificates work. As a Canadian citizen, I have been issued a Canadian passport that verifies that I am a certain person and that I am a citizen of Canada. When I cross the border into the United States, I can show my passport to the Customs official as proof of my identification and citizenship. This passport is deemed to be valid only if two conditions are met: The passport must be authenticated by the Canadian government (which is done through special security coding on the passport documents), and the Customs official must recognize the Canadian government as being trusted to make assertions about me. If the passport is deemed to lack authenticity or if the Customs official does not recognize the Canadian government as a trusted authority in passport issues, my passport is not acceptable for the purposes of identification.

Computer certificates work in much the same way a passport does. A server certificate issued to a Web server identifies that server as being a particular entity. This certificate must be authenticated by a third party (not me and not the server itself). This authenticating party is referred to as the Certificate Authority (CA). An example of a CA that is commonly used is Verisign. The authentication is only half of the requirement in order to create a trusted environment; my Web browser must trust Verisign to make assertions about servers. Fortunately, all current browsers are configured to trust certain CAs, of which Verisign is one. Once my browser and the Web server have verified that the server is who it says it is, a security negotiation can take place, thus enabling encrypted transmissions to take place.

Client certificates, on the other hand, are used to verify the identity of a person using a Web browser. Just as a server certificate allows a server to be identified, a client certificate allows a browser client to be identified. As with a server certificate, a client certificate must be authenticated by a third party, and that third party must be trusted by the server. If that is the case, the identity of a browser client can be established without sending a password over the Internet; all that is sent is the certificate information that identifies the particular user. This identification is made possible by incorporating the client certificate into the Web browser and then exporting the certificate to the IIS server. The certificate is then mapped to an account recognized by the IIS server and, when the certificate is seen in the future, it is recognized as being verification of a specific user. From that point, all permissions that apply to the user are applied to the holder of the certificate. Certificates can be mapped on a one-to-one basis with each being mapped to a unique user account, or a group of certificates can be mapped to a single account that has access to a Web site or set of data.

The use of Server certificates enables encryption of Web transmissions by way of secure sockets layer (SSL). The use of Client certificates enables password-free authentication of browser clients. These two certificate uses can be used independently or together.

Certificates can be obtained by purchase from a third party or they can be created by the Windows 2000 Certificate Services (a product that used to be part of IIS but which, because of its use throughout Windows 2000 security, has now been unbundled from IIS and can be installed as a separate operating system component). For Internet applications, third-party certificates are most often used because all browsers trust the third-party certificate vendors and, therefore, no browser configuration is required (except for installing the 128-bit security upgrade if you require it). For Intranet applications, you can use the Windows 2000 CA, but all your browsers must be configured to trust your root certifier.

Securing Web Access Using Server Certificates and SSL

SSL is an encryption methodology that relies on a server certificate to establish server identity and form the basis for encryption. As was mentioned in the introduction above, a certificate held by a server that comes from a CA trusted by a browser client can be used to guarantee a server's identity. In addition, with SSL enabled, it can be used to negotiate an encryption scheme between the browser and the server that ensures secure transmission of data. Under this system, clear text authentication is no longer a security hazard because the clear text password is being encrypted by the SSL connection and, therefore, is not clear text at all. This allows for not only the secure transmission of passwords but also for secure transmission of other confidential information (like credit card numbers on an e-commerce site). In addition, SSL transmissions can pass through firewalls, providing that TCP port 443 is open.

Step by Step 2.30 demonstrates the process of adding a server certificate to a Web site.

FIGURE 2.45
Server certificates can be added from the Directory Security tab of the Web site's Properties dialog box sheet.

STEP BY STEP

2.30 Adding a Server Certificate to a Web Site

1. Obtain a digital certificate from a trusted source.

2. From the Start menu, choose Programs, Administrative Tools, Internet Services Manager.

3. In the IIS Console window, you can locate your Web site by expanding the Console Root, Internet Information Services, and Your Server. When you see your Web site in the tree under the name of your server, right-click it and choose Properties from the menu that appears.

4. In the Web Site Properties window, on the Directory Security tab, click the Server Certificate button in the section labeled Secure Communications (see Figure 2.45).

5. When the Certificate Wizard appears, click Next to continue.

6. On the Server Certificate page, select the method you are going to use to obtain a server certificate (see Figure 2.46). If you already have a certificate, choose Assign an Existing Certificate. Click Next to continue.

7. On the Available Certificates page, select the certificate you want to assign to this server (see Figure 2.47). Then click Next.

8. Click Next at the summary page, and click Finish at the completion page.

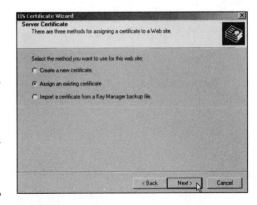

FIGURE 2.46
If you already have a certificate, you can add it to the server.

After the server certificate has been added to your site, you must configure your server for certificate authentication. The following Step by Step shows how to do that.

STEP BY STEP

2.31 Configuring Secure Communications on a Web Site

1. Open the properties for your Web site.

2. From the Start menu, choose Programs, Administrative Tools, Internet Services Manager.

3. In the IIS Console window, you can locate your Web site by expanding the Console Root, Internet Information Services, and Your Server. When you see your Web site in the tree under the name of your server, right-click it and choose Properties from the menu that appears.

4. From the Secure Communications dialog box, select Require Secure Channel (SSL) (see Figure 2.48).

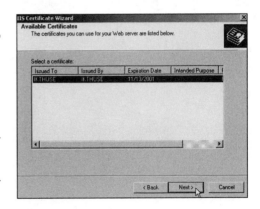

FIGURE 2.47
Select a certificate from the available certificates list.

continues

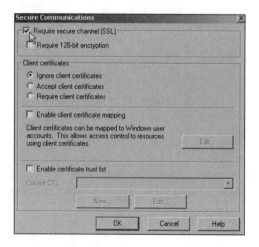

FIGURE 2.48
After a certificate has been added, you can secure your site using SSL.

continued

5. If you want to enable extra security, you can select Require 128-Bit Encryption. This kind of encryption can be imported to and enabled by people in all countires except for those that have state-supported terrorism. As of the time of this writing, this list includes Cuba, Iran, Iraq, Libya, North Korea, Syria, Sudan, Serbia, and Taliban-controlled areas of Afghanistan. If your Web site supports e-commerce or banking, you should enable this security.

Enabling Client Authentication Using Client Certificates

Client certificates are an alternate form of authentication to the ones described in the previous sections. What sets this form of authentication apart from the others is that no passwords are required by the client when a browser connects to a site requiring authenticated access. Instead, the browser sends certificate information that the Web server has mapped to a certain user account. Using this method, any browser can be used to connect to a site requiring authentication, without having to allow clear-text passwords and without requiring the user to actually log on using a user name and password.

The steps for configuring authentication using client certificates are straightforward. First, the server must have a certificate installed issued by the same CA that the clients' certificates are coming from. This will enable you to set the configuration to allow for client certificates for authentication.

Next, your clients must have a certificate installed on their browser. Like server certificates, these certificates need to be authenticated by a trusted source. If the browsers are connecting to an intranet, you could use the Certificate services to generate a root certifier and client certificates. If the connection is to an Internet site, the clients will most likely use a third-party certificate vendor like Verisign.

Finally, after clients have certificates installed, these need to be exported to the Web server and mapped to user accounts. Once the mapping has occurred, the server will be able to authenticate the client as being a particular user simply by being shown the client certificate. When the user is authenticated, access to resources is the same as that of any other authenticated user.

The next Step by Step shows how to enable client certificates for authentication.

STEP BY STEP

2.32 Configuring a Web Server to Accept Client Certificates for Authentication

1. Install a server certificate on your Web server (see Step by Step 2.31).

2. From the properties of the Web site for which you want to enable client certificate authentication, click the Directory Security tab.

3. On the Directory Security tab, click Edit in the Secure Communications section.

4. In the Secure Communications dialog box, you can select Accept Client Certificates or (if SSL has been enabled) Require Client Certificates. Accept allows, but does not require, a browser to attempt to authenticate with this Web server using a client certificate. Require Client Certificates forces a browser to attempt to authenticate with this Web server using a client certificate; failure or lack of certificate causes authentication to fail.

5. In the Secure Communications dialog box, select the check box labeled Enable Client Certificate Mapping, and then click the Edit button next to it. You can then add mappings between exported client certificates (provided by the clients) and user accounts (one-to-one mapping), or you can add a mapping between a root certifier and a user account (many-to-one mapping). A mapping between a root certifier and a user account ensures that anyone authenticating with a certificate from a specific root certifier will be given the same access on the Web site.

continues

continued

> **6.** In the Secure Communications dialog box, you can also enable a Certificate Trust List (CTL). A CTL is a list of certifiers you trust. If a client tries to authenticate with a certifier not in the CTL, that certificate will be rejected.
>
> **7.** When configuration is complete, click OK to exit.

Troubleshooting Web Site Access

Web site access is about two things: access to a running server and security.

Troubleshooting lack of access because of a server not running was covered in the earlier section "Troubleshooting Sharing."

Lack of access because of security issues revolves around all the topics that have been covered in this section. Look for TCP port incompatibilities and fix them if uncovered.

If a user is getting "Access denied" messages, check for authentication methods and underlying NTFS permissions. In addition, check for client certificates and see whether they are required. IP address restrictions may also cause these kinds of messages so check for these, too.

If a user can get to your site but cannot do what is desired (like upload files or execute scripts), check for those permissions and adjust them if necessary.

CONFIGURING AND MAINTAINING PRINTERS

Monitor, configure, troubleshoot, and control access to printers.

Next to accessing data, access to printers is probably the most important need for users. Most often, having a print device physically attached to every person's workstation is impractical, so a shared solution is desired. Windows 2000 Server provides you with the ability to host one or more print devices and to make them accessible to users.

Before you get into the mechanics of setting up printers and administering them, first look into the processes and terminology.

The Printing Process

You will rarely print from an application running directly on your Windows 2000 server. Instead, from a client computer, you will print to a printer that is shared on a Windows 2000 server. The act of sharing a printer on a Windows 2000 server denotes that server as a print server (a title which is descriptive, not prescriptive).

The process of printing can be broken down into discrete steps:

1. The client application requests to print to a printer defined on the network (which has been configured on the local client).

2. If the client operating system is Microsoft 32-bit, the following things happen locally on the client:

   • A local printer driver formats the request and sends it to a local spooler. If the client operating system is Windows 2000 or Windows NT 4.0, the client also contacts the print server to ensure that it has the most recent version of the printer driver; if it does not, that server's version of the printer driver is downloaded to the client.

   • A remote procedure call is used to contact the print server and to transfer the print job to the server. If the print server cannot be contacted, the print job is held in the local spooler until the print server can be contacted.

3. If the client operating system is not Microsoft 32-bit (or if it is configured to send only RAW), a local printer driver formats it into a RAW (printable) format and sends it to the print server.

4. When the print server receives the job, it is in RAW format. The job is written directly to disk in the spooler file in preparation to be sent to the print device. If it is not in RAW format, the print job may be modified to include separator pages and to print in duplex modes. This happens in the spooler file.

Printer Terminology   Terminology is very important, especially for the exam. Keep in mind that when the exam makes reference to a printer, it is talking about a software interface, not a physical device. The device is called a "print device"; all the software that you install and the icon you see in the Printers window is referred to as a printer. In order to make this clearer, I will often refer to this as the "virtual printer." The term "virtual printer" has been known to show up in Microsoft documentation, but I don't envision it making its way to the exam.

5. When the job arises next in the print queue, the job is sent to the print device, and it is converted into a bitmap format and is printed.

A *printer driver* is a piece of software responsible for communicating specific commands to a print device. Each driver is a little different because each print device is different.

A *spooler* is a file on a hard drive, which is the location that a client or a server uses to store print jobs that are pending printing. The print queue is the list of jobs stored on the spooler; this queue can be observed through the print manager.

As you can see from the previous points, Microsoft 32-bit operating systems maintain their own spoolers and keep their own copies of the printer drivers. In this way, the client can ensure that most of the work is done in the printing processes before the job gets sent to the print server. In addition, it also ensures that jobs can "print" even if the printer cannot be contacted at the time the job is submitted. In that case, the job simply sits on the local spooler until the print server can be contacted.

There is a difference between Windows NT and Windows 2000 clients and Windows 9x clients. The difference is that NT and 2000 clients have a mechanism to automatically update their versions of the print driver. When a job is to be submitted, the print server is contacted, and the print drivers are compared. If the server's driver is newer than the one on the client, the client's driver is updated automatically. Not so with Windows 9x clients. When a Windows 9x client establishes a connection to a network printer, the driver is installed (either from the print server or from the Windows 9x CD) and is not automatically updated.

On non-32-bit clients (like Windows 3.11, DOS, or UNIX clients), the print job is completely formatted at the client and sent to the server. There is no spooler on the client, and if the print server cannot be contacted, the print process fails at the client side.

Configuring the Print Server

The print server is the collection of software routines that provides print capabilities either locally or over a network. It is configured from the Printers folder, which is accessible either from the Control

Panel (double-click the Printers icon) or via Start, Settings, Printers. Once the Printers folder has been opened, you can get to the properties of the print server by choosing File, Server Properties.

The properties of the print server configuration dialog box are divided into four tabs: Forms, Ports, Drivers, and Advanced.

The Forms Tab

The Forms tab is used to create new form (paper size and format) configurations (see Figure 2.49). These forms are applied globally to the print server and can be made available to any virtual printer defined in it.

A number of forms are predefined, and you cannot modify or delete them. In addition, if you have a need to define a form that is not present, you can do so by selecting Create a New Form check box and then filling in a new name, dimensions, and margins for it. When you click on the Save Form button, the form will be available to any virtual printer that is configured on your server.

The advantage of forms is that they can be assigned to different paper trays on your printer (if you have more than one) and can be used to ensure that a user printing from an application will always print on the right size paper.

The Ports Tab

From the Ports tab, you define output locations for print jobs (see Figure 2.50). When you define a printer on your server, it must print to a location, like a data pipe. When information goes into the pipe, it is assumed that there is a print device at the other end. Ports enable you to define the openings into which print data is poured.

A number of ports come predefined in Windows 2000 Server. Not all of these ports actually define physical connections; these are defined by default, and it is up to you to configure the ones that will actually be used. Most frequently, print devices are physically connected to an LPT (parallel) port.

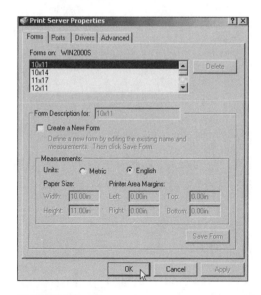

FIGURE 2.49
The Forms tab of the Properties dialog box is used to create, modify, and delete printer forms.

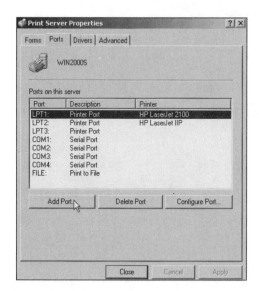

FIGURE 2.50
On the Ports tab of the Properties dialog box, you can define connections to output devices (real or virtual).

The default ports cannot really be configured. However, if you require more IRQ's, you could delete them using the Hardware Manager. A parallel port has only one configurable parameter: the retransmission retry in seconds when the print device is unavailable (like when it is out of paper).

This is the place where you can create your own ports and configure them. You might create new ports when you want to create a connection pipe that is not physical or at least not physically connected to a print device attached to your computer. This is done when you want to output print jobs to files, output to printers with network cards, or forward to other print servers (whether or not they are Windows-based).

With no additional services installed on your Windows 2000 server, you have two port types available: Local and Standard TCP/IP (other port types may show up if you have specific print services installed).

A local port defines a connection to a printer that's physically connected to your server (like on a parallel port), a test connection, an infrared connection (accessible through a UNC name), or a local file.

When you define a new local port, you are prompted for the name of the port. The answer you give determines where the print output will be directed. The following list outlines the possible answers and what they indicate:

◆ *A filename (like c:\printout\job.txt).* This defines a file to redirect the jobs to. Each subsequent print job will overwrite the previous.

◆ *The share name of a printer defined on another computer (like \\server1\hpprinter).* This will redirect the output to a shared printer or another print server. This is often used when a print device goes down and you want to allow clients to continue to print without having to reconfigure all the clients to print to a different print device. When requests come in, they are redirected to the other printer.

◆ *The word "NUL."* Jobs sent to the null port will be immediately deleted. This port type is used to test whether a client can print without having to waste paper or to queue up in front of other print jobs.

◆ *The word "IR."* This defines a connection to an infrared port to allow you to print to infrared capable printers.

Step by Step 2.33 demonstrates how to add a new local port to a
Windows 2000 computer.

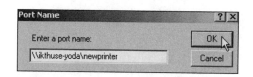

FIGURE 2.51
A new local port can connect to a shared
printer on another server.

STEP BY STEP

2.33 Adding a New Local Port

1. From the Print Server properties dialog box, select the
Ports tab and click the Add Port button.

2. In the Printer Ports dialog box, select Local Port and click
New Port.

3. In the Port Name dialog box (see Figure 2.51), enter a
local port name and click OK.

4. Exit the local port configuration dialog box.

A Standard TCP/IP port is used to connect directly to a network
printer that supports TCP/IP communication. This kind of printer
has a network card in it and acts much like a regular computer on
the network. When you configure a Standard TCP/IP port, you
define the connection via the TCP/IP address of the printer, and
requests to print on this printer will be redirected to its TCP/IP
address. The configuration of such a port will generally vary depending on the printer type. Some print devices have special software
that you can install on your print server that gives you a console
from which to do administration. If you use the standard Windows
2000 TCP/IP port configuration, you will need to know the TCP/IP
address of the print device (however that is determined).

The next Step by Step walks you through the configuration of a
Standard TCP/IP port.

> **NOTE**
>
> **Printing Directly to a Print Device**
> Many TCP/IP capable printers will
> allow you to print to them directly
> without having to have the jobs medi-
> ated through a Windows 2000 server.
> The disadvantage of this is that you
> do not get the benefits of Windows
> 2000 printer security, scheduling, or
> administration.

STEP BY STEP

2.34 Configuring a Standard TCP/IP Port

1. From the Print Server properties dialog box, select the
Ports tab and click the Add Port button.

continues

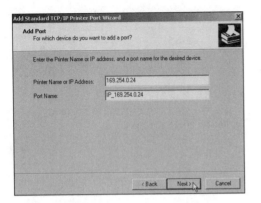

FIGURE 2.52
A TCP/IP printer (or network connected print server) has its own network card and TCP/IP address.

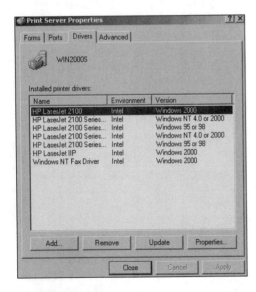

FIGURE 2.53
You should have drivers available for all the clients who will access this printer.

continued

2. In the Printer Ports dialog box, select Standard TCP/IP Port and click New Port.

3. When the Add Standard TCP/IP Printer Port Wizard appears, click Next.

4. In the Add Port dialog box, enter the TCP/IP address and a Port Name for the new port (see Figure 2.52). The port name will automatically default to IP_*ipaddress*. Click Next to continue.

5. When the Completing the Add Standard TCP/IP Printer Port Wizard dialog box appears, click Finish to complete the port configuration.

After ports have been configured, you can then install printers to print to them.

The Drivers Tab

Drivers are the software components responsible for converting high-level requests for printing into commands the processor can execute (see Figure 2.53). These commands are specific to the print device, the operating system that is requesting a print service, and the processor that is in the computer requesting the print service. As a result, a very large number of print drivers are available.

When you install a printer on your Windows 2000 server, the driver for your print device that is specific to an Intel-based Windows 2000 server is installed on your print server. The driver for this installation is obtained from the drivers.bin file local on your Windows 2000 computer (you should never have to produce the Windows 2000 CD-ROM to do a printer installation). However, there are reasons for installing more drivers. As was indicated already, when a client configures connectivity to a network printer, the first check made is to see if the driver is available from the print server. If it is not, the client is prompted to produce the driver (usually from a CD-ROM). You can avoid the users' questions and problems by ensuring that the most up-to-date drivers are available to your clients; this can be done by installing the platform-specific (hardware and software) drivers on your server.

Although Windows 2000 does not support the Compaq Alpha hardware platform, Windows NT 4.0 did. Therefore, you may need to install drivers for Windows 3.5x, Windows NT Alpha, and Windows 9x on your print server.

Step by Step 2.35 outlines the procedure for installing a printer driver on a Windows 2000 server.

STEP BY STEP

2.35 Installing a Printer Driver

1. From the Print Server properties dialog box, select the Drivers tab and click the Add button.

2. When the Welcome to the Add Printer Driver Wizard screen appears, click Next to continue.

3. At the Add Printer Driver Wizard dialog box, choose the printer manufacturer and model of your printer (see Figure 2.54). If the model is not available, you must provide a driver yourself. To do this, click the Have Disk button and browse to the location of your driver (on a disk, hard drive, network drive, CD-ROM, or Internet location). When you have provided the model, click the Next button to continue.

4. In the Environment and Operating Systems dialog box, select the correct environment (hardware platform) and operating system (software platform) combination (see Figure 2.55). Then click Next to continue.

5. At the Completing the Add Printer Driver Wizard dialog box, click Finish to continue.

6. You may be prompted to insert one or more CD-ROMs depending on the platform(s) you are installing.

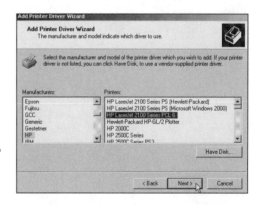

FIGURE 2.54
Identify the printer manufacturer and model.

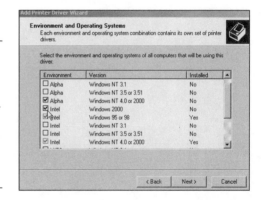

FIGURE 2.55
Identify the operating systems that will host clients for this printer.

In addition to adding a new driver, you might need to update a driver. When new versions of the drivers are created, it is a good practice to update your drivers with the new versions. For Windows 9.x clients, updating a driver requires actually installing the new driver manually on the computers. For Windows 2000 and NT clients, the new drivers will be automatically downloaded during the printing process.

A walk-through of the procedure for updating printer drivers is shown in Step by Step 2.36

STEP BY STEP

2.36 Updating a Printer Driver

1. From the Print Server Properties dialog box, select the Drivers tab, select the driver you want to update, and click the Update button.

2. When prompted, confirm that you really want to update the driver you selected.

3. When prompted, insert the CD-ROM or browse to the location of the new drivers, and then click OK to update the drivers.

If you find that a driver is no longer required, it is prudent to remove it from your print server. This is especially helpful when you upgrade your printing hardware and the drivers installed are for printers no longer accessible from the print server. Removing a driver is covered in the following Step by Step.

STEP BY STEP

2.37 Removing Printer Drivers

1. From the Print Server Properties dialog box, select the Drivers tab, select the driver you want to remove, and click the Remove button.

2. When prompted, confirm that you want to remove the driver by clicking the Yes button.

The Advanced Tab

The Advanced tab allows you to set such global defaults as the location of the spooler file, whether events having to do with the spooler are logged to the event log, and whether users are informed when documents have finished printing (see Figure 2.56).

The location of the spooler file is important, especially when the default drive is running out of space. By moving the spooler folder to a drive with more free space, you can save yourself a lot of troubleshooting problems. It is important to mention at this point that a change to the path of the spooler folder will result in immediate change. This change will prevent any documents that are pending printing from printing. To avoid this, it is best to change the spooler folder location when no one is printing to the printer.

The other options available on the Advanced tab of the Properties dialog box can be divided into logging, error notification, and print notification areas.

The first three check boxes define the level of event logging that is done for the printer. You can log errors, warnings, and information. If you do not want your event log to include information about when the printer is working correctly, you might remove logging of informational events.

The fourth check box, Beep on Errors of Remote Documents, instructs the server to beep when printing errors occur.

The last two check boxes have to do with notification of print job completion. If you select Notify When Remote Documents Are Printed, the user (if logged on) who sent the print job will be informed via a popup message when the print job has completed. If you also select Notify Computer, Not User, When Remote Documents Are Printed instead of a specific user being notified, the computer from which the print job was sent will be notified, regardless of who is logged on to it at the time.

When the print server has been configured, you can begin to consider installing printers on your server.

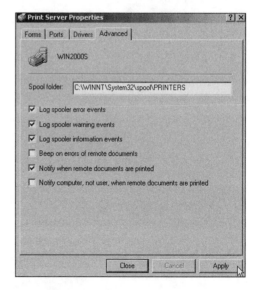

FIGURE 2.56
Advanced settings are modified on the Advanced tab of the Properties dialog box.

N O T E   **Remove Availability by Removing Sharing**   You can make a printer unavailable on the network by removing the sharing. After you change the spooler folder's location, you can again share the printer, and the documents held in local spool files will be transmitted to the print server.

Installing a Local Printer on a Windows 2000 Server

The underlying assumption of the printer server is that one or more local print devices will be accessible from virtual printers installed on a Windows 2000 server. From those virtual printers, you can configure availability and access to the print devices. This section will examine the installation of virtual printers (icons giving access to print to physical print devices) and their configuration.

You add and configure virtual printers through the Printers folder. This folder can be accessed from the Control Panel; by choosing Start, Settings, Printers (refer to Figure 2.49); or from the Printers share on the server (this share allows you to access the Printers folder even when you do not have local access to the server).

You already have been exposed to this folder because it is from here that you were able to configure the print server itself. From this folder, you can also add new printers (local and network), share printers for client access, and remove printers. Step by Step 2.38 walks you through installing a local printer.

STEP BY STEP

2.38 Installing a Local Printer

1. From the Start menu, choose Settings, Printers.

2. In the Printers window, double-click the Add Printer icon.

3. At the Welcome to the Add Printer Wizard screen, click Next to continue.

4. At the Local or Network Printer dialog box, select Local Printer (see Figure 2.57). If your printer is Plug and Play compliant, you can (optionally) select the Automatically Detect and Install My Plug and Play Printer check box. If your server detects the printer, it will install the appropriate driver for it (and skip to the end of this procedure). Click Next to continue.

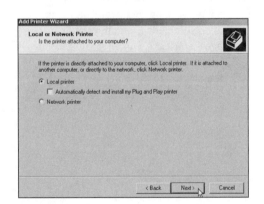

FIGURE 2.57
Identify the printer as connecting through a local port.

5. At the Select the Printer Port dialog box, shown in Figure 2.58, choose the port the printer is attached to (frequently it is LPT1). If you want to, you can create a new port (the procedure is outlined in Step by Steps 2.33 and 2.34). After choosing the port, click Next to continue.

6. At the Add Printer Wizard dialog box, enter the manufacturer and model of the printer you are connecting to (see Figure 2.59). If the model you have is not listed, or if you think that you have a more recent driver than Windows 2000 has, you can browse to the location of the driver by clicking the Have Disk button. Alternatively, you can also go to the Windows Update Web site to search for an updated driver by clicking the Windows Update button (you must have Internet access for this to work). After selecting the appropriate printer, click Next to continue.

7. At the Name Your Printer dialog box (see Figure 2.60), you can enter an intuitive printer name (something that describes its location, function, and/or ownership) and specify whether this is the default printer for this server (whether this device should be printed to if no specific printer is chosen by the user). Click Next to continue.

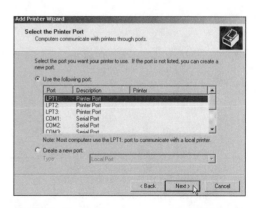

FIGURE 2.58
Specify the local port to connect through.

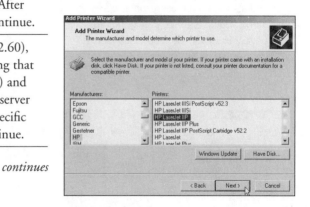

FIGURE 2.59
Identify the manufacturer and the model of the print device.

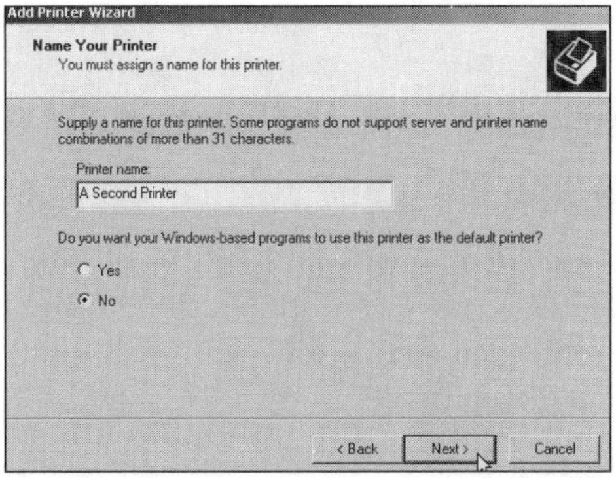

continues

![Add Printer Wizard - Name Your Printer dialog]

FIGURE 2.60
A printer should have an intuitive name describing its location, function, or ownership.

continued

8. In the Printer Sharing dialog box, you can choose to share this printer. This Step by Step assumes this is a local printer installation (sharing will be described in a later Step by Step). Select Do Not Share This Printer and click Next.

9. In the Print Test Page dialog box, you can choose to test your configuration and connection by printing a sample page. It is recommended that you do print a test page, especially if this is the first printer you have configured on a certain port or on a certain print server or of a certain type. This will ensure that the driver you have chosen works and that you have connectivity to the print device. Click Next to continue.

10. At the Completing the Add Printer Wizard screen, click Finish to complete the user interaction portion of the installation.

It is important to note at this point that many virtual printers can be configured for a single print device. As you move to the configuration section, I will point out why this is advantageous in many circumstances.

Configuring a Local Printer on a Windows 2000 Server

After you have added a printer to the Printers window, you can configure it. To do so, access the printer's Properties dialog box by right-clicking the printer you want to configure and choosing Properties from the menu that appears.

As you can see from Figure 2.61, the printer's Properties dialog box is divided into six tabs: General, Sharing, Ports, Advanced, Security, and Device Settings. This section covers all the tabs except Sharing; it will be covered in a later section.

> **N O T E**
>
> **Different Properties for Different Printers** The property sheets that appear in Figure 2.61 are the default tabs for a simple print device. Some print devices have more complex configurations, so you can expect to see some additions to the configuration pages. However, the tabs discussed in this section should always be present.

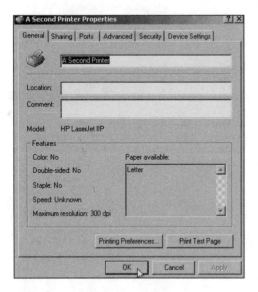

FIGURE 2.61
All printer properties can be accessed from the printer's Properties dialog box.

The General Property Sheet

The General property sheet (refer to Figure 2.61) is used to configure the printer's name and fill in information about its location and general comments. In addition, this property sheet also shows a summary of the features present on the printer.

There are two buttons at the bottom of the page: Printing Preferences and Print Test Page. Clicking the Print Test Page button sends a test job for printing. This is used to confirm connectivity and configuration. The Printing Preferences button allows you to set the default print specifications for jobs sent to the printer without the user indicating any special settings.

The Special Settings button brings up a Preferences dialog box. On it, you can set paper orientation, page order, and the number of document pages to print per piece of paper. In addition, you can set advanced settings like the print resolution (dpi) and any advanced features that might be supported by the print device.

The Ports Properties Sheet

The Ports properties sheet has the same configuration as the Ports properties sheet that's accessible from the Server Properties dialog box. With one exception, its configuration options are the same as those described in the section called "The Ports Tab" in the "Configuring the Print Server" section (see Figure 2.62). The exception is the check box labeled Enable Printer Pooling.

Printer pooling is the ability to have two or more print devices accessible from a single virtual printer. The advantage of this can be compared to the checkout line at a supermarket. When you go to the supermarket, you find a number of checkers each with their own line. People wanting to purchase groceries survey the lines looking for queue length and checker speed to determine which line they want to enter. (My wife and I usually enter separate lines and then move to the one that gets to the checker the fastest!) The fundamental problem with this scenario is that a person who got in line after me might get service sooner because I was unable to accurately judge the speed of the line I got stuck in (there is always some person who insists on dumping out a change purse to get the exact combination of coins—no matter how painfully slow the process is). Obviously, a

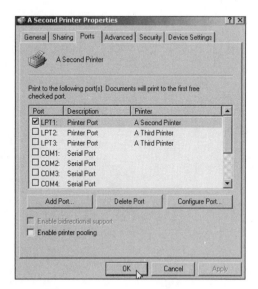

FIGURE 2.62
This property sheet is almost identical to the Ports sheet in the Print Server properties.

better solution would be to have a single line with multiple checkers at the end (which is typical of the setup at a bank or an airport). Then we would all be serviced in the order that we came into the line, and the next free checker would be assigned to the next person in line.

If you apply this to printing, you have the same issues. Let's say that accounting has a print device and so does maintenance. Accounting uses their printer almost continuously, whereas maintenance prints only the occasional memo. Here we have two lines (accounting and maintenance) at two devices; one line is almost always empty, and the other is almost always full of jobs to be printed. Printer pooling solves this problem by creating a single line; a print job may come out on the accounting printer or the maintenance printer depending on which one happens to be free at the time the job is sent. Because there is only one queue (line), all jobs will be serviced in the order they went into the queue.

To make printer pooling work effectively, a number of guidelines must be followed. First, the print devices must be the same or, at the very least, they must use the same print drivers. That is because there is only one configuration location and only one place to configure the driver. If the print devices are not the same, half the time the jobs will come out garbled because they will be printed using the wrong driver for that device.

Second, the print devices must all be accessible from ports on a single print server. You cannot pool resources from multiple servers unless you configure your server to treat a remote device as a local one.

Third, you must physically locate the print devices in close proximity. It is important that the people printing be able to find their print jobs because there will be no way to determine which print device the job was sent to except through visual inspection. For the mental health of your users, it is not a good idea to locate one print device on the fifth floor and another on the second floor because the users will have to run around the office looking for their printouts. Instead, put all the devices in a single room.

The following Step by Step describes how to set up a printer pool.

STEP BY STEP

2.39 Configuring a Printer Pool

1. Physically connect two or more print devices to your print server (or ensure that they are available on the network and that there are ports configured on the print server to access them).

2. Create a local virtual printer to connect to one of the print devices (refer to Step by Step 2.38).

3. From the Printers dialog box, right-click the printer you created in step 2 and select Properties from the menu that appears.

4. From the Properties dialog box, click the Ports tab.

5. On the Ports property sheet, select the Enable Printer Pooling check box and then select the ports that the print devices are accessible through (see Figure 2.63). The order in which these devices are selected is the order in which they will be checked when a job is sent to the pool.

6. Click the OK button to establish the pool.

   When you revisit this tab you will see that multiple ports have the same printer name associated with them (refer to Figure 2.63). This represents the printer pool.

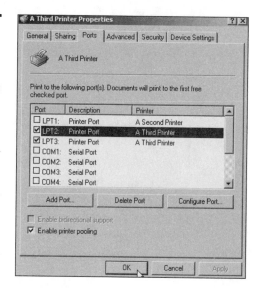

FIGURE 2.63
Enable printer pooling and then choose multiple ports to print to.

The Advanced Property Sheet

The Advanced property sheet allows you to configure a number of miscellaneous advanced functions of the printer (see Figure 2.64).

The first is printer availability. The default for this feature is to have a specific printer always available, and that is frequently the way this option is left. However, you can also configure a printer to be available only at certain times. When a print job is sent to a printer that is not available at that time, the job is held in the queue until the printer becomes available, and then the job will begin to print. I will give two examples of how this feature can be used.

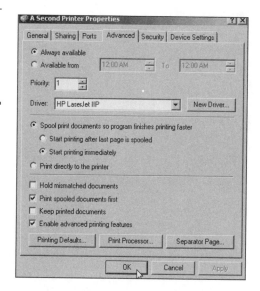

FIGURE 2.64
Advanced properties include availability and spooling settings.

In the first example, a specific department is prone to printing large jobs at certain times of the month. These jobs are generally hundreds of pages long and tie up a print device for hours at a time. This has obvious implications for other jobs that need to be printed. If the print jobs can be deferred to an evening print, that will benefit everyone greatly. To do that, you can create two virtual printers accessing the same print device. You could call one Batch and tell people to send large print jobs (anything larger that 100 pages, for example) to it. The virtual printer called Batch would have its availability set to 12:00 AM – 6:00 AM. This means that any jobs sent to it would stay in the queue until midnight, at which time they would print. Education and time would then help people to remember to send large jobs to that printer, which would free up the print device during the day by ensuring that large jobs printed automatically at night.

In the second example, two departments, Accounting and Maintenance, have their own print devices. Because the Maintenance device is not used all the time, you want to be able to make it available to Accounting at certain times of the day, such as from 2:00 PM until Midnight. Through the use of security (see the following section) and availability, you could make sure that the Maintenance print device is available to people in maintenance all the time but is also available to Accounting from 2:00PM to 12:00AM.

The second configuration option is priority. The priority sets the default importance of documents being printed from a specific virtual printer to a certain print device. The priority of a specific print device can be set anywhere from 1 to 99 with 1 being highest priority. To understand the importance of this, we must again look at the case of two virtual printers printing to a single print device. The print device has only one spool file; that means that all jobs for that device will accumulate in the same print queue. When a job goes into the queue, it jumps over all jobs that have been submitted (but are not currently printing) that have a lower priority that it does. If one virtual printer has a priority of 1 and another has a priority of 2, all the jobs submitted via the first printer will be printed before the jobs submitted via the second. In conjunction with security (see the following section), this can be used to control access to certain print devices and ensure that certain groups get print priority over others.

The third configuration option is the driver being used by this virtual printer. This option is set when you install the virtual printer, and it is usually not changed. You might want to change it if the name of the printer was to remain the same but the print device was changed. However, for the most part, you want to leave that option alone.

The fourth configuration has to do with spooling. The two spooling options allow you to either spool the documents (Spool Print Documents So Program Finishes Printing Faster) or not spool them (Print Directly to the Printer). You would normally want to spool documents, so unless spooling does not work properly, you would never choose to print directly to the printer.

If you choose to spool documents before printing, you can choose the priority of print jobs. You can either begin to print the print job immediately as it begins to spool, or you can wait until the entire document has been spooled before it begins to print. There are tradeoffs to both methods. If you wait until a job is spooled before printing, a large job may take longer to print because it must first be spooled before it prints. This might also allow other jobs to begin printing sooner even though they were submitted after it because if they are smaller jobs, they will be spooled sooner (this can be either a plus or a minus). On the other hand, if you choose to begin to print the job as soon as it begins spooling, it will finish printing sooner. The default is to allow jobs to begin to print as soon as they begin to spool.

At the bottom of the Advanced tab are a collection of check boxes that turn certain features on and off. Hold Mismatched Documents allows the spooler to check to see that the format of the document submitted is the same as what the printer accepts. If this check box is selected, mismatched documents will be held in the queue; otherwise, they will be discarded.

Print Spooled Documents First allows you to increase the efficiency of the printing process. Documents that have completely spooled are given priority over documents that are still being spooled to the print server. In addition, it also gives smaller documents priority over larger documents because they will spool faster. All of this is irrespective of the priority of the documents. If this option is not selected, priority is completely dependent on the priority of the documents.

Keep Printed Documents allows you to hold copies of documents in the queue even after they have printed. The default is to delete the documents from the print queue after they have printed (which increases the print environment security). However, keeping copies of the documents in the queue means that documents that take a long time to produce can be reprinted easily if necessary. In addition, keeping copies in the queue allows auditing of all printing for that device.

Enable Advanced Printing Features allows such features as booklet printing to be turned on. Normally, you would leave this option on unless it causes problems in the printing process, at which point you would turn it off.

There are also three buttons at the bottom of the Advanced property sheet. The first, Printing Defaults, sets exactly the same properties that the Printing Preferences button on the General property sheet does. Refer to the section "The General Property Sheet" for more information.

The second button is the Print Processor button. Unless the software being used to render print jobs requires some special print processor, you should not change the default settings.

The final button is Separator Page. In some offices, the volume of jobs and the number of people printing to a specific device makes it prudent to separate the jobs from one another. A separator page is a printed page identifying certain characteristics of the document being printed (like the owner). By clicking the Separator Page button, you can browse to a separator page file on your hard drive. You can use the separator files provided by Windows 2000 in the System32 folder on the Boot partition, or you can create your own files. The separator page you choose or create must be selected based on the class of printer you are using (PCL, Postscript, and so on). If no file is specified, no separator page will be printed.

The Security Property Sheet

When it comes to controlling access to your printers, nothing beats a good security model. Security on printers is very much like local file security through NTFS permissions on files; it applies whether you are accessing a printer locally (logged on to the server) or remotely (over the network). In fact, there is no such thing as shared permissions on a printer, and that makes it easier for you to administer because you do not have to worry about two levels of security interacting.

The basic security model has three levels, with a few more granular modifications that can be adjusted through advanced settings. These levels are:

◆ Print

◆ Manage Printers

◆ Manage Documents

Like NTFS permissions, security is managed through a DACL associated with the printer. Print gives users the ability to print to the printer. Manage Documents gives the assigned user or group the ability to manipulate documents in the print queue; this means the user can adjust the properties of and delete documents in the queue. Manage Documents does not automatically give the right to print to a printer; the Print permission must be given in addition to Manage Documents. Manage Printers not only gives all rights of Print and Manage Documents, but also gives the ability to modify the properties of the printer itself and to take ownership of the printer. In addition, Manage Printers gives the ability to manage the security of the printer through adjustment of the DACL.

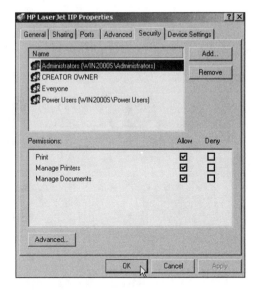

Figure 2.65 shows the default security configuration for a newly installed printer. Listed are the Administrators of the print server, Power Users of the print server, the CREATOR OWNER of the print jobs, and the Everyone group. Both the Administrators and the Power Users have all three permissions. These groups will be able to print to the printer, manage all the documents, and change the ACL of the printer. The CREATOR OWNER (the person who created the specific print job being manipulated) has Manage Document permission (to manage the documents that he or she creates). In addition, CREATOR OWNER also gets the permissions that the Everyone group gets (Print permissions).

FIGURE 2.65
Users and groups can be added, and permissions can be given to each.

The default settings provide a good jumping-off place for a discussion of combined permissions on a printer. Like NTFS permissions and shared access permissions, the effective printer permission is the combination of all the permissions granted. Therefore, although the CREATOR OWNER has only explicitly been given Manage Documents permission, because she is a member of the Everyone group, she also has Print permission. Also like NTFS and shared access permissions, explicit denial of a permission takes precedence over explicit allowance. So if a user belongs to a group given Manage Documents access but is explicitly denied Manage Documents access, that user would not have Manage Documents access.

The next Step by Step demonstrates the procedure for changing printer security settings.

STEP BY STEP

2.40 Changing Security Settings on a Printer

1. In the Printers dialog box, locate the printer you want to maintain, right-click it, and choose Properties from the menu that appears.

2. In the Properties dialog box, click the Security tab.

3. On the Security property sheet, click the Add button to add a new user to the list. If you want to remove a user, select the user in the list and click the Remove button.

4. After all users are added, either allow or deny the permissions desired.

5. Click OK to apply the changes and exit the Properties dialog box.

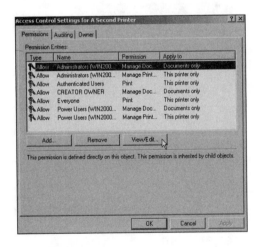

FIGURE 2.66
Special permissions allow more granular control over printer access.

As with NTFS security, advanced settings can also be applied to printer security. From the Security property sheet, you can click the Advanced button to access those properties (see Figure 2.66).

The advanced permissions break down the permissions set on the Security property sheet into their component parts. You can modify the permissions for a specific user or group by adding that user to the list (by using the Add button—as you did on the Security property sheet) and then clicking the View/Edit button.

As you can see in Figure 2.67, the advanced permissions add to the basic permissions set on the Security tab. Added to the basic permissions are Read Permissions, Change Permissions, and Take Ownership. Read Permissions allow a user to see the current security configuration of a printer. Change Permissions allows a user to modify permissions for a printer. Take Ownership allows a user to become the owner of a printer. By default, the owner of a printer has the ability to change permissions.

To take ownership of a printer you must have the advanced permission Take Ownership. Even if a user has no permissions other than Take Ownership, that user will still be able to access the Security property sheet and modify ownership. Taking ownership of a printer is outlined in the following Step by Step.

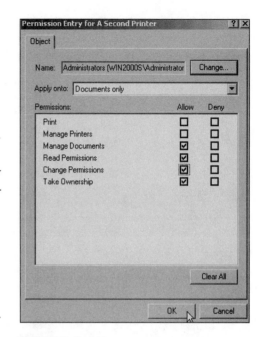

FIGURE 2.67
Special permissions can be explicitly given or denied.

STEP BY STEP

2.41 Taking Ownership of a Printer

1. From the Printers dialog box, right-click the printer you want to take ownership of and select Properties from the menu that appears.

2. From the Properties dialog box, click the Security tab. Regardless of the permissions you have, you will be able to read the DACL settings (even if you do not have Read Permissions permission). You may be informed that you only have permission to view the current security information on the printer. If a dialog box with this information appears, click OK to continue.

3. From the Security properties page, click the Advanced tab.

4. In the Access Control Settings dialog box, click the Owner tab.

continues

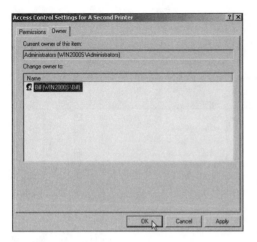

FIGURE 2.68
Every printer has an owner, and permission can be granted for another user to take ownership.

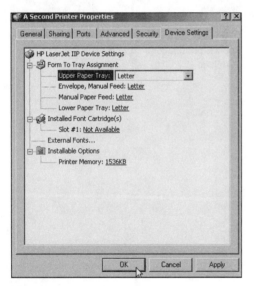

FIGURE 2.69
The device settings are specific to each printer. A wide variety of features can be expected.

continued

    5. On the Owner properties sheet, you will be presented with a list of users or groups that you can set ownership to. Usually there will only be one thing in the list: your name (see Figure 2.68). However, if you are a member of the Administrators group, you will also see that group listed in addition to your account in the list. You can set ownership to any person or group in the list. When you finish, click OK to apply that permission.

The Device Settings Properties Sheet

The Device Settings property sheet has contents that are very specific to the particular printer model you are configuring (see Figure 2.69). Generally, there will be options for assigning specific forms to paper trays, configuring installed font cartridges, and configuring other installable options. However, because this configuration page is so varied and idiosyncratic to specific printers, no further information on setting these options will be given.

Sharing a Printer on a Windows 2000 Server

If a print server is to truly live up to its name, it must give general access to print resources across a network. On a Windows 2000 server, this requires that you share one or more printers.

Sharing can be configured when you install a printer or after the fact. The next Step by Step describes how to configure sharing for a printer you have already installed.

STEP BY STEP

2.42 Sharing a Printer

    1. In the Printers dialog box, right-click the printer you want to share and select Sharing from the menu that appears.

2. From the Sharing property sheet, select the Shared As radio button and fill in the share name for the printer (see Figure 2.70). This share name will default to the name of the printer, but you do not have to leave it at that.

3. If you want this printer to be listed in Active Directory, select the List in the Directory check box. This box is selected by default and, if selected, ensures that users can search for the printer when configuring a network printer to connect to.

4. If you have clients who use operating systems other than Windows 2000, you can click the Additional Drivers button to add new client drivers (refer to Step by Step 2.34 for more information).

5. Click OK to apply the changes and exit.

Because all the security is configured from the local printer, there is no need to set up shared access after the printer has been shared.

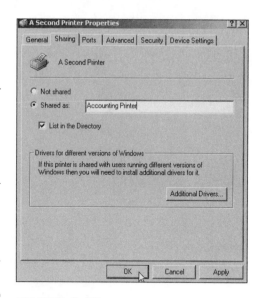

FIGURE 2.70
A shared printer's share name should be intuitive to any client connecting to it.

Maintaining Documents on a Windows 2000 Print Server

After printers have been configured, they will run without too much intervention (other than adding paper and toner). However, there are times when the printer and the documents in the queue must be managed. This management includes pausing a printer for maintenance, redirecting documents when a printer stops functioning, removing documents from the print queue, and changing the properties of documents in the print queue.

All ongoing printer maintenance is handled from the print queue for that printer. Double-click the printer for which you want to see the print queue, and a dialog box opens, showing the queue.

Many of the features of the print queue are accessible from the menus. The Printer menu allows you to change access and configuration for the printer; the Document menu allows you to change access and configuration for documents. To manipulate the printer, you must have Manage Printer permissions for the printer. To manipulate all the documents, you must have Manage Documents permissions for the printer. Anyone can manipulate his or her own documents because the CREATOR OWNER account is assigned Manage Documents permission.

In the event that you need to temporarily stop a printer from sending print jobs to a print device, you can select the Pause Printing option in the Printer menu. You might do this, for example, if you see that print jobs are being printed on company letterhead by mistake and you want to stop printing so you can change paper.

In the event that all jobs need to be removed, you can select Cancel All Documents from the Printer menu. This will delete all documents from the queue.

Whereas the Printer properties allow you to adjust options for all the documents being printed, the Document menu allows you to adjust properties for a document one at a time (you can also access these by right-clicking the document and choosing from the menu that appears). The Document menu allows you to pause a document from printing, resume a document's printing, and restart a document's printing (something that is very handy in the case of a paper jam). In addition, from the Document menu, you can access the Document properties dialog box. Finally, the Document menu also allows you to Cancel (delete) a document.

The Properties dialog box has three property sheets: General, Layout, And Paper/Quality. Of the three, only the General property sheet has properties that can actually be changed; the other two have read-only attributes.

On the General property sheet, you can change the person who is notified when the job is complete, the priority for the current document, and the time at which the document is printed (see Figure 2.71).

Although these properties may be adjusted by the owner of the document, the priority will not affect anything except those documents that belong to the same owner unless that person also has been explicitly assigned the Manage Documents permission. To get to the point, simply because a user knows how to change document properties does not mean that he or she can leapfrog his or her documents over others in the queue.

FIGURE 2.71
Document properties can be set to override the default printer settings.

Managing a Windows 2000 Printer from a Browser

If you have Internet Information Server (IIS) installed on your Windows 2000 server, you can manage the print queue of any shared printer from a browser. From a browser window, you can pause and resume a printer; view, pause, resume, and cancel documents; and view the properties of your printers. These capabilities are explored in Step by Step 2.43.

STEP BY STEP

2.43 Managing a Windows 2000 Printer from a Browser

1. Start a Web browser.

2. In the Address line, type **http://*servername*/printers** (where *servername* is the name of your print server). Figure 2.72 shows the result of this action.

continues

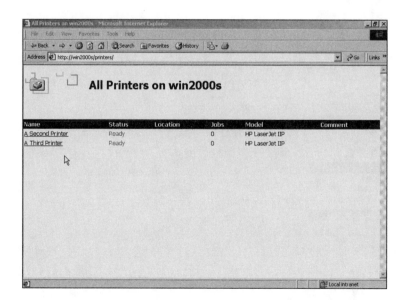

FIGURE 2.72
From a browser, you can see all the shared printers on a server running IIS.

continued

3. From the printers window, you can manage any of your shared printers by selecting the link representing the printer (see Figure 2.73). When you finish making changes, close the printers window.

Auditing a Windows 2000 Printer

Suppose you want to track access to a specific printer so you can determine who modifies permissions (or tries to) or who tries to access a printer and fails because of access restrictions. Auditing writes entries to the Security log, and you can access it at your convenience.

Auditing can watch for both success and failure of a specific type of access. Usually, you will want to audit only failures because they are the ones that will help you spot unauthorized people trying to access your printers. If you audit successful accesses, you will get a huge number of audit records—usually more than you want to sift through.

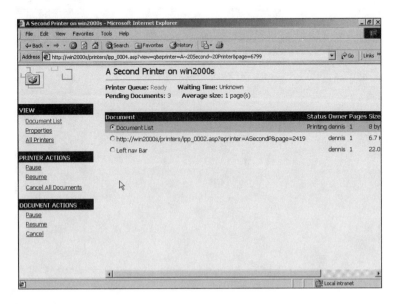

FIGURE 2.73
Documents on a selected printer can be managed from a browser.

Setting up auditing is a two-step process. First you configure your server to watch for audit events, and then you configure your printer to generate audit events for certain access types. Step by Step 2.44 walks you through this process.

STEP BY STEP

2.44 Configuring Auditing on a Windows 2000 Server

1. From the Start menu, choose Administrative Tools, Local Security Policy.

2. In the Security Settings console, expand Local Policies and click Audit Policy to expose the auditable types on the right (see Figure 2.74).

3. In the right pane, right-click Audit Object Access and choose Security from the menu that appears; turning on Audit Object Access will also enable the auditing of files and folders on NTFS partitions.

continues

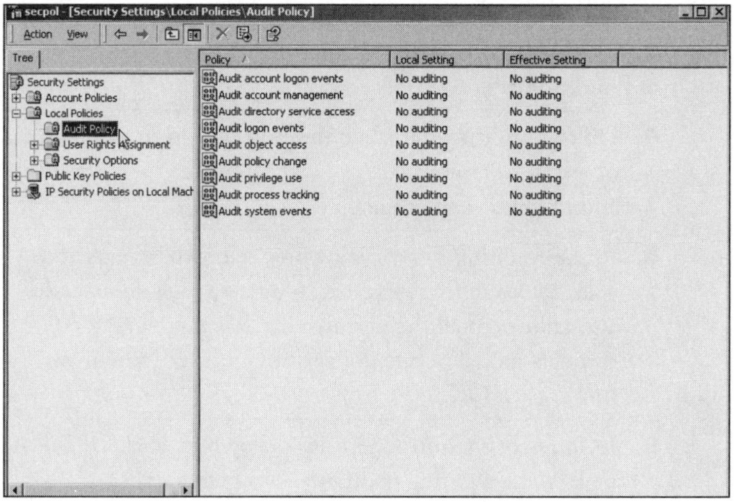

FIGURE 2.74
To enable auditing of print resources, you must configure it in the computer policies.

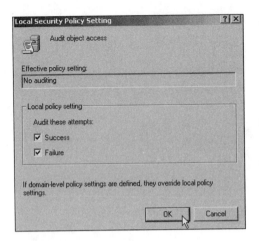

FIGURE 2.75
You can choose to audit successful and failed device access.

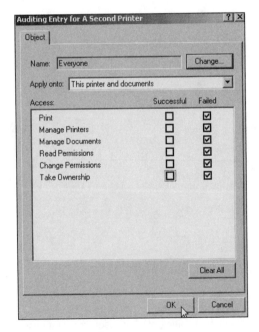

FIGURE 2.76
You can configure specific events to audit for each individual printer.

continued

4. In the Local Security Policy Setting dialog box, select Success and/or Failure to define the kind of events you want to audit (see Figure 2.75). Click OK to continue.

5. Close the Security Settings console.

After you configure your server to watch for audit events, you have to set up your printer(s) to define which events will trigger recording audit information. This is covered in Step by Step 2.45.

STEP BY STEP

2.45 Configuring Auditing for a Windows 2000 Printer

1. From the Printers dialog box, right-click the printer you want to configure for auditing and select Properties from the menu that appears.

2. Click the Security tab, and then click the Advanced button.

3. In the Access Control Settings dialog box, select the Auditing tab.

4. On the Auditing tab, click the Add button to add a user or group to monitor (if you want to watch for all events, add the Everyone group).

5. In the Auditing Entry dialog box, select the events you want to watch (see Figure 2.76). These include successes and failures of all the permissions that can be granted through special permissions for the printer. When you finish, click OK.

6. In the Access Control Settings dialog box, click OK to make these auditing configurations permanent.

Now that auditing is configured and your server is collecting information, you will want to check the logs to see whether events are
being generated. These events will be logged in the Security log,
which is accessible from the Event Log console. Step by Step 2.46
shows you how examine the Event Log.

STEP BY STEP

2.46 Examining the Event Log

1. From the Start menu, choose Programs, Administrative
Tools, Event Viewer.

2. From the log list (upper-left side), select the Security Log
(see Figure 2.77).

continues

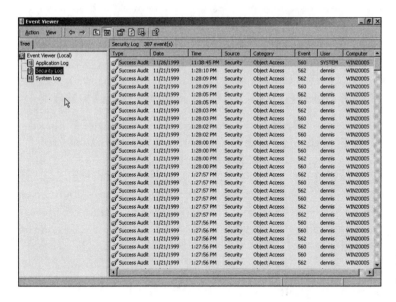

FIGURE 2.77
The Security log records all events configured
for auditing.

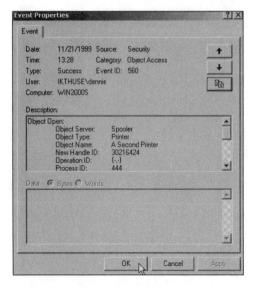

FIGURE 2.78
A security event shows the object you are auditing and the event that's recorded.

continued

3. Double-click the entry on the right that represents the event you want to examine (see Figure 2.78).

NON-WINDOWS OPERATING SYSTEM INTEROPERABILITY

Install and configure network services for interoperability.

In many network environments, Windows 2000 is not the only operating system in use. In those cases, some level of interoperability must be attained between Windows 2000 and the other operating system in order to share information effectively. Windows 2000 Server provides a number of services that allow for interoperation with network operating systems such as NetWare, AppleTalk, and UNIX.

Interoperation with Novell NetWare

At this time, Microsoft sees Novell NetWare as its major PC-based network operating system competitor. As a result, it has invested many years of research and development into creating tools to interoperate with NetWare as well as to migrate from it. This discussion focuses primarily on the tools that come with Windows 2000 Server, but for the sake of well-rounded knowledge and because other issues may crop up on the exam, the discussion touches briefly on some of the add-ons.

Installing and Configuring the NWLink Protocol

Although TCP/IP is available for NetWare and is becoming popular, especially on NetWare 5 servers, the proprietary IPX/SPX protocol suite is still the mainstay of NetWare network communications. As a result, in order to have any level of interoperability with NetWare servers, a compatible protocol must be installed on Windows 2000 Server machines. Microsoft's implementation of the IPX/SPX protocol is called NWLink IPX/SPX/NetBIOS Compatible Transport Protocol, and it is fully compatible with IPX/SPX, thus ensuring baseline communication with NetWare servers.

With NWLink installed on a Windows 2000 computer, you are able to connect to client/server applications running on NetWare servers. This is apart from any functionality gained by installing additional services.

To install NWLink, follow the steps in Step by Step 2.47.

STEP BY STEP

2.47 Installing the NWLink Protocol

1. Right-click the My Network Places icon on your desktop and choose Properties from the menu that appears (alternatively, double-click the Network and Dialup Connections icon in the Control Panel).

2. In the Network and Dialup connections window, right-click the connection that represents the network on which you want to connect to a NetWare server, and then choose Properties from the menu that appears.

3. In the Network Connection Properties dialog box, click the Install button (see Figure 2.79).

4. In the Select Network Component Type dialog box, click Protocol, and then click the Add button (see Figure 2.80).

5. From the Select Network Protocol dialog box (shown in Figure 2.81), select NWLink IPX/SPX/NetBIOS Compatible Transport Protocol, and then click OK.

continues

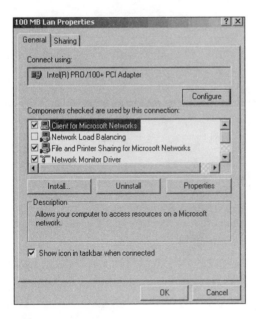

FIGURE 2.79
You can install a new protocol from the properties of your LAN connection.

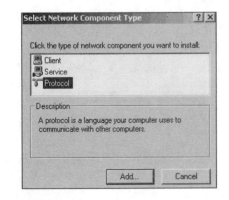

FIGURE 2.80
Choose to install a protocol.

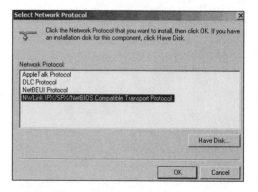

FIGURE 2.81
Select NWLink, the Microsoft implementation of the IPX/SPX protocol suite.

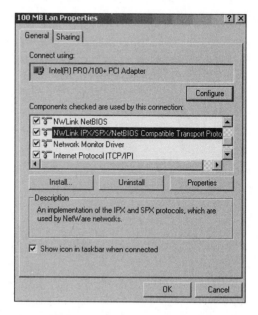

FIGURE 2.82
Frame type is a property of the NWLink protocol.

continued

6. When you're returned to the Network Connection Properties dialog box, close the window to complete the installation.

After installing NWLink, you might need to configure it. Whether or not you need to configure it depends on how many different kinds of NetWare servers you have in your environment. Different versions of NetWare (and NetWare servers using different network types, for example, Ethernet versus Token Ring) use different frame types (think of this as a dialect of IPX/SPX). These frame types are not compatible with one another. If you have only one frame type, NWLink will detect it and automatically configure itself. If there is more than one frame type (your NetWare Administrator will be able to tell you this), you will have to manually configure the frame types. If you do not, only one frame type will be used, and the others will be ignored (the frame type used will be either 802.2 or the first one detected if 802.2 is not detected on your network).

To manually configure frame types for NWLink, follow Step by Step 2.48.

STEP BY STEP

2.48 Manually Configuring NWLink Frame Types

1. Right-click the My Network Places icon on your desktop and choose Properties from the menu that appears (alternatively, double-click the Network and Dialup Connections icon in the Control Panel).

2. In the Network and Dialup Connections window, right-click the connection that represents the network with NWLink installed on it.

3. In the network connection Properties dialog box (shown in Figure 2.82), select NWLink IPX/SPX/NetBIOS Compatible Transport Protocol and click the Properties button.

4. In the NWLink IPX/SPX/NetBIOS Compatible Transport Protocol Properties dialog box, select the Manual Frame Type Detection radio button and then click Add (see Figure 2.83).

5. In the Manual Frame Detection dialog box, select the frame type you want to add, type in the external network number associated with that frame type, and then click OK (see Figure 2.84). The external network number defines routing characteristics for the connection, and each frame type will require a unique one. If you do not know the network number, consult with your NetWare administrator.

6. Repeat steps 4 and 5 until all the required frame types have been added. Then exit from the protocol configuration.

Although the NWLink protocol will give you basic connectivity to a NetWare server, that is often not sufficient for interoperation with a NetWare environment. The Gateway Service for NetWare (GSNW) provides further connectivity.

Installing and Configuring the Gateway Service for NetWare (GSNW)

Gateway Service for NetWare (GSNW) provides two connectivity services for Windows 2000 Servers. First, it provides connectivity to a NetWare server's printers and files through the installation of a NetWare Client for Windows 2000 (this is the same client that is installed on Windows 2000 Professional when Client Services for NetWare is installed). The client service will allow a Windows 2000 server to log into a NetWare server and access files and printers based on the permissions assigned to the account used to connect to the NetWare server.

Although the client portion of GSNW is useful, the full functionality of GSNW is the connectivity it can provide to other Microsoft clients through its gateway to NetWare resources.

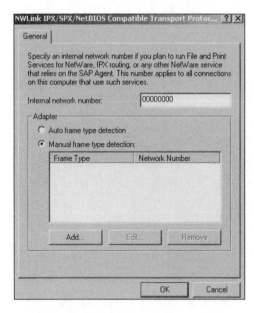

FIGURE 2.83
If you use more than one frame type, you need to configure each one manually.

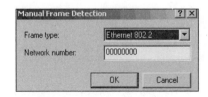

FIGURE 2.84
Specify the frame type present on your network.

After GSNW has been configured, it can be used to provide virtual folders on a Windows 2000 server that can be accessed by anyone with access to the Windows 2000 server. These virtual folders are really connections to folders on a NetWare 3.x or 4.x server (note that 5.x is supported with this service only if IPX/SPX has been installed on it because GSNW will not work over TCP/IP, which is the default protocol for NetWare 5.x). A Microsoft client sees a regular share on a Windows 2000 server, but access to that share causes the Windows 2000 server to retrieve information from the corresponding NetWare server.

The advantage of using the GSNW is that it ensures that you do not have to configure NWLink on all your Microsoft clients and that you do not have to install a NetWare client on those machines either. There is also no need for them to authenticate with the NetWare server. All your Microsoft clients can continue to operate the way they used to except that they now have access to some additional shared folders on a Windows 2000 server.

Because GSNW is a gateway, you must ensure that clients are using it only periodically. If people need frequent access to large amounts of data on a NetWare server, you might be better off to configure the client to directly access the NetWare server than to go through the gateway.

In order to set up a gateway, you must perform three basic steps:

1. Configure the NetWare server.

2. Install GSNW.

3. Configure GSNW.

The following must be done on a NetWare server to prepare it to be accessed by a Windows 2000 server running GSNW.

1. Designate an existing account as a Gateway account or create one or more accounts for that purpose.

2. Create a group called NTGATEWAY and populate it with the account(s) you identified or created in step 1.

3. Grant the NTGATEWAY group permission to access the resources that need to be available to clients connecting through the Windows 2000 server running GSNW.

The following Step by Step will guide you through installing GSNW on a Windows 2000 Server machine.

STEP BY STEP

2.49 Installing GSNW on a Windows 2000 Server

1. Right-click the My Network Places icon on your desktop and choose Properties from the menu that appears (alternatively, double-click the Network and Dialup Connections icon in the Control Panel).

2. In the Network and Dialup Connections window, right-click the connection that represents the network on which you want to connect to a NetWare server and choose Properties from the menu that appears.

3. In the Network Connection Properties dialog box, click the Install button.

4. In the Select Network Component Type dialog box, click Client and then Add (see Figure 2.85).

5. In the Select Network Client dialog box, select Gateway (and Client) Services for NetWare and click OK (see Figure 2.86).

6. In the Select NetWare Logon dialog box, choose either a NetWare server or a Tree and Context in which to log on (see Figure 2.87). The former is used with NetWare 3.x servers (or higher running Bindery emulation). The latter is used for NetWare servers running NDS (4.a and 5.x). Your NetWare Administrator will be able to tell you which is appropriate for your context. In addition, if login scripts need to be run on login, you can select the Run Login Script check box. Then click OK to continue.

7. When prompted, shut down your server and restart.

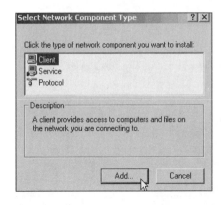

FIGURE 2.85
Gateway service is available as a client installation.

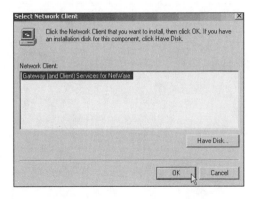

FIGURE 2.86
Select GSNW to install it.

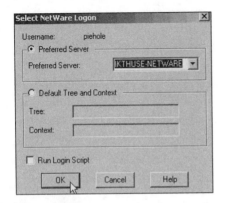

FIGURE 2.87
You must configure your NetWare logon.

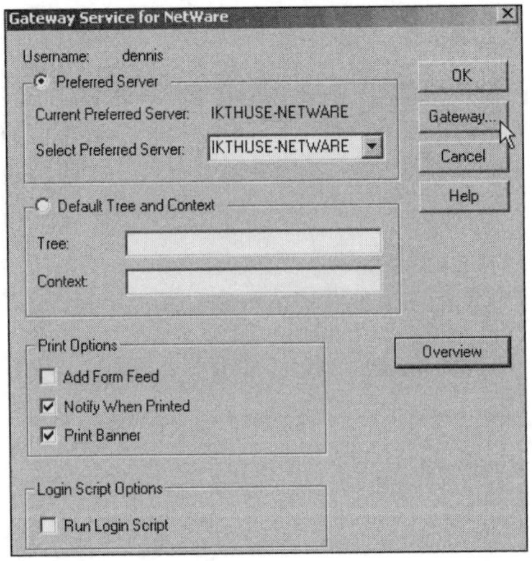

After installing GSNW, you have to configure it. You do this by creating virtual shares on your server that map to file resources on the NetWare server. You can also configure security on those shares at the same time using share-level security as you would on shared folders that are actually on your server.

Step by Step 2.50 demonstrates how to configure Gateway Service for NetWare.

STEP BY STEP

2.50 Configuring Gateway Service for NetWare

1. In the Control Panel, double-click the GSNW icon.

2. From the Gateway Service for NetWare window, click the Gateway button (see Figure 2.88).

3. In the Configure Gateway window, enter one of the accounts that was made a part of the NTGATEWAY group on the NetWare server and its password (see Figure 2.89). Then click the Add button to configure a virtual share point.

FIGURE 2.88
After you configure the NetWare logon, you have to configure the gateway.

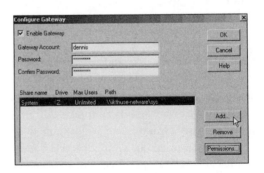

FIGURE 2.89
Define logon by specifying the gateway account and password.

4. In the New Share dialog box (shown in Figure 2.90), enter a name for the share (this is what users connecting to your Windows 2000 server will see), the network path to the NetWare server, and the drive letter that will be mapped to the share from the Windows 2000 server. In addition, if desired, restrict the number of concurrent users by typing a number into the Allow field. When you finish, click OK.

5. To configure share permissions, select the share you want to secure and then click the Permissions button. Configure user and group permissions as you would for any network share. Due to the interaction between these permissions and permissions for the gateway account, the effective permissions will be the more restrictive of the two.

6. Repeat steps 4 and 5 for all shares you want to map from your Windows 2000 server to your NetWare server. When you finish, close the window to exit.

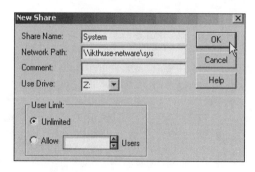

FIGURE 2.90
Create a virtual share by connecting to a shared NetWare resource.

From a client, the list of shares on the server configured in the preceding steps appears like that shown in Figure 2.91. Note the presence of the share called System, which is a gateway share to a NetWare server.

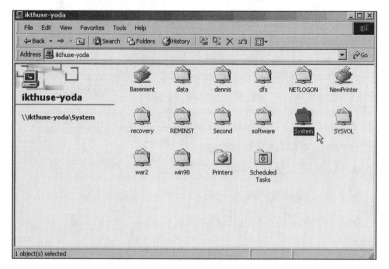

FIGURE 2.91
The shares listed when you browse a server running GSNW include the virtual shares that are redirected to the NetWare server.

NOTE

Most Restrictive Rights Apply You cannot give more share-level permission to the gateway shares than the Gateway account has been given to the NetWare shares. For example, suppose that on the NetWare server, your Gateway account has been given only Read access. You can configure Full Access from the gateway share, but the effective permission to the resource will be Read. To avoid this, it is recommended that the Gateway account be given Full Access on the NetWare side and that access be controlled from the share at the Windows 2000 Server. If the NetWare administrator is uncooperative in this regard, the next best thing is to attempt to match the shared permissions with those the gateway account has on the NetWare resource. That way there will never be any unexpected restrictions in data access.

As we have seen, through GSNW, Microsoft clients can be configured to obtain occasional access to NetWare servers. However, it may be the case that you have NetWare clients who want access to Windows 2000 files and printers. To provide this access, you must install File and Print Services for NetWare (FPNW).

File and Print Services for NetWare

File and Print Services for NetWare provide NetWare clients running IPX with access to Windows 2000 resources hosted on a Windows 2000 server. This tool is not provided with Windows 2000 Server; it must be purchased separately. It is ideal for environments in which Windows 2000 is in the minority but your clients need access to its resources.

Like Gateway Services for NetWare, FPNW functions using only NWLink. Therefore, any NetWare client attempting to use FPNW must be running IPX/SPX, not TCP/IP.

Because this is an add-on to Windows 2000, the exam will not ask any questions about it except for those that require you to show a basic understanding of the function of the product. You will not be required to know how to install or configure it.

Interoperation with Apple Macintosh

Although Apple Macintosh does not hold an overwhelming share of the personal computer market, it is still supported in many organizations. Because of its strengths in desktop publishing and graphic manipulation, it has earned itself a place in a niche market of the computer industry. As a result, many companies with Windows 2000 servers also have one or more Apple Macintosh computers. For this reason, under Windows 2000 Microsoft continues to support three tools for Macintosh interoperability:

◆ File Server for Macintosh

◆ Print Server for Macintosh

◆ The AppleTalk Protocol

Installing and Configuring the AppleTalk Protocol

The AppleTalk protocol is the proprietary Macintosh protocol designed to allow Macintosh computers to communicate in their own workgroups. To provide interoperability with Macintosh machines, AppleTalk is required.

Step by Step 2.51 outlines the procedure for installing this protocol.

> **NOTE**
>
> **The Protocol and the Services** The AppleTalk Protocol does no good without the accompanying services. Moreover, if you install the accompanying services, AppleTalk will be installed automatically as part of the process.

STEP BY STEP

2.51 Installing the AppleTalk Protocol

1. Right-click the My Network Places icon on your desktop and choose Properties from the menu that appears (alternatively, double-click the Network and Dialup Connections icon in the Control Panel).

2. In the Network and Dialup Connections window, right-click the connection that represents the network on which you want to connect to a NetWare server and choose Properties from the menu that appears.

3. In the Network Connection Properties dialog box, click the Install button.

4. In the Select Network Component Type dialog box, click Protocol and then click the Add button.

5. In the Select Network Protocol dialog box, select AppleTalk Protocol and then click OK.

6. When you're returned to the Network Connection Properties dialog box, close the window to complete the installation.

After the protocol has been installed, you might need to configure it. Macintosh machines divide themselves up locally through the use of zones (like Windows workgroups). To make a computer part of a zone, its AppleTalk protocol must be configured to participate in the zone of choice, as demonstrated in Step by Step 2.52.

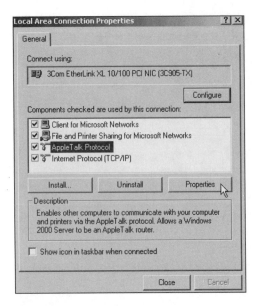

FIGURE 2.92
Configure the properties of the AppleTalk protocol.

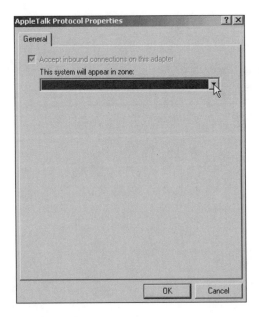

FIGURE 2.93
Add the Windows 2000 computer to an AppleTalk zone.

STEP BY STEP

2.52 Configuring AppleTalk Zones

1. Right-click the My Network Places icon on your desktop and choose Properties from the menu that appears (alternatively, double-click the Network and Dialup Connections icon in the Control Panel).

2. In the Network and Dialup Connections window, right-click the connection that represents the network with AppleTalk installed on it.

3. In the Network Connection Properties dialog box, select AppleTalk Protocol and then click the Properties button (see Figure 2.92).

4. In the AppleTalk Protocol Properties dialog box, choose the zone this Windows 2000 computer will participate in from the list of detected zones (see Figure 2.93). Then click OK.

Installing and Configuring the File Server for Macintosh

The File Server for Macintosh allows your Windows 2000 computer running AppleTalk to act as a file server for Macintosh computers. In order to act as a Macintosh file server, your Windows 2000 server must have NTFS volumes available on which to create a Macintosh-accessible volume.

The next Step by Step identifies the process for installing a file server for Macintosh.

STEP BY STEP

2.53 Installing a File Server for Macintosh

1. From the Control Panel, double-click Add/Remove Programs.

2. In the Add/Remove Programs dialog box, click the Add/Remove Windows Components icon to invoke the wizard.

3. In the Windows Components Wizard, click the Other Network File and Print Services option, and then click the Details button (see Figure 2.94).

4. From the Other Network and File and Print Services dialog box, select File Services for Macintosh (see Figure 2.95) and click OK. When you return to the Windows Components Wizard, click Next to continue.

5. When the Completing the Windows Components Wizard dialog box appears, click Finish to complete the task.

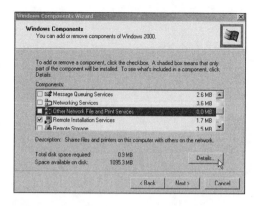

FIGURE 2.94
Add the Other Network File and Print Services.

Having installed the File Services for Macintosh, you now need to create a Macintosh-accessible volume. Step by Step 2.54 guides you through this process.

STEP BY STEP

2.54 Creating a Macintosh Accessible Volume

1. Create a folder on an NTFS volume that will become the root of a Macintosh-accessible volume.

2. From the Start Menu, choose Programs, Administrative Tools, Computer Management.

3. In the Computer Management console, expand the Shared Folders line (double-click). Then right-click Shares and choose New, File Share from the menu that appears (see Figure 2.96).

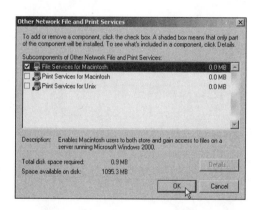

FIGURE 2.95
File services for Macintosh allow you to host a Mac-accessible volume.

continues

continued

FIGURE 2.96
Unlike other folder sharing, Mac-accessible volumes must be configured from the Computer Management console.

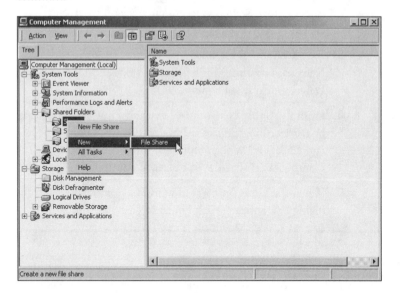

FIGURE 2.97
A specific Windows 2000 folder is designated as the root of the Mac-accessible volume.

4. In the Create Shared Folder dialog box, enter (or browse to) the location of the folder you created in step 1, type in a share name, and (optionally) enter a description for the share. Finally, in the Accessible from the Following Clients section of the dialog box (see Figure 2.97). Click Next to continue.

5. From the next dialog box, configure share-level security on the new folder (see Figure 2.98). Then click Finish.

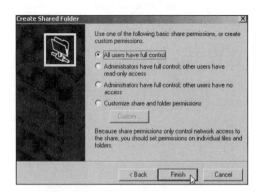

FIGURE 2.98
Like other shared folders, Mac-accessible volumes have a type of share-level security.

After you create a Mac-accessible share, you will need to secure it.
The next Step by Step shows you how to do this.

STEP BY STEP

2.55 Securing a Macintosh-Accessible Volume

1. From the Start Menu, choose Programs, Administrative
   Tools, Computer Management.

2. In the Computer Management console, expand the
   Shared Folders section and select Shares. Then right-click
   the Macintosh share you want to secure and choose
   Properties from the menu that appears (see Figure 2.99).

3. In the share's Properties dialog box, you can configure a
   special password in the SFM (Services for Macintosh)
   Volume Security section (see Figure 2.100). When Mac
   users attempt to connect to the volume, they will be
   prompted for this password. You can also configure the
   volume to be Read-Only for Mac users, and you can
   configure guest (unauthenticated user) access. When you
   finish, click OK.

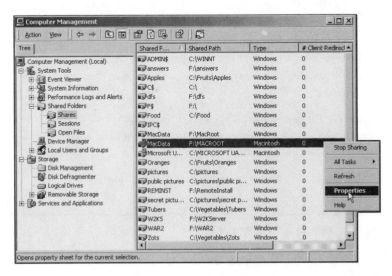

FIGURE 2.99
You can adjust Mac security after you create a
Mac-accessible volume by defining its proper-
ties in the Computer Management console.

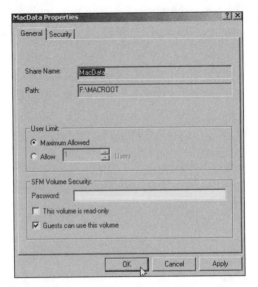

FIGURE 2.100
You can configure user authentication by defining a password that Macintosh users must provide in order to access the folder.

As this section comes to a close, there are some things worth mentioning. First, when a Macintosh-accessible volume is created, Windows users can access the volume by using regular network share access. To Windows users, these volumes appear as result shares.

Second, in order for a Macintosh client to access data on a Windows 2000 server, it must pass authentication. It is advisable to install Microsoft's User Authentication Manager (UAM) on your Macintosh clients. This UAM is present on your server in a folder called Microsoft UAM Volume, which is installed when you installed the File Services for Macintosh. The reason for installing this UAM instead of leaving the Macintosh one in place is that the Macintosh UAM allows the saving of account and password information (bad security) and transmits the credentials in clear text (even worse security). The UAM presents a Windows dialog box where the Mac user fills in his name and password.

Finally, although it was mentioned that AppleTalk must be installed to use the Macintosh services, if it is not installed before the services are installed, it will be installed automatically as part of the installation of either of the Macintosh services.

Installing and Configuring the Print Server for Macintosh

Print Server for Macintosh (PSFM) provides for two functions on a network: 1) the ability for Macintosh clients to print to printers controlled by Windows 2000 print servers, and 2) the ability for Windows clients to connect to Macintosh printers through a Windows 2000 Print Server.

To configure this functionality, you must install the AppleTalk protocol and the Print Server for Macintosh (AppleTalk is automatically installed when you install PSFM).

The next Step by Step takes you through installing PSFM.

STEP BY STEP

2.56 Installing Print Server for Macintosh

1. In the Control Panel, double-click Add/Remove Programs.

2. From the Add/Remove Programs dialog box, click the Add/Remove Windows Components icon to invoke the wizard.

3. In the Windows Components Wizard, click the Other Network File and Print Services option and click the Details button.

4. From the Other Network and File and Print Services dialog box, select Print Services for Macintosh and click OK. When you return to the Windows Components Wizard, click Next to continue.

5. When the Completing the Windows Components Wizard dialog box appears, click Finish to complete the task.

After the Print Services for Macintosh are installed, you will be able to install a local Macintosh print device or connect to a shared Macintosh printer. When installing a local Macintosh print device, you can create a new port for that device with the type set as AppleTalk Printing Devices.

Interoperation with UNIX

Seen by some as strictly a mainframe (and therefore obsolete) operating system, UNIX still has a large number of supporters. Through its many variations (not the least of which is Linux), it is making a strong comeback into the corporate market. As a result, Microsoft is actively developing interoperability tools for UNIX.

Because many of the TCP/IP based tools in Windows 2000 were modeled after tools that were originally part of UNIX systems, interoperability through that protocol was a natural path to take. Interoperability with UNIX consists of the use of the following Windows 2000 components: the TCP/IP protocol (see Chapter 6, "Configuring and Troubleshooting Windows 2000 Network Connections," Print Services for UNIX, and Microsoft Windows Services for Unix 2.0 (in beta as of this writing).

Installing and Configuring Print Services for UNIX

After you install Print Services for UNIX (PSU), Windows 2000 servers can connect to printers hosted by UNIX computers as well as allow UNIX clients to connect to printers hosted on the local Windows 2000 server.

UNIX machines support a variety of print utilities. Some of the supported ones under the Print Services for UNIX are line printer remote (LPR), which allows a client to send print jobs to a remote printer; line printer daemon (LPD), which allows a UNIX server to receive print job requests (and print them); and line printer queue (LPQ), which allows an administrator to review the items in an LPD print queue. The Print Services for UNIX provide all these utilities running on a Windows 2000 server. This means that with PSU running on your Windows 2000 server, you will be able to create a local printer (which you can share to your Windows clients) that connects through the local LPR service (LPRMON) to a UNIX printer hosted on a UNIX computer running an LPD. In addition, through the local LPD service (LPDSVC), a UNIX client running an LPR service would be able to connect to a printer configured locally on a Windows 2000 server.

To start either of these services, you must first install them. Step by Step 2.57 leads you through that process.

STEP BY STEP

2.57 Installing the Print Services for UNIX

1. In the Control Panel, double-click Add/Remove Programs.

2. In the Add/Remove Programs dialog box, click the Add/Remove Windows Components icon to invoke the wizard.

3. In the Windows Components Wizard, click the Other Network File and Print Services option and click Details.

4. From the Other Network and File and Print Services dialog box, select Print Services for UNIX and click OK. When you've returned to the Windows Components Wizard, click Next to continue.

5. When the Completing the Windows Components Wizard dialog box appears, click Finish to complete the task.

When the Print Services have been installed, UNIX clients will be able to connect to any of your printers. In addition, you will be able to add an LPR port on your server to redirect print jobs to an LPD service hosted an a UNIX computer. When installed on this port, a printer will be able to be shared on your server and will appear as any other printer to your Windows clients. All jobs submitted to it will be forwarded to a spooler on the UNIX server. In addition, UNIX clients will be able to connect to the IP address of the Windows 2000 UNIX Print server and then to the specific queue.

In addition to the standard print services, there are also file services that will allow your Windows clients to connect to data hosted on a UNIX server, much like GSNW allows clients to connect to data on NetWare servers.

Windows Services for UNIX

Windows Services for UNIX (an additional utility that can be purchased from Microsoft) gives you some additional interoperability options. This package provides you with Client Services for UNIX, Gateway Services for UNIX, Directory Synchronization for UNIX, and many other helpful utilities. These function in much the same way as the NetWare Services described in the previous sections.

CASE STUDY: WORDS, WORDS, WORDS

ESSENCE OF THE CASE

This case requires that the following end results be satisfied:

▶ The production printers should be configured so that the most efficient use can be made of all of them at all times.

▶ The administrative printer should be configured so that non-administrative personnel cannot direct print jobs to it.

▶ Areas on the servers that can hold confidential documents should have restricted access, so that only certain people can get any access to those files.

SCENARIO

Words, Words, Words, Inc. is a publishing company whose primary business is to reprint classic works of literature. As a result, much of what they produce is stored in digital form on servers. They have a local area network with five Windows 2000 servers performing print and file services. They have called you in to resolve two problems.

The first problem relates to five high-speed printers they purchased last year. Four of these printers were purchased for the document processing departments and are used to print draft copies of books they are reformatting for print. All four of these printers are located centrally in the building and are readily accessible by all departments. The fifth printer is used by the accounting and human resources departments to print administrative documents and reports. The four production departments cooperate quite well, and because the various production schedules are not the same, when one printer is not being heavily utilized by one department, people from another will redirect their print jobs to that printer. The problem is that only some of the production employees understand how to redirect print jobs (most of them just click the Print button), and those who do sometimes accidentally send large jobs to the administration printer. You have been asked to resolve the problems related to redirecting jobs from printer to printer and to prevent jobs from being sent to the administrative printer by unauthorized users.

CASE STUDY: WORDS, WORDS, WORDS

The second issue has to do with confidential information that is held on some of the print servers. Although most of the documents are accessible by everyone, some are confidential, and access to those needs to be restricted. Company managers understand that you can prevent remote access to files by not sharing them, but they want security against access by some of the people who can get local access to the servers. Some users who perform delegated administrative duties (but who are not full-blown administrators) have rights to log onto the servers, and they have been caught browsing through confidential information. The company wants to put an end to this.

ANALYSIS

In this case, analysis and solutions will fall into two categories: printer security and configuration; and local file security. You are dealing with four departments with four identical printers. Moreover, these departments already have a good cooperative relationship. These printers were all purchased at the same time and, therefore, are probably all the same. As a result, printer pooling is a good solution to the problem of different usage patterns. By placing all the print devices in the same place and then implementing printer pooling, you can ensure that each device is used the same amount and that jobs will always go to the

print device that is currently free. With this solution in place, users will no longer have to decide where their jobs are to be sent because sending it to the default printer (which is now the printer pool) will cause the job to be printed on one of four print devices, which are all located together.

The second problem is one of restricted access to the administrative print device. You can easily solve this problem by removing the default print access from the printer (Everyone: Print) and replacing it with Print access for a local server group that includes only members of the Human Resources and Accounting departments. Doing this will ensure that even if other employees try to direct jobs to this print device, they will fail to print.

The third problem involves the configuration of local security on certain files or folders on the servers. For this to be possible, NTFS partitions must be present. If they are not, you will first have to convert the FAT volumes to NTFS. Then you can modify the DACLs of the files or folders to remove the Everyone group from having Full Control and add a group (or groups) representing the people who ought to have access to the data. This ensures that whether or not the folders are ever shared, only the correct people will have access to the files and folders.

The following table summarizes the solution.

continues

CASE STUDY: WORDS, WORDS, WORDS

continued

OVERVIEW OF THE REQUIREMENTS AND SOLUTIONS IN THIS CASE STUDY

Requirement	Solution Provided By
Access to a number of print devices	Moving the print devices into physical proximity and configuring a printer pool on the server
Secure the Administration printer	Creating a local group representing all the people who should have access to the print device and modifying the print device's DACL to allow Print access to only people in that group
Secure files and folders on the servers	Converting partitions to NTFS and using local groups and file/folder DACLs to restrict access to only group members

CHAPTER SUMMARY

KEY TERMS

- Discretionary Access Control List (DACL)
- local group
- local user account
- Security Identifier (SID)
- NTFS permissions
- local file access
- CONVERT.EXE
- ownership
- Distributed file system (Dfs)

Summarized briefly, this chapter covered the following main points:

- *Making files available on a Windows 2000 Server.* This includes sharing folders using network shares and sharing folders using IIS Web sharing. It also includes using Dfs to make shares on other servers available at a central Windows 2000 file server.

- *Securing files on a Windows 2000 Server.* This includes implementing security on network shares, local security using NTFS permissions, and security on Web sites using a variety of methods.

CHAPTER SUMMARY

◆ *Managing and configuring printers on a Windows 2000 Server.* This includes installing printers and configuring availability (including sharing and securing). It also includes configuring printer pools, available times, and priorities, as well as managing printers both locally and from a Web browser.

◆ *Configuring interoperability with non-Windows operating systems.* This includes ensuring interoperability with NetWare, UNIX, and Macintosh computers. It includes configuring access to non-Windows resources from Windows clients through gateways. In addition, it includes making Windows 2000 resources available to non-Windows clients through file and print services for NetWare, UNIX, and Macintosh.

Configuring proper access to resources is a very important part of an administrator's job. As a result, you can expect a number of questions in these areas. Because data and printer availability are often the most critical part of what user's need, this information must be well understood by any Windows 2000 administrator.

KEY TERMS

- fault-tolerant Dfs
- Web sharing
- Internet Information Services (IIS)
- TCP port
- anonymous access
- basic authentication
- digest authentication
- Integrated Windows authentication
- Secure Socket Layer (SSL)
- printer
- print device
- spooler
- printer driver
- printer pooling
- NWLink
- Gateway Service for NetWare (GSNW)
- AppleTalk
- Macintosh-accessible volume

Exercises

2.1 Sharing and Securing a Local Folder

In this exercise, you learn how to share a local folder and secure it with shared and local (NTFS) permissions. To do this, you will also touch on the process for converting a FAT/FAT32 volume to NTFS and the process for creating local user accounts.

Estimated Time: 10 minutes

1. Log on as Administrator.

2. Create two local user accounts: User1 and User2.

   A. From the start menu, choose Programs, Administrative Tools, Computer Management.

   B. In the Computer Management console, expand the Local Users and Groups tree, right-click Users, and choose New User from the menu that appears.

   C. In the New User dialog box, fill in this information:

User Name	User1
Full Name	User One
Password	password
Confirm Password	password

   Deselect the User Must Change Password at Next Logon option, select the Password Never Expires option, and click Create.

   D. In the New User dialog box, fill in this information:

User name	User2
Full name	User Two
Password	password
Confirm password	password

   Deselect the User Must Change Password at Next Logon option, select the Password Never Expires option, and click Create.

   E. In the New User dialog box, click Close.

   F. Close the Computer Management console.

3. From a Windows 2000 server, locate an NTFS volume. If you do not have one, proceed to step 4 to convert a current FAT volume to NTFS, otherwise, skip to step 5.

4. Convert a FAT or FAT32 volume to NTFS.

   A. From the Start menu, choose Run.

   B. In the Run dialog box, type **convert** *drive***:** **/fs:ntfs** (where drive represents the letter of the drive you want to convert to NTFS; no data loss will occur).

   C. If the drive is currently in use, you will be informed that the conversion will take place at next reboot. If this is the case, restart your machine now to convert.

5. Log off as Administrator and log on as User1.

6. Create a folder called SecurityTest on the drive you just converted to NTFS and create a file called Testing.txt in it (you can use Notepad to create a .TXT file).

7. Modify the NTFS permissions to allow only User1 to have access to the SecurityTest folder.

   A. Open a window in which you can see the SecurityTest folder (use Windows Explorer or My Computer), right-click the folder, and choose Properties from the menu that appears.

APPLY YOUR KNOWLEDGE

B. In the Properties dialog box, click the Security tab (you will most likely see that the Everyone group has Full Control of the folder).

C. Click the Add button and then, in the dialog box that follows, double-click User1 in the directory list (the users are listed after all groups and computers). Click OK.

D. With User1 selected in the dialog box, click the box at the bottom that allows Full Control for your user name (this will cause all the check boxes to be filled in the Allow column).

E. Deselect the check box at the bottom of the dialog box (to remove inheritance of permissions from the folder). When you're prompted to do so, choose to Remove the inherited permissions (this will remove the Everyone group from the DACL list). Select the Everyone group in the top list, and then click the Remove button to its right. (You might have to first deselect the check box at the very bottom of the dialog box to prevent this folder from inheriting permissions from its parent. This will let you deviate from the parental permissions.) When you finish, the only user listed in the ACL should be you with Full Control.

F. Click OK to exit the SecurityTest Properties dialog box.

8. Log off the server and log back on as User2.

9. Check access to the SecurityTest folder.

A. Navigate to SecurityTest.

B. Try to open the folder to modify the file inside. Because you do not have permission to access the folder, you will not be able to access the file. Neither will you be able to create new files or delete the one that is there.

10. Log off and log back on as Administrator.

2.2 Configuring a Standalone Dfs

This exercise shows you how to install and configure a standalone Dfs on a Windows 2000 server. The step-by-step procedure is based on Step by Steps 2.13 and 2.14. This exercise assumes that you have done Exercise 1.2 in the previous chapter. There you installed a Windows 2000 server and called it WIN2000S. If you are doing this exercise on anther machine, adjust the instructions to reflect your server's name.

Estimated Time: 20 minutes

1. Create a folder called TestFiles on your server and copy some files into it. Ensure that it is shared using default properties.

2. Create another folder on your server called DFSRoot and share it with default share properties. Do not put any files into it.

3. From the Start menu, choose Programs, Administrative Tools, Distributed File System.

4. At the main Dfs screen, create a Dfs root by selecting New Dfs Root from the Action menu (this will invoke the New Dfs Root Wizard).

5. At the Welcome to the New Dfs Root Wizard screen, click Next.

6. At the Select the Dfs Root Type screen, choose Create a Standalone Dfs Root. Click Next to continue.

APPLY YOUR KNOWLEDGE

7. At the Select the Host Server for the Dfs Root screen, accept the default name (which will be the name of the machine you are configuring Dfs on). Click Next to continue.

8. At the Specify the Dfs Root Share screen, choose DFSRoot from the Use an Existing Share pull-down menu. Click Next to continue.

9. At the Name the Dfs Root screen, click Next to continue.

10. At the Completing the New Dfs Root Wizard screen, click Finish.

11. Right-click the name of the Dfs root you just created and choose New Dfs Link from the menu that appears.

12. In the New Link dialog box, enter Testing DFS in the Link Name field and type **WIN2000S**
TestFiles in the Send the User to This Shared Folder field. Click OK.

13. Test your Dfs by performing the next three steps.

14. From the Start menu, choose Run.

15. In the Run box, type **WIN2000S\DFSRoot**.

16. Open the Testing DFS folder that you see, and the files you copied into the folder should be present.

    You have just connected to your folder through the Dfs server.

2.3 Creating and Configuring a Shared Printer

In this exercise, you learn how to create and configure a shared printer on a Windows 2000 server. To do this exercise, you might need the Windows 2000 Server CD-ROM to provide the printer drivers.

Estimated Time: 10 minutes

1. From the Start menu, choose Settings, Printers.

2. In the Printers folder, double-click the Add Printer icon to start the wizard.

3. At the Add Printer Wizard dialog box, click the Next button.

4. At the Local or Network Printer dialog box, ensure that Local Printer is selected and click Next.

5. In the Select the Printer Port dialog box, select the port called LPT1: and click Next. If you are already using LPT1, choose any available LPT port.

6. In the Add Printer Wizard dialog box, select HP as the manufacturer and HP LaserJet 6P as the Printer to install. Click Next to continue.

7. In the Name Your Printer dialog box, type **Test Printer** as the printer name. Click Next.

8. In the Printer Sharing dialog box, select Share As and replace the default share name with **Shared Printer**. (When you see a prompt that says this name is not accessible from a DOS client, click Yes to accept the name anyway.)

9. At the Location and Comment dialog box, click Next to continue.

10. At the Print Test Page dialog box, click Next to continue.

11. In the Completing the Add Printer Wizard dialog box, click Finish.

12. In the Printers dialog box, right-click the printer you just created and choose Properties from the menu that appears.

APPLY YOUR KNOWLEDGE

13. Right-click your printer and choose Pause Printing from the menu that appears (this will prevent your server from trying to print test documents to this printer).

14. Start Notepad and type your name in the new document.

15. From the File menu in Notepad, choose Print. In the Select Printer box, choose Test Printer and click Print.

16. Close Notepad; do not save the document you just created.

17. In the Printers dialog box, double-click Test Printer to open the print queue. Note the presence of the document you just printed.

18. Double-click the document in the queue and examine the properties. Note your ability to change who is notified when the document is printed, as well as the priority and schedule. Click OK to exit.

19. Remove the document from the queue (cancel printing) by selecting the document and choosing Cancel from the Document menu. The document will disappear from the queue. Close the print queue.

2.4 Configuring a Secure Web Site

In this exercise, you learn how to install IIS and modify the TCP port on which the Web site is listening. In addition, you modify the authentication method required by enabling Integrated Windows authentication. This exercise presupposes that you installed Windows 2000 Server using the exercise in Chapter 1. If so, the IIS has not been installed. If you already have IIS installed, you can skip right to step 2, creating a unique home page.

Estimated Time: 30 minutes

1. Install IIS.

   A. From the Start menu, choose Settings, Control Panel.

   B. From the Control Panel, double-click the Add/Remove Programs icon. When the Add/Remove Programs folder appears, click the Add/Remove Windows Components button on the left side.

   C. In the Windows Components window, select Internet Information Services and then click the Details button.

   D. Deselect all components except Common Files, Documentation, Internet Information Services Snap-In, and World Wide Web Server. Click OK to return to the wizard.

   E. Click Next to continue.

   F. When prompted, insert the Windows 2000 Server CD and click OK.

   G. At the Completing the Windows Components Wizard screen, click Finish.

   H. Close the windows you opened to install IIS.

2. Create a unique home page for your IIS Web site.

   A. Using Windows Explorer or My Computer, navigate to the path c:\InetPub\wwwRoot (this was created when you installed IIS).

   B. In the folder c:\InetPub\wwwRoot, create a text document with the sentence "Cave ne ante ullas catapultas ambules" as its only content. (By the way, this is Latin for "If I were you, I wouldn't walk in front of any catapults.")

APPLY YOUR KNOWLEDGE

C. Rename the document you created to default.html.

D. Double-click the icon for default.html to ensure that it opens an Internet Explorer window and that the phrase "Cave ne ante ullas catapultas ambules" appears.

E. Close IE.

F. From the Start menu, choose Programs, Administrative Tools, Internet Services Manager.

G. Expand the tree on the left side to show the label Default Web Site, and then right-click that label and choose Properties from the menu that appears.

3. Set the default document to default.html.

A. In the Properties dialog box, click the Documents tab.

B. In the Documents property sheet, remove each document name by selecting each one and then clicking the Remove button.

C. Click the Add button and type `default.html` in the dialog box that appears. Click OK.

D. Click the Apply button to apply the default document change. If you're prompted for inheritance rules, click OK.

4. Confirm that the default document comes up when you access the site.

A. From the Start menu, choose Run.

B. In the Run dialog box, type `http://localhost` and click OK (localhost is predefined to mean your local machine).

C. When IE opens, verify that the text *Cave ne ante ullas catapultas ambules* appears and that you were not asked to log into the site.

D. Close IE and return to the Web Site Properties dialog box.

5. Modify the port that the IIS server is listening on.

A. Click the Web Site tab to display the Web Site property sheet.

B. In the TCP Port field, replace the default 80 with 2580.

C. Click Apply.

6. Verify that the site no longer works by default but does work when you specify the port.

A. From the Start menu, choose Run and type `http://localhost` into the dialog box. You should see a page saying that the page you selected cannot be displayed.

B. Modify the address in IE to read `http://localhost:2580` and press Enter to reload. The default page will now be displayed.

C. Close Internet Explorer and return to the Web Site properties.

7. Modify the security settings to prevent anonymous access and require Integrated Windows authentication.

A. Click the Directory Security tab to display the Directory Security property sheet.

B. Under the Anonymous Access and Authentication Control heading, click the Edit button.

APPLY YOUR KNOWLEDGE

C. In the Authentication Methods dialog box, deselect Anonymous Access. At the bottom of the dialog box, select Integrated Windows authentication. Then click OK.

D. Click OK to apply the changes and exit the IIS Manager.

8. Finish things up.

A. Using My Computer or Windows Explorer, modify the NTFS security for the c:\InetPub\wwwRoot folder to allow only the Administrator to access the folder and its file content.

B. Log off the server and log on as User1.

C. From the Start menu, choose Run and type **http://localhost:2580** in the dialog box.

D. When the Enter Network Password dialog box appears, enter the name and password for the user you are currently logged in as (this should not work, and the dialog box will reappear).

E. When the dialog box appears a second time, enter the name and password of the user that was given access to the wwwroot folder. The Web page will now appear.

F. Close all applications and folders and log back on as your administrative user.

2.5 Configuring Gateway Service for NetWare (GSNW)

In this exercise, you learn how to configure GSNW to connect to a NetWare server. To do this exercise, you need the following items: a Windows 2000 server, a NetWare 4.x server running bindery emulation (configured appropriately as identified in the section "Installing and Configuring the Gateway Service for NetWare (GSNW)," earlier in this chapter), and a network through which the two can communicate. If you do not have the NetWare server, you will be able to configure the gateway, but you will not be able to start it due to a lack of logon authentication with the NetWare server you claim to be communicating with.

Estimated Time: 30 minutes

1. Install the GSNW client on your Windows 2000 server.

A. Right-click the My Network Places icon on your desktop and choose Properties from the menu that appears.

B. In the Network and Dialup Connections window, right-click the connection that represents the network on which you want to connect to a NetWare server and choose Properties from the menu that appears.

C. From the Network Connection Properties dialog box, click the Install button.

D. From the Select Network Component Type dialog box, click Client and then click Add.

E. From the Select Network Client dialog box, select Gateway (and Client) Services for NetWare and click OK.

F. From the Select NetWare Logon dialog box, choose either a NetWare server or a Tree and Context in which to log on (your NetWare Administrator will be able to tell you which is appropriate for your context). Then click OK.

G. When prompted, shut down your server and restart.

APPLY YOUR KNOWLEDGE

2. After logging back in, configure the gateway on your server.

   A. From the Control Panel, double-click the GSNW icon.

   B. From the Gateway Service for NetWare window, click the Gateway button.

   C. From the Configure Gateway window, enter one of the accounts that was made a part of the NTGATEWAY group on the NetWare server and its password. Then click the Add button to configure a virtual share point.

   D. In the New Share dialog box, enter `NetWareShare` as the name for the share you will see when connecting to your Windows 2000 server, the network path to the NetWare server (\\netwareservername\sys), and the drive letter that will be mapped to the share from the Windows 2000 server. When you finish, click OK.

   E. Click OK to complete the GSNW configuration.

3. Test the GSNW configuration.

   A. From the Start menu, choose Run. In the Run dialog box, type `\\WIN2000S` and click OK. A dialog box appears, showing you all the shares. One of the shares will be called NetWareShare.

   B. Double-click the NetWareShare folder, and it will open to show you the content of the sys volume on the NetWare server.

   C. Close the folders.

Review Questions

1. What is the default authentication method for an IIS server, and what changes are made to your Windows 2000 security to allow this access?

2. What do you need to do to your servers to enable local security on files and folders?

3. If you have share-level permissions enabled on a folder and NTFS permissions enabled on the same folder, what are the effective permissions to the folder over the network? What are the effective local permissions?

4. If you want to enable Web sharing of a folder, what must be present on the computer you are doing this on?

5. What is the difference between a standalone Dfs and a domain-based Dfs?

6. What is GSNW, and how does it allow for simplification of administration?

7. How is a print device distinguished from a printer?

Exam Questions

1. You are an IIS 5.0 Web site administrator. Your Web site has three groups of users: internal company users on your LAN, internal company users outside the firewall protecting your LAN, and public users who are not part of your company. Currently, company users on your LAN can connect to this server and, when presented with the Security dialog box, they are able to access NTFS secured areas of the site. In addition, public users are able to access the non-secure parts of your site. However, company users outside your firewall

APPLY YOUR KNOWLEDGE

cannot authenticate. Of the options presented in Figure 2.101, what change must be made to allow these users to authenticate across the firewall yet still provide the maximum authentication security and retain public users' access?

   A. Deselect Anonymous access.

   B. Select Basic Authentication.

   C. Select Digest Authentication.

   D. Deselect Anonymous Access and select Basic Authentication.

2. You are a Windows 2000 server administrator tasked with the job of providing connectivity to a folder on a NetWare 4.11 server. The server, NWSERVER1, holds some accounting information that you have not yet brought over to your Windows 2000 server. As a result, you must allow your users continued access to this information. Currently, all your clients can access your Windows 2000 server but none can access the NetWare server.

FIGURE 2.101
Use this figure with question 1.

Required Result:

To allow members of your accounting department access to modify the files on the NetWare server.

Optional Results:

To allow company employees as a whole access to view the file contents.

To provide for the least possible configuration of individual Windows clients to gain access.

Proposed Solutions:

Configure the folder on the NetWare server with Read access for Everyone.

Set up the NTUSERS group on the NetWare server to include the account names of all the users in your organization who need access to the accounting resources.

Install and configure GSNW on your Windows 2000 server to connect to your NetWare server with a valid user account that is a member of the NTUSERS group.

Configure a share within the GSNW that gives Accounting users Change access and Everyone Read access.

Which result(s) does the proposed solution produce?

   A. The proposed solution produces the required result and both optional results.

   B. The proposed solution produces the required result and one of the optional results.

   C. The proposed solution produces the required result but does not produce either of the optional results.

   D. The proposed solution does not produce the required result.

APPLY YOUR KNOWLEDGE

3. You are a Windows 2000 server administrator tasked with the job of providing connectivity to a folder on a NetWare 4.11 server. The server, NWSERVER1, holds some accounting information that you have not yet brought over to your Windows 2000 server. As a result, you must allow your users continued access to this information. Currently, all your clients can access your Windows 2000 server, but none can access the NetWare server.

Required Result:

To allow members of your accounting department access to modify the files on the NetWare server.

Optional Results:

To allow company employees as a whole access to view the file contents.

To provide for the least configuration of individual Windows clients as possible to gain access.

Proposed Solution:

Configure the folder on the NetWare server with Full access for everyone.

Set up the NTGATEWAY group on the NetWare server to include the account names of all the users in your organization who need access to the accounting resources.

Install and configure GSNW on your Windows 2000 server to connect to your NetWare server with a valid user account that is a member of the NTGATEWAY group.

Configure a share within the GSNW that gives Accounting users Change access and gives Everyone Read access

Which result(s) does the proposed solution produce?

A. The proposed solution produces the required result as well as both optional results.

B. The proposed solution produces the required result and one of the optional results.

C. The proposed solution produces the required result but does not produce either of the optional results.

D. The proposed solution does not produce the required result.

4. George is a help desk support person. He gets a call from a user in a remote location who is trying to install a printer for a new print device. The user cannot find a driver for Windows 2000 and wants to know if a Windows 95 driver will work. Which of the following describes the relationship between drivers for different operating systems?

A. Windows 95 drivers will function properly when loaded on a Windows 2000 server.

B. Windows 98 drivers will function properly when loaded on a Windows 2000 server.

C. Any Windows 9x driver will function properly when loaded on a Windows 2000 server.

D. There is no compatibility between non-Windows 2000 drivers and Windows 2000 servers.

5. Emma is a network administrator in a Windows 2000 network. She is configuring a print device in the Sales Office that is connected to a Windows 2000 print server.

APPLY YOUR KNOWLEDGE

Required Result:

Provide a way for users to direct large jobs to print between 6:00 p.m. and 6:00 a.m. and to direct small jobs to print immediately.

Optional Desired Results:

Configure the managers' small print jobs to take priority over all other users' jobs.

Prevent people in the Accounting department from using the print device.

Proposed Solution:

Install three printers on the print server, all of which print to the port the print device is connected to. Configure the first printer so that only the Managers group has Print access and the Administrators group has Full Control. Give this printer a priority of 99.

Configure the second printer so that the Everyone group has Print access and the Administrators group has Full Control. Give this printer a priority of 1.

Configure the last printer so that the Everyone group has Print access and the Administrators group has Full Control. Leave the print priority at default and make it available only between 6:00 p.m. and 6:00 a.m.

Tell the managers to print regular documents to the first printer and large documents to the third. Tell all other Sales people to print regular documents to the second printer and large documents to the third.

Analysis:

Which result(s) does the proposed solution produce?

A. The proposed solution produces the required result as well as both optional results.

B. The proposed solution produces the required result and one of the optional results.

C. The proposed solution produces the required result but does not produce either of the optional results.

D. The proposed solution does not produce the required result.

6. Noah is a network administrator for a Windows 2000 network. He is configuring a print device in the Sales Office that is connected to a Windows 2000 print server.

Required Result:

Provide a way for users to direct large jobs to print between 6:00 p.m. and 6:00 a.m. and to direct small jobs to print immediately.

Optional Desired Results:

Configure the managers' small print jobs to take priority over all other users' jobs.

Prevent people in the Accounting department from using the print device.

Proposed Solution:

Install three printers on the print server, all of which print to the port the print device is connected to. Configure the first so that only the Managers group has Print access and the Administrators group has Full Control. Give this printer a priority of 99.

Configure the second printer so that the Everyone group has Print access, the Accounting group is explicitly denied Print access, and the Administrators group has Full Control. Give this printer a priority of 1.

APPLY YOUR KNOWLEDGE   ○

Configure the last printer so that the Everyone group has Print access, the Accounting group is explicitly denied Print access, and the Administrators group has Full Control. Leave the print priority at default and make it available only between 6:00 p.m. and 6:00 a.m.

Tell the managers to print regular documents to the first printer and large documents to the third. Tell all other Sales people to print regular documents to the second printer and large documents to the third.

Analysis:

Which result(s) does the proposed solution produce?

A. The proposed solution produces the required result as well as both optional results.

B. The proposed solution produces the required result and one of the optional results.

C. The proposed solution produces the required result but does not produce either of the optional results.

D. The proposed solution does not produce the required result.

7. You have two groups of users who need to print to the same printer. However, one group's print jobs must have priority over the other group's print jobs. What's the best way to accomplish this arrangement?

A. You must install two separate printing devices and assign each group to print to one of the printing devices.

B. Make the users that need the higher printing priority Printer Operators so they can adjust the order of print jobs in the print queue.

C. Set up a printing pool with multiple printers.

D. Install two printers that are connected to the same printing device. Assign different priorities and groups to each printer.

8. Some of the downlevel clients (pre-Windows 2000) users on your network habitually select the incorrect printer driver when printing to your laser printer. How can you make sure that improperly formatted documents don't print on the printer and possibly cause it to hang?

A. Tell the users to always check the printer driver they've selected before printing their documents.

B. Install a printer that supports both PostScript and PCL printing definition languages.

C. Select the Hold Mismatched Documents option in the printer's Properties dialog box. This tells the Windows 2000 print server to hold any documents that don't match the printer language.

D. You shouldn't have to worry about it. The newer printer drivers can automatically translate page formatting language to match the printer.

9. Alexander is in charge of supporting the administrators in a large corporate office. There are three HP LaserJet 2100 printers in the office. The problem is that two of the devices are heavily used, but the other is hardly used at all. Alexander has been asked to resolve the problem in the most effective way.

Required Result:

Ensure that all three printers are used equally.

APPLY YOUR KNOWLEDGE

Optional Desired Results:

Make the user intervention in the use-balancing process as small as possible.

Ensure that Alexander's manual intervention in balancing is kept to a minimum.

Proposed Solution:

Set up all three print devices in a central place in the office and connect them to three ports on the same print server.

Configure a printer pool to allow a single printer to print to whichever print device is available at the time.

Analysis:

Which result(s) does the proposed solution produce?

A. The proposed solution produces the required result as well as both optional results.

B. The proposed solution produces the required result and one of the optional results.

C. The proposed solution produces the required result but does not produce either of the optional results.

D. The proposed solution does not produce the required result.

10. Marvin is the administrator of a Windows 2000-based LAN. The folder named Secret is secured as described here:

    NTFS: Susan – Read & Execute

    Managers – Modify

    Bill – Full Control

    Share: Susan – Full Control

    Managers – Change

    Bill – No Access

Susan is a member of the Managers group. What effective level of access does Susan get over the network and locally, respectively?

A. Network = Full Control, Locally = Full Control

B. Network = No Access, Locally = Full Control

C. Network = Full Control, Locally = Modify

D. Network = Modify, Locally = Modify

11. Marvin is the administrator of a Windows 2000-based LAN. The folder named Secret is secured as described here:

    NTFS: Susan – Read & Execute

    Managers – Modify

    Bill – Full Control

    Share: Susan – Full Control

    Managers – Change

    Bill – No Access

Bill is not a member of the Managers group. What effective level of access does Bill get over the network and locally, respectively?

A. Network = No Access, Locally = Full Control

B. Network = No Access, Locally = No Access

C. Network = Full Control, Locally = Full Control

D. Network = No Access, Locally = No Access.

APPLY YOUR KNOWLEDGE

12. Simon is the administrator in a network with a Windows 2000 server but with clients hosted on a variety of operating systems. Simon needs to provide print services to all his clients, but he does not have the budget to purchase new software. Which of the following client combinations can Windows 2000 Server support without resorting to third-party or purchased software?

    A. Macintosh, UNIX, OS/2 Warp, and Windows 3.1

    B. Macintosh, UNIX, Windows NT 4.0, and Windows 3.1

    C. MS-DOS, Macintosh, Windows NT 4.0, and Amiga

    D. Windows NT 3.51, Windows NT 4.0, Commodore 64, and Windows 3.1

13. Horace needs to update all his Windows 2000 Professional clients with new versions of a printer driver for a print device controlled by a Windows 2000 print server. What is the most efficient way for Horace to do this?

    A. Install the driver on all the clients manually.

    B. Send the CD-ROM to all the users and have them install it manually.

    C. Install the driver on the server and have the clients download it the next time they print.

    D. Create an SMS package to deliver the driver to the clients.

14. Gerry has configured a GSNW on his Windows 2000 server to connect to a NetWare 4.1 server. What factor or factors control the effective permissions that his Windows users have to the data obtained via the gateway server?

    A. The version of the NetWare client they are running

    B. The more restrictive of the NetWare and Windows 2000 share permissions

    C. The Windows 2000 share permissions

    D. The NetWare permissions

15. Maurice is the administrator for a Windows 2000-based Web server. He has been told that changing the port on which the server runs is an effective form of security. Which of the following most accurately describes the effect of changing the port number for a Web server?

    A. No users will be able to get to the Web site unless Maurice tells them the port number.

    B. The Web server is hidden to the general public, but it's not impossible to find it.

    C. The Web server is completely secure because it cannot be accessed except by a special port/password combination.

    D. The Web server is neither hidden nor secure because changing the port number does not change access at all.

16. Herbert is the administrator of a Windows 2000-based Web server. He has decided to implement Integrated Windows authentication in addition to Anonymous access. Which of the following is true of this security model?

    A. All browsers can be used to access such a site secured in this way.

    B. Passwords provided to the dialog box travel over the Internet in an encrypted form.

APPLY YOUR KNOWLEDGE

C. All access to the server will produce a security dialog box.

D. Such security will work under all circumstances as long as the user is using Internet Explorer 4.0 or 5.0.

17. Angela is the administrator of a Windows 2000 network in which domain-based Dfs is being implemented. What advantage does domain-based Dfs have over standalone Dfs?

   A. Domain-based Dfs servers never go down because they are hosted by domain controllers.

   B. Domain-based Dfs servers allow you to configure multiple child nodes.

   C. Domain-based Dfs servers can work independently of the Active Directory instead of being tied to it as standalone Dfs servers are.

   D. Domain-based Dfs can have multiple root servers configured for the same hierarchy, thus enabling fail-over in the case of root server failure.

18. What two changes does the installation of IIS make to a Windows 2000 server?

   A. Creates an INETPUB folder and an anonymous user account.

   B. Creates an INETPUB folder and converts the host drive to NTFS.

   C. Converts the host drive to NTFS and creates an anonymous user account.

   D. Creates an INETPUB folder and installs TCP/IP on the server.

Answers to Review Questions

1. By default, an IIS server is configured to allow anonymous users to access the Web site without being prompted for a password in the event that NTFS security does not prevent it; otherwise, Integrated Windows authentication is used. To facilitate the identification of anonymous users, a special local account is created called IUSR_*SERVERNAME*. Any user connecting to the server is automatically assigned the rights this user has to the Web site. For more information, see the section "Controlling Web Site Access Through Authentication Methods."

2. To enable local security, you must host your folders and files on NTFS partitions and you must set the DACLs on resources to be secured. If your partitions are FAT, you can convert to NTFS without data loss by using the convert command. For more information, see the section "The NTFS File System."

3. When both share-level and local permissions are applied to a folder, the effective permissions when accessing over the network are the more restrictive of the two sets of permissions. When accessing locally, the NTFS permissions are all that apply. For more information, see the section "When Local File Security Interacts with Shared Folder Security."

4. To enable Web sharing of a folder, you must have a way to publish it to the Web. This requires that IIS be installed on the machine you want to Web share on, and directory browsing must be enabled in the IIS configuration. For more information, see the section "Preparing for Web Sharing."

APPLY YOUR KNOWLEDGE

5. The essential difference between a standalone Dfs and a domain-based Dfs is that the root servers in a domain-based Dfs are published to the Active Directory. This enables redundant copies of the root to be configured, thus ensuring that if the root server goes down, clients will be automatically directed to a functioning root when they try to connect. For more information, see the section "The Distributed File System (Dfs)."

6. The GSNW (Gateway (and Client) Services for NetWare) allows for occasional access of NetWare file resources by Windows clients through a Windows 2000 server. The GSNW makes administration simpler by ensuring that client systems do not need to be reconfigured to allow for access to NetWare resources. If the user can connect to the Windows 2000 server, the user has access to the NetWare resources. For more information, see the section "Installing and Configuring the Gateway Service for NetWare (GSNW)."

7. A print device is the physical device that paper spews out of, whereas a printer is a software interface that is configured to allow control of the device. For more information, see the section "The Printing Process."

Answers to Exam Questions

1. **C.** The key to this question is that you want to maintain maximum security while providing public access. This means that some combination of anonymous access and authentication is required. Digest authentication provides better authentication security than basic does, and it also provides secure access. That means it is preferred. Therefore, leaving the configuration as is and adding Digest authentication provides the best solution to this problem. For more information, see the section "Controlling Web Site Access Through Authentication Methods."

2. **D.** The required result is that members of the accounting department be able to modify the files on the NetWare server. However, none of the users are part of the NTGATEWAY group, they are part of NTUsers. This means that no access will be given to any of the users because one of the basic infrastructure requirements have not been met. Regardless of the access that is given out at the Windows 2000 side, the NetWare server will not allow any users to access. For more information, see the section "Interoperation with Novell NetWare."

3. **A.** This solution provides all desired results. When Full access is configured at the NetWare side, the control of access is dependent on the share-level permissions on the Windows 2000 end. By configuring Accounting users to have Change access, you have provided resolution to the required result. By configuring Everyone to have Read access, you have provided resolution to optional result 1. Finally, by using GSNW, you have provided resolution to optional result 2. For more information, see the section "Interoperation with Novell NetWare."

4. **D.** You can load the drivers for 9x clients at the server for use by 9x clients. The 9x drivers cannot be used by a 2000-based computer. For more information, see the section "Configuring and Maintaining Printers."

5. **B.** The configuration allows for large jobs to be printed at night and small jobs to be printed anytime. It also allows for managers' jobs to be

APPLY YOUR KNOWLEDGE

printed before everyone else's. However, because the Everyone group was given Print permission, it does not restrict the Accounting group from printing to the printer. For more information, see the section "Configuring and Maintaining Printers."

6. **A.** As in the previous scenario, the proposed solution allows for printing at different times and with different priorities. However, in this case, because the Everyone group is given access and the Accounting group is explicitly denied access, everyone will be able to print to the printer except the Accountants. For more information, see the section "Configuring and Maintaining Printers."

7. **D.** You can install more than one printer that is configured to print to the same print device. These printers can then be configured with different print priorities and groups, and the users who need to be able to access each printer can be created and assigned Print permissions to only their printers. Documents sent to the printer with the highest printing priority will always take precedence over waiting jobs that come from the lower priority printer. For more information, see the section "Configuring a Local Printer on a Windows 2000 Server."

8. **C.** Holding mismatched documents is one way to prevent documents formatted for one printer from printing on another print device. For more information, see the section "Configuring a Local Printer on a Windows 2000 Server."

9. **A.** A printing pool can be successfully implemented only if the printers all use the same printer driver, are controlled by the same print server, and are in close proximity to one another.

The first two are criteria of the operating system; the last is a criteria of your users. For more information, see the section "Configuring and Maintaining Printers."

10. **D.** Local access is determined by combining Susan's NTFS permission and share permissions. Because she is a member of the Managers group, she gets Modify access (the greater of Read & Execute and Modify). Her network permission is Full Control, but her effective permission over the network is the lesser of her share permissions and her NTFS permissions. Because she has only Modify permission locally, she cannot have any more than Change permission when accessing the folder over the network. For more information, see the section "When Local File Security Interacts with Shared Folder Security."

11. **A.** Bill's local access is Full Control, but his network access is No Access. Therefore, when accessing the folder locally, he has Full Control, but his effective permission when he accesses over the network is No Access (the more restrictive of his share and NTFS permissions). For more information, see the section "When Local File Security Interacts with Shared Folder Security."

12. **B.** A Windows 2000 server will support all Windows clients, both old and new, without any additional configuration. In addition, by installing Print Services for Macintosh and Print Services for UNIX (both of which come with Windows 2000), Simon can provide support for those operating systems as well. There is no built-in support for OS/2, Commodore-64, or Amiga clients. For more information, see the sections "Configuring and Maintaining Printers," "Interoperation with Apple Macintosh," and "Interoperation with UNIX."

APPLY YOUR KNOWLEDGE

13. **C.** Windows 2000 clients automatically check their printer driver against the printer driver on the Windows 2000 server. If the server driver is newer than the client driver, the driver from the server is automatically downloaded locally. For more information, see the section "Configuring and Maintaining Printers."

14. **B.** The effective permissions that Windows users get is the more restrictive of the permissions granted on the NetWare server and the permissions granted on the Windows 2000 server running GSNW. As a result, it is most effective to give Full Control at the NetWare side and control access from the Gateway Server. For more information, see the section "Installing and Configuring the Gateway Service for NetWare (GSNW)."

15. **B.** Changing the port effectively makes finding the Web server like finding a needle in a haystack. However, that does not really secure the site because anyone who knows the port will be able to connect to the server. No password is associated with port configuration, and for best results, port changes should be coupled with some sort of authentication. As an alternative, SSL could be enabled to allow for encrypted transmissions regardless of the browser client being used. For more information, see the section "Controlling Access to Web Sites."

16. **B.** The only browser capable of providing user access to a site protected with Integrated Security is IE 3 and higher. That is because Integrated security requires that a secure channel be established between the browser and the server. The user will be prompted for a password if the site has been secured with NTFS permissions and that user is not given access to the site, but not if Anonymous access is allowed for file. In addition, by using Integrated Security, IE can read the user's access token to determine if access should be allowed, and in that case, no dialog box will appear. In addition, IE 4.0 and 5.0 will not pass Integrated Security information through a firewall. For more information, see the section "Controlling Access to Web Sites."

17. **D.** Domain-based Dfs has its configuration stored in the domain's Active Directory. When a client goes to connect to a resource through the Dfs, the Directory is consulted to determine where it should go. You can configure multiple root servers so that if one goes down, clients will be redirected to another. This is not possible with standalone Dfs. For more information, see the section "Domain-Based Dfs (Fault-Tolerant Dfs)."

18. **A.** The installation of IIS creates a folder called INETPUB for the storage of WWW and FTP sites, and it creates an anonymous user account whose credentials are assigned to any authenticated user. For more information, see the section "Controlling Access to Web Sites."

APPLY YOUR KNOWLEDGE

Suggested Readings and Resources

The following are some recommended readings in the area of Resource Access:

1. Microsoft Windows 2000 Server Resource Kit: *Microsoft Windows 2000 Server Internetworking Guide* (Microsoft Press)

    • Chapter 11: Services for UNIX

    • Chapter 12: Interoperability with NetWare

    • Chapter 13: Services for Macintosh

2. Microsoft Windows 2000 Server Resource Kit: *Microsoft Windows 2000 Server Deployment Planning Guide* (Microsoft Press)

    • Chapter 22: Defining a Client Connectivity Strategy

3. Microsoft Windows 2000 Server: *Operations Guide* (Microsoft Press)

    • Chapter 4: Network Printing

4. Microsoft Internet Information Services 5.0: *Resource Guide* (Microsoft Press)

    • Chapter 9: Security

5. *Microsoft Windows 2000 Professional Resource Kit* (Microsoft Press)

    • Chapter 14: Printing

    • Chapter 24: Interoperability with NetWare

    • Chapter 25: Interoperability with UNIX

6. Microsoft Official Curriculum course 1556: *Administering Microsoft Windows 2000*

    • Module 6: Administering Printer Resources

7. Microsoft Official Curriculum course 1557: *Installing and Configuring Microsoft Windows 2000*

    • Module 5: Configuring Network Protocols

    • Module 11: Installing and Configuring Printers

    • Module 13: Installing and Configuring Web Services

8. Microsoft Official Curriculum course 2152: *Supporting Microsoft Windows 2000 Professional and Server*

    • Module 3: Connecting Windows 2000 Clients to Networks and the Internet

    • Module 7: Managing Data by Using NTFS

    • Module 8: Providing Network Access to File Resources

    • Module 9: Configuring Printing

9. Microsoft Official Curriculum course 2153: *Supporting a Microsoft Windows 2000 Network Infrastructure*

    • Module 11: Configuring a Web Server

    • Module 16: Configuring Network Connectivity Between Microsoft Windows 2000 and Other Operating Systems

10. Web Sites

    • www.microsoft.com/windows2000

    • www.microsoft.com/train_cert

Microsoft provides the following objectives for "Configuring and Troubleshooting Hardware Devices and Drivers":

Configure hardware devices.

▶ This objective is necessary because someone certified in the use of Windows 2000 Server technology must understand the methods for configuring the hardware in a Windows 2000 Server computer. This includes not only getting such devices to function, but also getting them to function well.

Configure driver signing options.

▶ This objective is necessary because someone certified in the use of Windows 2000 Server technology must understand the implications of driver signing. This includes understanding how driver signing can increase system reliability, protect a server against corrupted and/or virus-stricken device drivers, and ensure that fraudulent drivers are not loaded by mistake.

Update device drivers.

▶ This objective is necessary because someone certified in the use of Windows 2000 technology must be able to update the device drivers. This includes knowing where to obtain new drivers, what the procedures are for updating them, and what the implications are of upgrading or not upgrading these drivers.

Troubleshoot problems with hardware.

▶ This objective is necessary because someone certified in the use of Windows 2000 Server technology must be able to effectively troubleshoot problems with hardware. This includes detecting and solving problems using system tools, logic, intuition, and past experience.

CHAPTER 3

Configuring and Troubleshooting Hardware Devices and Drivers

STUDY STRATEGIES

▶ Although this is the shortest chapter in this book, it contains its fair share of testable Windows 2000 features. When you go through this material, make sure that you have a good knowledge of Plug and Play, driver signing, and the Hardware Compatibility List. Any of these are possible topics for exam questions.

▶ To prepare for the questions that may arise from the objectives, you should, of course, study the conceptual material presented in the chapter. In addition, you should also do the labs (Steps by Steps and Exercises), which will introduce you to most of this material in a hands-on fashion.

▶ Finally, and probably most importantly, you should try to gain experience with the installation and configuration of as many hardware devices as possible in Windows 2000 servers. This may include (but should not be limited to) video cards, sound cards, modems, and network cards. Try to find some legacy hardware so that you can experience the challenge (and sometimes the frustration) of manually installing and configuring drivers for hardware that is not configured automatically by the Plug and Play manager.

INTRODUCTION

This chapter will help you prepare for the "Configuring and Troubleshooting Hardware Devices and Drivers" section of Microsoft's Exam 70-215. Every Windows 2000 server has hardware. Drivers are the software that allow your operating system to talk to the physical devices. Therefore, it is imperative that your drivers are well-chosen, tested, and reliable in order to get good hardware functionality.

This chapter will provide you with an overview of drivers, their place in the Windows 2000 architecture, and the new signing options that guarantee driver authenticity and reliability.

HARDWARE AND DRIVERS IN WINDOWS 2000

To understand what drivers are and how they function, you must have a grasp of how a Windows 2000 server is constructed. Figure 3.1 shows the architectural components of Windows 2000.

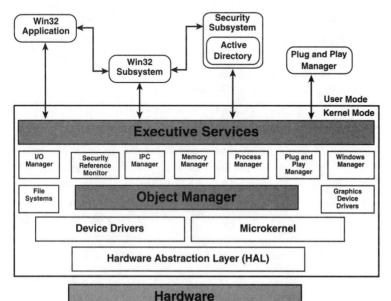

FIGURE 3.1
The Windows 2000 architecture is divided into user mode and kernel mode.

The Windows 2000 operating system is divided into two major operating environments called modes. *User mode* is where all user interaction happens; this includes logon and the Win32 subsystem, in which 32-bit programs are run (see Chapter 4, "Managing, Monitoring, and Optimizing System Performance, Reliability, and Availability"). The other mode is called *kernel mode.* The kernel is the essential core of the Windows 2000 operating system. All essential processes run in this mode. Processes in the kernel mode are protected from direct user interaction, ensuring that you (and your software) have very limited ability to cause system crashes or to compromise security.

The kernel mode consists of a number of components, including the Windows 2000 executive. This executive has a number of processes that control internal system functions. These processes include the GUI manager, the virtual memory manager, and the device drivers. Most of these functions are beyond the direct scope of this book, but suffice it to say that a wide variety of control systems are hidden from your direct manipulation.

To make access to hardware by processes in user mode (programs that a user runs) as simple as possible, a set of hardware interfaces (drivers) have been established, which reside in kernel mode (refer to Figure 3.1). A driver creates a standard programmer interface for directing output from and receiving input into a program. Programmers do not want to have to write a separate program (or subroutine) for every possible video card that might be installed in a system running their software. So, they simply ask for things to be displayed in a generic way. The device drivers convert those generic requests into specific requests to the hardware that they are configured to support.

Because so much is riding on the correct functioning of the interface between the user mode and the hardware, it is essential that drivers work properly with Windows 2000 and with the devices they are designed to interface with. As a result, Microsoft has created standards that define what the generic interface to the user mode should look like. Standards also define how the driver should position itself (and function) within the kernel mode processes.

One particular new feature in the Windows 2000 operating system was available in the Windows 9x clients and existed in a less-than fully functional form in Windows NT 4.0. This feature is called Plug and Play. The addition of a Plug and Play manager (with a component in both the user mode and the kernel mode) makes it much easier to configure hardware devices than it was previously. Now many devices will be automatically detected, and the drivers will be installed for you.

To summarize, proper functioning of drivers in Windows 2000 is essential for the proper functioning of the hardware devices they control. These drivers ensure that when programs manipulate hardware devices you get the proper results.

CONFIGURING HARDWARE DEVICES

Configure hardware devices.

The ability to configure your server hardware properly is essential to a smooth-running operating system. Windows 2000 makes the configuration of hardware devices much easier through the implementation of the Plug and Play manager. This manager ensures that all Plug and Play compatible devices are automatically detected and that their drivers are installed. Even devices that are not Plug and Play may still be located by Windows 2000. Their drivers will be installed just as Windows NT used to install them. This will reduce the amount of time you will spend manually configuring the drivers and the resources required by the hardware. Of course, despite all these new features, you will still need to do your homework before trying to install a new device. All devices must be on the Windows 2000 HCL or have a driver supplied by a third party vendor (adherence to the Windows 2000 HCL cannot be stressed strongly enough). You can go to http://www.microsoft.com/windows2000/upgrade/compat/search/devices.asp to search for your device compatibility using an online tool. You can also go to http://www.Microsoft.com/hcl for a current version of the Windows 2000 HCL. In addition, you can check the file \support\hcl.txt on the Windows 2000 Server CD.

The sections that follow will introduce you to two tools: the System Information reports and the Device manager. These two tools can be accessed together in the Computer Management console. These two tools allow you to view configuration information as well as install and update new devices.

Even with the new features, you still need to manually configure some hardware. In some cases, your server may not have sufficient IRQs (or resources) for all your devices. You might have to manually disable one device in order to enable another. In addition, you might want to configure a legacy device that is not properly detected by Windows 2000. Finally, you might want to have some devices accessible under certain circumstances while not under others. For those situations, you might find that a hardware profile or two is helpful (these will be discussed in a later section).

Viewing Installed Devices

You can view and change the properties of devices and drivers that are installed on your Windows 2000 server through the Computer Management console (see Figure 3.2). Among other things, this console allows you to access two tools: the Device manager and System Information. The Device manager allows you to view, add, and configure hardware devices. (You can also access the Device manager on its own through the Windows 2000 System Properties; right-click the My Computer icon and choose Properties or double-click the System icon in the Control Panel, and then click the Hardware tab.) System Information allows you to access a variety of reports showing the allocation of system resources to specific devices and software.

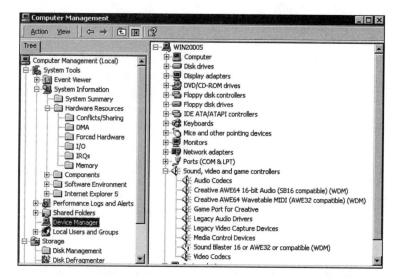

FIGURE 3.2
The Computer Management console with System Information expanded and the Device manager selected.

System Information takes the place of what used to be called the Windows NT diagnostic program WINMSD and the old DOS version called MSD. From this area of the Computer Management console, you can see information on IRQs, memory locations for devices, and hardware and software components on your system. All of these reports are read-only, so they are good only for reporting purposes. Figure 3.3 shows a System Information report.

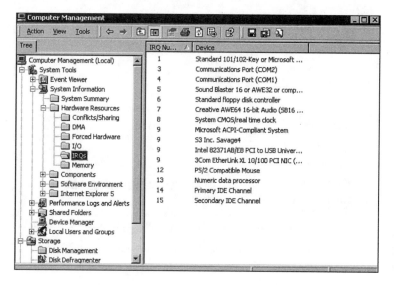

FIGURE 3.3
The System Information section of the Computer Management console is shown here with the IRQ report displayed.

The other area of interest is the Device manager (refer to Figure 3.2). The Device manager allows you to see the categories of devices installed on your server and the specific devices that have been installed or detected. In addition, you can also tell from the Device manager whether all the devices are functioning properly. When you expand any of the device categories, you will either see the device name by itself or the device name with a yellow exclamation point on it. If it has an exclamation point, there is some sort of problem with the device. The problem might be that the drivers could not be found or that the device could not be started for some reason. Figure 3.4 shows the Device manager screen for a Windows 2000 computer in which a sound card has been configured wrong, thus preventing it from starting properly.

From the Device manager, you can also see the specific properties of a device and, for some properties, change them. Double-click the device's name, and the properties for the device appear in a Properties dialog box. The Properties dialog box frequently consists of four tabs: General, Advanced, Driver, and Resources (see Figure 3.5). This is not universal, however, because some devices have additional or fewer configuration options.

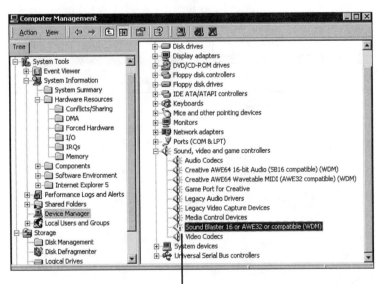

FIGURE 3.4
Devices with problems are identified with a yellow circled exclamation point.

The yellow exclamation point indicates a problem.

The General Property Tab

The General tab shows information such as the device name, its type, and its manufacturer. Also note that there is a button to invoke the device troubleshooter in the case of device malfunction. Finally, a pull-down list at the bottom allows you to enable (the default setting) or disable the device.

The Advanced Property Tab

The Advanced property tab may be available for some devices (see Figure 3.6). It allows you to set specific properties for the device that are not available on the other tabs. These properties will differ from device to device (or might not be present at all).

The Driver Property Tab

The Driver tab (shown in Figure 3.7) gives you information about the device and allows you to configure the driver software installed for the device. It identifies the source of the driver, when it was created, what version you have installed, and whether the driver is signed (see "Configuring Driver Signing Options" for more on signing).

At the bottom of the Driver tab are three buttons: Driver Details, Uninstall, and Update Driver. Driver Details lets you see the physical

FIGURE 3.5
In this Properties dialog box for a network card, the General tab shows information about the device, including its status.

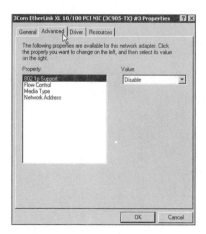

FIGURE 3.6
If present, the Advanced property tab allows you to set a number of advanced parameters for the device.

FIGURE 3.7
The Driver property tab tells you the source of the driver and whether it is digitally signed.

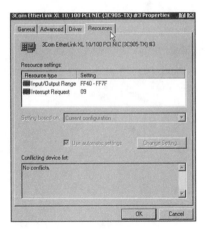

FIGURE 3.8
The Resources property tab identifies the resources being used by the device and whether there are conflicts with other devices.

location of the driver. Uninstall allows you to remove the driver from your server. Update Driver allows you to replace the current driver with another (presumably newer) version.

The Resources Property Tab

The Resources property tab shows you the resources being used by the device (see Figure 3.8). This includes, but is not limited to, the IRQ and memory address. It also shows you if the settings for this device are conflicting with those for another device. For some devices, you can change these settings manually. To do so, clear the Use Automatic Settings check box, and then click the Change Setting button.

Configuring a Hardware Device

Windows 2000 Server fully supports Plug and Play technology. Most of your hardware should be automatically detected and configured, and your drivers should be installed. As a result, the need to manually configure a new device occurs much less frequently than it did in Windows NT 4.0. However, devices are not always detected and might have to be manually installed and configured.

Installing a new device begins when your server is prompted to begin a hardware scan. This normally is initiated at startup, but it can also be initiated manually. The following Step by Step walks you through initiating a hardware scan.

STEP BY STEP

3.1 Initiating a Hardware Scan

1. From the Start menu, choose Programs, Administrative Tools, Computer Management.

2. In the Computer Management console, select Device Manager on the left to display a list of devices on your computer on the right.

3. In the right panel, right-click the name of your computer and, from the menu that appears, select Scan for Hardware Changes (see Figure 3.9).

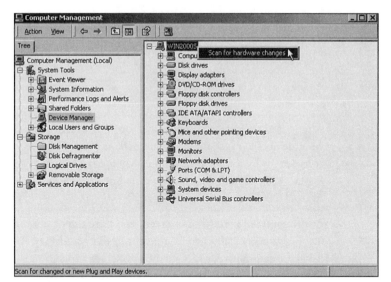

FIGURE 3.9
Right-click on the server name to initiate a scan
for Plug and Play hardware.

Many legacy devices will not be detected by a hardware scan.
Therefore, those devices must be configured manually. This configuration cannot be done from the Device manager. The Device manager will allow you to configure only those devices that have already
been installed.

To manually install and configure a device, you must bring up the
System Properties dialog box. This dialog box contains general information about your system, as well as specific configuration options
dealing with hardware (see Figure 3.10).

Step by Step 3.2 walks you through the manual installation of a
hardware device.

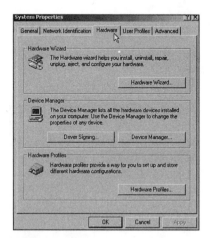

STEP BY STEP

3.2 Manually Installing a Hardware Device

1. Right-click the My Computer icon and choose Properties
   from the menu that appears.

2. In the System Properties dialog box, click the Hardware
   tab to access the Hardware page.

3. On the Hardware page, click the Hardware Wizard button.

FIGURE 3.10
The Hardware tab of the System Properties
dialog box is where you begin to install new
non-Plug and Play hardware.

continues

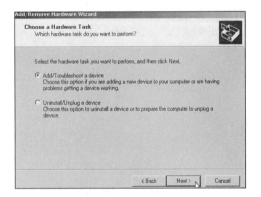

FIGURE 3.11
Choose to add a new device.

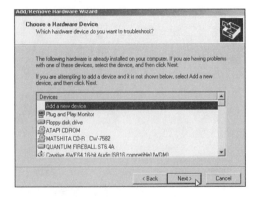

FIGURE 3.12
Choose to add a new device.

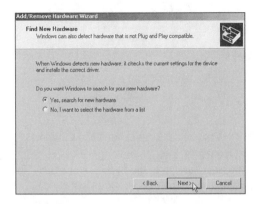

FIGURE 3.13
It is best to begin by allowing Windows 2000 to try to find your hardware device.

continued

4. At the Welcome to the Add/Remove Hardware Wizard page, click Next to continue.

5. At the Choose a Hardware Task page (see Figure 3.11), select Add/Troubleshoot a Device and click Next.

6. The wizard will begin a detection process to determine what devices are installed on your system. When it is complete, a list of detected devices will appear (see Figure 3.12). To add a new undetected device, select Add a New Device and click Next.

7. At the Find New Hardware screen, you have the option of having Windows 2000 try to detect non-Plug and Play devices (see Figure 3.13). Generally, you would have Windows 2000 try to detect hardware. However, if you know that a particular device is not going to be detected, you can choose No, I Want to Select the Hardware from a List instead of choosing Yes, Search for New Hardware. (For this example, click Yes…. After you make your selection, click Next to continue.

Windows 2000 will attempt to locate hardware that it is able to identify (see Figure 3.14). This process might take several minutes.

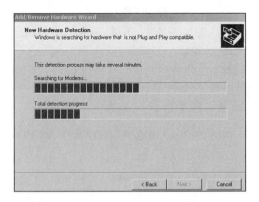

FIGURE 3.14
Windows 2000 will probe for all devices it knows in order to find non-Plug and Play devices.

8. If no new hardware is detected, you will have to manually install the device. At the Hardware Type screen, select the category of device you are installing (see Figure 3.15) and click Next.

9. At the Select a Device Driver screen, choose a manufacturer and model for the device you are installing (see Figure 3.16). If the appropriate choice is not available and you have the driver on disk or other media, click Have Disk and provide the path to the driver files. Click Next to continue.

10. At the Start Hardware Installation screen (shown in Figure 3.17), click Next to continue.

11. When the Completing the Add/Remove Hardware Wizard screen appears, click Finish to complete. You will have to restart your computer for the device to be detected by Windows 2000.

After you manually install a device, you can configure it through the Device manager.

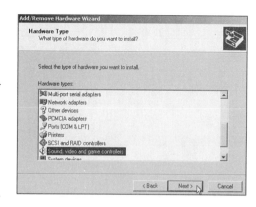

FIGURE 3.15
Choose the type of device you are installing.

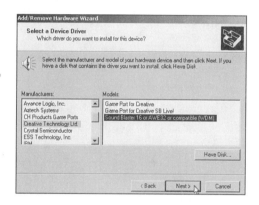

FIGURE 3.16
Specify the manufacturer and model of the device you are installing.

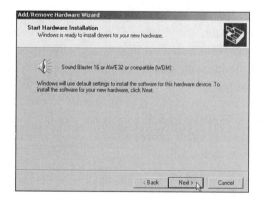

FIGURE 3.17
Click Next to start the installation.

Creating Hardware Profiles

Hardware profiles are configuration groupings that define which hardware devices are to be started under certain circumstances. Hardware profiles are very common on a Windows 2000 professional machine that is being docked and undocked from a docking station. There are also times, particularly in a test lab, when you might want to create profiles for your Windows 2000 server.

The idea of the hardware profile is simple. Under certain circumstances you do not want certain hardware devices to start, but you do not want to go through the work of physically removing the devices. The idea behind the profile is that drivers are software and, if they're not loaded and started, the drivers do not provide an interface to the devices. Without an interface, the devices might as well not be installed at all.

After multiple hardware profiles have been created, at system startup you will be prompted to choose one. You can configure which profile is the default and how long the system will wait before defaulting to that profile.

Hardware profiles are user independent and, therefore, are available to all users at system startup.

Hardware profiles can be configured from the Device manager. Each device can be associated with one or more hardware profiles. The actual hardware profiles are identified by name. When a profile is created, each device is, by default, started in conjunction with that profile. At that point, you can disable certain devices for certain profiles. With multiple profiles created, at boot you will be given the choice of what profile to load. If you choose a profile that does not start certain devices, those devices will not appear available to you when your server is started.

Step by Step 3.3 shows how to create a hardware profile in Windows 2000.

STEP BY STEP

3.3 Creating a Hardware Profile

1. Right-click the My Computer icon and choose Properties from the menu that is presented.

2. From the System Properties dialog box, click the Hardware tab.

3. On the Hardware tab, click the Hardware Profiles button.

4. A new profile always begins as a copy of an existing profile. Select the profile you want to copy and click the Copy button (see Figure 3.18).

5. In the Copy Profile dialog box, type a new profile name and click OK.

6. If the Windows 2000 computer for which you are configuring the profile is a laptop, click the Properties button. This will bring up the properties sheet for the new profile (see Figure 3.19). On this sheet, you can configure the profile to recognize the machine as a portable, and you can configure the docking status of the machine when the profile is selected. This configuration allows Windows 2000 to determine whether to start services and devices related to a docked state (like networking, for example).

7. When your new profile has been created, you can select it and use the up and down arrows on the right to determine which will be the default profile (the one at the top is the default profile).

8. In the Hardware Profiles Selection area at the bottom of the dialog box, you can choose how long the computer will wait before selecting the default profile. If you choose Wait Until I Select a Hardware Profile, system startup will pause until you select a profile. If you choose Select the First Profile Listed If I Don't Select a Profile in xx Seconds, you must specify how many seconds you want the computer to wait before starting the default profile.

FIGURE 3.18
Select the profile that you want to copy and click the Copy button.

FIGURE 3.19
For laptops, you can create a hardware profile related to the current docking state of the machine.

After you create a hardware profile, you must determine which devices are to be excluded from the profile. By default, all devices are included in any profile you create. Therefore, if you don't want certain devices (or even services) to start under certain circumstances, you have to manually configure that. Step by Step 3.4 shows you how.

STEP BY STEP

3.4 Configuring a Hardware Profile

1. Restart your computer and select the hardware profile you want to configure from the hardware profile list.

2. From the Start menu, choose Programs, Administrative Tools, Computer Management.

3. Select the Device manager from the system tools list. Expand the list of devices on the right until you find the device you want to exclude from this hardware profile.

4. Right-click the device you want to disable for this profile and choose Properties from the menu that is presented.

5. At the bottom of the General property tab is a pull-down list labeled Device Usage (see Figure 3.20). Click on the down arrow and choose Do Not Use This Device in the Current Hardware Profile (Disable). Click OK to make this change permanent.

6. Repeat steps 4 and 5 for each device you want to disable for this profile. Close the Device manager when you finish.

FIGURE 3.20
Disable desired devices in the current profile.

Although it's not strictly a hardware issue (and definitely not occurring on the exam), you can also configure certain services not to start when a particular hardware profile is selected on system startup. To do this, you start up the Computer Management console and navigate to the Services and Applications, Services section. This lists all the services that are available on your computer. Right-click a service and choose Properties to bring up the Properties dialog box. At the bottom of the Log On tab, you can select a hardware profile and then click the Enable or Disable button to choose when it is to start.

R E V I E W   B R E A K

To review, the configuration of hardware devices involves two tools: the System Information reports and the Device manager. These two tools can be accessed together in the Computer Management console. You need to understand the following specific tasks for the exam:

▶ Viewing device status using System Information and the Device manager

▶ Installing new devices (both automatically using Plug and Play, and manually)

▶ Configuring hardware profiles

If you understand and can perform these tasks, you will have the skills required to answer the exam questions related to hardware configuration.

CONFIGURING DRIVER SIGNING OPTIONS

Configure driver signing options.

Drivers are the crux of communication between your applications/operating system and your hardware. It is essential that they function properly. To this end, Microsoft has implemented driver signing in Windows 2000. The concept is straightforward. Each driver that Microsoft creates or verifies is digitally signed by them. As a result, that driver is guaranteed to work with Windows 2000

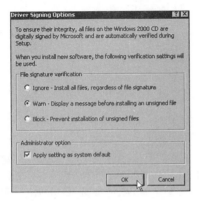

FIGURE 3.21
You can choose to verify digital signatures before a driver is installed.

and is verified to be free of corruption. Because that is the optimal state, you want all (or as many as possible) of your drivers to be signed. As new drivers are created by hardware vendors, they will be signed by Microsoft (or other trusted sources) and released. This section describes how to configure your system to watch for signed drivers and to respond appropriately when unsigned drivers are detected.

As a system administrator, you can implement a local security policy that checks for signatures on your drivers. You have three choices when it comes to signatures (see Figure 3.21).

◆ *Ignore.* You can ignore signatures and allow the installation of drivers without checking them.

◆ *Warn.* You can have the system check signatures on drivers when they are installed and warn you if they are not signed (this is the Windows 2000 default). This gives you a chance to reconsider your decision to install an unsigned driver.

◆ *Block.* You can block the installation of unsigned drivers to ensure that your system is free of unsigned and possibly corrupt drivers.

In addition, as you can see in Figure 3.21, as an administrator you can prevent anyone else who has access to this Windows 2000 server from modifying these signing properties. Filling in the checkbox for Apply setting as system default ensures that the integrity of your drivers is maintained.

Of course, for all good things there is usually a price, and signing is no exception. Many unsigned drivers are still required to get certain pieces of hardware to operate. If you require that all drivers be signed, you might end up in the situation where you are throwing the proverbial baby out with the bath water. To maintain such strict operating system integrity, you might prevent yourself from using certain pieces of hardware. Some might argue that this is the price you have to pay for the increased peace of mind, but that is sometimes debatable. Whether or not that is the case, you still must take that into account when deciding whether to maintain a strict policy of driver signing.

The following Step by Step outlines how to configure driver signing options.

STEP BY STEP

3.5 Configuring Driver Signing Options

1. Right-click the My Computer icon and choose Properties from the menu that appears.

2. Click the Hardware tab.

3. On the Hardware tab, in the Device Manager box, click the Driver Signing button.

4. In the Driver Signing Options dialog box, choose the desired file signature verification option. If you want to prevent other non-Administrators from overriding your option, select the Apply Setting As System Default check box. When you finish, click OK.

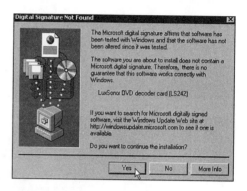

FIGURE 3.22
A warning is presented that you can choose to ignore.

After driver signing options have been configured, the installation of an unsigned driver will have one of three results. If you choose to ignore signatures, any driver you supply will be installed without question. If you choose to be warned when an unsigned driver is installed, a warning dialog box like the one shown in Figure 3.22 will appear. You will have the option of installing the driver or exiting the installation.

If you choose to block the installation of unsigned drivers, a warning dialog box like the one shown in Figure 3.23 will appear when you try to install an unsigned driver. You will not have the option to install; the installation will simply fail.

To summarize, driver signing ensures that device drivers will function—and function well. Windows 2000 has configuration options to protect you against unsigned drivers (or at least to warn you before you install one).

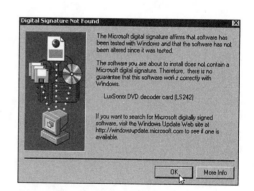

FIGURE 3.23
A warning is presented that you cannot ignore or bypass.

UPDATING DEVICE DRIVERS

Update device drivers.

Like any software, drivers are never static. As the underlying operating system changes and improvements are made to hardware, the drivers change. In addition, some drivers are discovered to have bugs and are fixed. Therefore, you might find that drivers need to be updated occasionally. These updates might come from Microsoft or from the hardware vendor. They might come to you on floppy disk or on CD-ROM, or they might be downloadable from the Internet. Whatever their source, updating them generally provides more stability in the operation of your hardware devices. In addition, these updates may increase driver speed and sometimes add new functionality. All of these results benefit you. All these driver issues are covered in this section.

You can update drivers from the Device manager. The process for updating a driver is covered in Step by Step 3.6.

STEP BY STEP

3.6 Updating a Device Driver

1. Right-click the My Computer icon and choose Properties from the menu that appears.

2. From the System Properties dialog box, click the Hardware tab and click the button labeled Device Manager.

3. From the Device Manager dialog box, expand the categories until you locate the device whose driver you want to update. Right-click on it and choose Properties from the menu that appears.

4. From the Properties dialog box of the hardware device, click the Driver tab and click the Update Driver button (see Figure 3.24).

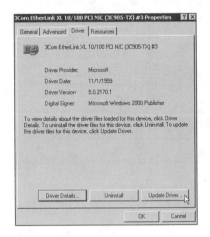

FIGURE 3.24
Update the driver from the device properties.

5. When the Update Device Driver Wizard appears, click Next to continue.

6. On the Install Hardware Device Drivers page, select the appropriate search mechanism for finding a new driver (see Figure 3.25). If you select Search for a Suitable Driver for my device, Windows 2000 will search your system for a new driver in the locations you indicate. If you select Display a List of the Known Drivers for This Device So I Can choose a Specific Driver, you will be shown a list of drivers that Windows 2000 recognizes. This option is not generally chosen because an updated driver is one that is new, not one that would have loaded from the CD automatically. When you finish here, click Next to continue.

7. On the Locate Driver Files dialog box (shown in Figure 3.26), choose the location you want to search. Then click Next to continue.

8. The system may prompt you for a location if you selected the Specify a Location check box on the previous step. If so, enter a location and click Next.

9. If a suitable driver is located, you will be informed of that. Click Next to continue.

10. On the Completing the Upgrade Device Driver Wizard screen, click Finish.

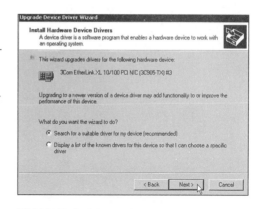

FIGURE 3.25
It is recommended that you tell Windows 2000 where to look for a new driver instead of letting it show you the drivers it knows about.

FIGURE 3.26
You can tell Windows 2000 where to look for a new driver.

Device drivers will occasionally need to be updated. Knowing the need for updates and how to update will ensure that you keep your hardware running at peak efficiency.

TROUBLESHOOTING HARDWARE PROBLEMS

Troubleshoot hardware problems.

Trouble with hardware comes from a number of sources. The device might be installed improperly or be faulty. If the device is not Plug and Play compliant, it might have been configured improperly.

If a device is Plug and Play compliant, an incorrect driver might have been manually installed for that device or someone might have tried to manually configure it when it would have been better to let auto configuration do so (this can specifically be an issue if another device is installed and auto configuration tries to assign resources to it that have been manually assigned to another device). The device may not have an IRQ assigned to it, so it might not function due to lack of resources. These and other topics are covered in this section.

There are two main sources for troubleshooting hardware problems: the system log in the Event Viewer and the Device manager.

Troubleshooting Using the System Log

Problems that stem from a device not starting will sometimes cause a message to be displayed on startup telling you that a service failed to start (see Figure 3.27). This is especially true when the failure is in the network card, because that device's starting is the precursor to the starting of all the networking services. These messages will have corresponding entries in the system log describing the nature of the problem.

In order to solve problems of this kind, you need to be able to find and interpret log entries. Step by Step 3.7 describes this process.

FIGURE 3.27
A warning message like this is often the first sign that something is wrong.

STEP BY STEP

3.7 Opening the System Log

1. From the Start menu, choose Programs, Administrative Tools, Event Viewer.

2. On the left side of the Event Viewer console, select System Log, and a list of events will appear on the right (see Figure 3.28).

3. Find the event you are interested in and double-click it to open it and see its details.

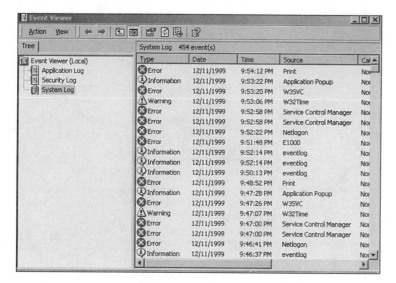

FIGURE 3.28
Three levels of messages are presented: Errors, Warnings, and Information.

As you can see in Figure 3.28, log entries come in three levels of severity. A fatal error is indicated by a red circle with an X in it. Fatal errors generally result in something failing. A warning is indicated by a yellow triangle (yield sign) with an exclamation point in it. Warnings indicate a problem that may have serious ramifications, but they do not necessarily indicate that a problem must be corrected. Informational entries indicate that something happened successfully.

Figure 3.29 shows a typical log entry. Much of it is obscure, but in this case, what is clear is that there is something wrong with the network adapter. This should be enough to suggest that the next likely source of troubleshooting information should be the Device manager.

Troubleshooting Using the Device Manager

When you know which device is causing your problem, the Device manager is the place to go. It shows you all the devices you have installed, as well as the status of each.

As you can see in Figure 3.30, a yellow circle with an exclamation point in it is displayed over the name of the device that is not functioning properly. Any device that is not functioning will be identified in that way.

N O T E

Event Log Event Indicates Starting of Server If you want to know what events have occurred since you last restarted, look for the Information event with a source of `eventlog`. This shows when the event log started. No entries are recorded until the event log starts. As you can see in Figure 3.28, the most recent event log entry was recorded at 9:52:14 PM. After the event log was started, the errors begin to surface.

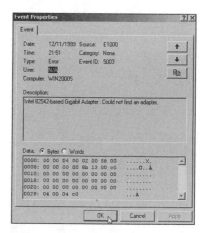

FIGURE 3.29
Log entries are sometimes obscure, but they generally have a nugget of information that is useful to the average administrator.

FIGURE 3.30
The network adapter is not functioning properly.

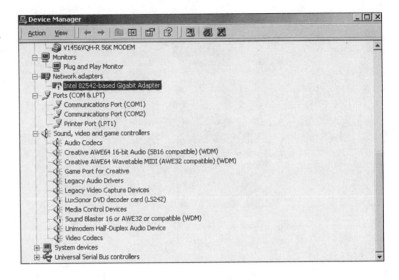

In this case, you can see that in addition to some other faulty devices, the network adapter is not functioning properly. You can double-click it to see its properties (see Figure 3.31).

The properties can tell you a number of things. The General property tab will tell you the status of the device. From here, you can also invoke the Troubleshooter, which will lead you through a text-based analysis of the problem with your device. The Driver property tab will tell you if the driver is signed by Microsoft and, therefore, whether it is certified to function properly. The Resources property tab will tell you if there are memory or IRQ conflicts with other devices.

Step by Step 3.8 walks you through the process of examining a device's properties.

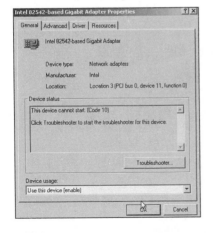

FIGURE 3.31
The device status might tell you what the problem is with the device.

STEP BY STEP

3.8 Opening a Device's Properties

1. Right-click My Computer and select Properties from the menu that is presented.

2. Click the Hardware tab.

3. On the Hardware tab, click the Device Manager button.

4. From the Device manager, locate the device you want to investigate and double-click it.

A major problem with devices is misconfiguration or malfunction. In many cases, reinstalling or updating the driver can fix the problem. In some cases, especially with graphics drivers, removal of the current driver is required, followed by a reboot to allow Plug and Play to redetect and reinstall the driver. In other cases, you might have to replace the device. This is often the solution when no reconfiguration has been done to a system that used to work but no longer functions.

Troubleshooting skills are essential for maintaining any Windows 2000 computer. The ability to use the event logs and the Device manager is essential in these skills. However, do not discount instinct and experience as you troubleshoot; and do not be afraid to ask someone with more experience than you for help.

CASE STUDY: GOTHIC CLOTHIERS

ESSENCE OF THE CASE

This case requires that the following end results be satisfied:

▶ You need to ensure that the drivers installed are safe for the system and will function properly.

▶ You need to ensure that Wanda can continue to do her other duties (including, in some cases, installing drivers).

SCENARIO

Gothic Clothiers is a small garment manufacturing company with 30 employees. Boris is the defacto network administrator, mainly because no one else knows as much about computers as Boris. A consultant came into the plant and set up a small LAN with five Windows 98 workstations and a Windows 2000 file and print server to store their documents. Lately, one of the other employees, Wanda, has been experimenting with the server and has added a new video card and a modem. Although Boris would like to take Wanda's privileges away, she has Power User status because she needs to do server maintenance. It is not what she is doing that concerns Boris, but the lack of concern that she has about the possible ramifications. He heard of another company whose server was devastated by a virus introduced through a driver downloaded from the Internet. Boris wants to make sure that this will not happen to his server. He calls you to get your advice on how to solve his dilemma.

continues

CASE STUDY: GOTHIC CLOTHIERS

continued

ANALYSIS

The issue here is being able to control the installation of bad drivers, while at the same time ensuring that Wanda can still perform her other duties. This means that you cannot simply take away her rights as a Power User. Of course, education in matters of downloading and installing drivers on a public server is necessary, but Boris needs to put driver signing into place to eliminate the possibility that invalid drivers can be installed. In addition, he needs to configure this driver signing to be the system default to ensure that Wanda cannot simply remove the requirement for driver signing. By blocking all unsigned drivers from being installed, Boris can ensure that the server is safe from corruption and malfunction. This will probably necessitate paying a little more for components that have signed drivers. Although most hardware will have drivers that are signed by Microsoft, the expense is worth the safety that is required in this case.

The following table summarizes the solution.

OVERVIEW OF THE REQUIREMENTS AND SOLUTIONS IN THIS CASE STUDY

Requirement	Solution Provided By
Wanda maintains her ability to perform tasks, including installing new hardware.	Maintaining Wanda's Power User status.
No one can install unsigned drivers.	Implement driver signing to block all unsigned drivers.
	Set this as the default Windows 2000 setting to ensure that no users can go in and change the driver signing options.

CHAPTER SUMMARY

Summarized briefly, this chapter covered the following main points.

- ◆ **Installing, configuring, and updating devices.** This includes the recognition of Plug and Play for most new devices, the presence of the Device manager, and the ability to manually install and configure non-Plug and Play devices.

- ◆ **Configuring driver signing options.** This allows you, the administrator, to create a policy on the need for drivers to be signed to ensure validity and to enforce such a policy to keep corrupt or non-verified drivers from being installed.

- ◆ **Troubleshooting hardware problems.** This is required whenever you encounter problems with drivers. This may be the result of drivers that have been manually misconfigured, drivers for legacy hardware that require configuration, or hardware that has malfunctioned.

Drivers are very important. Both Plug and Play and driver signing are new for Windows 2000. You can expect to see at least a couple of questions dealing with them.

KEY TERMS

- user mode
- kernel mode
- driver
- Device manager
- driver signing
- system log

APPLY YOUR KNOWLEDGE

Exercises

3.1   Updating and Troubleshooting Device Drivers

In this exercise, you learn how to update a device driver, how to troubleshoot the mistake you made, and how to repair the problem. This exercise assumes that you do not have a 3Com EtherLink XL 10/100 PCI NIC (3C905-TX) network card. If you do, substitute another driver when you apply the incorrect one.

Estimated Time: 30 minutes

Open the Device manager to investigate the current properties of your network card.

1. Right-click My Computer and choose Properties from the menu that appears.

2. Click the Hardware tab in the System Properties dialog box and click the Device Manager button.

3. In the device list, locate the Network Adapters section and expand it to display your network card.

4. Double-click the entry for your network card to display its properties.

5. Record the name of the driver that appears at the top of the General tab. An example would be 3Com EtherLink XL 10/100 PCI NIC (3C905-TX).

"Update" your network card driver with an incorrect one to create a driver error.

1. From the Device Properties dialog box, click the Driver tab.

2. At the bottom of the Driver tab, click the Update Driver button.

3. At the Welcome to the Upgrade Device Driver Wizard screen, click Next.

4. At the Install Hardware Device Drivers screen, select Display a List of the Known Drivers for This Device So That I Can Choose a Specific Driver. Then click Next.

5. At the Select Network Adapter screen, select Show All Hardware of This Device Class and then, when the full list appears, select Intel from the Manufacturers list and Intel 82542-based Gigabit Adapter under Network Adapter. Click Next to continue.

6. A message appears, indicating that Windows 2000 does not recommend that you install this driver. Click Yes to continue.

7. At the Start Device Driver Installation screen, click Next.

8. At the Completing the Upgrade Device Driver Wizard screen, click Finish.

9. Restart your computer.

Use the system log to examine the error that was produced.

1. When the Service Control Manager gives you an error, click OK to acknowledge it.

2. From the Start menu, choose Programs, Administrative Tools, Event Log.

3. On the left side, select System Log to display the system errors at the right.

4. Locate the error message with a source of E1000 and double-click it. It indicates that Windows 2000 is having trouble finding the Intel 82542-based Gigabit Adapter; it should have trouble

APPLY YOUR KNOWLEDGE

because you do not have that adapter. Click OK to close the message, and then close the Event Viewer console.

Use the Device manager to examine the error.

1. Right-click the My Computer icon and select Properties from the menu that appears.

2. Click the Hardware tab, and then click the Device Manager button.

3. Locate the Network Adapters section and expand to find the Gigabit Adapter; there is a warning symbol on it to show that the device is not functioning.

4. Double-click the Gigabit Adapter entry to bring up its properties. Note that the device status reads "This device cannot start."

Reinstall the original driver to repair network problems.

1. Click the Driver tab, and then click the Update Driver button.

2. At the Update Device Driver Wizard screen, click Next.

3. At the Install Hardware Device Drivers screen, select Display a List of the Known Drivers for This Device So That I Can Choose a Specific Driver. Then click Next to continue.

4. If your network card was originally detected by Windows 2000, at the Select Network Adapter screen, you can select the network adapter that has been located and click Next. Otherwise, you will have to show all the devices and choose yours from the list. This exercise assumes the former.

5. At the Start Device Driver Installation screen, click Next to install the new driver.

6. At the Completing the Upgrade Device Driver Wizard screen, click Finish.

3.2 Modifying Driver Signing Options

This exercise shows you how to modify the driver signing options to prevent the installation of unsigned drivers.

Estimated Time: 5 minutes

1. Right-click the My Computer icon and select Properties from the menu that appears.

2. In the System Properties dialog box, click the Hardware tab and click the Driver Signing button.

3. In the Driver Signing Options dialog box, select Block and click the OK button.

4. Exit the System Properties dialog box.

Review Questions

1. What major change has been made to the Windows 2000 architecture to make installation and configuration of drivers easier?

2. What are the implications of using each of the three levels of driver signing?

3. What utility shows you the Event Viewer, the System Information, and the Device manager all in one place?

4. Under what circumstances will you have to manually install and configure a hardware driver?

APPLY YOUR KNOWLEDGE

5. What indispensable source of information can be used to determine whether hardware is certified for use with Windows 2000? Where can you obtain this information?

6. Under what circumstances will you update a device driver? What are the possible benefits of doing so?

Exam Questions

1. Jamie is the network administrator in charge of maintaining a Windows 2000 file server. The network card just failed, and in the middle of the night, she is forced to repair the problem. She took the network card out of an old machine that she found in the office, but when she restarted Windows 2000, the card was not recognized by the Plug and Play administrator. What should she do to get this card working?

   A. Jamie will not be able to get this card working because no non-Plug and Play devices are supported under Windows 2000.

   B. Jamie should download a BIOS upgrade for the card, which will make it Plug and Play compatible. Then she must restart the server.

   C. Jamie should go to the Internet, download a Windows 2000 compatible driver for the card, and manually install it through the Hardware Wizard.

   D. Jamie should go to the Internet, download a Windows 2000 compatible driver for the card, and manually install it through the Device manager.

2. When Jamie tries to install a driver for the card she installed in question 1, a dialog box appears, telling her she is not allowed to install unsigned drivers on her Windows 2000 server. The installation fails. What must she do to install this driver?

   A. Log on as an Administrator and change the Driver Signing Options from Ignore to Block.

   B. Log on as an Administrator and change the Driver Signing Options from Block to Warn.

   C. Log on as an Administrator and change the Driver Signing Options from Warn to Ignore.

   D. Log on as an Administrator and change the system policy to allow anyone to install unsigned drivers.

3. What are the two primary tools for troubleshooting driver problems?

   A. Driver Signing and Device manager

   B. Device manager and Hardware Profiles

   C. Hardware Profiles and User Profiles

   D. System Log and Device manager

4. Pauline is a technician tasked with testing a piece of software in a number of hardware configurations. Unfortunately, she has only one Windows 2000 server on which to perform her tests, but she has five different hardware configurations to test. The main core of the computer can remain the same because what she is testing is peripherals (like network cards, video cards, and modems) for software compatibility.

Required Result:

Pauline needs to be able to test all five hardware configurations.

Optional Results:

Pauline wants to do as little physical installation and removal of hardware as she can get away with.

Pauline wants to avoid buying four additional test servers.

Proposed Solution:

Configure the single server with each hardware configuration in turn by installing the peripherals and then removing them before the next configuration.

Which result(s) does the proposed solution produce?

A. The proposed solution produces the required result and both optional results.

B. The proposed solution produces the required result and one of the optional results.

C. The proposed solution produces the required result but does not fulfill either of the optional results.

D. The proposed solution does not produce the required result.

5. Pauline is a technician tasked with testing a piece of software in a number of hardware configurations. Unfortunately, she has only one Windows 2000 server on which to perform her tests, but she has five different hardware configurations to test. The main core of the computer can remain the same because what she is testing is peripherals (like network cards, video cards, and modems) for software compatibility. Her test computer is capable of having all the hardware that needs to be tested installed on it.

Required Result:

Pauline needs to be able to test all five hardware configurations.

Optional Results:

Pauline wants to do as little physical installation and removal of hardware as she can get away with.

Pauline wants to avoid buying four additional test servers.

Proposed Solution:

Configure the single server with five hardware profiles, and invoke each one before the test for that hardware configuration.

Which result(s) does the proposed solution produce?

A. The proposed solution produces the required result and both optional results.

B. The proposed solution produces the required result and one of the optional results.

C. The proposed solution produces the required result but does not fulfill either of the optional results.

D. The proposed solution does not produce the required result.

APPLY YOUR KNOWLEDGE

6. With reference to Figure 3.32, what is the next step toward updating the driver for this network card?

   A. Go to the General tab and click the Update Driver button.

   B. On this page, select Media Type from the Property list and type in the location of the new driver in the resulting dialog box.

   C. Go to the Driver tab and click the Update Driver button.

   D. Exit this dialog box and open the Device manager.

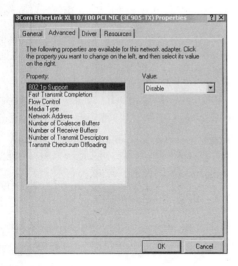

FIGURE 3.32
This is the Properties dialog box for an Ethernet network card.

7. What circumstance will produce the message shown in Figure 3.33?

   A. You just changed the driver signing options to Block.

   B. The driver signing option is Block, and you have tried to install an unsigned driver.

   C. The driver signing option is Ignore, and you have tried to install an unsigned driver.

   D. The driver signing option is Warn, and you have tried to install an unsigned driver.

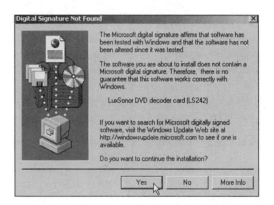

FIGURE 3.33
Figure for Question 7.

8. Bazyl is studying for his MCSE exams. He has configured a Windows 2000 server that he is using as a test machine. His video card stopped functioning, and not having sufficient funds to purchase a new one, he took one out of an old 486 machine that he had in his basement. After installing the hardware in his server, he started his machine but could only get 16 colors and could only change his screen resolution to 640×480. What can Bazyl do to get his video card to function properly?

APPLY YOUR KNOWLEDGE

A. Open the Device manager and have Windows 2000 scan for hardware.

B. Create a hardware profile that starts the driver for his card.

C. Adjust driver signing to allow for the installation of unsigned drivers, thus allowing the Plug and Play manager to install the video driver.

D. Use the Hardware Wizard to manually install the drivers for this non-Plug and Play device.

9. Misty is the administrator for a small Windows 2000-based network. She was browsing the 3Com site on the Internet and discovered a new driver for her server's network card. She downloaded the driver, but how can she ensure that her card now uses the new driver?

A. If she places the new driver in the *systemroot*\System32 folder, the Plug and Play manager will automatically install it the next time she reboots.

B. Open the Properties dialog box for the network card in the Device manager and use the Update Driver button to replace the old driver with the new one.

C. Use the Services Manager to configure the network card to start with the new driver.

D. Install a new occurrence of the network card using the new driver, and then let the Hardware Abstraction Layer automatically remove the old driver.

10. Lewis is the network administrator for a small civic government department. He is responsible for the maintenance and administration of 10 Windows 2000 servers. After a power failure, he arrived at the office to find that one of the servers was displaying a dialog box that read in part "At least one service of driver failed during system startup." What troubleshooting tool should he consult first to determine the source of this error?

A. The Device manager

B. The System Log in the Event Viewer

C. The Security Log in the Event Viewer

D. The Application Log in the Event Viewer

Answers to Review Questions

1. The new addition is the Plug and Play manager, which allows full support for Plug and Play devices. For more information, see the section "Hardware and Drivers in Windows 2000."

2. The three levels of driver signing are Ignore, Warn, and Block. Ignore means that no warning will be issued when an unsigned driver is installed, which could allow the installation of corrupt or unstable drivers. Warn means that when an unsigned driver is installed, a warning will be issued, but the user will be able to continue with the installation or abort it. Block means that no unsigned drivers can be installed on the system. A warning will be issued, but no possibility for override will be possible. For more information, see the section "Configuring Driver Signing Options."

3. The utility that allows for all the main system configuration utilities to be displayed in one place is the Computer Management console. For more information, see the section "Viewing Installed Devices."

APPLY YOUR KNOWLEDGE

4. Most hardware will be installed and configured by the Plug and Play manager. The only time you will have to manually configure is for legacy devices that are not Plug and Play. For more information, see the section "Configuring a Hardware Device."

5. A certified hardware list is available in the Hardware Compatibility List (HCL). This list is available both on the Internet (http://www.Microsoft.com/hcl) and on the Windows 2000 Server CD (HCL.TXT). For more information, see the section "Configuring Hardware Devices."

6. Devices drivers should be updated whenever a new version becomes available (provided that it has been thoroughly tested by the manufacturer and, if possible, signed by Microsoft). Updates to device drivers often fix possible bugs in the software and increase reliability, functionality, and speed. As a result, the benefits are more stable access to hardware and a more reliable Windows 2000 server. For more information, see the section "Updating Device Drivers."

Answers to Exam Questions

1. **C.** Jamie needs a driver for this non-Plug and Play device. If she can obtain one, Windows 2000 will allow her to install it. When she gets the driver, she will go to the Hardware Wizard to install it. Although the Device manager will allow you to do many things, you cannot use it to install non-Plug and Play devices. If she has time, it would be advisable for Jamie to check for this network card on the Hardware Compatibility List to ensure that, although it's not Plug and Play compatible, it is certified by Microsoft for reliable use with Windows 2000. For more information, see the section "Configuring a Hardware Device."

2. **B.** Because Jamie cannot install unsigned drivers, you know the signing option is set to Block. She must set it to something that will allow her to bypass that block. Answer B is the only choice that recognizes the current condition (Block) and provides an option that will allow her to install (Warn). For more information, see the section "Configuring Driver Signing Options."

3. **D.** The two primary tools are the System Log in the Event Viewer (which will allow you to see what system errors have occurred) and the Device manager (which will allow you to see what devices are having problems and will allow you to fix those problems). For more information, see the section "Troubleshooting Hardware Problems."

4. **B.** Because Pauline still has to swap hardware in and out of the server, she has not fulfilled the first optional result. However, she has fulfilled the required result, and she does not have to buy additional servers. For more information, see the section "Creating Hardware Profiles."

5. **A.** Not only does using multiple hardware profiles provide Pauline with a way to test, but she does not have to swap hardware or purchase other servers. For more information, see the section "Creating Hardware Profiles."

APPLY YOUR KNOWLEDGE

6. **C.** The Driver tab contains the Update Driver button, and it is from there that you can modify the installed driver for a device. For more information, see the section "Updating Device Drivers."

7. **D.** This dialog box was produced by an attempt to install an unsigned device driver. As you can see at the bottom of the dialog box, you have the option of continuing the installation or stopping it. This means that the device driver options have been set to Warn, exactly what this dialog box is doing. For more information, see the section "Configuring Driver Signing Options."

8. **D.** Bazyl will have to manually install the device driver for the video card from the Hardware Wizard. Answers A and C are invalid because both imply that the Plug and Play manager is capable of detecting and installing the card and that, for some reason, it is not doing so. Cards that old are not likely to be Plug and Play compliant and, as a result, cannot be detected and

installed by the Plug and Play manager. Answer B is incorrect because hardware profiles can start only those devices that they know about, and this device has not yet been detected or installed. For more information, see the section "Configuring a Hardware Device."

9. **C.** Misty must install the new driver using the Update feature in the Device manager. The new driver will not install itself under any circumstances, nor can the Services Manager start the card with the new driver without it being installed first. For more information, see the section "Updating Device Drivers."

10. **B.** The rest of the message would have read, "Use Event Viewer to examine the event log for details." The portion of the event log that contains information regarding the starting or failure to start of devices is the system log. For more information, see the section "Troubleshooting Using the System Log."

Suggested Readings and Resources

1. Windows 2000 Server Resource Kit: *Microsoft Windows 2000 Server Operations Guide,* Microsoft Press, 2000.

    • Chapter 14: Troubleshooting Strategies

2. *Microsoft Windows 2000 Professional Resource Kit,* Microsoft Press, 2000.

    • Chapter 6: Setup and Startup

    • Chapter 19: Device Management

3. Microsoft Official Curriculum course 2152: Supporting Microsoft Windows 2000 Professional and Server

    • Module 2: Configuring the Windows 2000 Environment

    • Module 11: Maintaining the Windows 2000 Environment

4. Web Sites

    • www.microsoft.com/windows2000

    • www.microsoft.com/train_cert

This chapter will help you prepare for the "Managing, Monitoring, and Optimizing System Performance, Reliability, and Availability" section of the exam.

Microsoft provides the following objectives for "Managing, Monitoring, and Optimizing System Performance, Reliability, and Availability":

Monitor and optimize usage of system resources.

▶ This objective is necessary because someone certified in the use of Windows 2000 Member Server technology must be able to use Performance Monitor to effectively monitor the use of the server and be able to adjust hardware and system usage to maximize performance.

Manage processes.

- **Set priorities and start and stop processes**

▶ Anyone certified in the use of Windows 2000 Member Server technology must understand how to adjust the priority of processes and how to start and stop them through the Task Manager.

Optimize disk performance.

▶ To be competent in this area of Windows 2000 Server technology, you must be able to monitor how hard drives are being used by users and the system and be able to configure them for optimal performance.

CHAPTER 4

Managing, Monitoring, and Optimizing System Performance, Reliability, and Availability

Manage and optimize availability of system state data and user data.

▶ You must be able to use backup strategies effectively to ensure that both system and user data is available at all times.

Recover systems and user data.

- **Recover systems and user data by using Windows Backup.**

- **Troubleshoot system restoration by using Safe Mode.**

- **Recover systems and user data by using the Recovery console.**

▶ When disaster strikes, you must be able to recover from system failure. This failure might come in the form of catastrophic disk or system failure or temporary failure resulting from incorrect configuration.

STUDY STRATEGIES

▶ As in other chapters, this chapter covers two new features: Recovery console and Safe Mode. The Recovery console is by far the more significant of the two.

▶ As it pertains to the other objectives, here are some tips. Understand application priority and, specifically, how to change foreground boost. Also understand how to change application priority both at the time an application begins and while it is running (using the Task Manager). Experiment with applications run at different priorities and with changing their priorities through Task Manager.

▶ Understand how the Performance console is set up and what the component parts are. Know how to create a system monitor, how to create counter and trace logs, and how to configure alerts. Know the main counters involved in the Processor, Memory, Network, and Disk (physical and logical) as outlined in this chapter. It is not likely you will be tested on counters, but you should be aware of them.

▶ As it pertains to system recovery, know the various mechanisms for saving system information and when each would be used. Know the limitations of Last Known Good Configuration and the Emergency Repair Disk. Know how to save this information using Windows 2000 Backup because that has always been a popular question.

▶ As it pertains to data backup and recovery, know how Windows Backup and Restore work, how to invoke them, and how the scheduler works.

▶ As usual, you should know the content of this chapter and work through the exercises and questions at the end. These have been designed to reinforce important concepts, so you should at least have a good look at them. In addition, going through the Step by Steps as you read the chapter will help to reinforce the concepts presented.

INTRODUCTION

The purpose of a member server is to provide services as diverse as printing, data storage, application hosting, and Web services. What these things have in common is a requirement for availability and performance. A file server that is capable of storing all the corporate data is not of much use if its hard drive has just crashed and you cannot recover the information. A Web server that can't keep up with client demands is of little value.

This chapter covers three main topics: controlling program execution and priority, monitoring and optimizing system performance, and recovery from failure (catastrophic or minor).

For the exam, you need to be familiar with all these topics.

MAINTAINING WINDOWS 32-BIT APPLICATIONS

Manage processes.

The execution of applications is very important on a Windows 2000 server, especially if its primary role is that of Applications server. An Applications server is one dedicated to providing services in the form of applications execution, like an Exchange server providing mail services, an IIS server providing Web and FTP services, or a SQL server providing database management.

In this section, you will be introduced to multitasking and the concept of the process. In addition, you will also see the priority levels that can be assigned to a process and how they can be assigned at the time the process is started. The section will also discuss the idea of the priority boost (extra processing cycles that can be given automatically to a foreground application). Finally, Task Manager utilities for changing priorities and starting and stopping processes will be covered.

Windows 2000 allows for multiple processes to run at once through the use of multitasking. This means that, regardless of the number of processors in a Windows 2000 server, more than one process appears to execute at one time. This is made possible by fast processors and a specific kind of multitasking called *preemptive multitasking*. Preemptive multitasking is used as opposed to the cooperative multitasking used in Windows prior to Windows 95.

The fundamental concept in a cooperative multitasking environment is that each process has access to the processor until the process decides to relinquish control of the processor. This is cooperative only as long as the process with control of the processor is in a generous mood. Otherwise, it is much like children saying, "This toy is mine until I don't want it anymore; then you can have it!" The problem with cooperative multitasking is that no independent, impartial judge can determine how long a process ought to keep control of the processor, and if a process fails while it is executing, it can cause all other processing to hang.

Preemptive multitasking solves the problem of processor access by letting the operating system control which processes (or threads) get access to the processor and for how long. This determination is made through the assignment of priorities to each process. The higher the priority that is assigned to a process, the longer (and more frequent) its processor access is. But lest you fear that some processes will never get any resources, Windows 2000 ensures that a process's priority is adjusted from its base priority enough to get access to the processor, even if it is only infrequently. This ensures that no process will be completely ignored as slices of the processor time are given out.

Windows 2000 is also capable of being a multiprocessor operating system. This completely depends, of course, on having multiple processors installed on the motherboard. Windows 2000 Server supports up to four processors. Windows 2000 Advanced Server supports up to eight processors. The multiprocessor capabilities use a system called *symmetric multiprocessing*. Symmetric multiprocessing systems like Windows 2000 allocate processor time from any available (or the least busy) processor. This is as opposed to asymmetric processor systems in which one processor (the master) is responsible for switching between tasks, regardless of how busy (or idle) that processor is at any given time.

Although it happens infrequently on any Windows 2000 computer, you are given the capability to modify the base priority at which an application runs. Process priorities, which can be set either manually (at startup or during execution) or through the application itself, are given a numbered priority between 0 and 31. In this priority scheme, 0 is the least likely to run and consume the processor, and 31 is the most likely to run.

Figure 4.1 illustrates how processes are divided into four categories: idle, normal, high, and real-time. Each of these categories is given a range of numbers in which they operate. In addition, each also has a base priority. The base priority is the priority that a process running in that category gets by default. As you can see, idle ranges from 0 to 6, normal from 6 to 11, high from 11 to 15, and real-time from 16 to 31. In Figure 4.1, the normal priorities are identified above the priority line.

Priorities can be manually assigned to processes for the purposes of making them more or less likely to consume the processor. In addition, the effective priority of an application can change, simply based on whether or not the window in which it is running is in the foreground.

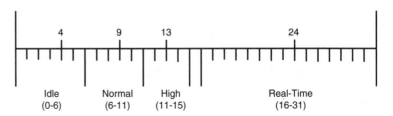

FIGURE 4.1
All application priorities fall on the scale between 0 and 31.

Controlling Normal Priority Applications

Windows 2000 can be configured to put higher priority on processes that are running in the foreground than those that are running in the background; this is called a *priority boost*. This means that if you start your word processor and then start your spreadsheet, the spreadsheet runs in the foreground and will get more processor time than the word processor. This is very reasonable when the applications you are running interact with a user. However, this is not so desirable when the background process is not sitting idle and waiting for user input, but is actively doing some processing (like a large statistical calculation).

Windows 2000 Server can be configured either to treat all normal priority applications the same whether they're in the foreground or the background or to boost the priority of foreground applications by 2.

By default, Windows 2000 Server does not boost foreground applications, but Windows 2000 Professional does. This reflects the typical uses of each operating system. On a Windows 2000 Professional machine, the focus is on user interaction with applications, whereas an application in the background is usually left idle. On the other hand, on a Server, most of the processes running (take services for instance) run in the background with no user interaction.

If you want to configure your Windows 2000 server to boost the priority of foreground applications (or to return it to the default), follow Step by Step 4.1.

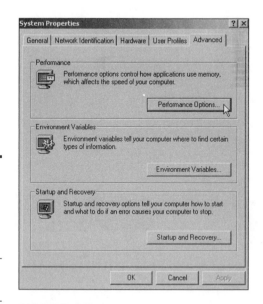

FIGURE 4.2
Default application priority is a performance characteristic.

STEP BY STEP

4.1 Configuring Normal Priority Boost

1. Right-click the My Computer icon and select Properties from the menu that appears.

2. From the System Properties dialog box, click the Advanced tab (see Figure 4.2).

3. Click the Performance Options button. The Performance Options dialog box appears.

continues

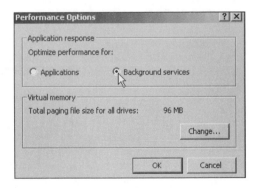

FIGURE 4.3
You can optimize for foreground or background performance.

continued

> **4.** Under Optimize Performance For:, choose either Applications or Background Services (see Figure 4.3).
>
> **5.** Click OK to exit, and then exit the System Properties.

Most applications will run just fine at normal priority. There are times when you will want to relegate a process to low (idle) priority or to a high priority. Microsoft recommends that you not run applications at real-time priority unless they were specifically designed as real-time applications. You must be an Administrator to run a process at real-time priority.

Assigning Priorities at Run Time

To invoke an application with a priority other than normal, use the following syntax from the Run command, in a command prompt, or in the shortcut associated with the application:

```
start /priority application.exe
```

In this syntax, /*priority* represents one of these options: /low, /normal, /high, or /realtime. For example, if you wanted to start Word at low priority, you would use the command start /low winword.exe.

In addition to being able to start a process with a certain priority, you can also adjust the priority while a process is running. This is done in the Task Manager. When you adjust the priority, you are presented with a list of options. Table 4.1 provides numerical interpretations of the various priority names.

TABLE 4.1

PRIORITY NAMES AND THEIR VALUES

Priority	*Numeric Value*
Realtime	24
High	13
AboveNormal	10

Priority	Numeric Value
Normal	8
BelowNormal	6
Low	4

Step by Step 4.2 describes how to adjust a process's priority while it is running.

STEP BY STEP

4.2 Adjusting a Process's Priority

1. Right-click the taskbar and choose Task Manager from the menu that appears (see Figure 4.4).

2. Click the Processes tab to see a list of processes.

3. Right-click the process you want to adjust, choose Set Priority from the menu that appears, and then select the priority from the list (see Figure 4.5).

FIGURE 4.4
The Task Manager can be invoked from the taskbar.

In addition to adjusting the priority of a process, you might want to start a new one or stop one that cannot be closed normally. The Task Manager is also the tool to use for those tasks.

Stopping and Starting Processes with the Task Manager

The Task Manager is a very versatile tool. You can use it to manage (start, stop, switch to) applications. You can use it to see various properties of processes and set their execution priorities, as well as to stop and start them. In addition, Task Manager can also be used as a performance monitor, displaying in both graphical form and text the current resources that are consumed and available on your server.

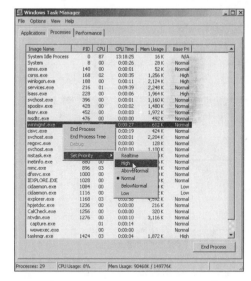

FIGURE 4.5
Process priority can be adjusted at run time.

Exercise Caution When Stopping Processes Although Microsoft wants you to know how to stop processes using the Task Manager, you must be *very* careful when actually doing so. Unlike applications, processes (which are simply threads of execution that might be a small part of a total application) do not have names that allow you to determine their purpose. This means you might stop a process that's vital to the proper functioning of the operating system and cause a server crash. In addition, if you stop a process related to an interactive application, like a word processor, you will not have the opportunity to save your work before exiting. As a result, you should not stop a process unless you are sure that you know and understand the ramifications of your action.

Of particular interest in this section is the ability to stop and start processes using the Task Manager.

A *process* is a single thread of execution, often associated with an application. However, the relationship between applications and processes is not one to one. Some applications spawn more than one process in order to do one thing in the background while doing something else in the foreground (like printing in the background while allowing you to format text). In other cases, a process may be running that has no discernable associated application.

When an application hangs, the first response is generally to try to close it using the "X" in the upper-right corner of the application window. If that is unsuccessful, you might try to open the Task Manager, go to the application's tab, and stop the application from there. However, that is not always completely successful. Some applications leave residual processes running even after the application stops. This, however, is generally an error condition and is not the norm. Some applications start a process that never quite initiates properly and prevents the application from starting at all. In such cases, you might need to manually end the process in order to clean up your system and allow applications and processes to run again.

Step by Step 4.3 demonstrates how to end a process using the Task Manager.

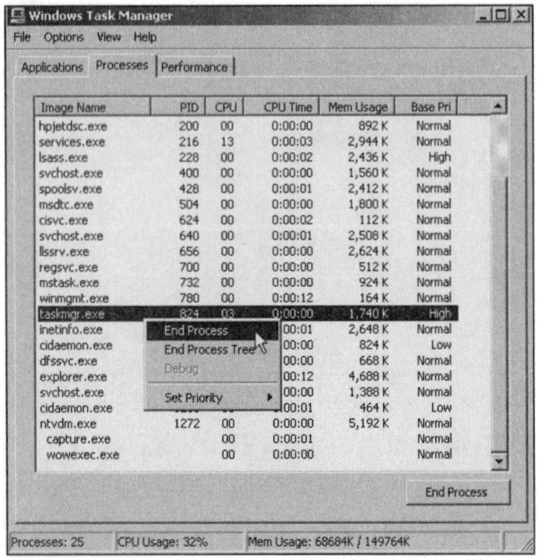

FIGURE 4.6
A process can be terminated from the Task Manager.

STEP BY STEP

4.3 Ending a Process Using the Task Manager

1. Right-click the taskbar and choose Task Manager from the menu that appears.

2. Click the Processes tab and locate the process you want to stop.

3. Right-click the process you want to end and choose either End Process (to stop just that specific process) or End Process Tree (to end that process and all the other processes it spawned in its lifetime). Figure 4.6 shows the shortcut menu for this step.

4. When the warning box appears, click Yes to end the process.

In addition to being able to stop processes, you can also start
processes either by typing a command or by browsing for an application file. Just as in the Run dialog box, however, you must know the
name of the process you want to start. The next Step by Step shows
you how to start a new process using the Task Manager.

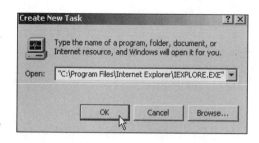

STEP BY STEP

4.4 Starting a New Process Using the Task Manager

1. Right-click the taskbar and choose Task Manager from the
   menu that appears.

2. From the File menu, choose New Task (Run . . .).

3. In the Create New Task dialog box, type a command or
   browse to an application (see Figure 4.7). Click OK to
   start the new process.

FIGURE 4.7
You can start a new task through a dialog box
much like the Run dialog box.

At this point you should understand the concepts of the process and
multitasking. In addition, you should be able to invoke the Task
Manager to start and stop processes. Finally, you should understand
the different process priorities and how foreground boost (or lack of
it) can influence the effective priority a process gets.

MONITORING AND OPTIMIZING SYSTEM RESOURCE USE

Monitor and optimize usage of system resources.

Optimize disk performance

Administering a Windows 2000 server is not simply about making
sure that people have access to it and that information is secure. The
question administrators ask themselves is not just, "Is it running?"
but should also be "Is it running well?" Of course, "well" is relative
and cannot really be quantified outside of your individual context.

This section will cover topics related to the assessment of server performance. This will include a variety of monitoring and logging utilities found in the Performance console. In addition, it discusses some tips on how to tune your server before problems occur and what devices should be monitored when they do. Because the optimization of system resources and the optimization of disk usage cannot really be separated (the disk, after all, is one of the system resources), both exam objectives will be covered in this section.

Periodic monitoring of your Windows 2000 server is important to the process of optimization. Monitoring helps to overcome the feeling-based assessment of your users. For example, by comparing current network performance against a previously established baseline, you have more information than the anecdotal "The network is slow today!" to base your actions on. By gathering current information and comparing it against established norms for your systems (a baseline), you can detect bottlenecks and identify those system components that are slowing down server performance, and fix them before they become a problem to your users.

Although the actual procedure for creating a baseline is outlined later in this section, it is important to discuss the concept of a baseline here because it is the first thing you will do in practice, even if it is not the first concept that is presented here. A baseline is an established norm for the operation of your server as determined by normal load. This baseline can then be used as a basis of comparison for future performance to see if repairable problems exist. As the configuration of your server changes (when, for example, a processor is added or RAM is added), new baselines are established to reflect the new expected performance.

The importance of establishing a baseline before beginning to monitor performance cannot be overstated. Although there are some guidelines as to what absolute performance numbers indicate, it is as you compare current performance against past performance (the baseline) that you will really be able to evaluate how well current demand is being met and whether you require more resources on your server. In addition, it is imperative that a baseline be established before problems begin to occur. If users are already beginning to complain "The network is slow," it is too late to establish a baseline because the statistics gathered will include whatever performance factors are contributing to the dissatisfaction.

It is important to monitor the following components of a Windows
2000 server: the hard disk(s), the processor(s), the memory, and the
network card(s). Regardless of what kind of services the server is
providing, these four areas will interact to make your server efficient
(thereby appearing fast) or inefficient. The actual speed or efficiency
of each of the components will vary in importance depending on
the application. In some applications, memory is more important
than processor speed or availability. In other applications, disk speed
and availability is more important than fast network access.

The Performance Monitor will allow you to watch various facets of
your system, whether you are looking for real-time graphical views
or a log that you can peruse at your convenience, the Performance
Monitor can provide the kind of data you need to evaluate performance and recommend system modification if necessary.

Collecting Data Using Performance Monitor

Monitoring performance begins with the collection of data. There
are four methods available for collecting data: the System Monitor,
counter logs, trace logs, and alerts.

The data collected by Performance Monitor is broken down into
objects, counters, and instances. An *object* is the software or device
being monitored, like memory or processor. A *counter* is a specific
statistic for an object. Memory has a counter called "Available
Bytes," and Processor has a counter called "% Processor Time." An
instance is the specific occurrence of an object you are watching; in a
multiprocessor server, you will have three instances, 0, 1, and _Total.

Using System Monitor

System Monitor enables you to view statistical data either live or
from a saved log. You can view the data in three formats: graph,
histogram, or report. Graph data is displayed as a line graph.
Histograms are displayed as bar graphs. Reports are text-based and
show the current numerical information available from the statistics.

The basic use of the System Monitor is straightforward. You decide which object/instance/counter combinations you want to display and then configure the monitor accordingly. At that point, information begins to appear. You can also change the properties of the monitor to display information in different ways.

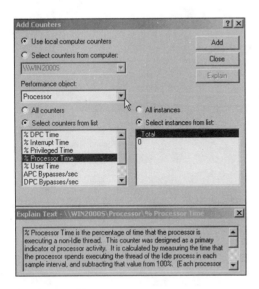

FIGURE 4.8
Adding a Processor counter in the Add Counters dialog box.

Figure 4.8 shows a typical Add Counter dialog box. At the top of the dialog box is a set of radio buttons with which you can obtain statistics from the local machine or a remote machine. This is useful when you want to monitor a computer in a location that is not within reasonable physical distance from you. Under the radio buttons is a pull-down list naming the performance objects that can be monitored. What performance objects are available depends on the features (and applications) you have installed on your server. For example, if you install Network Monitor, you can monitor specific network segments instead of the network card in general. Also, some counters come with specific applications. When you install a Lotus Domino server onto a Windows 2000 server, you have the option of installing performance counters with the software. These performance counters allow you monitor statistics relating to that application from the Performance Monitor.

When you first start the Performance Monitor, you will add counters for Memory, Processor, Hard Disk, and Network. Your increasing knowledge will enable you to fine-tune your approach by monitoring other objects.

Under the performance object is a list of counters. When applied to a specific instance of an object, counters are what you are really after, and the object just narrows down your search. The counters are the actual statistical information you want to monitor. Each object has its own set of counters from which you can choose. Counters allow you to move from the abstract concept of an object to the concrete events that reflect that object's activity. For example, if you choose to monitor the processor, you can watch for the average processor time, how much time the processor spent doing non-idle activity. In addition, you can watch for %user time (time spent executing user application processes) versus %privileged time (time spent executing system processes).

To the right of the counter list is the instances list. If applicable, instances enumerate the physical objects that fall under the specific object class that you have chosen. In some cases, the instances list is not applicable. For example, there is no instances list with memory. In cases where the instances list is applicable, you will see two instance variables. One variable represents the average of all the instances, and one variable represents the values for the first physical object (number 0). For example, if you have two processors in your server, you will see (and be able to choose from) three instance variables: _Total, 0, and 1. This allows you to watch each processor individually and to watch them as a collective unit.

The next Step by Step shows how to add a counter to the system monitor.

STEP BY STEP

4.5 Adding a Counter to the System Monitor

1. From the Start menu, choose Programs, Administrative Tools, Performance Monitor.

2. In the Performance console, click System Monitor to bring up the System Monitor panel on the right side.

3. Right-click the panel on the right side and choose Add Counters from the menu that appears (see Figure 4.9).

continues

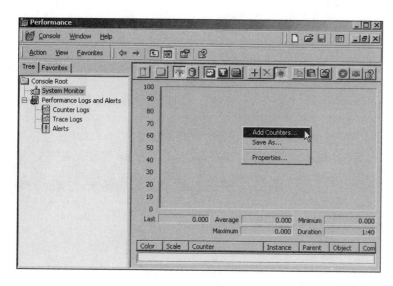

FIGURE 4.9
You can add a counter from the view you want to affect.

continued

4. In the Add Counters dialog box, choose the computer you want to monitor, as well as the object, counter, and instance. Then click Add. If you need help understanding what a certain counter does, click the Explain button, and an explanation will appear under the dialog box. As you add counters, your graph will begin to display data in real time (see Figure 4.10).

5. Repeat step 4 until you have added all the counters you want. Then click the Close button.

You can make a number of modifications to the System Monitor to improve how it functions in your environment. The properties allow you to change the look, the data source, and how the data is to be displayed.

To access the properties for the System Monitor, right-click on the graph and choose Properties from the menu that appears.

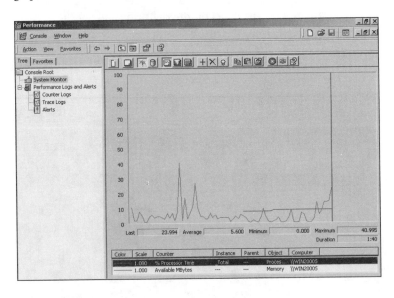

FIGURE 4.10
As you add counters in graph view, the current statistics begin to appear.

The General property tab allows you to change such features as the view, what shortcut elements are displayed, and appearance (see Figure 4.11). There are three views: graph, histogram, and report. Graph displays a line graph, histogram displays a bar graph, and report displays text. The frequency of reporting is based on the check box and field at the bottom of this sheet. You need to specify how often you would like this information updated. Simply check Update Automatically Every XX and indicate the update interval by entering a number between 1 and 9999999 seconds.

The Report and Histogram data sections allow you to specify what value will actually be displayed for reports and histograms. This is necessary because unlike the graph view, these other two do not show running results; instead they display only the current reporting interval. The only unusual choice in this list is Default. Default changes depending on the source of the data. If you are looking at live data, the default is current. Current data is the data generated since the last reporting period. If you are looking at data retrieved from a log, which is static, the default shows the average across the time you are evaluating.

The Source property tab allows you to indicate the source of the graph (see Figure 4.12). The default is to get the current system data according to the time interval specified on the General property sheet. However, you also have the option of displaying logged data from a file. If you choose to get logged data, you can also specify the time slice that you want to examine. Logged data may span many days or weeks. Looking at logged data will be discussed in the upcoming section "Using Counter Logs."

FIGURE 4.11
The General property tab for the System Monitor properties.

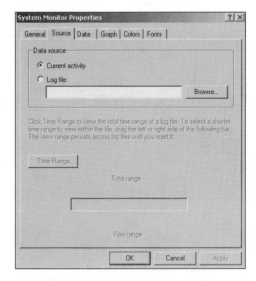

FIGURE 4.12
The Source property tab for the System Monitor properties.

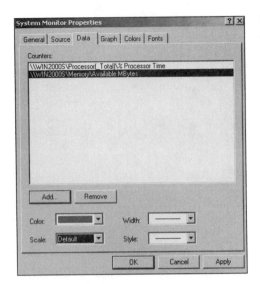

FIGURE 4.13
The Data property tab for the System Monitor properties.

The Data property tab displays the counters that are currently active for your monitor (see Figure 4.13). In addition, you can add or remove counters from this sheet. One feature that is only available here is the ability to change the scale of any active counter. This will allow you to see the values for a particular counter more clearly when it is presented in your view. You can also change the color, width, and style of the lines displayed in the graph view.

The Graph property tab allows you to customize the view you have chosen (see Figure 4.14). You can annotate the graph with a title, and you can label and choose a scale for the vertical axis.

The Colors property tab allows you to modify the colors that are used to highlight the data displayed on the graph (see Figure 4.15).

The Fonts tab allows you to modify the font faces, sizes, and styles (see Figure 4.16). Any change you make here modifies all text on the graph.

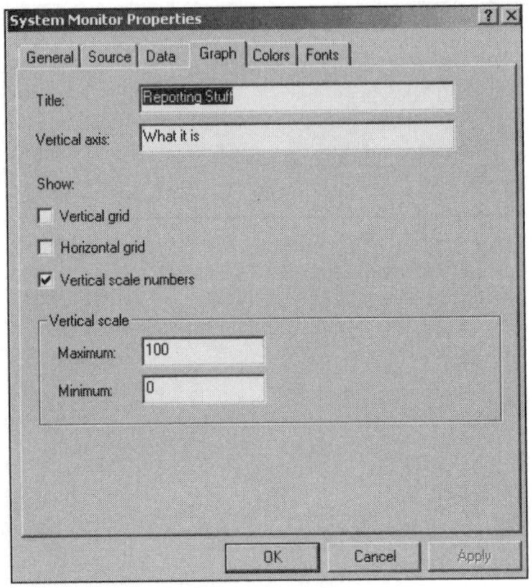

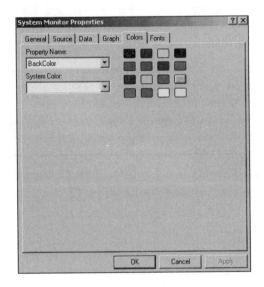

FIGURE 4.15
The Colors property tab for the System Monitor properties.

FIGURE 4.14
The Graph property tab for the System Monitor properties.

Using Counter Logs

While the System Monitor is useful for immediate analysis of a performance problem, it is not very useful as a real-time tool for bottleneck analysis. In order to get a good picture of the way resources are used on your server, you need to be able to examine data collected over a long period of time. The data collection needs to be long enough to allow you to take periodic spikes in usage into consideration. For example, it would be a mistake to analyze the need for more system resource solely by looking at system performance between 8:30 a.m. and 9:30 a.m. This is the time when everyone is logging on, and one could expect the system to be loaded more than average at that time. Similarly, you would not want to check system performance between 12:00 p.m. and 1:00 p.m. The load might be unusually low because people are having a lunch break. To determine system performance and the need for upgrades, you will want to collect data over a long period of time. This precludes using the System Monitor in real-time mode; you would have to sit in front of the console for long periods of time recording the current statistical results.

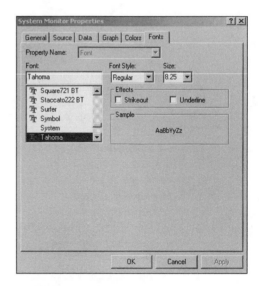

FIGURE 4.16
The Fonts property tab for the System Monitor properties.

A solution to this dilemma is to use *counter logs*. A counter log takes the same information that is captured by the System Monitor and, instead of displaying it in a graph, records it in a file. You can set the log to run and then come back to it in a week (or a month) to see general trends. After the log has been created, you can use the System Monitor in a static mode to look at the data collected by the log.

When configuring a counter log, you have the same choices for monitoring as you do with the System Monitor. You can choose specific objects, as well as counters and instances associated with those objects. Unlike System Monitor, using logs you can log all counters and instances for a specific object. This is a good feature to use when you do not know, or do not have available, the counters you want to monitor when you set up the log. In addition, you can also choose the interval at which to poll the system for information. You will poll at a frequency much less than every second. In fact, if you are logging over a long period of time, a polling time per minute is likely to give you good data without taking up your hard drive with log files.

One of the advantages of logging is that it can be configured to automatically start and stop itself at specific times and on specific days. If all you are interested in logging is system performance between 1:00 a.m. and 5:00 a.m., you can set the log to begin at 1:00 a.m. and then turn itself off at 5:00 a.m. Meanwhile, you're asleep at home.

You can configure as many simultaneous logs as you like. Logging does not create much system overhead, and as a result, it will not really affect the results you get from the logging process. What you do need to be careful of is how much data you collect and where you put the collected data. It is recommended that when you log, you create a partition that contains nothing but log data. In this way, if the log fills the disk, the only thing it will affect is logging. It will not choke out any other applications or the operating system itself.

> **A Sample Configuration** For your convenience, a sample log configuration has been created for you, and it is installed automatically with Windows 2000 Server. You can activate it and begin logging right away, even if you do not fully understand the logging process.

When you create a log, you are presented with a dialog box with three property sheets. On these property sheets, you can configure the data to capture, the place to put the data, and the schedule by which to run the logging process.

As you can see in Figure 4.17, the General property tab allows you to configure the log with the counters you want to track and the interval at which you want to collect information. To add counters, click the Add button. The dialog box that appears is the same as what you saw when you added counters to the System Monitor (refer to Step by Step 4.5).

In addition to adding counters, you can set the interval at which information is gathered. The interval can be set as high as 999,999, and the units can be set to seconds, minutes, hours, or days. Despite the large number the interval can be set to, it can never exceed 45 days. The rule of thumb is generally that the longer you are going to log, the larger the interval should be to prevent your log file from getting too large. However, there may be times when you want to log for a long time but still get finely generated data through the use of short intervals.

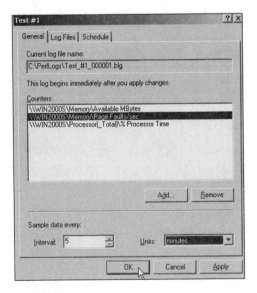

FIGURE 4.17
The General property tab.

On the Log Files property sheet, you can specify the filename and path for the log (see Figure 4.18). You can have the logs uniquely identified using a suffix of a number (nnnnnn) or a date in any one of six different formats.

The log file type defines the format of the log content. CSV and TSV are text formats that you can read with the System Monitor. You can also import this data into tools such as Microsoft Excel and Microsoft Word. CSV is comma delimited, and TSV is tab delimited. Binary files can be read only by the System Monitor or a third–party tool designed to analyze binary log files. Binary circular format is a binary format in which the log file overwrites itself from the beginning when it reaches its maximum size. Cyclical logging is useful when you are concerned about data overflowing the allotted drive. With cyclical logging, when the maximum size is reached, the log is overwritten from the first data samples to the last.

The final option on this property sheet is the size of the log file. You can set the limit to no limit (Maximum Limit). This means the log file will grow until you stop it or until the disk on which it resides is full. If you set a limit, a new log file will be created when the limit is reached. If you have chosen Binary Circular, the file will begin to overwrite itself.

On the Schedule property tab, you can configure the start and stop time for logging (see Figure 4.19). If both start and stop are set to manual, the log starts when you choose. It will continue logging until you manually stop it or the size limit is reached. You can also set logging to begin at a certain time and either go for a specific interval or go until a certain stop time.

When the log file is full, you can choose to begin a new log file and/or execute a command to do some post-logging processing.

Step by Step 4.6 shows you how to create a counter log.

STEP BY STEP

4.6 Creating a Counter Log

1. From the Start menu, select Programs, Administrative Tools, Performance Monitor.

2. From the Performance console, expand the section called Performance Logs and Alerts, right-click Counter Logs, and choose New Log Settings from the menu that appears.

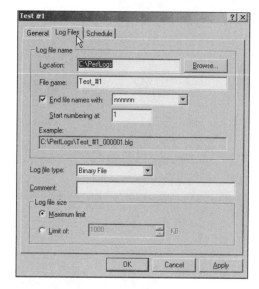

FIGURE 4.18
The Log Files property sheet.

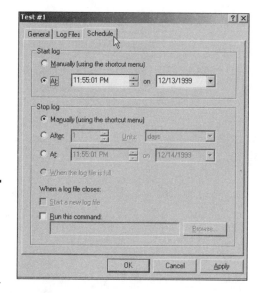

FIGURE 4.19
The Schedule property tab.

continues

continued

3. When prompted, type in a name describing the purpose of this log.

4. On the General property sheet, add the counters you want to log by clicking the Add button and filling in the Select Counter dialog box.

5. On the General property sheet, select the time interval you want to log at.

6. Click the Log Files tab to move to that property sheet.

7. Type in a location, a filename, and a log file suffix (if desired).

8. Specify the log file type and the maximum size.

9. Click the Schedule tab to move to that property sheet.

10. Define the start and stop times for logging and the When a Log File Closes parameter.

11. Click OK to save the log configuration.

If you configured your log to start manually, you will have to start it before logging will begin. A stopped log is marked with a red icon next to the log definition name. A green icon indicates that the log is active or is waiting for its scheduled time to start.

The next Step by Step illustrates how to start a log manually.

STEP BY STEP

4.7 Manually Starting a Log

1. From the Start menu, select Programs, Administrative Tools, Performance Monitor.

2. From the Performance console, expand the section called Performance Logs and Alerts, and then click Counter Logs to view the existing logs on the right side.

3. Right-click a log definition with a red icon and choose Start from the menu that appears.

After a log has been created, you can analyze it in a number of ways. You can open binary formats in the System Monitor. Excel will recognize and open files in CSV format. Any word processor or spreadsheet will open a TSV file, but you'll have to give it formatting information upon import.

Opening a binary file using the System Monitor is much the same as creating a real-time graph. The exception in this case is that the data is static, and you cannot add counters to the view that are not contained in the log. With this in mind, it is better to log more information than you think you'll need in case you find you really do need it in the end.

Step by Step 4.8 describes the process for opening a log file using the System Monitor.

STEP BY STEP

4.8 Opening a Log File with System Monitor

1. From the Start menu, choose Programs, Administrative Tools, Performance Monitor.

2. In the Performance console, click System Monitor to bring up the System Monitor panel on the right side.

3. Right-click the System Monitor window and choose Properties from the menu that appears (or click on the Properties icon).

4. Click the Source tab to move to that property sheet.

5. On the Source property sheet, type in (or browse to) the name of the log file (binary, CSV, or TSV) that you want to graph (see Figure 4.20).

6. If you want to see only a portion of the total time the log file spans, click the Time Range button. On the bar that appears below it, click and drag the blocks on the end toward the center until you reach the desired range.

7. Click the Data tab to move to that property sheet.

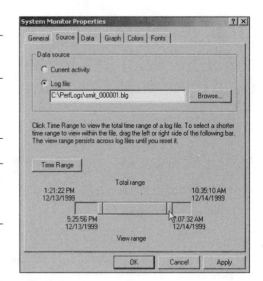

FIGURE 4.20
Choose the log file to get data from, and adjust the time if desired.

continues

continued

8. On the Data property sheet, add or remove counters as desired.

9. Click OK to return to the graph you have created.

You can create a similar graph by importing a CSV text file into a spreadsheet (like Microsoft Excel, for example). When you import, the results come in as headers with numeric data. You can then graph the results by hand. The advantage of this method over System Monitor is that these results can be pasted into word processors and very easily included in reports using OLE conventions.

Step by Step 4.9 shows you how to analyze log data in Microsoft Excel.

STEP BY STEP

4.9 Analyzing Log Data in Microsoft Excel

1. Open Microsoft Excel and open the CSV log you want to examine.

2. Select the extent of the imported data, invoke the chart wizard, and use the options of your choice (see Figure 4.21).

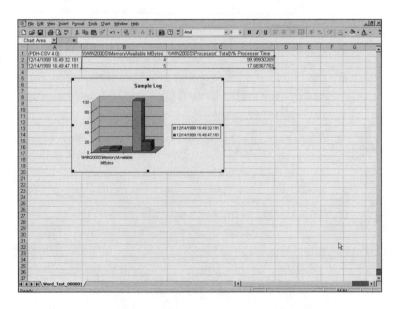

FIGURE 4.21
You can chart performance data in a spreadsheet like Microsoft Excel.

Creating Trace Logs

The subject of trace logs might show up on the exam simply because the feature is new for Windows 2000 and is a bit different from counter logs. There probably will not be more than one question, however, because you must have special third-party tools to analyze them. Therefore, they are generally not very useful to a system administrator (not until some good tools are built, that is).

The difference between a trace log and a counter log is the trigger that causes data collection. With a counter log, the trigger of data collection is a time interval. If you set the time interval to 10 seconds, you will get data every 10 seconds whether or not there is any change to the data from the last interval. With a trace log, the trigger of data collection is the occurrence of an event. For example, if you want to track user log in, you can set the Active Directory or the Local Security Administrator (depending on whether you are tracing login in a domain or on a local server) to watch for the event. When a user log in occurs, the trace process will collect the data.

The options for a trace log are much the same as those for a counter log. The biggest difference is that instead of configuring the log to monitor certain counters, you configure a trace provider to monitor certain events. In addition, you can configure advanced options. Specifically, you can configure how large the memory buffer is for collecting data before data is written out to the log file.

The General property tab allows you to configure the trace provider, as well as the event types to watch for and log (see Figure 4.22). A trace provider is a piece of software that can be either provided in the operating system like the system provider is or an additional utility created to watch for certain event types. Three providers are included with Windows 2000 Server: the Windows 2000 Kernel Trace Provider (system provider); the Active Directory: NetLogon provider; and the Local Security Authority (LSA). Each of these tracks different events. The system provider allows you to watch for processes and threads being created or destroyed, disk input or output, network traffic, memory page faults, and file I/O (reads and writes). Active Directory allows you to track user logon events at the domain level. LSA allows you to track user logon events at the local level.

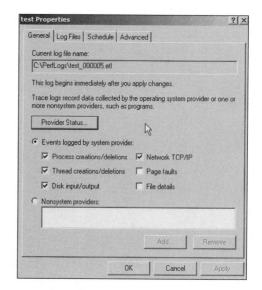

FIGURE 4.22
The General property tab.

Any trace log can track either the system provider or one or more nonsystem providers. If you need to track with more than one provider, you will have to create more than one trace log. One trace log must be created for the system events, and one or more trace logs must be created for the nonsystem events. The Provider Status button shows you which of the providers are enabled for logging through the creation of a trace log. This keeps track of all the trace logs. The result is cumulative across all trace logs you create for a specific server.

The Log Files page of the trace log configuration is nearly identical to that of the counter log. The difference between the two log files pages is that the trace log file time can only be a sequential trace file or circular trace file. This format is proprietary to the trace log. No utilities are provided with Windows 2000 for reading the .ETL files created by the log. Like the counter log, a circular trace file will begin to write over itself from the beginning once it is full.

The Advanced tab allows you to configure memory buffer number and size. These memory buffers are where the event data is initially captured before being written to the log file.

You can create a new trace log by right-clicking the Trace Logs header in the Performance console and choosing New Log Settings. You can then start or stop a trace log manually by right-clicking the log entry and choosing Start or Stop depending on the current state of logging.

Creating Alerts

It is probable that, over the long term, you do not want logging enabled all the time. However, that will necessitate that you check the system periodically to ensure that it is working efficiently and that potential problems are not sneaking up on you. Alerts are used to configure "watchers." These watchers can be used to watch certain objects reaching or crossing pre-defined thresholds. For example, if you decide that disk utilization greater than 80% is a serious condition, you can configure an alert to watch for disk utilization crossing this threshold. When this threshold is reached, an action that you configure will occur.

The alert configuration dialog box consists of three pages: General, Action, and Schedule. Schedule is just like the Schedule page for counter and trace logs, so it will not be discussed further here.

The General page allows you to configure multiple counters and the thresholds for each (see Figure 4.23). In addition, you can configure the polling interval. It is important to note that if you create more than one counter, the thresholds are ORed; that is, if any of the thresholds are crossed, an alert is generated. In addition, if a condition is present for 20 polling intervals in a row, 20 alerts will be generated.

The Action page is used to configure what happens in response to an alert (see Figure 4.24). As you can see from Figure 4.24, there are a variety of responses. The default is to write a message to the application log (accessible from the Event Viewer console). In addition (or alternatively), you can have a message sent to a specific computer in the form of a pop-up window. You can also have the Performance Monitor begin a specific counter log (thus, making the alert a trigger for starting the collection of data about a specific set of circumstances through a log). Finally, you can also have the program of your choice run. In conjunction with the running of a program, you can send the program some arguments from the alert. These arguments can be configured in the form of pieces of text that you set up in the Command Line Arguments dialog box (see Figure 4.25).

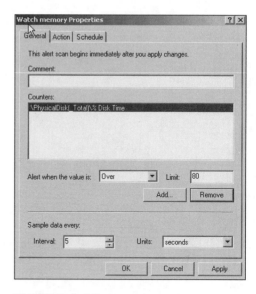

FIGURE 4.23
The General property tab.

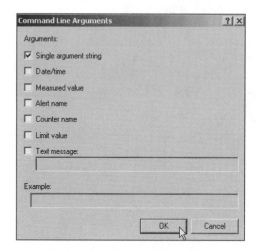

FIGURE 4.25
Command line arguments allow you to send information to a program when they're triggered.

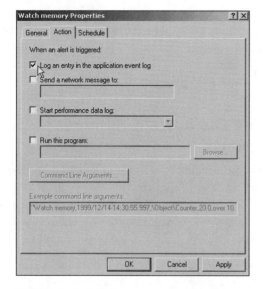

FIGURE 4.24
The Action property sheet.

The advantage of using these command line arguments is that you do not have to re-configure the exact information sent to a program that is executed. All you configure is the type of data; then the alert controls the specific data based on the current time or the trigger value. Receiving the data could be a Visual Basic, C++, or Java program that accepts the parameters you send to it.

Optimizing System Resource Availability

Now that you have seen how to collect statistical data, you need to understand how to use it. Your server is not a set of isolated processes and resources with which users interact. Your server is a dynamically changing entity that has weaknesses in some areas. A server that appears to have a disk problem, thrashing every time a user tries to read something, may, in fact, have too little RAM. Unless you have an understanding of how the major subsystems interact, you will not be able to effectively optimize your server. Furthermore, unless you know what are acceptable levels associated with the counters, all the statistics in the world will not help you troubleshoot the present or plan for the future.

Although there are dozens of objects and ten times that number of counters to sift through, four primary subsystems interact to make a server appear either fast or slow. These subsystems are: disk, memory, processor, and network. Of course, other objects are important, but these four form the core of server performance. The performance of these four subsystems will affect all other objects.

Changing the System to Increase Performance

Even before you begin to monitor your system to increase performance, there are some things that you can do proactively. In fact, even if you do not experience a lack of performance in any area, performing some basic tasks will ensure that it will be longer until you do experience problems than if these were left undone.

Three major areas of system cleanup and tuning are identified here: removal of unneeded components, tuning of the paging file, and tuning of the server service.

Remove Unnecessary Software Components

Begin attempting to improve system performance by removing
unnecessary software components: devices, protocols, and services.
Unnecessary components are those that were loaded for some reason
in the past, but they no longer have a use. Perhaps you have a device
installed that you no longer use. If that device was installed manually, the driver may still load into memory when your server starts.
You can use the Device manager to be ensure that the driver is no
longer installed.

Network protocols are another software component that may have
become unnecessary. If you used to have a NetWare server that you
communicated with, you might still have NWLink installed. If you
no longer have that NetWare server, you should uninstall the protocol.
Unused protocols not only use more system memory, they also
increase the network traffic that your communications generate and
increase the likelihood that a security breach will happen at an unexpected entry point.

Finally, you should look at unnecessary services. By default,
Windows 2000 Server installs IIS. If you are not using any of the
Web-related services, you should uninstall IIS. You will no longer
have software running in the background listening for something
that it will never hear.

Tuning the Size and Location of the Paging File

The next system configuration setting that might impact performance, is the size and location of the paging file. The paging file is
the disk location facilitating Windows 2000's virtual memory
model. In that model, RAM is simulated through a swapping
process that moves information from physical memory into virtual
memory residing in a file on the hard drive.

If this file is too small or if it resides on a disk with a lot of activity,
you could get a reduction in server performance. The paging file
starts at a certain size and is configured to expand as memory needs
increase. Every time the paging file expands, it takes system
resources to resize the file. One recommendation is that you watch
your server under typical load and then note the size of the paging
file. If the paging file is larger than the minimum size, you should
change the settings to make sure the paging file starts out at that
size. This will use up a bit more disk space, but you will increase the
efficiency of the server.

In addition to changing the size of the paging file, you might think about moving it from one disk to another. Because paging is a disk-intensive process, you might find that your server ends up waiting to swap in and out of the paging file because other processes are accessing the disk. The default location for the paging file is the Boot partition, the place where your WINNT folder is. This tends to be a fairly active drive, so you might benefit from moving the paging file to another location. If you choose to move your paging file, make sure you do not move it to another logical drive on the same physical disk. That will only guarantee more activity on that hard drive. If you have only one drive, leave the paging file where it is; if you have a second physical disk, you should consider moving your paging file to that location. If you have a server with a large amount of RAM (1GB or more), you may also consider purchasing a separate hard drive (or even RAID-5 array) to house the paging file. Because disk hardware is very inexpensive and systems with that much RAM often use the paging file considerably, you will find that spending a little money will improve performance noticeable.

Step by Step 4.10 identifies the steps for resizing a paging file.

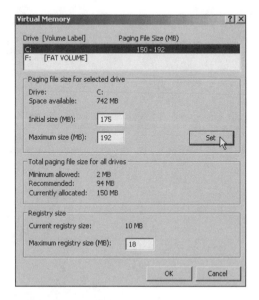

FIGURE 4.26
Change the minimum and maximum to define the limits of the paging file size.

STEP BY STEP

4.10 Resizing the Paging File

1. Right-click the My Computer icon and choose Properties from the menu that appears.

2. In the System Properties dialog box, click the Advanced tab.

3. On the Advanced property sheet, click the Performance Options button.

4. On the Performance Options dialog box, click the Change button (under the heading Virtual Memory).

5. In the Virtual Memory dialog box, select the current location for the paging file (at the top), enter new initial and maximum sizes, and then click the Set button (see Figure 4.26).

6. Click OK to set the paging file size and exit. (The paging file will automatically resize; you do not need to reboot.)

In case you decide to relocate your paging file, the next Step by Step will show you how.

STEP BY STEP

4.11 Relocating the Paging File

1. Right-click the My Computer icon and choose Properties from the menu that appears.

2. In the System Properties dialog box, click the Advanced tab.

3. On the Advanced property sheet, click the Performance Options button.

4. On the Performance Options dialog box, click the Change button (under the heading Virtual Memory).

5. Select the disk to which you want to move the paging file, enter the initial and maximum sizes into the fields, and click Set. Select the disk from which you want to move the paging file, clear the initial and maximum sizes, and click Set. A warning appears, telling you that the paging file will not be the same size as physical RAM appears.

6. Click the OK button to complete the process. Restart the server when prompted. (Removing the paging file from the boot partition requires a restart.)

Tuning the Server Service

The final system configuration option you need to look at is the configuration of the Server service. The Server service is responsible for responding to all incoming network requests for file, print, and named pipe sharing. This means that access to all shared files and printers is handled by the Server service. Without the Server service running, no inbound connections for those purposes are possible. The Server service can be set for specific kinds of applications. It can be configured to perform optimally in a file and print sharing environment. The Server service can also be configured to perform optimally in an application serving environment, like an Exchange or SQL server. When you open the Server Optimization dialog box (as demonstrated in Step by Step 4.12), four settings are presented: Minimize Memory Used, Balance, Maximize Data Throughput for File Sharing, and Maximize Data Throughput for Network Applications. The first two are not applicable to Windows 2000 server implementations; they are used for Windows 2000 Professional computers. The other two are significant and will be discussed here briefly.

Both of the "Maximize Data Throughput" settings adjust how a memory cache is used. If you select Maximize Data Throughput for File Sharing, the memory cache used to enhance data transfer is the system cache, which is controlled by the Windows 2000 operating system. For these kinds of network transactions, it makes more sense to allow Windows 2000 to take care of caching.

If you select Maximize Data Throughput for Network Applications, you indicate that the memory cache maintained by the application (Microsoft SQL Server, for example) is to be used for data transfer instead of the system cache. This makes sense because it is the application that is processing the data (and the data request), and it is in the best position to cache data and process it.

Step by Step 4.12 outlines how to change the properties for the Server service.

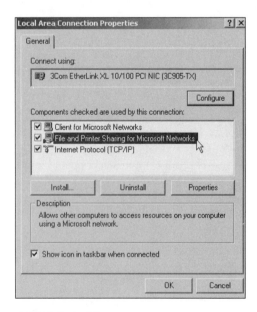

FIGURE 4.27
File and Printer Sharing is the common name for the Server service.

STEP BY STEP

4.12 Tuning the Server Service

1. Right-click the Network Places icon and choose Properties from the menu that appears.

2. Right-click the network connection for which you want to modify Server service performance, and choose Properties from the menu that appears.

3. In the Connection Properties dialog box shown in Figure 4.27, double-click the entry labeled File and Printer Sharing for Microsoft Networks (this is the Server service).

4. In the File and Printer Sharing for Microsoft Networks Properties dialog box (see Figure 4.28), choose Maximize Data Throughput for File Sharing if this server is used primarily as a file and print server. Choose Maximize Data Throughput for Network Applications if this server is used primarily as an applications server.

5. Click OK to exit the dialog box.

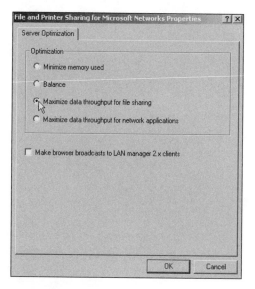

Using Performance Monitor to Discover Bottlenecks and Optimize Resource Utilization

Every chain, regardless of its strength, has its weakest link. When pulled hard enough, some point will give before all the others. Your server is much the same as a chain. When it's under stress, some component will not be able to keep up with the others. This will result in a degradation of overall performance. The weak link in the server is referred to as a *bottleneck* because it's the component that slows everything else down. As an administrator responsible for ensuring efficient operation of your Windows 2000 server, you need to determine the following two things:

◆ Which component is causing the bottleneck?

◆ Is the stress on the server typical enough that action is warranted either now or in the future?

FIGURE 4.28
Each option allows you to tune the server for a different number of users or different types of applications.

As was mentioned above, under normal operation, only four system components will affect system performance: memory, processor, disk, and network card. Therefore, you will be looking to monitor the counters that will tell you the most about how those four components affect system performance so you can determine the answer to the two diagnostic questions.

The biggest problem in monitoring is not collecting the data, it is interpreting it. Not only is it difficult to determine what a specific value for a particular counter means when taken in isolation, it is also difficult to determine what it means in the context of other counters. The biggest problem is that no subsystem (disk, network, processor, memory) exists in isolation. As a result, weaknesses in one might show up as weaknesses in another. Unless you take them all into consideration, you might end up adding another processor when all you needed was more RAM.

Understanding how the subsystems interact is important to understanding the significance of the counter values that are recorded. For example, if you detect that your processor is constantly running at 90%, you may be tempted to go out and purchase a faster processor (or another processor if you have a system board that will accommodate more than one). However, it is important to look at memory utilization and disk utilization. If you do not have enough memory, the processor will have to swap pages to the disk frequently. This will result in high memory utilization, high disk utilization, and higher processor utilization. By purchasing more RAM, you could alleviate all those problems.

That one example illustrates how no one piece of information is enough to analyze your performance problems or your solution. You must monitor the server as a whole unit by putting together the counters from a variety of objects. Only then will you be able to see the big picture and solve problems that may arise.

The recommended method of monitoring is to use a counter log. This will help you eliminate questions of whether or not the stress on the server is typical. If you log over a period of a week or a month and you consistently see a certain component under excessive load, you can be sure the stress is typical.

By default, there are counters available to monitor the physical disk object. This means that you can watch to see just how much activity is taking place on a physical disk. Although these counters are generally sufficient for monitoring disk performance, in some rare cases you may also want to monitor the performance of logical partitions. To modify the disk counters available, you need to use the `diskperf` command. This is the basic syntax of `diskperf`:

```
diskperf -switch
```

A number of `diskperf` switches allow you to start and stop different counters. Table 4.2 outlines the switches and their functions.

TABLE 4.2

DISKPERF SWITCHES AND THEIR FUNCTIONS

Switch	Function
No switch	Identifies which counters are turned on (if any).
-y	Enables all disk counters (both logical and physical) at next restart.
-yd	Enables physical disk counters at next restart (this is the default).
-yv	Enables logical disk counters at next restart.
-n	Disables all disk counters (both logical and physical) at next restart.
-nd	Disables physical disk counters at next restart.
-nv	Disables logical disk counters at next restart.

> **NOTE**
>
> **Windows 2000 Disk Counters Differ from Those in NT 4.0** Windows NT 4.0 users are aware that no disk counters were initialized on startup. With Windows 2000, disk counters are initialized on startup for the physical counters, but not the logical counters. The –yd switch is loaded by default, and it starts only the physical counters.

In addition to disk counters, you may find it valuable to enable the network segment monitors. Network segment counters are beyond the scope of the Windows 2000 Server exam because they require an add-on utility that is available only in System Management Server (SMS) 2.0. However, because you may find that their statistics are valuable, they will be discussed anyway. (Just remember, you do not have to know about the implementation or counters involved with network segment monitors for the exam.)

You can monitor two kinds of network counters when analyzing network performance: network interface counters and network segment counters. Network interface counters are those that trace actual information passing in and out of the network interface card being monitored. These counters will be useful only when monitoring the network performance as it relates to the specific card in question. On the other hand, network segment counters allow you to monitor the performance of the entire physical network segment the card is attached to. This is useful for monitoring network bandwidth utilization. However, in order to monitor this, you must install the full version of Network Monitor and the corresponding Network Monitor driver. Unfortunately, this Network Monitor does not ship with Windows 2000. Instead of the full version, you get a simplified version. The full Network Monitor allows you to scan the entire network segment your machine is sitting on and pick up packets and traffic information, regardless of the source or destination. The

Windows 2000 Network Monitor allows you to observe only network traffic for which your computer is the source or the destination. The result is that it cannot give you statistics on the network segment.

The full Network Monitor is available with the BackOffice product called Systems Management Server (version 2.0 at time of this printing). If you can get hold of it, the package itself will do wonders for administration. The Network Monitor is a big asset, especially when you need to analyze network usage.

In case you can get the full version of Network Monitor, Step by Step 4.13 shows you how to install it.

STEP BY STEP

4.13 Installing Network Monitor 2.0 and Network Monitor Drivers v.2 to Enable Network Segment Counters

1. Make sure you do not have the Windows 2000 Network Monitor or the Network Monitor Drivers installed on your Windows 2000 server.

2. From the SMS 2.0 CD, run \NMEXT\I386\Setup.exe and follow the instructions for installing the Network Monitor.

3. Right-click the My Network Places icon and choose Properties from the menu that appears.

4. In the Network and Dial-up Connections dialog box, right-click the connection for which you want to enable the Network Segment counter and choose Properties from the menu that appears. Typically, you will want to do this for all the connections.

5. In the Connection Properties dialog box, click the Install button and choose Protocol from the Select Network Component Type dialog box. Then click Add.

6. From the Select Network Protocol dialog box, select Network Monitor Agent v2 Driver and click OK to begin the installation (see Figure 4.29).

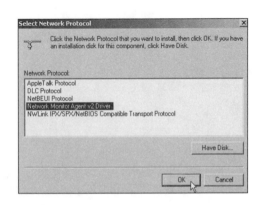

FIGURE 4.29
After you install the Network Monitor Agent v2 Driver, you can monitor the network segment.

As was indicated at the beginning of the section titled "Monitoring and Optimizing System Resource Use," baselines need to be established long before you begin to encounter problems. Once you have all your counters enabled, creating a baseline is the next step in the process of monitoring. Remember, a baseline is a set of typical readings that define "normal" for your server. What is normal is obviously open to interpretation, but one could say that normal is a server providing users with what they want in a time frame that they think is reasonable (oh no, another vague term!). If your system is already to the point where you are seeing system degradation, it is really too late to establish a baseline.

To establish a baseline, you will pick a time (or duration of time) that represents typical user interaction with the server. Then you will create a log of important counters for the duration you have decided on. These counters will be described in the next section. The log you create should be stored away in a safe place to ensure that you can refer to it in the future. Every time you do a major hardware upgrade (like increasing RAM or adding a processor), you will create a new baseline and delete the old one.

Which actual counters you want to monitor are based on the particular applications running on your server and the requirements you will have for the server. Although some recommendations are given in Table 4.3, you may want to watch other objects as well if you have specific applications installed. In addition, and as a point of clarification to the table, the second column provides an indication as to whether the counter is used to simply watch the component in question (usage), or whether that counter is used to determine if the component is a performance bottleneck.

> **EXAM TIP**
>
> **Counters Are Not Likely to Be on the Exam**   These counters and figures are for informational purposes only. It is extremely unlikely that you will be asked any questions about counters or thresholds.

TABLE 4.3

COUNTERS TO MONITOR

Component	Monitoring	Recommended Counters
Disk	Usage	Physical Disk\Disk Reads/sec
		Physical Disk\Disk Writes/sec
		Logical Disk\% Free Space
		Logical Disk\% Disk Time
		Logical Disk\% Idle Time

continues

TABLE 4.3 | *continued*

COUNTERS TO MONITOR

Component	*Monitoring*	*Recommended Counters*
Disk	Bottlenecks	Physical Disk\Avg. Disk Queue Length (all instances)
Memory	Usage	Memory\Available Bytes
		Memory\Cache Bytes
	Bottlenecks	Memory\Pages/sec
		Memory\Page reads/sec
		Memory\Transition Faults/sec
		Memory\Pool Paged Bytes
		Memory\Pool Nonpaged Bytes
		Paging File\% Usage (all instances)
		Cache\Data Map Hits %
		Server\Pool Paged Bytes
		Server\Pool Nonpaged Bytes
Network	Usage	Network Segment\% Net Utilization
Network	Throughput	Network Interface\Bytes total/sec
		Network Interface\Packets/sec
		Server\Bytes Total/sec
Processor	Usage	Processor\% Processor Time (all instances)
	Bottlenecks	System\Processor Queue Length (all instances)
		Processor\Interrupts/sec

As it pertains to the above table, the following are descriptions of some of the counters.

◆ **Physical Disk\Disk Reads/sec.** How many disk reads occur per second. This is a measure of the read activity on the disk.

◆ **Physical Disk\Disk Writes/sec.** How many disk writes occur per second. This is a measure of the write activity on the disk.

◆ **Logical Disk\% Free Space.** The ratio of free space total disk space on a logical drive. This is a measurement of remaining capacity on your logical drives. You will generally want to track this for each logical drive. To prevent excessive fragmentation, the value here should not be allowed to drop below 10%.

◆ **Physical Disk\% Disk Time.** The ratio of busy time to the total elapsed time. This represents the percentage the disk is servicing read or write requests. You will generally want to track this for each physical drive. If one drive is being used a lot more than another, it may be time to balance the content between the drives. The lower this number, the greater the capacity a disk has to do additional work.

◆ **Physical Disk\Avg. Disk Queue Length.** The average number of read and write requests that are waiting in queue. Optimally, this number should be no more than two because a larger number means the disk is a bottleneck; it is unable to service the requests placed on it.

◆ **Memory\Available Bytes.** This is the total amount of physical memory available to processes running on the computer. This number's significance varies as the amount of memory in the computer varies, but if this number is less than 4MB, you generally have a memory deficiency.

◆ **Memory\Cache Bytes.** The amount of cache memory available to processes running on the computer.

◆ **Memory\Pages/sec.** The number of hard page faults occurring per second. A hard page fault occurs when data or code is not in memory and must be retrieved from the hard drive. Each time this happens, disk activity is required, and process is temporarily halted (because disk access is momentarily slower than RAM access). A bottleneck in memory is likely when this number is 20 or greater.

◆ **Memory\Page reads/sec.** The number of times the disk needed to be read to resolve a hard page fault. Unlike Memory\Pages/sec, this counter is not an indicator of the quantity of data being retrieved but rather the number of times the disk had to be consulted. This counter may give a general feeling of a memory bottleneck, whereas Memory\ Pages/sec gives a more quantifiable value to the bottleneck.

◆ **Memory\Transition Faults/sec.** The number of times page faults were recovered by locating the material somewhere else in memory than where it originally was marked to be. This is usually caused by modifications to the data. Transition faults can be tolerated in large numbers because their resolution does not require disk access. However, a large number can be cause for concern, especially if it's accompanied by other memory issues.

◆ **Memory\Pool Paged Bytes.** The number of bytes of memory taken up by system tasks that can be swapped out to disk if needed. Although this counter is not a direct indicator of a memory bottleneck, if the number of Pool Paged Bytes is large, it may indicate a lot of system processes. If this number is a significant percentage of total memory, you may need to increase RAM to allow for these tasks to remain in RAM instead of being swapped out.

◆ **Memory\Pool Nonpaged Bytes.** The number of bytes of memory taken up by system tasks that cannot be swapped out to disk. This figure can indicate a bottleneck in memory, especially if the figure is a significant percentage of the total amount of RAM. Because these processes cannot be swapped out, they will continue to take up RAM for as long as they are running.

◆ **Paging File\% Usage.** The ratio of the amount of paging files being used to the total size of the paging file. A high number is desired here because it indicates that the paging file is sized correctly for the system. If this number is low, either the paging file has been set too large (and is, therefore, consuming more disk space than is necessary), or the paging file has been recently resized. It is the long-term value that you are looking for. Setting the initial size of the paging file(s) can resolve this bottleneck.

◆ **Cache\Data Map Hits %.** The ratio of positive hits to memory for data trying to be retrieved. A memory bottleneck may be the problem if this number is small. A small number indicates that a large percentage of the time, data had to be recovered from the disk rather than from memory. This counter may be useful in analyzing memory bottlenecks, but it must be taken in the context of other memory counters.

◆ **Server\Pool Paged Bytes.** Indicates the amount of paged memory (memory that can be swapped out to the hard drive) that is being consumed by the Server service. This is an indication of the amount of memory being used by network requests, and in conjunction with Memory\Pool Paged Bytes, it can be an indication of where the majority of a memory bottleneck is located.

◆ **Server\Pool Nonpaged Bytes.** Indicates the amount of memory being consumed by the Server service that cannot be paged. In conjunction with Memory\Pool Nonpaged Bytes, this can show how much permanent memory is allocated to processes and can be an indication of memory bottlenecks.

◆ **Network Interface\Bytes Total/sec.** This is an indication of the total throughput of the network interface. It can be used for general capacity planning and does not necessarily indicate a network bottleneck.

◆ **Server\Bytes Total/sec.** The number of bytes the Server service is sending to and receiving from the network. This is a general indication of how busy the Server service is (and correspondingly gives an indication of how busy the server is, depending, of course, on how many other tasks the server is performing).

◆ **Processor\% Processor Time.** The amount of time the processor spends executing non-idle threads. This is an indication of how busy the processor is. The processor for a single-processor system should not exceed 75% capacity for a significant period of time. The processors in a multiple-processor system should not exceed 50% for a significant period of time. High processor utilization may be an indication of processor bottlenecks, but it could also indicate lack of memory.

◆ **System\Processor Queue Length.** The number of processes that are ready but waiting to be serviced by the processor(s). There is a single queue for all processors, even in a multi-processor environment. A sustained queue of more than two generally indicates processor congestion.

◆ **Processor\Interrupts/sec.** The number of hardware requests the processor is servicing per second. This is not necessarily an indicator of system health but, when compared against the baseline, it can help to determine hardware problems. Hardware problems are sometimes indicated by a device dramatically increasing the number of interrupts it sends.

All this information goes to show you that monitoring is not a strict science. There are indicators to watch for and specific counters you should probably monitor. But in the end, your experience and intuition will tell you as much about what a specific counter means as specific numerical comparisons do.

REVIEW BREAK

To review the main points, you have been introduced to a variety of tools and techniques for analyzing performance problems with your server. You began with the importance of establishing a baseline and progressed through the variety of monitoring tools available in the Performance console. Finally, you learned about a number of recommended counters. The final thing to be aware of in performance monitoring is that, although there is some science involved, much of it is intuitively and situationally assessed; you need to do it to understand it fully.

MAINTAINING SYSTEM RECOVERY INFORMATION

Manage and optimize availability of system state data and user data.

Making your Windows 2000 server run efficiently is only part of your task as a server administrator. In the back of every administrator's mind is the inevitability of data loss, either through user error or through catastrophic hardware failure. The systems you put in place to recover from these situations may well make or break your standing as an administrator (if not your job, at least the way people perceive your competence).

A number of available tools enable you to recover your system and your data in the case of loss. Of course, recovery presupposes that you use the tools, and this section talks about how to do just that. The next section will deal with the actual recovery processes themselves.

Loss of data can take a variety of forms and, from a recovery point of view, can have a range of implications from mild to serious. Regardless of the severity of the loss, your job is to ensure that the

server is completely recoverable. To ensure this, you can use a variety
of tools. By using all of the tools identified, you ensure that you can
recover from any situation.

The list that follows identifies the tools available and what kinds of
loss each will allow you to recover from.

◆ **Last Known Good Configuration.** This allows you to recover
from configuration changes that affect Registry settings for
devices (like installing an incorrect video driver or configuring
it incorrectly). This tool has only a limited window of effectiveness; once you successfully log on locally to a Windows
2000 computer, this will no longer function.

◆ **Emergency Repair Disk.** This enables you to recover from
Registry settings that render your system inoperable. This
might be misconfiguration that could not be caught with the
Last Known Good Configuration, or it might be deleted user
accounts or other Registry changes.

◆ **Windows 2000 Backup.** This is useful for recovering other
Registry settings as well as user data. This option allows for the
widest breadth of recovery but also takes the most time.

Each of these tools will be covered in this section. How to recover
your system using them will be covered in the next.

System state, simply put, is the current configuration of your
Windows 2000 server. "Current configuration" refers to any information required to bring the operating system from a newly
installed state to the configuration that it currently is in. System
state does not include the installation of applications, nor does it
include user data; those need to be dealt with through backups of
file data.

Three tools available in a standard Windows 2000 Server installation
can save system state data and user data. These three are Last Known
Good Configuration, Emergency Repair Disk, and Windows 2000
Backup.

Before looking into the ways that system information and data can
be saved, let's digress into the kinds of failures you are protecting
against. There are all kinds of ways that data on your Windows
2000 server can become corrupt and non-functional.

Saving System State with Last Known Good Configuration

The first mechanism for saving system state data is the easiest to use. In fact, you do not have to do anything at all to save this information. Windows 2000 automatically does it for you. All the current information about system configuration is stored in a Registry location called the current control set. The current control set defines your hardware configuration, the protocols installed, the drivers installed, and other configurations in those kinds of categories. Each time you successfully log into your Windows 2000 server (that is, when, as a user, you complete the name and password dialog box locally on the server), the current configuration is written into the backup configuration. This backup configuration becomes the Last Known Good Configuration.

In the event that you make a change you regret (like removing all your network protocols), you can invoke the Last Known Good Configuration to recover the backup control set. The backup control set allows you to reset your machine's configuration to the last good configuration. Recovery based on the Last Known Good Configuration is discussed in the section "Recovering System State with Last Known Good Configuration."

Although it's useful, Last Known Good Configuration has a number of limitations, not the least of which is that the "system backup" is overwritten every time you log into the system. Further, Last Known Good Configuration does not save a number of pieces of useful information. This configuration does not save system files used to load Windows 2000, nor does it save the boot sector, which is used to actually start loading Windows 2000. Finally, Last Known Good Configuration does not save the startup environment, which, in a multi-boot system, defines which partition to boot each operating system from.

Saving System State with Emergency Repair Disk

Another mechanism for saving system state data is the Emergency Repair Disk. The emergency repair information is stored in a folder in the path %systemroot%\repair. %Systemroot% is the location of your Windows 2000 operating system files, usually WINNT. Repair information is automatically written into the repair folder when the system is installed.

If you choose, you can create a backup of the Registry into the repair folder as well. This backup information can be used to restore your Registry if it becomes corrupt. This information is useless if the hard drive on which the backup was done has failed. This backup offers a quick way of restoring your Registry, but it should never take the place of a real Registry backup (that is, one that is stored on a removable media). A real Registry backup is done when you back up all the files on your Windows 2000 server or when you take the file from the emergency repair directory and create an Emergency Repair Disk from it.

The Emergency Repair Disk can be used to facilitate some system repairs on your Windows 2000 server. Essentially, the disk can be used to repair startup problems, like when essential startup files are not present and your Server refuses to boot.

The next Step by Step shows how to create an Emergency Repair Disk.

STEP BY STEP

4.14 Creating an Emergency Repair Disk

1. From the Start menu, choose Programs, Accessories, System Tools, Backup.

2. On the Welcome tab of the Backup dialog box, click the Emergency Repair Disk icon (see Figure 4.30).

FIGURE 4.30
Start the Emergency Repair Disk creation from
the Backup dialog box.

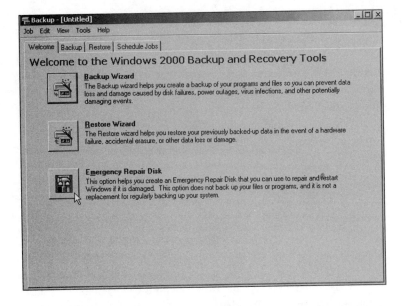

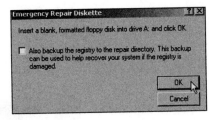

FIGURE 4.31
A disk is required to create an Emergency
Repain Disk.

3. When prompted, insert a blank floppy disk into the drive
   (see Figure 4.31). If you want to create a backup of the
   current state of the Registry, you can select the Also
   Backup the Registry to the Repair Directory check box.
   This will place current Registry information in a subfolder
   of Repair called RegBack.

4. Click OK to continue.

Instructions on how to repair your system with an Emergency
Repair Disk will be provided in the upcoming section "Recovering
System State with Emergency Repair Information."

Saving System State and User Data with Windows 2000 Backup

The most robust method of saving both system state and user data is
to use Windows 2000 Backup. This backup facility is much improved
over the one that came with Windows NT 4.0. It allows full backup
of all system state information at the click of a check box, as well as
the scheduling of backup times and dates.

The importance of regular backups cannot be overstated. The ability to recover from catastrophic failure or user error depends on your backups being up-to-date and secure from theft and physical damage. At some point, all servers are guaranteed to fail. Your ability to get your system running in short order often depends on the presence of a good backup.

What follows is first, a discussion of backup in general, and second, a discussion of backup using Windows 2000 Backup. The former will cover backup processes that would apply to any computerized environment where data and system recovery were important. The second will cover the backing up of information to allow the recovery of data and systems.

Elementary Backup Theory

The theory of backups, the how's and the why's have not really changed since the backup was invented. Regardless of the backup software you choose, the main features remain the same. There are essentially five backup types or five ways to determine what should be backed up and how this affects further backups. These five types are normal (or full), incremental, differential, copy, and timeframe (backups that are done on some regular interval; Windows 2000 implements this daily).

On a Windows 2000 server, each file residing on a FAT, FAT32, or NTFS partition has an archive bit that identifies whether that particular file has been backed up. An archive bit set to False means the file has been backed up and has not been modified since it was backed up. If a file has been modified since the last backup, its archive bit will be set. If the file has not been modified, its archive bit will not be set. This shows that the file should now be backed up. The backup types are differentiated by what they do to the archive bit and how they respond to the archive bit.

Normal (sometimes called *full*) *backups* save all files regardless of the state of the archive bit. While saving the files, normal backups set the archive bit to False to indicate that the files have been backed up. This means that if you were to do two normal backups in a row, both would save all the data, and both would set the archive bits to False.

Incremental backups look to see the current status of the archive bit before backing up data. If the archive bit is False, an incremental backup will skip the file because it has been backed up. If the archive bit is True, an incremental backup will save the file and set its archive bit to False. If you change a file and then run two incremental backups in a row, only the first will back up the file. The second will encounter the False archive bit set by the first incremental backup and will skip the file.

Differential backups also look at the current status of the archive bit before backing up data. As with an incremental backup, if the archive bit is False, a differential will skip the file, and if the archive bit is True, the differential backup will save the file. However, it will not set the archive bit to False. This means that two differentials in a row will both back up the same changed file because the first backup will not set the archive bit to tell the second to skip the file.

Copy backups are like normal backups in that they back up all data regardless of the state of the archive bit. However, they do not set the archive bits to True after backing up the data. They have no effect on any other backup processes. If you did two copy backups in a row, both would back up all the information, but the archive bits would be left as they were before the backups were done.

Timeframe backups are like copy backups. Timeframe backups back up all data regardless of the state of the archive bit, but they also look at the date a file was changed. As an example, daily backups (a type of timeframe backups) back up only those files modified on a specific day.

Now that you know the backup types, the next step is to see how they are put together. The copy backup is used only to make periodic copies of the data without affecting any other backup processes and, therefore, is the exception to the rule. You can do a copy backup anytime you want for any reason. The copy backup will not be factored into this discussion because it does not affect any other backup rotation.

General backup theory indicates that there are three types of ongoing backup strategies: normal only, normal/incremental, and normal/differential. The decision to use one over the other is determined by a number of factors. The first factor is how much time you have to do backups on any given day. If you have the time to do a complete

backup of all your systems every day, that is definitely the best
option. Using a normal only strategy ensures that all your data is
backed up at the end of every day. This means recovery requires that
only one backup set be available and ensures that if any tape fails,
you only have to go to the previous day's backup to completely
recover all the information available on that tape.

Unfortunately, time is often a factor. In some cases, the amount of
time available to do backups is exceeded by the amount of time it
would take to do a normal backup every day. In these cases, the next
decision is to determine which is more important: to save time on
the backup end or on the recovery end. If the backup end requires
quick backups, you probably want to choose normal/incremental.
These strategies make backup faster, because you only back up data
that has changed since the last incremental (or normal) backup.
However, this strategy makes for slower recovery because there are
more tapes to apply. On the other hand, normal/differential strategies make backup slower because each day's backup is saving all data
that has changed since the last normal backup. However, recovery is
faster than normal/incremental because to recover to any specific
day, you have to apply only one tape after the normal backup.

Figure 4.32 shows three successive weeks of backups. Note that a
normal/incremental scheme is being used. Several noteworthy things
can be seen in this example. First, note that the normal backup is
being done on a Friday. The reason for this is simple: Friday is typically the end of the work week, and you would want your backup
done as soon after that as possible. Many organizations choose not
to do backups on weekends. Conducting a backup on Sunday or
Monday runs the risk of a weekend crash, destroying Friday's data.

Second, note how the tapes are being used in the backup process.
Each day's backup is done on a tape separate from any other day.
Tape #1 is a normal backup. Tapes 2–7 are incremental backups. For
security of data, an incremental backup is done each night on a different tape. This ensures that the same tape does not stay in the tape
drive for a whole week, which would increase the likelihood that an
environmental disaster (like a fire) or a tape drive failure would
destroy the tape.

FIGURE 4.32

A sample normal/incremental backup scheme.

Friday	Saturday	Sunday	Monday	Tuesday	Wednesday	Thursday
Normal Tape #1	Incremental Tape #2	Incremental Tape #3	Incremental Tape #4	Incremental Tape #5	Incremental Tape #6	Incremental Tape #7

Friday	Saturday	Sunday	Monday	Tuesday	Wednesday	Thursday
Normal Tape #8	Incremental Tape #2	Incremental Tape #3	Incremental Tape #4	Incremental Tape #5	Incremental Tape #6	Incremental Tape #7

Friday	Saturday	Sunday	Monday	Tuesday	Wednesday	Thursday
Normal Tape #1	Incremental Tape #2	Incremental Tape #3	Incremental Tape #4	Incremental Tape #5	Incremental Tape #6	Incremental Tape #7

Third, pay particular attention to how the tapes are recycled. On alternate Fridays, the same tape is being used for the normal backup, but not on successive Fridays. This ensures that if a failure occurs in the middle of a normal backup, the previous normal backup has not been destroyed. The incrementals are used again, but only after a normal backup has been done. If recovering your system is your main concern, if a failure happens during the incremental on Saturday in the second week, you can restore from Tape #8, and you do not need the incremental from the previous Saturday.

A normal/incremental cycle such as this makes the backups process go very quickly. Incremental backups will record only those files that have changed that day. Therefore, the backup can be performed reasonably quickly.

Normal/differential cycles back up Monday's data on Tuesday, Wednesday, and Thursday, which makes the backup take longer each night. However, as you will see in the section on backup recovery, differential backups make recovery faster and more convenient.

The final thing to note about backups is the storage of the tapes or other backup media. It is essential that you get the backup tapes into a physically and environmentally secure environment as soon as possible after the backup is complete. Servers sometimes fail because of environmental factors like water or fire damage. If the backup itself is in the same place as the server, it will be destroyed, too. Your choices for backup storage should be as follows (in this order): 1) secure and environmentally safe off-site location; 2) secure and environmentally safe on-site location; 3) secure off-site location. If you choose to use a third party to store your tapes, ensure that you inspect their facility and have assurances (in writing) that their storage is secure and environmentally safe. If you choose to store your tapes on site, keep them in a media fire-proof safe. It needs to be "media" fireproof because "paper" fireproof will not protect your backup media (a tape will melt and be damaged long before paper will burn).

Backing Up System State and User Data Using Windows 2000 Backup

Now that you understand generic backup theory, you're ready to move to the specific implementation that you find in Windows 2000 Server. Windows 2000 Backup is really a pared-down version of BackupExec, a product supplied to Microsoft by Veritas, Inc.

Under Windows 2000, there are three ways to invoke a backup. You can configure a backup with the GUI and start it immediately. You can schedule it to start at another time as either a single job or a repeating one. You can configure a backup to start from a command line. In the first two cases, a wizard walks you through the configuration.

Windows 2000 Backup allows you to back up to either a file or a tape drive.

Windows 2000 Backup allows you to back up files from either the local machine or remote computers, provided that you have access to the files you want to back up on the remote computer. The limitation of backing up a computer remotely is that system state information cannot be saved.

To perform a backup, you must have Read access to the files or the user right of Backup and Restore Files, which is granted by default to Administrators and Backup Operators.

Special permissions are granted the Administrators and Backup Operators groups to access all files for the purposes of doing backups. Even if members of these groups cannot access the data as users, they will be able to back it up.

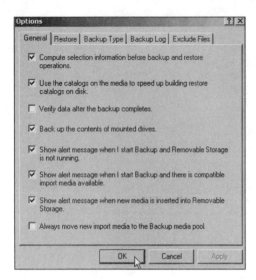

FIGURE 4.33
The General property tab.

Before beginning a backup, you will need to set the general backup options. These allow you to configure defaults, system responses, logging sensitivity, and files to be excluded from backups. When you bring up the backup options, you are presented with five property tabs that define these options: General, Restore, Backup Type, Backup Log, and Exclude Files.

The General property tab lets you configure some default properties, as well as some alert messages that have to do with removable storage (see Figure 4.33).

The bulleted list that follows shows the options on the General property tab and gives a brief explanation of each.

◆ **Compute Selection Information Before Backup and Restore Operations** shows the number of files and bytes that will be backed up or restored given the current selections.

◆ **Use the Catalogs on the Media to Speed Up Building Restore Catalogs on Disk** indicates that when you restore data from a backup, the catalog built at backup time should be used. This catalog tracks the files and paths that were backed up and should be used to display what can be restored. The alternative to this is having the Restore program build the catalog from scratch by consulting the backup itself. This could take many hours for a large backup. You would normally select this option; however, if the backup is damaged or the catalog is not available, you would want to deselect it to make sure a new catalog is built.

◆ **Verify Data After the Backup Completes** indicates that, by default, data on the backup should be checked against the content of the hard drive files before the backup is deemed to be complete. This adds a considerable length of time to the backup process. It is recommended that you do this at least once a week during the normal backup. If this is not possible due to the size of your backup window, you may need to do it less frequently, but verification is a piece of insurance that will makes your backups work when you need them.

◆ **Back Up the Contents of Mounted Drives** indicates that
mounted drives should be backed up when the drive they are
mounted to is backed up. A mounted drive is a drive that is
accessed from a folder defined on another drive. For example,
you could mount the CD-ROM drive (D:) into the folder
CDROM on the C: drive. If you did this, you could reference
the CD-ROM through the path C:\CDROM rather than by
D:\. If you select this check box, the content of the mounted
drive will be backed up when the parent drive is backed up.
Otherwise, only the path to the mounted drive will be backed
up, not the data.

◆ **Show Alert Message When I Start Backup and Removable
Storage Is Not Running** indicates that a message should be
displayed when the Removable Storage service is not running
when backup is started. If you use disk-based backups (to hard
drive, floppy, or network), do not select this box. You are not
using Removable Storage. If you use tape drives, this should be
checked.

◆ **Show Alert Message When I Start Backup and There Is
Compatible Import Media Available** indicates that a message
should be displayed if import media is available to use for the
backup. Import media is used with removable storage and is
an indication that media, like a tape that's used on another
computer, has been inserted into the tape drive. If you do
disk-based backups, it is not necessary to select this check box.

◆ **Show Alert Message When New Media Is Inserted into
Removable Storage** indicates that, when new media is available, you should be informed of that fact. If you do disk-based
backups, it is not necessary to select this check box.

◆ **Always Move New Import Media to the Backup Media
Pool** indicates that any import media should be made available to the backup program. If you do disk-based backups, it
is not necessary to select this check box.

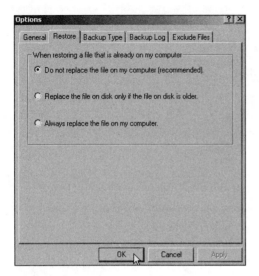

FIGURE 4.34
The Restore property tab.

FIGURE 4.35
The Backup Type property tab.

The Restore property tab contains options with which you define the defaults for restoring system state data and user data from backup (see Figure 4.34). The radio buttons define the action taken when a file that is being restored from backup is also present on the hard drive. You can choose never to restore, always to restore, or to restore only if the file in the backup set is newer than the one found on the hard drive.

The Backup Type property tab sets the default backup type (see Figure 4.35). If you do not choose the backup type from the advanced properties, the type of backup indicated here will be implemented.

The Backup Log property tab defines the amount of detail the log file should contain (see Figure 4.36). When you do a backup, the default is to create a log that tracks what happened during the backup. You can choose to log the name and path of each file backed up or skipped (making for a large log), or you can choose to log only key operations (like the backup starting and open files being skipped). You can also choose not to log at all.

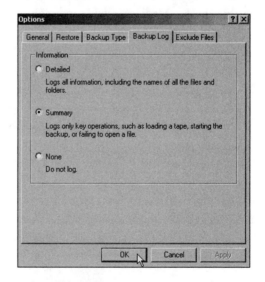

FIGURE 4.36
The Backup Log property tab.

The Exclude Files property tab lets you define the files that are never backed up (see Figure 4.37). This list can be configured for all users, as well as for the user who is doing the backup. The kinds of files that are excluded by default include the paging file and temporary Internet files.

Now that you know all the backup options, Step by Step 4.15 shows you how to change them.

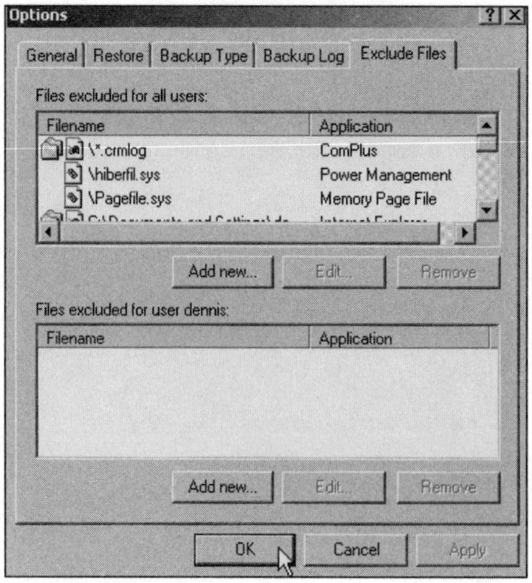

STEP BY STEP

4.15 Changing Backup Options

1. From the Start menu, choose Programs, Accessories, System Tools, Backup.

2. In the Backup dialog box, choose Tools, Options.

3. Change the options as desired, and then click OK to make them permanent.

FIGURE 4.37
The Exclude Files property tab.

Once the backup options have been set, it is time to do a backup. Step by Step 4.16 demonstrates how to configure a backup using the Backup Wizard.

STEP BY STEP

4.16 Backing Up Data using the Backup Wizard

1. From the Start menu, choose Programs, Accessories, System Tools, Backup.

2. At the Welcome page, click the Backup Wizard icon to start the configuration process (see Figure 4.38).

3. At the Welcome to the Windows 2000 Backup and Recovery Tools screen, click Next.

continues

continued

FIGURE 4.38
The Backup Wizard is invoked from the Welcome page of the Backup dialog box.

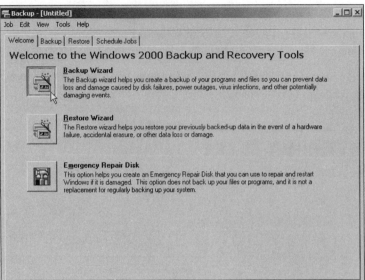

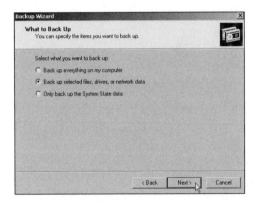

FIGURE 4.39
Choose how much of the local data you want to back up.

4. At the What to Back Up screen, choose Back Up Everything on My Computer; Back Up Selected Files, Drives, or Network Data; or Only Back Up System State Data (see Figure 4.39).

   If you choose to back up everything, Windows will back up all the data on the local machine. On a Windows 2000 server, system state data includes the Boot files, COM+ Class Registration Database, and the Registry. If you select either of these options, skip to step 6.

   If you choose to back up only selected files, you will have the option of choosing any local or remote files you want to back up. Continue to step 5.

5. At the Items to Back Up screen, you can choose which file, folders, drives, or remote data you want to back up. As you can see from Figure 4.40, you can back up mapped drives, system state data, or information from remote machines. A clear box with a blue check mark marks a drive or folder that has been chosen with all of its contents, including subfolders. A clear box with a gray check mark means that there are components in the tree that have been deselected. A box that is filled in with gray means that it is not possible to save all content, and you must descend farther in the tree to select files for backup. A clear box with no check mark indicates that no files from that tree will be backed up. Select the items you want to back up, and click Next.

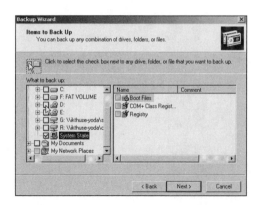

FIGURE 4.40
Select to back up remote drives, local drives, folders, and/or files.

6. At the Where to Store the Backup screen, choose the media type (file or tape) and the file name or media name (see Figure 4.41). If you are backing up to tape, you will notice that Backup remembers the backups that have been performed to tape. You have the option of backing up to a tape that you already created or backing up to a new tape. The assumption here is that you have specific tapes for specific purposes (which you should) and that you will always use the same media for the same backup task. If you choose a media name that you have already used, you will have the option of either overwriting the previous data on the tape or appending to the data that already exists.

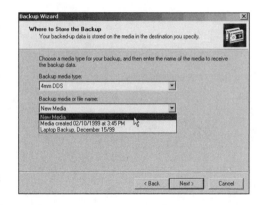

FIGURE 4.41
Choose the media type and the specific media to back up on.

7. At the Completing the Backup Wizard screen, either click Finish to begin the backup immediately with the default parameters or click the Advanced button to set the parameters of your backup (see Figure 4.42). These parameters are used if you want to deviate the current backup settings from the ones you established as the norms for your backup in Step by Step 4.15. If you click Finish, the backup will start immediately.

continues

FIGURE 4.42
The Advanced properties allow you to deviate
from your default backup settings.

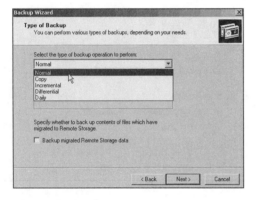

FIGURE 4.43
The type of backup defines what will be backed
up and how the archive bits are handled.

continued

8. At the Type of Backup screen, choose the backup type from the list (see Figure 4.43). In addition, you can choose to back up remote storage data. Remote storage allows you to migrate little-used data to a readily accessible archive, often centralized within your company. This is usually a tape or a group of tapes that are always mounted. When data is moved to remote storage, a pointer remains on the hard drive to allow access to the data in the future. Users do not know that the data has been archived, only Windows 2000 knows this. When you choose to back up remote storage data, the data is retrieved from the remote location and written to the backup tape or file. Choose the backup type you desire, and then click Next to continue.

9. At the How to Back Up screen, choose to turn on or off data verification and hardware compression (see Figure 4.44). Data verification reads back the data that was placed onto your backup media to make sure that it is the same as the file from which it is copied. This option adds time to the backup but ensures that all the data went onto the tape correctly. Hardware compression takes advantage of specific tape-drive hardware that supports additional compression of files as they go onto the tape. Although hardware compression will allow you to put more data onto a tape, you should exercise some caution when using this. Data saved with hardware compression will be readable only by using a similar tape device. Click Next to progress to the next page.

10. At the Media Options screen, you can choose to either append data to a currently existing file or tape or overwrite the current data, if any, with the new backup data (see Figure 4.45). If this is an overwrite or a new media, you will also be able to configure access restrictions.

If you select the Allow Only the Owner and the Administrator Access... check box, you ensure that data on the tape can be restored only by the person who made the backup (the owner) or a member of the Administrators group. This means that even if many people have physical access to the tape, only a select group will be able to retrieve data from it. Click Next to continue.

11. At the Backup Label screen, you can create labels for the backup and/or the media (see Figure 4.46). The media label is used for the first backup set placed into a file or onto a tape. The backup label is used when two or more backups are placed into a file or onto a tape. Click Next to continue.

12. At the When to Back Up screen, you can choose to begin the backup immediately or defer it to a scheduled time (see Figure 4.47). (For brevity, this Step by Step assumes you are backing up immediately; the next Step by Step covers the procedure for using schedules.) Click Next to continue.

13. When the Completing the Backup Wizard screen appears again, click Finish to begin the backup.

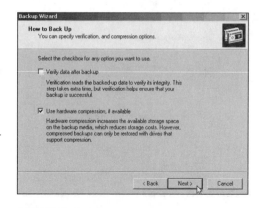

FIGURE 4.44
Do you want to verify the data or use hardware compression?

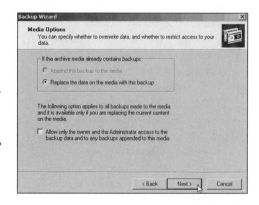

FIGURE 4.45
You can replace the data on the tape or append to it.

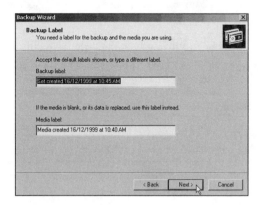

FIGURE 4.46
Enter a backup label and/or a media label.

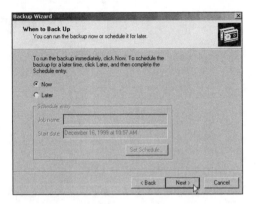

FIGURE 4.47
To perform a backup immediately, choose Now.

> NOTE
>
> **Windows 2000 Backup Does Not Back Up Open Files** Like many other backup programs, Windows 2000 Backup does not back up open files. This means you might have to stop some running processes in order to ensure that files accessed by them will be backed up. Files that are open when the backup process gets to them will be skipped, and that fact will be noted in the backup log (if you have logging configured).

One of the strengths of Windows 2000 Backup is the ability to schedule backups for times of low system usage—typically late at night. An administrator does not need to be present during the backup as long as the correct tape or tapes are mounted.

Scheduling a Backup Using the Backup Wizard

Scheduled backups can be created using the advanced features of the Backup Wizard. However, you can also invoke the scheduled Backup Wizard from the Schedule Jobs page of the Backup dialog box.

This page allows you to scan through a calendar and see which backups are schedule to run. By double-clicking on a date, you begin the Scheduled Jobs Wizard. Essentially, the wizard is the same as the Backup Wizard except that the advanced options are automatically presented to you. It is expected that you are going to create a scheduled backup rather than an immediate one.

The next Step by Step shows you how to use the Scheduled Jobs Wizard.

STEP BY STEP

4.17 Scheduling Jobs for Backup Using the Wizard

1. From the Start menu, choose Programs, Accessories, System Tools, Backup.

2. In the Backup dialog box, click the Schedule Jobs tab and navigate the calendar to find the date for which you want to schedule a backup (see Figure 4.48).

3. Double-click the date you want to schedule a backup for.

4. At the Welcome to the Windows 2000 Backup and Recovery Tools screen, click Next to continue.

5. At the What to Back Up screen, choose Back Up Everything on My Computer; Back Up Selected Files, Drives, or Network Data; or Only Back Up System State Data. If you choose either of the first two options, you will skip to step 7. If you choose to back up only select files, you will have the option of choosing any local or remote files you want to back up. Proceed with step 6.

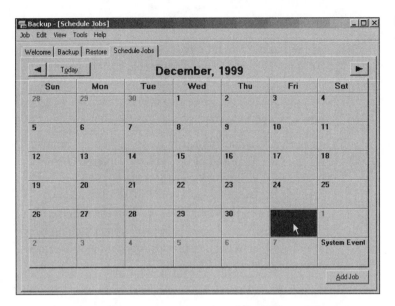

FIGURE 4.48
Select a date on which to schedule a backup.

6. At the Items to Back Up screen, you can choose which file, folders, drives, or remote data you want to back up. Select the items you want to back up, and then click the Next button to continue.

7. At the Where to Store the Backup screen, choose the media type (File or 4mm DAT) and the filename or media name. If you choose a media name that you have already used, you will have the option of either overwriting the previous data on the tape or appending to the data that already exists.

8. At the Type of Backup screen, choose the backup type from the list. In addition, you can choose whether to back up remote storage data. Choose the backup type you desire and click Next.

9. At the How to Back Up screen, choose to turn on or off data verification and hardware compression. Then click Next.

10. At the Media Options screen, you can choose to append data to a currently existing file or tape or to overwrite the current data, if any, with the new backup data. If this is an overwrite or a new media, you will also be able to configure access restrictions. Click Next to continue.

continues

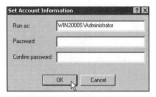

FIGURE 4.49
Enter the user name and password of a user with the rights to perform backups.

FIGURE 4.50
To defer the starting of the backup, choose Later and enter a job name.

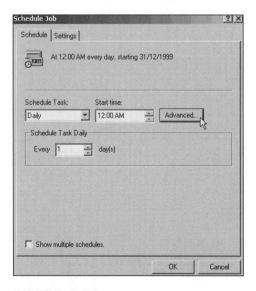

FIGURE 4.51
Choose a start time and a repeat interval.

continued

11. At the Backup Wizard screen, you can create labels for the backup and/or the media. The media label is used for the first backup set placed into a file or onto a tape. The backup label is used when two or more backups are placed into a file or onto a tape. Click Next to continue.

12. At the Set Account Information screen, you are prompted for the user name and password with which to begin the backup (see Figure 4.49). Because this backup will be invoked at a specific time in the future, the backup process must have the authority to perform the task. The user name you enter must be capable of performing backups on your server. Enter the appropriate name and password, and then click OK.

13. At the When to Back Up screen, make sure that Later has been selected and then type in a job name (see Figure 4.50). The job name will be used for reference on the Schedule Jobs page of the Backup dialog box, so it should accurately but succinctly describe the backup.

14. Click the Schedule button to set the schedule for the backup.

15. In the Schedule Job dialog box, specify the interval at which the backup is to occur: Daily, Weekly, Monthly, Once, At System Startup, At Logon, or When Idle (see Figure 4.51). You must also specify the time at which it is to occur if Daily, Weekly, or Monthly is chosen as the interval. You can then indicate how many of those intervals should occur before the next one. For example, daily with a multiple of 3 means every three days. If you are configuring Daily, Weekly, or Monthly, click the Advanced button to set an end time (see step 16); otherwise, move on to step 17.

16. In the Advanced Schedule Options dialog box, you can configure a start and end date for the schedule (see Figure 4.52). Actually, you can configure a number of other things, but none are really applicable to scheduling backups. Click the down-arrow to the right of the start and end date and choose dates from the calendars presented. When you finish, click OK.

17. Click the Settings tab to configure what to do when the task is complete (see Figure 4.53). At the top of the Settings page, you can specify whether to delete the task if it is not scheduled to run again or to stop the task if it runs for a predetermined length of time. There are some other options to configure on this page, but they deal with settings for computers on which interactive users are working or computers that use power management for batteries (like Windows 2000 Professional). Click OK to continue.

18. At the When to Back Up screen, click Next to complete the schedule.

19. At the Completing the Backup Wizard screen, click Finish to exit.

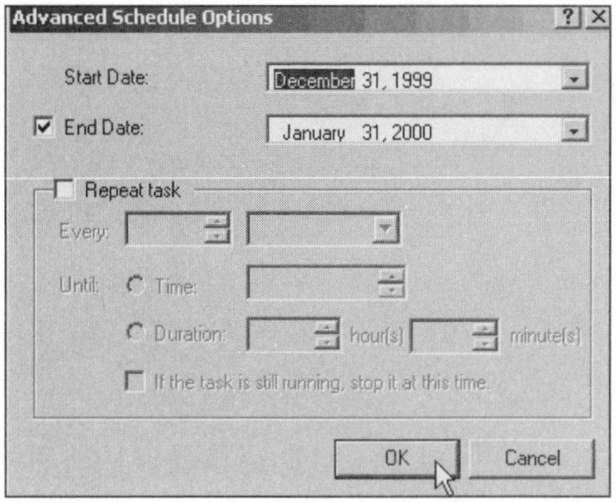

FIGURE 4.52
If you will want the backup to repeat, you can set the start and end dates to repeat between.

When you finish scheduling a backup, an icon appears on the calendar in every location where a backup is scheduled to occur (see Figure 4.54). A letter also appears beside the icon to indicate what kind of backup is scheduled to be performed on that date.

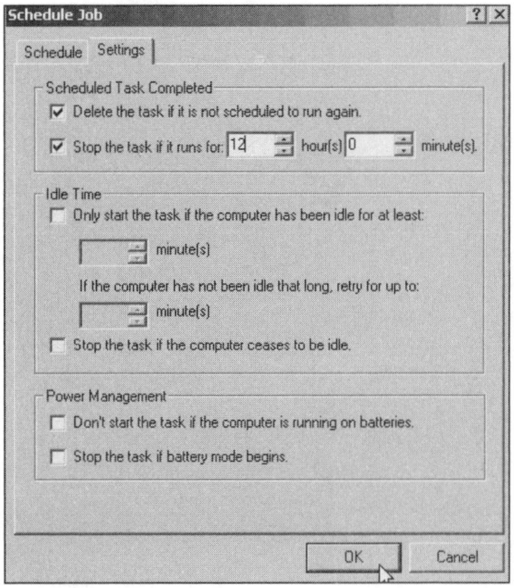

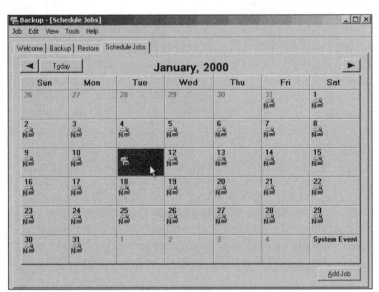

FIGURE 4.54
The calendar lets you see what backup events are scheduled.

FIGURE 4.53
Specify what to do when the task completes.

If you want to see the details of a job, double-click the icon. If you want to remove a job, double-click the icon and click Delete. If you delete a repetitive job, all repeated occurrences will be deleted as well.

At this point you have seen the backup types and have been given information that will help you determine what kind of backup procedures you need to put into place. You have also been introduced to the Backup Wizard and the processes for beginning an immediate backup and a scheduled backup using that tool.

What follows is the final backup method: starting a backup from the command line.

Configuring a Backup with a Command Line

The final method for invoking a backup is through a command line. A backup of any sort can be invoked using the NTBACKUP.EXE program and a set of command-line parameters that define how the backup is to progress. Under Windows NT 4.0, command line backups were very popular because there was no scheduler built into the backup program. Creating a batch file and then executing it using a scheduling program, like AT.EXE, was the only way to make a backup start on schedule.

A scheduling component is part of the Backup program for Windows 2000. However, there are still reasons to invoke a backup using a command line. The primary reasons are that you might need to perform a backup as one of a series of scheduled tasks, or you might need for some sort of processing to precede the backup. In these cases, you could configure a batch file with a command line backup and then have other commands execute from the same batch file. This batch file could be scheduled using the Windows 2000 Scheduler, found under Start, Programs, Accessories, System Tools, Scheduled Tasks.

Because the command-line parameters can get very complex and most of them will not be included on the exam, I will give an example of how to use the parameters to create a normal backup. I will then explain each component that I used in the command line.

```
Ntbackup backup "c:\backups\full backup.bks" /m normal /j
➥"Server Backup— Dec 31/99" /t "Normal Backup Tape" /d
"Server Backup" /v:yes /r:no /l:s /rs:no /hc:on
```

This command line reads as follows:

> Back up the set of files defined as the "c:\backups\full backup.bks" backup set file. Do a normal backup. In the log, call the set "Server Backup-Dec 31/99." Get a tape from the pool defined as the backup media. The name of the tape is to be set to "Normal Backup Tape," and the label for the backup set is "Server Backup." Verify the backup after it is complete; do not restrict the tape to just the owner or an administrator; do not back up the removable storage database; and turn hardware compression on.

The following command gives the full syntax of the command line backup, and Table 4.5 lists the switches and provides a brief description of each.

```
ntbackup backup [systemstate] "bks file name" /J {"job
➥name"} [/P {"pool name"}] [/G {"guid name"}] [/T { "tape
name"}] [/N {"media name"}] [/F {"file name"}] [/D {"set
➥description"}] [/DS {"server name"}] [/IS {"server name"}]
[/A] [/V:{yes|no}] [/R:{yes|no}] [/L:{f|s|n}] [/M {backup
➥type}] [/RS:{yes|no}] [/HC:{on|off}] [/UM]
```

TABLE 4.5

COMMAND LINE BACKUP SWITCHES AND THEIR MEANINGS

Parameter	*Numeric Value*
Systemstate	Specifies that you want to back up the system state data. This parameter forces the backup type to be normal or copy.
bks file name	Specifies the name of the backup selection file (.bks file) to be used for this backup operation. A backup selection file contains information on the files and folders you have selected for backup. You have to create the file using the graphical user interface (GUI) version of Backup. This switch can also be replaced by the path to the files you want to back up (for example, c:\data or \\server\pictures).
/J {"job name"}	Specifies the job name to be used in the log file. The job name usually describes the files and folders you are backing up in the current backup job, as well as the date and time you backed up the files.

continues

TABLE 4.5 | *continued*

COMMAND LINE BACKUP SWITCHES AND THEIR
MEANINGS

Parameter	Numeric Value
/P {"pool name"}	Specifies the media pool from which you want to use media. This is usually a subpool of the Backup media pool, such as 4mm DDS. If you select this, you cannot use the following switches: /A, /G, /F, or /T.
/G {"guid name"}	Specifies the tape you want to write to by its Globally Unique Identifier (GUID). The backup overwrites or appends to this tape. Do not use this switch in conjunction with /P.
/T {"tape name"}	Specifies the tape you want to write to by its name. The backup overwrites or appends to this tape. Do not use this switch in conjunction with /P.
/N {"media name"}	Specifies the new tape name. You must not use /A with this switch.
/F {"file name"}	Provides the logical disk path and file name. You must not use the following switches with this switch: /P, /G, or /T.
/D {"set description"}	Specifies a label for each backup set.
/DS {"server name"}	Backs up the directory service file for the specified Microsoft Exchange Server.
/IS {"server name"}	Backs up the Information Store file for the specified Microsoft Exchange Server.
/A	Performs an append operation. Either /G or /T must be used in conjunction with this switch. Do not use this switch in conjunction with /P.
/V:{yes|no}	Verifies the data after the backup is complete.
/R:{yes|no}	Restricts access to this tape to the owner or members of the Administrators group.
/L:{f|s|n}	Specifies the type of log file: f=full, s=summary, n=none (no log file is created).
/M {backup type}	Specifies the backup type. It must be one of the following: normal, copy, differential, incremental, or daily.
/RS:{yes|no}	Backs up the removable storage database.
/HC:{on|off}	Uses hardware compression, if available, on the tape drive.

Parameter	*Numeric Value*
/UM	Finds the first available media, formats it, and uses it for the current backup operation. You must use the /P switch to designate a device-type media pool when you use the /UM switch so that Backup searches for the appropriate type of media (for example, 4mm DDS). When you use the /UM switch, Backup will search the following media pools for available media: Free pool, Import pool, Unrecognized pool, and Backup pool. When available media is found, the search will stop, and the media will be formatted and used without prompting you for input. This command is not applicable to tape loaders and should be used only if you have a standalone tape device.

The above table made mention of a .bks file used to define the files to be included in the backup. Creating a .bks file is an easy way to make sure that the same set of data is backed up every time you execute a backup from the command line.

The next Step by Step shows you how to create a backup selection file.

STEP BY STEP

4.18 Creating a Backup Selection File (.bks)

1. From the Start menu, choose Programs, Accessories, System Tools, Backup.

2. In the Backup dialog box, click the Backup tab.

3. On the Backup page, select the locations (files, folders, local drives, network locations) that you want to include in your backup set. Also, select the system state if that is desired.

4. From the Job menu, select Save Selections and enter a path and file name that describes the purpose of the .bks file.

SERVER, SYSTEM STATE, AND USER DATA RECOVERY

Recover systems and user data.

If you are very fortunate, you will never have to recover any lost data or restore a server after a crash. In that case, the backups and repair disks you learned about in the previous sections are like insurance you will never use. They are not useful in a practical way, only as a source of peace of mind.

However, chances are unlikely that you will be so fortunate. If nothing else, you will encounter an end-user who has accidentally deleted a file and needs you to restore it. There's a good chance that a catastrophic accident will happen while you are an administrator, and you will need to recover from it. At that point, all the talk about saving data becomes practical and not simply theoretical; you had better hope that you've implemented a good strategy for saving system data.

As was mentioned at the beginning of the section "Maintaining System Recovery Information," each of the system tools used for recovery has a different function. Here again is the bulleted list to refresh your memory. Each of these will be covered to identify how to recover information.

- **Last Known Good Configuration.** This allows you to recover from configuration changes that affect Registry settings for devices (like installing an incorrect video driver or configuring it incorrectly). This tool has only a limited window of effectiveness; once you successfully log on locally to a Windows 2000 computer, this will no longer function.

- **Emergency Repair Disk.** This enables you to recover from Registry settings that render your system inoperable. This might be misconfiguration that could not be caught with the Last Known Good Configuration, or it might be deleted user accounts or other Registry changes.

- **Windows 2000 Backup.** This is useful for recovering other Registry settings as well as user data. This option allows for the widest breadth of recovery but also takes the most time.

Just as there are a number of ways to save data, there are also a number of ways to recover lost data. The first way is the easiest. You can use the Last Known Good Configuration.

Recovering System State with Last Known Good Configuration

As was mentioned in the section "Saving System State with Last Known Good Configuration," the Last Known Good Configuration is automatically saved whenever a user successfully logs on locally to the system. This state represents the last configuration settings that were able to support logon.

If you make a change to your system and want to be able to back out of it, you can do so at restart by invoking the Last Known Good Configuration. However, one of the problems is that you might not know anything is wrong until you log in again. One of the major indicators of poor configuration is that the Service Control Manager issues a message that a service failed to start. The problem with this warning is that, if you log in quickly, the message does not appear until after you have logged in. At that point, the Last Known Good Configuration represents your current configuration, which is not good at all.

One recommendation is that if you make changes to your system and then restart, wait a minute or two at the login dialog box to see if the Service Control Manager issues a message. If it does, restart your machine without logging in and either invoke the Last Known Good Configuration to back out of your changes or use one of the recovery techniques that follow. Step by Step 4.19 shows you one of the techniques, invoking Last Known Good Configuration.

STEP BY STEP

4.19 Invoking Last Known Good Configuration

1. Start or restart your server.

continues

continued

2. When the Hardware Profile/Configuration Recovery Menu screen appears (you are still in "text" mode at this point), press the L key on your keyboard.

3. Press Enter to continue the startup process.

Recovering System State with Emergency Repair Disk

The emergency repair folder and disk can be used to recover a variety of system files and configuration settings. It can be used to recover the Registry if it becomes corrupted. It can also be used to recover system files if they are accidentally deleted.

In order to recover, you must have three things. First, you must have a set of startup disks if your computer is not capable of booting from the Windows 2000 CD-ROM. You can create the startup disks using the Windows 2000 Server CD-ROM and any Windows-based computer with a CD-ROM drive. Second, you must have the Windows 2000 Server CD-ROM. Third, you must have an Emergency Repair Disk to direct the repair process to the location of your Windows 2000 installation. If you do not have the disk, a manual detection will be attempted.

Step by Step 4.20 demonstrates how to recover a lost system state using the emergency repair process.

STEP BY STEP

4.20 Recovering System State Using the Emergency Repair Process

1. Place the disk labeled Windows 2000 Setup Boot Disk into the disk drive and restart your server.

2. When prompted, insert the Windows 2000 Server Setup Disk #2 and press Enter to continue.

3. When prompted, insert the Windows 2000 Server Setup Disk #3 and press Enter to continue.

4. When prompted, insert the Windows 2000 Server Setup Disk #4 and press Enter to continue.

5. At the Welcome to Setup screen, press R to initiate the emergency repair process.

6. At the Windows 2000 Repair Options menu, press R to continue with the emergency repair process.

7. When prompted, choose either M to direct the repair process yourself or F to have Windows 2000 try to detect the problems and repair your system. Generally, you will want to perform a manual repair so that you can direct Windows 2000 to the problem. If you do not know the source of the problem, choose F, and the repair will progress without your intervention.

8. In the menu below, choose the appropriate areas of your server to repair. The Startup Environment includes files like BOOT.INI, NTDETECT.COM, and NTLDR. The System files include everything in the WINNT folder. The boot sector includes everything in the master boot record. This would be corrupted if you incorrectly installed a second operating system (like Windows 98) on your server trying to configure a dual boot.

As part of the repair process, Setup will perform each optional task selected below.

```
To have Setup perform the selected tasks, press
➥ENTER
To change the selections, use the UP or DOWN arrow
➥keys to select item, and then press ENTER

[X] Inspect startup environment
[X] Verify Windows 2000 system files
[X] Inspect boot sector
```

Make your choice and press Enter.

continues

continued

9. When the following menu appears, insert your Emergency Repair Disk and press Enter.

```
You need an Emergency Repair disk for the Windows
➥2000 installation you want to repair.
NOTE: Setup can only repair Windows 2000
➥installations.
 •If you have the Emergency Repair disk, press ENTER
 •If you do not have the Emergency Repair disk,
  ➥press L.
  Setup will attempt to locate Windows 2000 for you.
```

10. You might be asked to confirm the repair of files as your system is repaired. In addition, you may be asked to insert the CD-ROM if what you are repairing requires access to the installation files.

11. When the repair is complete, your server will restart automatically.

Recovering Systems with the Recovery Console

The Recovery console is a powerful text-based boot alternative for Windows 2000 Server. If your system becomes so corrupt that it will not boot and no other repair process will help, you can boot to the Recovery console and copy files to or from your server. In addition, you can stop and start services, if a service that you have installed causes problems with booting. There are two ways to boot to the Recovery console: using the setup disks or configuring the Recovery console as a secondary boot in the boot menu and choosing it at system startup.

Because the Recovery console is so powerful, when it starts you must log in as the administrator. The next Step by Step shows how to boot to this console.

STEP BY STEP

4.21 Booting to the Recovery Console with Setup Disks

1. Place the disk labeled Windows 2000 Setup Boot Disk into the disk drive and restart your server.

2. When prompted, insert the Windows 2000 Server Setup Disk #2 and press Enter to continue.

3. When prompted, insert the Windows 2000 Server Setup Disk #3 and press Enter to continue.

4. When prompted, insert the Windows 2000 Server Setup Disk #4 and press Enter to continue.

5. At the Welcome to Setup screen, press R to continue the repair process.

6. When the Windows Repair Options screen appears, press C to boot to the Recovery console.

7. When the following menu appears, type in the number of the Windows 2000 Server installation you want to log on to. In this case, there is only one. If you had your computer configured to multi-boot more than one operating system, you might have more than one separate installation of Windows 2000 from which to choose. Press Enter to continue.

```
Microsoft Windows 2000™ Recovery console.
The Recovery console provides system repair and
➥recovery functionality.
Type EXIT to quit the Recovery console and restart
➥the computer.

1. C:\WINNT

Which Windows 2000 installation would you like to
➥log on to (To cancel, press ENTER)?
```

8. When prompted for the Administrator password, type it in to log in.

continues

continued

9. When login is successful, you will be taken to a command prompt. You can now use the console as though it were a command prompt, with some restricted functionality. To get a full list of commands, type **HELP** and then type the name of the command to get help on. If you need to disable a service (or device) to prevent it from starting at the next reboot, type **DISABLE** *servicename*. For a list of services, type **LISTSVC**. If you need to copy files, all the drives (including the CD-ROM) should start as usual.

10. When you finish making repairs, type **EXIT** to reboot.

To make booting to the Recovery console more convenient, you can make it a boot item. The next Step by Step shows you how to install the Recovery console as a boot item.

STEP BY STEP

4.22 Installing the Recovery Console as a Boot Item

1. With Windows 2000 Server running, start a command prompt (select Start, Programs, Accessories, Command Prompt).

2. Navigate to the source of your Windows 2000 Server installation files (CD-ROM, network share, local folder) and change to the i386 folder.

3. From within the i386 folder, type **winnt32.exe /cmdcons**.

4. When prompted to install the console, confirm by clicking Yes.

5. When prompted that the console has been installed, click OK. If you restart your computer, you will see two choices during the text-mode section: Windows 2000 Server and Microsoft Windows 2000 Recovery Console. Choosing the Recovery console takes you to step 7 in Step by Step 4.21.

Troubleshooting with Safe Mode

Until Windows 2000, Safe Mode was available only in Windows 9x operating systems. As anyone who has used Windows 9x as an administrator knows, Safe Mode allows you to boot an operating system with a minimal set of generic drivers. This allows you to make changes to configurations that normally would prevent your system from starting or would make it start in an unusable condition. For example, suppose you change your video settings and do not test. Then you find that your screen is black. You will need to do something to fix your problem. You should be able to reboot and choose Last Known Good Configuration before you login. What if you forget to choose Last Known Good Configuration and login anyway? You have no way to recover your system. However, Safe Mode will allow you to restart and use a generic setting for your video that will allow you to repair your system.

When you boot with advanced options, you will be presented with three Safe Mode choices: Safe Mode, Safe Mode with Networking, and Safe Mode with Command Prompt. Choosing Safe Mode starts Windows 2000 using only basic files and drivers including mouse (except serial mice), monitor, keyboard, mass storage, base video, default system services, and no network connections. Choosing Safe Mode with Networking adds networking capabilities to the basic Safe Mode. Choosing Safe Mode with Command Prompt starts Windows 2000 in a text mode instead of a GUI mode. You will have to restart your computer to exit from the text mode.

Step by Step 4.23 illustrates how to boot to Safe Mode.

STEP BY STEP

4.23 Booting to Safe Mode

1. Start or restart your server.

2. During text mode, a screen appears with the message "For troubleshooting and advanced startup options for Windows 2000, press F8." Press F8.

continues

continued

3. When the Advanced Options menu (below) appears, use the arrow keys to move to the Safe Mode option you want, and then press Enter to continue.

```
Windows 2000 Advanced Options Menu
Please select an option:

        Safe Mode
        Safe Mode with Networking
        Safe Mode with Command Prompt
```

4. Log in when prompted. If you did not choose network support, you will be able to log on only with a local account. A domain controller will not be available to validate a domain login.

5. Modify the settings that are causing problems. Then restart your computer, choosing to start normally this time.

Recovering System State and User Data with Windows 2000 Backup

Most Windows 2000 Server implementations require that data be restored from backup at some point. Assuming that you have been using good backup methods, you should be able to quickly recover from any incident, whether it is a hard drive failure or a user deletion error.

The number of options for recovery of information are greatly reduced compared to options for saving information. In a simple recovery, you can indicate what needs to be restored and from what tape or file. Advanced options allow you to configure recovery in three ways. You can choose the location of recovered files. You can choose whether or not to overwrite existing files. There are also special options, which include restoring security, restoring the removable storage database, and restoring junction points to mounted volumes.

When setting file locations, you can choose to recover data to the original location. Another option is to recover data to an alternate location with the underlying tree structure preserved. A further option is to recover data to a single folder with all the files deposited without the original structure.

When setting overwrite policy, you have three choices for recovering information. You can choose never to overwrite a file that already exists, you can choose to overwrite a file that exists if the one on the backup is newer, or you can choose to always overwrite existing files.

When using special options for recovering information, you have three options. One of the special options allows you to define the recovery of security information: NTFS local permissions, auditing, and ownership. When restoring to an NTFS volume, you can recover NTFS permissions or leave them off. It is important to note that if you want full recovery of NTFS file properties, you must recover to an NTFS volume.

A second special option is the recovery of the removable storage database. This tracks what removable storage media were used for what purposes, including tracking where backups have been performed. This will replace the current removable storage database found in WINNT\System32\Ntmsdata with the one from the backup.

The final special option is the recovery of mounted volumes and their defining junction points. A mounted volume is essentially a pointer, or junction point, from a folder to a local drive or network location. You can choose to restore just the junction points (assuming the data is intact on the drive being pointed to). You can choose to restore both the junction points and the information on the mounted drive.

Step by Step 4.24 shows you how to recover information stored on backup tapes or files.

> **NOTE** **You Can Restore from GUI Only** Using the GUI program is the only way to restore data using Windows 2000 Backup. There is no command line interface, nor can it be scheduled.

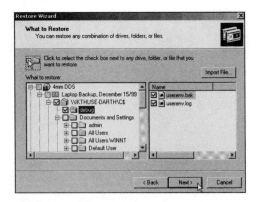

FIGURE 4.55
Choose the tape to restore from and the items to restore.

FIGURE 4.56
Clicking the Advanced button will allow you to deviate from the default restore settings.

STEP BY STEP

4.24 Recovering Data from Backup Tapes or Files

1. From the Start menu, choose Programs, Accessories, System Tools, Backup.

2. From the Welcome tab on the backup program, click the Restore Wizard icon.

3. At the Welcome to the Restore Wizard screen, click Next to continue.

4. At the What to Restore screen, choose the media type and the backup set from within that group (see Figure 4.55). Finally, expand the backup set and choose those files you want to restore. If your tape drive holds only a single tape, you will have to make sure you have the appropriate tape inserted into the drive. If you request to restore from a specific drive, it may take a minute or two to recover the folder list from the tape catalog before the tree is displayed. Click Next to continue.

5. At the Completing the Restore Wizard screen, review the settings. If they are acceptable, click Next. If not, click the Advanced button to set the advanced options (see Figure 4.56).

6. At the Where to Restore screen (see Figure 4.57), choose the location to restore to. If you choose Original Location, you can click Next. Otherwise, you will have to fill in the location to restore the files to a text box that appears on this page.

7. At the How to Restore screen (see Figure 4.58), specify what to do if the restore process detects a file in the restore location that is the same as a file trying to be restored. Click Next to continue.

8. At the Advanced Restore Options screen (see Figure 4.59), choose which special options you want, and then click Next.

9. When the Completing the Restore Wizard screen appears again, click Finish to begin restoring files.

10. At the Restore Progress screen, click Close to exit.

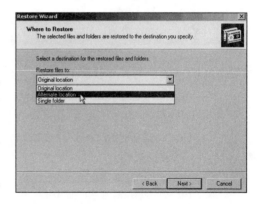

FIGURE 4.57
Select the restore location.

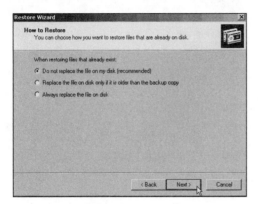

FIGURE 4.58
Define what to do if the restore process encounters a file on your hard drive that it is to restore from tape.

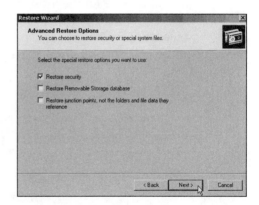

FIGURE 4.59
Define whether to restore security and what to do with removable storage and mounted drives.

CASE STUDY: WebCrazy Consulting

ESSENCE OF THE CASE

This case requires that the following results be satisfied:

- ▶ Devise a way to back up all Emilio's critical data.

- ▶ Make sure the backup strategy allows for storage on a single tape drive. Emilio does not want to buy more hardware.

- ▶ Make sure a clear schedule is devised that will provide for the most up-to-date backups with the least amount of inconvenience to Emilio.

SCENARIO

Emilio is the sole proprietor of a small home-based Internet consulting company called WebCrazy. He has a dedicated Internet connection, and he hosts his own Web page and those of some of his clients on a Web server running Windows 2000 Server, which is located in his basement. In addition, he has three other computers on a LAN in a workgroup configuration. Of these, one is a laptop on which he does most of his development; it runs Windows 2000 Professional. One computer is a test machine that he frequently formats and reinstalls. The other computer is one his family uses; it runs Windows 98.

Emilio knows that being able to recover data in the event of a hard drive crash is essential. Therefore, he purchased a 4mm DAT drive for his server. What he is unsure of is how to back up all the data on his server, laptop, and family machine from a single location—if that is possible at all. He also wants to know the recommended frequency for his backups and how many tapes he needs. He has called you to look over his network and advise him on a strategy.

ANALYSIS

Given the capabilities of Windows 2000 Backup and Emilio's network configuration, it is possible to fulfill all his backup needs with a minimum of hardware purchase. The only thing Emilio will have to buy is some tapes. The backup can also be configured with a minimum of interaction between Emilio and the system. However, he will have to change tapes occasionally.

CASE STUDY: WEBCRAZY CONSULTING

All Emilio's data can be accessed from a central location if the proper accounts have been created. In the case of the Windows 98 computer, the proper folder sharing must be put into place. It is recommended that Emilio create user accounts on both the server and the laptop that have the same name and password and that are in the Administrators group of the respective machines. In addition, on the Windows 98 computer, he should share the root of each hard drive (if there is more than one). This ensures that all data on all computers can be accessed from the server.

Because all the data is accessible from the server, Emilio can perform centralized backups from the server onto the DAT drive installed in it. By using Windows 2000 Backup, he can connect to the administrative shares on the laptop (C$, D$, and so on). Through those

shares, Emilio is an administrator on the laptop and the drives of the Windows 98 computer. This will allow him to back up all network data on a single tape.

Finally, you will recommend a backup procedure that includes scheduling incremental backups Saturday though Thursday nights and normal backups on Friday nights. Using a rotating tape system in which normal backups use two tapes (rotated each week), and incrementals use two more tapes (with all incrementals from one week on a single tape), Emilio needs only four DAT tapes to ensure that all his data is safe. In addition, using this procedure, he also ensures that he can go back to the previous week to recover data that might be accidentally deleted.

This table summarizes the solution.

OVERVIEW OF THE REQUIREMENTS AND SOLUTIONS IN THIS CASE STUDY

Requirement	Solution Provided By
Emilio's critical data must be backed up.	Using administrative shares on Windows 2000 and network shares on Windows 98 to provide access to all network data from the server.
Data must be saved at a central point.	Running Windows 2000 Backup on the server (from which we have access to all network data) is possible using the DAT drive Emilio already has.
Schedule needs to be automated.	Using the scheduling features of Windows 2000 Backup, all Emilio has to do is make sure the correct tape is present in the tape drive at the end of every day. (It would have to be changed on Friday and Saturday of each week.)

CHAPTER SUMMARY

KEY TERMS

Be sure you are familiar with the definitions of and concepts behind each of these key terms.

- applications server
- preemptive multitasking
- idle priority
- normal priority
- high priority
- realtime priority
- Task Manager
- Performance Monitor
- System Monitor
- counter log
- trace log
- alert
- counter
- object
- instance
- graph view
- histogram view
- report view
- trace provider
- bottleneck
- baseline
- normal backup

This chapter, "Managing, Monitoring, and Optimizing System Performance, Reliability, and Availability," outlined the main points for saving system configuration and data with an eye toward being able to restore those configurations and data should the need arise. Summarized briefly, this chapter covered the following main points:

- ◆ *Managing processes.* This includes setting application priorities through foreground boost and priority switches at run time and through the Task Manager. This also includes starting and stopping processes through the Task Manager.

- ◆ *Monitor and optimize usage of system resources.* This includes the use of Performance Monitor (System Monitor, counter logs, trace logs, and alerts) to gather information. In addition, it includes using the data gathered from Performance Monitor to isolate bottlenecks and improve performance.

- ◆ *Saving system state and user data.* This includes using the Last Known Good Configuration, emergency repair folder and disks, and Windows 2000 Backup to save critical system and user data.

- ◆ *Recovering system state and user data.* This includes using the Last Know Good Configuration, emergency repair folder and disks, Recovery console, Safe Mode, and Windows 2000 Backup to recover critical data that has been saved.

KEY TERMS   *continued*

- incremental backup
- copy backup
- NTBACKUP.EXE
- Recovery console
- Emergency Repair Disk
- Last Known Good Configuration

- differential backup
- daily backup
- backup selection file
- Safe Mode
- DISKPERF.EXE

APPLY YOUR KNOWLEDGE

Exercises

4.1   Set Application Priority

In this exercise, you learn how to set application priority at time of invocation and how to reset while it is running. You will also learn how to stop a process using the Task Manager. Note that this exercise will cause your server to stop responding, forcing you to power it off suddenly. Make sure you do not have any critical applications running when you do this exercise.

Estimated Time: 15 minutes

1. The CD-ROM that comes with this book contains a folder called Application Demo. Copy that folder to the hard drive on your Windows 2000 server.

2. From the Start menu, choose Programs, Accessories, Command Prompt.

3. From the Command Prompt, navigate to the location where you copied the Application Demo folder.

4. At the cursor, type **Start /Low Counter**. When it starts running, move the counter dialog box to the bottom of your screen. Note how quickly this program counts, even at low priority.

5. At the cursor, type **Start /Normal Counter**. When it starts running, move the second counter to the bottom of your screen. Note that this counter is counting quickly, but the low priority counter is no longer counting quickly.

6. Right-click the taskbar and choose Task Manager. Make sure that when it comes up, you can still see both counters (see Figure 4.60). Click the Processes tab on the Task Manager.

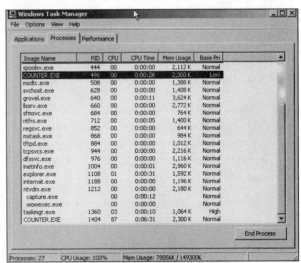

FIGURE 4.60
You can modify the data shown in the Task Manager by using the View menu.

7. From the View menu in the Task Manager, choose Select Columns. When the Select Columns dialog box appears, select Base Priority and click OK to exit. Expand the size of the Task Manager window to show the base priorities of each of the running applications.

8. Locate the version of COUNTER that is running at Low priority and right-click it. Choose Set Priority, Normal. When prompted to confirm that you want to reset the priority, click Yes. Note that the counters begin incrementing at roughly the same rate.

9. Change the priority of the same instance of COUNTER to High priority. Note that its counter starts running faster than the one running at Normal priority.

APPLY YOUR KNOWLEDGE

10. Right-click the instance of COUNTER that is currently running at Normal priority and choose End Process from the menu that appears. One counter will disappear because its process has just been terminated.

11. Change the priority of the remaining instance of COUNTER to Realtime. At this point, your server should effectively stop responding. The counter is now consuming CPU cycles faster than many of the system tasks.

12. Using the power button, restart your server.

4.2   Detect a Bottleneck Using System Monitor and Counter Logs

Exercise 4.2 shows how you can use Counter Logs and System Monitor to detect a bottleneck on your server. To do this, you will first artificially create a memory bottleneck. Then, using a counter log and the System Monitor, you will analyze the system performance during routine operation to detect the bottleneck.

Estimated Time: 30 minutes

1. Create a baseline log.

2. Create a folder called PerfLogs on the drive of your choice.

3. From the Start menu, choose Programs, Administrative Tools, Performance.

4. Expand Performance Logs and Alerts, right-click Counter Logs, and choose New Log Settings from the menu that appears.

5. When prompted, type **BASELINE** as the log name.

6. On the General page, click the Add button.

7. At the Add Counter dialog box, select the radio button labeled Use Local Computer Counters. Select the performance objects Processor, Memory, Paging File, and PhysicalDisk (in turn). Then select the All Counters radio button and click Add. When you finish, click Close.

8. Click the Log Files tab, make sure the location for the log file is "C:\Perflogs" (or wherever you put your Perflogs folder), and make sure the Log File Type is Binary File. Then click OK.

9. Open Notepad. Next, open Paint and spend a couple of minutes drawing. Then open Internet Explorer and go to the Microsoft Web site. Switch back to Notepad and type a few sentences.

10. After about 3–5 minutes, switch back to the Performance Monitor, right-click the Baseline log, and choose Stop from the menu that appears.

11. Close all the applications you started, including the Performance Monitor.

12. Change the BOOT.INI file, a startup file, to restrict the amount of memory your server is allowed to use.

13. Using My Computer or Windows Explorer, navigate to the root of the C: drive.

14. From the Tools menu, choose Folder Options.

15. At the Folder Options dialog box, click the View tab.

16. On the View property sheet, choose the radio button labeled Show Hidden Files and Folders and deselect the check box labeled Hide Protected Operating System Files. When prompted, confirm that you really want to do that by clicking Yes. Click OK to continue.

APPLY YOUR KNOWLEDGE

17. In the file window, locate the file named BOOT.INI, right-click it, and choose Properties from the menu that appears.

18. From the Properties dialog box, deselect Read-Only at the bottom and click OK.

19. Double-click the BOOT.INI icon to edit the file in Notepad.

20. In the BOOT.INI file, locate the line that begins "multi(0)" and move to the end of it.

21. At the end of the boot line, add a space and the text /MAXMEM:24.

22. Save and close the BOOT.INI file.

23. Restart your computer. The change to the BOOT.INI file will force your server to use only 24MB of the available RAM.

24. Repeat steps 3–11 above, substituting the name MEMORYTEST for BASELINE.

25. Edit the BOOT.INI file again as you did in step 12, and this time remove the memory restriction.

26. Restart your server.

27. Open the Performance console and select System Monitor.

28. Right-click the System Monitor view (on the right) and choose Properties from the menu that appears.

29. Click the Source tab, select the radio button labeled Log File, and type in the path to the BASELINE log file (or browse for it).

30. Click the Data tab and click the Add button at the bottom. Add the following counters: Memory\Pages/sec, Paging File\%Usage, PhysicalDisk\%Disk Time, and Processor\%Processor Time. Click Close.

31. Click OK to close the System Monitor Properties dialog box.

32. Note the condition of the graph. Although this was not a long test, you should see that the number of pages per second spiked when new applications were started (as did processor usage), but then paging dropped.

33. Right-click the graph and choose Properties. On the Source tab, enter the path to the MEMORYTEST log and click OK.

34. Note the condition of the graph. Although the processor stays at fairly low usage, the paging is high and fairly constant. The disk usage is also high and constant. It would be tempting to see this as a disk bottleneck, considering all the disk activity as you worked.

35. Close the Performance Monitor.

4.3   Repair Your Server Using the Recovery Console

This exercise shows how you can use the Recovery console to repair system files and allow your server to boot. To accomplish this, you will install the Recovery console as a separate boot option and then corrupt the BOOT.INI file to prevent the server from starting. To accomplish the fix, you must have a disk and a second computer to repair the BOOT.INI file. In case you do not, an alternate course of action will be given.

Estimated Time: 30 minutes

1. Install the System console as a secondary boot.

2. Insert the Windows 2000 Server CD-ROM into the CD-ROM drive.

APPLY YOUR KNOWLEDGE

3. From the Start menu, choose Run. In the Run dialog box, type **CDROMDRIVELETTER:\i386\winnt32 /cmdcons** (where *CDROMDRIVELETTER* is the letter assigned to your CD-ROM drive).

4. When prompted to install the console, confirm by clicking Yes.

5. When prompted that the console has been installed, click OK.

6. Using My Computer or Windows Explorer, make a copy of the BOOT.INI file and call it BOOT.OLD.

7. As you did in step 12 of Exercise 4.2, modify the BOOT.INI file to restrict the maximum amount of memory available. This time use /MAXMEM:8.

8. Restart your server. During system startup, the server will stop and display either a blue-screen (stop) error or an error during black-screen startup telling you that it cannot progress.

9. Restart your server. When you're presented with the menu that allows you to choose to boot to Windows 2000 Server or the Recovery console, choose the Recovery console (by using your up and down arrow keys to highlight Recovery console and pressing Enter).

10. When the Recovery console starts and you are prompted to choose the version of Windows 2000 that you want to start, choose the Windows 2000 Server installation you are working on (for most people, this will be number 1). Press Enter to continue.

11. When prompted, enter the password of the Administrator and press Enter.

12. Place a disk into the drive, type **COPY C:\BOOT.INI A:**, and press Enter.

If you do not have a disk and/or a second computer on which to edit the BOOT.INI file, type **DEL BOOT.INI**, press Enter, and then type **REN BOOT.OLD BOOT.INI**. Then skip to step 15.

13. Remove the disk, take it to another computer, and edit the BOOT.INI file to remove the memory restriction. Place the disk back into the drive of your server.

14. At the Recovery console, type **DEL C:\BOOT.INI** and press Enter, and then type **COPY A:\BOOT.INI C:** and press Enter.

15. Type **EXIT** to restart your server. Allow it to restart normally now.

4.4   Back Up and Restore Files Using Windows 2000 Backup

This exercise shows how you can use Windows 2000 Backup to save and then restore a file to your server. This exercise assumes you do not have a DAT (or other tape) drive available, so the backup will be to disk. It also assumes that you created a PERFLOGS folder in Exercise 4.1 and that it contains log files.

Estimated Time: 20 minutes

1. Back up the \PERFLOGS folder to file.

2. From the Start menu, choose Programs, Accessories, System Tools, Backup.

3. On the Welcome page, click the Backup Wizard icon.

4. At the Welcome to the Windows 2000 Backup and Recovery Tools screen, click Next.

APPLY YOUR KNOWLEDGE

5. At the What to Back Up screen, select Back Up Selected Files, Drives, or Network Data and click Next.

6. At the Items to Back Up screen, locate the PERFLOGS folder on the left side and select it (a blue check mark will appear in the box). Click Next.

7. At the Where to Store the Backup screen, make sure that File is chosen as the media type, and then type `c:\logbackups\logback.bkf` in the Backup Media or File Name field. Click Next.

8. At the Completing the Backup Wizard screen, click the Advanced button.

9. At the Type of Backup screen, make sure that Normal is selected and click Next.

10. At the How to Back Up screen, make sure no items are selected and click Next.

11. At the Backup Media Options screen, click Next.

12. At the Backup Label screen, type Performance Log Backups in the field labeled Media Label, and then click Next.

13. At the When to Back Up screen, make sure Now is selected and click Next.

14. At the Completing the Backup Wizard screen, click Finish.

15. When prompted to create the \LOGBACKUPS folder, click Yes.

16. When the backup is complete, click Close to close the Backup Progress dialog box, and then close the backup program.

17. Delete the \PERFLOGS\Baseline_000001.blg file.

18. Recover the \PERFLOGS\Baseline_000001.blg file.

19. From the Start menu, choose Programs, Accessories, System Tools, Backup.

20. From the Welcome page, click the Restore Wizard icon.

21. At the Welcome to the Restore Wizard screen, click Next.

22. At the What to Restore screen, expand File, Performance Log Backups, and C: (or whatever drive your PERFLOGS folder is in).

23. When prompted for the name of the backup file to catalog, make sure C:\logbackups\ logbackup.bkf is in the field and click OK.

24. Click the Perflogs folder on the left side and click baseline_000001.blg on the right. Then click Next.

25. At the Completing the Restore Wizard screen, click Finish.

26. When prompted for the name of the backup file you want to restore, make sure c:\logbackups\ logbackup.bkf is entered in the field, and then click OK.

27. When the restore is complete, click Close to close the Restore Progress dialog box, and then close the backup program.

28. Check to make sure that baseline_000001.blg has been restored.

APPLY YOUR KNOWLEDGE

Review Questions

1. What are the four application execution priorities, and what numeric ranges does each fall into?

2. Name three ways to change the execution priority of an application (whether it's running or not).

3. What are the two types of logs available in Performance Monitor, and how can you distinguish them from one another?

4. What is the purpose of an alert, and what are three of the actions that can be taken when one happens?

5. What limitation of Windows 2000 Backup should lead you to schedule backups for times when as few people are accessing the server as possible?

6. What are three ways to invoke the Windows 2000 Backup process?

7. How does the Recovery console differ from Safe Mode with Command Prompt?

8. What do you need to perform an emergency repair?

Exam Questions

1. Jim is the network administrator for two identical Windows 2000 servers in a high school. They both have SCSI CD-ROM drives, and all data is on NTFS partitions. He has just found one of his servers turned off. When he turns it back on, Jim gets an error that NTOSKRNL.EXE cannot be found and it will not boot. He suspects that a vandal in the school has deleted the file. He does not have the Windows 2000 Server CD-ROM, but he has disks and a CD-ROM writer. How can Jim recover his server?

    A. Boot his server to Safe Mode and then copy the NTOSKRNL.EXE file from the other server using a disk.

    B. Boot his server to the Recovery console using the setup disk set and copy NTOSKRNL.EXE using a disk.

    C. Boot his server to DOS and copy the NTOSKRNL.EXE from the other server using a CD-ROM with the file copied from the other server.

    D. Boot his server to the Recovery console using a secondary boot on the server and copy the NTOSKRNL.EXE using a CD-ROM with the file copied from the other server.

2. Pavel wants to determine whether or not his server is short of memory. Under light load, users get good response. However, as load increases, so does the lack of responsiveness. Which of the following counters will aid him in determining whether memory is the bottleneck in his system? (Choose two.)

    A. Memory\pages/sec

    B. Paging File\% Usage

    C. Processor\Interrupts/sec

    D. Network Segment\% Net Utilization

3. Christopher needs to back up the contents of a data folder on his server, but he does not have a tape drive. What other media can he use with Windows 2000 Backup?

APPLY YOUR KNOWLEDGE

A. CD-ROM.

B. Floppy disk.

C. Text dump.

D. No other media can be used.

4. Hikaru changed the driver for his video card and restarted his server. Now the display is garbled. Aside from rebuilding his server, what can he do to repair this problem?

A. Restart the server, and it will repair itself.

B. Restart the server, boot to the Repair console, and use the "Detect PNP" command to reinstall the video driver.

C. Restart the server, boot to the setup disks, and use the Emergency Repair Disk to repair the video settings.

D. Restart the server, boot to Safe Mode, and use the Device manager to choose a working driver.

5. Gene is the network administrator for a small company. Knowing that critical data must be recoverable, he has been doing normal backups every Friday night. Recently, he was forced to recover data lost on a Thursday from his last backup. Doing so has caused him to rethink the need for the frequency of backups. He has decided that he needs to back up his server every day. He does not care how long it will take to recover the data. However, he does want to minimize the time it will take to run the daily backup.

Required Result:

Data must be backed up at the end of every day.

Optional Desired Results:

Data must be recoverable in the shortest period of time possible (on average).

Data must be backed up in the shorted period of time possible (on average).

Proposed Solution:

Schedule a normal backup for each night.

Analysis:

Which result(s) does the proposed solution produce?

A. This solution produces the required result as well as both optional results.

B. This solution produces the required result and one of the optional desired results.

C. This solution produces the required result but does not fulfill either of the optional desired results.

D. This solution does not meet the required result.

6. Gene is the network administrator for a small company. Knowing that critical data must be recoverable, he has been doing normal backups every Friday night. Recently, Jean was forced to recover data lost on a Thursday from his last backup. Doing so has caused him to rethink the need for the frequency of backups. He has decided that he needs to back up his server every day. He would like the data to be recoverable in as short a period of time possible, but would rather minimize the time it will take to do the daily backup.

Required Result:

Data must be backed up at the end of every day.

APPLY YOUR KNOWLEDGE

Optional Results:

Data must be recoverable in the shortest period of time possible (on average).

Data must be backed up in the shorted period of time possible (on average).

Proposed Solution:

Retain the Friday schedule for normal backups and add an incremental backup.

Analysis:

Which result(s) does the proposed solution produce?

A. This solution produces the required result as well as both optional results.

B. This solution produces the required result and one of the optional desired results.

C. This solution produces the required result but does not fulfill either of the optional desired results.

D. This solution does not meet the required result.

7. Leonard wants to start an application, Grabber.exe, on his server that will capture and process environmental data in real time. However, he finds that the sampling rate is not fast enough. Other less important applications are running on his server in addition to this one. He does not want the other applications to stop altogether, but he wants to increase the priority of this application. How can he change the amount of processor time his application gets over the amount it gets when he invokes it from a command line?

A. Run it using this command line: `Start /Low Grabber.exe`

B. Run it using this command line: `Start /Normal Grabber.exe`

C. Run it using this command line: `Start /High Grabber.exe`

D. Run it using this command line: `Start /RealTime Grabber.exe`

8. Monty is the administrator for a Windows 2000 server. He has previously had servers fail because they have run out of disk space, so he wants to make sure the same thing will not happen in the future. How can he configure his server so that it lets him know when the amount of free disk space falls below 10%?

A. Configure alerts in Performance Monitor to warn him when any of the instances of the counter LogicalDisk\%Free Space fall below 10%.

B. Configure alerts in Performance Monitor to warn him when any of the instances of the counter PhysicalDisk\%Free Space fall below 10%.

C. Configure System Monitor to watch PhysicalDisk\%Free Space and check it every hour to see if it has fallen below 10%.

D. Configure a trace log to have the Windows 2000 Trace Provider watch the disk for %Free Space falling below 10%.

9. William has a batch file that contains the following code:

```
ntbackup restore [systemstate] /f
➥"D:\backup.bkf"
```

APPLY YOUR KNOWLEDGE

What will this code do?

  A. Restore the system state of the local computer from the file D:\backup.bkf.

  B. Restore all the data from the file D:\backup.bkf to the local computer.

  C. Save the system state data from the local server to a file called D:\backup.bkf.

  D. It will do nothing.

10. Beverly wants to create a baseline for her Windows 2000 server. However, when she tries to capture data for her logical disks, she finds that the counters are unavailable. What must she do to her server to enable the counters for that object?

  A. At the command line, type **DISKPERF -yd**.

  B. At the command line, type **DISKPERF -yd**. Then restart the server.

  C. At the command line, type **DISKPERF -nv**. Then restart the server.

  D. At the command line, type **DISKPERF -y**. Then restart the server.

11. Zephraim is doing his weekly log analysis. He notes that on Wednesday, the number of interrupts per second on his processor suddenly doubled and has remained high ever since. What does the increase in this counter likely mean?

  A. Nothing. It is normal for this counter to increase over time.

  B. It could mean that he has a potential hardware problem and that a piece of hardware is generating many more interrupts than normal.

  C. It indicates that the network card is the bottleneck in the system and should be replaced.

  D. It indicates that the CPU is the bottleneck in the system and should be replaced or upgraded.

12. Deanna needs to backup critical data on her server. However, she does not have enough DAT tapes to back up everything on her server. She wants to make sure that, in addition to the user data she is backing up, she backs up the Registry on her server. With reference to Figure 4.61, what should Deanna select in addition to those data files she wants to back up?

  A. Select C:.

  B. Select System State.

  C. Select My Documents.

  D. Select My Computer.

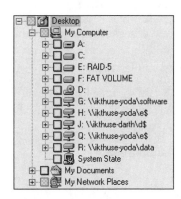

FIGURE 4.61
Figure for question 12.

APPLY YOUR KNOWLEDGE

13. Wesley is the IT Manager for a large Internet service provider. To make sure the Web servers (running Windows 2000 Server) are easily recoverable in the case of a hardware failure, he wants to set a policy regarding the recovery tools available at each server. Each of these servers is running Windows 2000 Server and has a 4MM DAT drive attached. Wesley's bottom line is that each server must be fully recoverable. In addition, he wants to be able to easily recover small errors caused by mistakes that people sometimes make or by corruption in operating system files. Unfortunately, he does not have budgeted funds to purchase any additional software or hardware.

Required Result:

All Web servers must be fully recoverable with data loss of no more than 12 elapsed hours of work.

No third-party tools can be purchased.

Optional Desired Results:

In the case of service errors preventing restart, servers must be recoverable without reinstallation of the operating system.

In the case of start file loss or corruption, servers must be recoverable without reinstallation of the operating system.

Proposed Solution:

Schedule a normal backup once a week for all servers. Configure all servers to boot to the Recovery console when chosen.

Analysis:

Which result(s) does the proposed solution produce?

A. This solution produces the required result as well as both optional results.

B. This solution produces the required result and one of the optional desired results.

C. This solution produces the required result but does not fulfill either of the optional desired results.

D. This solution does not meet the required result.

14. Tasha is the IT Manager for a large Internet service provider. To make sure the Web servers (running Windows 2000 Server) are easily recoverable in the case of a hardware failure, she wants to set a policy regarding the recovery tools available at each server. Each of these servers is running Windows 2000 Server and has a 4MM DAT drive attached. Her bottom line is that each server must be fully recoverable. In addition, she wants to be able to easily recover small errors caused by mistakes that people sometimes make or by corruption in operating system files. Unfortunately, she does not have budgeted funds to purchase any additional software or hardware.

Required Result:

All Web servers must be fully recoverable with data loss of no more than 12 elapsed hours of work.

No third-party tools can be purchased.

APPLY YOUR KNOWLEDGE

Optional Desired Results:

In the case of service errors preventing restart, servers must be recoverable without reinstallation of the operating system.

In the case of start file loss or corruption, servers must be recoverable without reinstallation of the operating system.

Proposed Solution:

Schedule a normal backup once a week for all servers. Schedule incremental backups every 12 hours for each server.

Analysis:

Which result(s) does the proposed solution produce?

A. This solution produces the required result, as well as both optional results.

B. This solution produces the required result and one of the optional desired results.

C. This solution produces the required result, but does not fulfill either of the optional desired results.

D. This solution does not meet the required result.

15. Gene wants to tune his server for optimum performance. Which of the following questions must he answer before beginning the process of server tuning?

A. How much money is in the budget?

B. What tasks is the server expected to perform?

C. What are the latest hardware breakthroughs?

D. What type of business is his company in?

Answers to Review Questions

1. The four priorities are Idle—sometimes called Low (0–6), Normal (6–11), High (11–15), and Realtime (16–31). For more information, see the section "Maintaining Windows 32-Bit Applications."

2. There are three ways to change the priority of an application. The first way is to start it at a command line (or from a shortcut) using the syntax **Start /priority applicationname.** The second way is to change its priority in the Task Manager while it is running. The third way is to set the foreground boost for all normal applications in the advanced page of the System Properties. For more information, see the section "Maintaining Windows 32-Bit Applications."

3. The two kinds of logs available in Performance Monitor are counter logs and trace logs. They are distinguished by their collection trigger and how much control you have over the information you collect. The collection of data in a counter log is controlled by time interval passing, and you can finely control the kind of data you collect through the application of object counters. The collection of data in a trace log is controlled by events that happen (like user logon), and you have little control over the specific information collected outside of a general category of data. For more information, see the section "Collecting Data Using Performance Monitor."

4. The purpose of an alert is to have Performance Monitor tell you when a critical situation happens so you don't have to check for it periodically. When an alert is triggered, you can have

APPLY YOUR KNOWLEDGE

Performance Monitor take one of the following actions: create an application log entry, send a network message, start a counter log, or run a program. For more information, see the section "Using Counter Logs."

5. The major drawback of Windows 2000 Backup is its inability to back up open files. That means that files that are open by system processes or by users when the backup process comes to them will be skipped over. Therefore, you should have as few people interacting with server data as possible when a backup is in progress. For more information, see the section "Saving System State and User Data with Windows 2000 Backup."

6. The three ways to invoke the Windows 2000 Backup process are: immediately through the GUI, on schedule through the GUI, and immediately through the NTBACKUP program at a command line. For more information, see the section "Saving System State and User Data with Windows 2000 Backup."

7. The Recovery console differs from Safe Mode with Command Prompt primarily in that it is a separate boot from the regular Windows 2000 Server boot process. Safe Mode requires that the server still be bootable in order for you to use it to effect changes. Recovery console can be used even if your Windows 2000 server is not bootable through normal means. In addition, Recovery console offers only a limited set of commands, whereas Safe Mode provides the full set of command-line commands. For more information, see the sections "Recovering Systems with the Recovery Console" and "Troubleshooting with Safe Mode."

8. To perform an emergency repair you must have the four-disk startup set. In addition it would be helpful (but not necessarily required) to have the Windows 2000 Server CD-ROM and an Emergency Repair Disk. If your system is capable of booting from its CD-ROM drive, you could do without the four-disk set and simply boot to the Windows 2000 Server CD. For more information, see the section "Recovering System State with Emergency Repair Information."

Answers to Exam Questions

1. **D.** The only answer that will work is to boot to the Recovery console and copy the file using a CD-ROM. Safe Mode will not work because you need to be able to boot to invoke Safe Mode. Booting to the Recovery console and copying from a disk will not work because NTOSKRNL.EXE is too large to fit on a disk. Booting to DOS will not work because DOS will not read NTFS partitions. For more information, see the section "Recovering Systems with the Recovery Console."

2. **A, B.** Page/sec shows you how many times per second your server had to go to the hard drive to recover information that it thought ought to be in memory but has been swapped out because of a shortage of memory. %Usage of the paging file can be an indicator of low memory because if it constantly decreases as applications run, the amount of RAM is not sufficient to fill the demand on the server, which is causing the paging file to be increased in size. Interrupts per second are generally an indication of hardware

APPLY YOUR KNOWLEDGE

performance, and %Net Utilization is an indicator of network saturation, neither of which is a memory problem. For more information, see the section "Optimizing System Resource Availability."

3. **B.** In addition to tape drives, Windows 2000 Backup can also store to any local or network drive. Floppy disk is the only choice available that is writeable. Text dump is not a backup option, and under NT 4.0 you could not write to anything but tape. For more information, see the section "Saving System State and User Data Using Windows 2000 Backup."

4. **D.** Safe mode is designed to allow repairs like the one Hikaru has to do. Although it is possible that the server will automatically give you a measure of functionality when booting (it can repair itself in some cases), it is not guaranteed to provide an environment where you can fix the problem. For more information, see the section "Troubleshooting with Safe Mode."

5. **B.** Doing a full backup at the end of every day will fulfill the required result. It also fulfills the optional result of being able to recover the data in the shortest period of time (on average). Because you only need to consult one tape to recover, this solution provides quick recovery. It does not provide quick backups, however, because he is saving all data every day. For more information, see the sections "Saving System State and User Data with Windows 2000 Backup" and "Recovering System State and User Data with Windows 2000 Backup."

6. **B.** By doing a normal backup once a week and incremental backups on all other days, he ensures that all the data is backed up. In addition, he

ensures that daily backups are quick because incremental backs up only changes made on the day it is invoked. It will not recover data quickly (on average) because he will generally have to recover from a normal backup and an incremental (at least one) to recover data. For more information, see the sections "Saving System State and User Data with Windows 2000 Backup" and "Recovering System State and User Data with Windows 2000 Backup."

7. **C.** Invoking an application from an icon will, by default, start it at Normal priority. That means neither A nor B can be the correct answer. He cannot start the application at a priority of Realtime because that process would consume so much of the processor resources it would make most the of the other processes effectively cease to function. The only choice he is left with is to start the application at high priority. For more information, see the section "Maintaining Windows 32-Bit Applications."

8. **A.** An alert is the only method that will tell Monty when something happens; System Monitor and trace logs will record the occurrence, but they are both passive and have to be checked. PhysicalDisk does not have a counter that monitors %Free Space, so he must use LogicalDisk. For more information, see the section "Monitoring and Optimizing System Resource Use."

9. **D.** William's batch file will do nothing. Restore is not an option available from the command line. For more information, see the section "Backing Up System State and User Data Using Windows 2000 Backup."

APPLY YOUR KNOWLEDGE

10. **D.** Beverly is correct in thinking she must run DISKPERF. The execution of DISKPERF sets a startup flag to turn on or off disk counters and must always be accompanied by a system restart. -yd is the default, and it starts only the physical counters. -nv turns off the logical disk counters. -y turns on both the physical and logical counters (-yv would have also worked because it turns on only logical counters). For more information, see the section "Monitoring and Optimizing System Resource Use."

11. **B.** The sudden increase in interrupts generally indicates that a piece of hardware has just gone into an altered state and should be repaired or replaced. For more information, see the section "Monitoring and Optimizing System Resource Use."

12. **B.** To back up (and hence recover) the Registry, you must back up the system state information for a local server. For more information, see the section "Saving System State and User Data with Windows 2000 Backup."

13. **D.** Although he is on the right track, Wesley has missed out on an important requirement: Data loss (and downtime) must never last more than 12 hours. By scheduling a backup for once a week, he cannot come anywhere near that promise unless the data loss occurred late in the day on the day the backup was done. For more information, see the section "Recovering System State and User Data with Windows 2000 Backup."

14. **A.** Through the use of correct backup schedules, Tasha has ensured that the required result is met. Without any other plans in place, she can also recover from start file loss by using the startup disk set and the emergency repair process (she does not need an ERD to do this). In addition, with the startup disks, she can also boot to the Recovery console to stop faulty services from starting. For more information, see the sections "Server, System State, and User Data Recovery."

15. **B.** Tuning means optimizing a server for its intended task. Although you may remove certain components or modify component properties because of security or other considerations, tuning needs to be done with reference to the expected tasks the server will perform. For more information, see the section, "Monitoring and Optimizing System Resource Use."

APPLY YOUR KNOWLEDGE

Suggested Readings and Resources

1. Microsoft Windows 2000 Server Resource Kit: *Microsoft Windows 2000 Server Operations Guide* (Microsoft Press)

   • Part 2 (Chapters 5–10): Performance Monitoring

   • Part 3 (Chapters 11–13): System Recovery

2. *Microsoft Windows 2000 Professional Resource Kit* (Microsoft Press)

   • Chapter 18: Removable Storage and Backup

   • Part 6 (Chapters 27–30): Performance Monitoring

3. Microsoft Official Curriculum course 1556: *Administering Microsoft Windows 2000*

   • Module 10: Backing Up and Restoring Data

4. Microsoft Official Curriculum course 1558: *Advanced Administration for Microsoft Windows 2000*

   • Module 10: Implementing Disaster Recovery

5. Microsoft Official Curriculum course 1560: *Updating Support Skills from Microsoft Windows NT 4.0 to Microsoft Windows 2000*

   • Module 16: Implementing Disaster Protection

6. Microsoft Official Curriculum course 2152: *Supporting Microsoft Windows 2000 Professional and Server*

   • Module 12: Monitoring and Optimizing Performance in Windows 2000

   • Module 13: Implementing Disaster Protection

7. Web Sites

   • www.microsoft.com/windows2000

   • www.microsoft.com/train_cert

This chapter will help you prepare for the "Managing, Configuring, and Troubleshooting Storage Use" section of the exam.

Microsoft provides the following objectives for "Managing, Configuring, and Troubleshooting Storage Use":

Configure and manage user profiles.

▶ This objective is necessary because someone certified in the use of Windows 2000 Server technology must understand how to create and manage local, roaming, and mandatory profiles.

Monitor, configure, and troubleshoot disks and volumes.

▶ This objective is necessary because someone certified in the use of Windows 2000 Server technology must understand both basic and dynamic disks. In addition, an understanding of the different partitions and volumes is necessary, as well as an understanding of the scenarios in which to use them.

Configure data compression.

▶ This objective is necessary because someone certified in the use of Windows 2000 Server technology must understand how NTFS volumes can support file compression. An understanding of how to apply compression and the implications of compressing a disk and folder is also necessary.

CHAPTER 5

Managing, Configuring, and Troubleshooting Storage Use

STUDY STRATEGIES

▶ In this chapter, two sections outline features of Windows 2000 that were not present in Windows NT: dynamic disks and disk quotas. You can definitely expect to see questions on these two topics on the Windows 2000 Server exam.

▶ As it pertains to profiles, you will need to understand the types of profiles and their function. You will need to understand the implications of using local versus roaming profiles and how each is configured. In addition, you will need to know how mandatory profiles can be configured and when you would want to use them. Furthermore, you need to know that mandatory profiles do not prevent users from making changes to their environments; it just prevents them from saving those changes to be used in their next session. Finally, you need to understand how to configure user accounts to use profiles.

▶ The exam questions regarding disks will almost exclusively be directed toward dynamic disks, the preferred disk type in Windows 2000. Be sure that you understand what each of the dynamic types are, how they are created, and what their properties are. In addition, you need to know their strengths and their limitations. You should also understand the concept of mounting volumes inside NTFS folders. Finally, you need to understand the recovery techniques for Mirror volume and RAID-5 volume failures.

▶ Data compression is not new to Windows 2000, but there is bound to be a question dealing with it. Make sure you know how to turn it on at the volume, folder, and file level and the implications of turning it on for each.

▶ Disk quotas are new, so you can expect one or two questions dealing with them. Understand the implications of imposing quotas and whom they apply to. In addition, know how to remove them if that becomes necessary.

▶ As with the other chapters, going through the material in this chapter is the beginning of understanding it. Then you should do the labs and return to the Step by Step examples and attempt to implement them. As I mention in every chapter, you need to do these things in order to understand the concepts. Having a server with a hard drive on which you can create, format, and delete partitions is essential to being able to apply and understand these concepts.

INTRODUCTION

Many Windows 2000 domain member servers function wholly or in part as data repositories (file servers). Many administrative tasks are required to manage this data. From creating volumes and partitions for storing this data, to setting quotas to prevent individual users from consuming all the available disk space, to recovering from disk failures, the tasks are diverse. This chapter deals with the theory and tasks required to maintain data on Windows 2000 servers. For the exam, you need to be familiar with all these topics.

CREATING AND MAINTAINING USER PROFILES

Configure and manage user profiles.

The idea that each user on a local area network has a single computer that only he or she logs in from is foreign to most network environments. Even if that is the rule in an organization, there will invariably be a time when one person logs on to the network from someone else's machine. The concept behind the user profile is that separate user settings are stored for each person, and that a user can maintain his or her own desktop settings without affecting other people who use the same computer. This can be taken a step further using roaming profiles. Roaming profiles allow the desktop settings a person has at one computer to be available at any computer to which that person logs on; no matter where he or she is, the desktop will always be the same.

Windows 2000 provides for three kinds of user profiles: local, roaming, and mandatory. *Local profiles* are stored on a specific computer and are available only from that computer. They are created automatically for each user who logs on and will retain desktop settings for each user from session to session.

Roaming profiles are stored in a central location (for example, on a file server) and accessed when a user logs on to any domain-activated machine. One roaming profile is created for each user, and it retains desktop settings from session to session.

Mandatory profiles are roaming profiles that have been designated read-only. When mandatory profiles are applied, they do not retain settings from session to session. A user's desktop will always appear the same upon logon, regardless of what he or she did to it in the last session. (No user changes are saved.)

Local User Profiles

Without any configuration, local user profiles are the norm for Windows 2000 logins. By default, Windows 2000 wants to allow each person who logs in to a specific machine to be able to maintain a unique desktop look.

Table 5.1 outlines the settings that are stored in a user profile.

TABLE 5.1

USER PROFILE COMPONENTS

Component	Contents
Application data	Information that is user-specific for particular programs. This might extend to things like special user-configured spell-check dictionaries. The amount of separate information stored in the user profile for an application is determined by the developers of the application, not by Windows 2000.
Cookies	User information and preferences as defined by Web applications.
Desktop	All desktop items including files, shortcuts, and folders.
Favorites	Internet shortcuts.
Local Settings	Application data, history, and temporary files.
My Documents	The My Documents folder and its contents.
My Network Places	Configuration of the network neighborhood.
Printers	Printer shortcuts.
Recent Documents	Shortcuts to recently accessed documents and folders.
SendTo	Configuration of the send-to menu.
Start Menu	Shortcuts to programs in the Start menu.
Templates	Any user templates.
NTUSER.DAT	The Registry settings that are included in a user's environment. This corresponds to the Registry subkey HKEY_CURRENT_USER.

The local user profile for a user is created in this way. The first time a user logs into a Windows 2000 computer, the default profile is copied into a profile with his or her user name associated with it. Then the All Users profile is consulted to determine what items are also to be applied to this user.

Local user profiles do not have to be maintained by an administrator because they are updated automatically by Windows 2000 when each user logs off. Local user profiles are stored in the Documents and Settings folder on the System partition.

Roaming User Profiles

Roaming user profiles perform the same function as local user profiles. The difference is that whereas local user profiles are always accessed locally on the machine a user is logging in on, roaming profiles are accessed over the network from a central location. This allows the same profile (and, therefore, the same configuration) to be accessed from anywhere on the network.

The creation of a roaming profile always follows the same basic steps:

1. Configure a shared folder on a server to hold the roaming profiles.

2. Create a folder within the shared folder for each user who is going to be roaming. The name of the folder should be the user's login name.

3. Copy an existing profile into the folder for each user. (If you do not do this, a profile will be created for the user using the default and All Users profiles of the machine being used.)

4. Configure the user's account to point to the roaming location.

To get a profile to copy into the roaming location, it is helpful to create a user account with a local profile that you can configure the way you want each roaming user's desktop to start out. If the user is being converted from a local profile to a roaming profile, copy that local profile to the user's roaming location. The following Step by Step illustrates how to do this.

> **NOTE**
>
> **Default Is Static; All Users Is Dynamic** The copying of the default user profile is a one-time-only task. If the default user profile is changed, it will not retroactively modify user profiles. On the other hand, the All Users profile is completely dynamic. Any modifications made to it will immediately result in changes to the current user's environment and will affect all users who subsequently log in.

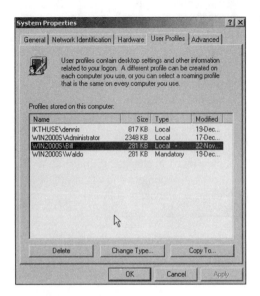

FIGURE 5.1
All the profiles created on this computer are listed here.

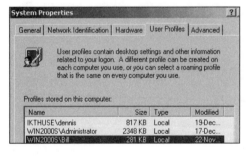

FIGURE 5.2
You can copy the profile to a local drive or to a network location.

STEP BY STEP

5.1 Copying a Local Profile to a Roaming Location

1. From the computer that holds the local profile you want to copy, right-click the My Computer icon and choose Properties from the menu that appears.

2. In the System Properties dialog box, click the User Profiles tab (see Figure 5.1).

3. From the User Profiles property sheet, select the profile you want to copy, and then click the Copy To button.

4. In the Copy To dialog box, type (or browse to) the path you want to copy the profile to (see Figure 5.2). You can also configure security on the new profile by clicking the Change button and selecting who will be allowed to access this profile. Click OK to continue.

5. Close the System Properties dialog box.

After you create the roaming profile, you must change the user account to point to that profile. This is slightly different depending on whether you are configuring roaming profiles for local users or domain users. Although this book does not deal with Windows 2000 Server as a domain controller, it is helpful to know this for both.

In both cases, you will have to modify the profile location for the user. Step by Steps 5.2 and 5.3, respectively, show you the procedures for pointing to a local Windows 2000 server and a Windows 2000 domain controller running Active Directory.

STEP BY STEP

5.2 Pointing a Local User to a Roaming Profile

1. From the Start menu, choose Programs, Administrative Tools, Computer Management.

2. Expand the tree Computer Management\System Tools\Local Users and Groups and click the Users folder. This will display the local users in the right panel.

3. Double-click the user you want to modify.

4. In the User Properties dialog box, click the Profile tab (see Figure 5.3).

5. On the Profile property sheet, type the path to the roaming profile in the Profile Path field Path. Click OK to continue.

6. Close the Computer Management console.

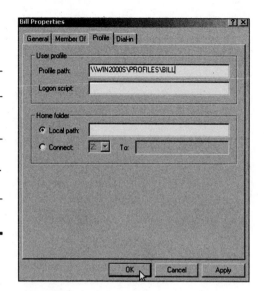

Pointing an Active Directory user to a roaming profile is done in almost the same manner.

FIGURE 5.3
The user's properties can include the path to a roaming profile.

STEP BY STEP

5.3 Pointing an Active Directory User to a Roaming Profile

1. From the Start menu, choose Programs, Administrative Tools, Active Directory Users and Computers.

2. In the Active Directory Users and Computers console, expand the Active Directory Users and Computers\ *yourdomain*\Users tree. This will display a list of Active Directory users in the right panel.

3. In the User Properties dialog box, click the Profile tab, and then enter the path to the roaming profile in the Profile Path text box. Click OK to continue.

4. Close the Active Directory Users and Groups console.

Mandatory User Profiles

There are some cases in which a user's profile should not be changed by a user. For times when company politics or procedures require that a user's desktop remain constant, a mandatory profile can be created.

Mandatory profiles are a special subclass of roaming profiles. It's important to note this for two reasons. First, the procedure for creating and accessing a mandatory profile is almost identical to that for creating and accessing a roaming profile. Second, configuring a local profile to be mandatory, although possible, will not work any differently than configuring a regular local profile (for example, the profile will still be changeable by the user).

There are two primary differences between a mandatory profile and a roaming profile. Mandatory profiles are read-only and are meant to be accessed by more than one user.

The reason for the roaming profile is that each user can have a configuration unique from everyone else's but can access it (and modify it) from any place on the network. With a mandatory profile, because it is read-only, it could be used by many users. In fact, if you group your users into functional groups, each functional group may require a different desktop, and you could be forced to create a mandatory profile for each group.

The creation of a mandatory profile always follows the same basic steps:

1. Configure a shared folder on a server to hold the mandatory profile(s). (It could be the same one that holds the roaming profiles.)

2. Create a folder within the shared folder for each mandatory profile.

3. Copy an existing profile into the folder.

4. Change the NTUSER.DAT file to NTUSER.MAN.

5. Configure each user's account to the mandatory location.

The key to the read-only status is the set of Registry entries held in the NTUSER.DAT file. The Registry contains the configuration settings that define most of the operations of your server. One component of the Registry is a tree (a set of Registry settings) called HKEY_CURRENT_USER. This set of Registry settings is represented on your hard drive by a file called NTUSER.DAT. This file is stored in each user's profile, and it defines the Registry settings for the user (which in turn defines the user's desktop environment).

To make this file read-only, simply change the extension from .DAT to .MAN, thereby making the file NTUSER.MAN. By doing this, you can ensure that users who access a profile with such a file will be able to change desktop settings but only for the duration of their login session. When the user logs out, the NTUSER.MAN file will not be updated, so the settings will not be changed. The user will be faced with the same initial desktop for every session. If you want to prevent the user from making changes in even the current session, you must implement local policies, which are discussed in Chapter 7, "Implementing, Monitoring, and Troubleshooting Security." To create a mandatory profile, follow these steps:

STEP BY STEP

5.4 Creating a Mandatory Profile

1. From the computer that holds the local profile you want to copy, right-click the My Computer icon and choose Properties from the menu that appears.

2. From the System Properties dialog box, click the User Profiles tab.

3. From the User Profiles property sheet, select the profile you want to copy, and then click the Copy To button.

4. In the Copy To dialog box, type (or browse to) the path you want to copy the profile to. You can also configure security on the new profile by clicking the Change button and selecting who will be allowed to access this profile (this works only when the profile is being held on an NTFS partition). Click OK to continue.

continues

continued

5. Close the System Properties dialog box.

6. Using My Computer or Windows Explorer, navigate to the Profiles share and open the folder that represents the profile you want to make mandatory.

7. Rename the file NTUSER.DAT as NTUSER.MAN.

The procedure for pointing a user to a mandatory profile is the same as pointing to a roaming profile.

CONFIGURING DISKS AND VOLUMES

Monitor, configure, and troubleshoot disks and volumes.

Before you can install and run a Windows 2000 server, you must begin with storage locations, and those usually happen on hard drives. As the size of a drive increases, you will sometimes find that having the entire drive as one huge partition is not practical or useful, so you need to be able to define smaller volumes that define logical disks, even when there is only one physical disk.

System and Boot Partitions

Two important terms you will hear (and probably be tested on) with reference to Windows 2000 Server are System partition and Boot partition. Because these terms are used quite often when referring to the location of specific files and with reference to certain functionality, it is important for you to understand the distinction.

When your Intel-based Windows 2000 server starts, the first thing that happens at the BIOS level is that the Master Boot Record is sought out. This record tells the computer what to do to get an operating system loaded. This Master Boot Record is always on the first sector of the hard disk with the partition table. The Master Boot Record points to the active partition on the hard drive. The

Active Partition can be set from within Windows 2000, but it is most often determined before Windows 2000 is even installed. Generally, utilities like FDISK will be used to set the active partition.

Windows 2000 refers to the location of the active partition as the System partition. When the BIOS of your computer determines which partition is the system partition, it looks to that partition to tell it how to begin operating system boot. On the System partition, there is a small amount of boot code that looks further to some special files Windows 2000 uses to start the operating system. These files are BOOT.INI, NTDETECT.COM, and NTLDR. The location of these files is the System partition.

When the System partition has been located and the operating system begins to start, the bootstrap code finds the location of the operating system files. It does so by consulting the BOOT.INI file, which indicates the physical location of the folder containing those files; usually it is WINNT. The partition on which that folder is located is referred to as the Boot partition. After the operating system has started, Windows 2000 no longer needs the files on the System partition; however, it needs the files on the Boot partition as long as the server is running.

The distinction between the System partition and the Boot partition is sometimes purely definitional. They are spoken of separately to distinguish the function of each group of files in the starting and running of Windows 2000. However, your server generally has only one partition (usually the C: drive), which is home to both the System and the Boot partition. However, for the exam, you will need to know how the two partitions can be distinguished.

ARC Paths and Volumes/Partitions

The BOOT.INI file (located on the System partition) contains the path to the Windows 2000 files (the Boot partition). To accurately define the location of these files, Windows 2000 uses a convention called ARC paths. Advanced RISC Computing (ARC) standards are conventions adopted by a variety of vendors that allow a piece of hardware to be defined by physical characteristics instead of by labels provided in the user interface of an operating system. As it relates to partitions and volumes in Windows 2000, it allows Windows 2000 to locate sections of a hard drive based not on an arbitrary lettering convention (F: defines a user handle to a volume, not a physical location) but on the physical location of a particular section of a drive.

The BOOT.INI file, in its simplest form, defines the location of a single operating system's boot files on a computer. More complex versions of BOOT.INI exist where more than one operating system is available to boot from. When more than one operating system is available, at system startup you will be presented with a menu that allows you to choose the operating system you want to start.

This is a sample BOOT.INI file:

```
[boot loader]
timeout=20
default=multi(0)disk(0)rdisk(0)partition(1)\WINNT
[operating systems]
multi(0)disk(0)rdisk(0)partition(1)\WINNT="Microsoft
➡Windows 2000 Server" /fastdetect
```

In the preceding example, the line beginning *timeout=* defines the length of time the system will wait before booting the default operating system. In the case of a single operating system to boot (like this example), the system will start Windows 2000 Server immediately; the 20 second delay will be invoked only if there is more than one operating system to choose from.

The next line, *default=*, defines the location of the default operating system; that definition is an ARC path to the WINNT folder. This line should correspond to an entry listed beneath the *[operating systems]* label. If it does not, when the system is started, a menu will appear showing *Windows 2000 Server* and *Default*. If that happens, the BOOT.INI file has been manually configured incorrectly, and you should repair it before starting your server again.

The entries under the label *[operating systems]* define the operating systems that are bootable from this BOOT.INI file. For Windows 2000 servers in production environments, the only other option you might see here is a boot to the *Recovery console*. Otherwise a single entry is all you should see. For Windows 2000 Professional or Windows 2000 computers in test labs, you might find numerous operating systems to boot.

The ARC specification for volumes and partitions (ARC path) defines physical location based on four parameters: the disk controller, the physical hard drive on the controller, the partition on the physical hard drive, and the folder on the partition.

The ARC path is organized in a tree. Each hard drive has its own partition 0, and each controller might have its own hard drives. This means that a unique ARC path requires each of the components (controller, drive, partition, folder) to be defined, not just one piece.

The full syntax for an ARC path can consist of one of two sets of parameters:

```
multi(0)disk(0)rdisk(0)partition(1)\Ospath
```

or

```
scsi(0)disk(0)rdisk(0)partition(1)\Ospath
```

The first one is far more common than the second, but you might encounter either one.

In an ARC path, the first parameter (multi or scsi) defines the type of controller to which the hard drive is attached. *Multi* indicates that the controller is either non-SCSI (IDE, EIDE, and so on) or is SCSI with the BIOS enabled. Most PC-based controllers fall into this category. *SCSI* indicates that the controller is SCSI with the BIOS disabled. This parameter's numbering scheme begins with 0, so the first controller is either *multi(0)* or *scsi(0)*.

The second ARC parameter is the number of the hard drive. This parameter consists of the pair of values *disk(x)rdisk(y)*. In this pair, only one value (either *x* or *y*) is significant. Which is significant depends on the controller type. If the controller is *multi*, the disk parameter to watch is *rdisk*. Conversely, if the controller is *scsi*, the disk parameter to watch is *disk*. Regardless of the controller type, both elements of the parameter pair must be present. Like the controller number, disk numbers begin with 0; the first disk on a controller is numbered 0.

The third ARC parameter is *partition(z)*. This defines the physical partition number of the volume that you want the path to point to. Unlike for the controller and drive, the numbering for partition begins at 1.

The final parameter is the folder on the partition that you want to point to. This is defined simply by using the name you would see when you looked in Windows Explorer or My Computer.

The numbers for controllers depend on the physical position in which they are installed in the computer. The numbers for hard drives are determined by their physical location on the cable attached to the controller. These two numbering systems are fixed unless you physically move components around in the computer.

Confusion inevitably arises when it comes to determining the number of the system partition from which Windows 2000 boots.

Only volumes or partitions with true ARC paths can be the location of the System or Boot partition for Windows 2000 operating systems. Moreover, the only volumes or partitions with true ARC paths must have at one time been a primary or logical partition on a basic disk (see the next section for details).

The exam does not deal with multiple boot scenarios because the idea of bringing a production server offline to boot another operating system is not reasonable. Moreover, the introduction of dynamic disks (to be covered in the upcoming section "The Dynamic Disk") makes the ARC path specification less useful as well for more than two partitions on each drive.

What is important to know is that each bootable partition has an ARC path defined, and that ARC path must be correct in the BOOT.INI file in order for Windows 2000 Server to start properly. If you have problems booting because the ARC path is incorrect, you can boot to the Recovery console and issue a MAP ARC command to find out what the ARC path is for your bootable partition. You can then copy a BOOT.INI file onto your hard drive that matches your hardware configuration.

As for the rest of the disk structure, all the storage areas on your hard drives are defined as either basic disks or dynamic disks. The next sections will define those terms.

The Basic Disk

The disk structure known as the basic disk is the industry standard for disk configuration across all PC operating systems. Whether you are working with OS/2, Windows 9x, or DOS, all support basic disk structures. This means that if you have a computer on which multiple operating systems are installed, all will be able to read the partition information. Because it is often useful to divide your disks into distinct logical units, basic disks support subdivision into two major types (or partitions): primary and extended. A *primary partition* is one that can be made bootable and is where the Active Boot record is stored for an operating system. As a result, every machine must have a primary partition, and the operating system is typically installed there. On most machines, this would be the C: drive.

A basic disk supports up to four primary partitions. In the history of such disks, having only four partitions on a hard drive was deemed to be too limiting. So another partition type was introduced into the standard—the *extended partition.*

On a single hard drive, you can have only one extended partition. Coupled with the fact that you can have only four partitions in total on a hard drive, this means you can combine partitions in only a limited number of combinations. Figure 5.4 shows two ways a disk could be configured using basic disk structures.

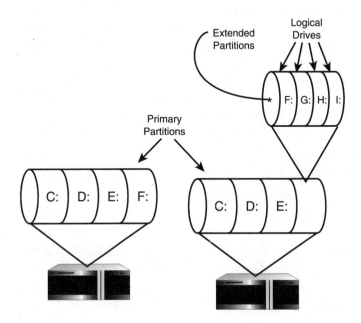

FIGURE 5.4

Using the basic disk structure, a physical disk can consist of up to four primary partitions or up to three primary partitions with one extended partition. An extended partition can be subdivided into an unlimited number of logical drives (theoretically).

Despite not being bootable, the extended partition has an advantage over the primary partition: In theory, it can be subdivided into endless numbers of logical drives. (Usually, you only subdivide into as many sections as there are letters to identify them with; however, with the new drive mounting features this is not necessary.) As a result, a system that had the capability of having only four partitions can now appear to have 10 or 20 because of logical drives.

All these partition and logical drive types can be seen by all operating systems, and this is the default structure on a hard drive under Windows 2000. If, however, you want to introduce fault tolerance into your disk system (which enables you to easily recover from disk failure), you will need to consider another disk type: the dynamic disk.

The Dynamic Disk

The term *dynamic disk* is new for Windows 2000, but the kinds of utilities available as a result are not new and have been available since the early days of Windows NT. A dynamic disk is one that consists of a single partition that is identified as dynamic (either when it's created or when it's converted from basic) and then subdivided into volumes. This can be done before or after a basic disk has been subdivided into partitions (the conversion program takes care of amalgamating the existing partitions and creating volumes out of them). A dynamic disk is a proprietary structure that is readable only by Windows 2000. Therefore, any data held on a dynamic disk cannot be read by other locally booting operating systems.

Within a dynamic disk, the following volume types can be created: Simple, Spanned, Mirrored, Striped, and RAID-5. Each of these has its advantages and disadvantages, which the following discussion will look at in depth.

As a production server, Windows 2000 Server will never be configured to dual-boot, so there is no reason not to immediately convert your basic disks to dynamic disks. Although this chapter will give you instructions on how to create partitions on a basic disk, it is recommended that you do not leave your disks as basic disks.

The Simple Volume

The simple volume is the most straightforward of the volume types. It is one or more segments of free space coming from a single hard drive with a letter identifying it. A simple volume is not fault tolerant because it is only a single entity and has no redundancy built into it. You can resize a simple volume by converting it to a spanned volume (provided that it was created originally as a simple volume). If it was created as a partition on a basic disk that was subsequently converted to a simple volume on a dynamic disk, it cannot be resized nor made part of a spanned volume.

A simple volume that was converted from a primary or logical partition on a basic disk has special properties. It is, in fact, the only partition type that can be home to the System or Boot partition of a Windows 2000 Server implementation. If you create a simple volume from scratch, it does not have a true ARC path and, therefore, cannot be booted from.

The Spanned Volume

The spanned volume is one that consists of fragments of disk space from between 2 and 32 different hard drives. These fragments of disk space are treated as a single drive and have a single letter associated with them. Spanned volumes are not fault-tolerant and, in fact, if any of the pieces are removed (either from disk failure or by manually breaking the volume), all the information is lost.

The fragments that are joined together do not have to be the same size. When the volume is filled, each piece is filled in turn before the space on the next is used.

Planning is important when you're thinking about spanned volumes. If you begin with a basic disk and format it using partitions (primary, extended, and logical), you can convert those partitions to simple volumes. However, once converted, these volumes can never become spanned volumes. For you to create a spanned volume, your volume must have been created as a simple volume, never as a basic disk partition that was converted to a simple volume.

The Mirrored Volume

A *mirrored volume* (sometimes referred to as RAID level 1) consists of two pieces of disk space on two hard drives. These two segments of space, like the spanned volume, are treated as a single drive and have a single drive letter associated with them. However, unlike the spanned volume, the total amount of storage space is not the accumulation of the two segments but the size of only one. Both pieces need to be the same size in a mirrored volume (but these pieces do not have to be taken from hard drives of the same size).

The basic function of mirroring is to provide redundancy and fault tolerance by writing the same information to two separate locations. One segment of space is used as a dynamic backup of the other. If the mirrored volume had a drive letter of D:, when a user wrote to the D: drive, two copies of the information would be written. This ensures that if either of the hard drives experiences a failure, there is always another copy of all the data available to recover from. In addition, mirroring also provides improved read capabilities because either disk could be accessed for information, and both could be concurrently accessed for different information, thus improving a disk's read throughput.

Any information can be stored on a mirrored volume, including the Boot and System partitions. However, in order for a mirrored volume to include the Boot or System partition, it must have been created from a volume that was originally a primary or logical partition.

One variation of the mirrored volume is referred to as a *duplexed mirror*. Duplexing, which is not software based but hardware based, is simply a mirrored volume that consists of disks controlled by different disk controllers. This ensures that a controller failure will not cause both disks to fail at the same time.

The Striped Volume

Striped volumes, like spanned volumes, consist of between 2 and 32 chunks of free space joined together. There are some differences between them, however. Whereas a spanned volume could consist of free space from a single hard drive, striped volumes must have free space from multiple hard drives. In addition, whereas the free space in spanned volumes does not need to be the same size, the pieces in a striped volume do. The reason for that comes down to the way in which the information is written to a striped volume. In a spanned volume, the information is written into one piece of free space at a time. The next segment of the spanned volume is not populated until the previous is full. In a striped volume, data is written to the volume in 64KB blocks across each segment of the volume. In this way, the stripes that are created span the volumes. Like the spanned volume, the removal of any free space causes all the data in the volume to be lost. Therefore, this kind of volume is not fault tolerant.

Like the spanned volume, a striped volume cannot hold the System or Boot partition of a Windows 2000 system.

The RAID-5 Volume

RAID-5 is a term that originally came from the hardware industry. The term RAID is an acronym for Redundant Array of Inexpensive Disks and was originally strictly implemented with hardware (multiple hard drives that functioned as one unit). RAID-5 is the implementation of a stripe set with parity to provide redundancy and recoverability in the case of a hard disk crash. The RAID-5 volume is the Windows 2000 implementation of stripe sets with parity and provides fault tolerance in systems where hardware RAID arrays are cost prohibitive or in other ways not desired. This volume type was referred to as a "stripe set with parity" in Windows NT.

RAID-5 volumes have all the features of the striped volume except that they require at least three hard drives (and as many as 32). What sets them apart is the presence of parity information written as part of each stripe. This parity information ensures that if a single hard drive is lost, the data on the remaining drives will continue to be available. Upon loss of a disk from the set, the volume will continue to be available, although performance is greatly reduced because of the calculations required to rebuild the missing drive from the existing data plus the parity. However, once repaired, the volume will operate as though no problem ever occurred.

The one drawback of the RAID-5 volume is the loss of some of the data area to this parity information. If x represents the total number of hard drives across which the RAID-5 volume is implemented, the total amount of usable space can be calculated with the following formula: $(x-1)/x$. For example, if you were to create a RAID-5 volume from five 1GB segments of free space, the usable area is (5–1)/5 or 80% of the total hard drive space. That would leave you with 4GB of the original 5GB because 1GB would be used to maintain the fault tolerance.

RAID-5 volumes have moderate write performance (reduced because the parity information must be calculated as the data changes) but excellent read performance because the data is stored on many hard drives, all of which can be accessed independently of one another.

Like striped volumes, RAID-5 volumes cannot be used to hold the System or Boot partition of a Windows 2000 installation.

IN THE FIELD

FAULT TOLERANCE PUTS STRAIN ON YOUR SERVER

All fault-tolerant disk volumes (mirrors and RAID-5) require additional overhead (processor and memory). This is a result of maintenance of the fault-tolerant data as it is being written to the volume. The performance change in your Windows 2000 server may or may not be significant to you or your user community. In a system dedicated to storage of data or retrieval of data, you may see noticeable increases or decreases in system performance when using this fault tolerance method.

In a system in which the primary operation a user performs is queries on a database, the increase in read performance may be significant in terms of throughput. If the system is designed to store data, mirroring may produce disk bottlenecks. You may only know whether these are significant by setting up two identical computers, implementing mirroring on one and not on the other, and then running Performance Monitor on both under simulated load to see the performance differences. For more information on monitoring, see Chapter 4, "Managing, Monitoring, and Optimizing System Performance, Reliability, and Availability."

REVIEW BREAK

Table 5.2 summarizes the characteristics of the partition and volume types described in the previous sections.

TABLE 5.2

PARTITIONS AND VOLUMES IN SUMMARY

Characteristic	Basic		Dynamic				
	Primary Partition	*Extended Partition*	*Simple Volume*	*Spanned Volume*	*Mirrored Volume*	*Striped Volume*	*RAID-5 Volume*
System partition	Yes	No	Yes	No	Yes	No	No
Boot partition	Yes	Yes	Yes	No	Yes	No	No
Fault tolerant	No	No	No	No	Yes	No	Yes
Space utilization	100%	100%	100%	100%	50%	100%	$(n/1)/n*100\%$
Drives required	1	1	1	2	2	2	3
Number of pieces that make it up	1	1	1–32	2–32	2	2–32	3–32
Pieces must be on different drives	n/a	n/a	No	Yes	Yes	Yes	Yes
Formats supported	All	All	All	All	All	All	All
Accessible locally by non-2000 OS if FAT	Yes	Yes	No	No	No	No	No
Read performance	Avg	Avg	Avg	Avg	Up	Up	Up
Write performance	Avg	Avg	Avg	Avg	Down	Up	Down

The Disk Manager

Partitions and volumes are more than theory. Of course, you need a tool to be able to create and manage partitions and volumes. That tool is the Disk Manager, and it is a sub-component of the Computer Management console.

The next Step by Step shows how to start the Disk Manager.

STEP BY STEP

5.5 Starting the Disk Manager

1. From the Start menu, choose Programs, Administrative Tools, Computer Management.

2. Under Computer Management, expand the Storage tree and click the Disk Management entry. This will display the disk configuration on the right side (see Figure 5.5).

3. If desired, change the disk view that is displayed in the top or bottom pane by right-clicking the Disk Management entry on the left, choosing Top (or Bottom), and then selecting the view you want to display.

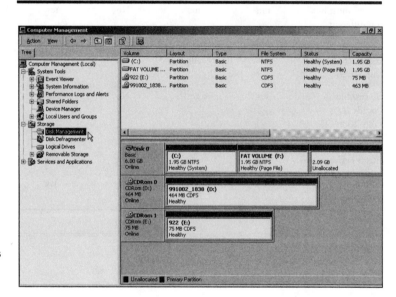

FIGURE 5.5
The Disk Manager consists of two panes. By default, the top one shows the lettered partitions and volumes; the bottom one shows the hard drives and the partitions and volumes on each.

Maintaining Partitions on Basic Disks

If you choose to keep your disks as basic, you will be able to maintain the logical drives as partitions. Partition maintenance involves the following tasks:

◆ Creating a new partition

◆ Deleting a partition

◆ Formatting a partition

◆ Changing the drive letter

◆ Marking a primary partition as active

Creating Partitions

Using the Disk Manager, you can create three kinds of partitions: primary, extended, and logical. You can create a primary partition in any free space, as long as that free space is not contained in an extended partition and as long as there are not already four primary partitions. A primary partition is created when you want to configure a partition to boot from or when you do not need more than four partitions on a disk in total.

Step by Step 5.6 walks you through creating a primary partition on a basic disk.

STEP BY STEP

5.6 Creating a Primary Partition on a Basic Disk

1. Open the Disk Manager.

2. Locate free disk space that is not contained within an existing extended partition, right-click it, and choose Create Partition from the menu that appears (see Figure 5.6).

continues

continued

FIGURE 5.6
Right-click on free space in a basic disk to create a new partition.

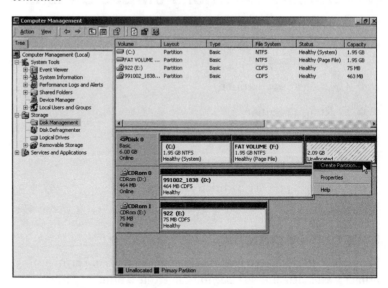

3. At the Welcome to the Create Partition Wizard screen, click Next.

4. At the Select Partition Type screen, choose the Primary Partition radio button (see Figure 5.7). Click Next to continue.

5. At the Specify Partition Size screen, enter a partition size between the minimum and maximum sizes displayed (see Figure 5.8). Click Next to continue.

6. At the Assign Drive Letter or Path screen, you can assign the next available letter or mount the partition in an empty NTFS folder on another driver, or you can leave the drive without a label (see Figure 5.9). Mounting will be discussed later in this chapter. Leaving the drive without a label will render it unusable until you assign a label to it. For the purpose of this Step by Step, select Assign a Drive Letter and click Next.

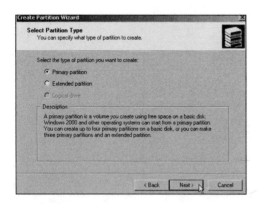

FIGURE 5.7
In unallocated free space, you can create a primary or an extended partition.

7. At the Format Partition screen (see Figure 5.10), choose whether you want to format the partition and, if you do, what file system you want to use. Whether you choose NTFS, FAT, or FAT32, you can then choose the Allocation Unit Size (a measure of how large the blocks of allocated space are) and the Volume Label. You can also choose whether to do a full format or a quick format (which simply writes a blank FAT instead of formatting it), and you can also enable compression. Because a later section will talk about the different formats, as well as compression, those features will not be discussed until then. Click Next to continue.

8. At the Completing the Create Partition Wizard screen, click Finish.

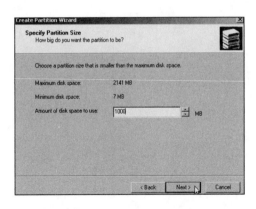

FIGURE 5.8
The partition can be any size up to the size of the free space in which you are creating it.

You might need to create an extended partition on a basic disk on which you want to create more than four partitions. An extended partition does nothing in itself, but it can be the container for a number of logical partitions (drives). Step by Step 5.7 outlines the process for creating an extended partition on a basic disk.

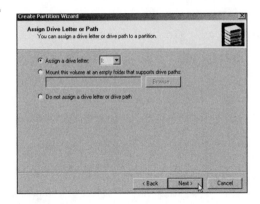

FIGURE 5.9
Most of the time, you will assign a letter to the new primary partition.

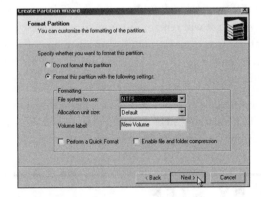

FIGURE 5.10
Choose the file system to format with: NTFS, FAT, or FAT32.

STEP BY STEP

5.7 Creating an Extended Partition on a Basic Disk

1. Open the Disk Manager.

2. Locate free disk space that is not contained within an existing extended partition, right-click it, and choose Create Partition from the menu that appears.

3. At the Welcome to the Create Partition Wizard screen, click Next.

4. At the Select Partition Type screen, choose the Extended Partition radio button. Click Next to continue.

5. At the Specify Partition Size screen, enter a partition size between the minimum and maximum sizes displayed. Click Next to continue.

6. At the Completing the Create Partition Wizard screen, click Finish.

If you created an extended partition, the new partition should appear in a different color than the primary partitions you already have. The free space will remain, but now if you look closely, you will see that the free space is contained inside a box of another color (by default, extended partitions are dark green, and the free space within is lime green).

Within an extended partition, you can create one or more logical partitions. The following steps illustrate the process of establishing such a partition.

STEP BY STEP

5.8 Creating a Logical Partition in an Extended Partition

1. Open the Disk Manager.

2. Right-click free space within an extended partition and choose Create Logical Drive from the menu that appears (see Figure 5.11).

3. At the Welcome to the Create Partition Wizard screen, click Next.

4. At the Select Partition Type screen, choose Logical Drive. Click Next to continue.

5. At the Specify Partition Size screen, enter a partition size between the minimum and maximum sizes displayed. Click Next to continue.

6. At the Assign Drive Letter or Path screen, you can assign the next available letter, or mount the partition in an empty NTFS folder on another driver, or you can leave the drive without a label. Click Next to continue.

7. At the Format Partition screen, choose whether you want to format the partition and, if you do, which file system you want to use. You can also choose whether to do a full format or a quick format, and you can enable compression. Click Next to continue.

8. At the Completing the Create Partition Wizard screen, click Finish.

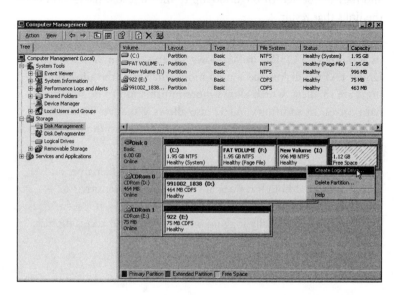

FIGURE 5.11

A logical drive (partition) can be created only in free space contained within an extended partition.

Deleting Partitions

Deleting a partition is not a complex process. What can be complex is recovering the data you lose if you delete a partition that you do not want to. Because deleting a partition deletes all the data that was on the partition, be careful when you delete partitions.

To delete a partition, right-click it and choose Delete from the menu that appears. When you're asked to confirm the deletion, click Yes.

Formatting Partitions

All drives must be formatted before information can be placed on them. Windows 2000 supports three kinds of file systems with which you can format drives: FAT, FAT32, and NTFS. In addition, Windows 2000 also supports CDFS for CD-ROMs, but you don't format drives with that file system. If you are planning to install more than one operating system on your computer (a plan that is ill-advised when talking about a server—unless it is a test machine), you will need to use FAT or FAT32. If you are not multi-booting, you should use NTFS.

FAT (File Allocation Table) was the original DOS file format. Is continues to be very popular for Windows and non-Windows operating systems alike. FAT uses a linked-list format to chain together files. A table contains pointers to the beginning of each list, and files are located through lookup to the table and navigation of the links that result.

FAT32 is simply an updated version of FAT that was implemented in Windows 95 OSR2, in Windows 98, and now in Windows 2000. Under FAT32, disk space is used more efficiently (the allocation units are smaller), which allows more information to be stored on hard drives. In addition, FAT32 also allows Windows 9x machines to create and use partitions larger than 2GB (something that was not possible under FAT).

Under Windows 2000, FAT/FAT32 supports long filenames and preserves case (although it does not recognize case sensitivity). FAT/FAT32 does not support local security—that is, not security as it pertains to users locally logging onto a system and accessing files.

Under NT 4.0, a case could be made for creating at least one FAT partition to enable access to the drives to solve boot problems. However, now that the Recovery console is available (see Chapter 4), that is not necessary. Under Windows 2000, FAT and FAT32 are recommended as file formats only if you are planning to install more than one operating system on your Windows 2000 machine. If, for example, you want to dual-boot Windows 2000 Server with Windows 98, you will need to format the active partition with FAT/FAT32. If you do not, Windows 98 will not be able to read from the hard drive and will not boot.

All the partition types can be formatted with FAT or FAT32. However, it is pointless to format any of the dynamic volume types as FAT because no other local operating system can read from them anyway.

NTFS is a proprietary file system that was introduced in the early days of NT. As a proprietary file system, it is readable by NT and Windows 2000 only. This means that in any multi-boot system, the non-NT or non-Windows 2000 operating system will not be able to read from a partition or volume formatted with NTFS. Under Windows 2000, the version of NTFS is 5. This version adds new features that were not present in Windows NT 4.0 (like file encryption). This means that not only does NTFS v.5 have advantages over FAT, but also has advantages over previous versions of NTFS.

NTFS has a number of advantages over FAT. One of the most significant is that NTFS is capable of locally securing files and folders on a partition or volume; this means that you can control who has access to files even when accessed locally by logging onto the machine.

Another feature that is significant is that built-in compression can be implemented at the directory and file levels (this contrasts with FAT compression methods, which must be done on a volume level). This compression is intrinsic to the file system and does not need to be installed. It provides on-the-fly compression and decompression with little loss of performance.

NTFS is, by its nature, a more efficient file storage medium than FAT. Using binary tree sorting, it can quickly store and retrieve data. In addition, it can theoretically be configured for partitions and

> **WARNING**
>
> **For Safety, Use FAT When Dual-Booting Windows 2000 and NT 4.0** Dual-booting an NT 4 system with Windows 2000 can be problematic. NTFS v4 (for Windows NT 4) and NTFS v5 (for Windows 2000) are only mostly compatible. That means new features used under Windows 2000 will render files inaccessible under NT 4. To ensure maximum compatibility, install the latest service packs on your Window NT 4.0 system. Microsoft recommends that to prevent surprises you use a FAT partition to share information.

volumes up to 16 exabytes (an exabyte is one billion gigabytes, or 2^{64} bytes). Practically, however, a partition of 2 terabytes (TB) is its upper limit. It is impossible to format a 1.44MB disk with NTFS, and it is recommended that you do not use it on partitions or volumes smaller than 500MB.

NTFS supports *sector sparing*, also known as *hot fixing*, on SCSI hard drives. If a sector fails on an NTFS partition of a SCSI hard drive, NTFS tries to write the data to a good sector (if the data is still in memory) and map out the bad sector so that it is not reused.

NTFS also keeps a transaction log while it works. If the power fails, leaving NTFS in a possibly corrupt state, the CHKDSK command, which executes when the system boots, attempts to either redo the transaction (in the case of a deletion, for example) or undo the transaction (in the case of a file-write where the data is no longer in memory).

One other new feature of NTFS under Windows 2000 is the ability to implement disk quotas to prevent users from using more than a specific amount of disk space on a server. In addition, local encryption is also available under NTFS in Windows 2000. This feature is supported by security subsystem enhancements and allows for files to be secured in such a way as to allow only the user who secured them to access those files. This feature is explained fully in Chapter 7.

You must use NTFS if you want to preserve existing permissions when you migrate files and directories from a NetWare server to a Windows 2000 Server system. In addition, if you want to allow Macintosh computers to access files on the partition through Windows NT's Services for Macintosh, you must format the partition for NTFS. And if you want a Windows 2000 server to support Windows 2000 domains and/or the Active Directory, you must use NTFS.

NOTE

Partitions Are Automatically Converted to NTFS v.5   If you upgrade a machine from Windows NT (SP3 or greater), all NTFS partitions will be automatically converted to NTFS v.5.

The following table shows a comparison in features between FAT and NTFS v.5 (the version available with Windows 2000) .

TABLE 5.3

A COMPARISON BETWEEN FAT, FAT32, AND NTFS

Feature	FAT	FAT32	NTFS (v. 5)
Maximum filename length	255	255	255
8.3 filename compatibility	Yes	Yes	Yes
Maximum file size	4GB	2TB	16EB
Maximum partition size	4GB	2TB	16EB
Recommended volume size	<500MB	512MB–32GB	>500MB
Directory structure	Linked list	Linked list	B-tree
Intrinsic local security	No	No	Yes
Intrinsic local encryption	No	No	Yes
Intrinsic compression	No	Yes	Yes
Supports disk quotas	No	No	Yes
Transaction tracking	No	No	Yes
Hot fixing	No	No	Yes
Overhead	1MB	1MB	4.5–10MB
Locally accessible MS-DOS	Yes	No	No
Locally accessible Win 95 OSR2	Yes	Yes	No
Locally accessible Win 98	Yes	Yes	No
Locally accessible OS/2	Yes	No	No
Locally accessible Windows 2000	Yes	Yes	Yes
Locally accessible Windows NT 4.0	Yes	No	Limited
Locally accessible Windows NT 3.5x	Yes	No	No
Case-sensitive filenames	No	No	POSIX only
Case-preserving filenames	Yes	Yes	Yes
Fragmentation level	High	High	Low
Used on floppy disk	Yes	No	No

Windows 2000 provides a utility called CONVERT.EXE that converts a FAT/FAT32 partition to NTFS. There is no utility for directly converting an NTFS partition to FAT. To change an NTFS partition to FAT/FAT32, you must back up all files on the partition, reformat the partition, and then restore the files to the reformatted partition.

Changing the Drive Letter of a Partition

In Windows 2000, drive letters are not fixed to specific partitions. Rather, they can be changed at any time. The only exceptions are the System and Boot partitions; you cannot change the drive letters of either of those special partitions. The problem is that some programs record their positions in the Registry using the drive letter they were installed on. If you change the drive letter of a partition, the references to it will not be updated, and many programs will no longer run. Therefore, you need to exercise caution when changing drive letters, and you should do it as soon as possible after you create the partition. The following Step by Step runs you through the change process.

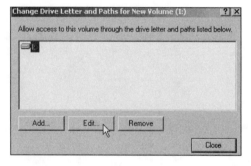

FIGURE 5.12
You can assign any unassigned letter to the drive.

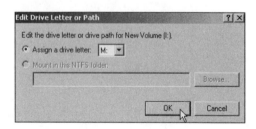

FIGURE 5.13
The drop-down list next to the drive letter shows which letters are available.

STEP BY STEP

5.9 Changing a Drive Letter

1. Open the Disk Manager.

2. Right-click the drive you want to change the letter for and choose Change Drive Letter and Path from the menu that appears.

3. At the Change Drive Letter and Paths dialog box, click the Edit button (see Figure 5.12).

4. In the Edit Drive Letter or Path dialog box, choose a new drive letter from the Assign a Drive Letter drop-down list (see Figure 5.13). Click OK to continue. When prompted, confirm that you really want to change the drive letter.

Marking a Primary Partition As Active

The active partition is the one your computer's BIOS will try to boot from. Therefore, you need to be careful when changing the active partition because it could render your server unable to boot.

The next Step by Step illustrates how to mark a primary partition as active.

STEP BY STEP

5.10 Marking a Primary Partition As Active

1. Open the Disk Manager.

2. Right-click the primary partition you want to mark as active and choose Mark Partition Active from the menu that appears.

Maintaining Volumes on Dynamic Disks

At Server installation, all disks are basic. To take advantage of any of the features of dynamic disks, you have to convert from basic to dynamic. You will then be able to perform the following tasks:

◆ Create a new simple volume

◆ Create a new spanned volume

◆ Create a new mirrored volume

◆ Create a new striped volume

◆ Create a new RAID-5 volume

◆ Delete a volume

◆ Format a volume

◆ Change the drive letter of a volume

◆ Mark a volume as active

Step by Step 5.11 shows you how to upgrade a basic disk to a dynamic disk using the Disk Manager.

STEP BY STEP

5.11 Upgrading a Basic Disk to Dynamic

1. Open the Disk Manager.

2. Right-click the disk indicator on the left side of the bottom pane and choose Upgrade to Dynamic Disk from the menu that appears (see Figure 5.14).

3. When you're prompted with the disk number of the disk you want to upgrade, click OK.

4. In the Disks to Upgrade dialog box, click Upgrade to upgrade the disk.

5. The Disk Management dialog box appears, warning you that no other versions of Windows will boot to this disk anymore (see Figure 5.15). Click Yes to continue.

6. In the Upgrade Disks dialog box, click Yes to continue.

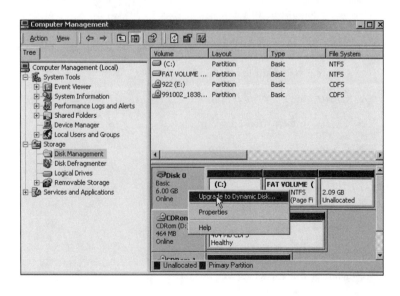

FIGURE 5.14

For most applications, updating from basic to dynamic disks is recommended.

7. In the Confirm dialog box, click OK to confirm that you know Windows 2000 will reboot to complete the upgrade (this will happen only if the partitions on the disk are currently being used—like the Boot partition).

8. After restart, log in.

9. When the Systems Settings Change dialog box appears, click Yes to restart your server again.

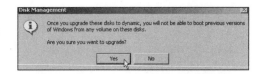

FIGURE 5.15
Because dynamic disks are unique to Windows 2000, converting will render them unreadable by any other local-booting operating systems.

Creating Simple Volumes on Dynamic Disks

As you perform ongoing maintenance of your dynamic disks, you might want to create new volumes. One advantage of a simple volume is that you can create it the size you want, and if you need more room in the future, you can expand it to a spanned volume without losing data. Creating a simple volume is covered in Step by Step 5.12.

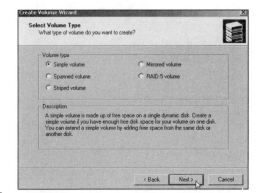

FIGURE 5.16
A simple volume consists of one or more blocks of free space on the same physical drive.

STEP BY STEP

5.12 Creating a Simple Volume

1. Open the Disk Manager.

2. Right-click the free space you want to create the volume in and choose Create Volume from the menu that appears.

3. At the Welcome to the Create Volume Wizard screen, click Next to continue.

4. At the Select Volume Type screen, select Simple Volume and click Next (see Figure 5.16).

5. At the Select Disks screen, enter the size for the partition you want to create in the For Selected Disk text box under the heading Size (see Figure 5.17). Click Next to continue.

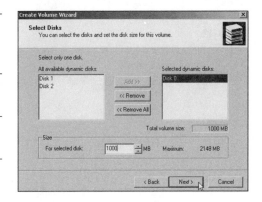

FIGURE 5.17
To keep this volume simple, you can choose free space from only one hard drive.

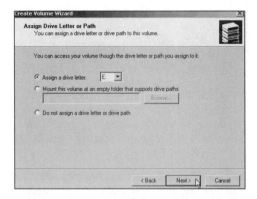

FIGURE 5.18
Generally, every new volume is given a label.

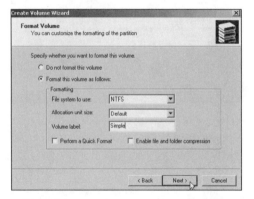

FIGURE 5.19
Because the volume cannot be read by any other locally booting operating system, you might as well choose to format with NTFS.

6. At the Assign Drive Letter or Path screen, choose the drive letter you want to assign to this volume and click Next (see Figure 5.18).

7. At the Format Volume screen, choose the file system and allocation unit size, and then enter a volume label (see Figure 5.19). Click Next to continue.

8. At the Completing the Create Volume Wizard screen, click Finish.

Creating Spanned Volumes on Dynamic Disks

As has already been mentioned, spanned volumes are single volumes that contain between 2 and 32 pieces of free space from one or more physical disks. Spanned volumes give you the ability to create large volumes out of small pieces and therefore give you usable storage space when each of the pieces would be useless because of its size.

You must exercise caution with spanned volumes because they are not fault tolerant; losing one piece will cause all the data in the volume to be lost. Good backup practices should always be used when handling data on spanned volumes.

Windows 2000 offers two ways to create a spanned volume. You can create it purely from free space (as demonstrated in Step by Step 5.13), or you can expand a simple volume into a spanned volume by adding more free space (as demonstrated in Step by Step 5.14).

STEP BY STEP

5.13 Creating a Spanned Volume from Free Space

1. Open the Disk Manager.

2. Right-click any free space you want to be part of the spanned volume. From the menu that appears, choose Create Volume.

3. At the Welcome to the Create Volume Wizard screen, click Next.

4. From the Select Volume Type screen, select Spanned Volume and click Next.

5. At the Select Disks screen (see Figure 5.20), from the All Available Dynamic Disks list choose the disks you want free space from to create the spanned volume. Then click the Add button to move those disks to the Selected Dynamic Disks list.

Select the disks in the Selected Dynamic Disks list and enter the amount of free space you want to allocate to the spanned volume. Click Next to continue.

6. At the Assign Drive Letter or Path screen, choose the drive letter you want to assign to this volume and click Next.

7. At the Format Volume screen, choose the file system and allocation unit size, and then enter a volume label. Click Next to continue.

8. At the Completing the Create Volume Wizard screen, click Finish.

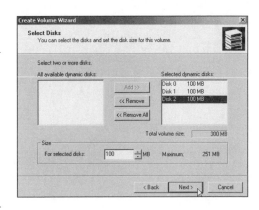

FIGURE 5.20
By definition, a spanned volume must contain blocks of free space spanning two or more physical drives.

STEP BY STEP

5.14 Expanding a Simple Volume to Create a Spanned Volume

1. Open the Disk Manager.

2. Right-click the simple volume you want to expand to form a spanned volume and choose Extend Volume from the menu that appears.

3. At the Welcome to the Extend Volume Wizard screen, click Next.

continues

continued

4. At the Select Disks screen, from the All Available Dynamic Disks lists, choose the disks you want free space from to add to the simple volume. Then click the Add button to move them to the Selected Dynamic Disks list.

Select the disks in the Selected Dynamic Disks list and enter the amount of free space you want to add to the simple volume. Click Next to continue.

5. At the Completing the Create Volume Wizard screen, click Finish.

Creating Mirrored Volumes

The mirror volume is the first fault-tolerant volume you will look at in this chapter. Mirror volumes are fault tolerant because they consist of two exact duplicates of the same data on two different drives. To create a mirror volume, you must have two physical drives with equal free space (the largest mirror you can create is equal to the smallest piece of free space provided).

Windows 2000 offers two ways to create a mirror volume. You can create it purely from free space (as demonstrated in Step by Step 5.15), or you can mirror an existing simple volume (as demonstrated in Step by Step 5.16). The second technique is safer for your data and will not cause data loss.

STEP BY STEP

5.15 Creating a Mirrored Volume from Free Space

1. Open the Disk Manager.

2. Right-click one of the pieces of free space that you want to create the mirror from and choose Create Volume from the menu that appears.

3. At the Welcome to the Create Volume Wizard screen, click Next to continue.

4. At the Select Volume Type screen, select Mirrored Volume and click Next.

5. At the Select Disks screen, move to the Selected Dynamic Disks list the disks that you want to be part of the mirror volume.

Enter the size of the mirror in the For Selected Disks text box under the heading Size (you do not need to do this for each disk because each portion of free space must be identical). Click Next to continue.

6. From the Assign Drive Letter or Path screen, choose the drive letter you want to assign to this volume and click Next.

7. At the Format Volume screen, choose the file system and allocation unit size, and then enter a volume label. Click Next to continue.

8. At the Completing the Create Volume Wizard screen, click Finish.

STEP BY STEP

5.16 Creating a Mirrored Volume from an Existing Simple Volume

1. Open the Disk Manager.

2. Right-click the simple volume you want to mirror and choose Add Mirror from the menu that appears.

3. In the Add Mirror dialog box, select a disk with sufficient free space to match the simple volume you are mirroring (see Figure 5.21). Click Add Mirror to continue.

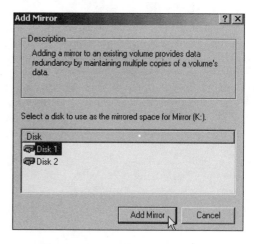

FIGURE 5.21

Choose a physical disk to mirror to. It must have as much free space available as the current volume is large.

Creating a Striped Volume

Striped volumes are like spanned volumes in that they combine many pieces of free space into a single volume that looks large. Like spanned volumes, they also allow you to combine between 2 and 32 pieces of free space. Also like spanned volumes, the loss of one of the pieces of free space causes the loss of all the data. Unlike spanned volumes, striped volumes must be created on at least two physical hard drives. Striped volumes are not fault tolerant; therefore, as with spanned volumes, you must make sure they are backed up regularly.

To create a striped volume, follow these steps:

STEP BY STEP

5.17 Creating a Striped Volume

1. Open the Disk Manager.

2. Right-click one of the pieces of free space that you want to create the Striped volume from and choose Create Volume from the menu that appears.

3. At the Welcome to the Create Volume Wizard screen, click Next.

4. From the Select Volume Type screen, select Striped Volume and click Next.

5. In the Select Disks screen, move to the Selected Dynamic Disks list the disks that you want to be part of the striped volume.

Enter the size of the free space you want to allocate from each selected disk in the For Selected Disks text box under the heading Size (you do not need to do this for each disk because each portion of free space must be identical). Click Next to continue.

6. At the Assign Drive Letter or Path screen, choose the drive letter you want to assign to this volume and click Next.

7. At the Format Volume screen, choose the file system and allocation unit size, and then enter a volume label. Click Next to continue.

8. At the Completing the Create Volume Wizard screen, click Finish.

Creating a RAID-5 Volume

RAID-5 volumes are the second kind of fault-tolerant volume. Using parity information, they create a system of disks that will tolerate the removal of one piece of the volume with continued operation. A RAID-5 volume requires at least 3 and as many as 32 physical drives. You can create a RAID-5 volume by following these steps:

STEP BY STEP

5.18 Creating a RAID-5 Volume

1. Open the Disk Manager.

2. Right-click one of the pieces of free space that you want to create the RAID-5 volume from and choose Create Volume from the menu that appears.

3. At the Welcome to the Create Volume Wizard screen, click Next.

4. At the Select Volume Type screen, select RAID-5 Volume and click Next.

5. In the Select Disks screen, move at least three disks to the Selected Dynamic Disks list to indicate that you want them to be part of the striped volume.

Enter the size of the free space you want to allocate from each selected disk in the For Selected Disks text box under the heading Size (you do not need to do this for each disk because each portion of free space must be identical). Click Next to continue.

6. At the Assign Drive Letter or Path screen, choose the drive letter you want to assign to this volume and click Next.

continues

continued

7. From the Format Volume screen, choose the file system and allocation unit size, and then enter a volume label. Click Next to continue.

8. At the Completing the Create Volume Wizard screen, click Finish.

Ongoing Maintenance of Volumes

All the maintenance tasks that you can perform on a partition, you can also perform on a volume. This includes formatting, changing the drive letter, and deleting. The procedures are the same as indicated in the section on partitions.

Mounting Partitions and Volumes in NTFS Folders

A new feature in Windows 2000 is the ability to mount volumes and partitions in NTFS folders. This allows you to reference a partition or volume by a folder name instead of a letter name. For example, you could create a folder called Data on the C: drive and then mount a 10GB simple volume into that folder. This would effectively increase the size of the C: drive and would make all that space available in the path C:\Data.

In addition, mounting can be used to increase space in commonly used folders without having to reformat drives and reinstall applications. For example, suppose you installed Windows 2000 Server on a 2GB hard drive, and you have been installing all your applications into the folder *C:\Program Files*. Now you have only 10MB of disk space available on your C: drive. You can buy a new hard drive, but you will have to do a lot of juggling to move everything over, and it will take a lot of time to do it. The solution is to install a new hard drive and create a new volume on it (let's say 2GB). Copy all the contents of the Program Files folder into this new volume. Then mount the volume into the C:\Program Files folder. Your applications have no idea that anything has changed because the mounting is transparent to all processes. All applications can still be accessed through C:\Program Files, and only you need know that there is another volume interacting in the process. Step by Step 5.19 shows you how to mount a volume or partition into an NTFS folder.

STEP BY STEP

5.19 Mounting a Volume or Partition in an NTFS Folder

1. Make sure the volume you want to create the mount in is formatted as NTFS (use convert.exe if the volume is FAT or FAT32).

2. Create a folder on the volume you want to create the mount point in. This folder must be empty or the mount will fail.

3. Open the Disk Manager.

4. Right-click the volume or partition you want to mount into the mount point prepared in step 2. Choose Change Drive Letter and Path from the menu that appears.

5. In the Change Drive Letter and Paths dialog box, click the Add button to add a new mount path to this volume (see Figure 5.22).

6. In the Add New Drive Letter or Path dialog box, either type the path to the mount point into the Mount in This NTFS Folder field or use the Browse button to locate or create the folder (see Figure 5.23). Then click OK.

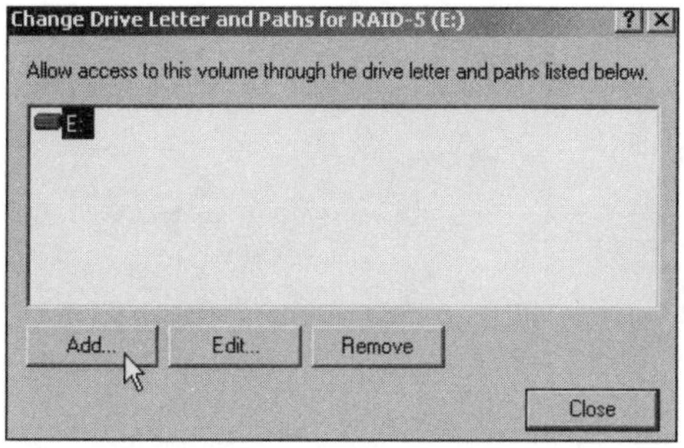

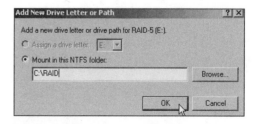

FIGURE 5.22
You can mount a drive into a folder on an NTFS volume.

Troubleshooting Problems with Disks and Volumes

There are really not very many problems that can arise with disks. Outside of the problems that arise when disks fail, you should not see very many problems. The following list contains some of the problems that may arise with disks and how you can remedy the

FIGURE 5.23
The drive can be mounted into any local folder on an NTFS partition on the server.

problems. It should be noted that many problems occur when certain volumes fail. These problems and their resolutions are covered in the upcoming section "Recovering from Disk Failures."

◆ *When booting to another operating system, the hard drive is not available.* This problem can occur for a couple of reasons. Either the file format being used on a Windows 2000 volume is not readable by the other operating system, or a dynamic volume is being used in Windows 2000, and it cannot be read by the other operating system. There really is no resolution to this problem short of re-creating the volume and/or formatting it with FAT or FAT32 (depending on the operating system). This is generally not a good solution, so this problem needs to be anticipated before disk formatting is done.

◆ *When booting, the System partition cannot be located* (this generally becomes evident when a message appears at boot indicating that the boot disk cannot be located). This problem usually indicates that your Boot.Ini has been modified to point to a partition that does not exist. You can repair this problem by booting to the Recovery console (see Chapter 4) and replacing the BOOT.INI file or by booting from a boot disk with a correct ARC path. This problem can also occur with some SCSI adapters when you add or remove a disk or tape drive; it can affect the order in which the OS numbers the available disks, making the BOOT.INI incorrect.

◆ *Data access to a RAID-5 volume is unusually slow.* This generally indicates that one of the partitions in the volume is no longer functioning. This problem can be repaired by replacing the faulty drive with a new one and then rebuilding the volume (see "Recovering from a RAID-5 Volume Failure").

◆ *Inability to install an additional copy of Windows 2000 on a dynamic disk.* This usually results from one of two conditions: 1) The dynamic disk type you are trying to install on cannot hold the boot partition of Windows 2000, or 2) The dynamic disk is not accessible via an ARC path. In the first case, there are enforced prohibitions against installing Windows 2000 on spanned, striped, or (software-based) RAID-5 volumes. As a result, these will not show up in the list of available partitions in the text-mode of Windows 2000 installation.

The second case is more abstract in its cause and is a result of a limitation of ARC paths as they relate to dynamic disks. In order to boot to a copy of Windows 2000 on your hard drive, the BOOT.INI file must be able to point to the partition on which Windows 2000 is installed. The problem is that only partitions created on basic disks are listed in the partition table on the hard drive; dynamic disks are not. Therefore, dynamic disks do not technically have ARC numbers. As a result, you will not be able to see dynamic volumes in the text-mode of the installation program unless those volumes were present before the disk was upgraded. For example, if a disk contained one partition and free space before it was upgraded to a dynamic disk, you would be able to install Windows 2000 on the first partition, and you would have the option of creating a new partition in the free space to install on. However, if you create a new partition in the free space, you will not be able to install Windows 2000 on it because it does not really have an ARC path, and therefore, the boot process will not be able to find it to boot to it.

You cannot fix this problem without destroying some dynamic volumes. You are best off to anticipate the possible problems rather than trying to fix them after they have occurred.

CONFIGURING DATA COMPRESSION

Configure data compression.

If a volume is formatted with the NTFS file system, it has a number of features that are not available on FAT or FAT32 volumes. One of those features is built-in compression. The reference to "built-in" simply means that compression is not an add-on feature, but is a property of any NTFS volume or folder or file on an NTFS volume.

Compression on an NTFS volume is drastically different from the compression you find employed in Windows 9x or products like PKZIP or WINZIP. In the case of Windows 9x, the compressed information is hosted in an uncompressed drive. All the data in the compressed drive is compressed; all that is not in the compressed drive is not. If you want to find out how much room there actually is left on your drive, you cannot because the amount of space depends on the amount of compression. And, inside a compressed drive, you no longer have the option of having files uncompressed.

Utilities like PKZIP and WINZIP are also different from NTFS compression. That is because they are statically compressed. The compressed files exist in a package that must be uncompressed manually before they can be used. This system is great for archiving data but has serious limitations when it comes to files that need to be accessed regularly.

NTFS compression does not have the limitations of either hosted compressed drives or static compression. On an NTFS volume, as much or as little of the drive can be compressed as you want. If you choose to compress only one file, that is all that will be compressed. On the other hand, if you compress the entire volume, the entire contents of the volume will be compressed (or at least you have the option). In addition, because compression is a property and not a new storage format, you do not need to apply an external process to the files to access them; you simply access them like any non-compressed file. Conversely, when you compress a folder or a disk, any new files placed into it are automatically compressed.

Compressing Objects Using the GUI Interface

Compressing a volume, folder, or file is as simple as ensuring that it is on an NTFS volume and selecting the correct property. If you compress a volume or a folder, you will have the option of cascading the compression down the tree to the lowest level files contained in it. Because, ultimately, compression is applied at the file level, you can uncompress any file without concern about whether the folder or drive it is on has its compression attribute set. Compressing an NTFS volume, compressing a folder on an NTFS volume, and compressing a file on an NTFS volume are described in the following three Step by Steps.

STEP BY STEP

5.20 Compressing an NTFS Volume

1. In My Computer or Windows Explorer, right-click the drive and choose Properties from the menu that appears.

2. At the Local Disk Properties dialog box, select Compress Drive to Save Disk Space check box (see Figure 5.24). Click OK to begin compression.

3. At the Confirm Attribute Changes dialog box, choose whether you want compression applied to the drive only or all its contents (see Figure 5.25). Click OK to continue.

STEP BY STEP

5.21 Compressing a Folder on an NTFS Volume

1. In My Computer or Windows Explorer, right-click the folder and choose Properties from the menu that appears.

2. At the Properties dialog box, click the Advanced button (see Figure 5.26).

3. Select Compress Contents to Save Disk Space check box (see Figure 5.27). Click OK to exit the advanced properties. Click OK again to begin compression.

4. In the Confirm Attribute Changes dialog box, choose whether you want to apply compression to the folder only or all its contents. Click OK.

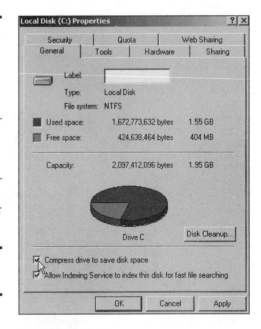

FIGURE 5.24
Compression is a property that can be applied to a volume.

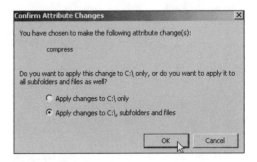

FIGURE 5.25
You can choose to have the compression property cascade to the entire folder and file tree within the drive.

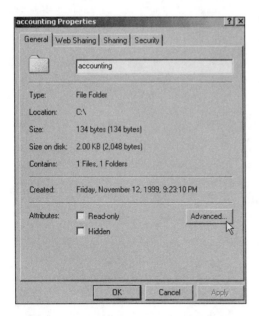

FIGURE 5.26
Compression is an advanced property of a folder.

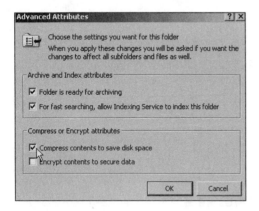

FIGURE 5.27
Select the compression check box to apply the property.

STEP BY STEP

5.22 Compressing a File on an NTFS Volume

1. In My Computer or Windows Explorer, right-click the file and choose Properties from the menu that appears.

2. In the Properties dialog box, click the Advanced button.

3. Select Compress Contents to Save Disk Space check box. Click OK to exit the advanced properties. Click OK again to begin compression.

Uncompressing an object is as simple as deselecting the check box in the Advanced Properties dialog box for any object.

Changing Views to Identify Compressed Objects

When these objects are compressed, by default, they do not look different from those that have not been compressed. However, this can lead to confusion when it comes to determining what is compressed and what is not. There is a view property you can set that allows you to change the color of a compressed object's label. If you have the property set, all compressed objects will be labeled with blue text. The color is not configurable, only presence or absence. Step by Step 5.23 outlines how to turn on this feature.

STEP BY STEP

5.23 Changing the View Properties to Identify Compressed Objects

1. From My Computer or Windows Explorer, select Tools, Folder Options.

2. In the Folder Options dialog box, click the View button.

3. At the View property page, select the check box labeled Display Compressed Files and Folders with Alternative Color and click OK.

Compressing Files Using the Command-Line Utility

Windows 2000 offers an alternative method of compressing files. That is to use the command line application called COMPACT.EXE. For most applications, you will find it most convenient to use the GUI to compress items. However, some useful features are available only when you use the command line method. For example, if you want to simply find out the compression status of a file, COMPACT will tell you that. In addition, if you want to compress only those files whose extension is .doc or .bmp, you can do that with COMPACT. Also, COMPACT will allow you to force compaction of files that Windows 2000 thinks are compacted but that really have not been because an error prevented them from being compacted completely. For example, if the power failed during compaction, a file's compacted attribute may have been set before the file was actually compacted.

The basic syntax of the COMPACT program is as follows:

```
COMPACT [/c or /u] [/s[:dir]] [/a] [/q] [/i] [/f]
➥[filename(s)]
```

Table 5.4 describes the parameters you can set when performing compression using the COMPACT program.

You can use the search function of Windows 2000 to select all the .doc or .bmp files and then modify their properties to compress them all at once.

TABLE 5.4

COMPACT PARAMETERS

Parameter	Function
none	Displays the compression state of the current folder.
/c	Compresses the specified folder or file.
/u	Uncompresses the specified folder or file.
/s:dir	Applies the compression or uncompression to the folder specified by *dir* (or, if *dir* is missing, applies to the current folder).
/a	Displays hidden or system files.

continues

TABLE 5.4	*continued*

COMPACT Parameters

Parameter	Function
/q	Does not report detailed progress information.
/i	Ignores errors during compression.
/f	Forces compression or uncompression even if the attributes indicate that the object(s) to be acted on are already in that state. (This allows for the repair of objects for which the compression attribute is incorrectly set due to system error during the last compression or uncompression attempt.)
/filename	Indicates the file or folder to compress. Many files or folders can be listed with spaces between them, and wildcard characters (* and ?) can be used. If you use wildcards, no folders in the tree will have their compression attribute set unless they conform to the wildcard format.

How Compression Is Applied to New Files in a Folder

Because compression can be added at the container (folder or volume) level, it needs to be made clear what happens to a file or folder when it is created in or moved into a container. The following five rules govern how compression attributes are applied when something arrives in a container:

1. Any object that is created inside a container gets the compression attribute of its direct container. That means that if a new text document is created in a folder with its compression attribute set, the document will also have its compression attribute set.

2. Any object that is copied into a container gets the compression attribute of its direct container. That means that if a folder is copied into a folder for which the compression attribute is set, that folder will also have its compression attribute set. In addition, all files and folders inside the folder will also have their compression attributes set (right down to every file in the whole tree).

3. Any object that is moved into a container from another volume gets the compression attribute of its direct container (moving from one volume to another really consists of a copy operation followed by a delete operation, so the above copy rule applies).

4. Any object that is moved into a container from the same volume retains its compression attribute (its attributes are unchanged).

5. Any object that is moved from an NTFS volume onto a FAT volume loses its compression attribute and will no longer be compressed (watch out when you move or copy files from compressed drives onto floppy disks).

MONITORING AND CONFIGURING DISK QUOTAS

Monitor and configure disk quotas.

Trying to monitor and control the amount of disk space users consume on server drives has always been a source of frustration for administrators. As soon as a location becomes available to a user to place files on, it seems as though the whole Internet gets downloaded into it, and every game and application gets copied into it.

Even when the location is used strictly for work-related files, the amount of "essential" information grows every day, and it seems as though it will never end. Moreover, after information has been copied onto a server, you're forced to try to convince people to delete or archive their information, which seems as painful to them as cutting off a body part or losing a beloved pet.

And if you try to manually monitor how much information people are storing and tell them that what they are storing is too large, you look like the bad guy (person) and you are the one "preventing me from doing my job!"

Disk quotas are a new feature in Windows 2000 that are designed to solve your storage and monitoring problems. Not only will they let you set storage boundaries, they will also inform users when they have reached those boundaries, which takes some of the heat off you and places it on "the system."

Quotas are set at the volume (or partition) level. To implement them, the volume must be formatted using the NTFS file format because FAT does not support quotas. Quotas are set for individuals and not for groups (the Administrators group being the one exception to this rule).

When creating quotas for a specific volume, you can set parameters for disk space usage, decide whether crossing those bounds results in a warning or a refusal to allocate space, and determine the default parameters for new users being added to the quota list.

By default, quotas are disabled for all volumes. However, after you enable quotas, the defaults are applied to every person who owns files on the hard drive. If you are the CREATOR OWNER of a file, its space is credited to you. You can then set specific users to whose quota is allowed to deviate from the defaults by adding them to the quota list and setting specific quota limits for them. Each user can be configured with different quota settings, so not everyone has to be treated the same. The only users who are exempt from quotas are the members of the built-in local Administrators group. The most that can be applied to them is a warning level at which an entry will be logged in the System log; they will never be denied disk space, regardless of the quotas applied to others.

As was already mentioned, quotas are applied at the volume level. The Properties dialog box of each NTFS volume has a tab labeled Quota, which contains the quota information for that volume. By enabling quota management (a check box on the property page), you have access to all the default quota management settings, as well as the specific quota settings for each user via the Quota Entries button (see Figure 5.28).

The first check box, Deny Disk Space to Users Exceeding Quota Limit, ensures that users who exceed their quota will not just have that fact logged but that disk space will be refused to them, and a message indicating a lack of free space on the volume will be displayed.

Under the heading Select the Default Quota Limit for New Users on This Volume, you can define the default disk usage limits that will be set for all users by default, whether they are in the quota list or not. Either limits are set to Do Not Limit Disk Usage, or you can set the space limit and the warning level limit. Both of these can be

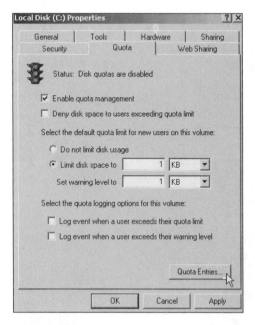

FIGURE 5.28
By enabling quota management, you can control the amount of disk space selected users are allowed to consume.

set to a number of kilobytes (KB), megabytes (MB), gigabytes (GB), terabytes (TB), petabytes (PB), and exabytes (EB). These limits do not define what users will get, they simply define the defaults for new users added to the quota list. If a user is not in the list, no quota is applied. If a user is added to the list, you can change the actual figures to deviate from the default.

Under the heading Select the Quota Logging Options for This Volume, you can specify whether an event is logged when a user hits his or her quota and/or warning level.

From this page you can also progress to actually adding people to the quota list. You do so by clicking the Quota Entries button. To enable disk quota management, follow the instructions in Step by Step 5.24.

STEP BY STEP

5.24 Enabling Disk Quota Management

1. From My Computer or Windows Explorer, right-click the hard drive you want to enable quota management for and choose Properties from the menu that appears.

2. In the Properties dialog box, click the Quota tab.

3. Select the check box labeled Enable Quota Management, and then define the default quota settings and logging options.

4. Click OK to enable quota management.

Once quota management has been enabled, Windows 2000 will go through a cataloguing process that tabulates how much space each user is currently using. This is then constantly maintained to determine whether quotas have been reached. Adding users to the quota list is illustrated in Step by Step 5.25.

STEP BY STEP

5.25 Adding Users to the Quota List

1. From My Computer or Windows Explorer, right-click the hard drive you want to enable quota management for and choose Properties from the menu that appears.

2. In the Properties dialog box, click the Quota tab.

3. At the bottom of the Quota property sheet, click the Quota Entries button.

4. From the Quota menu, choose New Quota Entry.

5. From the Select Users dialog box, choose the user (or users, using Ctrl-click) that you want to set a quota for and click the Add button. Click OK to continue.

6. In the Add New Quota Entry dialog box, enter the quota limit and warning threshold and click OK (see Figure 5.29). If multiple users were selected in step 5, the same limits will be set for all.

7. Close the Quota Manager.

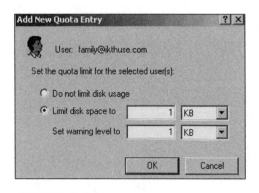

FIGURE 5.29

Assign a disk space limitation and a warning threshold for each user.

After you create quota entries, you can maintain them by returning to the Quota Manager and double-clicking the entry you want to modify. From there, you can change the quota for a specific user. You can also delete a user from the quota list, providing that the user is not currently using disk resources.

In Figure 5.30, you can see that beside each entry is a status that indicates whether a user is below the warning threshold (a green arrow), at the warning threshold but below the quota limit (a yellow triangle with an exclamation point in it), or at or above the quota limit (a red circle with an exclamation point in it).

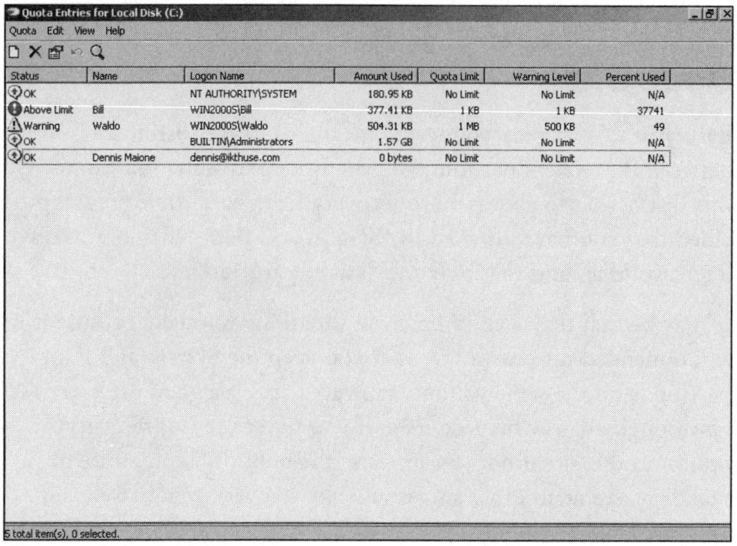

Quota Entries for Local Disk (C:)

Quota Edit View Help

Status	Name	Logon Name	Amount Used	Quota Limit	Warning Level	Percent Used
OK		NT AUTHORITY\SYSTEM	180.95 KB	No Limit	No Limit	N/A
Above Limit	Bill	WIN2000S\Bill	377.41 KB	1 KB	1 KB	37741
Warning	Waldo	WIN2000S\Waldo	504.31 KB	1 MB	500 KB	49
OK		BUILTIN\Administrators	1.57 GB	No Limit	No Limit	N/A
OK	Dennis Maione	dennis@ikthuse.com	0 bytes	No Limit	No Limit	N/A

5 total item(s), 0 selected.

FIGURE 5.30
The status icon indicates the current level of disk usage for each listed user.

RECOVERING FROM DISK FAILURES

Recover from disk failures.

A hard drive is a combination of metal and oxides spinning at thousands of revolutions per second in an almost total vacuum. The read-write heads float only microns above the drive surface. Although hard drive technology is extremely accurate, sophisticated, and robust, eventually every hard drive will fail. Either the heads will contact the drive surface, gouging out an area the size of the Grand Canyon, or the bearings will seize, sending smoke out through every crack in the server case. Whatever the cause, eventually something will happen to make your drives fail. When that happens, knowing about your recovery options will enable you to get your server running again in short order (if it has to come down at all).

This section will cover a variety of recovery techniques. Each of them relies on your forethought in preparing your system for the inevitability of a crash.

Recovering Using a Windows 2000 Boot Disk

Earlier in this chapter, you were introduced to the distinction between the System partition and the Boot partition. You can use this distinction to allow you to recovery from hard drive failure, provided that you have installed the System and Boot partitions as different volumes and that only the System partition fails.

It may be that this is an impractical situation, especially because it is recommended for practicality that you keep the System and Boot partitions on the same volume. However, this is a good exercise to go through anyway because, even if you never use this recovery option in this situation, you may use the boot disk you create to make it possible in other situations (like recovering from a mirror volume failure).

Although Windows 2000 cannot technically be booted from a floppy disk because of the size of the operating system and the limitation of the size of a floppy, you can, nonetheless, initiate boot from a floppy disk. If you recall the discussion of System and Boot partitions, you will remember that the System partition contains the files required to begin the boot process and to direct system start to the correct Boot partition. Well, the files required to perform that service can be copied onto a floppy disk, which can then serve as the System partition.

Before you copy any files onto the disk, make sure you format it under Windows 2000. If it has not been formatted under Windows 2000, when you try to boot using it, an error will appear telling you that the disk is not capable of booting Windows 2000.

The following essential files need to be copied onto a boot floppy: BOOT.INI, NTLDR, and NTDETECT.COM. Two other files may be needed to provide functionality. If you are using SCSI drives and they have the SCSI BIOS disabled, you must include a special driver called NTBOOTDD.SYS that is placed on the System partition. If this file exists, it must be copied onto the boot floppy. This file is actually the driver for the SCSI controller and will be a different file for different controller types. So you will need to copy it from a machine with the same SCSI adapter card.

The other file you might need is called BOOTSECT.DOS. This file provides non-Windows 2000 boot capabilities, whether you are booting to Windows 9x or DOS. If you need to preserve a boot to a non-Windows 2000 operating system, you will need to copy that file onto the floppy disk. This would presume that the system partition is FAT and is, therefore, accessible from DOS; any DOS boot disk would enable you to access this partition.

Step by Step 5.26 walks you through the procedure for creating the boot disk.

STEP BY STEP

5.26 Creating a Windows 2000 Boot Disk

1. Format a floppy disk using Windows 2000 formatting.

2. Copy the files BOOT.INI, NTLDR, and NTDETECT.COM from your Windows 2000 server to the floppy.

3. (Optionally) copy NTBOOTDD.SYS and BOOTSECT.DOS from your Windows 2000 server to the floppy.

You can (and should) test this disk by placing it in the floppy drive and restarting your server. To really test it, you can delete NTLDR from your hard drive and boot the disk again.

This disk will come in handy in a number of situations. If your System partition (which is separate from your Boot partition) fails, you can still boot to the Boot partition and operate your server. Second, if your system files become corrupt or are deleted, you can boot to the disk and copy the files back onto your hard drive. Third, if a mirror volume fails, you can use the disk to point to an alternate drive by adjusting the ARC path in the BOOT.INI file (you'll learn more on that later, in the section "Recovering from a Mirror Volume Failure").

Recovering Using Windows 2000 Backup

Windows 2000 Backup can be used as a source of recovery information, providing that the backups have been done and that they are current. Because Windows 2000 Backup does not back up at the sector level, it cannot be used by itself to recover a Windows 2000 system. Instead, you will have to rebuild the server by installing from a network share or CD-ROM and then applying the backup to it.

Recovering from a Mirror Volume Failure

Mirror volumes are fault tolerant: If one of the drives that makes up the set fails, the other will continue to operate. Because of the nature of the volume, users will be unaware that anything has happened.

Two scenarios exist in the configuration of a mirror volume that require two different approaches to recovery: mirror volumes that contain the System and/or Boot partitions and mirror volumes that do not.

Recovering from a Mirrored System or Boot Partition Failure

If a mirror volume that fails contains the System or Boot partition, possible restart problems exist if the failed drive is the first one (see Figure 5.31 for two scenarios). The BIOS of your computer looks to a specific physical drive to begin the startup process. If the System partition is on a mirror volume, and if the first volume of the set no longer exists, it will be impossible to start your server from the good component of the volume; this, despite the fact that it has all the correct information to start Windows 2000. Secondly, the BOOT.INI file points to a specific physical location for the Windows 2000 system folder (usually WINNT). If the physical location of the Boot partition is defined as being on the hard drive that no longer functions, again, your server will not start.

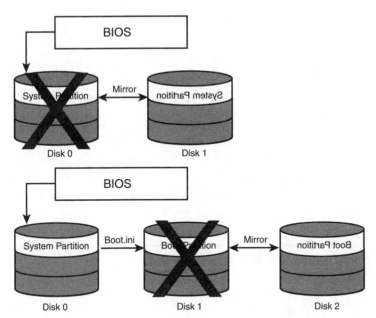

FIGURE 5.31
Special preparations must be made to recover from a mirror set failure that involves the System or Boot partition.

Both of these scenarios can be accounted for if you take the right steps to correct them.

In the first scenario in Figure 5.31, an alternate system partition is required to initialize Windows 2000. This can be provided via a Boot disk (see Step by Step 5.26 for instructions on how to create one). The boot disk contains a BOOT.INI file. To boot from it, make sure the BOOT.INI file defines the correct ARC path to the Boot partition that is functioning normally.

In the second scenario, the boot process will begin properly. However, system startup does not happen because the BOOT.INI file on the System partition points to a physical location that no longer exists. To start Windows 2000 properly, you will need to either correct the BOOT.INI file on the hard drive or modify the BOOT.INI file on your boot disk to point to the correct boot partition.

When you are set to boot Windows 2000 properly again, you can replace the failed hard drive and follow the mirror repair process outlined in the next section.

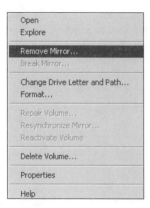

FIGURE 5.32
To repair a mirror, begin by removing it to isolate the good volume from the failed one.

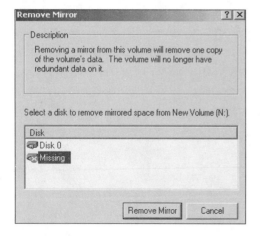

FIGURE 5.33
Choose the failed drive to remove it from the mirror volume.

Recovering from a Mirrored Data Volume Failure

Recovering a mirror volume that has failed is a relatively easy process if you do not have to deal with booting. A mirror can easily be regenerated after the failed drive has been replaced and your Windows 2000 server is restarted.

To repair a damaged mirror, you must first remove the mirror (isolating the functioning volume) and then re-establish the mirror to an alternate drive (a new one that replaced the failed drive or the equivalent free space on an existing drive). Regenerating a mirror volume is illustrated in the following Step by Step.

STEP BY STEP

5.27 Regenerating a Mirror Volume

1. Open the Disk Manager.

2. Right-click the mirror volume component on the disk that is still functioning and choose Remove Mirror from the menu that appears (see Figure 5.32).

3. In the Remove Mirror dialog box, choose the failed volume you want to remove from the mirror set. Click Remove Mirror to continue (see Figure 5.33). When prompted for confirmation, click Yes.

4. Right-click the remaining partition (now a simple volume) and select Add Mirror from the menu that appears.

5. In the Add Mirror dialog box, choose the disk to mirror the partition onto. Click Add Mirror.

Recovering from a RAID-5 Volume Failure

RAID-5 volumes have redundancy built into their structure. As a result, a RAID-5 volume will tolerate the failure on one of the hard drives that make up the set without a loss of data. Like in a mirror volume, repairs can be made to the volume that will restore it to full functionality.

To recover a RAID-5 volume when one hard drive fails, you must replace the drive and then manually invoke a RAID-5 volume regeneration. This will replace the data on the new drive with the data generated from the existing data and the parity information. This regeneration process may take a long time and is influenced by a number of factors, including how much data was on the drive and the total number of drives in the volume.

First, shut down the server and replace the defective drive. Then follow Step by Step 5.28 to regenerate the RAID-5 volume. Before you do that, you may have to restart your server to enable detection of the new hard drive.

STEP BY STEP

5.28 Regenerating a RAID-5 Volume

1. Start the Disk Manager.

2. Upgrade the new drive to a dynamic disk.

3. Right-click one member of the RAID-5 volume and select Reactivate Volume from the menu that appears (see Figure 5.34).

4. When the dialog box shown in Figure 5.35 appears, confirm that you want to reactivate the failed volume.

5. Right-click one member of the RAID-5 volume and select Repair Volume from the menu that appears (see Figure 5.36). When this step is complete, the volume will again be accessible.

FIGURE 5.34
A failed RAID-5 volume will automatically be deactivated, making it inaccessible; reactivate it to begin the recovery process.

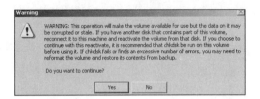

FIGURE 5.35
Verify that you want to reactivate the volume.

FIGURE 5.36
Begin the process of repairing the volume by right-clicking one of the remaining volume components.

continues

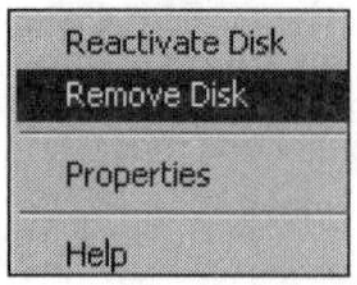

FIGURE 5.37
When the recovery is complete, remove the
failed disk from the Disk Manager.

continued

6. Indicate the disk you want to use to replace the failed one.
Then click OK to begin volume regeneration.

7. Right-click the label for the disk that has been replaced
and select Remove Disk from the menu that appears (see
Figure 5.37).

CASE STUDY: ROAMING PROFILES AND DISK QUOTAS

THE ESSENCE OF THE CASE

This case requires that the following results
be satisfied:

▶ Devise a way to ensure that users' desktops and settings follow them as they move from computer to computer.

▶ Place a cap on the amount of server storage space for each user.

▶ Separate the storage areas for users from different departments to eliminate the possibility that files of one department encroach on the available space for another.

SCENARIO

Claudio is the administrator of a Windows 2000 network. He manages five Windows 2000 servers, one of which functions as a file server for three departments. Lately, he is faced with two separate problems. First, a research library was just put into the building. It has two computers running Windows 2000 Professional, and users can log into them while they are doing research. They are automatically connected to a home directory on the server where the users can create documents based on their research findings. However, the users are finding that, when they move from the computers in their offices to the research computers, they have to reset their desktops, and if they create a shortcut on their office computers, they have to create the same shortcut on the research machines. The users are asking for a solution to this problem.

CASE STUDY: ROAMING PROFILES AND DISK QUOTAS

The second issue is one that the users are not complaining about (yet), but that is becoming a problem for Claudio. The users' home folders are stored on the file server. He periodically checks storage use and finds that some users are consuming a disproportionate amount of hard drive space on the server. In addition, this space usage is increasing dramatically over time. When he investigates, he finds that many users are downloading quite a large quantity of game demos and pictures, and these items are creating most of the storage consumption.

Claudio wants to be able to provide for the ongoing storage needs of the users while enforcing an upper limit on the amount of space any one user can consume. He also wants to be able to separate each department so that if the users in one department consume the maximum amount of space, that will not overrun the free space available to the users in another department. He currently has two hard drives with capacities of 10GB and 20GB, and he would like to allocate 10GB to each department.

You have been called in to analyze this situation and make recommendations.

ANALYSIS

Windows 2000 Server has features that will allow Claudio to solve all of his current problems. He can begin by creating a Profiles folder and sharing it on the server. He can then copy user profiles into this folder. Then when he configures the user accounts of each

of the users to point to that shared location, any changes users make to their desktops from any of the locations will follow them from computer to computer.

The problem of storage will take a bit more work. First, Claudio needs to isolate the storage locations of each department. He can do this by dividing the larger drive into two 10GB simple volumes. Then he can convert the three volumes to NTFS (if they are not already using that file system). He will then need to configure the user accounts to point to the new locations when users log into the network and secure the contents of the volumes so that only users from a specific department are allowed to access that volume.

The final issue can be solved by using disk quotas. For each of the volumes, he can configure quotas for the departmental users authorized to access that volume. At first, he will probably want to allocate the same amount of storage to each user. However, as time goes on, he may find that some users need more storage space than others, and the quotas can be modified accordingly.

Finally, Claudio needs to educate the users about the use of server space to store personal data. The quotas will help to reinforce the finite nature of storage space and the need to store only essential company data in home folders. He will also need to inform users of the implementation of quotas to prevent (or at least reduce) the users' surprise when they run out of space.

The following table summarizes the solution.

continues

CASE STUDY: ROAMING PROFILES AND DISK QUOTAS

OVERVIEW OF THE REQUIREMENTS AND SOLUTIONS IN THIS CASE STUDY

Requirement	Solution Provided By
Consistent user desktop	Implement roaming user profiles in a shared folder on the server and configure user accounts to use them.
Separate departmental storage	Configure three 10GB simple volumes with NTFS and secure each against write access by the other departments.
Storage space cap per user	Configure disk quotas on each volume for the users who will be accessing storage locations on it.

CHAPTER SUMMARY

KEY TERMS

- local profile
- roaming profile
- mandatory profile
- default user profile
- all users profile
- NTUSER.DAT
- NTUSER.MAN
- System partition
- Boot partition
- BOOT.INI
- ARC path

Summarized briefly, this chapter covered the following main points.

- ▶ *Creating and managing user profiles.* This includes recognizing local profiles and creating roaming and mandatory profiles stored on a Windows 2000 server.

- ▶ *Creating partitions and volumes.* This includes differentiating primary, extended, and logical partitions on basic disks from the volumes created on dynamic disks. This also includes understanding the different volume types (simple, spanned, striped, mirrored, and RAID-5) and their recommended uses.

- ▶ *Configuring data compression.* This includes configuring compression for disks, folders, and files. This also includes knowing the implications of moving an object into (or creating an object in) a container for which the compression attribute is set.

- ▶ *Creating and maintaining disk quotas.* This includes activating disk quotas and enforcing quotas for selected users.

- ▶ *Recovering from failed disks.* This includes recovering both fault-tolerant (mirror and RAID-5) as well as non-fault-tolerant volumes.

CHAPTER SUMMARY

KEY TERMS   *continued*

- basic disk
- primary partition
- extended partition
- logical disk
- dynamic disk
- simple volume
- spanned volume
- mirrored volume
- striped volume

- RAID-5 volume
- NTFS
- FAT
- FAT-32
- COMPACT.EXE
- disk quota
- quota limit
- quota warning threshold
- boot disk

APPLY YOUR KNOWLEDGE

Exercises

5.1 Configure Roaming Profiles

In this exercise, you learn how to configure roaming profiles on a Windows 2000 server.

Estimated Time: 15 minutes

1. Examine the current local profiles. Right-click the My Computer icon and choose Properties from the menu.

2. In the System Properties dialog box, click the User Profiles tab. Note the absence of a profile for a user called Elmo.

3. Close the System Properties dialog box.

4. Create a user named Elmo, and then log on as that user.

5. From the Start menu, choose Programs, Administrative Tools, Computer Management.

6. In the Computer Management console, expand the Local Users and Groups tree, right-click Users, and select New User from the menu that appears.

7. In the New User dialog box, fill in the fields with the information shown in Figure 5.38 and use the password "password."

8. Click Create to create the new user.

9. Click Close to close the New User dialog box.

10. Close the Computer Management console.

11. From the Start menu, choose Shut Down and log off as the current user.

12. Log on as Elmo.

13. Log off and log back on as the Administrator.

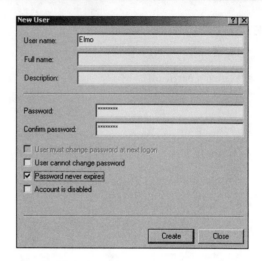

FIGURE 5.38
New User dialog box.

14. From My Computer or Windows Explorer, create a folder called Profiles and share it with default settings.

15. Examine the current profiles and copy the local profile for Elmo to the Profiles folder on the server. Right-click the My Computer icon and choose Properties from the menu that appears.

16. At the System Properties dialog box, click the User Profiles tab. Note the presence of a profile for a user called Elmo.

17. Select the entry for Elmo and click the Copy To button.

18. In the Copy To dialog box, type `\\`**servername**`\profiles\`**elmo** or browse for the shared folder (*servername* is the name of your server). Click OK to continue.

19. Click OK to exit the System Properties dialog box.

APPLY YOUR KNOWLEDGE

20. Change the user account Elmo to use the roaming profile when logging on. From the Start menu, choose Programs, Administrative Tools, Computer Management.

21. At the Computer Management console, expand Local Users and Groups, and then click Users.

22. Double-click the entry for Elmo.

23. In the User Properties dialog box, click the Profile tab to display that property sheet.

24. In the Profile Path field, type the same path you entered in step 18 (*servername*\profiles\elmo). Click OK to continue.

25. Close the Computer Management console.

26. Test the new profile by modifying it and logging on as Elmo. From My Computer or Windows Explorer, navigate to the Profiles\Elmo\Desktop folder. This folder defines the content of the desktop that is customized for this user.

27. Create a file called New Desktop Element.txt in this folder.

28. Log off the current user and log in as Elmo. Note the presence of the file New Desktop Element.txt on the desktop.

29. Log on as Administrator.

5.2   Create and Extend a Simple Volume

This exercise shows you how to create a simple volume and then how to extend it by adding free space. This exercise will require the existence of a dynamic disk, so you will also be walked through the upgrade process. This exercise assumes that you have 200MB of free space available on a hard drive attached to your server.

If you do not have 200MB of free space, adjust the numbers accordingly.

Estimated Time: 30 minutes

1. Start the Disk Manager. From the Start menu, choose Programs, Administrative Tools, Computer Management.

2. In the Computer Management console, click Disk Management.

3. To upgrade a basic disk to a dynamic disk, right-click the Disk label (on the left side of the bottom panel) for the disk you want to convert and choose Upgrade to Dynamic Disk from the menu that appears.

4. In the Upgrade to Dynamic Disk dialog box, select the disk you right-clicked on and click OK.

5. If prompted, restart your computer, log in as Administrator, and restart Disk Manager.

6. Next, create a 100MB simple volume. Right-click the free space on the drive you just upgraded and choose Create Volume from the menu that appears.

7. At the Welcome to the Create Volume Wizard screen, click Next.

8. At the Select Volume Wizard screen, select Simple Volume and click Next.

9. At the Select Disks screen, ensure that your disk is listed in the Selected Dynamic Disks list. Type **100** in the Size field and click Next.

10. At the Assign Drive letter or Path screen, accept the default drive letter by clicking the Next button.

APPLY YOUR KNOWLEDGE

11. At the Format Volume screen, accept the default format of NTFS by clicking the Next button.

12. At the Completing the Create Volume Wizard dialog box, click Finish.

13. Wait for the new volume to finish formatting before progressing to the next step.

14. Next, expand the simple volume by adding additional free space. Right-click the simple volume you just created and select Extend Volume from the menu that appears.

15. At the Welcome to the Extend Volume Wizard screen, click Next.

16. In the Select Disks screen, make sure the current hard drive is listed in the Select Dynamic Disks list and type **100** in the Size field. Click Next.

17. At the Completing the Extend Volume Wizard screen, click Finish.

18. Close the Computer Management console.

19. Next, test that a new volume is available with 200MB of free space. From My Computer or Windows Explorer, navigate to the new drive, right-click it, and choose Properties from the menu that appears.

20. In the Disk Properties dialog box, note that the capacity is 200MB (give or take a couple of MB) and that most of it is free space.

21. Close the Disk Properties.

5.3   Configure Data Compression on a Folder

This exercise shows how you can configure compression on a folder. It requires an NTFS volume. If you do not have one, you will have to convert one to NTFS prior to doing the exercise.

Estimated Time: 30 minutes

1. Create a folder called Compressed on the volume you created in Exercise 5.2. (If you did not do that exercise, make sure you create the folder on a drive formatted with the NTFS file system.)

2. Copy as many files into this folder as you can. Graphics files that do not use a compression scheme (like .BMP files) and word processing documents will give the most dramatic results. You want to have at least 20–30MB of data in the folder before the next step if possible. If you have no other source of files, copy a bunch from WINNT on the C: drive.

3. Right-click the folder called Compressed and choose Properties from the menu that appears. In the Properties dialog box, note that the number next to Size is very close to the same as the number next to Size on Disk. Size represents the number of bytes of data that are stored in the folder; Size on Disk represents the amount of disk space this data takes up on the volume. Size on Disk is what changes when you compress.

4. In the Folder Properties dialog box, click the Advanced button.

5. In the Advanced Attributes dialog box, select Compress Contents to Save Disk Space and click OK.

APPLY YOUR KNOWLEDGE

6. In the Properties dialog box, click OK to begin compression.

7. When the Confirm Attribute Changes dialog box appears, select the radio button labeled Apply Changes to This Folder, Subfolders, and Files and click OK.

8. When compression is complete, check the folder attributes again. There should be a marked difference between Size and Size on Disk. If you divide the difference between the two values by the original value, you will get the compression ratio for the files in the folder. (The compression ratio will vary depending on the kinds of files you have in a folder.)

5.4   Configure Disk Quotas

This exercise shows how you can enable disk quotas on a simple volume and then configure them to prevent excessive storage use by one user.

Estimated Time: 20 minutes

1. Start by enabling disk quotas and setting a quota for Elmo. In My Computer or Windows Explorer, navigate to the simple volume you created in Exercise 5.2. Right-click the volume and choose Properties from the menu that appears.

2. In the Properties dialog box, click the Quota tab.

3. Modify the Quota property sheet so it looks like that shown in Figure 5.39. This will limit all users to 1MB of disk storage.

4. Close the Properties dialog box. When prompted, click OK to begin the disk scan.

5. Log on as Elmo.

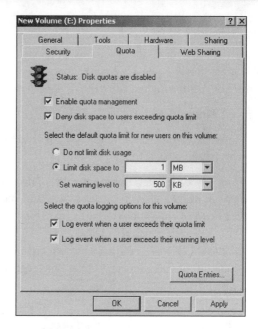

FIGURE 5.39
The Quota property sheet.

6. Using My Computer or Windows Explorer, navigate to the drive for which you enabled disk quotas. In the informational panel to the left of the drive contents, you should see that the amount of disk space available is 1MB.

7. Create a folder in the volume and call it Elmo's Stuff.

8. Copy the contents of the WINNT folder (on the C: drive) into the new folder. When 1MB of data has been transferred, you will get an error message indicating that you do not have enough disk space. This is the Quota Manager restricting the amount of disk space consumed by Elmo.

9. Log on as Administrator.

APPLY YOUR KNOWLEDGE

5.5 Create and Use a Boot Disk

This exercise shows how you can recover from corruption in the system files by using a boot disk. You will need a disk that you can format and convert to a boot disk.

Estimated Time: 15 minutes

1. From My Computer or Windows Explorer, format a disk.

2. From My Computer, navigate to the C: drive and copy all of the following files that you find on that drive to your floppy disk: BOOT.INI, NTDETECT.COM, NTLDR, NTBOOTDD.SYS. You may have to change the properties of your view to include both regular and hidden system files to see these.

3. On the C: drive, rename the file NTDETECT.COM to NTDETECT.OLD.

4. Remove the disk and restart your server. Boot will fail due to the absence of the NTDETECT.COM file.

5. Insert your boot disk into the floppy drive and restart your server (the boot disk is now your System partition).

6. Upon successful boot, rename the file NTDETECT.OLD back to NTDETECT.COM.

Review Questions

1. What are the three profile types, and how are they distinguished from each other?

2. What is the difference between a basic and a dynamic disk in Windows 2000?

3. What are the five volume types available on a dynamic disk? How are they defined? Which are fault tolerant, and how is their fault tolerance accomplished?

4. What is a disk quota and how is it enforced?

5. What are two methods for compressing a single file?

6. What is the process for recovering from a failed disk in a mirrored volume that does not contain the System or Boot partition?

7. What is a boot disk and how do you create one?

Exam Questions

1. Bendick is the System Administrator for a North American company with offices in Los Angeles, New York, Chicago, Toronto, and Vancouver. Each office has its own Windows 2000 server, and all the users in that office are connected to it by way of a LAN. The company has standardized their desktop on Windows 2000 Professional. The servers communicate via a medium speed WAN. Lately a number of complaints have come from the help desk saying that many users have non-standard desktop configurations, which makes it difficult to troubleshoot problems. To this point, desktop configurations have been up to the individual users with guidance from a document published by the IT department. Bendick wants to be able to configure logon properties to ensure that the desktop is the same every time.

APPLY YOUR KNOWLEDGE

Because the various offices have different desktop standards, he would also like (if possible) for the users in a specific office to all get the same desktop, and be configurable at that site to, perhaps, be different from the other offices.

In addition, he wants to reduce any WAN traffic that might result from getting central configurations from a single server.

Required Result:

Standard desktop on user logon

Optional Desired Results:

Different configurations in each office

Low WAN traffic

Proposed Solution:

Modify the local profiles on each server to change NTUSER.DAT to NTUSER.MAN

Analysis:

Which result(s) does the proposed solution produce?

A. This solution produces the required result as well as both optional desired results.

B. This solution produces the required result and one of the optional desired results.

C. This solution produces the required result but does not produce either of the optional desired results.

D. This solution does not produce the required result.

2. Luce is the System Administrator for a North American company with offices in Los Angeles, New York, Chicago, Toronto, and Vancouver.

Each office has its own Windows 2000 server, and all the users in that office are connected to it by way of a LAN. The company has standardized their desktop on Windows 2000 Professional. The servers communicate via a medium-speed WAN. Lately a number of complaints have come from the Help Desk that many users have non-standard desktop configurations, which make it difficult to troubleshoot problems. To this point, desktop configurations have been up to the individual users, with guidance from a document published by the IT department. Luce wants to be able to configure logon properties to ensure that the desktop is the same every time.

Because the different offices have different desktop standards, she would also like (if possible) for all the users in a specific office to have the same desktop, configurable at that site to be different from the other offices.

In addition, she also wants to reduce any WAN traffic that might result from getting central configurations from a single server.

Required Result:

Standard desktop on user logon.

Optional Desired Results:

A unique configuration for each office.

Low WAN traffic.

Proposed Solution:

Create a shared folder on each Windows 2000 server. Copy a local profile into this folder, and in it, change the NTUSER.DAT to NTUSER.MAN. Configure the properties of each user account to point to the profile for his or her office.

APPLY YOUR KNOWLEDGE

Analysis:

Which result(s) does the proposed solution produce?

A. This solution produces the required result as well as both optional desired results.

B. This solution produces the required result and one of the optional desired results.

C. This solution produces the required result but does not produce either of the optional desired results.

D. This solution does not produce the required result.

3. Dogberry is an application technician in the corporation described in question 2. He wants to ensure that the shortcut to a new application is available on the desktop of each user in Los Angeles. What is the best way to accomplish this?

A. Email each user in Los Angeles telling him or her how to add the icon to the desktop.

B. Modify the local profile for each client workstation to include the desktop icon.

C. Add the icon to the desktop folder of the profile identified as the mandatory profile for the Los Angeles users.

D. Add the icon to the desktop folder of the profile identified as Default User for the Los Angeles users.

4. Adriana just upgraded her server from Windows NT 4.0. After the upgrade, she found that the size of her System/Boot partition did not have sufficient free space to ensure abundant resources. To rectify the problem, Adriana upgraded the basic disks to dynamic disks (converting the System/Boot partition to a simple volume). However, when she tried to extend the simple volume, she was denied access to that function. Which of the following best explains why she could not do what she wanted to?

A. You cannot extend the System/Boot partition.

B. You cannot extend a simple volume that was originally created on a basic disk.

C. You cannot extend a simple volume.

D. She should have extended the volume before upgrading to a dynamic disk.

5. Puck wants to configure fault tolerance on his Windows 2000 server. Which of the following volume types gives the best data storage capacity while ensuring that a single disk failure will not destroy all data?

A. Spanned volume

B. Mirrored volume

C. Striped volume

D. RAID-5 volume

6. Amelia wants to configure data redundancy on her Windows 2000 server. Which of the following volume types gives the best data storage capacity while allowing her to make the System/Boot partition fault tolerant?

A. Spanned volume

B. Mirrored volume

C. Striped volume

D. RAID-5 volume

APPLY YOUR KNOWLEDGE

7. Oberon is the co-owner of a small home-based business. He has three workstations on a 10MB Ethernet network. Because he needed a Web/file server, he recently installed Windows 2000 on a machine that was formerly running Windows 98. When he installed Windows 2000, Oberon made no changes to the disk format characteristics of the drives, so they are as they were when Windows 98 was installed. He now wants to enable data compression on both hard drives. He is concerned that access to a folder that he reads from frequently will suffer performance problems if it is compressed, so he wants to be able to uncompress it if possible. He also wants to be able to establish disk quotas if that is possible.

Required Result:

Compress all files on both hard drives.

Optional Desired Results:

Allow for uncompressed folder on a compressed drive.

Allow for testing of disk quotas.

Proposed Solution:

Enable disk compression in the Properties dialog box of each disk. When prompted, specify that changes should be applied to all files and folders on the drives.

Disable compression on the folder he wants uncompressed by setting the Advanced property of the folder to Not Compress, and then specify that that property should be applied to all files and folders within the folder.

The ability to enable quotas is automatic when you install Windows 2000, so no additional configuration is necessary.

Analysis:

Which result(s) does the proposed solution produce?

A. This solution produces the required result as well as both optional desired results.

B. This solution produces the required result and one of the optional desired results.

C. This solution produces the required result but does not produce either of the optional desired results.

D. This solution does not produce the required result.

8. Rosaline is the co-owner of a small home-based business. She has three workstations on a 10MB Ethernet network. Because she needed a Web/file server, she recently installed Windows 2000 on a machine that was formerly running Windows 98. When installing Windows 2000, Rosaline made no changes to the disk format characteristics of the drives, so they are as they were when Windows 98 was installed. She now wants to enable data compression on both hard drives. She is concerned that access to a folder that she reads from frequently will suffer performance problems if it is compressed, so she wants to be able to uncompress it if possible. She also wants to be able to establish disk quotas if that is possible.

Required Result:

Compress all files on both hard drives.

Optional Desired Results:

Allow for uncompressed folders on a compressed drive.

Allow for testing of disk quotas.

APPLY YOUR KNOWLEDGE

Proposed Solution:

Convert the drive from FAT (or FAT32) to NTFS.

Enable disk compression in the Properties dialog box of each disk. When prompted, specify that changes should be applied to all files and folders on the drives.

Disable compression on the folder she wants uncompressed by setting the Advanced property of the folder to Not Compress, and then specify that that property should be applied to all files and folders within the folder.

The ability to enable quotas is automatic when you install Windows 2000, so no additional configuration is necessary.

Analysis:

Which result(s) does the proposed solution produce?

A. This solution produces the required result as well as both optional desired results.

B. This solution produces the required result and one of the optional desired results.

C. This solution produces the required result but does not produce either of the optional desired results.

D. This solution does not produce the required result.

9. Horatio just compressed the contents of his D: drive, and when prompted, he indicated that he wanted to cascade that property down to all files and folders in the drive. However, now that compression is complete, he cannot tell which objects have been compressed and which have not except by examining the properties. What can Horatio do to make the compressed objects more identifiable?

A. Log on as the Administrator, and the objects will appear blue.

B. Change the view properties of his folders to enable compressed objects to be displayed in alternate color.

C. Change the view properties of his folders to enable compressed objects to be displayed in alternate color and, when prompted, choose the color that best suits him.

D. Horatio cannot change how compressed objects are displayed.

10. Maria is the network administrator for a company with 2 member servers and 100 users on a single LAN. Each of her servers has three volumes, one that stores the System/Boot partitions, one that stores program files, and a third that stores user data. The divisions of sizes are 2GB, 5GB, and 20GB, respectively. Each volume is formatted with NTFS. An alert has just popped up on her computer telling her that the free space on one of her server's drives has fallen below 10%. Upon closer examination, she sees that certain users have been copying a tremendous amount of personal files onto the server to make space on their personal hard drives. Now she wants to cap the amount of storage each of the users has on the data volume of each server at 100MB. At this point, she will be satisfied just to be able to accomplish this task; however, she doesn't mind if the process takes a long time. In addition, she would like to be able to configure the cap for certain users to exceed 100MB and

for others to be less than 100MB, and she wants these caps to be easily configurable after they have been established.

Required Result:

Cap each user's disk space usage to 100MB on each server.

Optional Desired Results:

Achieve the required result in as efficient a way possible.

Allow for flexibility in the amount of storage space assigned to each user.

Proposed Solution:

Back up all the data onto tape.

Create 100 simple volumes of 100MB each from the 20GB drive.

Mount each simple volume into a folder in a 101st volume that is named for the user who is to access it. Secure the folder to allow access for that user only.

Expand the simple volumes into free space as the need arises.

Analysis:

Which result(s) does the proposed solution produce?

A. This solution produces the required result as well as both optional desired results.

B. This solution produces the required result and one of the optional desired results.

C. This solution produces the required result but does not produce either of the optional desired results.

D. This solution does not produce the required result.

11. Laertes is the network administrator for a company with 2 member servers and 100 users on a single LAN. Each of his servers has three volumes, one that stores the System/Boot partitions, one that stores program files, and a third that stores user data. The divisions of sizes are 2GB, 5GB, and 20GB, respectively. Each volume is formatted with NTFS. An alert has just popped up on his computer telling him that the free space on one of his server's drives has fallen below 10%. Upon closer examination, he sees that certain users have been copying a tremendous amount of personal files onto the server to make space on their personal hard drives. Now he wants to cap the amount of storage each of the users has on the data volume of each server at 100MB. At this point, he will be satisfied just to be able to accomplish this task; however, he would like the process to be as time consuming as possible. In addition, he would like to be able to configure the cap for certain users to exceed 100MB and for others to be less than 100MB, and he wants these caps to be easily configurable after they have been established.

Required Result:

Cap each user's disk space usage to 100MB on each server.

Optional Desired Results:

Achieve the required result in as efficient a way possible.

Allow for flexibility in the amount of storage space assigned to each user.

APPLY YOUR KNOWLEDGE

Proposed Solution:

Enable disk quotas on each of the 20GB drives with default quota limits at 100MB.

Add explicit quotas for those users who deviate from the default.

Analysis:

Which results does the proposed solution produce?

A. This solution produces the required result as well as both optional desired results.

B. This solution produces the required result and one of the optional desired results.

C. This solution produces the required result but does not produce either of the optional desired results.

D. This solution does not produce the required result.

12. Katherine has a mirror volume that contains only user data. One of the hard drives making up the volume has failed. How can she recover the data and re-establish the mirror?

A. Install a new hard drive, restore the data from tape, and invoke the Rebuild Mirror function from the functioning mirror volume.

B. Install a new hard drive and invoke the Rebuild Mirror function from the functioning mirror volume.

C. Install a new hard drive and invoke the Regenerate function from the functioning mirror volume.

D. Install a new hard drive, remove the old mirror, and add a new mirror from the functioning mirror volume to the new drive.

13. Rosencrantz restarted his Windows 2000 server and got this error message: "NTLDR is missing." Assuming that the System partition is intact except for the NTLDR file, which of the following will allow him to repair his server? Choose two.

A. Using the four disk set, boot to the Recovery console and copy NTLDR from a disk copied from another Windows 2000 server.

B. Using a startup disk, boot the server and copy NTLDR from the disk.

C. Boot to Safe Mode with Command console and copy NTLDR from the \Repair folder.

D. Copy NTLDR onto the server from backup tape.

14. Ariel has just had a disk fail on her server that was part of a RAID-5 volume. After replacing the faulty drive, she restarted her server and started Disk Manager. Which of the following puts the Disk Manager commands in an order that will allow her to restore the RAID-5 volume to full functionality?

A. Reactivate the volume, repair the volume, remove the failed disk.

B. Remove the volume, repair the volume, reactivate the volume.

C. Reactivate the volume, remove the volume, remove the failed disk.

D. Remove the failed disk, repair the volume, reactivate the volume.

15. Iago had two drives fail in his 32-drive RAID-5 volume. He now wants to repair the volume. Which of the following will allow him to repair the volume?

APPLY YOUR KNOWLEDGE

   A. Replace the faulty drives and repair the volume in the Disk Manager.

   B. Replace the first drive, repair the volume, replace the second drive, and repair the volume again.

   C. Replace the two drives, delete the volume, re-create the volume, and restore the data from backup.

   D. Repair the volume before replacing the drives, replace the drives, and repair the volume again.

Answers to Review Questions

1. The three profile types are local, roaming, and mandatory. Local profiles are created automatically when any user logs onto a Windows 2000 server. They are local to the machine onto which you are logging in and are not available anywhere else. Roaming profiles are pointed to from the properties of a user's account. These profiles are located centrally in a shared location and, therefore, are accessible from anywhere on the network. As a result, desktop settings are available from any machine a user logs into. Mandatory profiles are roaming profiles (with the same characteristics and configuration) but are read-only. This means that when changes are made to the desktop, they are not carried from session to session. For more information, see the section "Creating and Maintaining User Profiles."

2. The difference between a basic and a dynamic disk is that dynamic disks support volumes and can, therefore, be configured with simple, spanned, mirrored, striped, or RAID-5 volumes. Basic disks support only primary partitions and logical drives and will not, therefore, support

fault-tolerant configurations (except where they already existed in a version of NT that was upgraded) or expandable volumes. For more information, see the sections "The Basic Disk" and "The Dynamic Disk."

3. The five volume types are simple, spanned, mirrored, striped, and RAID-5. Simple volumes allow for a single non-fault-tolerant drive to be created from one or more blocks of free space on a single disk. Spanned volumes allow for a single non-fault-tolerant drive to be created from one or more (possible unequally sized) blocks of free space on more than one disk. Mirrored volumes allow for a single fault-tolerant drive to be created from two equal-sized blocks of free space on two disks. Striped volumes allow for a single non-fault-tolerant drive to be created from one or more equal sized blocks of free space on more than one disk. RAID-5 volumes allow for a single fault-tolerant drive to be created from three or more equal-sized blocks of free space on three or more disks. For more information, see the section "The Dynamic Disk."

4. Disk quotas are thresholds established on NTFS partitions that define the amount of disk space a user can consume. Total amount of storage attributed to a user is determined by the files of which a user is the owner. For more information, see the section "Monitoring and Configuring Disk Quotas."

5. A single file can be compressed by setting its advanced attribute Compress Contents to Save Disk Space. In addition, a single file can also be compressed with the COMPACT command from a command line, specifying the path to the file to be compressed. For more information, see the section "Configuring Data Compression."

APPLY YOUR KNOWLEDGE

6. To recover a mirror volume when one disk fails, do the following: shut down the server; replace the faulty drive; restart the server; in Disk Manager, remove the mirror; in Disk Manager, add a mirror to the functioning mirror volume and point it to the new disk for free space. For more information, see the section "Recovering from a Mirrored Data Volume Failure."

7. A boot disk is a disk that replaces the System partition for the purposes of booting a Windows 2000 server. You create a boot disk by formatting a disk under Windows 2000 and then copying the following files onto it: NTLDR, NTDETECT.COM, BOOT.INI, NTBOOTDD.SYS (optional), BOOTSECT.DOS (optional). For more information, see the section "Recovering Using a Windows 2000 Boot Disk."

Answers to Exam Questions

1. **D.** Although renaming NTUSER.DAT to NTUSER.MAN is the technique for making a profile mandatory, that technique works only if the original profile is roaming. Making a local profile mandatory has no effect. For more information, see the section "Mandatory User Profiles."

2. **A.** This solution will produce both the required and the optional requirements. When you make a profile roaming first and then rename NTUSER.DAT to NTUSER.MAN, it becomes mandatory. In addition, configuring each user to point to the server on his or her local LAN for the profile ensures that WAN traffic remains low. Finally, that configuration also allows for each office to have its own mandatory profile, which can be customized for the location. For more information, see the section "Creating and Maintaining User Profiles."

3. **C.** Having the users change their desktops will be ineffective because they will have to do that every time they log in due to the read-only nature of mandatory profiles. Modifying the local profile on the workstations is not only labor-intensive, it's also ineffective because the user accounts point to a mandatory profile, not to the local one. Redefining the default user will be ineffective because that is applied only when the user is created and not after the fact. It would not update the mandatory profiles for the Los Angeles users. The only option is to modify the Desktop folder in the mandatory profile for the Los Angeles users. For more information, see the section "Creating and Maintaining User Profiles."

4. **B.** Although it is true that you cannot extend the System/Boot partition, because that partition was once a basic disk that you cannot extend it. The only simple volumes that can be extended are those that were created after the disk was dynamic and not those that were converted in a disk upgrade. For more information, see the section "The Simple Volume."

5. **D.** Although mirror volumes are fault tolerant, they give only 50% return in storage for the total disk space they take up (50% of the volume is consumed in redundant data). RAID-5 volumes produce at least 66% usable space (where there are 3 disks) and will go up to 97% (where there are 32 disks). For more information, see the section "The Dynamic Disk."

APPLY YOUR KNOWLEDGE

6. **B.** Of the four choices, only mirror and RAID-5 are fault tolerant. However, of those two, only mirror volumes are capable of holding the System/Boot partitions. For more information, see the section "The Mirrored Volume."

7. **D.** Although the solution is sound, it misses one important fact: Oberon did nothing to the disk structure when he installed Windows 2000 Server, so it must be either FAT or FAT32 (the only format types Windows 98 supports). Neither of the FAT types is capable of supporting compression or quotas. For more information, see the sections "Configuring Data Compression" and "Monitoring and Configuring Disk Quotas."

8. **A.** Unlike Oberon before her, Rosaline converted to NTFS first and as a result was able to produce both the required and the optional desired results. For more information, see the sections "Configuring Data Compression" and "Monitoring and Configuring Disk Quotas."

9. **B.** Changing the display color of compressed objects is a property of the folder view. However, you cannot choose the color; it is always blue. For more information, see the section "Configuring Data Compression."

10. **B.** Surprisingly, this solution fulfills both the required result and one of the optional desired results. By creating individual drives for each user, Maria ensures that they cannot exceed a pre-scribed size. By mounting each drive in a folder, she can get around the need to be restricted to 26 drives (one for each letter). In addition, because these are simple volumes, they can easily be expanded to meet growing needs by certain users. The big problem is that this is a very tedious and labor-intensive solution. For more information, see the section "Configuring Disks and Volumes."

11. **A.** By configuring disk quotas, Laertes ensures that he can control disk usage and that he has the flexibility to configure any user to deviate from the default. Any user who does not deviate, does not have to be configured; he or she will get the default settings. This makes the configuration very efficient. For more information, see the section "Monitoring and Configuring Disk Quotas."

12. **D.** The proper order of tasks is this: Install a new hard drive, remove the old mirror (to isolate the good data in the remaining volume), and add a new mirror using free space from the new drive. Answers B and C do not work because the functions that are listed do not exist. Answer A is incorrect because there is no need to restore from backup when the data is preserved on the surviving member of the mirror volume. All that is necessary is that the mirror be re-established with a functioning drive. The mirror will then rebuild itself. For more information, see the section "Recovering from a Mirrored Data Volume Failure."

13. **A, B.** The Recovery console (see Chapter 4) will allow Rosencrantz to boot his server to a state where he can copy the NTLDR file back onto his System partition (the NTLDR is generic and can be obtained from any Windows 2000 server). In addition, a startup disk will allow you to boot by replacing the System partition with the files on the disk. Safe Mode will not work because it requires that your Windows 2000 server be able to boot unaided. Finally, recovering from tape is not possible because Windows 2000 Backup requires you to boot the server first. For more information, see the section "Recovering Using a Windows 2000 Boot Disk."

APPLY YOUR KNOWLEDGE

14. **A.** She reactivates the volume first to make it accessible. Then she repairs the volume using free space in the replaced drive. Finally, she removes the failed drive from the Disk Manager. For more information, see the section "Recovering from a RAID-5 Volume Failure."

15. **C.** RAID-5 volumes cannot tolerate the loss of two drives. Therefore, restoring the data from backup is the only solution. For more information, see the section "Recovering from a RAID-5 Volume Failure."

Suggested Readings and Resources

1. Microsoft Windows 2000 Server Resource Kit: *Microsoft Windows 2000 Server Deployment Planning Guide* (Microsoft Press)

   - Chapter 19: Determining Windows 2000 Storage Management Strategies

2. Microsoft Windows 2000 Server: *Operations Guide* (Microsoft Press)

   - Chapter 1: Disk Concepts and Troubleshooting

   - Chapter 2: Data Storage and Management

   - Chapter 3: File Systems

3. *Microsoft Windows 2000 Professional Resource Kit* (Microsoft Press)

   - Chapter 17: File Systems

   - Chapter 32: Disk Concepts and Troubleshooting

4. Microsoft Official Curriculum course 1556: *Administering Microsoft Windows 2000*

   - Module 4: Administering File Resources

   - Module 7: Managing Data Storage

5. Microsoft Official Curriculum course 1557: *Installing and Configuring Microsoft Windows 2000*

   - Module 4: Configuring Disks and Partitions

   - Module 10: Configuring File Resources

6. Microsoft Official Curriculum course 1560: *Updating Support Skills from Microsoft Windows NT 4.0 to Microsoft Windows 2000*

   - Module 14: Managing File Resources

   - Module 15: Performing Disk Management

7. Microsoft Official Curriculum course 2152: *Supporting Microsoft Windows 2000 Professional and Server*

   - Module 6: Configuring and Managing Disks and Partitions

   - Module 7: Managing Data by Using NTFS

8. Web Sites

   - www.microsoft.com/windows2000

   - www.microsoft.com/train_cert

This chapter will help you prepare for the "Configuring and Troubleshooting Windows 2000 Network Connections" unit of the exam.

Microsoft provides the following objectives for "Configuring and Troubleshooting Windows 2000 Network Connections":

Install, configure, and troubleshoot shared access.

▶ This objective is necessary because someone certified in the use of Windows 2000 Server technology must understand how to configure Internet connection sharing as well as how to use the NAT protocol to distribute access to a single Internet connection to a number of users.

Install, configure, and troubleshoot a virtual private network (VPN).

▶ This objective is necessary because someone certified in the use of Windows 2000 Server technology must understand how to configure remote access to a Windows 2000 LAN through a public Internet connection and a virtual private network. This includes both allowing access by way of PPP and securing that access through the use of the PPTP and L2TP tunneling protocols.

Install, configure, and troubleshoot network protocols.

▶ This objective is necessary because someone certified in the use of Windows 2000 Server technology must understand the commonly used protocols. This includes understanding how NetBEUI, NWLink, and TCP/IP are installed and configured, and under what circumstances they are commonly used.

C H A P T E R 6

Configuring and Troubleshooting Windows 2000 Network Connections

Install and configure network services.

▶ This objective is necessary because someone certified in the use of Windows 2000 Server technology must understand how to install and maintain network services. This includes installing and configuring the Dynamic Host Configuration Protocol (DHCP) service for automatic TCP/IP configuration in clients. In addition, it also includes name resolution services like DNS and WINS.

Configure, monitor, and troubleshoot remote access.

- **Configure inbound connections.**

- **Create a remote access policy.**

- **Configure a remote access profile.**

▶ This objective is necessary because someone certified in the use of Windows 2000 member technology must understand the various ways of implementing remote access via a dial-up connection.

Install, configure, monitor, and troubleshoot Terminal Services.

- **Remotely administer servers by using Terminal Services.**

- **Configure Terminal Services for application sharing.**

- **Configure applications for use with Terminal Services.**

▶ This objective is necessary because someone certified in the use of Windows 2000 Server technology must understand how to configure the server side of a Terminal Services-based network. This includes the installation of a Terminal Services server to host applications, as well as facilitate remote administration. In addition, it also includes an understanding of Terminal Services client installation.

Configure the properties of a connection.

▶ This objective is necessary because someone certified in the use of Windows 2000 Server technology must understand how to create connections through the network properties. These include not only network connections but also connections for dial-up access.

Install, configure, and troubleshoot network adapters and drivers.

▶ This objective is necessary because someone certified in the use of Windows 2000 Server technology must understand how to install and maintain the drivers for network adapters.

▶ This chapter is full of content that could be prime test material on the Windows 2000 exam. Because networking and its services are so important to the successful operation of a Windows 2000 server, you can expect the content of this chapter to play a major role on the exam.

▶ This chapter provides you with a lot of information; much of it is background that you need to understand in order to implement the solutions described. However, many of these components will not be tested on. For example, you are not likely to see questions on TCP/IP, NWLink, or NetBEUI as protocols. However, you are likely to see scenarios that use these protocols as components installed on servers. Be sure you know what the protocols are and what their characteristics are so you will be able to weed the irrelevant information from the relevant information on exam questions.

▶ Much of the content of this chapter deals with TCP/IP and the services that can be installed to support it. You should know the installation and implementation of DHCP in detail. Although they're very important in the scheme of things, WINS and DNS will not be a major focus on the exam. Because WINS has been largely replaced by DNS, and because DNS is likely to be covered on other exams in more detail, you will primarily be responsible for understanding what they do and when they are used, as opposed to in-depth understanding of their configuration (especially the complex WAN factors that are not covered in this book).

▶ Connection sharing and the NAT protocol are new for Windows 2000, so they are bound to find their way onto the exam. Expect a question or two on their configuration and use.

▶ Remote access has always been a major point on the Server exams; expect the Windows 2000 Server exam to be no different. Make sure you understand and can implement PPP servers and connections. In addition, understand the uses for PPTP and L2TP—how they are similar and how they are different.

▶ Terminal Services has changed from Windows NT, so it is a likely target for exam questions as well. Understand application and remote administration modes and how they are configured. In addition, understand the limitations of each and their licensing requirements. It would be good to know the list of Windows clients that can be configured as Terminal Services clients and how to configure them.

▶ As is usual for the study strategies, you are encouraged to know the content of this chapter, to do the labs and Step by Steps, and to test your knowledge with the review questions. Furthermore, creating a test lab with two or three networked computers will be helpful by allowing you to try test scenarios that might be beyond the direct scope of this book, but will reinforce the concepts covered in this chapter.

INTRODUCTION

Windows 2000 Server is about networking. Without a network, most of what Windows 2000 Server does would be useless. As a result, the importance of knowing how networking in Windows 2000 can be configured and maintained cannot be overestimated. The skills and knowledge required to do this have quite a range. From the underlying architecture, to network cards and drivers, to network support services, all the communication features are required knowledge. From there, you also have to know the different features for supporting client access. These include Internet connection sharing, virtual private networks, Remote Access Services, and Terminal Services. This chapter deals with all those topics, and the exam will too.

THE WINDOWS 2000 NETWORKING ARCHITECTURE

Although the hardware components and drivers of the Windows 2000 networking environment are installed and configured much like other hardware devices, the environment into which they are installed is unique unto itself. Because networking is such a vital part of the functioning of a Windows 2000 computer, it has its own specially developed architectural model—a model that it has inherited directly from its Windows NT predecessors. This model, based roughly around the OSI seven-layer model, is the basis for Windows 2000 networking (see Figure 6.1).

As you can see in Figure 6.1, the Kernel mode network architecture can be roughly divided into four sections. At the bottom is the Network Adapter Card. It is responsible for sending data out onto the network cable in the form of electrical signals (this corresponds to the OSI Physical layer).

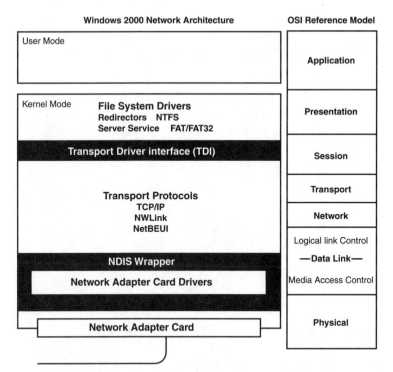

FIGURE 6.1

The architectural model of Windows 2000 networking alongside the OSI reference model.

The next level is the Network Adapter Card Driver (this and the NDIS Wrapper roughly correspond to the OSI Data Link layer). The driver, which is responsible for communication with the network card, is encased in a wrapper called the NDIS Wrapper. The NDIS Wrapper is a boundary layer that defines how drivers should talk to cards and how drivers should talk to transport protocols. Boundary layers are not network components as such, but are standards that tell the people who develop drivers what the connection point between their software and the rest of the architecture should look like. By writing drivers to conform to the NDIS standard, manufacturers can be sure that the drivers will be compatible with the rest of the network architecture, even if they don't know what that architecture looks like.

The next level up is the Transport Protocols. This level defines the communication languages that are used in the network architecture, and it roughly corresponds to the Network and Transport layers of the OSI model. As you will see later, this level uses most frequently (but not exclusively) the TCP/IP, NWLink, and NetBEUI protocols.

Between the Transport Protocols and the File System Drivers is another boundary layer: the Transport Driver Interface (TDI). Like NDIS, the TDI defines a set of specifications for communication at high levels in the network architecture.

The final level is the File System Drivers. This level defines the drivers responsible for accepting requests from the network, making requests to the network, and redirecting information requests to the appropriate file systems (like FAT and NTFS). These roughly correspond to the Session and Presentation layers of the OSI model.

Above the Kernel mode is the User mode. In User mode, the user interfaces to networking are created. Internet Explorer would be an example of such an application. Most of what it does involves passing information down through the network architecture and out onto the network. This corresponds to the Application layer of the OSI model.

INSTALLING AND CONFIGURING NETWORK ADAPTERS AND DRIVERS

Install, configure, and troubleshoot network adapters and drivers.

For the most part, the topic of network adapters and drivers was covered in Chapter 3, "Configuring and Troubleshooting Hardware Devices and Drivers," where hardware was discussed. Except for their function, not much differentiates a network adapter from any other piece of hardware in your server.

Like other hardware devices, many new network cards are Plug and Play compatible, so whether you have one or five cards installed, they should be detected by Windows 2000 and their drivers installed. Like other hardware, network cards have device drivers that allow Windows 2000 Server and the applications that run on it to communicate to the hardware.

See Chapter 3 for more information on hardware and drivers in Windows 2000.

CONFIGURING CONNECTIONS

Configure the properties of a connection.

Connections are what Windows 2000 uses to create all its network communication. When a network card is installed in a Windows 2000 server, a connection is created to allow communication on that card. From the connection, network protocols are installed, as are interfaces to other networks (like UNIX or NetWare).

In addition to LAN connections, which are created automatically, there are other kinds of connections (such as those for modems) that must be created manually.

Creating a New Connection

The Connections dialog box can be accessed from the properties of the My Network Places icon, which is on your desktop. When a new network adapter is installed in your server, a new connection icon automatically appears in this dialog box.

In addition to LAN connections, you can also manually create connections of other types. When you double-click the Make New Connection icon in the Connections dialog box, a wizard appears that allows you to create a new connection from the dialog box displayed in Figure 6.2.

Table 6.1 summarizes the potential connection types and their uses. The ones that are pertinent to a discussion of the Windows 2000 Server exam will be thoroughly dealt with in later sections of this chapter.

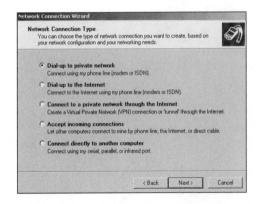

FIGURE 6.2

Five types of connection can be configured from the Network Connection Wizard.

TABLE 6.1

CONNECTION TYPES

Connection Type	*Function*
Dial-up connection	Dial-up connections allow you to establish a connection to a remote network using a modem, X-25, or ISDN connection. This includes the choices Dial-Up to Private Network and Dial-Up to the Internet (refer to Figure 6.2). This kind of connection relies on a modem, X.25, or ISDN connection to provide the ability to dial to a remote server. Each connection will have different dialing characteristics (like phone numbers) so, if you dial into a private network (like your company's network) and an Internet service provider (ISP), you will have two or more connections.
VPN connection	A VPN connection allows you to establish a secure connection on a public network (like the Internet). VPNs use an already existing connection (like a dial-up to an ISP) to piggyback secure transmissions. As such, they require either a dial-up or a LAN connection. This connection type is created via the radio button labeled Connect to a Private Network Through the Internet (refer to Figure 6.2).
Direct connection	A direct connection allows you to establish a connection from one computer to another without using a network interface card or cable. This can be done to allow connectivity between devices in close proximity on a temporary basis. You can use the serial or parallel ports on two computers to establish this connection. In addition, you can use infrared ports to connect directly. This would allow you to transfer information from one computer to another where no network exists. This connection type is created via the radio button labeled Connect Directly to Another Computer (refer to Figure 6.2).
Incoming connection	Using this kind of connection, you can establish a Windows 2000 Professional or Windows 2000 standalone server (one that is not in a domain) to be the host for an incoming connection. After you create such a connection, other computers will be able to connect to your computer (using a modem or other connection mechanism), and you will host their sessions. This connection type is created via the radio button labeled Accept Incoming Connections (refer to Figure 6.2). This method is not available to Windows 2000 servers that are member servers or domain controllers. Instead, you would use routing and remote access to fill that need.

Configuring a Connection in Windows 2000

After creating a connection, you can configure it from a number of dialog boxes accessible from the Network and Dial-Up Connections dialog box. You can reach configuration settings by choosing either the Advanced, Advanced Settings command or the Advanced, Optional Networking Components command. Alternatively, you can double-click the connection icon and modify the properties in the Status dialog box that appears. Finally, you can right-click the connection icon, choose Properties from the menu that appears, and adjust the settings in the Properties dialog box.

The Advanced Settings Dialog Box

To access the Advanced Settings dialog box, you choose the menu command Advanced, Advanced Settings in the Network and Dial-Up Connections dialog box. From the Advanced Settings dialog box, you can configure advanced properties of the network in general; all configuration settings apply to all the connections.

On the Adapters and Bindings property sheet, you can configure the order in which connections are used to perform network functions. Figure 6.3 shows a Windows 2000 server with two network adapters. Currently, network functions are attempted on the connection called 10MB Cable Modem, and if that is not successful, 100MB LAN is attempted. If the 100MB LAN connection is the preferred connection, you can use the up and down arrows on the right to change the order.

At the bottom of the Adapters and Bindings property sheet are the bindings for the connection selected at the top. A binding represents the protocols that function on a specific connection. When you install a new protocol, that protocol becomes available for communication on all network connections. However, you may not always want all installed protocols to be available on all connections. You can deselect a certain protocol from either the incoming or the outgoing components of the connection.

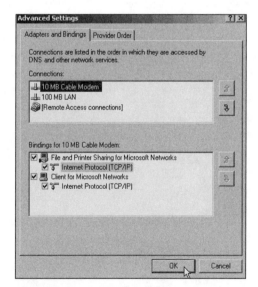

FIGURE 6.3
Bindings define the priority given to network protocols and services on a specific connection.

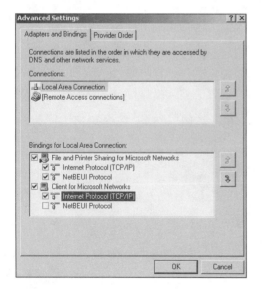

FIGURE 6.4
By unbinding a protocol from a service, you eliminate the network communication that uses it, as well as the network overhead associated with using it.

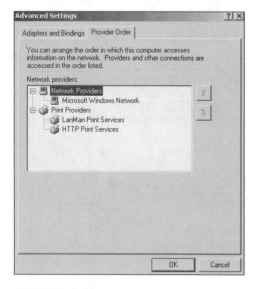

FIGURE 6.5
Provider order lets you give one network provider priority over another.

Figure 6.4 shows the Advanced Settings for a server with one LAN connection and both TCP/IP and NetBEUI installed. The File and Printer Sharing for Microsoft Networks entry represents the Server service for the connection. This service listens on that connection for requests for shared files or printers. Currently, the Server service will respond to requests from clients who ask for shared information with either TCP/IP or NetBEUI.

The Client for Microsoft Networks is the Workstation service for the connection. This service is responsible for initiating connections to network resources on other computers. In Figure 6.4, the NetBEUI protocol has been disabled for the Workstation service. This is probably because none of the NetBEUI clients are sharing information, which makes it undesirable to broadcast requests for information using both TCP/IP and NetBEUI because that causes twice as much traffic as is necessary.

The Provider Order property sheet allows you to set preferred order for accessing network resources with the providers installed. In Figure 6.5, there is only one network provider: Microsoft Windows Network. However, you could also install a NetWare provider, and then you would order the providers by importance; the first one listed would be tried first in any attempt to access resources. Similarly, the print providers can be put in order with the preferred provider at the top to make printing more efficient.

The Windows Optional Networking Components Wizard

The Windows Optional Networking Components Wizard (see Figure 6.6) is used to install additional networking services on your Windows 2000 computer. This wizard actually provides a subset of the options you can install from the Add/Remove Programs Wizard.

Specifically, the Windows Optional Networking Components Wizard can be used to install management and monitoring tools (like the Network Monitor), network services (like DHCP and DNS), and other file and print services (like File and Print Services for Macintosh and Print Services for UNIX). To install these services, invoke the wizard by choosing the Advanced, Optional Networking Components command from within the Network and

Dial-Up Connections dialog box. When you're prompted for the components to install, select the ones you want and continue with the installation. Most of the components you install here will require configuration after installation is complete.

The Status Dialog Box

The Status dialog box has three functions:

◆ To show you the status of the connection (complete with packets transferred and time the connection has been active)

◆ To disable the connection when you do not need it

◆ To access the properties (which will be discussed in the next section)

You can access the Status dialog box (see Figure 6.7) by double-clicking the network connection you want to configure. If you click the Disable button, the connection will be temporarily disabled. This will immediately disconnect all users connected and abort all network transfers on that connection. To enable the connection, you can double-click the icon again or restart your computer.

You can click the Properties button to access the Properties dialog box.

The Connection Properties Dialog Box

The Connection Properties dialog box is the place from which new protocols are installed and configured, where clients can be installed and configured, and where some network services can be installed and configured (see Figure 6.8). Note that you have already seen this dialog box; it was used to configure the GSNW in Chapter 2, "Installing, Configuring, and Troubleshooting Access to Resources."

You can access the Connection Properties by double-clicking on a connection and then clicking the Properties button in the Status dialog box. Alternatively, you can right-click the connection and select Properties from the menu that appears.

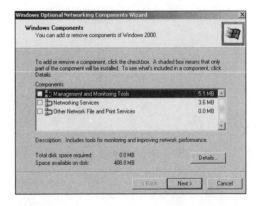

FIGURE 6.6
The Windows Optional Networking Components wizard gives you a subset of the options available in the Add/Remove Programs tool in the Control Panel.

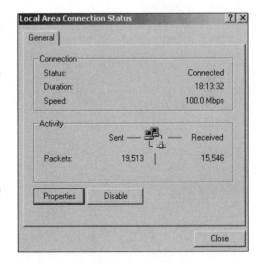

FIGURE 6.7
This dialog box shows the Sent and Received status and lets you disable a connection.

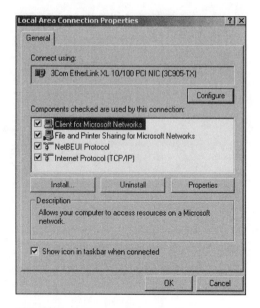

FIGURE 6.8
Connection properties can be used to add new clients, protocols, and network services.

From that point, you can choose to add new clients, protocols, and services by clicking the Install button and then following the instructions for each. The next section outlines the process for installation of network protocols from this dialog box.

In addition, when you select a component, you can also configure its properties by clicking the Properties button. You saw this in Chapter 2, when the properties of the Server service (File and Printer Sharing for Microsoft Networks) were discussed.

INSTALLING AND CONFIGURING NWLINK AND NETBEUI PROTOCOLS

Install, configure, and troubleshoot network protocols.

Although the test objective associated with this section deals with all network protocols, only three will be tested on: TCP/IP, NWLink, and NetBEUI. Moreover, because TCP/IP is such an important protocol in Windows 2000 networking, and because it has far reaching implications to other discussions in this chapter (like Network Services, for example) it has been split off into its own section. As a result, the complete discussion of network protocols spans this section and the section "Installing, Configuring, and Maintaining the TCP/IP Protocol Suite."

A network protocol is a collection of rules and procedures governing communication among the computers on a network. In a sense, a protocol is a language your computer uses when speaking to other computers. If two computers don't use the same protocols, they cannot communicate. Windows 2000 includes several protocols designed for different situations and different networking environments. Previous chapters have discussed some of those protocols (like NWLink and AppleTalk), but this section is dedicated to describing protocols in detail.

Three protocols are used for communication in a Windows 2000 network in which interoperability with other network types is not an issue:

◆ NWLink

◆ NetBEUI

◆ TCP/IP

Other protocols are used on Windows 2000. However, these are installed when there is a need for interoperability with other network types (like AppleTalk for example); these issues were already discussed in Chapter 2.

Installing and Maintaining the NWLink Protocol

One of the protocols used in Windows 2000 networks is the NWLink IPX/SPX/NetBIOS Compatible Transport Protocol, NWLink for short. This protocol is Microsoft's emulation of Novell's IPX/SPX protocol and was developed to enable interconnectivity between Microsoft and NetWare networks. NWLink is routable, meaning that it can be transferred from a local network to a remote one through a router. A router is a computer or dedicated hardware device that is able to look at the destination address on a network packet and determine (by looking at a routing table) if the information is destined for a computer on the local LAN or if it should be transferred (through a second network interface) to another network. NWLink configures its own routing tables, which makes it nice for small networks; however, it is not practical for large WANs like the Internet and cannot be used to connect directly to the Internet.

NWLink is used for three purposes in a Windows 2000 network environment. The first use is obvious: to enable communication with NetWare servers. The second reason to use NWLink is for connecting small, interconnected (routed) networks. Because NWLink is much easier to install and configure than TCP/IP, it is a choice when Internet access is not an issue. The third reason deals with security considerations. If you are concerned about attacks from malicious people via a TCP/IP connection and have no need for Internet connectivity, you can convert your network to NWLink. This would allow you to preserve the capability of routing while at the same time eliminating the capability for most hackers to get at your network data. Securing a network in this way would require that no connection to the Internet or other TCP/IP network be configured at all. Once a logical connection to a TCP/IP network is configured (through routing or conversion), the value of a NWLink-only network for security would be lost.

Installing NWLink

This installation was covered in detail in Chapter 2, in the discussion of connectivity with NetWare. However, to review, the NWLink protocol is installed via the properties for a connection. From the Properties dialog box, you can choose to install a new component; in this case, you would install the NWLink IPX/SPX/NetBIOS Compatible Transport Protocol. For a full discussion, see the section "Installing and Configuring the NWLink Protocol" in Chapter 2.

Configuring NWLink

The topic of configuration was also covered in Chapter 2. What is important in the configuration of NWLink is that the external network number and the frame type be the same as that of the other computers you desire to communicate with. These should not need to be changed in the average NWLink implementation. For a full discussion, see the section "Installing and Configuring the NWLink Protocol" in Chapter 2.

Troubleshooting NWLink

Although NWLink is primarily self-configuring, certain things that might go wrong can be repaired. Primarily, one of two things is causing the problem: NWLink is not bound to the network interface, or the network number and/or frame type is configured incorrectly.

In this case, "binding" refers to a protocol being configured to operate on a specific network card and with a specific service. Generally, when you install NWLink on a Windows 2000 computer, it is bound to all network adapters and all services on those adapters. However, bindings can be changed manually, and as a result, a specific protocol may not be transmitted (or received) by way of a specific adapter. Three problems can result: 1) you might not experience any NWLink traffic through a specific adapter, 2) you might be able to connect to network shares on other computers but no one can connect to your shares, or 3) others might be able to connect to your shares but you cannot connect to theirs. All three of those situations (especially the last two) indicate a problem with binding.

Bindings were discussed in the section titled "Configuring a Connection in Windows 2000," so the mechanics of configuring bindings will not be covered here. However, it is important that, in order for NWLink communication to occur, you make sure NWLink is bound to the network adapters connected to the NWLink network and that NWLink is enabled for the Server service (File and Printer Sharing for Microsoft Networks in the Adapters and Bindings dialog box) and the Workstation service (Client for Microsoft Networks in the Adapters and Bindings dialog box).

The second source of potential problems in an NWLink network is the external network number and frame type assigned to a network adapter. The external network number is (typically) an automatically configured number identifying all the computers on a LAN. The frame type is like a dialect of NWLink used by different network types (Ethernet vs. Token Ring, for example) or by different versions of NetWare (3.x or 4.x, for example). Frame types, like external network numbers, are also (typically) configured automatically.

The easiest way to determine if a problem with external network numbers and/or frame types is causing problems with NWLink communication is to use a command-line utility called IPXROUTE CONFIG. When executed from a Windows 2000 command prompt, this utility will identify the connection names, the external network number, the node number (a unique identifier for the local machine obtained from the hardware address of the network adapter), and the frame type.

When you enter the `IPXROUTE CONFIG` command, you will see information similar to this:

```
NWLink IPX Routing and Source Routing Control Program v2.00

Num  Name                    Network   Node           Frame
===============================================================
1.   IpxLoopbackAdapter      1234cdef  000000000002   [802.2]
2.   Local Area Connection 2 00000000  0050dab5c056   [802.2]
3.   NDISWANIPX              00000000  D86720524153   [EthII]
```

In this case, the connection to the LAN is represented by the name Local Area Connection 2. If you issue the same command on the other computer or computers you want to communicate with, you need to make sure the network number and frame type are the same. If they are not, one of two things must be done. Either you need to change the network numbers and frame types to all be the same, or you need to add a second network number and frame type to one or more of your machines. Sometimes more than one NWLink network is operating on the same physical LAN. This is usually the case when more than one NetWare server is present and they are of different versions (3.x and 4.x). In such a case, in order to preserve connectivity with both, you must configure multiple networks, each with its own frame type. The manual configuration of networks and frame types was discussed in Chapter 2, in the section "Interoperation with Novell NetWare."

Installing and Maintaining the NetBEUI Protocol

NetBEUI, also known as the NetBIOS Extended User Interface, is a non-routable network transport suite for use in small networks consisting of a single LAN with 50 or fewer computers. In the Microsoft networking world, NetBEUI was the primary protocol for Windows 3.11 (Windows for Workgroups). It is easy to work with, and may still be used where little network configuration is required and where you do not need to route to other networks or communicate with the Internet.

NetBEUI is easy to use because it is self-configuring. There is nothing to do except install it. It has limitations in that all network communication is done primarily by broadcast (rather than directed), and as a result, the larger the network, the more cumbersome network traffic becomes. In addition, because all computers have to be on the same LAN, it cannot be used in a WAN (wide area network) environment.

NetBEUI may be used in a Windows 2000 network where Windows 3.11 clients still exist and the 32-bit TCP/IP protocol has not been installed. However, in situations like that, you should investigate the practicality of upgrading the Windows 3.11 clients to Windows 98 or Windows 2000 Professional.

Installing NetBEUI

NetBEUI can be installed through the properties of the connection over which you want to communicate with NetBEUI.

Step by Step 6.1 illustrates how to install the NetBEUI protocol.

STEP BY STEP

6.1 Installing the NetBEUI Protocol

1. Right-click the My Network Places icon and select Properties from the menu that appears.

2. At the Network and Dial-Up Connections dialog box, right-click the connection for which you want to install NetBEUI and select Properties from the menu that appears.

3. At the Connection Properties dialog box, click the Install button.

4. In the Select Network Component Type dialog box, select Protocol and click Add.

5. At the Select Network Protocol dialog box, select NetBEUI Protocol and click OK (see Figure 6.9).

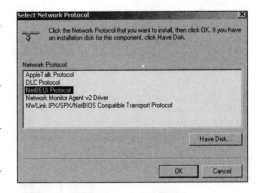

FIGURE 6.9
Select NetBEUI in the protocols list.

Troubleshooting NetBEUI

Because NetBEUI is such a simple protocol, and because it cannot be configured, very few things can go wrong with communication over NetBEUI. If you encounter a problem with NetBEUI-based communication, you should check the following three things:

◆ Check the network infrastructure, including network cards, cables, and drivers (through the Device manager).

◆ Check computer names to ensure that there are no duplicates on your network. The computer name (called the NetBIOS name) is located in the System Properties dialog box for your computer.

◆ Check network bindings to verify that the protocol is being used with the desired network adapters (see the section "Configuring a Connection in Windows 2000," earlier in this chapter, for information on configuring bindings).

Step by Step 6.2 demonstrates how to view and modify a computer's NetBIOS name.

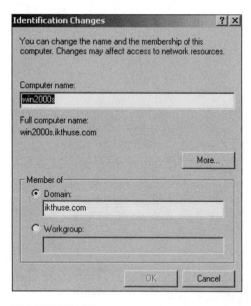

FIGURE 6.10
You can go through the System Properties dialog box to change a server's NetBIOS name.

STEP BY STEP

6.2 Viewing and Modifying a Computer's NetBIOS Name

1. Right-click the My Computer icon and select Properties from the menu that appears.

2. Click the Network Identification tab, and then click the Properties button.

3. In the Identification Changes dialog box, view the name in the Computer Name field and type in a new name if necessary (see Figure 6.10).

4. Click OK to apply the new name.

Installing, Configuring, and Maintaining the TCP/IP Protocol Suite

The Transmission Control Protocol/Internet Protocol (TCP/IP) is the global protocol. Every operating system vying for any appreciable market share has a built-in version of TCP/IP. However, TCP/IP is not the protocol of choice because of ease of use or ease of configuration; it is the protocol of choice because it is the protocol that defines Internet connectivity, because it is an open standard, and because it is scalable to accommodate even the largest WAN design.

Actually, to say that TCP/IP is a protocol is misleading. It is, in fact, a suite of protocols designed to ensure the most flexible network communication. Some components of the TCP/IP suite are designed purely for communication, others for ensuring proper information delivery, and others for troubleshooting. For simplicity, the protocol suite will often be referred to as the TCP/IP protocol, but you need to realize that it is much more than a single transport mechanism.

This section will deal with TCP/IP, its configuration, and the software available intrinsically and in Windows 2000 for implementing it. Because the concepts and tools behind TCP/IP are extensive, this section addresses only those features that directly pertain to understanding the basic functions of TCP/IP communication and that are bound to be on the Windows 2000 Server exam. Many features will be left unexplained; you will need to consult other resources to learn about them.

This section will cover the following TCP/IP topics:

- ◆ TCP/IP addresses and subnets
- ◆ TCP/IP name resolution theory
- ◆ Manual TCP/IP configuration
- ◆ Automatic TCP/IP configuration using DHCP
- ◆ Implementing DNS for name resolution
- ◆ Implementing WINS for name resolution

These topics will be discussed in the order presented above. This ensures that you are introduced to concepts and terminology at appropriate times and adheres to the structure of the exam objectives.

TCP/IP Addresses and Subnets

Ipv6   There is an evolving standard, Ipv6, that will greatly expand this configuration, but that is not the version of TCP/IP implemented in Windows 2000.

TCP/IP is most recognizable by its addressing scheme. TCP/IP addresses currently are defined by four octets separated by decimals (for example, 204.219.197.223). These octets, which are displayed as decimal numbers between 0 and 255, do not look much like sets of eight (which is what octet means), but that is because we generally do not look at them in a simple enough form. Each octet is really a binary number of eight digits that ranges between 00000000 and 11111111 (0 to 255). On the public Internet, each TCP/IP address uniquely identifies a specific computer, so no duplicate addresses are given out.

The TCP/IP address is not just a simple set of four decimal numbers, however. A TCP/IP address is really divided into two parts: the network address and the host address. If you think about house numbers on a suburban street, this might make more sense. My house number is 51, and I have a friend whose house number is also 51. When you mail a letter to me via the postal system (you remember, it used paper and stamps), how does the postal carrier know whether to deliver to my friend or me? Well, the house number is not all there is to my address; I also have a street, city, province (that's a state here in Canada), and country. The house number defines the specific house, but the rest of my address defines what area the mail should go to and what postal carrier will actually put the mail into my mailbox.

Delivery of information in a TCP/IP network is very much the same. The TCP/IP address is divided into two sections: the network and the host. The network address is always the high-order end of the address (some set of numbers beginning from the left side), and the host address is always the low-order end of the address (the rest of the numbers up to the end of the right side). The combinations are complex and are for another book; however, I will describe some of the common ones in just a few sentences. The problem is that the network needs to be told what part is the network address and what part is the host address (just like the mail carrier would need to be told which is my house number if my whole address were just a bunch of numbers). Another configured component of TCP/IP addressing takes care of network/host identification; that component is referred to as the "subnet mask." The subnet mask and the TCP/IP address define where information should be delivered (generally as well as specifically) and are the only two pieces of addressing information required to correctly configure a TCP/IP network that has no routers.

Because subnet theory can be very complex, let me give you some quick examples. Groups of TCP/IP addresses are defined by their class. Three classes are commonly used worldwide: classes A, B, and C. In class A addresses, the subnet mask indicates that the first octet is the network and the last three define hosts. In class B addresses, the subnet mask indicates that the first two octets are the network and the last two are the host address. In class C addresses, the subnet mask indicates that the first three octets are the network address and the last one is the host address.

As you may have already figured out, the fewer octets that are available for host addresses, the fewer host addresses a particular network can have. Class C "streets" are short, consisting of a maximum of 254 addresses (0 and 255 cannot be used as a host address for technical reasons). Class B networks are mid-sized, consisting of a maximum of 65,534 host addresses. Class A networks are very large, consisting of up to 16,777,214 host addresses.

The following is an example of a typical class C address with a subnet:

```
207.219.193.233
255.255.255.0
```

In this subnet mask, the first three 255s indicate that the 207.219.193 is the network and the 233 is the host number. Class B addresses have a subnet mask of 255.255.0.0, and class A addresses have a subnet mask of 255.0.0.0.

Subnet masks are necessary in TCP/IP addressing because TCP/IP is a routed protocol. This means that not every address is directly accessible by your computer. Instead, like directions from your house to the local shopping mall, you may get to certain (virtual) intersections and have to turn left or right; all roads do not lead

N O T E

Default Gateway Is the Path of Last Resort In networking environments in which a company has more than one internal subnet, computers may be configured to seek out more than one router in case the destination address is not on its subnet. In these cases, the default gateway is the route of last resort—the one to take if no other routed path can satisfy direction to the subnet required.

directly to the mall! When I try to access another computer running TCP/IP, the address that I am trying to get to is checked (using the subnet mask) to see if the network is the same. If it is, my computer knows that the destination machine is on the same LAN, and I can access it directly. On the other hand, if my computer determines that the other machine does not have the same network address, the communication will have to go through a router to get to the final destination. A router, in essence, is a hardware device that is responsible for directing network traffic from one network (subnet) to another. A router is configured with a set of network addresses and told where to direct network traffic that is destined for any of the networks the router knows about. As a result, if you are trying to set up communication on a LAN between a number of computers, not only do the network addresses have to be the same, but the subnet masks must also be the same. If they are not, your computer will always be trying to direct the communication through a router.

If information really does need to travel through a router out to another LAN, a third piece of information must be supplied in the configuration: the default gateway. That is generally the address of the router that directs information out of your LAN to the outside world.

TCP/IP, ARP, and Address Resolution

In a TCP/IP network, communication between computers does not actually happen based on the TCP/IP address. There is an identifier even more fundamental to network communication than the TCP/IP address; it is called the Media Access Control (MAC) address. An adapter's MAC address is universally unique and is assigned to the network card when it is manufactured. When communication occurs between two TCP/IP-based computers, some background communication must occur to determine if the MAC address of the network card is associated with a certain TCP/IP address. This communication happens via the Address Resolution Protocol (ARP). This concept is important because ARP can be used as a troubleshooting tool, and it is used by the automatic TCP/IP configuration utility (DHCP) to ensure that a specific TCP/IP address is not currently being used on a LAN.

When a computer resolves another machine's TCP/IP address to a MAC address, it is stored for between 2 and 10 minutes (depending on how many subsequent times it is used) in a local ARP cache. Because of this cache, if the same machine is contacted again within a short period of time, the MAC address does not have to be resolved by way of a network broadcast.

The MAC address of another machine (or even the local machine) can be determined using ARP and the ARP cache. The next Step by Step shows you how to use ARP to determine what is in the cache.

STEP BY STEP

6.3 Investigating the Contents of the Local ARP Cache

1. From the Start menu, select Programs, Accessories, Command Prompt to access a command prompt.

2. In the command prompt window, type **PING** *hostname* or **PING** *TCP/IP address* where *hostname* is the name of the machine you want to resolve the MAC address for or where *TCP/IP address* is the TCP/IP address of the network adapter for which you want to resolve the MAC address.

3. Immediately (within two minutes of step 2), type **ARP -a**. A list of one (or more) TCP/IP addresses will be displayed along with the physical (MAC) addresses of the network adapters associated with those addresses.

4. Close the command prompt window.

It is important to note that there is much more to ARP than what was covered here. However, other details of ARP are beyond the scope of the Server exam and this book.

TCP/IP and Name Resolution

As has been mentioned, TCP/IP identifies computers using numbers, which is fine for computers. However, people do not like to use numbers to identify things; it is completely non-intuitive. Instead, people prefer to identify objects, people, and servers by way of names. The world would be a hard place to communicate if all people were identified by their Social Security or Social Insurance numbers (only the Beagle Boys would find that comfortable).

As a result, people have found it convenient to give computers names. Two types of names are commonly given to computers: NetBIOS names (commonly referred to as the "computer name") and host names (the name associated with TCP/IP configuration). Of course, TCP/IP does not like to communicate with names; it wants addresses. If names are to be used, some way to map a specific name to a specific TCP/IP address is required.

There are five common ways to resolve names of servers to their TCP/IP addresses: Domain Name System (DNS), Windows Internet Name Service (WINS), HOSTS files, LMHOSTS files, and network broadcast.

DNS (which is used to resolve host names) and WINS (which is used to resolve NetBIOS names) will be discussed briefly here, and more fully in the section titled "Installing and Configuring Network Services" later in this chapter.

As with ARP, it must be noted that this chapter will not attempt to discuss every nuance of address resolution; rather, it covers only those areas that will be pertinent to the Windows 2000 Server exam.

Name Resolution Using DNS

DNS is unquestionably the most widely used name resolution mechanism on the planet, primarily because it is the resolution method used on the Internet. If you type www.microsoft.com, somehow your browser knows how to get to the Microsoft Web site—and this is a result of DNS. The power of the resolution capabilities of DNS is that many DNS servers (rather than a single one) are responsible for resolving names. Each Internet domain has at least one DNS server that is responsible for resolving the names of computers (hosts) within that domain. If there is more than one DNS machine for an

Internet domain, one of them is designated the Start of Authority (SOA). The SOA machine is the definitive expert on the domain, meaning that if you want to find a specific machine in a domain and the SOA for that domain does not know what you are looking for, the answer cannot be found using DNS.

If a client is using TCP/IP and is configured to use DNS to resolve host names, it will be configured with a DNS server to query should a name need to be resolved. If you consider that there are tens of thousands of Internet domains representing millions of individual hosts, it is obvious that each DNS server cannot know about all the other hosts worldwide. However, it is not necessary for each DNS server to know everything. Each DNS server knows about a certain set of hosts (the ones in its domain), and it knows about certain root DNS servers. The DNS structure of Internet names is set up in a tree. For example, the host www.IKTHUSE.com falls into a DNS structure (see Figure 6.11). As the figure shows, starting from the root (the "dot" server), each level has progressively more nodes in it (all the nodes are not shown, even in the second level). To get to www.IKTHUSE.com, you travel from the root (.) to COM to IKTHUSE to WWW.

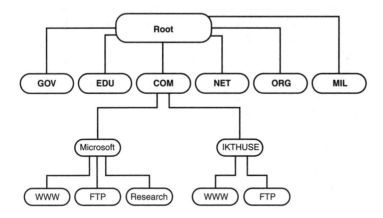

FIGURE 6.11
This is a small part of the global DNS tree.

If your computer queried its DNS to find out about www.IKTHUSE.com, it would come up empty-handed if it had to rely on its own local information to resolve that name (a recursive query). However, it does not. Instead, an iterative query is initiated. Without going into how many servers there are servicing the root or the .COM domains, the iteration goes as follows: Your client queries its designated DNS server. If that server cannot resolve the name, it queries the root. The root knows about only those name spaces that are directly below it. In effect, the root server would return back to your DNS with the message "I can't find it, but I know where COM is." At that point, your DNS server would be given the name of the nearest .COM server. Your DNS server would then query the .COM server for the host name. It would then get the response, "I can't find it, but I know where IKTHUSE is." Your DNS would then query the server that is the SOA for IKTHUSE, and it would return the TCP/IP address 24.66.33.130 as a resolution for www.IKTHUSE.com.

The strength of DNS is that the tree structure ensures quick resolution of names and ensures that the amount of information actually known by any one server is kept to a minimum.

There are three major drawbacks to the traditional implementation of DNS name resolution. First, it is complex to set up. In order to get it working, you must configure one or more DNS servers (depending on the size of your implementation). Second, it has been, to this point, a manually configured set of mappings. That means new hosts must be put into the DNS database as they are configured, or there will be no name resolution for those host names. Third, the DNS structure on a server is held in a text file that can be deleted or modified by anyone with sufficient access to it.

The implementation of DNS under Windows 2000 has solutions for all three of these problems. First, DNS is essential to the configuration of a Windows 2000 domain. Because DNS is used almost exclusively for name resolution under Windows 2000, it is a requirement for the configuration of Active Directory. As a result, configuring your DNS goes hand in hand with the configuration of Active Directory in your domain. Although this does not actually make the configuration of DNS any simpler, the complexity is coupled with other configuration and research you are doing to set up Active Directory, so it is not an isolated task.

Second, a new DNS standard allows for automatic configuration of DNS records through the cooperation of the DHCP service (a service installed on a Windows 2000 server for the automatic configuration of TCP/IP addresses on client machines; see the section "Installing and Configuring Network Services"). This standard allows much of the manual configuration of DNS entries to be avoided, replaced instead by automatic configuration when clients get TCP/IP addresses from the DHCP server.

Finally, the problem of security is alleviated somewhat through the use of DNS integrated into the Active Directory. When DNS is integrated into the Active Directory, the security is increased measurably, so many of the security issues have tools for resolution.

Name Resolution Using WINS

NetBIOS is a TCP/IP interface that operates at the Application layer of the OSI model. It was designed to provide a naming strategy for small networks. It consists of a flat namespace (names can only be used once in an organization) of up to 16 character names for devices.

Until Windows 2000, NetBIOS was required for networking with Windows operating systems. In a pure Windows 2000 network, NetBIOS is no longer required; however, in a network with a mixture of clients, support is still necessary.

Like the host names used in DNS, NetBIOS names need to be resolved to TCP/IP addresses if TCP/IP-based communication is to work. Microsoft implemented WINS, a variation on the standard TCP/IP name server standard, to allow for the automated resolution of NetBIOS names on TCP/IP networks.

In a simple WINS implementation (which is all that will be dealt with here), a single WINS server is installed. This WINS server has a database that is dynamically populated with the mapping of NetBIOS names with TCP/IP addresses as clients announce their presence on the network. In order to increase the efficiency of the WINS registration process, each WINS client has the TCP/IP address of its registration server configured into its TCP/IP properties. When a client is started, that client registers its name, function, and TCP/IP address with the WINS server.

When a client wants to locate another computer using its NetBIOS name, a request is made to its WINS server for the TCP/IP address corresponding to the name. If the WINS server has a mapping, the address is returned; if not, the resolution fails and the client may have to try another method (depending on how it was configured to resolve NetBIOS names).

To ensure that the WINS database is efficient and that names of NetBIOS computers that are no longer present on the network do not persist in the database, when a client machine is shut down using an appropriate method (as opposed to simply powering down the machine), it sends a message to its WINS server telling the server to remove its name from the WINS database. In addition, to ensure that WINS entries are removed even if clients are not shut down properly, the WINS server places a time limit (time to live) on the record that is created when the client registers. By default, this limit is six days. When the client registers itself, the WINS server sends back a message indicating the time to live (TTL) of the registration. At half of the TTL, the client sends a renewal notice to the WINS server to indicate that it is still present on the network, and the client is again issued a six-day TTL on its registration. If the WINS server does not try to contact the client to ensure that the registration is renewed, the client's entry is removed from the WINS database when the TTL expires.

Clients can be configured to use WINS in different ways to resolve NetBIOS names. As you will see when configuring DHCP (see the section "Installing and Configuring DHCP" to follow), a WINS client is given a node type to indicate what kind of NetBIOS name resolution will occur. These types always differentiate between a client using WINS to resolve NetBIOS names and using broadcast (simply calling out on the network to see if a client with a particular name responds). A client can be configured with one of four node types: B-node, P-node, M-node, or H-node. Table 6.2 shows the node types and their methods of name resolution.

TABLE 6.2

NETBIOS RESOLUTION NODE TYPES

Node Type	Resolution Method
B-node (broadcast)	B-node uses only broadcast to resolve NetBIOS names. Clients configured with B-node will never use WINS.
P-node (peer-to-peer)	P-node uses WINS only. It will never use broadcast, even if the WINS server cannot resolve the name.
M-node (mixed)	M-node uses a combination of broadcast and WINS. Clients configured to use M-node first use broadcast (B-node) to resolve; if that is unsuccessful, they query the configured WINS server (P-node).
H-node (hybrid)	H-node uses a combination of broadcast and WINS. Clients configured to use H-node first query the WINS server (P-node); if that is unsuccessful, they try broadcast (B-node) to resolve.

By default, Windows 2000 clients are configured to use B-node. However, if a client's TCP/IP configuration is changed to include the address of a WINS server, it changes to H-node.

Name Resolution Using HOSTS and LMHOSTS Files

Although DNS and WINS are both excellent ways of configuring for host and NetBIOS name resolution, there are times when such configuration is more than is necessary. In cases where it would be impractical or impossible to configure DNS and WINS servers to provide name resolution for all TCP/IP names, you can configure files on local computers to do name resolution. The HOSTS file can be configured to take the place of (or supplement) DNS host name resolution. This means it can be the sole method of host name resolution, or it can be a supplement to the DNS database for names that are not, or cannot, be configured there.

On the other hand, if resolution of NetBIOS names is required and there is no WINS server available (or if for some reason, the clients cannot or do not register their names with your WINS server), an LMHOSTS file can be configured to replace or supplement WINS.

On a Windows 2000 computer, both files are created and stored in the \WINNT\SYSTEM32\DRIVERS\ETC folder. To aid you in creating these files, there are samples of both in that folder under the names HOSTS and LMHOSTS.SAM. You can use these as templates for creating your own files, but the .SAM extension must be removed from the LMHOSTS.SAM file before it will function.

The HOSTS file, which is used when host name resolution is attempted, has entries that map TCP/IP addresses with host names. In the case of the HOSTS file provided, one mapping is already present, the one mapping 127.0.0.1 with the name localhost. Other entries can be configured simply by creating new lines with the TCP/IP address followed by a space and the host name (which can be a single name or an Internet host name like www.ikthuse.com).

The LMHOSTS file is configured in much the same way the HOSTS file is. It is used when NetBIOS name resolution is attempted. The sample file provided (LMHOSTS.SAM) outlines the configuration specifications for file entries. At its most basic, an LMHOSTS entry consists of a TCP/IP address followed by at least one space and a computer name (of up to 16 characters). There is, however, one additional setting that is worth mentioning: the #PRE designator.

When NetBIOS name resolution occurs, any resolved names go into a local NetBIOS name cache on the client machine. This local cache ensures that if resolution happens, it stores the result for 10 minutes and, therefore, does not need to be resolved again until that time. The entries in the LMHOSTS file are not placed into the NetBIOS name cache until resolution actually happens. If you want to preload the cache with values from the LMHOSTS file, you can suffix the LMHOSTS line with #PRE (for preload). This ensures quick resolution of those names.

Integration of Name Resolution Methods

Because of the variety of name resolution methods, you may find that more than one is suitable in your organization. For example, if your Windows 2000 network contains Windows 9x or Windows NT clients, you will have to retain support for NetBIOS name resolution as well as the default DNS used by Windows 2000. You may also find it helpful to populate HOSTS or LMHOSTS files on local client machines to supplement the other name resolution methods. In these cases, it is helpful to know how the name resolution methods interact with one another when many are present.

When a host name is being resolved (such as what happens when you try to connect using Internet Explorer), the following order is used in resolution:

1. Check to see if the name being referenced is the host name of the local machine.

2. Check to see if the name being referenced is in the local HOSTS file.

3. Check with the configured DNS server to see if it can resolve the name.

4. Check the local NetBIOS name cache for the name.

5. Check the configured WINS servers for the name.

6. Broadcast on the local LAN for the name.

7. Check the local LMHOSTS file for a match.

8. Return with a failure message.

The above steps are tried in order. If any of them successfully resolves the name, the resolution process ends, and network operation continues.

When a NetBIOS name is being resolved (such as when a NET command is issued at a command prompt), the following order is used in resolution:

1. Check to see if the name being referenced is in the local NetBIOS name cache of the local machine.

2. Check the configured WINS servers for the name.

3. Broadcast on the local LAN for the name.

4. Check the local LMHOSTS file for a match.

5. Check the local HOSTS file for a match.

6. Check with the configured DNS server to see if it can resolve the name.

7. Return with a failure message.

As with host name resolution, these steps are followed in order until the name is resolved or the failure message is generated.

Installing TCP/IP

TCP/IP is the default protocol installed when you install Windows 2000 Server. However, that does not mean every Windows 2000 server begins with TCP/IP installed. As a result, you might have to install TCP/IP on a Windows 2000 server.

Protocols are installed from the properties of the connection over which they are to be used to communicate. You must have access to the Windows 2000 Server installation files to be able to install the protocol and all its utilities. The following Step by Step leads you through the process of installing the TCP/IP protocol suite.

STEP BY STEP

6.4 Installing the TCP/IP Protocol Suite

1. Right-click the My Network Places icon and select Properties from the menu that appears.

2. At the Network and Dial-Up Connections dialog box, right-click the connection in which you want to install TCP/IP and select Properties from the menu that appears.

3. In the Connection Properties dialog box, click the Install button.

4. In the Select Network Component Type dialog box, select Protocol and click the Add button.

5. At the Select Network Protocol dialog box, select Internet Protocol (TCP/IP) and click OK (see Figure 6.12).

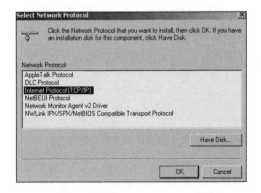

FIGURE 6.12
Many protocols are available to be installed. Here you choose TCP/IP.

Configuring TCP/IP

The only required information for TCP/IP is the IP address and
subnet mask. However, there is an additional requirement of a
default gateway for those networks that use a router. Even though
those three settings are the only required ones, other settings make
working with a TCP/IP network more user-friendly. These include
the DNS server and/or the WINS server a client will use.

Configuration of TCP/IP can be done in three ways:

◆ Manually

◆ Automatically via DHCP, or

◆ Automatically via system configuration

Manual configuration is the most labor-intensive configuration
method; it is also the most prone to misconfiguration. However, it is
inherently more secure than automatic configuration and requires no
infrastructure to support it; you just type in numbers.

Manually configuring a TCP/IP address requires that you open the
properties of the TCP/IP protocol on each machine and type in the
appropriate TCP/IP address, subnet mask, default gateway, and any
other configuration that you require. In order to configure the
TCP/IP properties on a computer, you have to be in the
Administrators local group.

Step by Step 6.5 demonstrates how to manually configure TCP/IP.

STEP BY STEP

6.5 Manually Configuring TCP/IP

1. Right-click the My Network Places icon and select
   Properties from the menu that appears.

2. At the Network and Dial-Up Connections dialog box,
   right-click the connection for which you want to configure
   TCP/IP from the menu that appears.

3. At the Connection Properties dialog box, double-click
   Internet Protocol (TCP/IP).

continues

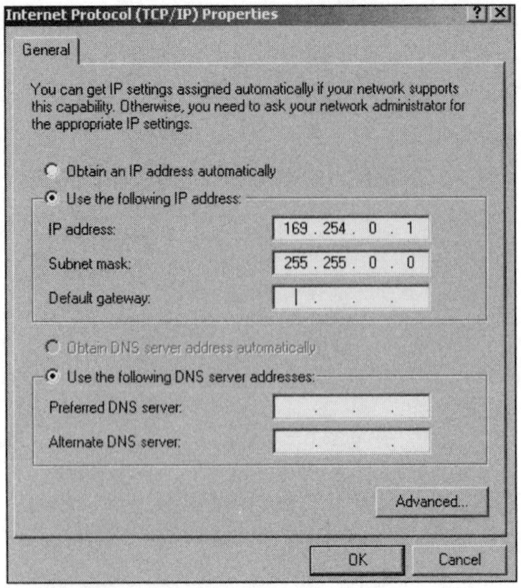

FIGURE 6.13
The required TCP/IP properties are the address
and subnet mask.

FIGURE 6.14
When a TCP/IP address conflict occurs, this
message is displayed on the screen of the person who is trying to use an allocated address.

continued

4. In the Internet Protocol (TCP/IP) Properties dialog box, select the radio button labeled Use the Following IP Address and fill in the TCP/IP address and subnet mask (see Figure 6.13). In addition, fill in a default gateway and a DNS server (if you have an address resolution server available).

5. Click OK.

Although manually configuring TCP/IP on a computer is relatively easy, it is generally avoided. It is labor-intensive and runs the risks of errors. First, you have to configure each machine separately, and that is a lot of configuration if you have 200 or 2,000 machines in your company. In addition, it is also labor-intensive to keep track of which addresses have been given out and which have not. If your organization's employee count numbers in the thousands, you might have someone working full-time just tracking TCP/IP addresses for you.

Manual configuration is also prone to misconfiguration. Keying errors occur, and when they do, a computer will not communicate to the rest of the network. In addition, errors can be introduced by people with good intentions (but little knowledge) who change their own TCP/IP addresses. (I know of organizations in which people routinely change their own TCP/IP addresses because theirs is too hard to remember!)

Finally, manual configuration can lead to duplicate addresses being assigned on your network. Duplicate addresses are problematic because the destination for network transmissions is ambiguous. As a result, the possibility exists for one machine to get information that is destined for another. This is not just inconvenient, it can also be insecure. If this happens, two dialog boxes will pop up.

On the computer where the TCP/IP address has been configured, the message box displayed in Figure 6.14 will appear, indicating that the TCP/IP address configured is already in use by another computer.

On the computer that originally had the TCP/IP address, the message box shown in Figure 6.15 will appear, indicating that another computer has been configured with its TCP/IP address. At this point, TCP/IP will be disabled on the computer with the illegal copy of the TCP/IP address.

Despite the problems that are associated with manual configuration, many large companies and agencies still use it. There are a number of reasons for doing this. First, assigning TCP/IP addresses manually increases security. Many government agencies use manual configuration because automatic configuration means that anyone who enters a location and can plug a laptop into the LAN will get a TCP/IP address and can begin the process of hacking into servers. Second, although manual configuration introduces administrative effort, it also eliminates the need for computers to give out addresses. This is especially important for networks with many subnets and few hosts in each, because a configuration server is required to be locally available on each subnet. (There is a way to avoid this by enabling the forwarding of BOOTP messages, but some organizations do not want this traffic travelling across their routers.) This is a financial outlay that many companies do not want to be burdened with just to have automatic configuration.

On the other hand, automatic configuration has many advantages and should be used in all but special circumstances. The basis of automatic configuration is DHCP, which can be set up on a Windows 2000 server. A DHCP server has a pool of addresses and is pre-configured to give out certain kinds of information that would normally be configured manually (like a subnet mask, default gateway, and name resolution servers).

When the TCP/IP protocol is set to get its configuration from a DHCP server, two types of address request situations are possible. You might obtain a TCP/IP address when none exists already, or you might get a TCP/IP address back after it has been obtained.

FIGURE 6.15
When a TCP/IP address conflict occurs, this message is displayed on the screen of the person who is currently using the address in question.

In the first situation, the client machine does not already have a TCP/IP address, and without one, it cannot communicate on the network using TCP/IP. The following steps are taken to obtain an address:

1. The client broadcasts a message using the DHCP protocol to the entire LAN to which it is connected, asking for an address from any DHCP server that can provide one.

2. All DHCP servers that are on the LAN receive the request and, if they have an address available, they broadcast a message back out onto the network, informing the machine that requested the address that there is one available. This message is directed back to the client using the hardware (MAC) address that it provided with its request. At this point, the DHCP servers responding have tentatively reserved the address being offered so that no other machine can grab it in the meantime.

3. The client receives the addresses offered. It sends a message back to each DHCP server that responded. To the first one it sends back a request for the address. To the others, it sends back a message that it does not need the addresses offered.

4. The DHCP server whose address was accepted makes a permanent entry in its database pairing the TCP/IP address it gave out with the hardware address of the machine that accepted it. All other DCHP servers remove the tentative reservation for the addresses they offered so that those addresses can be offered again.

5. The client receives the acknowledgement from the DHCP server whose address it accepted, and it begins to use the TCP/IP address configuration that was sent out (at least for the duration of the lease). The client can now communicate using TCP/IP.

Addresses given out by a DHCP server always have a lifetime associated with them; that is referred to as the *lease duration*. This lease duration defines the length of time a client is allowed to keep the address before it must give it back. In an attempt to continue to use the address, the client periodically tries to renew the address (and it is generally successful unless there are problems with the DHCP server). The only time renewal will not happen is when the lease is of infinite duration.

There are two instances in which a client will try to renew a lease. The first comes when a client computer is powered up, and the second occurs when the current lease has reached 50% of its life. In both cases, the DHCP server that issued the TCP/IP address is contacted directly, and the address is requested. Unless the server is unavailable, the address will generally be renewed. There are a few instances when a lease may not be renewed. For example, a lease will not be renewed if the client has been shut off for a period of time during which the lease expired. At that point, the address may have been given to another client. In addition, the lease might not be renewed if the DHCP server has deleted the reservation. Finally, the lease will not be renewed if the address requested is now in a part of the address range that is excluded from being given out after the initial offering. In all of these cases, the client must begin the lease discovery process again as though it were getting an address for the first time.

Step by Step 6.6 outlines the process for configuring a client to use DHCP to configure TCP/IP.

STEP BY STEP

6.6 Automatically Configuring TCP/IP Using DHCP

1. Right-click the My Network Places icon and select Properties from the menu that appears.

2. At the Network and Dial-Up Connections dialog box, right-click the connection for which you want to configure TCP/IP for and select Properties from the menu that appears.

3. At the Connection Properties dialog box, double-click Internet Protocol (TCP/IP).

4. At the Internet Protocol (TCP/IP) Properties dialog box, select the radio button labeled Obtain an IP Address Automatically, and then select the radio button labeled Obtain DNS Server Address Automatically (unless there is a reason to configure name resolution servers manually). This is shown in Figure 6.16.

5. Click OK.

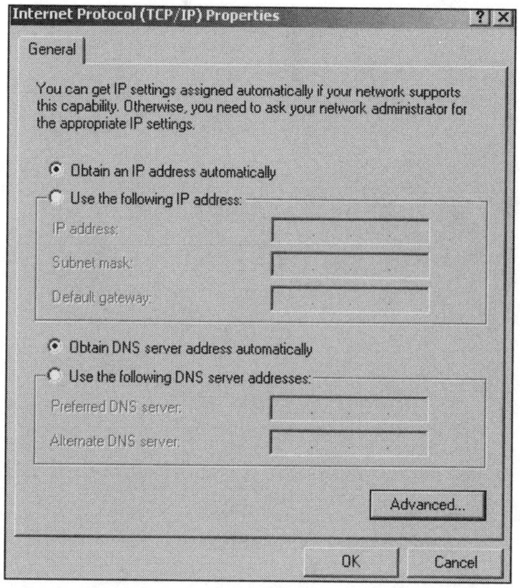

FIGURE 6.16
Choosing to obtain a TCP/IP address automatically reduces TCP/IP administration dramatically.

The final method for obtaining an address is to get one automatically when no DHCP server is available. This may occur when clients have inadvertently been set to obtain an address automatically but no DHCP server exists. It may also happen when all the TCP/IP addresses in the address pool to be given out by a DHCP server have been allocated to other clients.

If a client is configured to obtain an address automatically but a DHCP server cannot be contacted, it automatically configures its own TCP/IP address from the class B address reserved for general internal use: 169.254.x.x. Correspondingly, it configures itself with a subnet mask of 255.255.0.0 (the appropriate one for a class B address). The Internet community has reserved this set of addresses for internal use only. That means that addresses in this range should never be configured on the public Internet, only in network environments that do not directly interact with the public Internet.

To ensure that the address a client has autoconfigured is not being used by another client, the client sends out a network message (called a *gratuitous ARP*). You will recall that ARP is a tool used to resolve hardware addresses from TCP/IP addresses. The ARP sent here attempts to locate the network adapter with which a specific TCP/IP address is associated (in this case, the address that the client wants to assign to itself). The ARP is gratuitous because the client has no desire to resolve the address, only to determine if the address is in use. If no reply is received, the client knows that the address is not being used and it configures itself. The client will try up to 10 addresses before autoconfiguration fails. From the time an address has been autoconfigured, it will try to find the DHCP server every five minutes until a reply is received from the server offering a TCP/IP address.

Troubleshooting TCP/IP

TCP/IP configuration can be complex. Proper communication is dependant on the address and subnet mask being configured properly and on the default gateway being configured properly if information is ever to be sent to other networks. In addition, proper communication is also dependant on the proper configuration of every machine you are trying to communicate with.

Three tools are specifically designed for troubleshooting:

◆ IPCONFIG

◆ PING

◆ TRACERT

IPCONFIG

IPCONFIG is used for two things. First, it is used to determine the current TCP/IP configuration for the local computer. Second, it is used to manually release and renew DHCP addresses.

To obtain a summary of the current TCP/IP configuration of the local machine, you can go to a command prompt and type IPCONFIG. You should see something like the following listing:

```
Windows 2000 IP Configuration

Ethernet adapter Local Area Connection:

        Connection-specific DNS Suffix . .: ikthuse.com
        IP Address. . . . . . . . . . . .: 179.254.0.21
        Subnet Mask . . . . . . . . . . .: 255.255.0.0
        Default Gateway . . . . . . . . .: 179.254.0.1
```

This configuration indicates that my TCP/IP address is 179.254.0.21, my subnet mask is 255.255.0.0, and my default gateway is 179.254.0.1.

To obtain detailed information about the current TCP/IP configuration, type IPCONFIG /all. You should see something like the following listing:

```
Windows 2000 IP Configuration

        Host Name . . . . . . . . . . . : win2000s
        Primary DNS Suffix. . . . . . . : ikthuse.com
        Node Type . . . . . . . . . . . : Hybrid
        IP Routing Enabled. . . . . . . : No
        WINS Proxy Enabled. . . . . . . : No
        DNS Suffix Search List. . . . . : ikthuse.com
```

continues

continued

```
Ethernet adapter Local Area Connection:

       Connection-specific DNS Suffix . . : ikthuse.com
       Description . . . . . . . . . . . : 3Com EtherLink XL
    ➥10/100 PCI NIC (3C905-TX)
       Physical Address. . . . . . . . . : 00-60-97-D5-22-CA
       DHCP Enabled. . . . . . . . . . . : Yes
       Autoconfiguration Enabled . . . . : Yes
       IP Address. . . . . . . . . . . . : 179.254.0.21
       Subnet Mask . . . . . . . . . . . : 255.255.0.0
       Default Gateway . . . . . . . . . : 179.254.0.1
       DHCP Server . . . . . . . . . . . : 179.254.0.1
       DNS Servers . . . . . . . . . . . : 179.254.0.1
       Primary WINS Server . . . . . . . : 179.254.0.1
       Lease Obtained. . . . . . . . . . : Monday, December
    ➥27, 1999 11:55:57 AM
       Lease Expires . . . . . . . . . . : Tuesday, January
    ➥04, 2000 11:55:57 AM
```

It should be obvious that quite a lot more information is provided here than in the summary.

IPCONFIG is useful for troubleshooting because it not only allows you to see what your configuration is, it helps you determine whether you have a TCP/IP address at all. If communication with other computers fails, your first action should be to check your TCP/IP configuration using IPCONFIG. If the TCP/IP address is 0.0.0.0, you do not have an address. If your TCP/IP address begins with 169.254, you have a problem with your DHCP process because your client is not receiving addresses from your DHCP server.

IPCONFIG can also be used to force the DHCP server to renew your lease. At a command prompt, enter IPCONFIG /release to release your current address or enter IPCONFIG /renew to renew your address. This method is effective for renewing your lease and verifying that the DHCP server is responding. It will generally not get you a new TCP/IP address because, most often, you will receive your old address back.

PING

The PING command is also useful for troubleshooting. Whereas IPCONFIG tells you what your TCP/IP configuration is, PING tells you whether you can communicate with other computers using TCP/IP. The syntax of the PING command is PING *x.x.x.x*, where *x.x.x.x* is the address of the computer for which you want to test connectivity. The standard PING command sends a request for echo to other TCP/IP hosts. This request is sent four times, and a clear line will result in four responses. Where there is an intermittent connection (which sometimes occurs when you PING an Internet address), you might receive only two or three responses. A result of "unknown host" or "host unreachable" is a sign of a connectivity problem at your end, the remote end, or somewhere in between.

The following steps outline how to perform the standard connectivity test with PING:

1. PING the address 127.0.0.1. This is called the *loopback address*, and a response indicates that TCP/IP has been installed correctly on your computer.

2. PING the address of one of the adapters on the local computer. A response from this address indicates that the driver for the network card is functional.

3. PING the address of the default gateway (your router). A response from this address indicates that your interface to the outside world is reachable from your location.

4. PING the address of the external interface of the router. This is the interface that is connected to the outside world (or at least to other subnets). If a response comes back from that interface, your router is capable of routing packets properly.

5. PING the address of a remote host (something on the other side of the router). A response from this address indicates that the connection between your router's external interface and the next machine in the chain is functioning properly.

By following these steps, you can determine where the breakdown in communication is. If there is a problem at any point, you know where to go to determine what the problem is.

NOTE

PING by TCP/IP Address First It is important to begin the test by PINGing TCP/IP address to isolate connectivity issues from name resolution issues. For example, if I was trying to get to a Web site and was unable to, it would be better for me to try to PING it by TCP/IP address. That way I could eliminate problems with the translation between the name of the site (www.*site*.com) and the TCP/IP address associated with it. If I determine that I can get to the site by TCP/IP address, I can troubleshoot name resolution problems.

TRACERT

The third troubleshooting tool is called TRACERT. It is used to determine what route is being taken from one host to another. It is helpful when you have already established that there is a connectivity problem with that host (as determined by a PING test). The problem with PING is that it is an all-or-nothing proposition: once the echo request leaves your router, there is no way of telling where the problem is. On the other hand, TRACERT tells you what links can be successfully established and where communication is breaking down. This lets you know if the problem lies with your ISP, the remote host's ISP, or something in between, and you can determine whether you can take any course of action or whether you simply have to wait for connectivity to be re-established.

The syntax for TRACERT is TRACERT *ipaddress* or TRACERT *name*.

As an example, I live in Winnipeg, Canada, which is right in the center of the North American continent. I have a friend in Japan whose ISP is typhoon.co.jp. A TRACERT to his ISP results in the following:

```
C:\Tracert typhoon.co.jp

Tracing route to typhoon.co.jp [202.33.21.38]
over a maximum of 30 hops:

  1   10 ms    10 ms    10 ms    IKTHUSE-YODA [169.254.0.1]
  2   20 ms    20 ms    20 ms    24.66.36.1
  3   20 ms    20 ms    30 ms    24.66.63.3
  4   70 ms    40 ms    41 ms    cgdist1-f5-0-0.cg,sfl.net
➡[204.209.214.97]
  5   60 ms    40 ms    40 ms    cgcore2-f0-0-0.cg,sfl.net
➡[204.209.214.9]
  6   70 ms    40 ms    50 ms    205.150.143.17
  7   81 ms    70 ms    60 ms
➡h10.bb1.cal1.h810.bb1.van1.uunet.ca [205.150.241.73]
  8  130 ms   101 ms    90 ms    152.63.137.37
  9  120 ms    90 ms   100 ms    294.ATM2-
➡9.TR2.VAN1.ALTER.NET [152.63.136.154]
 10  120 ms    90 ms    90 ms    136.ATM7-
➡9.TR2.SEA1.ALTER.NET [152.63.10.105]
 11  150 ms   110 ms   110 ms    110.at-2-1-
➡0.TR4.SCL1.ALTER.NET [152.63.3.226]
 12  140 ms   120 ms   110 ms    399.ATM6-
➡0.XR2.SFO4.ALTER.NET [152.63.49.9]
 13  140 ms   110 ms   120 ms    190.ATM8-0-
➡0.GW5.SFO4.ALTER.NET [146.188.149.37]
 14  241 ms   110 ms   100 ms    att-gcs-
➡gw.customer.ALTER.NET [157.130.197.78]
```

```
15   120 ms    100 ms     90 ms    199.37.127.67
16   220 ms    201 ms    200 ms    205.174.74.66
17   220 ms    201 ms    200 ms    165.76.0.43
18   231 ms    200 ms    220 ms    att-r1.typhoon.co.jp
➡[202.33.21.194]
19   231 ms    210 ms    210 ms    storm.typhoon.co.jp
➡[202.33.21.38]
```

This tells me a number of things. First, it shows that any message I
send goes through 19 servers/routers to get to the destination.
Second, it shows the path that my communication takes (Winnipeg,
MB → Vancouver, BC → Seattle, WA → San Francisco, CA →
Tokyo, JP). Third, it tells me there is very little I can do if there is a
breakdown in communication because most of the path is beyond
my, or my friend's, control. Finally, and most importantly, because I
did not receive a "Request timed out" message, I know I do not
have a connectivity problem.

INSTALLING AND CONFIGURING
NETWORK SERVICES

Install and configure network services.

Windows 2000 network services provide support for optional functions that assist in the administration and management of the network. As such, many services are optional. This section discusses
three network services you might install on a Windows 2000 server:
DHCP, DNS, and WINS. These services have already been introduced to you in terms of their use on a TCP/IP network; this section will discuss how they are installed and configured. There are
many services in addition to these, but many are discussed in other
chapters of this book (or in other sections of this chapter). In addition, many configuration options related to these services will not be
discussed in this book. This section will focus on giving you enough
information to set up the services in a basic environment but will
not discuss the WAN or Active Directory implications of them.

N O T E

Verify That Servers Have Static TCP/IP Addresses   Although Windows 2000 Server will allow you to install DHCP and WINS on a computer that gets its address from a DHCP server, this may result in unstable performance (which you will be informed of if you try it). Before you install any of these services, you should make sure your server has a statically assigned TCP/IP address.

As was discussed earlier in the section on TCP/IP, DHCP is the process responsible for automatic configuration of the TCP/IP protocol on machines enabled for such. It is, therefore, extremely important on most Windows 2000 TCP/IP-based networks. As you will see, DHCP is also important for the new Dynamic DNS implemented in domain controllers.

DNS and WINS are two TCP/IP services designed to provide clients with name resolution (the ability to use meaningful names in place of TCP/IP addresses when communicating with servers). DNS is the preferred method and the one that takes the most work to configure. It is installed almost exclusively on domain controllers in a Windows 2000 network, so it will not be discussed in detail in this chapter. WINS will be used to provide name resolution service for non-Windows 2000 clients that require it.

The discussion of these services will not be complete. The Network Architecture exam and the book in this series deal with these services in a lot more depth. The intent of this discussion is to give you enough information to configure simple implementations of these services and, of course, enough information to pass the exam.

Installing and Configuring DHCP

When it comes to configuring TCP/IP on the clients in your organization, installing and configuring a DHCP server is arguably the most important administrative task you will perform. Notwithstanding the special cases in which DHCP is not recommended, DHCP is an essential part of administering a TCP/IP-based network.

The job of the DHCP server is threefold:

◆ It holds the configuration and the pool of addresses to give out to clients.

◆ It responds to client requests and sends address configuration.

◆ It updates the DNS server (to be discussed later) with the names and addresses of clients when they get leases.

After you have configured the address pool and the desired additional TCP/IP information, the DHCP server does its work independent of you. It needs very little maintenance and very little ongoing configuration. Therefore, what is essential is that the service is installed properly and configured properly. Everything else that happens is based on client request.

DHCP configuration begins with installing the service on your Windows 2000 server. Step by Step 6.7 walks you through the installation process.

STEP BY STEP

6.7 Installing DHCP on a Windows 2000 Server

1. Make sure your server has a statically assigned TCP/IP address on the network interfaces for which you intend to use DHCP.

2. Open the Control Panel and double-click the Add/Remove Programs icon.

3. In the Add/Remove Programs dialog box, click the Add/Remove Windows Components button.

4. At the Windows Components screen, scroll through the Components list, click on Networking Services, and click the Details button.

5. In the Networking Services dialog box, select Dynamic Host Configuration Protocol (DHCP) and click OK (see Figure 6.17).

6. At the Windows Components screen, click Next to continue.

7. At the Completing the Windows Components Wizard screen, click Finish.

8. Close the Add/Remove Programs dialog box.

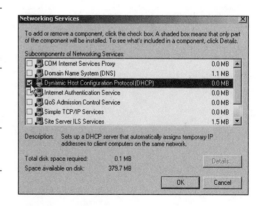

FIGURE 6.17
Select DHCP from the list of optional networking services.

After you install DHCP on your server, it needs to be configured. This configuration includes the pool of addresses from which dynamic addresses are to be allocated. Configuration also includes specifying the subnet mask and default gateway to assign to clients on your LAN. In addition, DHCP can be configured to give out a number of other TCP/IP configuration properties, such as a domain name.

DHCP can also be configured to update the DNS server database. DNS provides host name to TCP/IP address resolution for clients. This allows clients to use computer host names to access servers rather than having to use the TCP/IP addresses. In the past, DNS was a statically configured database, and each computer in an organization had to have an entry configured in the DNS database. This caused problems for DNS name resolution not only because the process of adding all the computer names to the database was tedious, but also because if DHCP was used to allocate TCP/IP addresses, the DNS entries for clients could quickly become obsolete.

Windows 2000 uses a dynamic DNS implementation that employs a combination of manually entered name/address pairs and dynamically configured entries. These dynamically configured entries are provided by the DHCP server as addresses are given out to clients. This ability can also be configured to provide support to those DHCP clients that are capable of updating the DNS and those that are not.

Step by Step 6.8 shows how to configure the DHCP scope on a Windows 2000 server.

STEP BY STEP

6.8 Configuring a DHCP Scope on a Windows 2000 Server

1. From the Start menu, choose Programs, Administrative Tools, DHCP.

2. On the DHCP console, right-click your server and choose New Scope from the menu that appears (see Figure 6.18).

3. At the Welcome to the New Scope Wizard screen, click Next.

4. At the Scope Name screen, type in a name and description to identify the pool of addresses and their purpose. The name may be as simple as *Dynamic Addresses for XYZ Co.* Click Next to continue.

5. At the IP Address Range screen, enter the starting and ending address in your address pool (see Figure 6.19). In addition, enter the subnet mask for your addresses. If you want, you can have Windows 2000 calculate your subnet mask by providing it with the number of bits that represent the network address of the TCP/IP addresses (typed into the Length field). Click Next to continue.

6. At the Add Exclusions screen (see Figure 6.20), you can specify any addresses or range of addresses in the address range you entered in step 5 that are not to be dynamically allocated; these addresses may be statically assigned to machines already. To exclude a range of addresses, enter a start and end address and then click Add. If you want to exclude only one address, enter the same address in both the start and the end address boxes. Click Next to continue.

continues

FIGURE 6.18
The first task in configuring a DHCP server is creating an address pool (scope).

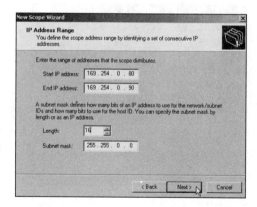

FIGURE 6.19
Enter the range of addresses and the subnet mask.

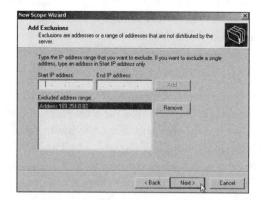

FIGURE 6.20
Addresses in the exclusions list are not allocated by the DHCP server; usually they are already statically assigned to computers on the network.

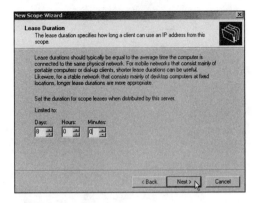

FIGURE 6.21
The lease duration determines the length of time a TCP/IP address is allocated to a client.

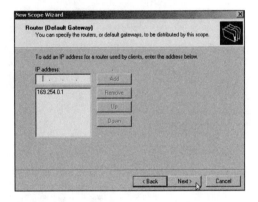

FIGURE 6.22
Enter one or more default gateways (routers) for clients to use to get to external networks.

continued

7. At the Lease Duration screen shown in Figure 6.21, enter the lease of an address (how long it will last before it expires, at which time the client is forced to discontinue use of the TCP/IP address). The duration of the lease determines how much network traffic DHCP clients generate because at the halfway point of the lease's life, a client will try to renew the lease by contacting the server it got the address from. In general, the lease duration should be the average length of time that clients spend connected to the network. If your network is very stable and clients rarely need configuration changes, you can increase the lease duration. You can configure an infinite lease by entering 0 as the duration lease. Click Next to continue.

8. At the Configure DHCP Options screen you can choose to configure additional TCP/IP properties that are to be given to clients that obtain addresses from this DHCP server. If you choose not to configure at this time, you can manually configure these options later. Choose an option and click Next to continue (this discussion assumes you choose Yes).

9. At the Router screen, you can enter one or more default gateways for clients. One value is typical here, but more than one can be entered (see Figure 6.22). If you enter more than one, when Windows 2000 determines to route out through the default gateway, it will choose which one to use based on current activity, not on the order they're listed. Enter the value(s) and click Next.

10. At the Domain Name and DNS Servers screen, enter the name of the Domain that these clients are a part of and the server that they will contact to resolve host names to TCP/IP addresses (see Figure 6.23). The TCP/IP configuration of DNS server requires a TCP/IP address. However, if all you know is the server's name, you can type it into the Server Name field and then click Resolve. This will result in the TCP/IP address being entered into the IP Address field and you can then use the Add button to enter it into the DNS server list. Click Next to continue.

11. At the WINS Servers screen, enter the TCP/IP address for the WINS server(s) on the network (see Figure 6.24). These servers are used to resolve NetBIOS names to TCP/IP addresses. WINS has, for the most part, been superceded by dynamic DNS, but some clients may only be able to use WINS, and therefore, a WINS server may be required. Click Next to continue.

12. At the Activate Scope screen, choose to either activate the scope or leave it inactive. If your server is already authorized in the domain (or if your server is not part of a domain), when you activate the scope, the DHCP server will be available to respond to client requests. Unless configuration changes need to be made before activation, you will want to activate the scope at this time. Click Next to continue.

13. At the Completing the New Scope Wizard screen, click Finish.

If your DHCP server is a member server in a Windows 2000 domain, it must be authorized in the Active Directory before it can give out addresses. This is a safety precaution to ensure that DHCP servers cannot be accidentally enabled on the network, thus throwing the configuration of TCP/IP addresses into chaos.

Step by Step 6.9 shows how to authorize a DHCP server in the Active Directory.

STEP BY STEP

6.9 Authorizing a DHCP Server in the Active Directory

1. Open the DHCP console and select the server.

2. From the Action menu, choose Authorize.

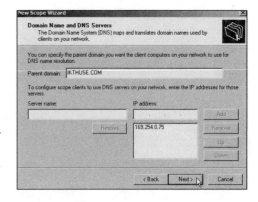

FIGURE 6.23
Enter the Domain name and DNS server address(es) for the client.

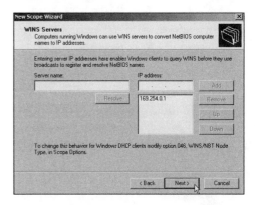

FIGURE 6.24
Enter the WINS server address(es) for the client.

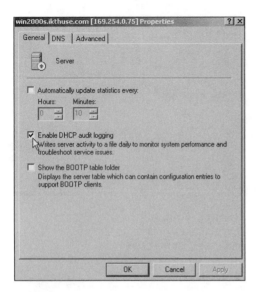

FIGURE 6.25
DHCP logging is enabled on the General property sheet.

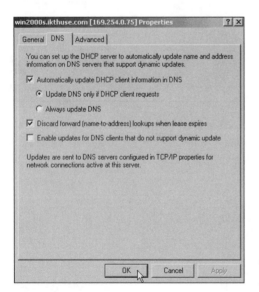

FIGURE 6.26
The DHCP server can be configured to update (and delete) DNS records for DHCP clients when addresses are allocated to or unallocated from them.

When the DHCP server has been configured and authorized, it will begin to give out addresses when requested by clients, sending the configuration properties that were specified when the scope was enabled. After it's enabled, you can make modifications to the configuration. Configuration properties are available for the DHCP server in general, for all scopes managed by the server and for a specific scope. Server scope configuration defines properties and settings for all scopes. However, if a specific scope has properties that contradict the server scope configuration, the specific scope settings will take precedence.

Regarding the general server properties, it's especially important that you know three things:

◆ How to enable logging for DHCP

◆ How DHCP is involved in the updating of DNS records for DHCP clients

◆ How conflict detection is configured

You can open the properties for the server by right-clicking on the entry for the server (defined by the name of the server in the DHCP console) and choosing Properties from the menu that appears.

On the General property sheet, you can configure DHCP logging by selecting Enable DHCP Logging (see Figure 6.25). This feature is enabled by default and will create a daily log file stored in the Audit Path as defined on the Advanced property sheet.

On the DNS property sheet, you can configure how DHCP interacts with DNS to make the DNS entries dynamic (see Figure 6.26). If Automatically Update DHCP Client Information in DNS is selected, DNS records for Windows 2000 clients will be updated automatically when addresses are leased. Whether the client updates the DNS record or the DHCP server updates it depends on whether Update DNS Only if SHCP Client Requests or Always Update DNS is selected. If the automatic update box is not selected, Windows 2000 clients never have DNS records created or updated when addresses are leased.

By default, when the client's lease expires, the DHCP server removes the DNS entry for the client. If you want the DNS entry to persist, you can clear the check box labeled Discard Forward (Name-to-Address) Lookups When Lease Expires.

Finally, you can configure the DHCP server to create and update DNS entries for non-Windows 2000 clients by selecting Enable Updates for DNS Clients That Do Not Support Dynamic Update. This option, which is deselected by default, ensures that legacy Windows clients will be registered in the Dynamic DNS.

On the Advanced property sheet, you can enable the Conflict Detection Attempts property (see Figure 6.27). This setting defines how many times the DHCP server PINGs the network for a response to an address that it is about to allocate to a client. If a response is detected, the DHCP server knows that another client is using the address and tries to allocate another. By default this property is not enabled (set to 0), but you can increase it to check addresses. On a LAN, one try should be sufficient to check for a duplicate address on the network.

Default TCP/IP configuration options for the server can be set in the DHCP console. These options apply to all scopes configured for this server unless the properties are specifically overwritten at the scope level. For example, if you want the DNS server to be the same across all scopes, you can configure it that way in the Server properties.

To configure the Server TCP/IP options, right-click the Server Options line and select Configure Options from the menu that appears.

The General property sheet provides a list of available options (see Figure 6.28). Select any of the options, and fields will appear for which you can configure values.

Although there are a number of options, most of them define DHCP options that are not applicable to Microsoft clients. The following properties are applicable to all Microsoft clients:

◆ Router

◆ DNS Server

◆ DNS Domain Name

◆ WINS Server

◆ NetBIOS Node Type

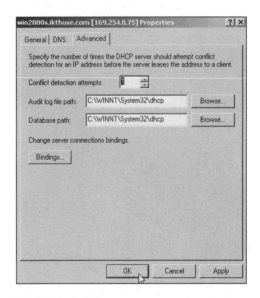

FIGURE 6.27
Conflict detection ensures that an about-to-be-allocated address is not already in use on the network.

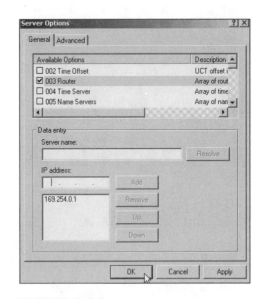

FIGURE 6.28
Server TCP/IP options set default options for the properties selected and configured.

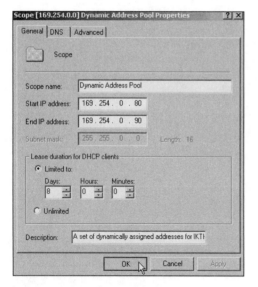

FIGURE 6.29
You can adjust the address pool and lease duration from the General property sheet.

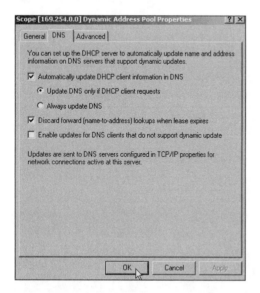

FIGURE 6.30
You can configure the DNS properties for this scope to override the DNS properties for the server.

In addition, Windows 2000 DHCP clients also accept configuration of Perform Router Discovery and Static Route. All other configuration settings will be ignored by Microsoft clients.

In addition to the options for the DHCP server in general, you can also set options for the specific scope(s) you have configured.

First, you can configure the general scope properties (including the address pool). To do so, right-click the scope and select Properties from the menu that appears. Of those properties, only the general and DNS property sheets are relevant to this discussion.

From the General property sheet, you can adjust the address pool and the lease duration after it has been originally configured (see Figure 6.29).

On the DNS property sheet, you can set the same properties you could for the server (see Figure 6.30). Any differences between the two will defer to the scope configuration (this one) for resolution.

You can also set specific TCP/IP options for the scope (which will override settings configured in the server scope). To set these, right-click the Scope Options and choose Configure Options from the menu that appears. The resulting dialog box is the same as the server options dialog box shown earlier in Figure 6.28.

Finally, you can also configure specific computers to get specific addresses when those machines request an address from the DHCP server. These address allocations are referred to as *reservations*. A reservation pairs the MAC address of a network card with a TCP/IP address. This has the effect of creating a static configuration without actually having to modify the TCP/IP properties on the client. Address reservations are useful in a number of situations. For example, if you have a network printer that obtains its TCP/IP address via DHCP but must always have the same address, you can use a reservation. In addition, if you want to explicitly set the TCP/IP address of a machine because it has a particular service installed but you want it to benefit from the other configuration parameters given out by the DHCP server, you could also use a reservation.

To create a reservation you need the hardware (MAC) address of the network card for which you want to reserve the address. The first is easy to get; the second can be obtained either locally at the computer with the network card or remotely. In both cases, the computer must have TCP/IP installed and must have a TCP/IP address. Locally, if you issue an IPCONFIG /all command at a command prompt, a line with the label *Physical Address* will be displayed with a number like *00-60-97-D5-22-CA* associated with it. That is the MAC address, and if you remove the hyphens, that is the number DHCP wants associated with the reservation.

If you cannot access the computer locally, you can determine the address remotely using the PING command and the ARP utility. ARP discovers and caches the hardware address associated with a TCP/IP address contacted by the local machine. If you PING the machine you are trying to configure and then check the ARP cache, you will discover the MAC address. This has already been illustrated in Step by Step 6.3.

When you have a TCP/IP address and the MAC address of the computer for which you want to create a reservation, you can create an address reservation. Follow these steps to create one:

STEP BY STEP

6.10 Configuring an Address Reservation

1. Open the DHCP console, select the server, expand the scope, right-click the Reservations line, and choose New Reservation from the menu that appears.

2. In the New Reservation dialog box, fill in the reservation name, the TCP/IP address reserved, and the MAC address of the card on the computer (see Figure 6.31). Click Add to continue.

3. Click Close to exit.

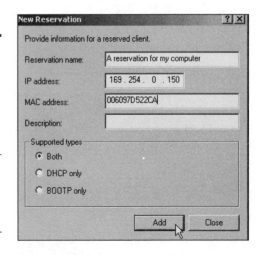

FIGURE 6.31
A reservation pairs a specific TCP/IP address with the unique hardware address of a network card.

Installing and Configuring DNS

As was discussed in the section titled "Name Resolution Using DNS," the DNS service is a very important part of Windows 2000 network communication—so much so that it is impossible to configure a Windows 2000 domain without a DNS server being present on the network somewhere. For security and reliability, DNS is usually configured on a domain controller. However, configuring a DNS server on a domain controller is not required, and that kind of configuration is beyond the scope of this book. From time to time DNS servers are configured on Windows 2000 servers instead of on domain controllers, and that is what this section will deal with.

DNS servers are installed as one of three types: primary name a server, a secondary name server, or a caching-only server. A primary name server is responsible for one zone and obtains its configuration from a local DNS file. A secondary name server obtains its configuration information from another name server using a process called zone transfer; these servers are used for load balancing, redundancy, and fast DNS lookup in remote locations. Finally, a caching-only server does not have a DNS file locally and is responsible only for resolving names and caching that information locally.

In a Windows 2000 DNS configuration, frequently DNS' configured on a Windows 2000 server will be either of the secondary or caching variety because of the benefits from integrating DNS with the Active Directory on a domain controller. However, in-depth coverage of this would require discussions on configuring zone transfers from primary servers that would, again be beyond the scope of this book. As a result, the Step by Steps that follow will show you how to configure a Windows 2000 server as the primary server in a domain.

To configure a Windows 2000 server as a primary DNS server, you first must install DNS. This is outlined in Step by Step 6.11

STEP BY STEP

6.11 Installing DNS on a Windows 2000 Server

1. From the Start menu, choose Settings, Control Panel.

2. From the Control Panel, double-click the Add/Remove Programs icon.

3. From the Add/Remove Programs window, click the Add/Remove Windows Components icon.

4. In the Windows Components dialog box, scroll down in the components list, select Networking Services, and click the Details button.

5. In the Networking Services dialog box, select Domain Name System (DNS) and click OK.

6. In the Windows Components dialog box, click Next.

7. In the Completing the Windows Components Wizard dialog box, click Finish.

8. Close the Add/Remove Programs dialog box.

Once the DNS service has been installed on your server, you can configure it. The basic configuration involves setting the DNS server up as a primary server and configuring a domain name that it is the start of authority for. In addition, it involves configuring a forward lookup zone and a reverse lookup zone. A *forward lookup zone* is one that maps a host name to a TCP/IP address. A *reverse lookup zone* is one that maps a TCP/IP address to a host name. You have the option of creating new zone files or using files that already exist (which you would do if a new server was being configured to take the place of an already configured server that was being decommissioned).

Step by Step 6.12 demonstrates how to configure a Windows 2000 server as a primary name server.

STEP BY STEP

6.12 Configuring a Server as a First Network DNS on a Windows 2000 Server

1. From the Start menu, choose Programs, Administrative Tools, DNS.

2. In the DNS console, select your server name, open the Action menu, and choose Configure the Server.

3. At the Welcome to the Configure the DNS Server Wizard, click Next.

4. At the Root Server dialog box, choose This Is the First DNS Server on This Network and click Next (see Figure 6.32).

continues

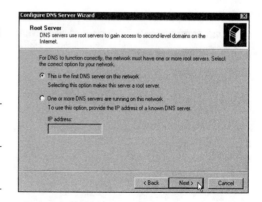

FIGURE 6.32
Create a new zone.

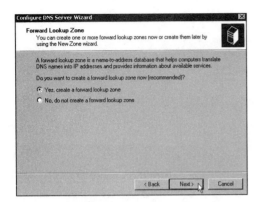

FIGURE 6.33
Create a forward lookup zone.

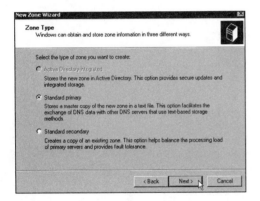

FIGURE 6.34
Set up a primary name server.

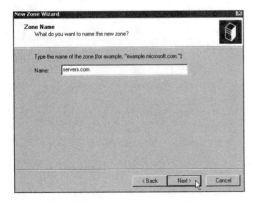

FIGURE 6.35
Identify the name of the new zone.

continued

5. At the Forward Lookup Zone dialog box, choose Yes, Create a Forward Lookup Zone and click Next (see Figure 6.33).

6. At the Zone Type dialog box, select Standard Primary and click Next (see Figure 6.34).

7. At the Zone Name dialog box, type in the name of the zone for which this server will be the Start of Authority (see Figure 6.35). Click Next to continue.

8. At the Zone File dialog box, either keep the zone filename the wizard suggests (recommended) or type in an alternate name (see Figure 6.36). If this server is to replace an existing DNS server, you can copy the DNS file from the other server and indicate that you want to use this existing file as the DNS database. Click Next to continue.

9. At the Reverse Lookup Zone dialog box, choose whether or not to create a reverse lookup zone (usually you do). If you choose not to create a reverse lookup zone, skip to step 13. Click Next to continue.

10. At the Zone Type dialog box, select Standard Primary and click Next.

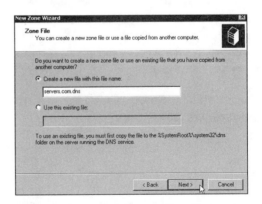

FIGURE 6.36
You can use the suggested filename, create a new one, or use an existing file.

11. At the Reverse Lookup Zone dialog box, type the network portion of the TCP/IP addresses that are resolvable through this reverse lookup (recommended), or type the name of the reverse lookup zone (see Figure 6.37). Click Next to continue.

12. At the Zone File dialog box, either keep the zone filename that the wizard suggests (recommended) or type in an alternate name. If this server is to replace an existing DNS server, you can copy the DNS file from the other server and indicate that you want to use this existing file as the DNS database. Click Next to continue.

13. At the Completing the Configure DNS Server Wizard dialog box, click Finish.

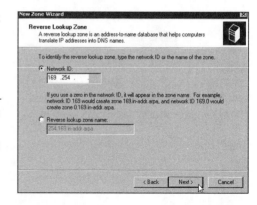

FIGURE 6.37
Identify the network ID or domain name of this reverse lookup zone.

Although, as was discussed in the section "Installing and Configuring DHCP," many of the DNS records on your name server will be automatically configured, there will still be times when you will have to manually configure records. For example, you might need to configure resolution for hosts that DHCP does not configure (like UNIX hosts on your network), or you might need to configure for special tasks that are not configured automatically (like the MX record to indicate the TCP/IP address for your mail server, Exchange, Lotus Notes, or others). Or, you might just want to configure for commonly used host name aliases that are not registered automatically. In all these cases and more, you will want to manually create records.

Step by Step 6.13 shows you how to create a variety of records. A host record is the mapping of a host name to a TCP/IP address. An alias record is the mapping of one host name (the alias) to another host name for which there is already a host record. A Mail Exchanger (MX) record is a record that defines the location of a mail server in this domain.

FIGURE 6.38
Choose the record type you want to create.

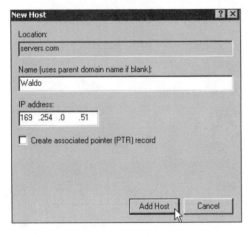

FIGURE 6.39
This is the dialog box for creating a new host record.

STEP BY STEP

6.13 Manually Adding a New Record to a DNS Server

1. Open the DNS console.

2. Expand the Forward Lookup Zones under the DNS server name and locate the name of the domain.

3. Right-click the domain name and, from the menu that appears, choose the record type you want to create (see Figure 6.38).

   If you choose to create a new host record, in the New Host dialog box, fill in the name of the host you want to add and the TCP/IP address of that host (see Figure 6.39). Click Add Host, and then click Done to exit.

   If you choose to create a new alias record, in the New Resource Record dialog box, fill in the alias name and the name of the host for which you are creating an alias (see Figure 6.40). Click OK.

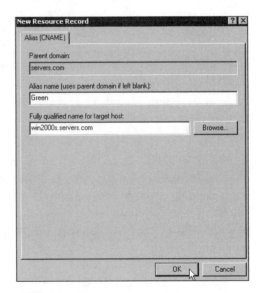

FIGURE 6.40
This is the dialog box for creating a new alias record.

If you choose to create a new Mail Exchanger (MX) record, in the New Resource Record dialog box, fill in the host or domain name (this indicates the mail domain that this mail server is servicing; leave it blank to indicate the parent domain defined in this DNS), the full name of the mail server, and its priority among other mail servers in this DNS domain (see Figure 6.41). Click OK.

4. Repeat step 3 for all static entries to the DNS you want to create.

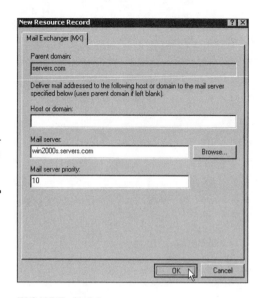

FIGURE 6.41
This is the dialog box for creating a new Mail Exchanger record.

Installing and Configuring WINS

As was explained in the section "Name Resolution Using WINS," the Windows Internet Name Service (WINS) is used to resolve NetBIOS names to TCP/IP addresses. In a Windows 2000 environment, WINS is used when clients and software require NetBIOS name resolution (rather than the host name resolution that DNS provides). Although dynamic DNS has superceded WINS in much functionality, there will still be times (at least in the foreseeable future) when NetBIOS name resolution is required because of down-level clients (Windows 9x and Windows NT, for example).

In the most straightforward case, WINS is very easy to configure. You simply install the service, and it begins to work. Then all you have to do is configure your client machines to use the WINS server you have configured. The best way to do that is by creating a WINS entry in the DHCP configuration.

Step by Step 6.14 shows you how to install WINS on a Windows 2000 server.

STEP BY STEP

6.14 Installing WINS on a Windows 2000 Server

1. Make sure your server has a statically assigned TCP/IP address.

continues

continued

2. From the Control Panel, double-click the Add/Remove Programs icon.

3. In the Add/Remove Programs dialog box, click the Add/Remove Windows Components button.

4. At the Windows Components screen, scroll through the components list, click on the Networking Services entry, and click the Details button.

5. In the Networking Services dialog box, select Windows Internet Name Service (WINS) and click OK.

6. At the Windows Components screen, click Next to continue.

7. At the Completing the Windows Components Wizard screen, click Finish.

8. Close the Add/Remove Programs dialog box.

INSTALLING, CONFIGURING, AND TROUBLESHOOTING SHARED ACCESS

Install, configure, and troubleshoot shared access.

Many offices—especially small ones—have a greater need for Internet access than they have connections. A home-based office might have a single dial-up connection (or ADSL, or a cable modem) and two or three computers on a LAN. In other cases, perhaps two or three Internet connections are available in an office, but there are ten machines on the company LAN. In both cases, connection sharing can be used to provide access to everyone who needs it.

Connection sharing provides access from one network to another through a single (or multiple) point(s) of contact. Connection sharing always involves a computer with two network cards: one to communicate with the internal network and the other to communicate with the Internet. In the simplest case, a computer is configured for con-

nection sharing, and all the other network infrastructure changes are
made automatically. In cases that are more complex, a number of
Internet addresses are made available through a special protocol
called Network Address Translation (NAT). However, in both situations, the same result is desired: to provide a number of users with
access to a network to which they do not have direct access without
creating a router to do it.

Shared Access Using Connection Sharing

In the simplest situation, a single TCP/IP address is available to a
small (perhaps home-based) office for Internet connectivity. This
address may be available through a dial-up connection (intermittent
or permanent) or through a LAN (like a cable-modem or ADSL
would provide). However it is made available, only one computer
has access to it. A second computer is then added to the equation
with a LAN connection between it and the first. In this scenario, the
second computer has LAN access to the first, and the first computer
has both Internet access and LAN access to the second, but the second
computer does not have Internet access. This is where the simplest
form of shared access can be implemented; Figure 6.42 shows that
configuration.

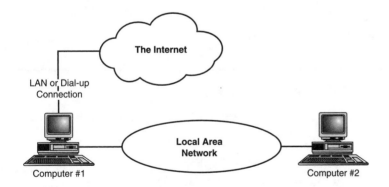

FIGURE 6.42
A shared connection allows one computer to
access the Internet through the connection
on another.

In this scenario, the solution is as simple as enabling automatic TCP/IP configuration on the second machine and enabling connection sharing on the first machine's Internet connection (LAN or dial-up).

When you enable connection sharing on the Internet connection, some configuration changes are made on your network. First, the TCP/IP address associated with the shared connection is changed to 192.168.0.1. Second, the computer with connection sharing enabled becomes the *de facto* DHCP server for all other computers on the network, providing them with TCP/IP addresses in the network 192.168.x.x.

As a result of the configuration changes that are made by default when connection sharing is enabled, you must ensure that there are no computers on the network with manually configured (static) TCP/IP addresses unless they are also in the 192.168.x.x range. In addition, there should be no active DHCP servers on the LAN.

Some network-based programs require extra configuration in order to operate properly through a shared connection. This configuration (which is unique to each program) is handled through the Settings dialog box.

If you are providing network services to users on the Internet side of your connection, you will have to enable those services to be accessed through the connection. This configuration is also done in the Settings dialog box.

Step by Step 6.15 demonstrates how to enable shared Internet access using connection sharing.

STEP BY STEP

6.15 Enabling Shared Access Via Connection Sharing

1. Right-click My Network Places and choose Properties from the menu presented.

2. In the Network and Dial-Up Connections dialog box, right-click the connection to be shared and choose Properties from the menu that appears.

3. In the Connection Properties dialog box, click the Sharing tab. On the property sheet that appears, select Enable Internet Connection Sharing for This Connection (see Figure 6.43).

4. If the connection is dial-up, select Enable On-Demand Dialing to ensure that the connection is available when requested by another user (see Figure 6.44).

5. If required, click the Settings button to configure applications to operate through the shared connection.

6. If you need to configure applications to work through the shared connection, click the Applications tab, click Add, and fill in the TCP port configuration (see Figure 6.45). Click OK to continue.

continues

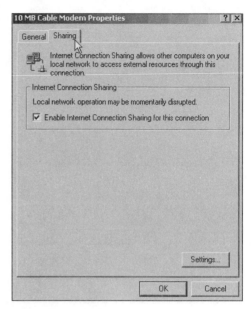

FIGURE 6.43
In a simple situation, you can enable connection sharing on the Sharing tab.

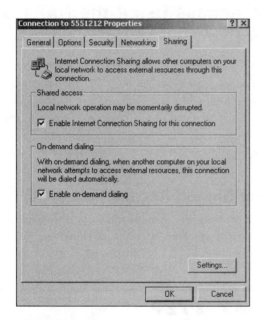

FIGURE 6.44
For dial-up connections to work properly, you must select Enable On-Demand Dialing.

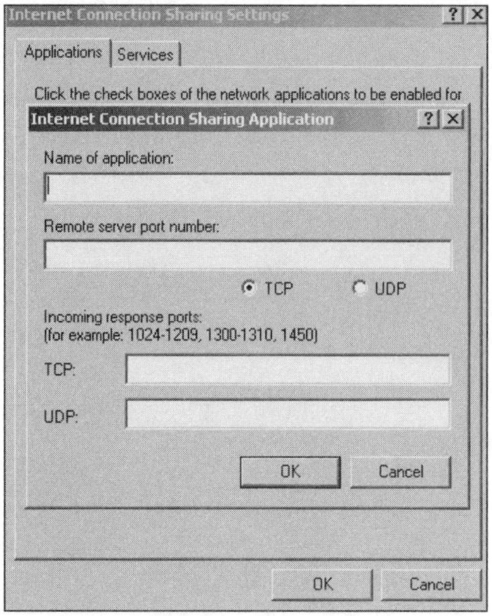

FIGURE 6.45
You can configure specific ports through the shared connection to allow network-based applications to function.

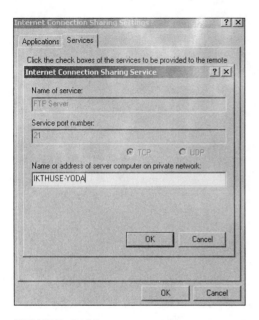

FIGURE 6.46
Internal network services (like Web and FTP servers) can be made available to users on the public side of the connection.

continued

7. If you need to configure access to internal applications through the shared connection, click the Services tab and select the predefined applications to which you want to provide access. When prompted, fill in the name or TCP/IP address of the server providing the application, or click the Add button to add an application to the list and then enable it (see Figure 6.46).

8. Click OK to continue.

9. When prompted to confirm the TCP/IP address changes, click Yes.

Shared Access Using the NAT Routing Protocol

The NAT Routing Protocol allows for the situation where a number of TCP/IP addresses are available, but there are not enough for all the clients who need addresses. Only a single special configuration is required of clients who use a NAT server to connect to the Internet: The clients must set their default gateway to the address of the NAT server.

Installing Shared Access Using NAT

For the NAT protocol to function, you must first enable sharing using NAT on a server. Step by Step 6.16 shows you how to do just that.

STEP BY STEP

6.16 Enabling Sharing Using NAT on a Member Server

1. On a domain controller for the domain, open the Start menu and choose Programs, Administrative Tools, Active Directory Users and Computers.

2. In the Active Directory Users and Computers manager, click the Computers entry. From the list of computers displayed on the right, right-click your member server and choose Properties from the menu that appears (see Figure 6.47).

3. In the Computer Properties dialog box, click the Member Of tab and click the Add button (see Figure 6.48).

4. In the Select Groups dialog box, scroll through the groups list and double-click RAS and IAS Servers (see Figure 6.49). Click OK to continue.

5. Click OK to exit the Computer Properties dialog box.

6. Close the Active Directory Users and Computers manager.

7. At the sharing server, open the Start menu and choose Programs, Administrative Tools, Routing and Remote Access.

continues

FIGURE 6.47
NAT is configured in the properties of the server.

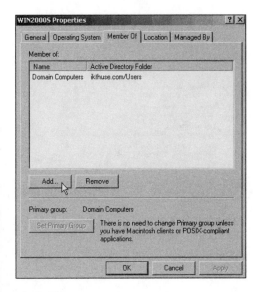

FIGURE 6.48
To enable a member server for NAT, you must change its group membership in the Active Directory.

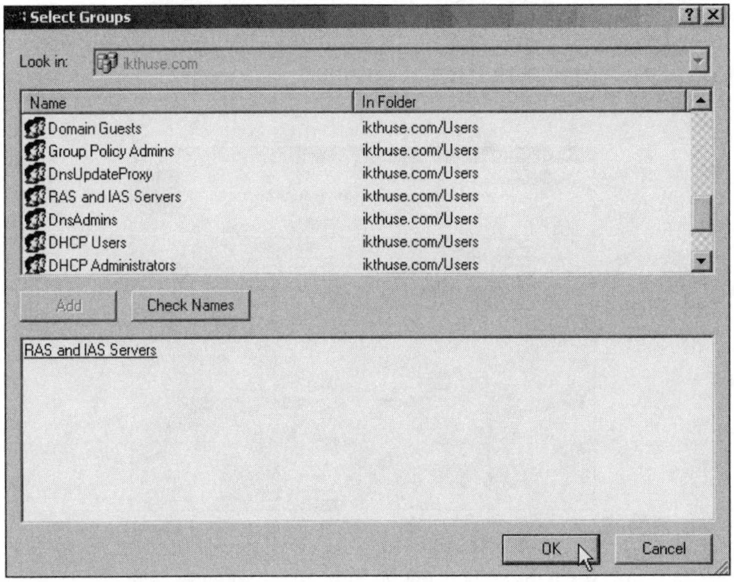

FIGURE 6.49
Add the potential NAT server to the RAS and IAS Servers group.

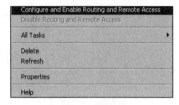

FIGURE 6.50
Routing and Remote Access is installed by default. You need to enable it to allow it to function.

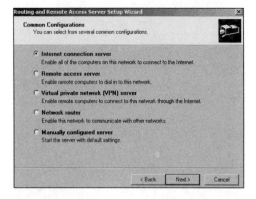

FIGURE 6.51
The Routing and Remote Access Server Wizard provides options with preconfigured settings for specific routing and remote access needs.

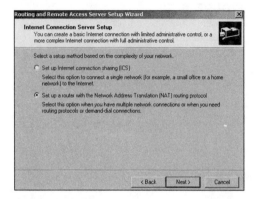

FIGURE 6.52
Of the two available connection sharing options, NAT gives you the most flexibility.

8. In the Routing and Remote Access manager, select the computer you want to enable for shared access, open the Action menu, and choose Configure and Enable Routing and Remote Access (see Figure 6.50).

9. At the Welcome to the Routing and Remote Access Server Setup Wizard screen, click Next.

10. At the Common Configurations screen, choose Internet Connection Server and click Next (see Figure 6.51).

11. At the Internet Connection Server Setup screen, select Set Up a Router with the Network Address Translation (NAT) Routing Protocol and click Next (see Figure 6.52).

12. At the Internet Connection screen (see Figure 6.53), if you have already configured a permanent connection to the Internet via a LAN, select Use the Selected Internet Connection and go to step 22. If you have a dial-up connection to the Internet, select Create a New Demand-Dial Internet Connection. Click Next to continue.

13. At the Applying Changes screen, click Next to continue.

14. At the Welcome to the Demand Dial Interface Wizard screen, click Next to continue.

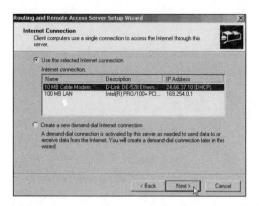

FIGURE 6.53
Choose the connection to enable for connection sharing; this must be the one connected to the public network.

15. At the Interface Name screen, enter a meaningful name for the new interface (see Figure 6.54). Click Next to continue.

16. At the Connection Type screen, select the kind of demand-dial connection you are using (see Figure 6.55). Choose either the Connect Using a Modem, ISDN, or Other Physical Device option, or choose the Connect Using Virtual Private Networking (VPN) option. VPN connect presupposes that a physical connection is always available and will be discussed in a further section. This Step by Step assumes you select the first choice. Click Next to continue.

17. At the Select a Device screen, select the device to use to demand dial (see Figure 6.56). This discussion assumes a modem. Click Next to continue.

continues

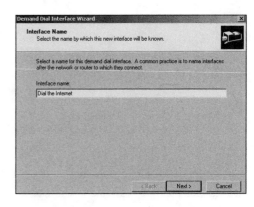

FIGURE 6.54

The interface name is just a text string to identify the connection that's being created.

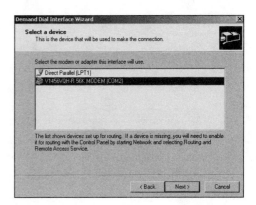

FIGURE 6.56

Select the device to use to connect to the public network from the list. If one is not available, you can create one from the Modems icon in the Control Panel.

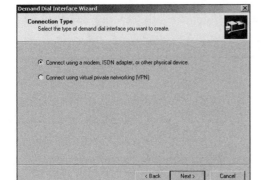

FIGURE 6.55

For NAT demand-dial routing, you will connect through a physical (rather than a virtual) connection.

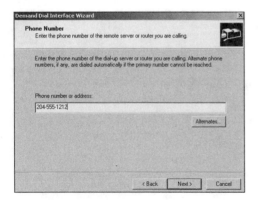

FIGURE 6.57
Demand-dial implies dialing a destination; enter the phone number here.

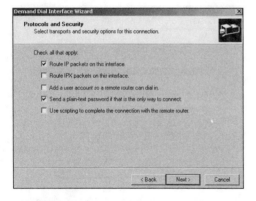

FIGURE 6.58
Specify what this new interface can be used to transmit and what its general security properties are.

continued

18. At the Phone Number screen, enter a phone number to dial for Internet service (see Figure 6.57). (If desired, you can enter multiple phone numbers in case the primary one does not connect; to do so, use the Alternates button.) Click Next to continue.

19. At the Protocols and Security screen, choose the protocols you want to route using this connection (TCP/IP and/or IPX) and the security options that are appropriate (see Figure 6.58). These options will be configured by your ISP or other network administrator. Click Next to continue.

20. At the Dial Out Credentials screen, fill in the user name, domain, and password required to connect to the remote network (see Figure 6.59). Click Next to continue.

21. At the Completing the Demand Dial Interface Wizard screen, click Finish.

22. At the Completing the Routing and Remote Access Server Setup Wizard screen, click Finish.

Your NAT server is now essentially ready to begin processing Internet access requests from clients. However, some configuration may be required for your specific situation. The next section talks about that.

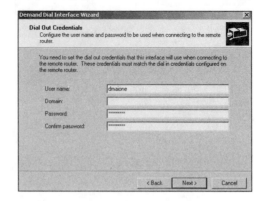

FIGURE 6.59
If you are required to log on to the dial-up computer, enter your credentials here.

Configuring Shared Access Using NAT

In simple scenarios, NAT configuration is complete as soon as it is installed. However, if the simplest situation was all you wanted, it would be more efficient to configure shared access using connection sharing because it is easier to set up.

NAT differs from connection sharing in that it is configurable. You can configure the internal addresses to be given out automatically. You can also configure more than one external address to use for communication (in the case where two or more addresses are provided by your ISP). In addition, you can also configure logging and statistical collection to define an ongoing log of NAT protocol translation.

Shared access using NAT is configured through the Routing and Remote Access manager. From that manager, you can configure a number of routing tasks including RRAS, which will be discussed in the next section.

In the Routing and Remote Access manager, you can configure the properties of the NAT protocol in general, as well as the properties of the connection that you are using to access the public network you are connecting to.

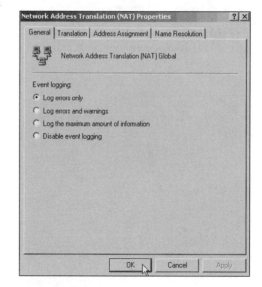

The Network Address Translation (NAT) Properties dialog box contains four property sheets:

◆ General

◆ Translation

◆ Address Assignment

◆ Name Resolution

The General property sheet allows you to define activity logging in the System log (see Figure 6.60). You can log from nothing (Disable Event Logging) to everything (Log the Maximum Amount of Information) or points in-between.

FIGURE 6.60
Logging detail is defined on the General property sheet.

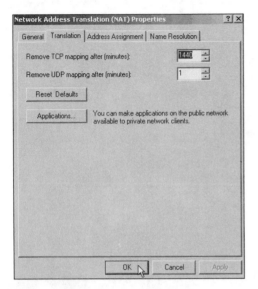

FIGURE 6.61
Mapping timeouts are configured on the
Translation property sheet.

The Translation property sheet defines the length of time that a mapping between a private (internal) address and a public (Internet) address is retained (see Figure 6.61). These mappings are disposed of at different times depending on whether the communication uses TCP or UDP.

Mappings enable NAT to maintain communication while using only one (or a few more) public TCP/IP addresses. If you think of the NAT as a Mandarin Chinese translator, imagine what chaos would result if 10 English-speaking people were having a conversation with 10 Mandarin speakers, and you were the translator. Not only are you responsible for translating 10 ongoing conversations, but you have to direct the translation to the correct person or the conversations are all pointless. Now, if we move back to the NAT, let's suppose you have 10 people on a private LAN browsing 10 Web sites through a NAT connection. Each user requests a Web page; those requests go out through the shared connection and have the public address of the NAT server on them (because that is the only address the Web servers are going to be able to send information back to). As a result, 10 HTML pages are transmitted back to the NAT server, and it has to figure out which of the private addresses to direct each transmission back to, or the person who tried to get to www.countingcrows.com will end up with the www.vegemite.com site on his screen.

To prevent such confusion, NAT not only maps the internal address with a destination TCP/IP address but also assigns a port number to the transmission. When a user connects to a Web site, it uses the outgoing port 80 and the return port 1025. When this gets to the NAT server, it forwards the request to the appropriate public address, but then it changes the return port to something else (say 5000). When the information comes back, it is destined for port 5000. The NAT server checks its map and finds out that transmissions from this server on port 5000 are really destined for port 1025 on the appropriate private addresses.

The timeout values are used to ensure that communication is complete before the mapping is removed. If the mappings stay forever, the table would quickly fill up with useless mappings. If the mappings stay for too short a time, the transmission from the destination server might not be complete before the NAT server was unable to resolve the transmission anymore (like a 12 hour download of some huge file on a slow dial-up link). The TCP timeout is longer because

TCP communication (browser traffic is one example) is connection oriented and, therefore, bound to be for a longer duration. The UDP timeout is short because it is connectionless and is typically used for test communications like the echo-response request sent by the PING utility.

The default values are 1440 minutes (24 hours) for TCP and 1 minute for UDP. It is not recommended that you change these values unless performance is suffering.

The Applications button is used to define special TCP/IP applications and the ports they communicate on. This allows internal clients to connect to external servers (like gaming hosts) without the fear of their ports being used for temporary mapping. It also ensures that the NAT server knows what to do with the transmissions.

The Address Assignment property sheet is used to configure the NAT server as a DHCP server to give out internal addresses (see Figure 6.62). Like DHCP, you can configure a pool of addresses and a subnet mask to be given out. By using the Exclude button, you can configure addresses in the pool that should be excluded because they are statically assigned. If you already have a DHCP server on the internal network, this should not be used unless the DHCP server has been configured to exclude the addresses given out by the NAT server.

The Name Resolution property sheet allows your NAT server to forward DNS name resolution requests to a public DNS server (see Figure 6.63). If that is configured, you can also indicate whether this resolution request is allowed to initiate a dial-up to the Internet through a demand-dial interface.

Step by Step 6.17 shows you how to open the NAT properties.

STEP BY STEP

6.17 Opening the NAT Properties

1. From the Start menu, choose Programs, Administrative Tools, Routing and Remote Access.

   ---

2. Expand the desired server, and then expand the IP

continues

> **NOTE**
>
> **You Can See the Current Mappings**
> You can see the current mappings for the NAT server by right-clicking the connection name (on the right side of the manager) and choosing Show Mappings from the menu that appears.

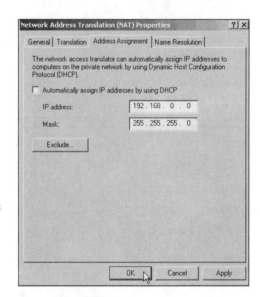

FIGURE 6.62
You can configure the NAT server to act as a pseudo-DHCP server by assigning a scope of addresses to allocate to clients.

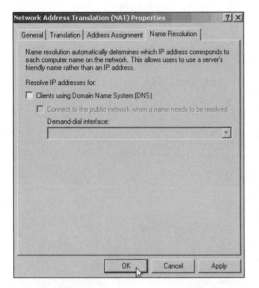

FIGURE 6.63
You can configure the NAT server to forward name resolution requests to a DNS server on the public side of the network.

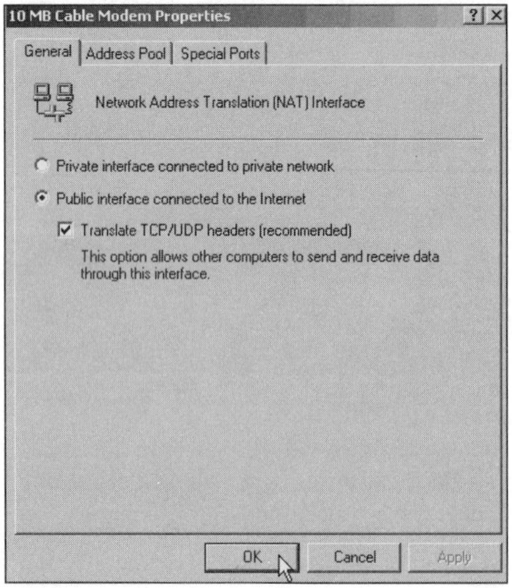

FIGURE 6.64
In order for NAT to work, one connection must be connected to the public network.

continued

Routing section.

3. Right-click the Network Address Translation (NAT) entry and choose Properties from the menu that appears.

The second configuration area is the configuration for the connection that is being used to connect to the public network. When the Routing and Remote Access manager is open and the NAT entry has been chosen, all the connections will be displayed in the right panel.

The Connection Properties dialog box has three property sheets: General, Address Pool, and Special Ports.

The General property sheet allows you to configure a connection to be used to route translated Internet traffic through (see Figure 6.64). This is selected automatically by the configuration wizard when you set up NAT connection sharing. This must stay as its configured in order for NAT to work.

The Address Pool property sheet allows you to define more than one accessible public address (see Figure 6.65). In this way, you can have network traffic translated to two or more addresses instead of just one. In addition, once the pool has been configured, you can also reserve a certain public address to be permanently mapped to a private address, thereby ensuring that certain private servers (like a Web server) are accessible from public locations without having to be on the public network.

The Special Ports property sheet allows you to redirect external requests to internal servers depending on the port being used to communicate (see Figure 6.66). With these settings, you could configure a mapping between port 80 and a Web server on the private network.

Troubleshooting Shared Access Using NAT

The proper functioning of shared access using NAT depends on a number of factors, all of which have been discussed here. If a client fails to connect to an external server, you need to check the following:

◆ There must be connectivity at the client; TCP/IP should be configured properly.

◆ There must be connectivity at the NAT server, both on the private network and the public network.

◆ The TCP/IP addresses for all the private computers must match the TCP/IP address for the private connection on the NAT server.

◆ Address translation must be enabled for the connection to the public network.

◆ If addresses are being assigned to private clients by the NAT server, there cannot be another DHCP server on the private LAN also giving out addresses in the same range unless it is configured to exclude addresses given out by the NAT server.

◆ If the NAT server is not enabled for DNS, it must be configured to forward DNS requests from the private clients to a public DNS server.

◆ If the public connection on the NAT server is dial-up, a demand-dial interface must be configured for it.

◆ If clients are connecting to application servers on the public network, they might need special ports configured on the NAT connection.

INSTALLING, CONFIGURING, AND TROUBLESHOOTING REMOTE ACCESS

Configure, monitor, and troubleshoot remote access.

◆ Configure inbound connections

◆ Create a remote access policy

◆ Configure a remote access profile

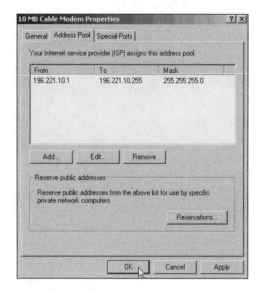

FIGURE 6.65
You can give the NAT multiple addresses to map to if multiple addresses have been allocated to you by your ISP.

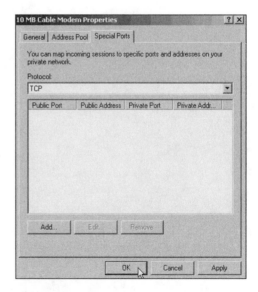

FIGURE 6.66
You can make private network services (like FTP and Web servers) available to public clients by mapping port communication to specific internal addresses.

Most corporate networks have at least one user with a laptop who travels. The idea of remote access is that a client should be able to connect to a remote access server and thereby be granted access to network resources.

The components of a remote access system are:

◆ A remote access server

◆ A remote access client

◆ A remote access security policy

The remote access server is responsible for accepting (or denying) an access request from a client and then directing that client to appropriate network resources as required. The remote access client is responsible for initiating a connection through an approved media (telephone, ISDN, and so on) to the remote access server and providing appropriate credentials to identify the remote access user. Finally, the remote access security policy defines valid users and the appropriate resources for them to access. All three of these must be functioning properly in order for remote access to work properly.

A Windows 2000 member server can supply two types of remote access connectivity: dial-up networking (DUN) and virtual private networking (VPN). Both provide for access to remote systems. However, their configurations are quite different. Dial-up networking is configured over a private communication link, like a telephone line, whereas virtual private networking is configured as a secured transmission over an already established communication link, like an Internet connection or a LAN.

Both remote access types require a server to receive and process requests and both create a connection to a network that is the same in functionality (but usually not in speed) as though the user were physically connected to the LAN. This section will discuss the configuration of remote access via dial-up networking, and the next section will discuss virtual private networks.

Dial-up networking is based on a dial-up connection. As such it supports connections over hardware such as packet switching networks (the phone line), IDSN, and X.25. In addition, for data transfers between computers in close physical proximity, you can use direct cable connections between parallel or serial ports (LPT or COM).

Two communication protocols are currently being used to facilitate dial-up networking: Point-to-Point Protocol (PPP) and Serial Line Interface Protocol (SLIP). PPP is a more robust protocol and has largely superseded SLIP. However, some dial-up servers still use SLIP technology (mainly UNIX machines). SLIP has not been supported by Windows servers since NT 3.51; therefore, SLIP clients cannot connect to Windows 2000 remote access servers.

PPP provides a variety of features in dial-up networking. It allows for the transmission of TCP/IP, IPX, NetBEUI, AppleTalk, and other protocols via the dial-up connection. In addition, it also supports the dynamic allocation of TCP/IP addresses to clients at connect time (much like DHCP). PPP also supports secured transmission although, for the most part, it is not required because the communication mechanisms are, by their nature, private.

Configuring Inbound Connections

The configuration of a remote access server requires two things: enabling of the Routing and Remote Access Service (RRAS) and configuration of at least one hardware device to accept incoming calls.

The Routing and Remote Access Service (which was introduced in the section "Shared Access Using the NAT Routing Protocol") is installed by default when you install Windows 2000 Server. However, it is not enabled until you manually select it. RRAS is used for a variety of functions, so it might already be enabled when you come to configure dial-up networking.

Step by Step 6.18 shows how to enable RRAS if it is not already enabled.

STEP BY STEP

6.18 Enabling the Routing and Remote Access Service (RRAS)

1. Ensure that the network card being used for RRAS uses a static TCP/IP address.

---

continues

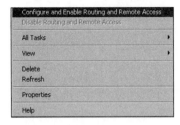

FIGURE 6.67
The Routing and Remote Access Service must be enabled before RRAS will work.

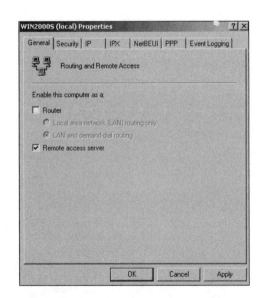

FIGURE 6.68
A server must be configured to be a remote access server before you can connect to it from a remote access client.

continued

2. From the Start menu, choose Programs, Administrative Tools, Routing and Remote Access.

3. On the Routing and Remote Access manager, right-click the server for which you want to enable RRAS and choose Configure and Enable Routing and Remote Access from the menu that appears (see Figure 6.67).

4. At the Welcome to the Routing and Remote Access Server Setup Wizard, click Next.

5. At the Common Configurations screen, select Manually Configured Server. Click Next to continue. It is recommended that you manually configure because then you can see all the changes that are made.

6. At the Completing the Routing and Remote Access Server Setup Wizard screen, click Finish.

7. The Routing and Remote Access dialog box appears, asking if you want to start the service. Click Yes.

If RRAS has already been enabled, the remote access portion can be disabled. If it is, your server will not accept any incoming dial-up networking connections. To enable the remote access feature of the server, follow Step by Step 6.19.

STEP BY STEP

6.19 Enabling the Remote Access on Your Server

1. From the Start menu, choose Programs, Administrative Tools, Routing and Remote Access.

2. On the Routing and Remote Access manager, right-click the server for which you want to enable RRAS and choose Properties from the menu that appears.

3. In the Server Properties dialog box, select Remote Access Server on the General property sheet (see Figure 6.68).

4. Close the Server Properties dialog box.

When RRAS has been started, you need to have a dial-in device configured. This could be a modem, an ISDN adapter, an X.25 connection, or a serial or parallel cable connected to a COM or LPT port. If you have a modem installed in your Windows 2000 server, it should have been detected by the Plug and Play manager and automatically configured. If it was not, you will have to install it manually. Step by Step 6.20 describes how to manually install a modem. The screen shots were taken installing a port to port connection via a null modem cable, but the same principle applies to any modem installation.

STEP BY STEP

6.20 Manually Installing a Modem

1. From the Control Panel, double-click the Phone and Modem Options icon.

2. In the Phone and Modem Options dialog box, click the Modems tab and then click the Add button on that property sheet.

3. At the Install New Modem screen, select the option labeled Don't Detect My Modem; I Will Select It from a List. Then click Next.

4. At the Install New Modem screen, select the manufacturer and model of the modem you want to install. If you have a driver on disk, click Have Disk and supply the disk when prompted. Click Next to continue.

5. At the Install New Modem screen, select the port that you are using to communicate externally with this device. Click Next to continue.

6. At the final Install New Modem screen, click Finish to exit.

7. Close the Phone and Modem Options dialog box.

All modem devices are automatically enabled for incoming traffic when RRAS is enabled. Any modems installed after RRAS is enabled are also automatically configured for RRAS. However, you may want to enable or disable one or more of these devices. In the RRAS manager, these devices are listed as ports, and you can configure the properties of each of the ports to allow or disallow routing or remote access.

Step by Step 6.21 shows how to enable a port for remote access.

FIGURE 6.69
Begin port configuration from the Properties dialog box.

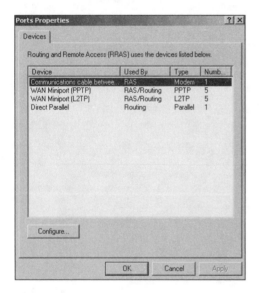

FIGURE 6.70
Select the device to enable for RRAS.

STEP BY STEP

6.21 Enabling a Port for Remote Access

1. From the Start menu, choose Programs, Administrative Tools, Routing and Remote Access.

2. On the Routing and Remote Access manager, expand the server you are configuring, right-click the Ports line, and select Properties from the menu that appears (see Figure 6.69).

3. In the Ports Properties dialog box, select the device you want to enable for remote access and click the Configure button (see Figure 6.70).

4. In the Configure Device dialog box, select Remote Access Connections (Inbound Only) and click OK (see Figure 6.71).

5. Close all open windows.

When you have enabled RRAS and configured an input device, you are ready to allow users to connect from remote dial-up locations. Before you do, though, both the user account configuration and server configurations should be done.

Configuring the Server for Security and Network Access

Once enabled, the server can be configured to fit the authentication, security, and logging needs of your organization. You can configure what protocols will be allowed to pass from the client, as well as how much of the network a remote user will be allowed to access. Both are configured from the server properties.

The server's Properties dialog box contains five or more property sheets (the "or more" depends on how many protocols are installed on the server). For example, if you have TCP/IP, NWLink, and NetBEUI installed, you will see seven property sheets; if only TCP/IP is installed, you will see only five.

The General property sheet allows you to configure the server for remote access.

The Security property sheet allows you to configure the authentication provider and methods, as well as the accounting provider (see Figure 6.72). For both configurations, either RRAS allows Windows 2000 to take care of the task, or it allows you to pass that responsibility to a Remote Authentication Dial-In User Service (RADIUS) server. RADIUS is an industry standard for centralized authentication and accounting in a remote access environment. These servers are generally used in large-scale dial-up environments such as those of an Internet service provider (ISP). Windows 2000 server has a RADIUS client that is capable of using the services of a RADIUS server.

In most non-ISP Remote Access Environments, Windows Authentication will be used to provide authentication services for dial-up clients. You can configure the types of authentication the Remote Access Services will accept by clicking the Authentication Methods button. Because authentication requires the passing of name and password information over a possibly insecure line, a variety of encryption schemes are available. You can make one or more of these methods available to your clients. The server and client will negotiate for the least common denominator between them and use

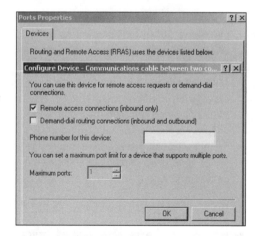

FIGURE 6.71
To allow clients to dial to a port, configure it to receive inbound connections.

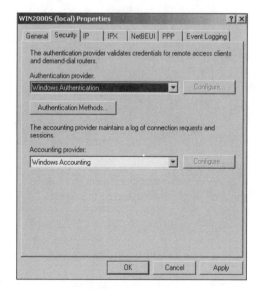

FIGURE 6.72
You can configure so that either Windows 2000 or a RADIUS server should provide authentication and/or Accounting services.

N O T E **Windows 2000 Can Function As a RADIUS Server** Windows 2000 does have the ability to function as a RADIUS server. This implementation is referred to as the Internet Authentication Services (IAS) and allows for the centralization of many remote access management functions in an enterprise or multiple enterprise environment.

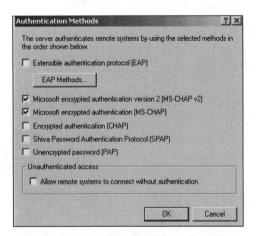

FIGURE 6.73
A variety of authentication methods are available, some of which are more secure than others.

that method to encrypt the password data being transmitted. If a client cannot provide the authentication method demanded by the server then the client will not be able to authenticate and will generally not be able to connect to the remote network. The exception to this is if you enable Allow Remote Systems to Connect Without Authentication. In this case, no user information is sent from the client, and there is no way for the server to know who the user is. This is potentially dangerous because server or network resources may be made available to unknown users without the ability to record or log user identification.

Figure 6.73 shows the list of authentication methods. Table 6.3 outlines the authentication methods available and the features of each.

TABLE 6.3

REMOTE ACCESS AUTHENTICATION METHODS

Connection Type	Function
EAP	The Extensible Authentication Method is an authentication method that leaves open-ended the forms of authentication available. Under EAP, the server and client negotiate the actual authentication used. This authentication may use smart cards or other authentication types. This authentication method can incorporate secondary checks like prompting the user for a PIN number to go with whatever authentication has been provided. This authentication method choice allows (through the click of the EAP Methods button) you to specify the particular methods that EAP encompasses in your implementation.
MS-CHAP v2	The Microsoft Challenge Handshake Authentication Protocol version 2 allows for challenge-response authentication based on a two-way encryption algorithm and the user name/password combination provided. MS-CHAP v2 eliminates some of the security holes in the original MS-CHAP authentication method. However, when used with dial-up networking, it is available to only Windows 2000, Windows NT 4.0, and Windows 98 clients (the NT and 98 clients must have the appropriate patches applied).

Connection Type	*Function*
CHAP	The Challenge Handshake Authentication Protocol method allows for encrypted authentication with non-Microsoft clients (or MS clients not capable of using MS-CHAP v2). This ensures that encrypted authentication can happen even with non-Microsoft dial-up clients. CHAP authentication relies on the MD5 hashing scheme and the storage of user passwords in a reversibly encrypted form in the Active Directory. Configuring reversibly encrypted passwords in the Active Directory was discussed in Chapter 2, in the section on interoperability with Macintosh clients ("Interoperation with Apple Macintosh").
SPAP	The Shiva Password Authentication Protocol is an encryption mechanism employed by Shiva. This method is more secure than sending passwords clear-text (no encryption) but not as secure as MS-CHAP or CHAP. Although the password is encrypted under this method, the same password is always encrypted the same way. This is a security risk because the password packets that are sent could be re-sent by a hacker to provide the appropriately encrypted password.
PAP	The Password Authentication Protocol is the least secure method of authentication available in dial-up access. Using this method, passwords are sent as plain text without any sort of encryption. This method should be left available only if authentication is required and the client has no way of providing encryption.

In addition to the authentication provider, you can configure an accounting provider for remote access sessions. This can be either a RADIUS server or the remote access server. If you configure Windows Accounting, then a record of connection requests and sessions is logged using the logging settings defined in the Routing and Remote Access manager (Remote Access Logging folder).

If your server is running the TCP/IP protocol, you have the option of making this protocol available for remote access communication (see Figure 6.74). To do that, you must select Allow IP-Based Remote Access and Demand-Dial Connections. If you enable TCP/IP, you have the option of defining the scope of network access using this protocol. If you want the connecting user to only be able to access resources located on the dial-up server, leave Enable IP Routing deselected. If you want DUN clients to be able to access the entire network, be sure to select Enable IP Routing.

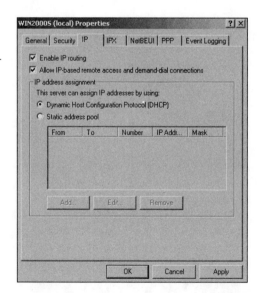

FIGURE 6.74
TCP/IP communication can be made available to remote access clients, as can the network beyond the remote access server.

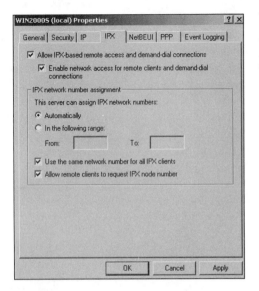

FIGURE 6.75
IPX communication can be made available to remote access clients, as can the network beyond the remote access server.

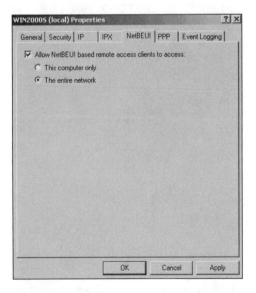

FIGURE 6.76
NetBEUI communication can be made available to remote access clients, as can the network beyond the remote access server.

When a user connects to your network using DUN and TCP/IP, his or her modem effectively becomes a network card. As such, that interface needs a TCP/IP address to communicate using the TCP/IP protocol. You can decide how a TCP/IP address is assigned to both the server's interface and the client's. If a DHCP server is available to the remote access server, then you could choose to assign addresses from the DHCP scope. In this case, the remote access server obtains two addresses from the DHCP server and sends one to the client. If you do not have a DHCP server available or if you do not want to use addresses from your LAN scope, you can give out addresses configured on this property sheet. You need to provide a range of addresses to give out. To do so, click the Add button and provide the range.

If your server is running the NWLink protocol, you have the option of making the IPX protocol available for remote access communication (see Figure 6.75). To do that, you must select Allow IPX-Based Remote Access and Demand-Dial Connections. If you enable IPX, you have the option of defining the scope of network access using this protocol. If you want the connecting user to only be able to access resources located on the dial-up server, leave Enable Network Access for Remote Clients and Demand-Dial Connections deselected. If you want DUN clients to be able to access the entire network, be sure to select that check box.

Like TCP/IP, IPX-configuration can be generated by the remote access server. You can have this configuration generate automatically or be generated within a certain address scope. Configure the options appropriately for your network environment.

If your server is running the NetBEUI protocol, you have the option of making that protocol available for remote access communication (see Figure 6.76). To do that, you must select Allow NetBEUI-Based Remote Access Clients to Access. Then you must choose either This Computer Only or The Entire Network to define the scope of network access.

Because NetBEUI has no configuration parameters, there are no other options for this protocol.

On the PPP property sheet, you can configure the remote access server to use PPP in advanced ways (see Figure 6.77). Multilink provides increased transmission bandwidth by combining multiple physical links into one virtual link. By configuring both the server and the client with multilink, you could turn two 56K connections into a single 112KB connection. This would require two phone lines and modems to be available on the both the server and the client side.

An enhancement to Windows 2000 over Windows NT 4.0 is the addition of the Bandwidth Allocation Protocol (BAP) and Bandwidth Allocation Control Protocol (BACP) to dynamically allocate lines to a connection as required.

You can also configure the use of Link Control Protocol (LCP) extensions from here. A discussion of LCP is beyond the scope of the book, but more information can be obtained in TCP/IP RFC 1570.

Finally, you can configure software compression of data sent over the dial-up connection.

On the Event Logging property sheet, you can configure logging of remote access events to the system log (see Figure 6.78). The settings range from not logging any information to logging most event information. You can also configure the logging of PPP events to a special PPP log by selecting the Enable Point-to-Point Protocol (PPP) Logging check box.

The next Step by Step shows how to modify the properties of the RRAS server.

STEP BY STEP

6.22 Modifying Remote Access Server Properties

1. From the Start menu, choose Programs, Administrative Tools, Routing and Remote Access.

2. On the Routing and Remote Access manager, right-click the server you are configuring and choose Properties from the menu that appears.

3. Modify the desired parameters and close the Server Properties dialog box.

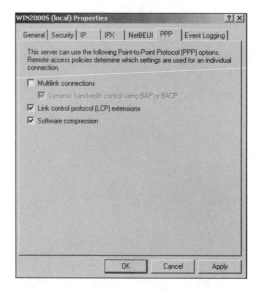

FIGURE 6.77
Multilink allows you to expand the incoming bandwidth that's available by combining two or more physical connections into a single virtual connection.

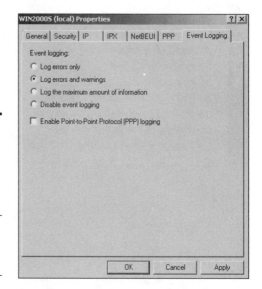

FIGURE 6.78
Logging of remote access events in the System log can take a variety of forms.

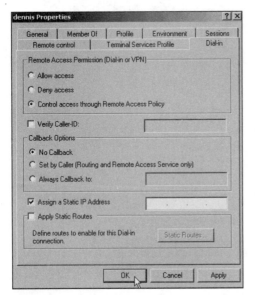

FIGURE 6.79
The user's properties must be configured to
allow remote access in order to be used.

Configuring User Accounts for Remote Access

Although remote access is automatically available once you have
enabled the Routing and Remote Access Service, all clients are, by
default, denied the ability to access the network using remote access.
This is a safety feature to prevent unauthorized access through inat-
tentive administration. Because in the average organization it is
likely that only a small fraction of the network user community uses
remote access, this is a reasonable policy.

Included in the dial-in properties for a user's account is the ability to
use remote access to get to the network.

In the property section headed Remote Access Permission (dial-in or
VPN), you can configure a user's ability to use remote access (see
Figure 6.79). In a Windows 2000 workgroup (for example, one in
which there are no Domain Controllers but Windows 2000
machines), the following apply: If Allow Access is selected and at
least one remote access policy exists, that user will be able to connect
using remote access. If Deny Access is selected, a user will always be
denied access to remote access. If Control Access through Remote
Access Policy is selected, whether a user can connect using remote
access will be subject to conformity to the policies governing remote
access users. These policies are discussed in the next section.

In addition to enabling or disabling remote access for a user, you can
configure a number of other properties. If you select Verify Caller-
ID and enter a telephone number, the remote access server will
check the caller's ID to ensure that the right source is being dialed
from. If a user dials from the wrong number, access will be denied.

The Callback Options allow the configuration of user callback. User
callback triggers the server to terminate an incoming call and then
call the dialer back at a predetermined number. This feature enables
two things. First, it ensures that dialup users can call from only one
location, thus securing the network against callers who have user
names and passwords but who are not calling from the right location. Second, it allows remote access clients to avoid large long distance charges by ensuring that only a nominal connection fee is
incurred, and that the bulk of the call's cost is billed centrally to the
server.

If you select Assign a Static IP Address and then configure a TCP/IP address, all other dynamic address allocation will be ignored for the user in favor of the address listed here.

If you select Apply Static Routes, you can define routes to other networks for dial-in clients.

To set the above properties on the local account for a server, open the Computer Management console, open the users list, and edit the user properties on the Dial-In property sheet. To set the above properties on an Active Directory account, open the Active Directory Users and Computers console, open the users list, and edit the user properties on the Dial-In property sheet.

> **WARNING**
>
> **Caller ID Must Be Supported** If you configure the caller ID setting and caller ID is not available to the server or is blocked by the user, access will be denied, regardless of the number from which the user is calling.

Creating a Remote Access Policy

Under Windows 2000, control of remote access is an elegant endeavor. As you saw in the last section, through the properties of the user's account, you can grant or deny access to remote access. However, it is in the remote access policy that the true power and flexibility of remote access control is found. Remote access policy is a set of rules that define a user's or group of users' ability to connect to a server by way of remote access. For example, perhaps a group of users should not be allowed to use remote access; you can create a remote access policy that denies access based on user group in the Active Directory. Perhaps certain users should be granted access but only during certain hours; you can configure a remote access Policy that defines those criteria. If you have more than one policy, each is designated with a number. The lower the number, the sooner it is evaluated. If a user is granted access based on one policy and denied access based on another, if the granting policy has a lower number, the user gets access. If it has a higher number the user is denied access.

One remote access policy is created by default. That policy denies access to all users at all times of the day. This policy ensures that, if user accounts are configured to grant access based on the remote access policy (as they are by default), no one gets access to the network by remote access. If you choose not to use policies at all, you can override this policy by granting explicit access through the user account properties. This is essentially the way things worked under

FIGURE 6.80
A remote access policy specifies rules for allowing or denying remote access.

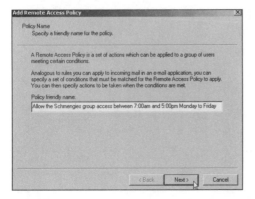

FIGURE 6.81
If you give the policy a meaningful name, you can easily tell its purpose by looking at the policy list.

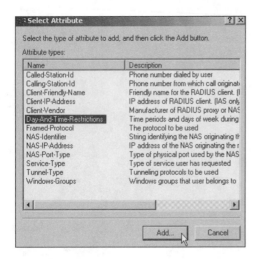

FIGURE 6.82
Many attributes can be added to the list of rules for a policy.

Windows NT 4.0. As a cautionary reminder, a warning in the last section indicated that the default policy should not be removed. If you have no policies at all, no one gets remote access regardless of the account properties, so be sure to override the policy. Do not delete it.

If you want your access policy to be more complex, you can modify the default policy to put rules in place and/or you can add more policies to control users or groups based on certain rules.

Step by Step 6.23 shows you how to create a remote access policy.

STEP BY STEP

6.23 Creating a Remote Access Policy

1. From the Start menu, choose Programs, Administrative Tools, Routing and Remote Access.

2. In the Routing and Remote Access manager, expand the Remote Access server section, right-click the Remote Access Policies entry, and choose New Remote Access Policy from the menu that appears (see Figure 6.80).

3. At the Policy Name screen, type in a meaningful name that fully describes the purpose of the policy such as "Allow the Schmengies Group Access between 7:00 a.m. and 5:00 p.m. Monday to Friday" for example (see Figure 6.81). Click Next to continue.

4. At the Conditions screen, click the Add button. Select the attribute type to add as a rule (see Figure 6.82), and then click Add to continue.

5. At the Constraints screen, enter the values appropriate to the attribute type to describe the allow or deny access condition (see Figure 6.83). This screen shot shows how you would modify the time parameters to allow access only between 7:00 a.m. and 5:00 p.m. on weekdays. Click OK to continue. Modify the desired parameters, and then close the Server Properties dialog box.

6. Repeat steps 4 and 5 until all the necessary rules have been added (see Figure 6.84). These rules are ANDed, and the policy applies only if all the rules produce a TRUE result. Click Next to continue.

7. At the Permissions screen, choose the radio button to indicate if a TRUE to all the rules explicitly grants or denies permission to use remote access (see Figure 6.85). Click Next to continue.

8. At the User Profile screen shown in Figure 6.86, click the Edit Profile button to configure the profile for users meeting the criteria (profiles are discussed in the next section). Then click Finish.

9. The policies are evaluated from the top down. If a client conforms to a policy, access is granted or denied, and policy evaluation ends. Put the existing profiles into an appropriate order by right-clicking the profile you want to move and choosing Move Up or Move Down (see Figure 6.87).

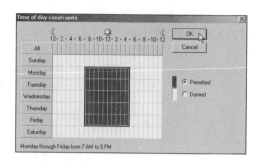

FIGURE 6.83
Once an attribute has been selected, properties for that attribute can be configured. Here, time of day constraints are being configured.

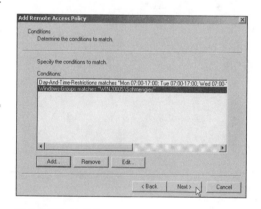

FIGURE 6.84
You can add a number of rules to a single policy.

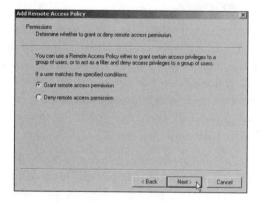

FIGURE 6.85
Conformance to the policy rules can either grant or deny access.

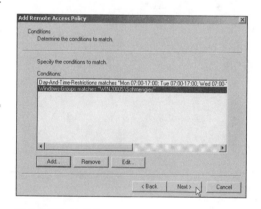

FIGURE 6.86
A profile defining remote access features available to the user can be associated with adherence to a specific policy.

FIGURE 6.87
The policies are evaluated from the top down.

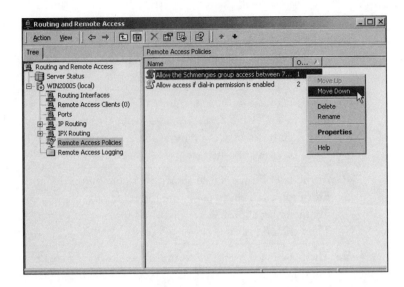

Configuring a Remote Access Profile

If remote access policies are the rules by which users are explicitly granted or denied remote access, remote access profiles define what the nature of the access is to be.

Remote access profiles are always associated with specific policies. A user will be granted remote access restricted by the definition in the policy. This may include placing a time limit on the connection or restricting the connection to a certain media type. Even if the user has been granted explicit access through account properties, a profile belonging to a policy that would have applied to the user will still be applied.

You can create profiles at the time you create a policy (see step 8 of Step by Step 6.23), or you can create/modify profiles afterward. Regardless, configuring the properties for a profile consists of addressing six property sheets:

- ◆ Dial-In Constraints
- ◆ IP
- ◆ Multilink
- ◆ Authentication
- ◆ Encryption
- ◆ Advanced

The Dial-In Constraints property sheet allows for the configuration of limitations on the ability for the session to initialize or to carry on indefinitely (see Figure 6.88). You can restrict the session to a certain amount of idle time before it's automatically disconnected or to be disconnected after a certain elapsed connection time. In addition, you can restrict the connection to only being allowed during certain times or on certain days of the week. You can also configure a specific number to dial from (which requires that the server be able to determine the number from which the client is dialing). You can even go so far as to restrict access from a specific media type (such as Ethernet or ISDN).

The IP property sheet allows for the configuration of the TCP/IP configuration parameters (see Figure 6.89). You can force the IP address to come from a specific source (client, server, or—the default—the server properties). In addition, you can filter the IP information that's sent to restrict communications to certain TCP/IP addresses or to allow only certain TCP/IP packet types between the client and a specific address.

The Multilink property sheet allows for the configuration of multilink for this connection (see Figure 6.90). You can allow the server properties to define multilink, disable multilink, or cap the number of ports multilink will function over. In addition, you can configure the BAP settings to drop multilink connections based on bandwidth usage.

The Authentication property sheet allows for the configuration of authentication methods used by this profile (see Figure 6.91). By doing this, you can require that certain authentication methods be available during the day (when connections can be monitored) but not at night. The options here are the same as the server properties, but these override the authentication methods allowed by the server.

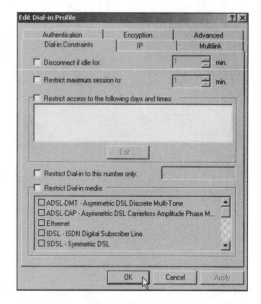

FIGURE 6.88
The dial-in constraints are restrictions placed on a client to whom the profile is applied.

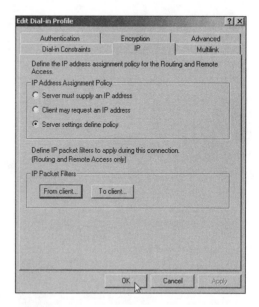

FIGURE 6.89
The IP properties define how TCP/IP addresses are allocated to the remote access client and whether filtering occurs.

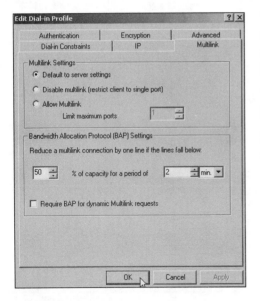

FIGURE 6.90
The Multilink properties define how multilink is used (if at all) and whether bandwidth is to be allocated or de-allocated dynamically.

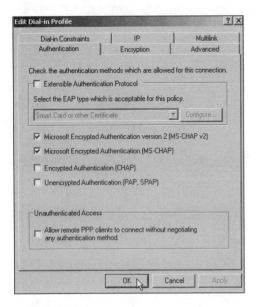

FIGURE 6.91
The Authentication properties define how authentication is to be handled for clients to whom this profile is assigned.

The Encryption property sheet allows for the configuration of levels of encryption allowed by this profile (see Figure 6.92). You can allow all encryption levels (from none to strong) or allow only certain levels of encryption.

The Advanced property sheet allows you to define the additional information supplied to the server by the client (see Figure 6.93).

Step by Step 6.24 shows how to edit a remote access profile for a remote access policy.

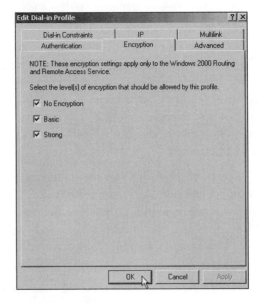

FIGURE 6.92
The Encryption properties define the levels of network encryption that should be applied to connections to which this profile is applied.

STEP BY STEP

6.24 Editing a Remote Access Profile for a Remote Access Policy

1. From the Start menu, choose Programs, Administrative Tools, Routing and Remote Access.

2. On the Routing and Remote Access manager, expand the Remote Access Server section, select the Remote Access Policies entry, and double-click the specific policy for which you want to edit the profile.

3. On the Policy Properties dialog box, click the Edit Profile button (see Figure 6.94).

4. Modify the Remote Access Profile settings, and then click OK.

5. Close the Policy Properties dialog box.

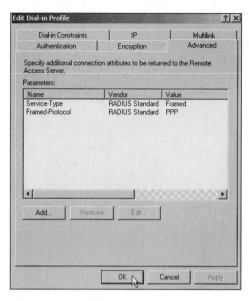

FIGURE 6.93
The Advanced properties define additional information supplied to the remote access server from the client.

INSTALLING, CONFIGURING, AND TROUBLESHOOTING VPNs

Install, configure, and troubleshoot a virtual private network (VPN).

Dialing from one computer to another through the phone system is a reasonably secure method of connection. After all, you are establishing a point-to-point connection over a media that requires special equipment to grab data. However, more and more communications are happening over less-secure channels (like the Internet). And even that point-to-point connection you established via the phone system is not really as secure as you might think. Anyone determined enough to grab your data will be able to get their hands on the tools necessary to capture your packets as they are being transferred.

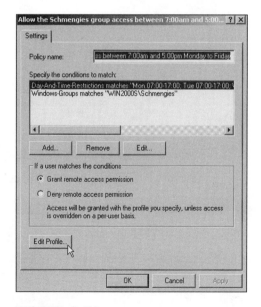

FIGURE 6.94
Profiles are associated with policies and are, therefore, accessed from the policies with which they are associated.

The idea of the virtual private network (VPN) is that a secure tunnel is established between one point and the next. This tunnel could be established through a dial-up connection, through an Internet connection established via an ISP, or on a local LAN. What is important is that a point-to-point connection already exists before the tunnel can be established. This tunnel can be established using a secure protocol that encapsulates encrypted data within it. This encrypted data may take the form of TCP/IP packets, NWLink packets, NetBEUI packets, or AppleTalk packets. Regardless of the data being sent, the communication is secure because, even if the tunneling packets are grabbed, they contain only encrypted data and are, therefore, useless to the grabber.

Two tunneling protocols are available under Windows 2000 Remote Access Services: Point-to-Point Tunneling Protocol (PPTP) and Layer Two Tunneling Protocol (L2TP).

PPTP is a tunneling protocol that was available in NT 4.0. It uses TCP/IP as a means of transporting encrypted packets containing the real network communication. As such, PPTP requires that a TCP/IP connection be established before communication can begin. However, when this TCP/IP session is established, the information contained in the PPTP packets can be from any supported protocol.

L2TP is a new tunneling protocol that is available in Windows 2000 only. Unlike PPTP, it does not require TCP/IP as a means of transportation and, therefore, can be used in Frame Relay, X.25, or ATM networks. However, also unlike PPTP, it does not have any inherent security. L2TP relies on cooperation with an encryption protocol, like IPSec (Internet Protocol Security), to provide encryption of data within the L2TP tunnel.

Table 6.4 compares the two protocols.

TABLE 6.4

PPTP/L2TP COMPARISON

PPTP	*L2TP*
Transit network must be TCP/IP	Transit Network can be TCP/IP, Frame Relay, X.25, or ATM
No header compression	Header compression for reduced overhead

PPTP	*L2TP*
No tunnel authentication	Tunnel authentication for increased security
Inherent encryption	No inherent encryption; requires IPSec for encryption

When Routing and Remote Access is enabled, five PPTP and five L2TP ports are created automatically. If you need more, you can easily create them by adjusting a property for each in the Ports properties. Step by Step 6.25 shows you how to create additional PPTP and L2TP ports.

STEP BY STEP

6.25 Creating PPTP and L2TP Ports

1. From the Start menu, choose Programs, Administrative Tools, Routing and Remote Access.

2. In the Routing and Remote Access console, expand the server you are working with, right-click the Ports entry, and choose Properties from the menu that appears.

3. In the Ports Properties dialog box, double-click either WAN Miniport (PPTP) or WAN Miniport (L2TP).

4. In the Configure Device dialog box, increase the Maximum Ports field to the maximum number of simultaneous connections required (see Figure 6.95). Click OK to continue.

5. Close the open dialog boxes.

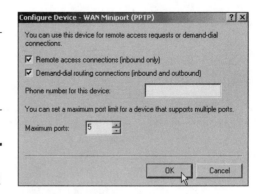

FIGURE 6.95
You can create new PPTP or L2PT ports by increasing the number of ports in the device configuration.

As has already been mentioned, VPN connections can be established via two transport mechanisms: through a direct LAN/WAN connection (like the Internet) or via a dial-up connection to the remote access server. Both pose problems in terms of control of the security being used. If a dial-up connection can be established, what requires the client to use PPTP instead of regular PPP? This problem is compounded when you consider a connection via the Internet because anyone with a TCP/IP address can potentially connect to your remote access server.

The solution to both of these problems rests in a remote access policy defining traffic of type PPTP and the filtering (and disposal) of non-PPTP or L2TP protocols from the remote access server. By creating a policy demanding a tunneling protocol, you ensure that all remote access traffic will be encrypted. In addition, by configuring your remote access server to ignore all packets that do not conform to PPTP or L2TP specifications, you ensure that no Internet traffic will be inadvertently passed on to your network.

Configuring a Remote Access Server for PPTP-Only Communication

To configure a RRAS server to allow only PPTP communication, you have to set some filters. PPTP communicates on port 1723. In addition, it uses a special protocol called the Generic Routing Encapsulation (GRE) protocol, which is assigned the identifier protocol 47. Both of these are present during communication using PPTP. If you want to eliminate all other traffic, you simply need to configure the RRAS server to drop all communication that does not use port 1723 and protocol 47. That procedure is outlined in the following Step by Step.

STEP BY STEP

6.26 Configuring a PPTP Remote Access Server

1. Configure a connection to the Internet from the remote access server. This will require you to configure an adapter to the Internet (T1, ISDN, and so on).

---

2. Configure a connection to the intranet (the internal network) from the remote access server. This will require a network card connected to the internal network.

---

3. Configure the remote access server to allow remote access clients to connect to the server. Begin by opening the Routing and Remote Access console.

4. Right-click the server and choose Properties from the menu that appears.

5. On the General property sheet, select Remote Access Server.

6. On the Security property sheet, configure an appropriate Authentication method for the clients expected. Also, configure an authentication provider and accounting provider appropriate for your remote access environment.

7. On the IP property sheet, ensure that the check boxes for both Enable IP Routing and Allow IP-Based Remote Access and Demand-Dial Connections are checked. Enable the appropriate address allocation method (use DHCP if you can).

8. Configure the remote access server to allow remote access clients to reach the internal network (enable the server as a router). Begin by opening the Routing and Remote Access console.

9. Right-click the server and choose Properties from the menu that appears.

10. On the General property sheet, select Router and select the radio button labeled LAN and Demand-Dial Routing.

11. Configure the PPTP ports to function as inbound remote access ports, and then adjust the number of ports if desired. Begin by opening the Routing and Remote Access console.

12. Expand the server, right-click Ports, and select Properties from the menu that appears.

13. On the Ports Properties dialog box, double-click the device entry WAN Miniport (PPTP).

continues

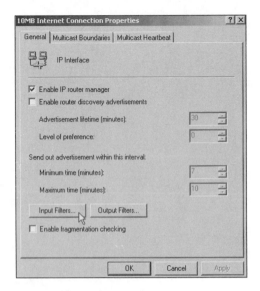

FIGURE 6.96
Input filters are accessible from the General tab of the Connection Properties dialog box.

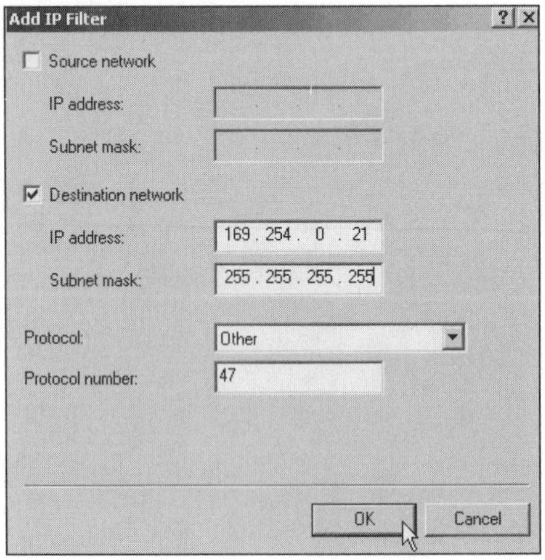

FIGURE 6.97
Allow all protocol 47.

continued

14. In the Configure Device-WAN Miniport (PPTP) dialog box, ensure that the check box for Remote Access Connections (Inbound Only) is selected. If desired, increase the number of PPTP connections available by changing the Maximum Ports from the default of 5.

15. Configure incoming and outgoing PPTP filters to eliminate Internet traffic from non-PPTP clients. Begin by opening the Routing and Remote Access console.

16. Expand the server and expand IP Routing.

17. Select General. Then, in the interface list, double-click the interface connected to the Internet.

18. At the Connection Properties dialog box, click Input Filters (see Figure 6.96).

19. In the Input Filters dialog box, click Add.

20. In the Add IP Filter dialog box, select Destination Network, type the TCP/IP address of the network card you are currently configuring, and enter a subnet mask of 255.255.255.255 (see Figure 6.97). In the Protocol list, select Other, and type 47 in the Protocol Number field. Click OK.

21. At the Input Filters dialog box, click Add.

22. In the Add IP Filter dialog box, select Destination Network, type the TCP/IP address of the network card you are currently configuring, and enter a subnet mask of 255.255.255.255 (see Figure 6.98). In the Protocol list, select TCP, type 1723 in the Source Port field, and enter 0 in the Destination Port field. Click OK.

23. At the Input Filters dialog box, click OK.

24. At the Connection Properties dialog box, click Output Filters.

25. At the Output Filters dialog box, click Add.

26. On the Add IP Filter dialog box, select Source Network, type the TCP/IP address of the network card you are currently configuring, and enter a subnet mask of 255.255.255.255 (see Figure 6.99). In the Protocol list, select Other, and type 47 in the Protocol Number field. Click OK.

27. At the Output Filters dialog box, click Add.

28. In the Add IP Filter dialog box, select Source Network, type the TCP/IP address of the network card you are currently configuring, and enter a subnet mask of 255.255.255.255 (see Figure 6.100). In the Protocol list, select TCP, type 1723 in the Source Port field, and enter 0 in the Destination Port field. Click OK.

continues

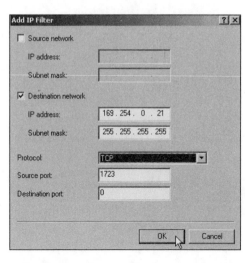

FIGURE 6.98
Allow all TCP packets originating on port 1723 and destined for port 0.

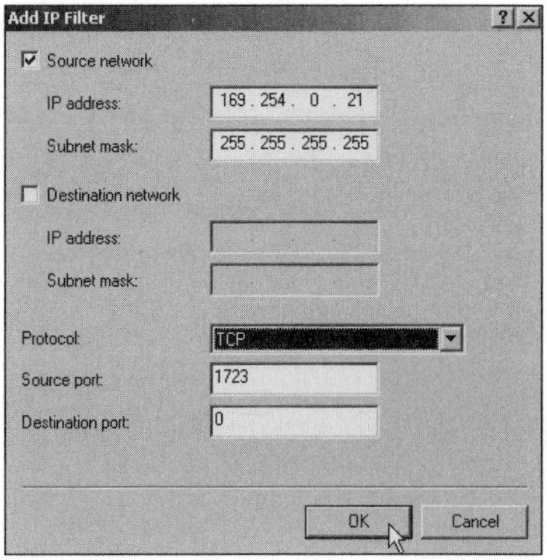

FIGURE 6.100
Allow all TCP packets from port 1732 to port 0.

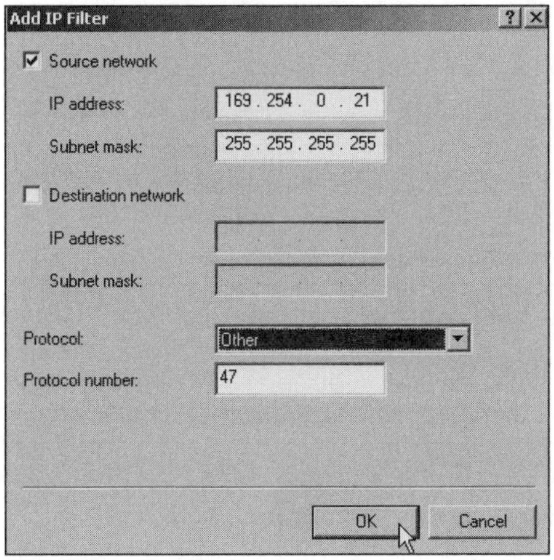

FIGURE 6.99
Allow all protocol 47 packets.

continued

29. At the Output Filters dialog box, click OK.

30. Configure remote access policies to allow only PPTP clients. Start by opening the Routing and Remote Access console.

31. Expand the server, right-click Remote Access Policies, and choose New Remote Access Policy from the menu that appears.

32. At the Policy Name screen, type in a meaningful name (like "PPTP Access Policy"). Click OK to continue.

33. At the Conditions screen, add the policy rules. Click Next to continue.

34. Click the Add button.

35. In the Select Attribute dialog box, select Tunnel-Type and click Add.

36. On the Tunnel-Type dialog box, locate Point-to-Point Tunneling Protocol in the Available Types list and double-click it. Click OK to continue.

37. Click the Add button.

38. In the Select Attribute dialog box, select NAS-Port-Type and click Add.

39. In the NAS-Port-Type dialog box, locate Virtual (VPN) in the Available Types list and double-click it. Click OK to continue.

40. At the Permissions screen, select Grant Remote Access. Click Next to continue.

41. At the User Profile screen, click Finish.

42. If desired, move the new policy up in the policies list to ensure proper order of processing.

Configuring a Remote Access Server for L2TP-Only Communication

Configuring a server for L2TP communication is a little more complex than configuring for PPTP. This is because the tunnel itself is not secure. As a result, you have to add an encryption protocol to the transmission to ensure security. The encryption protocol supplied with Windows 2000 is IPSec. Configuring a remote access server to provide L2TP plus IPSec security is beyond the scope of this book and the Windows 2000 Server exam.

INSTALLING, CONFIGURING, AND TROUBLESHOOTING TERMINAL SERVICES

Install, configure, monitor, and troubleshoot Terminal Services.

◆ Remotely administer servers by using Terminal Services

◆ Configure Terminal Services for application sharing

◆ Configure applications for use with Terminal Services

Terminal services is a session hosting service that allows a Windows 2000 server to provide environment resources (memory, processor, hard drive) so that a client needs to provide only minimal memory and processor resources. The end result is that both thin clients (like Windows CE machines and "dumb terminals") and fat clients (any PC running the Terminal Services client) will be able to use a Windows 2000 environment with little loss of performance over a Pentium machine with 64MB of RAM running the same applications.

This capability has obvious benefits. It means that legacy hardware can continue to be used, reducing the amount spent on hardware upgrades for old machines. It also means that legacy operating systems can continue to be used while, at the same time, taking advantage of 32-bit Windows 2000 applications. In addition, because all settings are hosted on a remote machine, control can be exercised over what software can be installed by clients and what applications can be run. Finally, through the Terminal Services administrator, you can take remote control of client sessions, which will make help desk functions much easier.

In addition to the regular client options, tools also exist for configuring remote administration on the server. This means that Terminal Services clients can be configured to remotely administer servers by providing live sessions on the server itself. This is much like the kinds of functionality that are provided by third-party products like *Remotely Possible*. Unlike the traditional approach to remote administration, where tools are installed on an administrator's machine, these sessions give local access to the server itself. That means processes can be terminated, software can be installed, services can be started and stopped, and so on.

The disadvantage of using the Terminal Services is that it uses server memory and sometimes increases network traffic. Because all the processing is happening on the server side, all that happens on the client is input from the keyboard and mouse and display of screen information. That means all keyboard and mouse commands have to be sent over the network to the server, and all display information must be sent to the client over the network. With some file-based database applications, network utilization can actually be reduced, and some of the network load implications can be overcome by creative subnetting. However, network bandwidth utilization should be monitored. In addition, memory needs to be increased in any server that is running the Terminal Services (slightly for simple administration hosting, much more for multiple-application user sessions) to allow for multiple sessions.

Terminal Services Hardware and Software

A terminal server implementation consists of two environments: the server environment and the client environment. The server environment is where the client session is hosted, and it must be robust enough to provide services to as many concurrent users as is permitted without loss of performance in other areas on the server. As a result, hardware requirements need to be carefully considered, and hardware may need to be upgraded before and during your terminal server implementation.

The Terminal Services Server

Terminal server requires a Windows 2000 server to host it. It is recommended that the server be a member server in a domain rather than a domain controller (a server that authenticates domain logon) because the Terminal Services may degrade the server's functions in other areas. Furthermore, if your implementation is large, you might need several terminal servers to service all your clients.

The primary hardware components to be managed in a terminal server environment are memory and processor power. Of course, the minimum memory requirements for Windows 2000 must be met (64MB), but on top of that, Microsoft recommends 4–8MB of RAM for every anticipated concurrent user. Failure to adhere to these guidelines will, at best, result in poor performance from the client's perspective and, at worst, render the clients unable to connect to the server at all (the client may get failure messages indicating that the server is too busy for the connection).

Like memory, processor requirements will scale linearly as the number of users increase. As a result, it is recommended that when you first implement terminal server, you use a server that is capable of being expanded to multiple processors in case additional processing power is required down the line.

Microsoft divides users into three categories:

◆ Task-based (those users who run a single data entry application)

◆ Typical (those users who run one or two simultaneous applications but whose data entry requirements are low; they may run a word processor and a browser)

◆ Advanced (those users whose requirements are heavy, running three or more simultaneous applications and/or doing large queries on databases)

The number of users that can be supported on any given server depend on the kinds of users being supported.

Based on data published by Microsoft, Table 6.5 provides a sample of terminal server users supported on given server hardware platforms.

TABLE 6.5

AVERAGE NUMBER OF USERS SUPPORTED ON SELECT SERVER PLATFORMS

Server Configuration	Task-based	Typical	Advanced
Single processor, Pentium Pro, 200MHz, 128MB RAM	25	15	8
Dual processor, Pentium Pro, 200MHz, 256MB RAM	50	30	15
Quad processor, Pentium Pro, 200MHz, 512MB RAM	100	60	30

In addition to memory and processor power, fast hard drives (preferably SCSI because they are supported under RAID and that can give performance benefits) are recommended, as is a network infrastructure tuned for maximum throughput (multiple network adapters are recommended and third-party NIC load balancing software really helps).

The Terminal Services Client

Because Terminal Services run almost exclusively on the server, the client can be much less powerful than would be necessary if the client were hosting applications itself. That fact is one of the benefits of using Terminal Services. In fact, Terminal Services allows a wide variety of clients to support Windows 2000 applications, as shown in the following list:

- Windows 2000 (all types)
- Windows NT (all types and versions running on Intel or Alpha processors)
- Windows 9x

◆ Windows for Workgroups (3.11)

◆ Windows CE clients (appropriately configured)

◆ Windows-based terminals ("thin clients")

To operate, all that is required is that certain minimum hardware specifications be met and that the terminal services client be installed on the computer. After that, when a session is opened, the user will be executing in a Windows 2000 window and will be able to work as though his or her local operating system were Windows 2000.

Table 6.6 lists the Windows operating systems on which terminal services clients operate and their minimum hardware requirements.

TABLE 6.6

MINIMUM HARDWARE REQUIREMENTS BY OPERATING SYSTEM

Operating System	RAM	Processor	Video Card
Windows 2000	32MB	Pentium	VGA
Windows NT	16MB	486	VGA
Windows 98	16MB	486	VGA
Windows 95	16MB	386	VGA
Windows 3.11	16MB	386	VGA
Windows CE	any	any	any

One more hardware requirement needs to be mentioned. Certain applications that are hosted from the terminal server may require special input devices (such as barcode readers) to function properly. Because all input comes from the client, two criteria must be met. First, the device must be installed on the client computer. Second, the device must operate as a keyboard-input device in order for its data to be recognized by the Terminal Services server.

Hosted Terminal Services Applications

As has been mentioned already, the environment that Terminal Services provides is Windows 2000. This means that any applications that are to be run by the Terminal Services client must be Windows 2000 compliant. If an application will not run under Windows 2000, it will not run hosted by a Terminal Services server. Although it is theoretically possible to run DOS, Windows 16-bit, and Windows 32-bit applications under Terminal Services, for best performance, Windows 32-bit applications are recommended.

Installing Terminal Services Server

When you install Terminal Services, you have three options in terms of the software to be installed. Of course, the Terminal Services server must be installed. In addition, you can install the Terminal Services client creator, used for creating client installation disks (not required if you are going to install the client software over the network). Finally, you can install the Terminal Services License Manager. You are required to install this software once for each enterprise in which applications are to run from Terminal Services clients.

During the installation process, you will be prompted for the kind of application your Terminal Services installation will have. You have two choices: remote administration and application server. Remote administration is used when the purpose for installing Terminal Services is to be able to open server consoles from remote machines in order to administrate the server. In installations like this, there will typically be only one user connected at a time—you or another administrator (two simultaneous connections).

Application server mode is used when the primary reason for installing Terminal Services is to host client sessions executing applications (this mode includes the ability to do remote administration of the server). In this case, the hardware requirements will be greater, but so will the administration. In addition to installing the applications for execution by the clients, you will also have to administer licensing of the clients.

Terminal Services licensing is not part of the license that you buy with the operating system your clients are running. As a result, you are required to install the Terminal Services License Manager on at least one computer in your company. When a client connects to a terminal server for the first time, it obtains and stores locally a license from the License Manager. On subsequent occasions, the local license is presented to the terminal server for validation. A terminal server will allow unlicensed clients to connect for 90 days, at which time it requires a License Manager with valid licenses in order to function. These licenses must be obtained from Microsoft.

The License Manager can be installed on a member server but, in order to work for all the users in your domain, it must be installed on a domain controller. Therefore, it is recommended that the License Manager always be installed on a domain controller. Moreover, if you want to use the same License Manager for your entire organization and you have multiple domains, you can install the manager as an enterprise manager so it can be accessed by any Windows 2000 domain in your organization.

The next two Step by Steps show you how to install Terminal Services to facilitate remote server administration and to run applications, respectively.

STEP BY STEP

6.27 Installing Terminal Services for Remote Server Administration

1. From the Control Panel, double-click the Add/Remove Programs icon.

2. At the Add/Remove Programs dialog box, click the Add/Remove Windows Components icon.

3. At the Windows Components screen, scroll down and select Terminal Services. Click Next to continue.

4. At the Terminal Services Setup screen, ensure that Remote Administration Mode is selected and click Next (see Figure 6.101).

5. At the Completing the Windows Components Wizard screen, click Finish.

6. When prompted, restart your server.

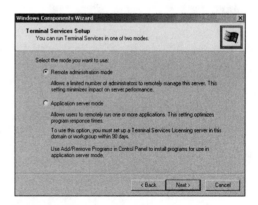

FIGURE 6.101
Remote Administration Mode allows for connection to a terminal server for the purposes of administering it.

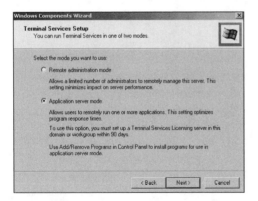

FIGURE 6.102
Application servers allow Terminal Services clients to connect and run programs. This server type requires that a License Manager be available.

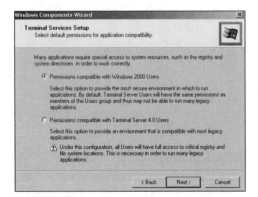

FIGURE 6.103
Choose the most restrictive permissions that will allow all your users to execute their applications.

STEP BY STEP

6.28 Installing Terminal Services for Application Server Operation

1. From the Control Panel, double-click the Add/Remove Programs icon.

2. At the Add/Remove Programs dialog box, click the Add/Remove Windows Components icon.

3. At the Windows Components screen, scroll down and select Terminal Services and Terminal Services Licensing. Click Next to continue.

4. At the Terminal Services Setup screen, ensure that Application Server Mode is selected and click Next (see Figure 6.102).

5. At the next Terminal Services Setup screen, choose the minimum permissions required to execute your applications (see Figure 6.103). If any of your applications require access to the Registry and system files to operate, you will have to choose Permissions Compatible with Terminal Server 4.0 Users; otherwise, choose Permissions Compatible with Windows 2000 Users. Click Next to continue.

6. At the next Terminal Services Setup screen, note any applications that are flagged as being potentially problematic. This list is compiled from your system, so yours will be different from what is shown in Figure 6.104. Applications listed may have to be reinstalled after Terminal Services is configured. Click Next to continue.

7. At the Completing the Windows Components Wizard screen, click Finish.

8. When prompted, restart your server.

If you need to reconfigure your server from one mode to the other (from Administration to Application or vice versa), you can do so through Add/Remove Programs applet in the Control Panel. Step by Step 6.29 illustrates this process.

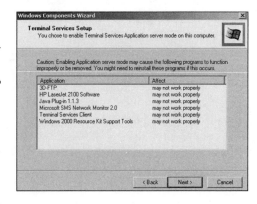

FIGURE 6.104
A list of applications with possible problems
is generated.

STEP BY STEP

6.29 Switching Between Server Modes

1. From the Control Panel, double-click the Add/Remove Programs icon.

2. At the Add/Remove Programs dialog box, click the Add/Remove Windows Components icon.

3. At the Windows Components screen, click Next to continue (there is no need to select or deselect any options at this time).

4. At the Terminal Services Setup screen, choose the mode you want to switch to and click Next. If you choose Administration, the wizard will complete the configuration. If you choose Applications, you will continue with steps 5–8 from Step by Step 6.28.

Configuring Terminal Services Server

Configuration of the Terminal Services server is done in two separate areas. First, the server itself is configured. Then, users are configured for Terminal Services sessions.

Terminal Services Server Configuration

Installed with the Terminal Services on the server is a Terminal Services Configuration Manager that allows you to set defaults for the operation of the terminal server. From that manager, you can configure the settings for the terminal server connection, and the settings for the terminal server itself.

All communications between Terminal Services clients and a Windows 2000 terminal server happen using the Remote Desktop Protocol-Transmission Control Protocol (RDP-Tcp). When the Terminal Server is activated on your server, a connection is created to use this protocol. Other connections can be created, but only for other terminal server types (a topic which is beyond the scope of this book and the Server exam).

When you open the properties for the RDP-Tcp connection, a dialog box with eight property sheets appears.

The General property sheet allows you to configure three things:

◆ A comment pertaining to the connection

◆ The encryption level of network data transmission

◆ Whether to always use standard Windows authentication

Because most of the activity that happens during a Terminal Services client session passes over the network, some level of encryption is necessary to preserve data integrity and secrecy (see Figure 6.105). Three levels of encryption are available:

◆ Low (only encrypt data from client to server but not the other way around)

◆ Medium (use 40- or 56-bit encryption in both directions)

◆ High (use 128-bit encryption if the server and client are so equipped)

Low encryption is used when security is not a large issue. It encrypts all data from the client to the server, ensuring that logon passwords are encrypted. Medium encryption is used when general network security is required. Medium security encrypts data to and from the client using either 40-bit (for pre-Windows 2000 Terminal Services clients) or 56-bit (for Windows 2000 Terminal Services clients).

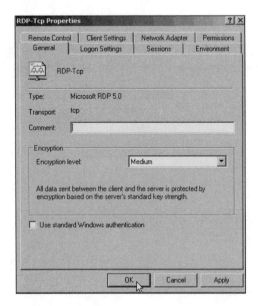

FIGURE 6.105

Client-server encryption defines the times at which encryption is applied to communication and how strong it is.

High encryption is used when security is very important. High encryption is available in all countries except those that have state-sponsored terrorism. At time of printing, this list included Cuba, Iran, Iraq, Libya, North Korea, Syria, Sudan, Serbia and Taliban-controlled areas of Afghanistan.

If Use Standard Windows Authentication is selected, Windows authentication is used even if another security provider is installed on the Windows 2000 terminal server.

The Logon Settings property sheet allows you to configure logon settings for users connecting to your server. You can have users provide their own logon (in which case, upon connection, users will be prompted to log on), or you can provide a single account that all users will connect to the server with (see Figure 6.106). The check box labeled Always Prompt for Password is significant only if you also select Always Use the Following Logon Information. In that case, you will not be able to provide a password to the logon account; the user connection will have to do that manually.

The Sessions property sheet allows you to set Terminal Services timeout and reconnection settings (see Figure 6.107). There are four user states with respect to a terminal server and a client:

◆ Active session

◆ Idle session

◆ Disconnected session

◆ Terminated session

An active session is one in which the client is working and keyboard or mouse information is being transferred to the server. An idle session is one in which no keyboard or mouse information is being transferred to the server. A disconnected session is one in which a user has exited the client software but has not logged off. The user can return to this session later as long as it is not terminated. Disconnected sessions take up resources on the server and, if the number of sessions is limited, may prevent other users from connecting. Terminated sessions are not sessions at all but are the absence of a session and the release of system resources formerly dedicated to a session.

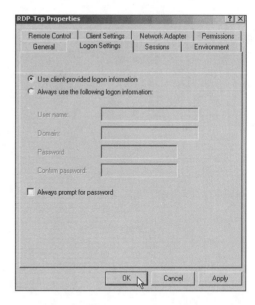

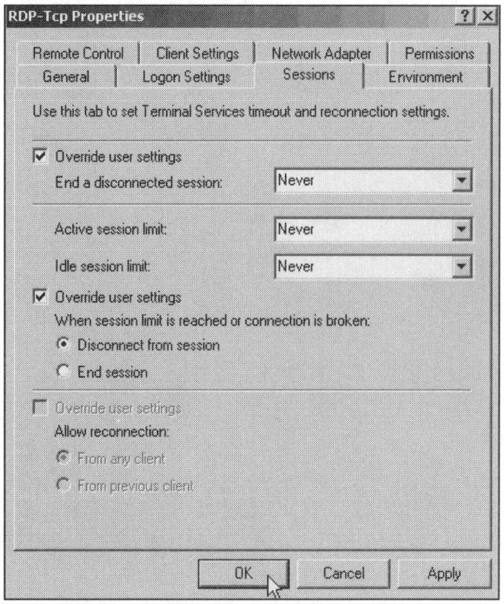

FIGURE 6.106
Configure the server to accept logon information from the client or to always use the same logon account.

FIGURE 6.107
Set timeout settings for server sessions.

Settings for what to do with disconnected sessions, active sessions, and idle sessions can be set for individual users (as they are in the properties of a user's account). Here, these user settings can be overridden with server settings.

If you change the End a Disconnected Session setting from Never to another value, when a session is disconnected, it must be reactivated within the time you specify or it will be terminated. You can either choose a time frame (from 1 minute to 2 days) or type in your own (using a number and the letter m for minutes, h for hours, and d for days). If you type in your own value, it cannot be greater than 49 days, 17 hours.

If you change the Active Session Limit setting from Never to another value, a session can only remain active for the length of time you specify. When the limit is reached, the session will be either disconnected or terminated (depending on the setting you choose for When Session Limit Is Reached Or Connection Is Broken). You can either choose a time frame (from 1 minute to 2 days) or type in your own (using a number and the letter m for minutes, h for hours, and d for days). If you type in your own value, it cannot be greater than 49 days, 17 hours.

If you change the Idle Session Limit setting from Never to another value, a session can remain idle for only the length of time you specify. When the limit is reached, the session will either be disconnected or terminated (depending on the setting you choose for When Session Limit Is Reached Or Connection Is Broken). You can either choose a time frame (from 1 minute to 2 days) or type in your own (using a number and the letter m for minutes, h for hours, and d for days). If you type in your own value, it cannot be greater than 49 days, 17 hours.

You can also choose to override the settings for what to do when a time limit on idle or active sessions has been reached (or when the network connection is broken between the client and the server). You can choose to either disconnect from the session and place the session into a disconnected state, or end session and release all session resources.

The Allow Reconnection Override setting does not apply to Windows 2000 clients, only to Citrix ICA-based clients; with respect to Windows 2000 clients, reconnection is allowed from any client. Therefore, this option will not be discussed here.

The Environment property sheet allows you to configure the initial program to run when a client is connected and whether wallpaper should be displayed (see Figure 6.108). Both of these settings are part of the configuration for the user account. These settings override what the user account settings specify.

The Start the Following Program When the User Logs On setting defines the shell the user will operate in (this replaces EXPLORER.EXE). If, for example, you configured this to run NOTEPAD.EXE, when a user logged in, Notepad would be displayed. When the user exited Notepad, the session would be terminated. You can also specify where the program should start—that is, what the default data directory is.

The property sheet also allows you to configure whether or not to display desktop wallpaper. Because wallpaper graphics tend to be large, this eliminates network traffic that is not related to functionality. This setting is often used when connecting over a slow link or where network bandwidth is at a premium.

The Remote Control property sheet configures the ability for administrators and help desk personnel to take control of a Terminal Services client's desktop (see Figure 6.109). When activated, it allows a remote administrator to connect to an active session and transmit mouse and keyboard commands. If Use Remote Control with Default User Settings is chosen, the configuration is deferred to the settings in the properties for the user account. If Do Not Allow Remote Control is set, none will be available under any circumstances. If Use Remote Control with the Following Settings is selected, you will be able to use a series of check boxes to configure the remote control parameters. These parameters include requiring the user's permission before taking control (a dialog box will appear on the user's screen asking for approval) and defining the level of interaction allowed (View the Session or Interact with the Session).

The Client Settings property sheet allows configuration of persistent settings from session to session and allows you to disable certain Windows features (see Figure 6.110).

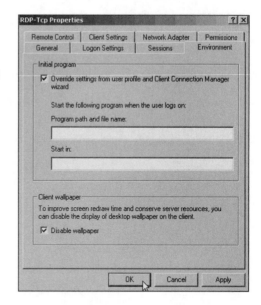

FIGURE 6.108
This property sheet allows automatic configuration of the Terminal Services client's environment after logging on.

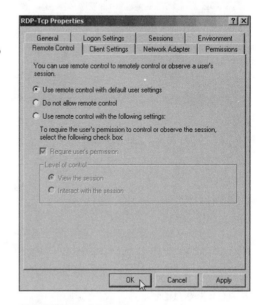

FIGURE 6.109
Configure the ability for administrators to watch or control client sessions.

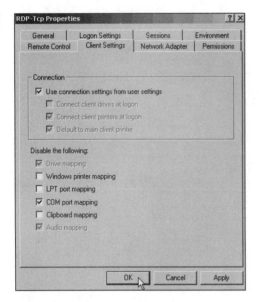

FIGURE 6.110
Configure persistent settings and hardware mappings from the client's computer.

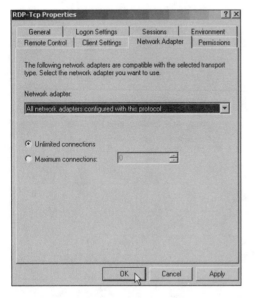

FIGURE 6.111
Configure the network adapter(s) to use for Terminal Services and the number of simultaneous client connections allowed.

If you deselect Use Connection Settings from User Settings, you will be able to set persistence of user-defined printer mappings (connections to network printers established manually) and default printer settings. The option to connect drives at logon is available to Citrix ICA-based clients only, so it is not discussed here.

You can choose to disable Windows printer mapping, which means that users will not be able to map to network printers; this is enabled (not checked) by default. You can choose to disable the client LPT port mapping, which means that users will not be able to print to local printers on their computers; this is enabled (not checked) by default. You can choose to disable the client COM port mapping, which means that users will not be able to connect to devices connected to their local COM ports; this is disabled (checked) by default. You can also choose to disable Clipboard mapping, which means that the user will not be able to copy things to the local Clipboard on his or her computer. If you disable this setting, a user will not be able to copy content from the Terminal Services window to local applications running on the client operating system. This feature is enabled (not checked) by default. Of course, with true thin clients, these functions cannot be made available anyway because there is no local operating system to interact with.

Two features are disabled (checked) by default and cannot be changed except on Citrix ICA-based clients. Those are drive mapping and audio mapping. As such, they are not discussed here.

The Network Adapter property sheet allows you to configure the network adapters on the server that are available for Terminal Services communication (see Figure 6.111). In addition, you can also configure the maximum number of simultaneous connections to allow. Throttling back the number of connections can be used to ensure that those clients who do connect will get satisfactory service from a terminal server that is underpowered for the total number of users trying to connect.

The Permissions property sheet allows you to configure which users or groups of users are allowed access to the terminal server and what they are allowed to do (see Figure 6.112).

Three levels of permissions are available:

◆ Full Control

◆ User Access

◆ Guest Access

Table 6.7 gives a breakdown of the rights given to each permission level.

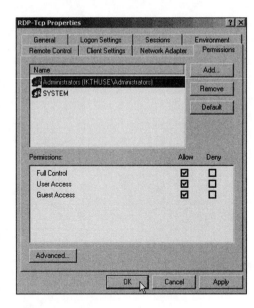

FIGURE 6.112
Configure permissions on the terminal server.

TABLE 6.7

RIGHTS BY CONNECTION PERMISSION LEVEL

Right	*Full Control*	*User*	*Guest*
Query session information	X	X	
Modify connection parameters			X
Reset (end) a session			X
Remote control another session		X	
Log on to a session on the server	X	X	X
Log another user off a session	X		
Send a message to another user's session	X	X	
Connect to another session	X	X	
Disconnect a session	X		
Use virtual channels (provide access from server program to client devices)	X		

By default, the local Administrators group and the SYSTEM get full control, the local Users group gets User access, and the Guest group gets guest access. You can configure permissions for any user or group that you have access to from the terminal server.

These settings are actually from the Registry, the interface is just a little more friendly.

In addition to the Connection Properties dialog box, you can also view and configure the server from the Server Settings window. You can double-click on any of the settings shown in Figure 6.113 to view the current configuration.

FIGURE 6.113
You view the current configuration of any of the settings by double-clicking them.

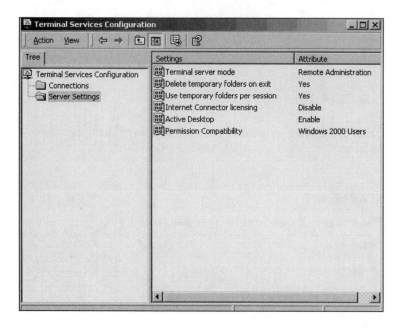

The Terminal Server Mode property indicates whether the Terminal Server is configured for Remote Administration or as an Application Server. You cannot change this setting from here; the mode must be set from the Add/Remove Programs icon.

The Delete Temporary Folders on Exit property can be set to Yes or No. If Yes, all folders created to facilitate a user's session will be deleted when the session is terminated.

The Use Temporary Folders Per Session property can be set to Yes or No. If Yes, a separate temporary folder will be created for every session established. If disk space is at a premium, you can set this to No and make all sessions share the same temporary folder.

The Internet Connector licensing property can be set to Enabled or Disabled. When Enabled, this property allows for up to 200 non-employees (domain authenticated users) to connect to the terminal server over the Internet. The purpose of this is to allow users to connect to an application that has not been configured for Internet (HTML, ASP, and so on) use but that needs to be accessed or demonstrated. You must purchase a separate license to legally enable this property. You cannot enable this feature while the server is in Remote Administration Mode.

The Active Desktop property can be enabled or disabled. By disabling this property, you eliminate the ability for users to enable the Active Desktop on their client sessions. This reduces the network traffic between the client and server.

The Permission Compatibility property can be set to either Permissions Compatible with Windows 2000 Users or Permissions Compatible with Terminal Server 4.0 Users. If possible, you want to leave the permissions as Windows 2000 because this restricts access to the Registry and system files. However, you may find that some legacy applications will not function with those restrictions and you have to reconfigure this setting.

Terminal Services User Account Configuration

The installation of Terminal Services server on a Windows 2000 server makes fundamental changes to the properties of the user accounts. These changes not only extend to the local accounts but, if the server is a member server in a domain, they also extend to the properties of the domain accounts.

The extension of the user properties takes the form of four property sheets that allow configuration of Terminal Services access. The four property sheets are:

◆ Terminal Services Profile

◆ Remote Control

◆ Sessions

◆ Environment

The Terminal Services Profile property sheet allows for the configuration of a special profile for use when connecting to a terminal server, a home directory for use when connecting to a terminal server, and a check box that labels a user as a potential Terminal Services client (see Figure 6.114).

Like a regular user profile, a Terminal Services profile allows you to configure the desktop environment for a Terminal Services user. By pointing the profile path to a shared location with a mandatory

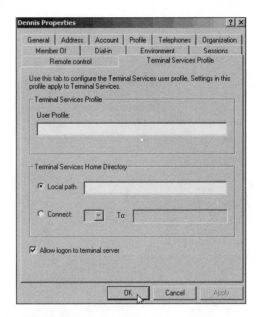

FIGURE 6.114
A separate profile can be configured when a user uses a Terminal Services client than when he uses local processing.

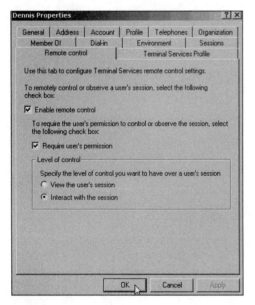

FIGURE 6.115
These remote control properties defined for the user are overridden by the server properties if those are set.

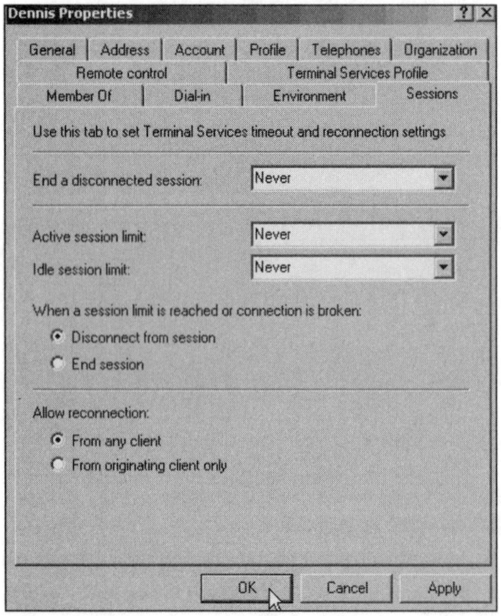

FIGURE 6.116
The user-specific session properties are overridden by the server settings if those are configured.

profile in it, you can ensure that Terminal Services clients can do what they need to without being able to make extensive (network-intensive) changes to their desktop settings. Of course, the profiles do not need to be mandatory; a simple roaming profile could be created instead.

To facilitate storing data from session to session, you can create home directories for users. These directories can be the same ones that a user uses when not connecting via Terminal Services (for those users who do both), or it can be separate. If you set a local path, it will connect to a local folder on the terminal server. If you set a connect path, the drive letter of your choice will be connected to a network share. It is advisable to use the same profile and home directory for terminal and normal windows use. This provides a consistent interface (desktop look and feel) with either connection type, lowering the learning curve and increasing the productive usage time.

Finally, on this property sheet you can configure access to Terminal Services in your environment. By selecting Allow Logon to Terminal Server, you enable a user to connect to terminal servers on your network. If this is not selected, that user will not be able to connect to any terminal servers. In conjunction with connection permissions, this setting can be used to enable a user to connect to all servers (in theory) but restrict access to only specific users (in practice).

The Remote Control property sheet enables you to set specific remote control properties for a specific user account (see Figure 6.115). If you have not configured these properties to be overridden in the connection properties for the server, these will take effect when a user connects to the terminal server.

The Sessions property sheet enables you to set session-specific time and disconnection options (see Figure 6.116). If you have not configured these properties to be overridden in the connection properties for the server, these will take effect when a user connects to the terminal server.

The Environment property sheet enables you to set the startup environment for the user (see Figure 6.117). If you have not configured these properties to be overridden in the connection properties for the server, these will take effect when a user connects to the terminal server.

Installing Terminal Services Client

In order to access the Terminal Services server from a user workstation, the Terminal Services client must be installed. The installation files can be distributed either on a floppy disk set (for 16-bit or 32-bit Intel) or via a network share (for any of the platforms).

When you install Terminal Services on a Windows 2000 server, a folder is installed into the system root (WINNT) folder that contains the installation files for 16-bit Intel, 32-bit Intel, and 32-bit Alpha clients. In addition, within the selection to install Terminal Services is the option to install the Client Creator Files that installs the program to create setup disks.

To enable installation of the Terminal Services client over the network, share the appropriate client installation files from the path \WINNT\System32\clients\tsclient. Also, ensure that at least Read access is configured for all users who need to install the client.

Step by Step 6.30 describes how to create a Client Installation Disk Set. Step by Step 6.31 describes how to install a Terminal Services client using that disk set.

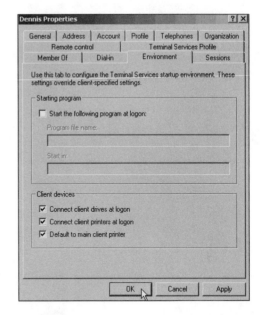

FIGURE 6.117
The user-specific environment settings are overridden by the server settings if those are configured.

STEP BY STEP

6.30 Creating a Client Installation Disk Set

1. From the Start menu, choose Programs, Administrative Tools, Terminal Services Client Creator.

2. At the Create Installation Disks(s) dialog box, select the kind of client you are going to install the Terminal Services client on (see Figure 6.118). Select a destination drive, and if the disks are not blank, select the Format Disk(s) check box. Click OK to continue.

3. When prompted, label a disk Terminal Services for 32-bit x86 Windows DISK1 and insert it into the disk drive. Click OK to continue. If formatting, confirm the format by clicking Yes when prompted.

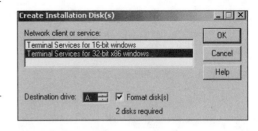

FIGURE 6.118
Installation disk sets can be created for 16-bit or 32-bit clients.

continues

continued

4. When prompted, label a disk Terminal Services for 32-bit x86 Windows DISK2 and insert it into the disk drive. Click OK to continue. If formatting, confirm the format by clicking Yes when prompted.

5. At the Network Client Administrator dialog box, click OK to confirm the creation of the installation disks.

6. Click Cancel to exit the Create Installation Disk(s) dialog box.

STEP BY STEP

6.31 Installing the Terminal Services Client

1. Either insert DISK1 of the Client Installation Disk set or connect to the appropriate network folder for the client type on the terminal server. Run SETUP.

2. At the Welcome to the Terminal Services Client Installation Program dialog box, click Continue.

3. At the Name and Organization Information dialog box, enter your name and organization. Click OK to continue. When asked to confirm the names, click OK.

4. At the License Agreement dialog box, click I Agree to continue.

5. At the Terminal Services Client Setup dialog box, specify the location to install the client in and click the button at the left of the dialog box.

6. At the Terminal Services Client Setup dialog box, click Yes to install the client into the All Users profile or click No to install the client into the profile of the current user (see Figure 6.119). If you choose No, you will be prompted for a location for the program group.

7. At the Terminal Services Client Setup dialog box, click OK.

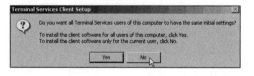

FIGURE 6.119
You can configure each user of the Terminal Services Client on a machine to have the same initial settings or to be unique to the user installing the client.

Connecting Using the Terminal Services Client

After the server has been configured and the client has been installed on a workstation, connecting to a terminal server is quite simple.

Step by Step 6.32 shows how to connect to a terminal server using the Terminal Services client.

STEP BY STEP

6.32 Connecting Using the Terminal Services Client

1. From the Start menu, choose Programs, Terminal Services Client, Terminal Services Client.

2. At the Terminal Services Client dialog box, set the properties of your current connection (see Figure 6.120). Start by choosing the terminal server you want to connect to. You can either type in the computer name or browse for the server.

3. Choose the screen area. It can be set to anything from 640×480 to the resolution your screen is currently set to. Lower resolutions should be used for slow network links.

4. If desired, select the Enable Data Compression check box. This is used to increase performance over a slow network link.

5. If desired, select the Cache Bitmaps to Disk option. This is another network saving feature that reduces the number of times bitmaps are send to the client from the server.

6. Click Connect to connect to the server.

7. Log in and work as usual from a Windows 2000 desktop session.

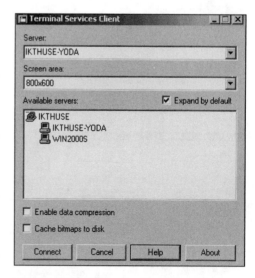

FIGURE 6.120
Set up the properties of the connection, and then attempt a connection to the server of your choice.

Locally Administering a Terminal Services Client

Although connecting to a terminal server is straightforward, a tool exists to make the connection process even simpler: the Client Connection manager. Using this tool, you can preconfigure connection settings and then invoke certain connections simply by choosing a menu option.

Step by Step 6.33 shows how to create a connection using the Client Connection manager.

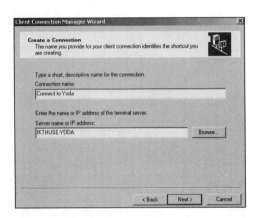

FIGURE 6.121
The connection begins with choosing a server to connect to.

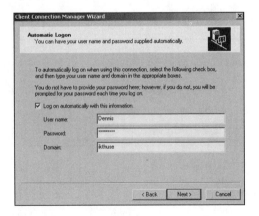

FIGURE 6.122
You can configure the client to automatically log on using a preset account and password.

STEP BY STEP

6.33 Creating Connections Using Client Connection Manager

1. From the Start menu, choose Programs, Terminal Services Client, Client Connection Manager.

2. At the Client Connection Manager dialog box, choose File, New Connection.

3. At the Welcome to the Client Connection Manager Wizard dialog box, click Next to continue.

4. At the Create a Connection screen, type in a meaningful name for the connection, and then type in or browse for a server to connect to (see Figure 6.121). Click Next to continue.

5. At the Automatic Logon screen, you can select Log On Automatically with This Information and then type in the user name and password you want to log in as (see Figure 6.122). If you log on as different users to the same server, you can leave this empty or create a connection for each user. If the server property Always Prompt for Password has been enabled, the automatic logon will not take effect; instead, a logon dialog box will be presented at connection time. Click Next to continue.

6. At the Screen Options screen, choose the screen area and whether you want the Terminal Services window to be initialized at full screen (see Figure 6.123). Click Next to continue.

7. At the Connection Properties screen, choose to Enable Data Compression and Cache Bitmaps if this connection will be used over a slow network link (see Figure 6.124). Click Next to continue.

8. At the Starting a Program screen, you can choose the user shell to start in (see Figure 6.125). This selection is over-ridden by the user account setting and the server setting. Click Next to continue.

9. At the Icon and Program Group screen, select a new icon (if desired) and a program group location for the new connection (see Figure 6.126).

10. At the Completing the Client Connection Manager Wizard screen, click Finish to create the new connection. This connection is now available from the program group you selected in step 9.

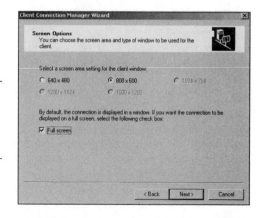

FIGURE 6.123
Configure the properties of the Terminal Services client window.

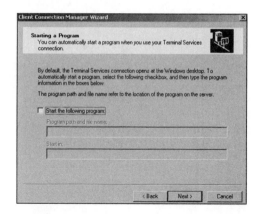

FIGURE 6.125
Configure the shell program to start on successful connection.

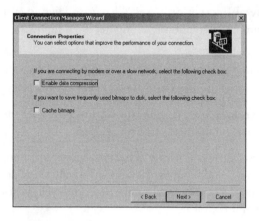

FIGURE 6.124
Configure bandwidth saving options.

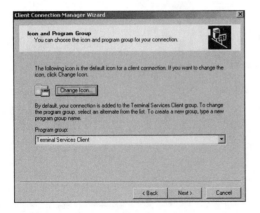

FIGURE 6.126
Configure the access location and icon for the Terminal Services client software on the local machine.

Remotely Administering Servers Using Terminal Services

Connecting to a terminal server allows you to log on to that server as though you were accessing it locally. As a result, if you log in with an administrative account, you will be able to do any administrative tasks you could do if you had logged on locally.

If you install Terminal Services on your servers only to facilitate administration, you should implement certain performance and security optimizations. On the properties of the RDP-Tcp Connection you should change the following settings:

- ◆ **Sessions\End a Disconnected Session:** Change to 1 minute to ensure that memory and resources are freed as soon as possible.

- ◆ **Sessions\Idle Session Limit:** Change to 5 minutes to ensure that sessions are ended promptly and you do not attempt to exceed the maximum number of sessions (2) by leaving a session running accidentally.

- ◆ **Environment\Disable Wallpaper:** Enable this option to ensure that unnecessary network traffic is not produced.

- ◆ **General\Encryption Level:** Change to High to ensure that maximum encryption is configured for administration.

- ◆ **Permissions:** Restrict access to only System and Administrators to reduce the possibility that unauthorized users get administrative access.

- ◆ **Network Adapter\Maximum Connections:** Set this to a low number to minimize security breaches.

- ◆ **Client Settings:** Disable Windows Printer Mapping, LPT Port Mapping, and Clipboard Mapping to reduce the possibility that confidential information is left on the client after the session is complete.

Configuring Terminal Services for Application Sharing

In order for a terminal server to host applications for Terminal Services clients, two things must be done. First, the terminal server must be put into Application Server Mode. Second, the License Manager must be configured in your domain or enterprise within 90 days after installation of the application server.

Step by Step 6.34 shows you how to install the Terminal Services License Manager.

STEP BY STEP

6.34 Installing Terminal Services License Manager

1. From the Control Panel, double-click the Add/Remove Programs icon.

2. At the Add/Remove Programs dialog box, click the Add/Remove Windows Components icon.

3. At the Windows Components screen, scroll down and select Terminal Services Licensing. Click Next to continue.

4. At the Terminal Services Licensing Setup screen, specify whether to install this computer as an enterprise manager or as a domain/workgroup manager (see Figure 6.127). Fill in the path to the license database and click Next to continue.

5. At the Completing the Windows Components Wizard screen, click Finish.

6. When prompted, restart your server.

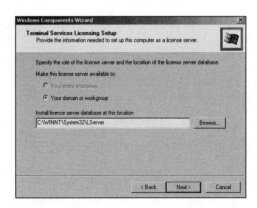

FIGURE 6.127
You can configure the scope of the License Manager and the location of the licenses.

Configuring Applications for Use with Terminal Services

Applications must be configured properly to work for all clients as though they were being executed on their local machines. You first need to ensure that they are installed using the right method. Then you may have to execute a script after installation to ensure that the applications have been tuned for Terminal Services execution.

Installing Applications on a Terminal Server

Any application that is installed on a terminal server could be available to all users on that server. You must ensure that they are available, including shortcuts in the Start menu to invoke them. In addition, you must ensure that when each new user uses the application, he starts with his own settings, which are maintained independent of everyone else's.

The tool for doing this is the `change user` command. When invoked at a command line with the `/install` switch, it puts the system into a "watch" mode that tracks the initial settings for an application and records them. If you install an application in this mode, all pertinent data can be recorded and made available to all users. To complete the process, you then must invoke the `change user/execute` command, which then exits you out of the watching mode.

This may seem like a complex process to go through every time you install an application. In order to make the process easier, it is done automatically for you when you install applications as an administrator through a Client Services session.

Step by Step 6.35 demonstrates how to install an application through a Terminal Services client session.

STEP BY STEP

6.35 Installing Applications Through a Terminal Services Client Session

1. Establish a connection to the terminal server and log on as an Administrator.

---

2. From the Control Panel, double-click the Add/Remove Programs icon.

3. Navigate to the Setup program and install the software.

4. The After Installation screen shown in Figure 6.128 will appear just before the Setup program begins. Leave it in the background until the installation is complete. At that time, click Next.

5. At the Finish Admin Install screen, click Finish to switch back to change user/execute mode.

FIGURE 6.128
Do not click Next until the application is completely installed on the server.

Occasionally, an application cannot be installed through Add/Remove Programs. For example, when you are browsing with Internet Explorer, you are frequently prompted to install plug-in software. To ensure that the settings are recorded properly for Terminal Services clients, before proceeding with the installation, switch to a command prompt and run change user/install. When the installation is complete, run change user/execute.

Using Application Compatibility Scripts to Fine-Tune Application Execution

Microsoft has provided some Application Compatibility Scripts for common applications in order to fine-tune the installations for use with Terminal Services. These scripts will modify settings to ensure that applications are set for optimal execution under Terminal Services.

The Application Compatibility Scripts are available in the path WINNT\Application Compatibility Scripts\Install.

The next Step by Step outlines the process for running Application Compatibility Scripts.

NOTE

Not All Application Scripts Are Provided Although a number of application compatibility scripts are provided by Microsoft, not all applications have scripts. Many popular Microsoft applications and some applications by other vendors are provided. At this point, for example, Office 2000 is notably absent. In fact, it will not install under terminal server at all unless you install the Terminal Services components available in the Office 2000 Resource Kit. For more specific information on Office 2000 in a Terminal Services environment, go to http://www.Microsoft.com/office/ork/2000/two/30t3.htm.

STEP BY STEP

6.36 Running Application Compatibility Scripts

1. Install the application.

2. In the *WINNT\Application Compatibility Scripts\Install* folder, locate the script for the application you are installing (if one is not available, check the Microsoft Web site or the Web site of the application vendor). Edit the script to modify any paths that need to be customized for your environment.

3. Open a command prompt and run the script

4. If there is a logon script for the application in the *WINNT\Application Compatibility Scripts\Install* folder, edit it and modify the paths to suit your environment.

5. Edit the file User.cmd in the *WINNT\Application Compatibility Scripts\Install* folder. Add a call for each logon script that you are using (there is a sample call in the existing User.cmd file).

6. Remove the REM command in front of the lines corresponding to the application you are installing.

7. Copy User.cmd to the *WINNT\System32* folder. (This only has to be done once on your system; subsequent installations should modify this copy of User.cmd rather than the one in the Install folder.)

8. At the command prompt, run User.cmd.

CASE STUDY: IN YOUR TOWN INC.

THE ESSENCE OF THE CASE

This case requires that the following results be satisfied:

- ▶ Allow Isaiah to connect to head office servers to do administration when he is on the road.

- ▶ Secure the communications between his laptop and servers while administration is going on.

SCENARIO

Isaiah is the network administrator for In Your Town Inc. (IYT), a national company with 30 regional offices in the United States and Canada. Although IYT has a number of national locations, it has very few employees and a small IT staff (Isaiah and two technical assistants), who works out of the head office in New Orleans, Louisiana. As a result, Isaiah finds himself traveling a great deal to service servers in different locations (there is at least one Windows 2000 server in each regional office). When he is on the road, Isaiah would like to be able to administer the Windows 2000 servers at the head office from his laptop.

Not only does Isaiah want to be able to do simple administration (like creating new users and checking printer queues), he also wants to be able to start and stop services, start performance monitors, observe running tasks, and restart servers that may have problems.

Because security is an issue with IYT, a firewall is configured to protect the head office servers. In addition, any communication between Isaiah's laptop and the head office servers must be done over some kind of secured connection.

You have been called in to analyze this situation and make recommendations.

continues

CASE STUDY: IN YOUR TOWN INC.

continued

ANALYSIS

Windows 2000 Server has features that will allow Isaiah to satisfy both his accessibility and his security issues. First, he can install the Terminal Services component of Windows 2000 Server and configure it to operate in Administration mode. This, coupled with the installation of the Terminal Services client on his laptop, will enable him to connect remotely to a local session on each server. This feature will work as long as he is inside the firewall. However, on the road, the firewall will prevent direct access to his servers from his laptop. That can be overcome by installing the RRAS services on a server inside the firewall (or by configuring a new server to be an RRAS server). Finally, in order for Isaiah to connect to the RRAS server, he will need to do three things: configure the RRAS server to accept VPN connections (PPTP), configure his laptop to connect to the RRAS server to establish VPN sessions, and open port 1723 in the firewall to allow the VPN traffic to pass through.

Using this configuration, Isaiah will be able to use any Internet connection to establish a VPN connection through his firewall to his RRAS server at his head office. Having established that connection, he can then use the Terminal Services client to establish a session with any of his servers, and he will be able to perform secure administration of his servers.

The following table summarizes the solution.

OVERVIEW OF THE REQUIREMENTS AND SOLUTIONS IN THIS CASE STUDY

Requirement	Solution Provided By
Access to server sessions	Installing Terminal Services on servers in Administration mode; installing Terminal Services client on roaming laptop
Secure connection to his network	Configuring an RRAS server to accept PPTP connections via a VPN connection and placing this server inside the firewall
Allow secure connection through the firewall	Opening port 1723 in the firewall to allow PPTP traffic to pass

CHAPTER SUMMARY

Summarized briefly, this chapter covered the following main points:

◆ *Configuring the infrastructure for network communications on a Windows 2000 server.* This includes network adapters and drivers, network protocols, and network connections.

◆ *Installing and configuring network services.* This includes DHCP (for automatic configuration of TCP/IP on clients) and WINS (for NetBIOS address resolution).

◆ *Installing and configuring the Routing and Remote Access Services.* This includes shared Internet connections, dial-up networking, and virtual private networking.

◆ *Installing and configuring Terminal Services.* This includes installing Terminal Services to provide remote server administration as well as application hosting. It also includes configuring Terminal Services clients.

KEY TERMS
- remote access policy
- remote access profile
- virtual private networking
- PPTP
- L2TP
- IP filter
- Terminal Services
- Remote Administration Mode
- Application Server Mode
- remote control
- terminal services profile
- Terminal Services License Manager
- Application Compatibility Script

KEY TERMS
- connection
- binding
- protocol
- TCP/IP
- NWLink
- NetBEUI
- subnet mask
- DHCP
- DHCP lease
- IPCONFIG
- TRACERT
- PING
- scope
- Dynamic DNS
- WINS
- connection sharing
- NAT
- Demand Dial Interface
- remote access server
- Dial-Up Networking
- RADIUS server
- EAP
- MS-CHAP v2
- multilink
- BAP/BACP

APPLY YOUR KNOWLEDGE

Exercises

6.1 Install, Configure, and Test DHCP Service

In this exercise, you learn how to install and configure the DHCP service on a Windows 2000 server. You will also learn how to configure the TCP/IP properties on a Windows 2000 client and to test DHCP configuration of that client's TCP/IP stack.

In order to do this lab, you need one Windows 2000 server and one Windows 2000 client (Server or Professional).

Before you begin this lab, make sure no other DHCP servers are running on your network. If they are, you should stop them to ensure that the results of this lab are not influenced by outside servers.

Estimated Time: 45 minutes

1. Install the DHCP service on a Windows 2000 server.

   A. From the Start menu, choose Settings, Control Panel.

   B. In the Control Panel, double-click the Add/Remove Programs icon.

   C. In the Add/Remove Programs dialog box, click the Add/Remove Windows Components icon.

   D. In the Windows Components dialog box, scroll down in the Components window until you locate Networking Services. Click on the label (not in the check box) and click the Details button.

   E. In the Networking Services dialog box, select the check box next to Dynamic Host Configuration Protocol (DHCP) and click OK.

   F. In the Windows Components dialog box, click the Next button to continue.

   G. If you are presented with a dialog box indicating that your server is currently using DHCP, follow steps H–K. Otherwise, skip to step 2 now.

   H. In the Optional Networking Components dialog box, click OK to acknowledge that you must change from a dynamic to a static address on your DHCP server.

   I. At the Connection Properties dialog box, select Internet Protocol (TCP/IP) and click the Properties button.

   J. In the Internet Protocol (TCP/IP) Properties dialog box, select Use the Following IP Address. For the IP Address, enter **169.254.0.50**, and for the subnet mask, enter **255.255.0.0**. Click OK to continue.

   K. At the Connection Properties dialog box, click OK.

   L. At the Completing the Windows Components Wizard, click Finish.

   M. At the Add/Remove Components dialog box, click Close.

2. Configure the DHCP service.

   A. From the Start menu, choose Programs, Accessories, Command Prompt.

   B. In the Command Prompt window, type **IPCONFIG** and make a note of your server's IP address and subnet mask. (This is important because when you configure your DHCP server, you want the clients to get addresses that will communicate with the server.) Close the Command Prompt window.

C. From the Start menu, choose Programs, Administrative Tools, DHCP.

D. In the DHCP Management console, choose Action, Add Server.

E. In the Add Server dialog box, type the name of your server into the This Server field and click OK.

F. Right-click the server entry that now appears under the DHCP heading and choose All Tasks, Start from the menu that appears. If the icon next to the server entry does not change, you will have to reboot your server at this point.

G. Right-click the server entry and choose New Scope from the menu that appears.

H. At the Welcome to the New Scope Wizard dialog box, click Next.

I. In the Scope Name dialog box, type `Windows 2000 Scope` in the Name box and type `A Test Scope` in the Description box. Click Next to continue.

J. In the IP Address Range dialog box, enter the following information in the fields (if your server already had a static IP address before step 1J, you will need to add a range of addresses that are compatible with your server's address).

Start IP Address: 169.254.0.200

End IP Address: 169.254.0.210

Length: *leave as is*

Subnet Mask: *leave as is*

Click Next to continue

K. In the Add Exclusions dialog box, click Next to continue.

L. In the Lease Duration dialog box, click Next to continue.

M. In the Configure DHCP Options dialog box, select No, I will configure these options later and click Next.

N. At the Completing the New Scope Wizard screen, click Finish.

3. Check current status and enable the DHCP scope.

A. Expand the newly created scope entry and click on the Address Leases line. Note that, currently, there are no leases.

B. Right-click the scope entry and choose Activate from the menu that appears.

4. Configure your client to configure TCP/IP via DHCP (do this on your Windows 2000 client machine).

A. Right-click the My Network Places icon on the desktop and choose Properties from the menu that appears.

B. In the Network and Dial-Up Connections dialog box, locate the icon for your LAN connection, right-click it, and choose Properties from the menu that appears.

C. In the Connection Properties dialog box, double-click the component that reads Internet Protocol (TCP/IP).

D. In the Internet Protocol (TCP/IP) Properties dialog box, select the radio button labeled Obtain an IP Address Automatically and click OK.

APPLY YOUR KNOWLEDGE

E. In the Connection Properties dialog box, click OK.

F. From the Start menu, choose Programs, Accessories, Command Prompt.

G. In the Command Prompt window, type **IPCONFIG /all.**

H. Verify that for your LAN network connection, the IP address falls within the scope you configured for your DHCP server. Also verify that the DHCP server's address is the address of your DHCP server. (If it is not, you have—or had—another DHCP server running on your network; if all DHCP servers are stopped except yours, type **IPCONFIG /renew** to obtain an address from your server.)

5. Verify that you can see the lease given out to your client machine (do this on your DHCP server).

A. From the Start menu, choose Programs, Administrative Tools, DHCP.

B. Expand the following tree: DHCP, server, Scope.

C. Select the Address Leases line. On the right, note that a lease has been created for the address given to your client machine.

D. Close the DHCP management console.

6.2   Install RRAS and Configure a VPN Connection

This exercise shows you how to install and configure Routing and Remote Access on a Windows 2000 server with the objective of configuring a VPN server. In addition, you will also configure a Windows 2000 client to use a VPN to connect to the server.

In order to do this lab, you need one Windows 2000 server and one Windows 2000 client (Server or Professional). You also need one null modem cable connecting the COM ports of the two computers.

Note: Due to limitations of the technology being used, it will not be possible to test the security of the VPN that is established.

Estimated Time: 45 minutes

1. Enable and configure remote access (do this on the RRAS server).

A. From the Start menu, choose Programs, Administrative Tools, Routing and Remote Access.

B. Right-click the computer name and choose Configure and Enable Routing and Remote Access from the menu that appears.

C. At the Welcome to the Routing and Remote Access Server Setup Wizard, choose Next.

D. At the Common Configurations menu, choose Manually Configured Server and click Next.

E. At the Completing the Routing and Remote Access Server Setup Wizard, click Finish.

F. If you're presented with a dialog box warning that this server cannot be added as an RRAS server to the directory, click OK. This is beyond the scope of this exam to configure.

G. When you're presented with a dialog box asking if you want to start RRAS, click Yes.

H. When the Routing and Remote Access console returns, do not close it.

APPLY YOUR KNOWLEDGE

2. Create a direct-connection interface to allow a simulated Internet client to connect (do this at the RRAS server).

   A. From the Start menu, choose Settings, Control Panel.

   B. At the Control Panel, double-click Phone and Modem Options.

   C. If you're prompted with the Location Information dialog box, fill in the fields and click OK to continue.

   D. In the Phone and Modem Options dialog box, click the Modems tab, and then click the Add button.

   E. In the Install New Modem dialog box, select the check box labeled Don't Detect My Modem; I Will Select It from a List. Then click Next.

   F. At the second Install New Modem dialog box, select (Standard Modem Types) as the Manufacturer and Communications Cable Between Two Computers as the Model. Click Next to continue.

   G. At the third Install New Modem dialog box, choose a free COM port to install to (if you are in doubt, choose COM1 and, if that fails, return and change to COM2). Click Next to continue.

   H. At the final Install New Modem dialog box, click Finish to exit.

   I. At the Phone and Modem Options dialog box, click OK to exit.

3. Verify the inbound connection configured for the new modem you installed.

   A. At the Routing and Remote Access console, right-click the Ports entry (on the left side) and choose Properties from the menu that appears.

   B. In the Ports Properties dialog box, double-click the device that begins "Communications cable."

   C. In the Configure Device dialog box, verify that Remote Access Connections (Inbound Only) is selected and that Demand-Dial Routing is deselected. Click OK to exit.

   D. At the Ports Properties dialog box, click OK to exit.

4. Configure the RRAS server to only allow access to the local machine (not to the LAN) and to give out a specific range of TCP/IP addresses to RRAS clients.

   A. On the Routing and Remote Access console, right-click the RRAS server name and choose Properties from the menu that appears.

   B. In the Server Properties dialog box, on the General tab, deselect the check box labeled Router and make sure the check box labeled Remote Access Server is enabled.

   C. In the Server Properties dialog box, on the IP tab, select Static Address Pool (in the IP Address Assignment section). Click the Add button. In the New Address Range dialog box, type **169.254.0.240** in the Start IP Address field and enter **5** in the Number of Addresses field (the End IP Address will be filled in for you). Click OK to continue.

   D. In the Server Properties dialog box, click OK to continue.

APPLY YOUR KNOWLEDGE

E. If you're prompted to restart the router, click Yes.

5. Create a local VPN user on the RRAS server and enable it for dial-in.

A. From the Start menu, choose Programs, Administrative Tools, Computer Management.

B. In the Computer Management dialog box, expand the section labeled Local Users and Groups, right click on Users, and choose New User from the menu that appears.

C. In the New User dialog box, type `VPNUser` in the User Name field, type `password` in both the password fields, clear the check box labeled User Must Change Password at Next Logon, and select the check box labeled Password Never Expires. Click Create to continue.

D. Click Close to exit the New User dialog box.

E. Click the Users entry on the left side of the Computer Management console (under Local Users and Groups).

F. On the right side of the console, double-click the entry for the user VPNUser.

G. In the VPNUser Properties dialog box, click the Dial-In tab.

H. On the Dial-In tab, under Remote Access Permissions (Dial-In or VPN), select Allow Access. Click OK to exit.

I. Close the Computer Management console.

6. Repeat step 2 on the RRAS client.

7. Create a dial-in connection on the RRAS client.

A. From the desktop, right-click the My Network Places icon and choose Properties from the menu that appears.

B. In the Network and Dial-Up Connections window, double-click the Make New Connection icon.

C. At the Welcome to the Network Connection Wizard dialog box, click Next.

D. At the Network Connection Type dialog box, choose Connect Directly to Another Computer, and then click Next.

E. At the Host or Guest dialog box, choose Guest and click Next.

F. At the Select a Device dialog box, choose the device labeled Communications Cable Between Two Computers and click Next.

G. At the Connection Availability dialog box, click Next.

H. At the Completing the Network Connection Wizard dialog box, click Finish.

I. If the Connect Direct Connection dialog box appears, click Cancel to cancel the connection at this time.

8. Create a VPN connection on the RRAS client.

A. In the Network and Dial-Up Connections window, double-click the Make New Connection icon.

B. At the Welcome to the Network Connection Wizard dialog box, click Next.

C. At the Network Connection Type dialog box, choose Connect to a Private Network Through the Internet and click Next.

D. At the Public Network dialog box, ensure that Automatically Dial This Initial Connection is selected and that your Direct Connection connection (created in step 7) is selected as the connection to dial before the VPN connection is established. Click Next to continue.

E. At the Destination Address dialog box, type the name of your RRAS server and click Next.

F. At the Connection Availability dialog box, click Next.

G. At the Internet Connection Sharing dialog box, be sure that Connection Sharing is not enabled and click Next.

H. At the Completing the Network Connection Wizard dialog box, click Finish.

I. If the Initial Connection dialog box appears, click No to prevent connection at this time.

9. Test the VPN dial-in.

A. Connect the COM ports of the client and the server with a null-modem cable.

B. Disconnect the LAN cable from the network card on the client only (this allows you to determine if communication is really happening over the dial-up connection).

C. On the client, double-click the Virtual Private Connection icon in the Network and Dial-Up Connections window.

D. In the Initial Connection dialog box, click Yes to establish the dial-up connection.

E. At the Connect Direct Connection dialog box, enter the user name **VPNUser** and the password **password** and click Connect.

F. If you're presented with a second login dialog box, type the name of the RRAS server in the Logon Domain field and click OK.

G. Repeat steps E and F for the VPN connection.

H. At the Connection Complete dialog box, click OK.

I. From the Start menu, choose Run, type **servername** (where *servername* is the name of your RRAS server), and click OK. After a short pause, a window appears, showing the network shares enabled on your RRAS server.

10. Verify that both the dial-in and VPN connections are active on the RRAS server (do this on the RRAS server).

A. Open the Routing and Remote Access console.

B. Select the Ports entry.

C. Verify that the status of your Communications cable and one VPN (PPTP) connection are Active.

11. Disconnect the connections on the client.

A. From the Network and Dial-Up Connections window, right-click the VPN Connection icon and choose Disconnect from the menu that appears.

B. From the Network and Dial-Up Connections window, right-click the Direct Connection icon and choose Disconnect from the menu that appears.

APPLY YOUR KNOWLEDGE

6.3   Install, Configure, and Test Terminal Services in Administration Mode

This exercise shows how to install Terminal Services on a Windows 2000 server and to configure it for Administration mode. In addition, you will also configure a Windows 2000 machine with a Terminal Services client, and you will demonstrate administration via that connection.

In order to do this lab, you need one Windows 2000 server and one Windows 2000 client (Server or Professional).

Estimated Time: 45 minutes

1. Install Terminal Services on your Windows 2000 server.

    A. From the Start menu, choose Settings, Control Panel.

    B. From the Control Panel, double-click the Add/Remove Programs icon.

    C. From the Add/Remove Programs window, click the Add/Remove Windows Components button.

    D. In the Windows Components dialog box, scroll through the Components list and select the check box labeled Terminal Services. Click Next to continue.

    E. At the Terminal Services Setup dialog box, make sure that Remote Administration Mode is selected, and then click Next. If, during installation, you are asked to insert the Windows 2000 CD-ROM, please do so.

    F. At the Completing the Windows Components Wizard dialog box, click Finish to exit.

    G. When prompted, click Yes to restart your computer.

2. Add a new user and make that user part of the local Administrators group to test Terminal Services.

    A. From the Start menu, choose Programs, Administrative Tools, Computer Management.

    B. In the Computer Management dialog box, expand the section labeled Local Users and Groups, right-click on Users, and choose New User from the menu that appears.

    C. In the New User dialog box, type `TerminalU` in the User Name field, type `password` in both password fields, clear the check box labeled User Must Change Password at Next Logon, and select the check box labeled Password Never Expires. Click Create to continue.

    D. Click Close to exit the New User dialog box.

    E. Click the Users entry on the left side of the Computer Management console (under Local Users and Groups).

    F. On the right side of the console, double-click the entry for the user TerminalU.

    G. In the TerminalU Properties dialog box, click the Member Of tab.

    H. On the Member Of tab, click the Add button, double-click the Administrators group, and click the OK button.

    I. At the TerminalU Properties dialog box, click OK.

    J. Close the Computer Management console.

3. Share the Terminal Server client files on the terminal server machine.

    A. Navigate to the WINNT\System32\Clients\ tsclient folder on your server.

    B. Right-click the win32 folder and share it with default settings. Click OK to continue.

4. Configure the terminal server client (on the Windows 2000 client machine).

    A. From the Start menu, choose Run.

    B. In the Run dialog box, type **servername**\ **win32\disks\disk1\setup** (where *servername* is the name of your terminal server) and press Enter.

    C. In the Terminal Services Client Setup dialog box, click Continue.

    D. In the Name and Organization Information dialog box, type your name and organization (make one up if you have to) and click OK.

    E. In the Confirm Name and Organization Information dialog box, click OK.

    F. In the License Agreement dialog box, click I Agree.

    G. At the second Terminal Services Client Setup dialog box, click the button on the left side to begin installation (if you want, you can choose an alternate installation location).

    H. At the third Terminal Services Client Setup dialog box, click Yes.

    I. At the final Terminal Services Client Setup dialog box, click OK to complete the setup.

5. Use the Client Connection Manager to create a connection configuration (do this on the Terminal Services client machine).

    A. From the Start menu, choose Programs, Terminal Services Client, Client Connection Manager.

    B. At the Client Connection Manager console, select File, New Connection.

    C. At the Welcome to the Client Connection Manager Wizard, click Next.

    D. At the Create a Connection dialog box, type **Administrative Connection** in the Connection name field and type the name of your server in the Server Name or IP Address field. Click Next to continue.

    E. At the Automatic Logon dialog box, select the check box labeled Log On Automatically with This Information. In the User Name field, type **TerminalU**; in the Password field, type **password**; in the Domain field, type the name of the Terminal Services server (because you created the TerminalU user local to that machine). Click Next to continue.

    F. At the Screen Options dialog box, choose a screen area setting and click Next.

    G. At the Connection Properties dialog box, click Next.

    H. At the Starting a Program dialog box, click Next.

    I. At the Icon and Program Group dialog box, click Next.

    J. At the Completing the Client Connection Manager Wizard, click Finish.

    K. Close the Client Connection Manager console.

APPLY YOUR KNOWLEDGE

6. Test the Terminal Services client.

   A. From the Start menu, choose Programs, Terminal Services client, Administrative Connection.

   B. When asked to log in as TerminalU, type **password** into the Password field and click OK.

   C. Scroll through the client window so you can see the taskbar of the Terminal Services window. Right-click that taskbar and choose Task Manager from the menu that appears (be sure that you are right-clicking the Terminal Services taskbar and not the one for your client machine).

   D. In the Windows Task Manager dialog box, click the Processes tab and, at the bottom of that page, select the check box labeled Show Processes from All Users.

   E. On the Terminal Services server machine, start the Paint program from the Start menu.

   F. On the Terminal Services client machine, scroll the Task Manager window until you see an entry for the process named MSPAINT.EXE. Select that process and click the End Process button.

   G. In the Task Manager Warning dialog box, click Yes to end the process. Note that the Paint window disappears from the Terminal Services server machine.

   H. Enable a second concurrent session to the server from this client by following steps A and B again. You can now switch back and forth between the two sessions (this would be possible to do between administrative sessions for two different machines).

   I. Disconnect each session by choosing Start, Shut Down and choosing Log Off TerminalU. This must be done from within each session that you have open with the terminal server.

Review Questions

1. What service is available to automatically configure TCP/IP addresses on client machines? What are some advantages to using this kind of configuration over manual configuration?

2. What are the two main reasons for using the NWLink protocol?

3. What two mechanisms are available for sharing a single connection to the Internet among a number of client machines on a LAN? What are the main differences between the two?

4. Before connecting to an RRAS server over a VPN, what must already be established from the client to that server?

5. What two protocols are available under Windows 2000 for use with VPNs? How do their security mechanisms differ?

6. What are the two modes in which Terminal Services can run on a Windows 2000 server? What are the licensing requirements of each?

7. What Windows operating systems can support the Terminal Services client, and what is the minimum hardware required?

Exam Questions

1. Ehud is the network administrator for a snake-breeding farm in Michigan that employs 200 people. He is responsible for installing a Windows 2000 network consisting of three servers and 100 Windows 2000 Professional clients. Each user requires Internet access. At this point, security is not an issue. He also wants the cheapest and most efficient way of configuring this.

   Required Result:

   Enable Internet access on all clients and servers.

   Optional Desired Results:

   Find an inexpensive way of enabling Internet access.

   Find an efficient way of configuring the clients.

   Proposed Solution:

   Lease a class-C TCP/IP license and purchase router.

   Configure one of the servers as a DHCP server to automatically configure the client's TCP/IP protocol suite.

   Analysis:

   Which of the following statements best describes the proposed solution?

   A. This solution fulfills the required result, as well as both optional results.

   B. This solution fulfills the required result and one of the optional results.

   C. This solution fulfills the required result, but does not fulfill either of the optional results.

   D. This solution does not meet the required result.

2. Ehud is the network administrator for a snake-breeding farm in Michigan that employs 200 people. He is responsible for installing a Windows 2000 network consisting of three servers and 100 Windows 2000 Professional clients. Each user requires Internet access. At this point, security is not an issue. He also wants the cheapest and most efficient way of configuring this.

   Required Result:

   Enable Internet access on all clients and servers.

   Optional Desired Results:

   Find an inexpensive way of enabling Internet access.

   Find an efficient way of configuring the clients.

   Proposed Solution:

   Lease a single cable-modem connection.

   Configure one of the servers as a DHCP server to automatically configure the client's TCP/IP protocol suite.

   Configure the same server with two network cards, connect the cable-modem connection to the second card, and enable connection sharing.

   Analysis:

   Which result(s) will the proposed solution produce?

   A. The proposed solution produces the required result, as well as both optional desired results.

   B. The proposed solution produces the required result and one of the optional results.

APPLY YOUR KNOWLEDGE

C. The proposed solution produces the required result, but does not fulfill either of the optional desired results.

D. The proposed solution does not produce the required result.

3. Eve is the network administrator in a small bank. She currently supports a NetBEUI workgroup of 15 computers (five Windows 3.11; seven Windows 95; and three Windows 98). She is contemplating installing a Windows 2000 domain controller to make the move to domain-based security and administration. She wants to remove NetBEUI from all the machines and use strictly TCP/IP; however, she is concerned about the amount of broadcast traffic that will result from name resolution attempts. She wants TCP/IP configuration to be efficient, but reducing broadcast traffic is more important at this time. In addition, she would like to be able to ensure that TCP/IP addresses are automatically configured and that the addresses of any name resolution servers are automatically configured in the client.

Required Results:

Allow all clients to resolve names to IP addresses with minimal broadcast required.

Optional Desired Results:

Configuration of TCP/IP addresses on the client machines is done automatically.

Configuration of name resolution server addresses on the client is done automatically.

Proposed Solution:

Install both DNS and WINS on her server.

Analysis:

Which result(s) will the proposed solution produce?

A. The proposed solution produces the required result, as well as both optional desired results.

B. The proposed solution produces the required result and one of the optional results.

C. The proposed solution produces the required result, but does not fulfill either of the optional desired results.

D. The proposed solution does not produce the required result.

4. Eve is the network administrator in a small bank. She currently supports a NetBEUI workgroup of 15 computers (five Windows 3.11; seven Windows 95; and three Windows 98). She is contemplating installing a Windows 2000 domain controller to make the move to domain-based security and administration. She wants to remove NetBEUI from all the machines and use strictly TCP/IP; however, she is concerned about the amount of broadcast traffic that will result from name resolution attempts. She wants TCP/IP configuration to be efficient, but reducing broadcast traffic is more important at this time. In addition, she would like to be able to ensure that TCP/IP addresses are automatically configured and that the addresses of any name resolution servers are automatically configured in the client.

Required Results:

Allow all clients to resolve names to IP addresses with minimal broadcast required.

APPLY YOUR KNOWLEDGE

Optional Desired Results:

Configuration of TCP/IP addresses on the client machines is done automatically.

Configuration of name resolution server addresses on the client is done automatically.

Proposed Solution:

Install DNS on her server for address resolution.

Install DHCP and configure to allocate TCP/IP addresses to clients as well as the DNS server address.

Analysis:

Which result(s) will the proposed solution produce?

A. The proposed solution produces the required result, as well as both optional desired results.

B. The proposed solution produces the required result and one of the optional results.

C. The proposed solution produces the required result, but does not fulfill either of the optional desired results.

D. The proposed solution does not produce the required result.

5. Adam is the network administrator in a small synagogue. He supports one Windows 2000 server and three Windows 2000 Professional clients configured as a workgroup. The server has a modem, and they have a dial-up connection to the Internet through a local Internet service provider. He wants to be able to configure connection sharing on this server but does not want to leave the Internet connection open all the time. How can Adam accomplish this task?

A. Configure connection sharing on the dial-up connection.

B. Configure connection sharing on the dial-up connection and enable on-demand dialing.

C. Configure Connection sharing on the dial-up connection, enable on-demand dialing, and enable on-demand routing.

D. It is not possible to implement connection sharing without a constant connection to the Internet

6. Cain is the network administrator for a vegetable farm in Illinois. He supports three Windows 2000 servers and 25 Windows 98 clients. He has three dedicated TCP/IP addresses available and needs to be able to share them all with all the machines on his network. Currently, one of the servers has two network cards and is connected to the Internet through one and to the internal network through the other; however, none of the client machines is able to access the Internet through this setup. He would like to be able to create a solution that provides maximum flexibility in the use of the addresses (perhaps he does not want to use them all for client Internet access in the future). He also wants to be able to implement a solution that will require him to purchase as little new hardware as possible.

Required Result:

Allow all clients to access the Internet.

Optional Desired Results:

Avoid hardware purchases.

Provide for maximum address usage flexibility.

APPLY YOUR KNOWLEDGE

Proposed Solution:

Add a second network card to each of the two servers that have only one.

Configure the second card on each server with a dedicated TCP/IP address.

Analysis:

Which result(s) will the proposed solution produce?

A. The proposed solution produces the required result as well as both optional desired results.

B. The proposed solution produces the required result and one of the optional results.

C. The proposed solution produces the required result but does not fulfill either of the optional desired results.

D. The proposed solution does not produce the required result.

7. Cain is the network administrator for a vegetable farm in Illinois. He supports three Windows 2000 servers and 25 Windows 98 clients. He has three dedicated TCP/IP addresses available and needs to be able to share them all with all the machines on his network. Currently, one of the servers has two network cards and is connected to the Internet through one and to the internal network through the other; however, none of the client machines is able to access the Internet through this setup. He would like to be able to create a solution that provides maximum flexibility in the use of the addresses (perhaps he does not want to use them all for client Internet access in the future). He also wants to be able to implement a solution that requires him to purchase as little new hardware as possible.

Required Result:

Allow all clients to access the Internet.

Optional Desired Results:

Avoid hardware purchases.

Provide for maximum address usage flexibility.

Proposed Solution:

Configure the server that has two network cards with NAT, which will enable all three addresses for translation.

Analysis:

Which result(s) will the proposed solution produce?

A. The proposed solution produces the required result, as well as both optional desired results.

B. The proposed solution produces the required result and one of the optional results.

C. The proposed solution produces the required result, but does not fulfill either of the optional desired results.

D. The proposed solution does not produce the required result.

8. Abel is the network administrator for a sheep ranch in Wyoming. He has configured RRAS to allow shepherds with laptops and cellular phones to dial into the network while watching their flocks at night. Abel wants to ensure that the shepherds can access both the RRAS server and the network on which the RRAS service is connected. Which of the following RRAS server configurations will allow Abel to accomplish his goal?

A. Enable the RRAS server as a router for LAN routing.

APPLY YOUR KNOWLEDGE

B. Enable the RRAS server as a router for LAN routing and enable IP Routing.

C. Enable the RRAS server as a router for LAN and demand-dial routing.

D. Enable the RRAS server as a router for LAN and demand-dial routing and enable IP Routing.

9. Zillah is the network administrator of a widget manufacturer in Sweden. This company has a number of employees that dial into the RRAS server from home or from off-site locations. The users can be grouped together, and each group has different requirements and restrictions on their remote access sessions. What is the most efficient way for Zillah to configure her RRAS server to account for the differences?

A. Configure RRAS policies and apply them to the appropriate user groups.

B. Configure each user independently because RRAS policies will not work in this situation.

C. Create policy memos for each group and instruct them to follow the policy guidelines sent out regarding RRAS connections.

D. Configure System Policies and restrict access to RRAS connections by way of groups.

10. Jubal is the network administrator for a contractor working for the Canadian Department of National Defense. He has a number of employees that use the Internet to connect to his servers and some that connect on X.25 networks. Due to a recent barrage of hacking attempts, he has been directed to tighten security; either he secures

server access, or all outside lines will be removed. Which of the following provides a solution that will both ensure that all his users can still connect and ensure that RRAS traffic is secure?

A. Enable a VPN using PPTP.

B. Enable a VPN using L2TP.

C. Enable a VPN using L2TP with IPSec.

D. Leave the system like it is because the current traffic is encrypted automatically by Windows 2000.

11. Abraham is the Terminal Services administrator for a small manufacturing company. He has a number of thin network clients, and on March 23, 2000, he configured a terminal server in Application Mode to host their applications. Initially, everything ran very smoothly. However, on June 21, 2000, all the clients received messages that there were not enough client licenses, and their applications failed to run. What should Abraham have done to prevent this problem?

A. He should have configured his terminal server in Administration mode because there are no licensing requirements.

B. He should have purchased more Windows 2000 client licenses for his server running Terminal Services.

C. He should have installed Terminal Services License Manager.

D. He should have installed Terminal Services License Manager and purchased licenses for his Terminal Services clients.

APPLY YOUR KNOWLEDGE

12. Sarah is using Windows 2000 Professional to run a Terminal Services client session. She wants to shut down her computer for lunch (as is the company policy) but does not want to end her Terminal Services session. With reference to Figure 6.129, which Shut Down option can she choose to accomplish her goal?

    A. Log off

    B. Shut Down

    C. Restart

    D. Disconnect

13. Isaac has just installed a new network adapter in his Windows 2000 server. He now wants to create a network connection for it. Which of the following best describes the process he needs to follow?

    A. Open Network and Dial-Up Connections and create a new LAN connection using the wizard.

    B. Open Network and Dial-Up Connections and create a new LAN connection using the Advanced, Create LAN Connection menu command.

    C. Open the Device manager, right-click the network card, and choose Create Connection from the menu that appears.

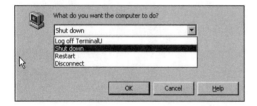

FIGURE 6.129
One of these options leaves the session running.

    D. He does not have to create a connection; one is created automatically.

14. Jacob is one of three network administrators of a Windows 2000 domain. He configured three Windows 2000 Professional workstations with TCP/IP as the only protocol and chose to have TCP/IP configured using DHCP. The address range that is used in Jacob's company is 10.10.10.0 to 10.10.10.100. Unbeknownst to Jacob, just before he began to configure the workstations, one of the other network administrators brought the DHCP server offline for the day. When the Windows 2000 Professional workstations are brought online, what will their TCP/IP status be, and who will they be able to communicate with?

    A. They will be unable to get TCP/IP addresses from the DHCP server, so they will be unable to communicate on the network.

    B. They will be unable to get TCP/IP addresses from the DHCP server, so they will revert to NetBEUI, which is a hidden protocol. The three workstations will be able to communicate only amongst themselves.

    C. They will be unable to get TCP/IP addresses from the DHCP server, so they will poll the network, detect the current address range in use, and self-configure. They will be able to communicate with all other computers on the network.

    D. They will be unable to get TCP/IP addresses from the DHCP server, so they will self-configure using addresses in the range 169.254.x.x. They will be able to communicate only amongst themselves.

15. Several salespeople dial in to your network via RRAS. How can you configure the security options in RRAS to minimize the users' long distance phone charges?

   A. Configure the user's Dial-Up Networking software to use PPTP, which bypasses the PSTN billing computers and gives the users free long distance service.

   B. Configure the RRAS service to perform a call-back based on the number specified by the user dialing in to the RRAS server. The server authenticates the logon and then disconnects and calls the user back at the specified number.

   C. Issue the users long distance calling cards and have their RRAS calls billed directly to the company.

   D. Make sure the users are calling only from public telephones and are making collect calls to the RRAS server. Then configure the RRAS server to accept collect calls.

Answers to Review Questions

1. The service available to automatically configure TCP/IP addresses on client machines is DHCP. DHCP has many advantages over manual configuration. Some of them include removal of the tedium of manually configuring clients with TCP/IP addresses; ability to automatically configure a wide variety of TCP/IP-based properties (including name resolution servers); and the ability to reduce TCP/IP conflicts on your network by keeping track of addresses allocated and by doing PING tests prior to allocating addresses.

For more information, see the sections "Installing, Configuring, and Maintaining the TCP/IP Protocol Suite" and "Installing and Configuring DHCP."

2. The two main reasons for using NWLink are to allow for communication with NetWare servers using only IPX/SPX and to increase security on Windows 2000 networks. Many NetWare servers still are configured to use only IPX/SPX and, therefore, interoperability with them requires a common protocol; NWLink is Microsoft's implementation of the IPX/SPX protocol. Security on Windows 2000 networks can be enhanced by replacing TCP/IP with NWLink. Because NWLink is routable, it can be used in WAN implementations. As long as there is no need for access to the Internet, NWLink can safely be used and will eliminate TCP/IP-based attacks on your network. For more information, see the section "Installing and Maintaining the NWLink Protocol."

3. The two mechanisms available for sharing a single connection to the Internet among a number of client machines are connection sharing and NAT. The main differences are ease of configuration and flexibility. Connection sharing can be configured simply by selecting a check box, whereas NAT requires that you configure RRAS. On the other hand, NAT is much more flexible, allowing a greater array of control mechanisms for incoming and outgoing information, as well as the ability to provide more than one address in a pool to share amongst internal clients. For more information, see the section "Installing, Configuring, and Troubleshooting Shared Access."

APPLY YOUR KNOWLEDGE

4. To establish a VPN connection, you must already have a connection the RRAS server established. This could be in the form of a direct connection via the Internet or via a dial-up connection. Because a VPN uses a tunneling protocol, the tunnel must have been established first. For more information, see the section "Installing, Configuring, and Troubleshooting Remote Access."

5. Two tunneling protocols are available for use with VPNs: PPTP and L2TP. These protocols differ in their security mechanisms. PPTP has built-in encryption, whereas L2TP requires a secondary encryption mechanism (like IPSec). For more information, see the section "Installing, Configuring, and Troubleshooting VPNs."

6. Terminal Services run in two server modes: Administration and Application. In Administration mode, a maximum of two connections can be established for the purposes of administering a server. These connections do not require client licenses. In Application mode, 90 days grace is given from the point when Terminal Services is placed into that mode. After that, licenses must be purchased from Microsoft and managed by the Terminal Services License Manager. These licenses are separate from client access licenses for regular connections to a server. For more information, see the section "Configuring Terminal Services for Application Sharing."

7. The following Windows operating systems can support Terminal Services clients: Windows 3.11, Windows 95, Windows 98, Windows NT 4.0, and Windows 2000. The minimum hardware is

supported under Windows 3.11. It consists of a 386 processor, 16MB of RAM, and a VGA video card. For more information, see the section "Terminal Services Hardware and Software."

Answers to Exam Questions

1. **B.** A class C license will allow enough addresses to provide each user with direct access to the Internet. In addition, the router will give all users a route to the Internet. This means that the required result has been fulfilled. In addition, the use of DHCP ensures that the clients are configured efficiently. However, a class C license and a router are not cheap; therefore, the first option result is not satisfied by this solution. For more information, see the sections "Installing, Configuring, and Maintaining the TCP/IP Protocol Suite" and "Installing and Configuring DHCP."

2. **A.** A single cable-modem connection to the Internet, coupled with the enabling of connection sharing, is sufficient for providing all users with access to the Internet. In addition, the use of DHCP ensures that clients are configured efficiently. Finally, because only one address is required and the only hardware needed was an extra network card, the solution is also cost efficient. For more information, see the sections "Installing, Configuring, and Maintaining the TCP/IP Protocol Suite," "Installing and Configuring DHCP," and "Shared Access Using Connection Sharing."

APPLY YOUR KNOWLEDGE

3. **C.** In the chapter, two name resolution methods were discussed: DNS and WINS. Although DNS is the primary name resolution method in a pure Windows 2000 network, any other Windows clients require NetBIOS name resolution, which is best provided via a WINS server. Because both DNS and WINS are installed in this solution, it fulfills the required result. However, TCP/IP must be manually configured on each machine, therefore neither of the optional results is satisfied. For more information, see the section "Installing and Configuring Network Services."

4. **D.** As was mentioned above, WINS is required to provide NetBIOS name resolution, something that all pre-Windows 2000 computers require. Because of not installing WINS, broadcasts will still be required to resolve NetBIOS names; therefore the required result has not been fulfilled. For more information, see the section "Installing and Configuring Network Services."

5. **B.** In order to share a single connection, either connection sharing or NAT is required. In this case, connection sharing is the mechanism used. However, in the case where a connection to the Internet is done via dial-up, on-demand dialing must be enabled. For more information, see the section "Shared Access Using Connection Sharing."

6. **C.** Although this solution provides access to the Internet for all users, it does not provide flexibility, nor does it eliminate the need to purchase new hardware. All three servers require a second network card. In addition, connection sharing is more inferior to NAT in its flexibility. For more information, see the section "Installing, Configuring, and Troubleshooting Shared Access."

7. **A.** By using NAT, Cain provides the mandatory access to the Internet for all users. In addition, because NAT performs the task using only one server, the need to purchase and install new hardware has also been eliminated. Finally, because NAT can be given a pool of Internet addresses to translate to and from, it proves the most flexible solution. All three addresses could be configured now, and one could easily be removed from the pool in the future with little loss of functionality from the users' perspective. For more information, see the section "Installing, Configuring, and Troubleshooting Shared Access."

8. **D.** In order for RRAS clients to get access to a TCP/IP network through a RRAS server, that server must be configured to be able to route for LAN users and dial-up users. In addition, the TCP/IP protocol must also be enabled for routing. For more information, see the section "Installing, Configuring, and Troubleshooting Remote Access."

9. **A.** The idea of RRAS policies is to provide for exactly the situation that Zillah is in. They allow rules to be created governing the RRAS abilities of specific users and groups of users. To configure each user separately is a waste of effort. To create paper memos to tell people how they should act is not a workable solution except in the most utopian environment. Finally, system policies do not apply here. For more information, see the section "Creating a Remote Access Policy."

10. **C.** In order to provide tunneling to both Internet and X.25 clients, L2TP must be used. However, L2TP does not encrypt network traffic on its own, so IPSec must be used in conjunction with it. For more information, see the section "Installing, Configuring, and Troubleshooting VPNs."

11. **D.** Terminal Services clients require separate licenses from regular network clients to a Windows 2000 server. There is a grace period of 90 days provided for the use of applications hosted on a Terminal Services server. If licenses have not been purchased by the end of 90 days, the clients will no longer be able to connect. For more information, see the section "Configuring Terminal Services for Application Sharing."

12. **D.** A Terminal Services client session will continue to be active even if the user shuts down her machine if the Disconnect option is used. If this option is used then the session is suspended, and the session can be resumed upon reconnection. Of course, this puts extra load on the Terminal Services server, so this feature should be used with caution. For more information, see the section "Installing, Configuring, and Troubleshooting Terminal Services."

13. **D.** Connections are created automatically for each network adapter added to the Windows 2000 computer. Other connections, such as dial-up, need to be configured manually. For more information, see the section "Configuring Connections."

14. **D.** DHCP clients that cannot obtain a TCP/IP address from a DHCP server will auto-configure themselves with an address in the 169.254.x.x range. As a result, they will only be able to communicate with other computers that have addresses in the same range (in this case, the other two Windows 2000 Professional computers). For more information, see the section "Installing, Configuring, and Maintaining the TCP/IP Protocol Suite."

15. **B.** By enabling callback from the server, the users will only incur a small initial connection charge. After a user's identity has been established, the server will disconnect and call the user back (hence the name, "callback"). For more information, see the section "Configuring User Accounts for Remote Access."

APPLY YOUR KNOWLEDGE

Suggested Readings and Resources

1. Microsoft Windows 2000 Server Resource Kit: *Microsoft Windows 2000 Server Internetworking Guide* (Microsoft Press)

   - Chapter 2: Routing and Remote Access Service

   - Chapter 3: Unicast IP Routing

   - Chapter 7: Remote Access Server

   - Chapter 8: Internet Authentication Service

   - Chapter 9: Virtual Private Networking

   - Chapter 16: NetBEUI

2. Microsoft Windows 2000 Server Resource Kit: *Microsoft Windows 2000 Server Deployment Planning Guide* (Microsoft Press)

   - Chapter 7: Determining Network Connectivity Strategies

   - Chapter 11: Planning Distributed Security

   - Chapter 16: Deploying Terminal Services

   - Chapter 17: Determining Windows 2000 Network Security Strategies

3. Microsoft Windows 2000 Server Resource Kit: *TCP/IP Core Networking Guide* (Microsoft Press)

   - Part 1 (Chapters 1–3): Windows 2000 TCP/IP

   - Chapter 4: Dynamic Host Configuration Protocol

   - Chapter 7: Windows Internet Name Service

   - Chapter 8: Internet Protocol Security

4. *Microsoft Windows 2000 Professional Resource Kit* (Microsoft Press)

   - Chapter 13: Security

   - Chapter 21: Local and Remote Network Connections

   - Chapter 22: TCP/IP in Windows 2000 Professional

   - Chapter 23: Windows 2000 Professional on Microsoft Networks

   - Chapter 24: Interoperability with NetWare

5. Microsoft Official Curriculum course 1557: *Installing and Configuring Microsoft Windows 2000*

   - Module 5: Configuring Network Protocols

   - Module 6: Enabling Dynamic IP Addressing by Using DHCP

   - Module 12: Configuring Remote Access to Windows 2000 Networks

   - Module 14: Installing and Configuring Terminal Services

   - Module 15: Enabling NetBIOS Name Resolution by Using WINS

APPLY YOUR KNOWLEDGE

Suggested Readings and Resources

6. Microsoft Official Curriculum course 1558:
   Advanced Administration for Microsoft Windows 2000

   - Module 2: Strategies for Administering a Windows 2000 Network

7. Microsoft Official Curriculum course 1560:
   Updating Support Skills from Microsoft Windows NT 4.0 to Microsoft Window 2000

   - Module 10: Installing and Configuring Terminal Services

   - Module 11: Configuring Remote Access

   - Module 12: Securing Windows 2000

   - Module 13: Supporting DHCP and WINS

8. Microsoft Official Curriculum course 1562:
   Designing a Microsoft Windows 2000 Networking Services Infrastructure

   - Module 3: Designing an Automated IP Configuration Service Using DHCP

   - Module 5: Designing a NetBIOS Name Resolution Service Using WINS

   - Module 6: Designing Internet Connectivity Using Network Address Translation

   - Module 9: Designing Remote User Connectivity

   - Module 10: Designing a Remote Access Solution Using RADIUS

9. Microsoft Official Curriculum course 2152:
   Supporting Microsoft Windows 2000 Professional

   - Module 14: Configuring Windows 2000 for Mobile Computing

   - Module 15: Installing and Configuring Terminal Services

10. Microsoft Official Curriculum course 2153:
    Supporting a Microsoft Windows 2000 Network Infrastructure

    - Module 2: Automating Internet Protocol (IP) Address Assignment

    - Module 4: Implementing Name Resolution Using WINS

    - Module 5: Configuring Network Traffic Security and Cross-Platform Authentication

    - Module 6: Configuring Remote Access to a Network

    - Module 7: Supporting Remote Access to a Network

    - Module 8: Extending Remote Access Capabilities Using RADIUS

    - Module 13: Integrating Windows 2000 Network Services

    - Module 14: Managing a Windows 2000 Network

11. Web Sites

    - www.microsoft.com/windows2000

    - www.microsoft.com/train_cert

This chapter will help you prepare for the "Implementing, Monitoring, and Troubleshooting Security" section of the exam.

Microsoft provides the following objectives for the "Implementing, Monitoring, and Troubleshooting Security" unit:

Encrypt data on a hard disk by using Encrypting File System (EFS).

▶ This objective is necessary because someone certified in the use of Windows 2000 Server technology must understand how to locally encrypt hard drive data for maximum security against data loss from people with malicious intent.

Implement, configure, manage, and troubleshoot policies in a Windows 2000 environment.

- **Implement, configure, manage, and troubleshoot Local policy in a Windows 2000 environment.**

- **Implement, configure, manage, and troubleshoot System Policy in a Windows 2000 environment.**

▶ This objective is necessary because someone certified in the use of Windows 2000 Server technology must understand how local and system policies are implemented on a Windows 2000 member server and how they affect user and server function.

Implement, configure, manage, and troubleshoot auditing.

▶ This objective is necessary because someone certified in the use of Windows 2000 Server technology must understand how to implement auditing for tracking resource access and failed access.

CHAPTER 7

Implementing, Monitoring, and Troubleshooting Security

Implement, configure, manage, and troubleshoot local accounts.

▶ This objective is necessary because someone certified in the use of Windows 2000 Server technology must understand how to create and manage local accounts.

Implement, configure, manage, and troubleshoot account policy.

▶ This objective is necessary because someone certified in the use of Windows 2000 Server technology must understand how local account policy can be configured and how it affects functionality.

Implement, configure, manage, and troubleshoot security by using the Security Configuration Tool Set.

▶ This objective is necessary because someone certified in the use of Windows 2000 Server technology must understand how to efficiently analyze and configure servers using the tools available in the Security Configuration toolkit.

OUTLINE	**STUDY STRATEGIES**

▶ In the exam, you can expect that the new features implemented in Windows 2000 server will be points of examination. For this chapter, that will include the Encrypting File System and the Security Configuration Tool Set. This is not to say that the other parts of the chapter will not be tested, but you can be sure that EFS and SCTS will be.

▶ As it pertains to local accounts, you will need to be familiar with the concept of the SID and how it identifies an account. You will also need to understand the implications of deleting an account.

▶ Be sure you understand the elements of local password policy and local lockout policy. Also, remember that domain policy will override these policies if they are set locally. You might see questions that provide domain policy alongside local policy and ask you to decide which is more effective.

▶ As far as local and system policies go, understand auditing as it pertains to the exercise of rights and the access of resources. Know, for example, that file auditing requires that NTFS be implemented first. You should also understand how to create the Group Policy console and how the user and computer templates affect local users.

▶ You must understand what EFS is, as well as the role of the recovery agent. Be sure to understand that EFS does not prevent deletion of files, just reading of files.

▶ You might be tested on the Security Configuration Tool Set. Be sure you know how to create the consoles for managing these tools. In addition, know how to create and use templates and configuration databases.

▶ Preparation for questions will involve being familiar with the material here and, as usual, doing the labs and walking through the Step by Steps.

▶ As has been mentioned in other chapters, nothing prepares you better than experience working with Windows 2000 servers. Try out as many as possible of these concepts with real machines before you attempt the exam.

INTRODUCTION

Security is a major concern in any network environment. Much of any company's critical, confidential, and proprietary data is stored on servers somewhere. As a result, the ability to control access to this data is of paramount importance. Even if there is no imminent threat from people outside your organization trying to break into your data, there is still the matter of people accessing it from within, either the malicious or the curious who need to have their access to certain data curbed if not completely restricted. This chapter deals with the central security mechanism in Windows 2000—the user account. From there, it will move to policies you can put into place to restrict what people can do with certain accounts.

Most of the security configuration in a Windows 2000 environment is handled by the domain controller in the Active Directory. Because this book deals with only Windows 2000 member servers, it does not talk directly about Active Directory. Where discussions of Active Directory are required to explain concepts in this chapter, it will be covered. However, material here will stay away from Active Directory whenever possible.

IMPLEMENTING, CONFIGURING, MANAGING, AND TROUBLESHOOTING LOCAL ACCOUNTS

Implement, configure, manage, and troubleshoot local accounts.

In a Windows 2000 network environment, every user has to log in to get access to network resources. Logging in is no more complex than providing a name the computer recognizes and a password that identifies you as being authorized to act as a certain person. Both of these things rely on the presence of user accounts.

There are two kinds of user accounts in Windows 2000 networking: domain accounts and local accounts. Domain accounts are held in the Active Directory and are managed by the domain controllers. These accounts are available for logon from any domain controller or any member server in the domain.

Local accounts are held in the security database of a member or standalone server (the difference between the two is that a member server is part of a domain and a standalone server is part of a workgroup). Local accounts are managed by a local server and can only be used to log on to a local machine; they are not useful on the domain as a whole.

Maintenance of local accounts on Windows 2000 member servers is done in the Computer Management console.

To allow a user to log into the server with a local account, you first need to create it. Step by Step 7.1 outlines that procedure.

STEP BY STEP

7.1 Creating a Local Account on a Windows 2000 Member Server

1. From the Start menu, choose Programs, Administrative Tools, Computer Management.

2. From the Computer Management console, open the tree Computer Management\System Tools\Local Users and Groups.

3. Right click the Users folder and select New User from the menu that appears.

4. In the New User dialog box, fill in (at minimum) the user name, the initial password, and a confirmation of that password (see Figure 7.1). In addition, you can also add the user's full name and a description of the user. There are also some check boxes at the bottom of the dialog box. If User Must Change Password at Next Logon is selected, the user will be forced to change to a new password before logging in for the first time. If User Cannot Change Password is selected, the user will not be able to change the account password from the one you configured. If Password Never Expires is selected, the user will never be required to change his or her password; this may override

continues

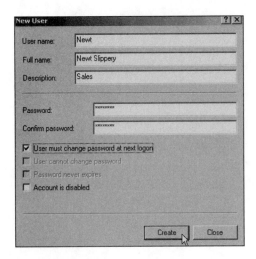

FIGURE 7.1
To create a new user account, you must provide at least a user name and password.

continued

> an account policy that's designed to force users to change passwords at regular intervals. If Account Is Disabled is selected, no one will be able to log onto the server with this account.

5. When you finish, click OK.

6. Click Close to exit.

Once an account has been created, you will eventually need to manage it. Account management requires the following tasks:

- ◆ Renaming
- ◆ Changing properties
- ◆ Resetting passwords
- ◆ Deleting

Renaming an Account

When an account is created, it is assigned a Security Identifier (SID). This SID is unique; no two accounts have the same one. The SID is the basis for all account recognition. This SID is to a server as your Social Security Number (or Social Insurance Number if you are Canadian) is to your government. Regardless of what you call yourself or how you change your name, you are still identified as the same person by this number. Of course, this is a very important feature that you can take advantage of in your network. When you give an account access to a particular resource, it is really the SID that is put into the Discretionary Access Control List (DACL), despite the fact that you use the account name. (In fact, if you are quick, when you open an ACL, you just might see the SID before Windows 2000 has a chance to resolve it.) The account name is just a convenience for you; it is irrelevant to Windows 2000.

As a result of all this, renaming is a trivial task. You simply rename the account, and everything else stays the same. When you open the ACLs of resources associated with the old name, the new name will show up. Step by Step 7.2 walks you through the process of renaming a local account.

STEP BY STEP

7.2 Renaming a Local Account on a Windows 2000 Member Server

1. From the Start menu, choose Programs, Administrative Tools, Computer Management.

2. From the Computer Management console, open the tree Computer Management\System Tools\Local Users and Groups\Users.

3. Right-click the user account that you want to rename and choose Rename from the menu that appears.

4. Type the new name over the old one and press Enter. To cancel the renaming procedure before you press Enter, press Esc instead.

Changing Account Properties

By default, four property sheets are associated with each account:

◆ General

◆ Member Of

◆ Profile

◆ Dial-In

The General property sheet is what you saw when you created the account. It contains the full name, description, and check boxes describing the password properties. However, it has one property that the original New User dialog box did not have: the Account Is Locked Out check box (see Figure 7.2) .

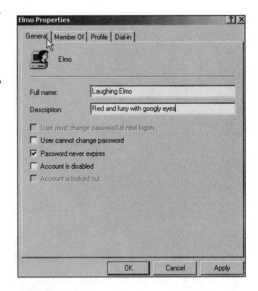

FIGURE 7.2
The differences between this property sheet and the one you filled in when creating the user account are that the user name is read-only and the "Account Is Locked Out" check box is present.

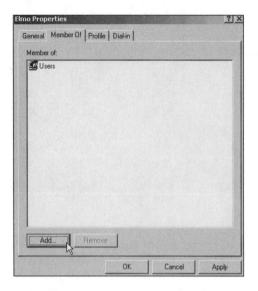

FIGURE 7.3
You can make a local user account the member of any local group.

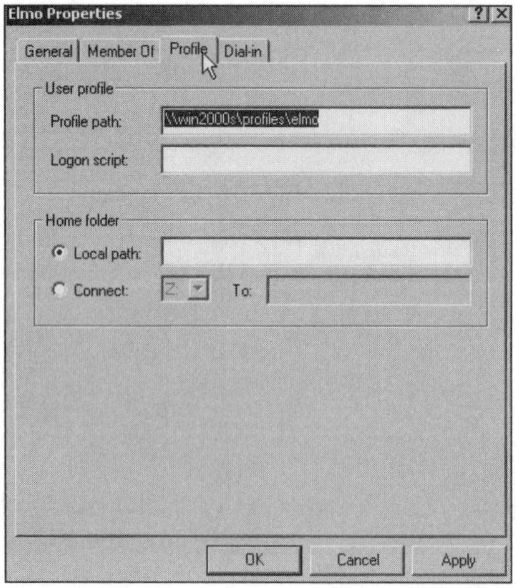

The Account Is Locked Out check box cannot be manually selected. It is normally gray until a user violates the Maximum Failed Passwords policy for the server. This policy, as you will see later, allows you to define the number of times a user can enter an incorrect password before the account becomes unusable. When an account gets locked, you (as an administrator) can unlock it; however, you cannot lock it manually.

The Member Of property sheet allows you to configure the group memberships a user has (see Figure 7.3). By placing users into groups, you can make security administration easier because any security authorization or restriction you place on a group will automatically be placed on all of its members. You can add a user to a group by clicking the Add button and then selecting the group or groups the user is to be a part of. If the groups are local to the member server, you need to be part of the Administrators group or the Power Users group. If the groups are in the Active Directory, you must be in the Domain Administrators or Account Operators group.

The Profile property sheet (see Figure 7.4) allows you to point to a roaming or mandatory profile that will be accessible to the users upon logon. This sheet also allows you to configure a home folder for the user. This home folder will be accessible when the user logs on. The folder you create can either be local (meaning that it is created on the server and is accessible only when the user logs onto the server locally—which is not of much use for most users), or it can be on the network. If you configure a Connect folder, the drive letter you choose will be connected to the folder you specify. Of course, in order for the profile and home folders to be accessible to the user, permissions must be configured to allow access.

The Dial-In property sheet allows you to configure dial-in ability and dial-in properties (see Figure 7.5). These options were discussed in Chapter 6, "Configuring and Troubleshooting Windows 2000 Network Connections."

FIGURE 7.4
You can point to a roaming or mandatory profile provided that it is in a shared folder on a server.

Step by Step 7.3 shows you how to configure local account properties.

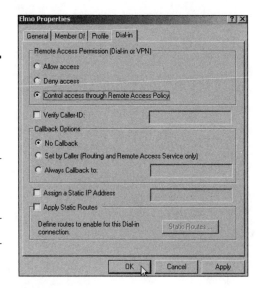

FIGURE 7.5
On the Dial-in property sheet, you can configure the ability (or inability) to dial-in to an RRAS server.

STEP BY STEP

7.3 Configuring Account Properties

1. From the Start menu, choose Programs, Administrative Tools, Computer Management.

2. From the Computer Management console, open the tree Computer Management\System Tools\Local Users and Groups\Users.

3. Double-click the user account you want to modify.

4. In the User Properties dialog box, adjust the desired properties and click OK to exit.

Resetting User Account Passwords

Occasionally (or maybe frequently, depending on your user community), a user will forget his or her account password. When that happens, the user becomes locked out of network access until a solution to the dilemma is found. As an administrator, you cannot find out what a user's password is. However, you can override the current password with a new one. If a user calls requesting that you find out the password or calls to tell you that he or she cannot remember an account password, follow Step by Step 7.4 to reset the password.

STEP BY STEP

7.4 Resetting an Account Password

1. From the Start menu, choose Programs, Administrative Tools, Computer Management.

2. From the Computer Management console, open the tree Computer Management\System Tools\Local Users and Groups\Users.

continues

continued

> **3.** Right-click the account you want to set the password for and choose Set Password from the menu that appears.
>
> **4.** In the Set Password dialog box, type the new password twice. Then click OK.

Deleting a User Account

Deleting a user account is a simple process. However, it is one that you should consider carefully before you do it. Most user account deletions occur because an employee ceases to work for a company or goes on short- or long-term leave (sabbaticals, maternity, disability). When an employee leaves permanently, the account becomes redundant. In the case of short- and long-term leave, the account is still useful. However, it is anticipated that it will be dormant for a significant period of time. In either case, the account offers a doorway back into the company's network, either for the employee or for a hacker looking for an idle account to try to break into. As a result, the tendency is to remove the account as soon as possible. The problem with that solution is that it tends to be short-sighted and will probably create a lot of work in the future for someone—probably you.

Usually, when an employee leaves a company, someone else is hired for the same position. Because the position is the same, the same resources are required for the new user as for the old. Similarly, if a user goes on leave, it may seem prudent to remove the account for security reasons even though the user will be returning. If you delete the user account, that user is removed from all the groups and the ACLs of all resources. That means that if a new employee is hired or an employee returns from a leave, you will have to create a new account and repopulate groups and ACLs with the new user's name. A better solution is to disable the user account while it's not needed. Then, when the new person is hired, you can simply rename and reconfigure the account and then re-enable it. This would be the same for someone on leave, only the account does not need to be renamed. This would ensure that all accesses the old user had, the new one will have as well.

However, sometimes you really do need to delete an account. If you've thought it through and you're sure you want to delete a user account, follow the process described in Step by Step 7.5

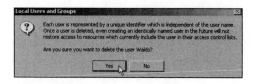

STEP BY STEP

7.5 Deleting a User Account

1. From the Start menu, choose Programs, Administrative Tools, Computer Management.

2. From the Computer Management console, open the tree Computer Management\System Tools\Local Users and Groups\Users.

3. Right-click the account you want to delete and choose Delete from the menu that appears.

4. A dialog box appears, warning you about the repercussions of deletion (see Figure 7.6). Click OK to delete the account anyway.

FIGURE 7.6
Deleting a user account can have negative long-term consequences, so you are warned before you actually take the action.

WINDOWS 2000 MEMBER SERVERS AND POLICIES

Policies in Windows 2000 define rules about how some aspect of user configuration or interaction works. For example, in Chapter 6 you saw how the Remote Access Policy defines rules by which users get remote access to a network.

The policies that are discussed in the next few sections define rules and parameters by which security is implemented in Windows 2000, specifically Windows 2000 member servers.

Two levels of policies apply to Windows 2000 member servers... those of the server and those of the domain. Becoming a member server in a domain means that a server loses some of its individuality and is, instead, subject to the rules of the domain. As a result, the domain rules will generally take precedence in cases where policies for the server and the domain conflict.

For most policy settings, when you view them, you will see two sets of values for the configuration: the local setting and the effective setting (see Figure 7.7). In this book, you will be introduced to the local setting because the Active Directory and its policies are beyond the scope of the exam. However, you must note that, when you set policies on the server, the effective policy will not change unless the domain policy is undefined. In that case, the local policy setting will be the effective setting.

It is not assumed that you have access to a Windows 2000 domain controller, either for learning purposes or in your work. However, if you are the manager of a Windows 2000 domain and the member servers within it, you will find it helpful to see the domain equivalents of the policy configurations you will see applied to a Windows 2000 member server. Therefore, this book includes directions in all cases as to how to perform the same functions in the domain. In some cases, explanations have been left out (such as what the purpose and implications of a domain group policy are, or how to create one), but the mechanics of how to get to the policy settings will be laid out so you can make the changes you see necessary.

For all the figures shown in the policy sections to follow, the domain policy has been disabled. As a result, the effective policy will always appear as the local policy. This will generally not be the case in real life, but it makes the policy settings less confusing while you are learning.

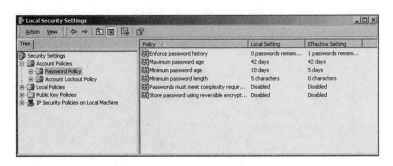

FIGURE 7.7
On a member server, the local properties are not always the effective ones.

IMPLEMENTING, CONFIGURING, MANAGING, AND TROUBLESHOOTING ACCOUNT POLICY

Implement, configure, manage, and troubleshoot account policy.

In Windows 2000 servers, account policy defines two separate policy areas: password policy and account lockout policy. Password policy defines how many characters passwords have to be, how long they can stay in effect until they have to be changed, and other related settings. Account lockout policies define at what point an account is locked after too many failed password attempts, how long the lockout lasts, and when the counter is reset. Because security of accounts depends on passwords being secure, these policies ensure that accounts are secure and prevents the use of an account for which security has been breached.

Implementing Local Password Policy

A Windows 2000 password policy consists of six settings:

- Password history
- Minimum age
- Maximum age
- Minimum length
- Complexity
- Reverse encryption storage

This policy allows you to ensure that users adhere to the password requirements for your organization. However, a policy cannot remove the disdain that users will have for you if the password policy is, in their minds, unreasonable. If, for example, you require a 14-character password that contains upper- and lowercase characters and numbers that must be changed every three days, you will quickly have a revolt on your hands (unless people understand the need for such an extreme policy). That means the user community

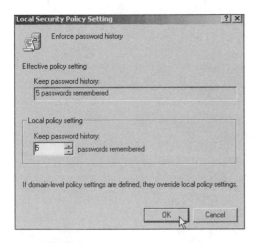

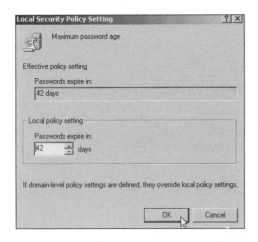

must be educated to the security requirements in your organization and the possibility of external vandals breaking into their systems. If the people acknowledge the need, it becomes their need and makes the requirement much easier for them to handle.

The following sections describe the six password settings and their uses.

Enforce Password History

Password history is a running list of the passwords that have been set for a particular account. The setting consists of a counter that's set between 0 and 24 (see Figure 7.8). This defines the number of passwords Windows 2000 will remember, the implication of which is that none of the remembered passwords can be used again. If, for example, the history is set to 3 and the history records passwords of *apple*, *orange*, and *banana*, those three words cannot be used until they are not in the history. If the same user changes the password to *cucumber*, *apple* will be forgotten and can be used again.

The reason for using a password history setting is to keep users from switching back and forth between two passwords when they are required to change them. Much manual password hacking is based on information known about a user. If a password becomes known and the user switches back to it in short order, it can be guessed again.

Maximum Password Age

Maximum password age is a numeric value between 0 and 999 days that defines how long a password can stay in effect before it must be changed (see Figure 7.9). This setting allows the administrator to exercise control over how long a user keeps the same password. Before the password expires, the user will be warned; if it does expire, the user will not be allowed to log on until the password is changed. If the value is set to 0, the password never expires (which is the same as selecting the account property Passwords Never Expire).

Minimum Password Age

Minimum password age is a numeric value between 0 and 999 days that defines the minimum length of time a password must be in place before a user can change it (see Figure 7.10). Although on the surface it looks as though this property contradicts the maximum age, they actually go together with the password history to form a complete package. Consider this scenario as an example. A password policy is set to keep five passwords in history with a maximum age of 20 days. Harold wants to keep his password of *banana* because it is easy to remember. Realizing that five passwords will be remembered, when the maximum age of 20 days is reached, he simply changes his password in quick succession as follows: *banana* → *apple* → *grape* → *tangerine* → *apricot* → *banana*. He has technically fulfilled the requirements of the policy: He changed his password after 20 days and did not use *banana* again until four other passwords had been used. However, he violated the spirit of the policy because he effectively kept his password the same all the time. In order to prevent this, you can set the minimum password age to 15 days. That way, Harold can change his password only once every 15 days. This will ensure that Harold cannot use his *banana* password again until at least 60 days have passed.

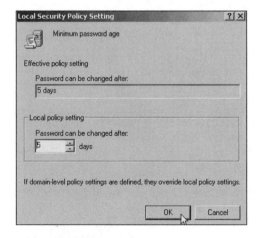

FIGURE 7.10
Minimum password age can be set between 0 and 999 days (inclusive).

Overcoming Minimum Age When Password Is Compromised   One possible problem with minimum password ages occurs when a user knows that his or her password has been compromised (someone knows what it is). In this case, the user wants to be able to change the password immediately to prevent the other person from using it to log into his or her account. This can be overcome in that the administrator can still change the account password in the Computer Management console (see Step by Step 7.4). The administrator must change the password, select the check box labeled "User Must Change Password at Next Logon," and then tell the user the new password. When the user logs on the next time, he or she will use the new password (the one set by the administrator) and then will be forced to change that password to something new. If this procedure is followed, the minimum password age will not apply in this case. When you decide to put a minimum password age into effect, you need to be aware of this security problem and be prepared to act promptly when a user calls requesting a new password.

Minimum Password Length

Minimum password length is a numeric value between 0 and 14 that defines the minimum length for an account password (see Figure 7.11). If the value is 0, an account password is optional.

This value allows you to enforce passwords that are simpler than a single character or a short word. The longer the password, the more difficult it is to guess it (at least in theory). However, this setting cannot require that a 14-character password be something other than a long string of the letter *a*.

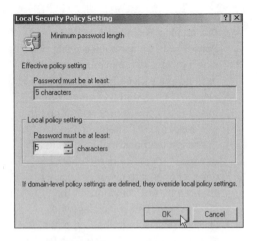

FIGURE 7.11
Minimum password length can be set between 0 and 14 (inclusive).

Passwords Must Meet Complexity Requirements

Password complexity requirements prevent a user from creating a password that is a long string of only a single letter or that uses only the person's full name. If password complexity is enabled (see Figure 7.12), the user must adhere to the following rules when assigning or changing the password:

◆ Passwords must be at least six characters long, regardless of the minimum length defined in the policy.

◆ Passwords must contain characters from at least three of the following four character groups:

• English uppercase characters (A, B, C...)

• English lowercase characters (a, b, c...)

• Westernized Arabic numerals (0, 1, 2...)

• Non-alphanumeric symbols like punctuation (!, @, $, and so on)

◆ Passwords may not contain the user's username or any single name portion of the full name.

Suppose complexity is enforced, and a user's username is *Bob* and his full name is *Bob Millar*. Table 7.1 lists some allowed and disallowed passwords.

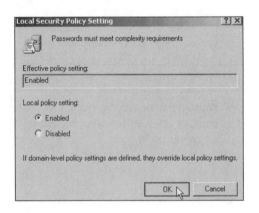

FIGURE 7.12
Complex passwords must contain at least six characters in three of the following categories: capital letters, small letters, numbers, special characters.

TABLE 7.1

VALID AND INVALID PASSWORDS FOR BOB MILLAR

Valid Passwords	Invalid Passwords
Aardvark1	Aardvark (only two kinds of characters)
IsaacNewton?	BobMillar2 (contains parts of full name)
A1aaaa	A1aaa (too few characters)

Complexity is only part of the password checking equation. If minimum length is 10, the password must be at least 10 characters despite the fact that password complexity requires only 6.

Store Password Using Reversible Encryption

This password storage feature is required for CHAP authentication for non-Windows clients (see Figure 7.13). It stores the passwords using a reversible encryption scheme that can be provided during the authentication process. For application of this, see the section "Interoperation with Apple Macintosh" in Chapter 2, " Installing, Configuring, and Troubleshooting Access to Resources" and the section "Installing, Configuring, and Troubleshooting Remote Access" in Chapter 6.

Step by Steps 7.6 and 7.7 show how to configure local password and domain password policies, respectively.

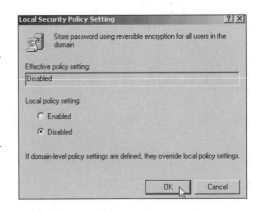

FIGURE 7.13
Enabling reversible encryption allows for CHAP authentication.

STEP BY STEP

7.6 Configuring Local Password Policy

1. From the Start menu, choose Programs, Administrative Tools, Local Security Policy.

2. Expand the navigation tree (on the left side) in the path Security Settings\Account Policies\Password Policy, and then click on Password Policy.

3. Double-click the policy on the right that you want to set, adjust the value, and close the dialog box.

STEP BY STEP

7.7 Configuring Domain Password Policy

1. On a domain controller, open the Start menu and choose Programs, Administrative Tools, Active Directory Users and Computers.

2. Right-click the domain name and choose Properties from the menu that appears.

3. At the Domain Properties dialog box, click the Group Policy tab.

4. On the Group Policy property sheet, double-click the Default Domain Policy displayed in the Group Policy Object Links box.

5. From the Group Policy dialog box, expand the tree Default Domain Policy\Computer Configuration\Windows Settings\Security Settings\Account Policies\Password Policy, and then click Password Policy.

6. Double-click the policy on the right that you want to set, adjust the value, and close the dialog box.

Implementing Local Account Lockout Policy

A Windows 2000 account lockout policy consists of three settings:

◆ Lockout duration

◆ Lockout threshold

◆ Counter reset

This policy allows you to ensure that you have control over how many times a user can enter an incorrect password and what happens at the point when you think that an attempt to crack your network is occurring. You can control how many bad passwords can be entered before the account is locked. You can control how long the counter tracking incorrect lockouts stays active. You can also control how long an account is locked before a user can access it again.

The following sections describe the settings and their uses.

Account Lockout Threshold

The Account Lockout Threshold allows you to define the number of incorrect password attempts that will cause the account to be unavailable to the user (see Figure 7.14). This number can be set from 0 to 999, where 0 represents an infinite number of attempts. The higher the security you want in your organization, the smaller this number should be (greater than 0, of course).

FIGURE 7.14
Lockout Threshold can be set between 0 and 999 tries (inclusive).

Account Lockout Duration

Account Lockout Duration allows you to define the length of time an account will remain locked before it is released (see Figure 7.15). This number can be set from 0 to 99999 minutes, where 0 represents an infinite time, which would require an administrator to manually unlock the account. The higher the security, the greater this number should be. When an account is locked, it can be unlocked from the General property sheet of the Properties dialog box for the user account.

Reset Account Lockout Counter After

The Reset Account Lockout Counter After parameter allows you to define the length of time Windows 2000 remembers failed logon attempts (see Figure 7.16). This number can be set from 1 to 99999 minutes. The implication of this setting is that after a user has typed his password in incorrectly a couple of times, he can wait a predefined length of time and try again, knowing that the previous two attempts will not be held against him. Regardless of this setting, a correct logon password will reset the counter back to zero.

FIGURE 7.15
Lockout Duration can be set between 0 and 99999 minutes (inclusive).

FIGURE 7.16
Reset Lockout Counter can be set between 0 and 99999 minutes (inclusive).

Step by Steps 7.8 and 7.9 (respectively) demonstrate how to configure lockout policy locally and in a domain.

STEP BY STEP

7.8 Configuring Local Account Lockout Policy

1. From the Start menu, choose Programs, Administrative Tools, Local Security Policy.

2. Expand the navigation tree (on the left side) in the path Security Settings\Account Policies\Account Lockout Policy, and then click on Account Lockout Policy.

3. Double-click the policy on the right that you want to set, adjust the value, and close the dialog box.

4. When you set a policy value, you may be presented with a dialog box suggesting recommended values for the other two settings. If this appears, click OK to accept the changes (you cannot progress with your change unless you accept the recommendations).

STEP BY STEP

7.9 Configuring Domain Account Lockout Policy

1. On a Domain Controller, from the Start menu, choose Programs, Administrative Tools, Active Directory Users and Computers.

2. Right-click the domain name and choose Properties from the menu that appears.

3. At the Domain Properties dialog box, click the Group Policy tab.

4. On the Group Policy property sheet, double-click the Default Domain Policy displayed in the Group Policy Object Links box.

5. From the Group Policy dialog box, expand the tree Default Domain Policy\Computer Configuration\ Windows Settings\Security Settings\Account Policies\ Account Lockout Policy, and then click Account Lockout Policy.

6. Double-click the policy on the right that you want to set, adjust the value, and close the dialog box.

7. When you set a policy value, you may be presented with a dialog box suggesting recommended values for the other two settings. If this appears, click OK to accept the changes (you cannot progress with your change unless you accept the recommendations).

Troubleshooting Account Policy

Most troubleshooting in the realm of policies involves understanding the implications of the different settings and how they interact with one another. If a user expresses concern about some phenomena he is experiencing, get as much information as possible about what is happening. Then go back to the policy and see how these phenomena could be produced. One of the biggest sources of trouble with account policy is the interaction of complexity requirements with the other settings (and with users). Be sure that users understand the requirements for passwords under an enforced complexity policy. This will prevent confusion when passwords are rejected for not conforming to the rules.

IMPLEMENTING, CONFIGURING, MANAGING, AND TROUBLESHOOTING LOCAL AND GROUP POLICIES

Implement, configure, manage, and troubleshoot policies in a Windows 2000 environment.

◆ Implement, configure, manage, and troubleshoot Local policy in a Windows 2000 environment.

◆ Implement, configure, manage, and troubleshoot Group policy in a Windows 2000 environment.

Local and group policies on a Windows 2000 member server allow you to control the environment a user is allowed to operate in. Whereas profiles record what a user *has* done and how the desktop has been configured, these policies define what a user *can* do. Policies may control user rights to log on to a server locally or to shut a server down. Policies may control whether the Run command is found in the Start menu and what wallpaper is present on the desktop.

As with other policies, because a member server is part of a domain, the local policy settings are subject to the Group policy settings and, as a result, the effective settings may not be those that were configured locally.

Configuring Local Policies on a Windows 2000 Member Server

Local policies on a Windows 2000 member server define three areas of configurations:

◆ Audit policy

◆ User Rights Assignment

◆ Security options

Implementing Audit Policy

Audit policy allows for the tracking of various resource access rights exercised on your server based on either successes or failures. Before any auditing can occur on a Windows 2000 server, the audit policy must be adjusted to allow auditing in that area. Figure 7.17 shows events marked for auditing.

Configuring a particular event or access to be audited is, for the most part, as simple as opening the entry and selecting Success and/or Failure. Success auditing tracks every time a specific event occurs successfully (for example, every time someone successfully logs on to the server). Failure auditing tracks only those events that did not happen because the user did not have sufficient rights or permissions to do what he or she tried to do (for example, every time someone tries to access a folder for which NTFS security settings disallow access to that user).

One audit setting, Audit Object Access, requires a little more configuration. Object access applies to printers, files, and folders. For access to specific objects to be audited, the object has to be enabled for auditing, and auditing has to be enabled in the general policy of audit access. This will be touched on again in the section "Implementing, Configuring, Managing, and Troubleshooting Auditing," later in this chapter.

Step by Steps 7.10 and 7.11 walk you through setting up local audit and domain audit policies, respectively.

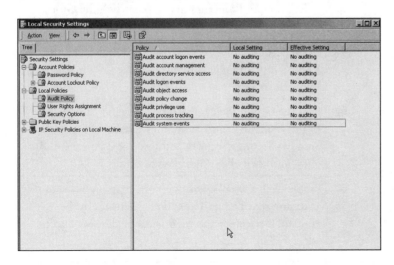

FIGURE 7.17
You can audit a variety of event types, which is configured by the audit policy.

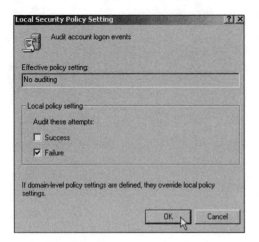

FIGURE 7.18
You can audit for success, failure, or both.

STEP BY STEP

7.10 Configuring Local Audit Policy

1. From the Start menu, choose Programs, Administrative Tools, Local Security Policy.

2. Expand the navigation tree (on the left side) in the path Security Settings\Local Policies\Audit Policy, and then click on Audit Policy.

3. Double-click the policy on the right that you want to set, and then select or deselect Success and/or Failure (see Figure 7.18). Click OK.

STEP BY STEP

7.11 Configuring Domain Audit Policy

1. On a domain controller, open the Start menu and choose Programs, Administrative Tools, Active Directory Users and Computers.

2. Right-click the domain name and choose Properties from the menu that appears.

3. At the Domain Properties dialog box, click the Group Policy tab.

4. On the Group Policy property sheet, double-click the Default Domain Policy displayed in the Group Policy Object Links box.

5. From the Group Policy dialog box, expand the tree Default Domain Policy\Computer Configuration\ Windows Settings\Security Settings\Local Policies\Audit Policy, and then click Audit Policy.

6. Double-click the policy on the right that you want to set. Make sure that Define These Policy Settings in the Template is selected, and then select or deselect Success and/or Failure. Click OK.

Implementing User Rights Assignment

Assigning user rights allows the administrator to control who is allowed to perform special tasks or have special privileges on the server. Most tasks a user would want to undertake are covered under the User Rights Assignment policy. This policy covers all the administrative tasks and some of the mundane tasks that might be carried out on a server.

Unlike the other policies you have seen so far, the assignment of a user right is based on inclusion in the list of SIDs that have been assigned that user right.

The following list contains some user rights that you might find helpful:

- ◆ **Access This Computer from the Network.** Defines a user's ability to log on to and access resources from the network. By default, everyone has this right.

- ◆ **Back Up Files and Directories.** Defines who can perform backups on the computer. This right allows the specified users to bypass local security to place files onto backup tape.

- ◆ **Log On Locally.** Defines which user accounts will be allowed to authenticate locally at a Windows 2000 standalone server. Although the default setting is to allow everyone to log on locally, you might want to remove the Users group from this list to increase security.

- ◆ **Restore Files and Directories.** Defines who can restore information to the server from a backup.

- ◆ **Take Ownership of Files or Other Objects.** Defines who can take ownership of any files or objects on the server. By default, all people in the local Administrators group have this right.

Step by Steps 7.12 and 7.13 define the procedures for configuring a local user right and a domain user right, respectively.

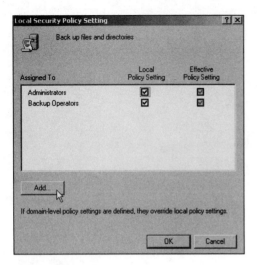

FIGURE 7.19
The right to perform certain system functions can be given to (or taken away from) any group or user.

STEP BY STEP

7.12 Configuring a Local User Right

1. From the Start menu, choose Programs, Administrative Tools, Local Security Policy.

2. Expand the navigation tree (on the left side) in the path Security Settings\Local Policies, and then click on User Rights Assignment.

3. Double-click the right you want to set to open the dialog box.

4. At the Local Security Policy Setting dialog box, you can add or remove the user right from any user (see Figure 7.19). To add a user to the list, click the Add button and locate the user to add. To remove a user from the list, click the check box in the Local policy Setting column beside the user name.

5. Click OK to exit the Local Security Policy Setting dialog box.

STEP BY STEP

7.13 Configuring a Domain User Right

1. On a domain controller, open the Start menu and choose Programs, Administrative Tools, Active Directory Users and Computers.

2. Right-click the domain name and choose Properties from the menu that appears.

3. At the Domain Properties dialog box, click the Group Policy tab.

4. On the Group Policy property sheet, double-click the Default Domain Policy displayed in the Group Policy Object Links box.

5. From the Group Policy dialog box, expand the tree Default Domain Policy\Computer Configuration\ Windows Settings\Security Settings\Local Policies, and then click User Rights Assignment.

6. Double-click the right you want to set to open the dialog box.

7. At the Template Security Policy Setting dialog box, make sure the Define These Policy Settings in the Template check box is selected. To add a user to the list, click the Add button and locate the user to add. To remove a user from the list, select the user and click the Remove button.

8. Click OK to exit the Template Security Policy Setting dialog box.

Implementing Security Options

Security options define the basic and complex security settings that can be configured on a system-wide basis. These options create a number of security restrictions or perform system tasks to ensure a secure environment. These options are settings-oriented, generally not pointed toward specific users. Where they are, lists of users will be provided as the properties for the option.

The following list contains the security options you might find helpful:

◆ **Clear Virtual Memory Pagefile When System Shuts Down.** Ensures that when a server is shut down, the page file is deleted. This prevents the pagefile from being examined after a reboot.

◆ **Do Not Display Last User Name in Logon Screen.** Defines whether the user name of the last person to log onto a Windows 2000 machine is displayed for logon convenience. If you enable this option, the User Name field always comes up blank.

◆ **Message Text for Users Attempting to Log On.** Defines the text of a special security dialog box that appears just before the Logon dialog box. This text box is used to make it clear to users who owns the system and who is welcome and who is not. For example, you might configure a message like this: "Network access is restricted to Company XYZ Inc. employees only!"

Step by Steps 7.14 and 7.15 show you how to configure a local security option and a domain user right, respectively.

STEP BY STEP

7.14 Configuring a Security Option

1. From the Start menu, choose Programs, Administrative Tools, Local Security Policy.

2. Expand the navigation tree (on the left side) in the path Security Settings\Local Policies, and then click on Security Options.

3. Double-click the option you want to set to open the dialog box.

4. At the Local Security Policy Setting dialog box, set the value as you like (see Figure 7.20). Click OK to exit.

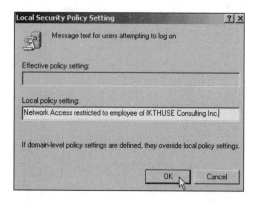

FIGURE 7.20
Set the value for a specific security policy setting; here a text value is being entered.

STEP BY STEP

7.15 Configuring Domain User Right

1. On a domain controller, open the Start menu and choose Programs, Administrative Tools, Active Directory Users and Computers.

2. Right-click the domain name and choose Properties from the menu that appears.

3. At the Domain Properties dialog box, click the Group Policy tab.

4. On the Group Policy property sheet, double-click the Default Domain Policy displayed in the Group Policy Object Links dialog box.

5. From the Group Policy dialog box, expand the tree Default Domain Policy\Computer Configuration\ Windows Settings\Security Settings\Local Policies, and then click Security Options.

6. Double-click the security option you want to set to open the dialog box.

7. At the Template Security Policy Setting dialog box, make sure the Define This Policy Setting in the Template check box is selected. Set the value for the option. Click OK to exit.

Configuring Group Policy on a Windows 2000 Member Server

Windows 2000 allows you to tune system configuration settings via the Group Policy snap-in (commonly referred to as the Group Policy Editor). In a domain environment, the Group Policy Editor allows computer and user settings to be configured for a Group Policy Container (sites, domains, and organization units). On a member server, the Group Policy Editor can be focused on the Local Computer object to configure the Local policy for the computer and user of the computer.

To edit the Local policy of a computer, you must create a console that has the Group Policy snap-in loaded. You can do this by creating a new console or by adding the Group policy to one that already exists. Step by Step 7.16 describes how to add the snap-in.

STEP BY STEP

7.16 Creating a Group Policy Console

1. From the Start menu, choose Run. In the Run dialog box, type **MMC** and press Enter.

2. At the Console dialog box, select Console, Add/Remove Snap-In.

3. In the Add/Remove Snap-In dialog box, click the Add button.

4. In the Add Standalone Snap-In dialog box, double click Group Policy.

5. At the Select Group Policy Object screen, Local policy will show up as the Group Policy Object. Click Finish to continue.

6. Click Close to exit the Add Standalone Snap-In dialog box.

7. At the Add/Remove Snap-In dialog box, click the OK button.

8. At the Console dialog box, select Console, Save. When prompted, enter the name **Group Policy** for the new console and click Save.

After you create the console, as described in Step by Step 7.16, you can access it by choosing Start, Programs, Administrative Tools, Local policy.

As you can see in Figure 7.21, the Group Policy console consists of two sections: the Computer Configuration and the User Configuration.

An administrator can manage specific Registry settings by configuring Administrative templates for computer configuration (when the Registry settings are applied to the HKEY_LOCAL_MACHINE Registry key) or for user configuration (when the Registry settings are applied to the HKEY_CURRENT_USER key).

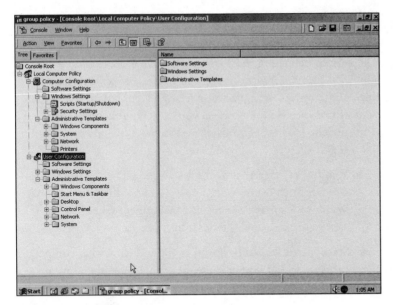

FIGURE 7.21
The Group Policy console allows for configuration of the various security administrative templates for the computer and users.

Administrative Templates in Computer Configuration

Administrative templates for computer configuration are divided into four sections:

◆ **Windows Components.** Allows you to define settings for the configuration and operation of NetMeeting, Internet Explorer, Task Scheduler, and Windows Installer.

◆ **System.** Allows you to configure logon, disk quotas, DNS client configuration, Group Policy configuration, and Windows file protection.

◆ **Network.** Allows you to configure network operations in areas pertaining to offline files, and network and dial-up connections.

◆ **Printers.** Allows you to configure computer properties pertaining to printers and printing.

Administrative Templates in User Configuration

The settings defined in the Administration Templates for users are applied to every user who logs on to the member server. These settings primarily have the effect of removing icons and tools from sight or from access (for example, you can disable access to the Control Panel). These administrative templates include the following:

- ◆ **Windows Components.** Allows you to set configuration settings for such components as NetMeeting, Internet Explorer, Windows Explorer, Microsoft Management Console (MMC), Task Scheduler, and Windows Installer.

- ◆ **Start Menu & Taskbar.** Allows you to define what components show and do not show on the Start menu and what kinds of functions can be performed from the Start menu.

- ◆ **Desktop.** Allows you to customize the desktop, including which icons will be displayed.

- ◆ **Control Panel.** Allows you to define which components (if any) of the Control Panel are accessible and which options function.

- ◆ **Network.** Allows you to configure network operations in areas pertaining to offline files, and network and dialup connections.

- ◆ **System.** Allows you to define how the system looks to the user, including using a custom shell that replaces Explorer, and how logon/logoff functions work.

Modifying the Local Policy

When you modify the Administrative Templates in the Group Policy console, two files are created. A file called NTUSER.POL is created in the profile location for the current user. In addition, a file called REGISTRY.POL is created in the path \WINNT\System32\GroupPolicy\User.

The following Step by Step describes how to change the Local policy.

STEP BY STEP

7.17 Modifying Local Policy

1. From the Start menu, choose Programs, Administrative Tools, Group Policy (assuming you created the Group Policy console in Step by Step 7.16).

2. At the Group Policy console, expand the section Local Computer Policy\Computer Configuration\Administrative Templates or Local Computer Policy\User Configuration\Administrative Templates. Navigate to the policy you want to modify and double-click the policy entry on the right side (for example, you can select the Disable Logoff policy).

3. In the Policy Properties dialog box, adjust the setting to the value desired and click OK (see Figure 7.22).

4. When you finish configuring settings, exit the Group Policy console.

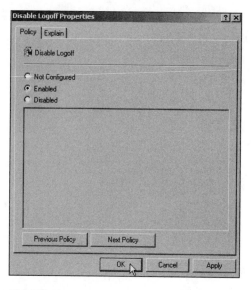

FIGURE 7.22
Adjust the Disable Logoff policy as desired.

IMPLEMENTING, CONFIGURING, MANAGING, AND TROUBLESHOOTING AUDITING

Implement, configure, manage, and troubleshoot auditing.

Auditing is the process by which you track access to system resources. The access that you track may be general (like logging on) or specific (like access to a specific file), and it may be successful access or unsuccessful access.

Auditing is done mainly when you are concerned about people trying to access specific resources that they are not supposed to access. However, it is sometimes necessary to check resource usage and to track that usage.

Auditing and the Audit Policy

Configuring auditing begins with an audit policy. That policy will encompass all the facets of system use that you desire to track. The method for setting up an audit policy was discussed in this chapter in the section "Implementing Audit Policy." However, here you will look more closely at the kinds of events you can audit and what configuration settings are required in order to audit (specifically as it relates to object access).

In Figure 7.17, you saw that the audit policy was made up of nine areas. Table 7.2 lists those areas and describes the kinds of activities covered by each area.

TABLE 7.2

AUDIT POLICY AREAS

Audit Policy Area	Encompasses
Account Logon	Requests made to validate user accounts.
Account Management	Modification of a user account or group. This includes adding and deleting accounts and changing passwords or other account properties.
Directory Service Access	Access to Active Directory objects. This does not apply to audit policy on member servers.
Logon	The actual logging on or off of a user. This also includes making a network connection to a computer, which requires validating access rights on that machine.
Object Access	User gained access to a file, folder, or printer to perform any action (read, write, delete, manage, and so on).
Policy Change	Modification to any of the security policy properties, user rights, or audit policies.
Privilege Use	The exercise of any user right (like changing system time or shutting down a server).
Process Tracking	Actions performed by a program. This is generally only of interest to programmers who want to track certain events that their programs are causing.
System	Server was started or stopped, or the security log filled up and entries have been discarded.

When you have decided which area you want to audit, you must determine whether you are interested in successful access or unsuccessful access. You should audit successful access when you are interested in knowing each time a resource (like a specific financial report) is accessed. You should audit unsuccessful access if you are interested in knowing every time someone tried to access a resource but failed because of insufficient rights. This could be used in the case of a financial report, or it could be used to determine if someone is trying to hack into your system by manually (or automatically) trying to guess an account password.

Most audit configurations are as simple as enabling success or failure auditing. The exception is the auditing of object access. Object access is not an event that can be grouped into one convenient package. You might have thousands of files on your server, and each of those can be monitored for access. In addition, you might have hundreds or thousands of users, and you might want to watch only some of them for resource access. Finally, resource access itself is a broad concept: You might be interested in modification of a resource as opposed to read access. Therefore, object access is a finely tunable audit event. When the audit policy is in place, you must configure the individual objects (files, folders, printers) for the kind of events you are looking for and the people you want to watch. Finally, to add one more variable, you can only audit file objects on NTFS volumes.

The following Step by Step describes how to configure file resource auditing.

STEP BY STEP

7.18 Configuring File Resource Auditing

Enabling Auditing of Object Access

1. From the Start menu, choose Programs, Administrative Tools, Local Security Settings.

2. At the Local Security Settings console, expand the tree Security Settings\Local Policies and click Audit Policy.

3. On the right side, double-click Audit Object Access.

continues

continued

4. At the Local Security Policy Setting dialog box, select Success and/or Failure and click OK.

Enabling Auditing of a Specific NTFS File Object

1. Using My Computer or Windows Explorer, navigate to the object you want to audit, right-click it, and choose Properties from the menu that appears.

2. At the Object Properties dialog box, click the Security tab.

3. On the Security property sheet, click the Advanced button.

4. In the Access Control Settings for Object dialog box, click the Auditing tab.

5. On the Auditing property sheet, click the Add button.

6. In the Select User, Computer, or Group dialog box, choose the person or group you want to watch for access to this object.

7. In the Auditing Entry for Object dialog box, select Successful or Failed for every type of access you want to watch (see Figure 7.23). What actually gets logged will depend on these settings and the setting for the object audit profile; you can watch for success here, but if your audit policy says to watch only object access for failure, only failures will be logged. When you finish, click OK.

8. In the Access Control Settings for Object dialog box, click OK.

9. Click OK to close the Object Properties dialog box.

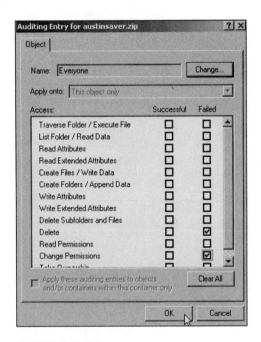

FIGURE 7.23
You can watch for success and/or failure for a variety of object access types.

When you have an audit policy in place, you will need to check on the logged events occasionally. It is a good idea to regularly do this because you cannot know what is happening unless you take time to look at the logs.

Auditing and the Security Log

Audit events are written into the security log on the local machine. This Security log can be accessed from the Event Viewer, which is a part of the Administrative Tools. You need to be aware of certain properties of the Security log if you are implementing auditing in your organization (see Figure 7.24). First, it is configured with a maximum size (by default that size is 512KB), and you can store about three events per kilobyte.

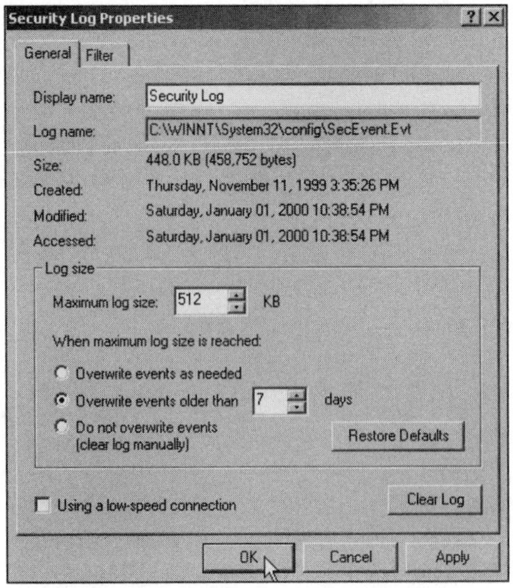

Second, you can configure what to do when the log fills up. Your choices are to overwrite old events, to overwrite old events only if they are beyond a certain age, or to never overwrite old events. In a high security environment, you don't want events to ever be over-written; instead, you will have to manually archive logs when they reach capacity. In fact, if security is a big enough issue, you may want to enable the security policy item that shuts down the server when the Security log is full (this will prevent anyone from accessing anything if it cannot be tracked).

Finally, you can archive log entries at any time so you can have a permanent record of all log entries made throughout history.

Step by Steps 7.19 and 7.20 show how to configure the Security log properties and how to archive log entries, respectively.

FIGURE 7.24
In the Security Log Properties dialog box, you can adjust the log size and what will happen when that size is reached.

STEP BY STEP

7.19 Configuring Security Log Properties

1. From the Start menu, choose Programs, Administrative Tools, Event Viewer.

2. At the Event Viewer console, right-click Security Log and choose Properties from the menu that appears.

3. In the Security Log Properties dialog box, adjust the settings as desired and click OK.

STEP BY STEP

7.20 Archiving Log Entries

1. From the Start menu, choose Programs, Administrative Tools, Event Viewer.

2. At the Event Viewer console, right-click Security Log and choose Save Log File As from the menu that appears.

3. In the Save Security Log As dialog box, enter a name and location for your log file, and then click OK.

4. Right-click Security Log and choose Clear All Events from the menu that appears. This removes the archived events from the active log.

The Security log tracks all events produced by auditing and records them as either success audit or failure audit. When you open the Security log, you may be presented with a daunting list of events to sift though. To save you time and effort, you can use filters to go through the events. You can choose to see only certain event types; in the case of security, you can see either successes or failures. You can also choose to filter out events that fall outside of a particular time range. Step by Step 7.21 shows you how to view and filter events in the log.

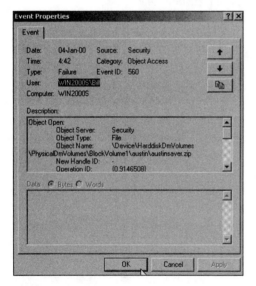

FIGURE 7.25
This event shows that a user named Bill has tried to access a file called AustinSaver.zip (he was actually trying to delete it).

STEP BY STEP

7.21 Viewing and Filtering Security Log Entries

1. From the Start menu, choose Programs, Administrative Tools, Event Viewer.

2. At the Event Viewer console, click Security Log.

3. On the right side, you can see the Security log with either Failure Audit or Success Audit in the Type column. Double-click an event to see its details (as shown in Figure 7.25). Then click OK to continue.

4. Filter the events as desired. Right-click Security Log and choose Properties from the menu that appears.

5. In the Security Log Properties dialog box, click the Filter tab.

6. On the Filter property sheet, configure the filter to show only the items you want to see (see Figure 7.26). Click OK to continue.

7. When you want to see all the events again, remove the filter by opening the Filter property sheet and clicking the Restore Defaults button.

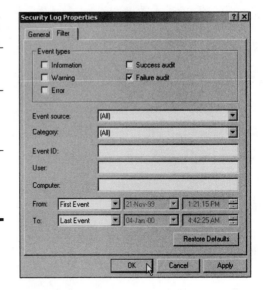

FIGURE 7.26
Configure the filter to show only what you want to see. This filter eliminates everything but the failure events.

Troubleshooting Auditing

Problems with auditing usually occur for one of three reasons:

◆ You are collecting too much data.

◆ You are collecting too little data.

◆ You are not collecting the right data.

To get auditing configured right, you have to begin with a goal. The goal should never be to collect information; information gathering is only a tool that helps you reach your goal. If, for example, your goal is to investigate how many attempts are made to hack into your server at night, you will want to audit failed logon attempts and then filter the results to show only those that occurred during certain hours.

The point is, when you know what the purpose is, you will be in a better position to determine what audit policy you should use to get the kind of information you need to fulfill your goal. Troubleshooting auditing always comes down to you understanding what the policies are and then applying what you know about them to the goal you want auditing to help you reach.

ENCRYPTING DATA USING THE ENCRYPTING FILE SYSTEM

Encrypt data on a hard disk by using Encrypting File System (EFS).

One of the issues with NTFS file security on Windows 2000 volumes is that it is dependent on the drive being in the computer on which the files were created. You can gain access to NTFS files if you can steal the hard drive out of the computer because, by putting the drive into another computer, that local administrator can take ownership of the files and access the data.

Local encryption has long been available through third-party software as a way of ensuring that only the user who encrypts files can access them. EFS is built into NTFS version 5, so no add-ons are required. When EFS is in place, encryption and decryption of data happens transparently to the user.

Although encryption is extremely useful for locally securing data, it comes with a price. Encrypted data cannot be used on file systems except NTFS version 5; this means that it cannot be applied to FAT and FAT32 partitions. In addition, encrypted files are secure only on the hard drive; if you access an encrypted file over the network, the network transmission of the data is not secure unless you also use network encryption like IPSec. Finally, encryption is not compatible with compression; if you encrypt a compressed file, the compression will be removed.

Although encryption prevents data from being accessed, that does not eliminate the need for NTFS security. Encryption prevents a file's contents from being viewed or modified; however, it does not prevent the file from being deleted. In order to ensure the best security, make sure that both encryption and NTFS security are applied.

The following principles apply to the encryption attribute:

◆ You can designate a folder as being encrypted by setting its Encryption attribute; however, the folder is not actually encrypted, only its contents are.

◆ If a folder is encrypted, all new content created in it, copied into it, or moved into it, the folder will also be automatically encrypted.

◆ If a file is encrypted and is copied or moved into an unencrypted folder, the Encryption attribute is retained unless the folder is located on a non-NTFS partition, in which case the encryption is removed.

◆ When a file is encrypted, the file can only be decrypted by the user who encrypted the file and by a designated *recovery agent.* (For more information on how EFS works, see the upcoming section titled "Understanding EFS Encryption."

Step by Step 7.22 outlines how to encrypt a file or folder.

STEP BY STEP

7.22 Encrypting a File or Folder

1. Using Windows Explorer or My Computer, navigate to the file or folder you want to encrypt.

2. Right-click the object to be encrypted and choose Properties from the menu that appears.

3. In the Properties dialog box, click the Advanced button.

4. In the Advanced Attributes dialog box (see Figure 7.27), select the Encrypt Contents to Secure Data check box, and then click OK.

5. Click OK to exit the Properties dialog box.

For your convenience, Windows 2000 also offers a command-line utility called CIPHER.EXE that encrypts files and folders with your encryption key. For most applications, you will find it more convenient to use the GUI to encrypt. However, some useful features are found only in the command-line version. For example, CIPHER allows you to encrypt only those files with the .DOC extension. CIPHER will also allow you to force encryption of files that Windows 2000 thinks are encrypted but that have not been because an error prevented them from being encrypted completely. (For example, if the power failed during encryption, a file's Encryption attribute might have been set before the file was actually encrypted.)

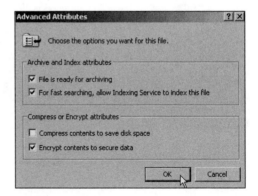

FIGURE 7.27
Encryption is inherent to NTFS and, therefore, can be implemented through the setting of a file property.

The basic syntax of the CIPHER program is as follows:

```
CIPHER [/e or /d] [/s:dir] [/i] [/f] [/q] [filename(s)]
```

Table 7.3 lists the parameters you can set when performing encryption using the CIPHER program.

TABLE 7.3

CIPHER PARAMETERS

Parameter	Function
none	Displays the encryption state of the current folder.
/e	Encrypts the specified folder or file.
/d	Decrypts the specified folder or file.
/s:*dir*	Applies the encryption or decryption to the folder specified by *dir*, or if *dir* is missing, applies to the current folder; this applies to all files and subfolders as well.
/i	Ignores any errors during encryption (by default, an error causes encryption to fail).
/f	Forces encryption or decryption even if the attributes indicate that the objects to be acted on are already in that state. (This allows for the repair of objects for which the Encryption attribute is incorrectly set due to system error during the last encryption or decryption attempt.)
/q	Does not report detailed progress information.
/*filename*	Indicates the file or folder to encrypt. Many files or folders can be listed with spaces between them, and wildcard characters (* and ?) can be used. If you use wildcards, no folder in the tree will have its Encryption attribute set unless it conforms to the wildcard format.

Understanding EFS Encryption

The EFS encryption process is outlined in the following steps (see Figure 7.28) :

1. EFS encryption encrypts the data file using a file encryption key (FEK).

2. The FEK is stored in a header attached to the encrypted data file known as the data decryption field (DDF). The DDF is encrypted so that only the user who encrypted the file can decrypt the FEK. When the user has decrypted the FEK, he or she can then decrypt the data file using the FEK.

3. The FEK is also stored in a second header known as the data recovery field (DRF). The DRF is encrypted so that only the designated recovery agent can decrypt the FEK. After the recovery agent decrypts the FEK, he or she can decrypt the data file using the FEK.

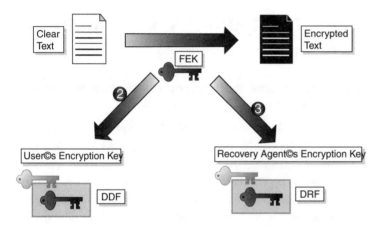

FIGURE 7.28
The EFS encryption process.

Implementing an EFS Recovery Policy and Recovering Encrypted Files

With encryption-based security comes a large inherent weakness: If a user's account is deleted, the ability to decrypt data can be lost if a recovery agent is not defined. Therefore, it is imperative that before encryption starts to be used in your organization, a recovery policy must be put into place. Such a policy designates someone as a recovery agent and allows that account to decrypt any encrypted data.

When a Windows 2000 server is installed, a default recovery policy is put into place. In fact, without such a policy, encryption is not possible on the machine at all. This policy consists of the designation of the local administrator as the recovery agent. This user is capable of recovering files encrypted by any user on the local machine.

To recover a file that has been encrypted with an encryption key that is no longer available, that file must be sent to the recovery agent, who is authorized to decrypt any file. When it is decrypted, the file can then be sent back to the original location.

USING THE SECURITY CONFIGURATION TOOL SET

Implement, configure, manage, and troubleshoot security by using the Security Configuration Tool Set.

Security is an all-pervasive part of Windows 2000 Server. Hardly an area in the administrative structure is not impacted by security in some way. Windows NT (the precursor) always had good security tools; the problem was you had to go all over the place to configure security. As a result, configuring security meant knowing a bunch of tools and a number of interfaces, and knowing which tool did what.

The Security Configuration Tool Set is an integrated tool for analyzing and configuring your servers and workstations. It provides a way to analyze security configuration against predefined baselines. In addition, it allows you to configure the servers and workstations to those baselines. Finally, it allows you to create baselines that can be used as the basis for configuring other servers and workstations.

All the security tools discussed in this chapter (and more) are in the Security Configuration Tool Set. It includes analysis and settings for the following security areas:

- Account Policies
- Local Policies
- Event Log
- Restricted (System) Groups

◆ System Services

◆ Registry

◆ The File System

Using the Security Configuration Tool Set is straightforward. After you start it, you can load a predefined security setting. This setting can be either a provided settings file or one that you've created specifically for the servers, workstations, or domain controllers in your environment. The settings files define the recommended security settings in a number of areas for computers in specific roles with specific security requirements (generally security is defined as basic, secure, and high-secure). These .INF files can be used to check your Windows 2000 machines against the recommended setups and then, if desired, configure the settings on your machines to conform to the settings. If you want, you can create your own configuration files to define the particular security settings for your domain controllers, servers, and workstations and then apply those settings to all the machines in your organization. By going through this exercise, you can ensure that all your domain controllers, servers, and workstations are configured the same without having to write down and implement all the settings manually.

When you install Windows 2000, a number of security templates are installed in the \WINNT\Security\Templates folder. Some of those templates are described in Table 7.4.

TABLE 7.4

PREDEFINED SECURITY TEMPLATES

Template File Name	*Description*
BASICDC.INF	A basic security domain controller. Specifies default security settings for all security areas, with the exception of user rights and group memberships. Designed for low-to-medium security environments.

continues

TABLE 7.4	*continued*

PREDEFINED SECURITY TEMPLATES

Template File Name	Description
SECUREDC.INF	A secure domain controller. Beginning from default settings, this increases security settings for account policy, auditing, and Registry keys. This template assumes that BASICDC.INF was installed before it.
HISECDC.INF	A high security domain controller. This assumes a network environment containing only Windows 2000 servers and workstations because the security precludes communication with any other machines. This template defines security for network communications that are digitally signed and encrypted.
BASICSV.INF	A basic security Windows 2000 Server (non-domain controller). Same as BASICDC.INF only for standalone or member servers.
BASICWS.INF	A basic security Windows 2000 Professional client. Same as BASICDC.INF only for workstations.
SECUREWS.INF	A secure Windows 2000 Professional client. Same as securedc.inf only designed for workstations.
HISECWS.INF	A high security Windows 2000 Professional client. Same as HISECDC.INF only designed for workstations.

Creating the Security Configuration Tool Set Console

In order to access the Security Configuration Tool Set, you first have to create an MMC that includes the Security Configuration and Analysis snap-in. Setting up the console is illustrated in the following Step by Step.

STEP BY STEP

7.23 Creating the Security Configuration Tool Set Console

1. From the Start menu, choose Run. In the dialog box that appears, type **MMC** and press Enter.

2. In the Console dialog box, select Console, Add/Remove Snap-In.

3. At the Add/Remove Snap-In dialog box, click the Add button.

4. In the Add Standalone Snap-In dialog box, scroll through the list and double-click Security Configuration and Analysis (see Figure 7.29). Click Close to continue.

5. Click OK to close the Add/Remove Snap-In dialog box.

6. At the console, choose Console, Save. In the Save As dialog box, type a meaningful name for the new console (like `Security Configuration and Analysis`) and click Save.

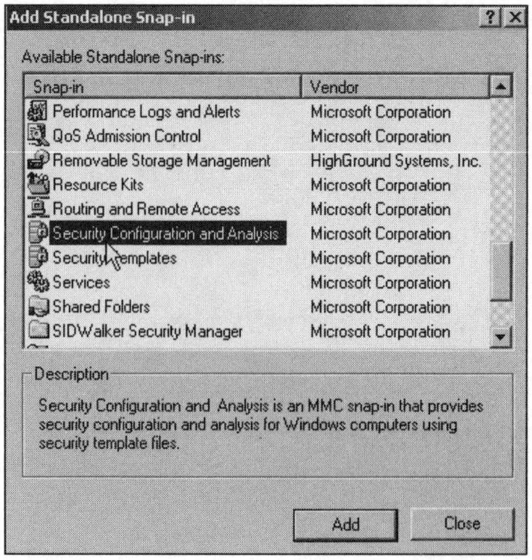

FIGURE 7.29
Adding the Security Configuration and Analysis snap-in creates a new tool for you to use.

After you create the console as described in Step by Step 7.23, you will be able to access it by choosing Start, Programs, Administrative Tools, Security Configuration and Analysis.

Analyzing Your Server

Analyzing a server begins with a configuration database, which you create by applying one or more templates to a blank configuration. This database can be saved and used to analyze the server again and again. In addition, you can export its settings to create a new template you can then use to create databases for the analysis of other servers.

When a database is first created, a template configuration must be imported into it. At that point, additional template configurations can be added until the configuration database is complete.

Step by Step 7.24 shows how to create and configure a configuration database.

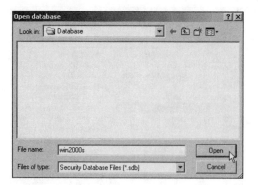

FIGURE 7.30
You create a new database by "opening" one that does not exist.

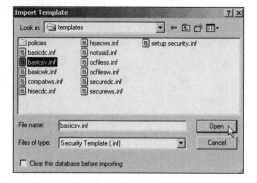

FIGURE 7.31
Importing a template sets the current database configuration to be consistent with a predetermined level of security.

STEP BY STEP

7.24 Creating and Configuring a Configuration Database

1. Open your Security Configuration and Analysis console.

2. Right-click Security Configuration and Analysis, and then choose Open Database from the menu that appears.

3. In the Open Database dialog box, type a name into the File Name field (see Figure 7.30). This name should represent the name of the server (if this is to be the only configuration database for the machine). Click Open to continue.

4. At the Import Template dialog box, select a template to begin the configuration with (see Figure 7.31). Click Open to continue.

5. If desired, add more templates (the configuration is saved as you configure it). To do this, right-click Security Configuration and Analysis, and choose Import Template from the menu that appears.

6. In the Import Template dialog box, choose the template to add to the current configuration (any current settings that are also in the new template will be overwritten). If you want to clear out the database and make this the only template present, select the Clear This Database Before Importing check box at the bottom of this dialog box. Click Open to continue.

7. Repeat steps 5 and 6 until all desired templates have been added.

After you create the configuration database, you are ready to analyze the local computer with it. Step by Step 7.25 describes this process.

STEP BY STEP

7.25 Analyzing a Server with a Configuration Database

1. Open your Security Configuration and Analysis console.

2. Right-click Security Configuration and Analysis and choose Open Database from the menu that appears.

3. In the Open Database dialog box, select the database you want to open and click Open.

4. In the Security Configuration and Analysis console, right-click Security Configuration and Analysis and choose Analyze Computer Now from the menu that appears.

5. When the Perform Analysis dialog box appears, either accept the default location for the analysis log or type in your own. Then click OK.

When the analysis is complete, you can examine the results in the GUI interface by expanding the security sections and comparing the Database Setting with the Computer Setting for the same policy entries. An icon is displayed next to each property to help you. An icon with a green check mark means there is a setting in the database, and it is the same as the computer setting. A red circle with a white X in it indicates there is a setting in the database, and it is not the same as the computer setting (see Figure 7.32). An icon with neither a check mark nor an X indicates the setting is not defined in the database or on the server.

If, after the analysis, you decide that a database entry should be changed, you can change it by double-clicking the entry and filling in the value you desire. As the notes on the dialog boxes indicate, this will change only the database and not the system configuration.

FIGURE 7.32
A red circle with a white X in it indicates a
contradiction in settings.

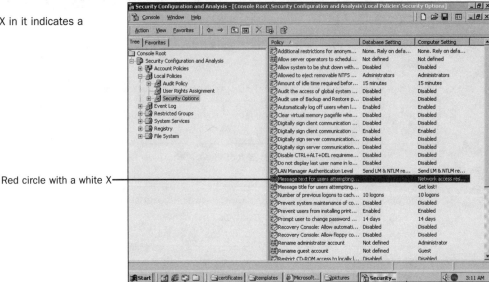

Red circle with a white X ⟶

Creating a New Configuration Template

There are two ways to create a new configuration template. Either you can modify a current template, or you can export a current database's settings to a template file. If your template will differ only slightly from an existing template, you might find it easiest to create a copy of an existing template and then modify it using the Security Templates snap-in. That process is illustrated in the following Step by Step.

STEP BY STEP

7.26 Modifying an Existing Template

1. In the WINNT\Security\Templates folder, make a copy of an existing template.

2. Create a new console (as described in Step by Step 7.23) and add the Security Templates snap-in, or add that snap-in to the Security Configuration and Analysis console you have already configured.

3. Open the Security Templates console.

4. Expand the console tree Security Templates*templates path**newtemplate*, and then modify the desired settings by double-clicking them (in the right panel) and editing the setting values (see Figure 7.33).

5. Modify the description of the template. Right-click the template filename (on the left side) and choose Set Description from the menu that appears.

6. At the Security Template Description dialog box, type in a text string that defines the attributes and purpose of the template.

7. Click OK to continue.

8. Right-click the template filename (on the left side) and choose Save from the menu that appears.

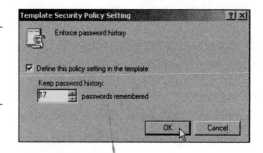

FIGURE 7.33
Modify the template by adjusting the policy settings.

On the other hand, if your configuration includes a number of templates and some manual modifications, you are well advised to configure a database and then export it. This process is illustrated in Step by Step 7.27.

STEP BY STEP

7.27 Exporting a Database Configuration to a Template

1. Configure a configuration database as outlined in Step by Step 7.24.

2. Right-click Security Configuration and Analysis and select Export Template from the menu that appears.

3. In the Export Template To dialog box, enter a name that adequately describes the purpose of the template and click Save. (It might take a while to create the template from the database.)

Configuring a Server Using a Configuration Database

With a configuration database that has been created for your server, you can easily configure your server to conform to the database. This ensures that the server meets the minimum security standards for your organization. In addition, by leaving server-unique settings undefined in the database, you can allow for some flexibility on the part of individual administrators for special properties.

The following Step by Step demonstrates how to export a configuration database to a template.

STEP BY STEP

7.28 Exporting a Configuration Database to a Template

1. Open a pre-configured database in the Security Configuration and Analysis console.

2. Right-click Security Configuration and Analysis and select Configure Computer Now from the menu that appears.

CASE STUDY: PAYROLL IS US

THE ESSENCE OF THE CASE

This case requires that the following results be satisfied:

▶ Force users to change passwords more frequently.

▶ Adjust other password options as necessary.

▶ Determine who is accessing critical files.

▶ Determine who is printing critical files and when.

SCENARIO

Matthew is the network administrator for Payroll Is Us (PIU), a North American payroll company specializing in custom payroll solutions for companies with 1,000 or more employees. Security is a major issue at PIU—physical security, that is. The company has locks on the doors and uses guards with guns and armor-plated trucks. However, to this point, their network security has been rather lax. A survey of the 500 employees indicates that many have not changed their password since the day they were hired, and many have the password "password," which is the default for new accounts. Even the Administrator password for the domain is easy to remember (and guess): "payroll."

What has really brought this issue to a head is the apparent leak of confidential information from the company's databases and from people's network shares. Confidential memos are being referred to in the newspaper, and PIU's clients are getting calls from businesses that seem to know how many employees they have and what those employees' salaries are (more than a little disconcerting for the clients and the management of PIU). They think that access to this data is coming primarily from people on the outside hacking into the corporate network using passwords that have been guessed.

Your job is to tighten security. At this point, the security needs to focus on passwords and auditing, but you will be given more latitude to make further changes if you prove to be successful at this task.

CASE STUDY: PAYROLL IS US

ANALYSIS

Through the judicious use of policies, Matthew can attain all the stated goals. He can begin by applying account policy. In this way, he can control how many characters passwords must contain, how often passwords need to be changed, how long they must be in place before they can be changed again, and how many passwords are remembered to prevent duplicates too often. In addition, he can put lockout policies in place to prevent brute-force attacks on the logon process (creating programs to send random passwords at the logon to attempt to guess the password), or at the very least, to prevent those attacks from succeeding. These policies might in fact eliminate the current visible problems.

To satisfy the requirements of determining who is accessing and printing critical files, Matthew can implement an audit policy. This allows him to determine what level of auditing he wants (whether to watch for reads or writes or changes) and which files to audit. Of course, in order for these audits to work, he must make sure all the hard drives are converted to NTFS. He can also apply auditing to printers to determine who is using them and when and what is being printed when they are being used. The System log can then be monitored periodically to determine who is accessing resources.

The following table summarizes Matthew's solution.

OVERVIEW OF THE REQUIREMENTS AND SOLUTIONS IN THIS CASE STUDY

Requirement	Solution Provided By
Force users to change passwords.	Implement account policies to force passwords to be changed frequently.
Implement other password controls.	Implement account policies to save history, control password age, and configure lockout policies.
Determine who is accessing files.	Configure audit policies on critical files to watch for access.
Monitor printing of critical files.	Configure audit policies on printers.

CHAPTER SUMMARY

Summarized briefly, this chapter covered the following main points:

◆ *Creating and managing local accounts.* This includes creating, renaming, configuring, and deleting local user accounts.

◆ *Establishing and maintaining account policy.* This includes configuring password length, history, age, and complexity and using reversible encryption. This also includes configuring lockout polices for accounts and recovering locked out accounts.

◆ *Configuring Local and Group policies.* This includes configuring audit policy and user rights and configuring and using computer and user configuration templates.

◆ *Configuring and managing auditing.* This includes creating and activating an audit log and investigating the Security log.

◆ *Encrypting data using the Encrypting File System.* This includes implementing EFS locally and recognizing the implications of doing so.

◆ *Using the Security Configuration Tool Set.* This includes creating the Security Configuration Tool Set console, implementing server configuration analysis, creating and modifying Configuration Templates, and setting up server configuration using configuration databases.

KEY TERMS

Before taking the exam, make sure you are familiar with the definitions and concepts behind each of the following key terms.

- local account
- Security Identifier (SID)
- local password policy
- password history
- password age
- account lockout
- audit policy
- user rights
- Group policy
- configuration templates
- Security log
- Encrypting File System (EFS)
- Security Configuration Tool Set
- security configuration template
- security configuration database

APPLY YOUR KNOWLEDGE

Exercises

7.1 Create and Maintain Local Accounts

In this exercise, you learn how to create and maintain
a local account. You will create an account, adjust its
properties, and assign it to the DACL of an NTFS
folder (it is assumed that your WINNT folder is on
an NTFS partition). Then you will rename the account
and see how the DACL changes to reflect the
new name.

Estimated Time: 15 minutes

1. Create a new local account.

    A. From the Start menu, choose Programs,
       Administative Tools, Computer Management.

    B. In the Computer Management console,
       expand the Local Users and Groups line.
       Then right-click the Users entry and choose
       New User from the menu that appears.

    C. In the New User dialog box, enter the field
       values shown in Figure 7.34. The password is
       "password." When you finish, click Create
       and then Close.

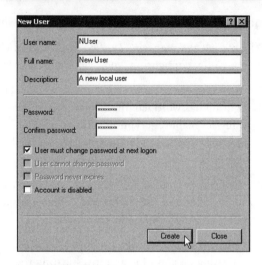

FIGURE 7.34
This figure shows the configuration of the
NUser account.

2. Add the new user to the DACL of a file resource.

    A. Navigate in the file system to the WINNT
       folder (which should be on your C: drive).

    B. Right-click the WINNT folder and choose
       Properties from the menu that appears.

    C. In the WINNT Properties dialog box, click
       the Security tab.

    D. On the Security tab, click the Add button.

    E. In the Select Users, Computers, or Groups
       dialog box, select your server from the Look
       In pull-down menu. Then locate the NUser
       name and double-click it. Click OK to con-
       firm your choice.

APPLY YOUR KNOWLEDGE

F. In the WINNT Properties dialog box, change the permissions by selecting NUser and then selecting Full Control in the Allow column. Click OK.

3. Change the name of NUser to NewUser and investigate how the change looks in the DACL of WINNT.

   A. Open the Computer Management console, locate the NUser account, right-click it, and choose Rename from the menu that appears.

   B. Type `NewUser` as the new name and press Enter.

   C. Navigate to the WINNT folder on your hard drive, right-click it, and choose Properties from the menu that appears.

   D. In the WINNT Properties dialog box, select the Security tab.

   E. Note that the entry for NUser has been changed to NewUser.

   F. Exit the WINNT Properties dialog box.

7.2   Create and Test a Local Account Policy

This exercise shows you how to create a local account policy. Then it shows you how this policy affects users who log onto your server. It is assumed that you have already created the NewUser account as described in Exercise 7.1.

To ensure that settings configured in the following exercises are not influenced by domain policy, make sure you follow step 1 to remove the computer from the domain if your server is a member of a domain. Normally, you would not do this; however, to avoid having to discuss and deal with Active Directory policy issues, this step is necessary for lab purposes.

Estimated Time: 30 minutes

1. Make sure that the server is not a member of a domain. (Do this step only if your Windows 2000 server is currently a member of a domain.)

   A. From the desktop, right-click the My Computer icon and choose Properties from the menu that appears.

   B. From the System Properties dialog box, select the Network Identification tab and click the Properties button.

   C. In the Identification Changes dialog box, click the Workgroup radio button (in the Member Of section) and enter `Workgroup` as the workgroup name. Click OK to continue.

   D. After a pause, you should be welcomed to the Workgroup workgroup and prompted to restart your computer. Do so and log on as Administrator.

2. Adjust the password policy to remember two passwords and require a minimum length of five characters.

   A. From the Start menu, choose Programs, Administrative Tools, Local Security Policy.

   B. On the Local Security Settings console, expand the Account Policies section to reveal the Password Policy. Select the Password Policy.

   C. On the right, the current password policies are displayed (the column labeled Effective Setting does not apply here because no domain policy is in effect). Double-click the Enforce Password History policy.

APPLY YOUR KNOWLEDGE

D. In the Local Security Policy Setting dialog box, change the value in the Enforce Password History box to 2. Click OK to continue.

E. Change the Minimum Password Length policy to 5.

F. Close the Local Security Settings console and log off the Administrator account.

3. Log on as NewUser and change from password to test policy.

A. Log on as NewUser with a password of "password."

B. When you're prompted to change your password, try to change it from "password" to "1234." You will be told that this violates the policy. Change it to "12345" instead.

C. Upon successful logon, press Ctrl+Alt+Del to invoke the Windows Security dialog box, and then click the Change Password button.

D. In the Change Password dialog box, type in the old password (12345) and type **password** as the new password. Click OK to continue.

E. When the Change Password Error message appears, click OK to continue. You cannot change your password back to the most recent one because the password history setting prevents it.

F. When the Change Password dialog box appears again, change the password from "12345" to "54321." You will be informed that your password has changed. Click OK to clear the informational dialog box and return to the Windows Security dialog box.

G. Click the Change Password button again and change your password from "54321" back to "password." This time you will be successful.

H. In the Windows Security dialog box, click the Cancel button to return to the desktop.

4. Log off as NewUser and log on as Administrator.

7.3   Configure and Test a Local Account Lockout Policy

This exercise shows how you can configure a local account lockout policy to prevent more than three incorrect password attempts. It also shows how to unlock an account that's locked and how to reset a user account password.

It is expected that you have already completed Exercises 7.1 and 7.2.

Estimated Time: 30 minutes

1. Open the Local Security Policy console on your server.

2. Expand the Account Policies section and select the Account Lockout Policy.

3. On the right, change the Account Lockout Threshold to 3. Windows 2000 will then automatically set the other two lockout policies.

4. Close the Local Security Policy console and log off as Administrator.

5. Lock out the NewUser account by entering an incorrect password.

A. In the Log On to Windows dialog box, type **NewUser** as the User Name and then enter three incorrect passwords in a row. Although you cannot tell yet, the NewUser account becomes locked out.

APPLY YOUR KNOWLEDGE

B. On the fourth attempt, correctly type in the password ("password"). You will be told that the account is locked out.

6. Log in as Administrator.

7. Open the Computer Management console, expand the Local Users and Groups section, and select Users.

8. Double-click the NewUser account.

9. Clear the check box labeled Account Is Locked Out. Select the check box labeled User Must Change Password at Next Logon (this will allow NewUser to change his or her password to a known value). Click OK to continue.

10. In the Computer Management console, right-click the NewUser account and choose Set Password from the menu that appears.

11. In the Set Password dialog box, type **password** into both fields. Click OK.

12. Close the Computer Management console and log off the Administrator account.

13. Log on as NewUser using the password "password." When prompted, change your password.

7.4 Configure and Test Local System Policy

This exercise shows how you can modify Local System policy. In this case, you will modify user rights for NewUser to prevent her from logging in to the server locally, and when that user is able to log in, she will be prevented from shutting down the server.

Estimated Time: 20 minutes

1. Create and configure a system policy.

A. Open the Local Security Policy console.

B. In the console, expand the Local Policies section and select the User Rights Assignments.

C. Locate the Deny Logon Locally policy, double-click it, and add NewUser to the list. This will override the Log On Locally policy setting.

D. Locate the Shut Down the System policy and verify that neither NewUser nor the Users group (of which NewUser is a part) has the right to shut down the system.

E. Close the Local Security Policy console and log off the Administrator account.

2. Attempt to log on as NewUser.

A. In the Log On to Windows dialog box, attempt to log in as NewUser.

B. When logon fails, log on as Administrator.

3. Open the Local Security Policy console and adjust the user rights to allow NewUser to log onto the server locally. To do so, clear the check box in the policy.

4. Log on to the server as NewUser.

5. Attempt to shut down the server.

A. From the Start menu, choose Shut Down. Note that all you can do is log off this account.

B. In the Shut Down Windows dialog box, click Cancel.

C. Press Ctrl+Alt+Del to bring up the Windows Security dialog box.

APPLY YOUR KNOWLEDGE

D. In the Windows Security dialog box, click the Shut Down button. Note that the Shut Down Windows dialog box appears, and you do not have the option to shut down the system.

E. In the Shut Down Windows dialog box, click Cancel.

F. In the Windows Security dialog box, click Cancel to return to the desktop.

6. Log off the NewUser account.

7.5 Enable and Examine the Effects of File Auditing

This exercise shows how you can enable auditing on a file and how you can examine the Security log to determine what access has been made to that file. This exercise requires an NTFS partition.

Estimated Time: 15 minutes

1. On your C-drive, create a folder called AuditMe and create (or copy) a text file in this folder called WatchThis.txt.

2. Configure audit policy to audit logon events and object access.

   A. Open the Local Security Policy console, expand the Local Policies, and select the Audit Policy.

   B. Double-click Audit Logon Events. Then in the Local Security Policy Settings dialog box, select the Success check box and click OK.

   C. Double-click Audit Object Access. Then in the Local Security Policy Settings dialog box, select both the Success check box and the Failure check box. Click OK.

   D. Close the Local Security Policy console.

3. Configure the WatchThis.txt file for object auditing.

   A. Navigate to the WatchThis.txt file in the AuditMe folder.

   B. Right-click the WatchThis.txt file and choose Properties from the menu that appears.

   C. Select the Security tab, click the Add button, and add Administrator to the Name list.

   D. Give the Administrator full control access by selecting the Administrator in the Name list and then selecting the check box next to the Full Control permission in the Allow column.

   E. Adjust the permissions of the Everyone group to only allow Read permission of the file. Because the current permissions for Everyone are inherited from the parent folder, you will have to first deselect the check box labeled Allow Inheritable Permissions from Parent to Propagate to This Object (when the dialog box appears, click Copy). Then select the Everyone group in the Name list and deselect all the check boxes in the Allow column except the one labeled Read.

   F. Click the Advanced button at the bottom of the dialog box.

   G. In the Access Control Settings for WatchThis.txt dialog box, select the Auditing tab.

   H. On the Auditing tab, click the Add button and add the Everyone group to the list.

   I. In the Auditing Entry for WatchThis.txt dialog box, select the check boxes for Successful and Failed next to the Create Files/Write Data access type. Click OK to continue.

J. Click OK to exit the Access Control Settings for WatchThis.txt dialog box.

K. In the WatchThis.txt Properties dialog box, click OK.

4. Log on as NewUser and try to write to the WatchThis.txt file.

A. Log on as NewUser.

B. Navigate to the WatchThis.txt file and double-click it to open it in Notepad.

C. In the WatchThis.txt – Notepad dialog box, type "**Anything you can do I can do better**" and choose File, Save.

D. When the Save As dialog box appears, click Cancel.

E. Exit Notepad, discarding any changes you tried to make to the file.

5. Log off as NewUser and log on as Administrator.

6. Open the Event Viewer and examine the Security log for audit entries.

A. From Start menu, choose Programs, Administrative Tools, Event Viewer.

B. In the Event Viewer console, select Security Log.

C. Because you are auditing both Logon/Logoff events and access failures, you will see events of both types. Double-click an entry that is of type Failure Audit; this should be the entry that was generated when you tried to save changes to a file you had only Read access to.

D. As you can see in Figure 7.35, the Event Properties dialog box identifies the user (WIN2000S/NewUser), as well as the name of the object that you were trying to access (C:\AuditMe\WatchThis.txt).

E. Close the Event Properties dialog box and close the Event Viewer console.

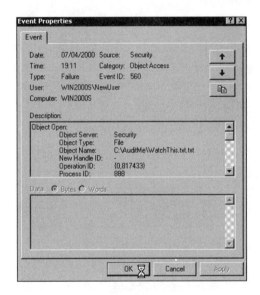

FIGURE 7.35
The Event Properties dialog box shows the event and the user that caused the event, and it gives details about the event.

APPLY YOUR KNOWLEDGE

7.6   Enable EFS, Examine Its Effects, and Use the Default Recovery Agent to Recover an Encrypted File

This exercise shows how you can enable EFS on a file and what its effect is. In addition, it shows how to use the default recovery agent (the Administrator) to recover an encrypted file. This exercise requires an NTFS partition.

Estimated Time: 15 minutes

1. Create a new user called InTheDark using the Computer Management console. Ensure that this user is not part of the Administrators group.

2. Log on to the Server as NewUser.

3. Create some data to test encryption with.

    A. Create a folder on the C: drive and call it SecretStuff.

    B. In the SecretStuff folder, create a document called ThisIsSecret.txt. If you want, edit it with Notepad and put some text into it.

    C. In the SecretStuff folder, create a document called ThisIsNotSecret.txt. If you want, edit it with Notepad and put some text into it.

4. Enable encryption on the ThisIsSecret.txt file.

    A. Right-click the ThisIsSecret.txt file and choose Properties from the menu that appears.

    B. In the Preoprties dialog box, click the Advanced button at the bottom of the General tab.

    C. In the Advanced Attributes dialog box, select the check box labeled Encrypt Contents to Secure Data and click OK.

    D. In the Properties dialog box, click OK.

    E. When the Encryption Warning dialog box appears, select the radio button labeled Encrypt File Only and click OK.

    F. Open and close both files to ensure that the encryption and decryption is transparent to the user.

5. Log off NewUser and log on as InTheDark to test the encryption.

    A. Log on as in InTheDark.

    B. Navigate to the SecretFiles folder and double-click ThisIsNotSecret.txt. The file will open, and you can make changes and save it.

    C. Double-click the ThisIsSecret.txt file. When the error message appears, click OK and close Notepad.

6. Recover the encrypted file by using the default recovery agent, the Administrator.

    A. Log on as Administrator.

    B. Navigate to the SecretFiles folder and double-click ThisIsSecret.txt. The file will decrypt and open. Close Notepad.

    C. Right-click the ThisIsSecret.txt file and choose Properties from the menu that appears.

    D. In the Properties dialog box, click the Advanced button and deselect the Encryption check box.

E. Click OK to exit the Properties dialog box. The file is now decrypted.

7. Log on as InTheDark and open the ThisIsSecret.txt file to verify that encryption has been removed by the default recovery agent.

7.7 Examine Your Server Using the Security Configuration Tool Set

This exercise shows how you can examine your server's configuration against predefined guidelines stored in a security template.

Estimated Time: 15 minutes

1. Log on as Administrator.

2. Create a Security Configuration Tool Set console.

   A. From the Start menu, choose Run. In the dialog box that appears, type **MMC** and press Enter.

   B. In the Console dialog box, select Console, Add/Remove Snap-In.

   C. In the Add/Remove Snap-In dialog box, click the Add button.

   D. In the Add Standalone Snap-In dialog box, scroll through the list and double-click Security Configuration and Analysis. Double-click Security Templates. Click Close to continue.

   E. In the Add/Remove Snap-In dialog box, click OK.

   F. At the console, choose Console, Save. When the Save As dialog box appears, enter **Security Configuration and Analysis** and click Save.

G. Expand the internal window in the Security and Configuration Analysis console.

3. Create and modify a Custom Security template for your Windows 2000 Server configurations. You will configure the account lockout policy to allow only two invalid logon attempts.

   A. Expand the Security Templates item and select the entry beneath. (This is the path to the templates on your hard drive.)

   B. In the template list, locate basicsv, right-click it, and choose Save As from the menu that appears.

   C. In the Save As dialog box, type **customsv** in the File Name field and click Save.

   D. Double-click the entry for customsv to display the configuration options.

   E. On the left in the tree, expand the customsv entry to display the following tree: customsv, Account Policies, Account Lockout Policy.

   F. Select the Account Lockout Policy tree, and then double-click the policy Account Lockout Threshold (on the right).

   G. In the Template Security Policy Setting dialog box, set the Lockout Threshold to 2 and click OK. When the Suggested Value Changes dialog box appears, click OK to accept the changes.

   H. Right-click the entry for customsv and choose Save from the menu that appears.

APPLY YOUR KNOWLEDGE

4. Create a configuration database to analyze your server.

   A. In the Security Configuration and Analysis console, right-click the Security Configuration and Analysis item and choose Open Database from the menu that appears.

   B. In the Open Database dialog box, type the name of your server (for example, WIN2000S) in the File Name field and click Open.

   C. In the Import Template dialog box, double-click customsv. This will allow you to analyze your configuration against the custom template you created (a basic server with the lockout policy modified).

5. Analyze your server's configuration against the template.

   A. Right-click the Security Configuration and Analysis item and choose Analyze Computer Now from the menu that appears.

   B. When the Perform Analysis dialog box appears, click OK to accept the default log path.

   C. When the analysis is complete, expand the Security Configuration and Analysis tree to view the account policies. You will probably see non-conformance from some of the Password Policy settings, and you will see that the lockout threshold currently set does not conform to the template (see Figure 7.36). You can tell that some policy setting does not conform because there is a red circle with a white X in it.

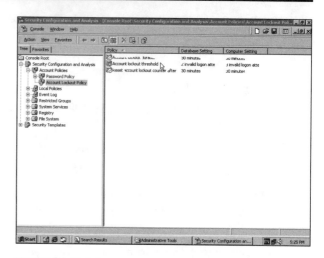

FIGURE 7.36
A red circle with a white "X" in it indicates a deviation in the current configuration from the template being used for the analysis.

6. Configure your server using the template.

   A. Right-click the Security Configuration and Analysis item and choose Configure Computer Now from the menu that appears.

   B. When the Perform Analysis dialog box appears, click OK to accept the default log path.

7. Verify the configuration using the Local Security Policy.

   A. From the Administrative Tools, open the Local Security Policy console.

   B. Expand the Account policies, select the Account Lockout Policy, and note that the Account Lockout Threshold has been changed from 3 to 2.

8. Close the consoles.

APPLY YOUR KNOWLEDGE

Review Questions

1. How are accounts identified internally by Windows 2000, and what is the implication of deleting an account?

2. When a Windows 2000 server is part of a domain, what is the interaction between domain policy and local policy?

3. What criteria apply to an account password when complexity rules are enforced?

4. Logically, what is the rationale for denying most users in your organization the right to log onto a server locally?

5. In order to audit access to a specific file on a Windows 2000 server, what three administrative tasks must first be done?

6. To ensure that all files encrypted by EFS on a Windows 2000 computer can be accessed by at least one person, a recovery agent must be designated. Who is the default recovery agent on a Windows 2000 server?

7. What steps are required for automating the configuration of a Windows 2000 server to a specific security specification using the Security Configuration Tool Set?

Exam Questions

1. Mark is the administrator for a small board games manufacturer. Many of his 20 users are new to computers and have a difficult time understanding the need for security. Mark wants to set up an account policy to ensure that the users must change their passwords once a month and that they cannot reuse a password more than once a year. Which of the following will allow him to do that?

   A. Set the password history to 12 and set the maximum password age to 30.

   B. Set the password history to 12 and set the minimum password age to 30.

   C. Set the maximum password age to 30 and the minimum password age to 28.

   D. Set the password history to 12, the minimum password age to 28, and the maximum password age to 30.

2. Luke is the network administrator for a pharmaceutical company. He has set the account policy to require complex passwords and to require passwords of at least five characters. Using the default Windows 2000 definition of a complex password, which of the following passwords is permissible? (Choose all that apply.)

   A. Kumquat

   B. Tiger359

   C. Pt109

   D. 33b!!bb

3. John is the network administrator of a large multinational oil and gas company. One of the users in the company, Mary Green, just got married and is now Mary Green-Smith-Widget. Mary has access to a number of system resources under her previous name and, of course, needs to continue to access them. What procedure will John have to take in order to ensure that Mary can continue to access the resources she did before?

APPLY YOUR KNOWLEDGE

A. Rename her account from MGreen to MGreenSmithWidget.

B. Rename her account from MGreen to MGreenSmithWidget and update her group memberships to reflect her new name.

C. Rename her account from MGreen to MGreenSmithWidget, update her group memberships to reflect her new name, and update all the DACLs that contain her old name.

D. Delete the MGreen account, create an MGreenSmithWidget account, update her group memberships to reflect her new name, and update all the DACLs that contain her old name.

4. Pricilla is the network administrator for a real estate company. Herod, an unscrupulous agent, has just been fired, and Pricilla must make sure he does not have access to any Windows 2000 resources. Given that Herod's job will be filled in the near future, which is the best course of action for Pricilla to take?

A. Delete Herod's account.

B. Disable Herod's account.

C. Lock Herod's account.

D. Change the password to Herod's account.

5. Paul is the security administrator for a large Windows 2000 domain. He sets the local policy for a Windows 2000 server to allow certain users to log on locally to a print server to do maintenance. However, when these users try to log on, they are presented with the dialog box shown in Figure 7.37. What is the likely cause of the lack of rights for these users?

FIGURE 7.37
This error message appears when a user tries to log in.

A. You cannot grant the right for users to log on locally to a Windows 2000 print server.

B. A domain policy is overriding the local policy.

C. Only Administrators are allowed to log on locally, regardless of the policy settings.

D. A local audit policy is overriding the user rights assignment.

6. Drusilla is the network administrator for a high-fashion clothier. She is responsible for securing a number of Windows 2000 print and application servers. All the print servers need the same security configurations. In addition, all the application servers need the same security configurations, which differ from the print servers. Drusilla needs to ensure that all print servers are configured the same and all application servers are configured the same. In addition, she wants to be able to easily check to see if a server's configuration has been modified from the security plan and to reset it easily. She also would like to be able to hire a student each summer to do an audit without having to do extensive Windows 2000 training.

Required Results:

Ensure that all servers are configured correctly for their function type (application or print).

APPLY YOUR KNOWLEDGE

Optional Desired Results:

Easily check and modify security settings.

Ensure that a person with a minimum of training can audit settings.

Proposed Solution:

Create a security configuration template for each server group (application and print).

Create a configuration database on each server using the appropriate template.

Analyze and configure each server using the configuration databases.

Analysis:

Which result(s) will the proposed solution produce?

A. The proposed solution produces the required result, as well as both optional desired results.

B. The proposed solution produces the required result and one of the optional results.

C. The proposed solution produces the required result, but does not produce either of the optional desired results.

D. The proposed solution does not produce the required result.

7. Drusilla is the network administrator for a high-fashion clothier. She is responsible for securing a number of Windows 2000 Print and Application servers. All the print servers need the same security configurations. In addition, all the application servers need the same security configurations, which differ from the print servers. Drusilla needs to ensure that all print servers are configured the same and all application servers are configured the same. In addition, she wants to be able to easily check to see if a server's configuration has been modified from the security plan and to reset it easily. She also would like to be able to hire a student each summer to do an audit without having to do extensive Windows 2000 training.

Required Results:

Ensure that all servers are configured correctly for their function type (application or print).

Optional Desired Results:

Easily check and modify security settings.

Ensure that a person with a minimum of training can audit settings.

Proposed Solution:

Document the current required settings through written security proposals.

Check each server against the documents and update settings.

Give student auditors the security proposal documents and allow them to audit security settings.

Analysis:

Which result(s) will the proposed solution produce?

A. The proposed solution produces the required result, as well as both optional desired results.

B. The proposed solution produces the required result and one of the optional results.

C. The proposed solution produces the required result, but does not produce either of the optional desired results.

D. The proposed solution does not produce the required result.

APPLY YOUR KNOWLEDGE

8. Felix is the network administrator for the British royal family. He wants to audit access to all files on the central file server. Which of the following are required to configure auditing? (Choose all that apply.)

   A. Use NTFS partitions.

   B. Enable object auditing.

   C. Enable auditing for at least Read events on all files.

   D. Enable auditing for the Everyone group on all files.

   E. All of the above.

9. Timothy is the network administrator for Gulliver's Travels, a small travel company working primarily in the Mediterranean. He has configured auditing on his servers to monitor failed logon access. Which of the following logs will he need to archive regularly to ensure that he can keep an accurate historical record of logon failure?

   A. Application log

   B. System log

   C. Access log

   D. Security log

10. Festus is the network administrator for Clones Are Wee, a sheep manufacturing plant in Edinburgh. He wants to be able to encrypt some of his critical (and sensitive) data on his hard drive. Which of the following represents the elements required for EFS to function properly?

    A. Recovery agent, NTFS partition

    B. Recovery agent, NTFS partition, Certificate Authority

    C. NTFS partition, Certificate Authority

    D. Recovery Agent, Certificate Authority

11. Martha is the network administrator for a house-cleaning company. She wants to be able to create a batch file that encrypts files in the path C:\Data on all ten of her Windows 2000 file servers. Which command should she use to perform this task?

    A. ENCRYPT /e /a c:\data

    B. ENCRYPT /d /a c:\data

    C. CYPHER /e /a c:\data

    D. CYPHER /d /a c:\data

12. Bartholemew is the network administrator for a hat manufacturer. To facilitate the assignment of user rights, a number of global groups are being used at the local computer level. In addition, both domain policy and local policy have been created with respect to rights on local servers. James is in the Maintenance group, which is a global group. Table 7.5 shows the configurations that are interacting. Given that configuration, what is James' effective ability to log on locally to servers in the domain?

TABLE 7.5

DOMAIN AND LOCAL POLICY

Domain Policy	Local Policy
Log on Locally = Maintenance	Log on Locally = James
Deny Logon Locally = James	Deny Logon Locally = not set

APPLY YOUR KNOWLEDGE

A. Maintenance, including James, can log on locally to all servers.

B. Maintenance, with the exception of James, can log on locally to all servers.

C. Maintenance, including James, is denied the ability to log on locally to all servers.

D. Maintenance, with the exception of James, is denied the ability to log on locally to all servers.

13. Peter is the network administrator for a fish processing plant. To facilitate the assignment of user rights, a number of global groups are being used at the local computer level. In addition, both domain policy and local policy have been created with respect to rights on local servers. Jude is in the Maintenance group, a global group. Table 7.6 shows the configurations that are interacting. Given that configuration, what is Jude's effective ability to log on locally to servers in the domain?

TABLE 7.6

DOMAIN AND LOCAL POLICY

Domain Policy	Local Policy
Log on Locally = Maintenance	Log on Locally = Jude
Deny Logon Locally = not set	Deny Logon Locally = Maintenance

A. Maintenance, including Jude, can log on locally to all servers.

B. Maintenance, with the exception of Jude, can log on locally to all servers.

C. Maintenance, including Jude, is denied the ability to log on locally to all servers.

D. Maintenance, with the exception of Jude, is denied the ability to log on locally to all servers.

14. Joseph is the network administrator for a furniture manufacturing company. He wants to be able to configure a number of servers using a configuration database populated with a custom .INF file. What snap-ins are required to be able to perform this configuration? (Choose all that apply.)

A. Security Configuration and Analysis

B. Security Configuration Tool Set

C. Security Templates

D. Security Manager

15. Anna is a technical assistant responsible for server configuration in a large organization. While running an analysis on one of her servers, she found that some of the policy settings have no icons beside them. What does the absence of an icon in an analysis indicate?

A. The server policy deviates from the template in that area.

B. Neither the server policy nor the template policy have that area defined.

C. The server policy is the same as the template policy in that area.

D. The server policy has been changed to reflect the template policy in that area.

Answers to Review Questions

1. Accounts are identified internally using a SID. These SIDs are assigned object access and user rights. Because the SID and not the user name is effectively given access to resources, if an account is deleted, that SID ceases to exist and object access is effectively terminated for that user. If a user account is created with the same user name, the SID will be different, so that account will not have the same access to the resources, and all DACLs and rights must be reassigned. For more information, see the section "Implementing, Configuring, Managing, and Troubleshooting Local Accounts."

2. When a Windows 2000 server is part of a domain, the domain policy settings (when configured) become the effective policy settings. When a policy setting is not configured at the domain level, the local policy becomes the effective policy setting. For more information, see the section "Windows 2000 Member Servers and Policies."

3. Enforcing complexity rules ensures that passwords must conform to three of the following four criteria: lowercase characters, uppercase characters, numbers, and symbolic characters. In addition, these passwords must be at least six characters long and cannot contain any parts of the user name. For more information, see the section "Implementing Local Password Policy."

4. Denying local logon access to servers is recommended because it reduces the local access a user has to a server. Local access is always a potential security problem because it allows access to files on FAT and FAT32 partitions. Removing local logon also means that users will not be tempted to use the server as a workstation. For more information, see the section "Configuring Local Policies on a Windows 2000 Member Server."

5. To audit access to file resources, three things must be done. First, the partition on which the files are located must be (or must be converted to) NTFS. Second, local (or domain) policy must be set to enable auditing of object access. Third, each file resource must have its audit settings configured for the type of access to be audited. For more information, see the section "Implementing, Configuring, Managing, and Troubleshooting Auditing."

6. The default EFS recovery agent on a Windows 2000 server is the local administrator. This person has the ability to decrypt any file encrypted using EFS on that server. For more information, see the section "Encrypting Data Using the Encrypting File System."

7. Before you can automate the configuration of a Windows 2000 computer, you must take the following steps. First, if required, create and configure a custom configuration template. Second, create a configuration database using a predefined or a custom configuration template. Third, configure the server using the configuration database. For more information, see the section "Using the Security Configuration Tool Set."

Answers to Exam Questions

1. **D.** To produce the result required, Mark must implement minimum age, maximum age, and history. Maximum age ensures that passwords are changed at regular intervals. Minimum age ensures that passwords are not changed and then immediately changed back. Finally, history ensures that passwords are not used more than once every 12 cycles (in this case, no more than once a year). For more information, see the section "Implementing Local Password Policy."

2. **B, D.** Complex passwords must be at least six characters long and be a combination of three of the following: uppercase characters, lowercase characters, numbers, and symbols. "Kumquat" does not contain enough variety of characters and "Pt109" does not contain enough characters. For more information, see the section "Implementing Local Password Policy."

3. **A.** Changing Mary's name is sufficient to give her continued access to all the resources she could access before the name change. Because it is the SID of her account, and not her user name, that is actually used to identify her, changing her user name has no effect as far as Windows 2000 is concerned. For more information, see the section "Renaming an Account."

4. **B.** Because Herod will be replaced by another employee, it is not advisable to delete his account. If it is kept in place, changing the name to that of his replacement will ensure that the new employee will have all Herod's old resource access and rights. Herod's account cannot be locked by an administrator, it can only be unlocked. A change in Herod's account password

leaves the opportunity for Herod to try to guess the new password and obtain access to company resources again. Disabling Herod's account is the only reasonable course of action for Pricilla to take. For more information, see the section "Implementing, Configuring, Managing, and Troubleshooting Local Accounts."

5. **B.** Because the rights were granted to the users, the only reason the users would be prevented from logging on is if some other right were overriding it. Because there is no mention of a local policy having been set to disallow local login, the reasonable solution is to suspect that local login has been prevented in the domain policy. For more information, see the section "Windows 2000 Member Servers and Policies."

6. **A.** The solution Drusilla proposes will fulfill the required result as well as the optional results. Not only will she be able to configure each server for its function, she will also be able to easily check and modify both existing and future server security settings. Finally, with a minimum of training, she can show a summer student how to use a configuration database to compare the security settings of the servers against the ideal configuration. For more information, see the section "Using the Security Configuration Tool Set."

7. **C.** Although "easily" is a subjective term, here it can be evaluated objectively. For configuration and auditing to be easy, the information must be readily available, and the configuration must be able to be set with a minimum of effort. Neither of these is the case with written proposals. Although written proposals will ensure that the proposed configurations are documented, and therefore reproducible, checking and configuring

APPLY YOUR KNOWLEDGE

are far from easy. In addition, teaching knowledge of Windows 2000 policies on how to locate policy settings and to check each setting will not be a trivial task either. For more information, see the section "Using the Security Configuration Tool Set."

8. **A, B, C.** To enable auditing, the file resources must be on NTFS partitions, and auditing on objects must be enabled. Finally, at least Read access must be audited for on each file resource. It is required that someone be audited; however, it could be individuals or groups other than the Everyone group so neither D nor E applies. For more information, see the section "Implementing, Configuring, Managing, and Troubleshooting Auditing."

9. **D.** Auditing creates entries in the Security log. To keep an ongoing record of audit results, this log must be archived regularly. For more information, see the section "Implementing, Configuring, Managing, and Troubleshooting Auditing."

10. **A.** All that is needed to implement EFS is a recovery agent (which is the local administrator, by default) and an NTFS (version 5) partition. A Certificate Authority is not required because, in the absence of one, the local server generates its own certificate for EFS encryption. For more information, see the section "Understanding EFS Encryption."

11. **C.** The command-line executable for encrypting is CYPHER. The /e switch indicates encrypt (the /d indicates decrypt). The /a switch indicates the path in which files are to be encrypted. For more information, see the section "Encrypting Data Using the Encrypting File System."

12. **B.** Because domain policy overrides local policy, the Maintenance group is given the right to log on locally. However, because Deny Logon takes precedence over Allow Logon, James is prevented from logging on locally despite his membership in the Maintenance group. For more information, see the sections "Windows 2000 Member Servers and Policies" and "Configuring Local Policies on a Windows 2000 Member Server."

13. **C.** Because domain policy overrides local policy and Deny overrides Allow, the Maintenance group is both allowed to log on as well as denied that right. Therefore, the entire Maintenance group, Jude included, is denied the right to log on locally. For more information, see the sections "Windows 2000 Member Servers and Policies" and "Configuring Local Policies on a Windows 2000 Member Server."

14. **A, C.** Joseph's task is twofold: He must configure custom templates, and he must create and use a configuration database. For the first task, he needs the Configuration Template snap-in, and for the second, he needs the Security Configuration and Analysis snap-in. For more information, see the section "Using the Security Configuration Tool Set."

15. **B.** Two symbols are displayed after an analysis has been performed. Policy settings that conform to the database are indicated with check marks. Policy settings that deviate from the database are indicated with "X"s. Policy settings that are not defined in the database or the server policy have no symbol. For more information, see the section "Analyzing Your Server."

APPLY YOUR KNOWLEDGE

Suggested Readings and Resources

1. Microsoft Windows 2000 Server Resource Kit: *Microsoft Windows 2000 Server Deployment Planning Guide* (Microsoft Press)

    • Chapter 11: Planning Distributed Security

2. Microsoft Windows 2000 Server Resource Kit: *Microsoft Windows 2000 Server Distributed Systems Guide* (Microsoft Press)

    • Chapter 15: Encrypting File System

    • Chapter 22: Group Policy

3. *Microsoft Windows 2000 Professional Resource Kit* (Microsoft Press)

    • Chapter 7: Introduction to Configuration and Management

    • Chapter 13: Security

    • Chapter 23: Windows 2000 Professional on Microsoft Networks

    • Chapter 24: Interoperability with NetWare

4. Microsoft Official Curriculum course 1556: *Administrating Microsoft Windows 2000*

    • Module 2: Setting Up User Accounts

    • Module 5: Administering User Accounts

    • Module 7: Managing Data Storage

5. Microsoft Official Curriculum course 1557: *Installing and Configuring Microsoft Windows 2000*

    • Module 10: Configuring File Resources

6. Microsoft Official Curriculum course 1558: *Advanced Administration for Microsoft Windows 2000*

    • Module 8: Implementing Security in a Windows 2000 Network

7. Microsoft Official Curriculum course 1560: *Updating Support Skills from Microsoft Windows NT 4.0 to Microsoft Windows 2000*

    • Module 12: Securing Windows 2000

8. Microsoft Official Curriculum course 2152: *Supporting Microsoft Windows 2000 Professional*

    • Module 4: Creating and Managing User Accounts

    • Module 10: Implementing Windows 2000 Security

9. Web Sites

    • www.microsoft.com/windows2000

    • www.microsoft.com/train_cert

FINAL REVIEW

Fast Facts

Study and Exam Prep Tips

Practice Exam

The seven chapters of this book cover the objectives for the Windows 2000 Server exam. After having read those chapters, you might be wondering what are the important points that you really need to know? What should you review in that last hour prior to walking into the testing center to take your first (or next) Microsoft certification exam?

The following sections cover the most significant points of the previous seven chapters and provide some insight into the information that makes particularly good exam material. There is no substitute for real-world hands-on experience. However, knowing what to expect on the exam will go a long way towards a passing score. The information that follows provides the material you must know to pass the exam. Don't memorize the concepts given; make sure you understand them, and you will have no difficulty passing the exam.

INSTALLING WINDOWS 2000 SERVER

This section will review information you are required to know about the installation of Windows 2000 Server.

General Installation Notes

When installing, you must remember these things first:

- ◆ The Windows 2000 installation CD-ROM is bootable.

- ◆ You can start Setup by running the command `<CD-ROM drive letter>\i386\WINNT.EXE` from MS-DOS or Windows 3.1.

Fast Facts

INSTALLING, CONFIGURING, AND ADMINISTERING MICROSOFT WINDOWS 2000 SERVER, EXAM (70-215)

◆ Setup can also be started with the command `<CD-ROM drive letter>\i386\WINNT32.EXE` from Windows 9x or Windows NT.

◆ You can also start Setup by running setup.exe in the root of the CD-ROM drive.

◆ Setup boot disks are now made with the `<CD-ROM drive letter>\BOOTDISK\MAKEDISK.EXE` command instead of `WINNT /OX`, and there are four disks.

◆ Minimum requirements are a Pentium 133, 256MB of RAM, and a 1GB disk with 650MB of free space.

◆ Alpha CPUs are not supported.

◆ The Hardware Compatibility List (HCL) should always be checked prior to the purchase of hardware.

◆ The `/CHECKUPGRADEONLY` switch can be used to see if your currently installed software is compatible with Windows 2000.

◆ The System partition is where the BIOS boots from (C:), but the Boot partition is where Windows 2000 system files are located (the partition with the \WINNT directory).

◆ Upgrades may be done from Windows 9x, Windows NT 4, or Windows NT 3.51. Windows NT 3.1 computers will have to be upgraded to Windows NT 3.51 first.

◆ Servers can be licensed either Per Server (limited concurrent connections to the server) or Per Seat (client can connect to unlimited servers).

◆ The default computername is made up from the first eight letters of the company name and a randomly generated name.

◆ The Administrator password and all passwords should be more than seven characters and contain uppercase letters, lowercase letters, and numbers for stronger security.

◆ Windows 2000 computers can be part of a Windows 2000 Active Directory, a Windows NT domain, or a workgroup.

Unattended Installations and Installation Tools

The following are important facts to remember about unattended installations:

◆ Installation scripts (UNATTEND.TXT) can be created using the Setup Manager application, which is found in `<CD-ROM drive letter>\SUPPORT\TOOLS\DEPLOY.CAB`.

◆ Setup Manager can be used to create scripts for the following types of installations: Windows 2000 unattended install, Sysprep install, and Remote Installation Services.

◆ Sysprep removes computer-specific information from an installation so that it can be duplicated using third-party copying utilities.

◆ Remote Installation Services (RIS) requires Active Directory, an authorized DHCP server, a configured DNS server, and a minimum 1GB NTFS partition to be installed on.

◆ An RIS client must meet the Net PC specification, have a PXE compliant network card, or be booted with a RIS Remote boot disk.

◆ Unattended installations can be started using the command `WINNT /U:<scriptname>` or `WINNT32 /UNATTEND:<scriptname>`.

- User interaction for unattended installations can range from providing defaults only to providing no information at all (it's completely unattended). The options are Provide Defaults, Fully Automated, Hide Pages, Read Only, and GUI Attended.

Upgrading a Server from Microsoft Windows NT 4.0

You can upgrade Microsoft Windows NT 4.0 member servers at any time during the deployment of Windows 2000 and Active Directory. Windows 2000 servers are able to be part of a workgroup, a Windows NT domain, or Active Directory.

The upgrade to Windows 2000 can be started with either WINNT32 or the SETUP program or by using the CD Autorun.

The Report System Compatibility option will provide a detailed report of which components on your system might not function after the upgrade.

Deploying Service Packs

Service packs under Windows 2000 are similar to service packs under Windows NT 4.0. Support for the /slip switch allows for the service pack to be applied to the installation source.

Troubleshooting Failed Installations

The /checkupgradeonly switch for WINNT32.EXE allows you to detect potential problems prior to the installation.

Reasons for failed installs include the following:

- Minimum hardware requirements not met
- Hardware not on the HCL
- Media errors on installation media
- Failure of a dependency service to start
- Inability to connect to the domain controller
- Automated installation script errors
- RIS installation requirements not met

INSTALLING, CONFIGURING, AND TROUBLESHOOTING ACCESS TO RESOURCES

This section will review components that are required for access to network resources.

Group Management in Windows 2000

The types of groups that exist in Windows 2000 are listed in Table 1.

TABLE 1
TYPES OF GROUPS THAT EXIST UNDER WINDOWS 2000

Group	*Location*	*Contains*	*Used*
Universal	Active Directory	Domain users from any domain. Domain global groups from any domain. Universal groups from any domain.	To create single groups that are accessible from any domain in Active Directory, which contains users or groups from several domains.
Global	Active Directory	Domain users from own domain. Domain global groups from own domain.	To group common users together.
Domain Local	Active Directory	Domain users from any domain. Domain global groups from any domain. Universal groups from any domain.	To grant permissions to domain or local resources.
Local	Local PC	Domain users from any domain. Domain global groups from any domain. Universal groups from any domain.	Same as domain local groups. Should only be used when domain local groups have not been created or when the computer is not a member of Active Directory.
Security	Active Directory	N/A	Used to assign permissions and rights. Security groups can also be used as email distribution lists.
Distribution	Active Directory	N/A	Used as an email distribution list.

Universal groups and group nesting is available only when Active Directory domains are running in Native mode. Only local and global groups are available when the domain is running in Mixed mode.

Always try to place user accounts into global groups, place global groups into domain local groups, and apply permissions to the domain local group. (Use AGLP and UGLP as mnemonic devices to help you remember this strategy).

Domain local groups can be used on member servers or workstations that are part of Active Directory.

Network Printer Management

Default permission to share directories are granted to these groups:

◆ Administrators

◆ Server Operators

◆ Power Users

Print Operators have the right to share printers.

Share Management

Any user that is given the right to Create Permanent Shared Objects may also share directories.

Users may be granted or denied access to a share through three permission levels:

- Full Control
- Change
- Read

If a user is denied access at a specific level, he is denied that level of permission, regardless of other granted permissions. The denial of access overrides all other permissions.

Hidden shares can be created by appending a dollar sign ($) to the end of the share name.

NTFS Security

NTFS permissions are applied at a file or folder level. These permissions apply to both local users on the PC, and users accessing through shared directories across the network.

NTFS permissions can only be applied on NTFS partitions. You can convert other partitions to NTFS but keep data intact by using the CONVERT command.

Basic folder-level NTFS permissions:

- Full Control
- Modify
- Read & Execute
- List Folder Contents
- Read
- Write

Advanced permissions allow you to be more granular in your permission assignments.

Basic file-level permissions do not include List Folder Contents.

When accessing files from across the network, you will require the permission at both the Share level and the NTFS File level. For example, to read a file, you would have to be granted the Read permission at both levels.

Distributed File System (Dfs)

Distributed file system (Dfs) hides the physical layout of the network from users.

Windows 95 requires Dfs client software. Windows NT 4.0, Windows 2000, and Windows 98 already have a client built into the OS.

Dfs roots look like shared directories, and Dfs links point to existing shared directories on other servers.

Standalone Dfs is implemented outside of Active Directory.

Domain or Fault-Tolerant Dfs can be implemented only on servers that are part of an Active Directory domain. It also provides replication of data and load balancing between specified replica servers.

Working with Web Services

Windows 2000 includes Internet Information Server (IIS) 5. When it is installed, two service accounts are created:

- IUSR_<*SERVERNAME*> is used for directory access by the IIS service when anonymous connections are made to the server.
- IWAM_<*SERVERNAME*> is used when the server has to start out-of-process applications.

Directories can be published for HTTP access either through the Web Sharing tab of the folder's Properties dialog box or through Internet Services Manager.

You can specify any of the following options when creating a virtual directory:

◆ Read

◆ Write

◆ Script Source Access

◆ Directory Browsing

◆ Application Permissions (Script or Execute)

Directories that are published for Web access are similar to shared directories in that you must have the permissions (like Read) granted to all Web users, and you must have equivalent NTFS permissions.

Virtual Web servers can be accessed and identified by IP address, by TCP port number (default 80), or by a Host Header (DNS name).

The Administration site is assigned a random TCP port number between 2,000 and 9,999.

Execute and Script permissions on Web directories are considered to be a security risk. These permissions are required on directories that contain Active Server Pages (ASP).

There are four type of authentication for Web server access:

◆ *Anonymous* uses the IUSR_<SERVERNAME> account.

◆ *Basic Authentication* uses clear text passwords using an authentication domain.

◆ *Digest Authentication for Windows Domain Servers* uses a hashed password.

◆ *Integrated Windows Authentication* uses Windows NT Challenge Response.

Access to your Web site can be restricted or granted by IP address, IP address and subnet mask, or Internet domain name.

Secure access to your Web site can also be granted through SSL and a Certificate Authority. Windows 2000 can act as a Certificate Authority.

When troubleshooting access problems, check the NTFS permissions granted to IUSR_<SERVERNAME>, IP address or domain name restrictions, and configured authentication methods.

Local Printer Management

You should know the following printing system terminology:

◆ *Printer.* Software that is installed on your computer that interfaces with a physical printing device (equivalent to a print queue).

◆ *Printing device.* A physical device that transfers an electronic image onto print media.

◆ *PCL (Printer Control Language).* A language or protocol that is used to communicate with a printer. Developed by Hewlett-Packard, PCL is predominant in Windows-based laser printers.

◆ *Postscript.* Another language that is used to communicate with printers. Postscript is used with Windows-based printing, but is predominant in Macintosh and UNIX printing.

◆ *RAW.* Formatted in the printer's native language.

◆ *EMF (Enhanced Metafile).* A graphic format that acts as an intermediary stage between the application and RAW output. EMFs are used to speed up the time is takes for an application to finish processing a document.

Standard TCP/IP ports are used to print to TCP/IP-based printers, such as UNIX print servers and HP JetDirect printers. When printing to UNIX print servers, it is better to install Print Services for UNIX and print using an LPR (Line Printer Remote) port. Print Services for UNIX will also allow UNIX clients to print to Windows 2000 shared printers.

When sharing a printer, Windows 2000 is capable of deploying drivers for these other operating systems: Windows 95, Windows 98, Windows NT 4.0, Windows NT 3.51, Windows NT 3.5, and Windows NT 3.1. The client must first attempt connection to the printer on the Windows 2000 server.

Printer pooling allows you to use one printer to print to several identical devices.

You can set up several printers to print to the same printing device, which allows you to schedule jobs at different priorities.

Printer permissions:

◆ Print

◆ Manage Printers

◆ Manager Documents

The default permissions on a printer give everyone the permission to print and give creator owner the permission to manager documents.

You can access a printer using one of three distinct methods:

◆ Through the standard Printer dialog box.

◆ Through a normal network browse statement like
   \\<servername>\<printer>.

◆ Through a Web browser by connecting to
   http://<servername>/printers.

Access to this virtual Web directory is restricted to valid Windows 2000 accounts. The Windows 2000 computer acting as the print server for the print device must also be running IIS 5.

Interoperability with NetWare

All communications from Windows 2000 to Novell NetWare still require the IPX/SPX or NWLink protocol.

With NWLink installed, you will be able to communicate with client/server applications running on a NetWare server or have NetWare clients connect to client/server applications that are running on your server.

Gateway Services for NetWare (GSNW) or Client Services for NetWare (CSNW) is required to access file and print resources on a NetWare server.

GSNW allows your server to act as a gateway by providing access to NetWare resources through shares that appear on your Windows 2000 server. This allows computers that have neither IPX/SPX or a NetWare client to access the Novell systems through the Windows 2000 server.

The gateway requires a user account to be created on the NetWare server. This account should have supervisor permissions and be placed in a group named NTGATEWAY.

File and Print Services for NetWare (FPNW) allows NetWare clients to access shared resources on your Windows 2000 server. These resources are shared specifically to NetWare clients through the Create Shared Folder Wizard, which is launched from the Shared Folders object in the Computer Management tool.

Interoperability with Apple Macintosh

When you install File and Print Services for Macintosh, the AppleTalk protocol is also installed.

The name of the server might appear different to Macintosh clients than it does to Windows clients. To configure the server name, right-click on the Shared Folders object in the Computer Management tool.

Print Services for UNIX

Print Services for UNIX allow you to print to UNIX Line Printer Daemons (LPD) and allow UNIX clients to print to your printers using their Line Printer Remote clients (LPR).

The LPD service under Windows 2000 is also called Print Services for UNIX.

CONFIGURING AND TROUBLESHOOTING HARDWARE DEVICES AND DRIVERS

This section will review the configuration of hardware devices and their drivers.

Configuring Hardware Devices

Windows 2000 has two separate processing areas, Kernel mode and User mode. Applications run in User mode, and most drivers load into Kernel mode.

Windows 2000 supports Plug and Play (PNP). This means that a specific manager service allocates hardware resources like IO addresses, IRQs, and DMA channels.

The Device manager is used to view and modify settings for most drivers.

You can use hardware profiles when you need to maintain several different hardware configurations. This is often the case with laptop computers where, for example, you might or might not be plugging into a docking station.

Configuring Driver Signing Options

Windows 2000 supports a feature called Driver Signing. This allows vendors of products to send their drivers to Microsoft for testing.

An administrator gets to set one of the following policy options for driver signing:

◆ Install the Driver, Signed or Not Signed

◆ Warn When Installing Unsigned Drivers

◆ Only Install Signed Drivers; Prevent the Installation of Unsigned Drivers

Updating Device Drivers

The Device manager is used to update drivers to newer versions. These drivers may be accessed from one of the following media:

◆ Floppy disk

◆ CD-ROM

◆ Hard drive or UNC pathname

◆ Windows Update (a special location on Microsoft's Web site)

Troubleshooting Problems with Hardware

Most hardware problems fall into three categories:

◆ Improperly installed or configured hardware

◆ Hardware resource conflicts

◆ Incorrect or outdated drivers

Most hardware errors are logged into the system log. This information usually includes the driver that is having the problem and a short description of the problem. These messages will occur before the first Event log item and will have red Xs in front of the messages.

The Device manager displays each non-functioning device with a red X in front of it.

MANAGING, MONITORING, AND OPTIMIZING SYSTEM PERFORMANCE, RELIABILITY, AND AVAILABILITY

Windows 2000 supports both multiprocessing and multitasking.

Most multitasking is pre-emptive. Cooperative multitasking occurs when multiple 16-bit Windows applications run in a common application memory space.

Table 2 lists the number of processors supported in different versions of Windows 2000.

TABLE 2
PROCESSOR SUPPORT UNDER WINDOWS 2000

OS Version	Number of Processors Supported
Windows 2000 Professional	2
Windows 2000 Server	4
Windows 2000 Advanced Server	8
Windows 2000 Datacenter Server	32

Managing Processes

Applications run at one of 32 priority levels that range from 0 to 31.

Priorities of 16 and above are not normally used by applications.

Applications with the highest priority get the most processing time.

Task Manager can be used to examine and change application priorities, and Performance Monitor can be used to examine application priorities.

Table 3 contains a list of priority names and the base values for the priority levels.

TABLE 3
PRIORITY LEVELS UNDER WINDOWS 2000

Level Name	Priority Base
Real Time	24
High	13
Above Normal	10
Normal	8
Below Normal	6
Low	4

You can set priorities at runtime by using the START command (for example, START /ABOVENORMAL WORDPAD.EXE).

Optimizing Disk Performance

You can optimize disk performance by using some of the following options:

◆ Investing in a hardware RAID solution

◆ Implementing a Windows 2000 software RAID solution

◆ Organizing files that are used by the operating system and its services to reduce disk contention

◆ Setting up regular defragmentation of disks to allow for quicker access to files

Monitoring and Optimizing

Performance Monitor supports three views:

◆ Chart View

◆ Histogram View

◆ Report View

Counter logs and trace logs can be use to record performance counters so they can be viewed or analyzed later.

Counter logs can be viewed with the System Monitor snap-in or other applications, depending on the format the log is saved in:

◆ *Text file.* Comma-Separated Values (CSV)

◆ *Text file.* Tab-Separated Values (TSV)

◆ *Binary file.* Readable in System Monitor

◆ *Binary Circular file.* Same as above, but reuses the log file as needed to keep file sizes down

Trace logs can be read by third-party applications, and logging is based on computer activity.

Alerts can be configured to monitor server performance and alert administrators.

Only physical disk performance counters are enabled by default; to enable logical disk performance counters you must run DISKPERF -Y or DISKPERF -YV from the command prompt.

To use the Network Segment data counters, you need to install the Network Monitor Agent. This will allow you to monitor the performance of traffic going to or coming from the local network segment.

The following resources are critical to the monitor:

◆ Memory

◆ Disks

◆ Processor

◆ Network

Refer to Table 4.3 in Chapter 4, "Managing, Monitoring, and Optimizing System Performance, Reliability, and Availability" to familiarize yourself with some of the available counters. Specific counters will not likely be on the exam.

Managing System State Data and User Data

System state can be backed up using the Windows 2000 Backup utility. The system state backup contains the following:

◆ Active Directory service

◆ Boot files

◆ Certificate Services

◆ Cluster service information

◆ COM+ Class Registrations

◆ Registry

◆ SYSVOL directory

The Registry can also be backed up by creating an Emergency Repair Disk (ERD) and restored by booting into the Last Known Good Configuration or by using the Emergency Repair process.

To recover system state and user data, it must have been backed up. The Backup utility provided with Windows 2000 offers five types of backups:

◆ Normal backup

◆ Copy

◆ Incremental

◆ Differential

◆ Daily copy

Windows 2000 Backup Utility (NTBACKUP.EXE) is a smaller version of BackupExec from Veritus software.

NTBackup supports several command-line switches.

When booting a system, you will have the option of pressing F8 to view a Windows 95-like Boot menu. It includes options for starting the computer in the following modes:

◆ Safe Mode

◆ Safe Mode with Networking

◆ Safe Mode with Command Prompt

◆ Enable Boot Logging

◆ Enable VGA Mode

◆ Last Known Good Configuration

◆ Directory Service Restore Mode

◆ Debugging Mode

Several of these boot modes can be used to recover components of your system.

The Recovery console allows for the running of several command-line utilities that can be used to repair your system. It can be accessed from the boot menu if it was previously installed. If the Recovery console is not installed, you can still access it by booting from the Windows 2000 CD.

MANAGING, CONFIGURING, AND TROUBLESHOOTING STORAGE USE

Storage use covers all areas that deal with magnetic and optical media and the ways that data is loaded on that media.

User Profiles

User profiles contain settings that are specific to individual users.

There are three types of user profiles:

◆ Local profiles

◆ Roaming personal profiles

◆ Roaming mandatory profiles

You create mandatory profiles by renaming a roaming profile's NTUSER.DAT file to NTUSER.MAN. If this profile is not available at logon, a local profile will be used, but changes will not be saved.

Mandatory profiles can also be created by placing a MAN extension on the folder that contains the profile. If this profile is not available, the user will be denied a logon.

The All Users profile is added to all other loaded user profiles.

Working with Disks and Volumes

This section will review important facts with regard to how disks and volumes may be implemented on your system.

Upgrading basic disks to dynamic disks requires 1MB of unallocated space on the disk.

Booting Windows 2000

The master boot record is found on the System partition. Windows 2000 loads the operating system kernel from the Boot partition. The Boot partition contains the WINNT directory.

This is the boot order of the system files on the System partition:

- ◆ NTLDR
- ◆ BOOT.INI
- ◆ NTDETECT.COM
- ◆ NTBOOTDD.SYS

NTLDR is responsible for controlling the boot process until NTOSKRNL takes over the job.

BOOT.INI is used by NTLDR to display the boot loader menu.

NTDETECT.COM conducts hardware detection and returns the results to NTLDR.

NTBOOTDD.SYS is the SCSI driver for a SCSI adapter. This file will exist only if you chose to install Windows 2000 on a SCSI disk that has a controller with the SCSI BIOS disabled.

ARC pathnames are used to identify the location of the boot files that NTLDR is to load. A typical ARC pathname identifies a disk controller, disk, partition, and directory from which to load the OS. This is a typical ARC pathname: multi(0)disk(0)rdisk(0)partition(1)\ <OS_Path>.

ARC paths will start with either "scsi" (for SCSI controllers that have their BIOS disabled) or "multi" (for all other drives).

Disk Volumes

Windows 2000 supports disk features like limited RAID and volume sets by using modified partition tables on a disk. These updated disks are referred to as dynamic.

Basic disks are used to support backward compatibility.

The following types of volumes are supported on dynamic disks:

- ◆ Simple
- ◆ Spanned
- ◆ Mirrored (RAID-1)
- ◆ Striped (RAID-0)
- ◆ Striping with Parity (RAID-5)

Only Mirrored and RAID-5 volumes are fault tolerant and protect your data.

Mirrored volumes can also be referred to as RAID-1 volumes; striped volumes can also be referred to as RAID-0 volumes.

Only Mirrored and Simple volumes can contain the System and Boot partitions.

The Disk Management snap-in is used to manage disk partitions. It is part of the Computer Management snap-in.

Partitions Under Windows 2000

New partitions can be assigned a drive letter, left without a drive letter, or mounted into an empty folder on an NTFS volume.

Partitions can be formatted as FAT, FAT32, or NTFS.

There is a 32GB limit for FAT32 partitions that are created on Windows 2000.

NTFS partitions will be required to support the following features:

◆ NetWare Migration

◆ Services for Macintosh

◆ File and Print Services for NetWare

◆ Extending Spanned Volumes

◆ Active Directory

◆ Remote Installation Services

◆ Disk Quotas

◆ Compression

◆ Encryption

CONVERT.EXE can be used to convert other file systems to NTFS.

Configuring Data Compression

Compression can be used to save disk space, but it may decrease access time and overall server performance.

Compression is a file-level or folder-level attribute, like NTFS permissions. The settings for enabling compression are stored in the property pages of both files and folders.

Compression can be enabled at the command prompt with COMPACT.EXE. This utility can also be used to report on the amount of compression that was achieved.

Certain files (mostly OS files) that are always in use cannot be compressed.

You can have the names of compressed files displayed in blue by changing your viewing options.

Compression settings are always inherited from the parent folder. Files that are *moved* into a folder (not copied) retain their compression settings when moved within the same partition or volume.

Monitoring and Configuring Disk Quotas

Disk quotas are enabled in the properties of a disk.

Quota settings for all new users of a drive are enabled on the Quota tab of the disk properties. Quota entries can also be configured for individual users.

You can configure warning levels for disk quotas, and you can specify whether or not to enforce the quota limits.

Quota violations can be written to the event logs.

Quotas cannot be set for groups (with the exception of the Administrators group).

Recovering from Disk Failures

To recover from boot sector problems, you can temporarily boot from a Windows 2000 boot disk that meets the following requirements:

◆ The disk was formatted on a computer running Windows 2000.

◆ The disk contains NTDLR, NTDETECT.COM, NTDLR, and NTBOOTDD.SYS. The last file is the computer-specific SCSI driver, which exists only on systems that have their SCSI BIOS disabled.

◆ The disk must have a BOOT.INI file with the machine-specific ARC settings.

You can often solve boot sector problems by running an Emergency Repair from the four server boot disks or by booting from CD.

To create the four required Setup disks, run `<2000_CD>\BOOTDISKS\MAKEBOOT.EXE` or `MAKEBT32.EXE`.

To restore a backup, you must have a working installation of Windows 2000.

To recover from one disk in a mirrored volume that's failing, replace the failed disk and choose to reactivate the disk. This presumes that the system is able to boot from the primary mirror or that the system has been reconfigured to do so.

To recover from one disk in a RAID-5 volume, replace the damaged disk and choose to repair the volume.

Configuring Windows 2000 Network Connections

Networking components operate in both Kernel mode and User mode.

Network connections are configured through the Network and Dial-Up Connections folder. Network adapters appear there by default, and the computer operator can add dial-up connections, VPN connections, and direct connections.

Configuring Shared Access

Shared access to networks can be configured through either Internet Connection Sharing or Network Address Translation (NAT).

NAT is a more robust and configurable routing protocol.

NAT is configured through the Routing and Remote Access snap-in.

NAT allows you to apply complex filtering based on protocol or port numbers.

Configuring a Virtual Private Network (VPN)

Windows 2000 supports two industry standard tunneling protocols: Point-to-Point Tunneling Protocol (PPTP) and Layer Two Tunneling Protocol (L2TP).

L2TP relies on protocols like IPSEC for its encryption, and it only provides a tunnel connection with authentication.

These technologies can be used with Routing RAS to provide secure demand-dial office connections.

Configuring Network Protocols

The following basic network protocols are supported for Windows 2000 communications:

◆ TCP/IP

◆ NWLINK (IPX/SPX)

◆ NetBIOS Frames (NetBEUI)

TCP/IP

TCP/IP assigns a unique 32-bit address to each system on a network.

The subnet mask is used to determine whether a communication partner is local or remote.

A gateway or router is used to forward remote data. TCP/IP is a routable protocol.

TCP/IP can be configured manually or dynamically through Dynamic Host Configuration Protocol (DHCP).

Table 4 lists useful TCP/IP utilities and their uses.

A single DHCP server can be configured to handle scopes for multiple segments. Each network segment requires a system to process DHCP traffic. This could be any of the following:

◆ DHCP server

◆ DHCP Relay Agent

◆ Router that supports Bootp forwarding

TABLE 4
TCP/IP TROUBLESHOOTING UTILITIES

Utility	Function
IPCONFIG (IP Configuration)	Used to see the current TCP/IP configuration. It can also be used to release and renew DHCP-based addresses.
Ping (Packet Inter-Network Grouper)	Used to test basic TCP/IP connectivity with other hosts. It can also display the first nine routers that are passed through.
NSLOOKUP (Name Server Lookup)	Used to troubleshoot DNS resolution problems. It can also display proper DNS names when provided an IP address.
TRACERT (Trace Route)	Used to display the full router path between your computer and a remote host. It will also let you see which routers are the busiest.
NBTSTAT (NetBIOS over TCP/IP Statistics)	Used to display and reset the NetBIOS name cache on your computer.
ARP (Address Resolution Protocol)	Used to display and modify the ARP cache on your computer.
NET	Used to establish connections with Windows-based servers. It also supports several switches that allow you to see the current configuration and statistics.

DNS servers resolve TCP/IP hostnames; WINS servers resolve NetBIOS names. Active Directory relies on DNS for name resolution services.

The four NetBIOS node types are:

◆ B-node (Broadcast)

◆ P-node (Peer)

◆ M-node (Mixed)

◆ H-node (Hybrid)

NWLINK (IPX/SPX)

NWLINK is used primarily for communicating with NetWare servers.

NWLINK runs a type of sub-protocol called a frame-type. Frame-types include the following:

◆ 802.2

◆ 802.3

◆ Ethernet II

◆ Ethernet Snap

◆ Token Ring

◆ Token Ring Snap

To communicate with NWLINK, computers must share a common frame-type or must be able to communicate with a router that supports both frame-types.

802.2 is the current industry standard frame-type.

NetBEUI

NetBEUI is a non-routable protocol.

NetBEUI is self configuring.

Network Monitor is required to do troubleshooting of NetBEUI because it does not have its own diagnostic utilities.

Configuring Remote Access

Remote access deals with most aspects of serial communication.

Configuring Inbound Connections

There are two major dial-up line protocols: SLIP (Serial Line Interface Protocol) and PPP (Point-to-Point Protocol). Windows 2000 is able to dial out using either of these protocols, but it will accept inbound connections only on PPP.

Authentication services for inbound connections can be provided by a Remote Authentication Dial-In User Service (RADIUS) server. Windows 2000 Server can act as a RADIUS server.

In addition to clear text, Windows 2000 supports the following dial-up authentication protocols:

◆ EAP

◆ MS-CHAP v2

◆ CHAP

◆ SPAP

◆ PAP

Multi-link allows multiple client modems to be dialed to multiple server modems to increase dial-in bandwidth.

Bandwidth Allocation Protocol (BAP) can be used to reduce the amount of bandwidth to some users so that all users get their share.

Creating a Remote Access Policy

Dial-in permissions can be granted to the user account, or they can be set for all users through the Remote Access Policy. The default setting for all users is to follow the RAS Policy.

If no Remote Access Policies are defined for a domain, all users will be denied access.

If Verify Caller ID is selected and the appropriate hardware is not installed, access will be denied.

Configuring Terminal Services

The inclusion of Terminal Services in the Windows 2000 operating system will greatly increase the popularity of these services.

Terminal Services are now included with the Windows 2000 operating system. Two remote administration user licenses are provided with the product.

Terminal Services License Server is required to run the Terminal Services in Application Mode.

Terminal Services allows a wide variety of clients including the following:

- ◆ Windows 2000 (all types)
- ◆ Windows NT 4.0
- ◆ Windows 9x
- ◆ Windows for Workgroups (3.11)
- ◆ Windows CE clients (appropriately configured)
- ◆ Windows-based terminals ("thin clients")

Terminal Services uses Remote Desktop Protocol-Transmission Control Protocol (RDP-TCP) for communications. Citrix ICA protocol support can be purchased from Citrix.

Client installation disks can be made with the Terminal Services Client Creator. The clients are also available in the \WINNT\SYSTEM32\CLIENTS directory.

All clients require the right to log in locally.

The Change User command or the Add/Remove Programs Control Panel should be used to install applications.

IMPLEMENTING, MONITORING, AND TROUBLESHOOTING SECURITY

This section will review several features of Windows 2000 that make it more secure.

Encrypt Data on a Hard Disk by Using Encrypting File System (EFS)

Encryption can be enabled on NTFS volumes.

When a file is encrypted, the public keys of the user who is encrypting the file, as well as all currently configured recovery agents, are included in the file.

The private key of a user or recovery agent is used to decrypt a file. Your key must be in the file originally in order for you to be able to decrypt the file.

The recovery agent is able to decrypt files to allow for increased recoverability of the files. By default, the local Administrator is the recovery agent.

CIPHER.EXE is a command-line utility to encrypt or decrypt files.

Encryption is an advanced file attribute of the file.

Encryption is inherited from the parent folder when a file is created in a folder or copied into a folder. If you move or copy a file into a folder, it retains its current encryption setting.

Encryption does not prevent a file from being seen and having its properties read, it only prevents the contents from being read. NTFS permissions are still required to prevent the file from being seen, examined, or deleted.

Policies in a Windows 2000 Environment

Policies can be managed locally or through Active Directory.

Policies are configured through the Group Policy snap-in.

ADM files act as templates for the Group Policy objects. POL files contain a list of Registry entries that are supposed to be applied.

Configuring Auditing

Auditing is usually implemented in two levels. Some items (such as logon success) can be enabled directly though the audit policy, whereas others (such as auditing the NT file system) require object-level configuration.

Audit results are stored in the audit log, which can be viewed with the Event Viewer.

Auditing can track failures as well as successes.

Auditing can be configured separately on individual computers, or it can be configured on all computers in a domain through a Group Policy Object (GPO).

The following items can be enabled through the Audit Policy:

- ◆ Account logon
- ◆ Account management
- ◆ Directory service access
- ◆ Logon
- ◆ Object access
- ◆ Policy change
- ◆ Privilege use
- ◆ Process tracking
- ◆ System

Configuring Accounts

Each user account is identified by a unique Security Identifier (SID).

An account can be renamed without losing the permissions associated with it.

Each of the users on a system should have his or her own account.

Administrator and Guest are the two default system accounts; they cannot be deleted but can be renamed.

Configuring an Account Policy

Account policies can be managed locally or through Active Directory.

Account policies enable you to set the following options:

- ◆ Password history
- ◆ Minimum age
- ◆ Maximum age
- ◆ Minimum length
- ◆ Complexity
- ◆ Reverse encryption storage
- ◆ Account lockout

Using the Security Configuration Tool Set

The Security Configuration Tool Set is used to create and apply security templates to your system. Windows 2000 ships with the following templates:

◆ Basicdc.inf

◆ Securedc.inf

◆ Hisecdc.inf

◆ Basicsv.inf

◆ Basicwk.inf

◆ Securews.inf

◆ Hisecws.inf

◆ Compatws.inf

This element of the book provides you with some general guidelines for preparing for a certification exam. It is organized into four sections. The first section addresses your learning style and how it affects your preparation for the exam. The second section covers your exam preparation activities and general study tips. This is followed by an extended look at the Microsoft Certification exams, including a number of specific tips that apply to the various Microsoft exam formats and question types. Finally, changes in Microsoft's testing policies, and how these might affect you, are discussed.

LEARNING STYLES

To better understand the nature of preparation for the test, it is important to understand learning as a process. You probably are aware of how you best learn new material. You may find that outlining works best for you, or, as a visual learner, you may need to "see" things. Whatever your learning style, test preparation takes place over time. Obviously, you shouldn't start studying for these exams the night before you take them; it is very important to understand that learning is a developmental process. Understanding it as a process helps you focus on what you know and what you have yet to learn.

Thinking about how you learn should help you recognize that learning takes place when you are able to match new information to old. You have some previous experience with computers and networking. Now you are preparing for this certification exam. Using this book, software, and supplementary materials will not just add incrementally to what you know; as you study, the organization of your knowledge actually restructures as you integrate new information into your existing knowledge base. This will lead you to a more comprehensive understanding of the tasks and concepts

Study and Exam Prep Tips

outlined in the objectives and of computing in general. Again, this happens as a result of a repetitive process rather than a singular event. Keep this model of learning in mind as you prepare for the exam, and you will make better decisions concerning what to study and how much more studying you need to do.

STUDY TIPS

There are many ways to approach studying just as there are many different types of material to study. However, the tips that follow should work well for the type of material covered on the certification exams.

Study Strategies

Although individuals vary in the ways they learn information, some basic principles of learning apply to everyone. You should adopt some study strategies that take advantage of these principles. One of these principles is that learning can be broken into various depths. Recognition (of terms, for example) exemplifies a more surface level of learning in which you rely on a prompt of some sort to elicit recall. Comprehension or understanding (of the concepts behind the terms, for example) represents a deeper level of learning. The ability to analyze a concept and apply your understanding of it in a new way represents a further depth of learning.

Your learning strategy should enable you to know the material at a level or two deeper than mere recognition. This will help you perform well on the exams. You will know the material so thoroughly that you can easily handle the recognition-level types of questions used in multiple-choice testing. You will also be able to apply your knowledge to solve new problems.

Macro and Micro Study Strategies

One strategy that can lead to this deeper learning includes preparing an outline that covers all the objectives and subobjectives for the particular exam you are working on. You should delve a bit further into the material and include a level or two of detail beyond the stated objectives and subobjectives for the exam. Then expand the outline by coming up with a statement of definition or a summary for each point in the outline.

An outline provides two approaches to studying. First, you can study the outline by focusing on the organization of the material. Work your way through the points and sub-points of your outline with the goal of learning how they relate to one another. For example, be sure you understand how each of the main objective areas is similar to and different from another. Then, do the same thing with the subobjectives; be sure you know which subobjectives pertain to each objective area and how they relate to one another.

Next, you can work through the outline, focusing on learning the details. Memorize and understand terms and their definitions, facts, rules and strategies, advantages and disadvantages, and so on. In this pass through the outline, attempt to learn detail rather than the big picture (the organizational information that you worked on in the first pass through the outline).

Research has shown that attempting to assimilate both types of information at the same time seems to interfere with the overall learning process. Separate your studying into these two approaches, and you will perform better on the exam.

Active Study Strategies

The process of writing down and defining objectives, subobjectives, terms, facts, and definitions promotes a more active learning strategy than merely reading the material. In human information-processing terms, writing forces you to engage in more active encoding of the information. Simply reading over it exemplifies more passive processing.

Next, determine whether you can apply the information you have learned by attempting to create examples and scenarios on your own. Think about how or where you could apply the concepts you are learning. Again, write down this information to process the facts and concepts in a more active fashion.

The hands-on nature of the step-by-step tutorials and exercises at the ends of the chapters provide further active learning opportunities that will reinforce concepts as well.

Common-Sense Strategies

Finally, you should also follow common-sense practices when studying. Study when you are alert, reduce or eliminate distractions, and take breaks when you become fatigued.

Pre-Testing Yourself

Pre-testing allows you to assess how well you are learning. One of the most important aspects of learning is what has been called "meta-learning." Meta-learning has to do with realizing when you know something well or when you need to study some more. In other words, you recognize how well or how poorly you have learned the material you are studying.

For most people, this can be difficult to assess objectively on their own. Practice tests are useful in that they reveal more objectively what you have learned and what you have not learned. You should use this information to guide review and further studying. Developmental learning takes place as you cycle through studying, assessing how well you have learned, then reviewing, and then assessing again until you feel you are ready to take the exam.

You may have noticed the practice exam included in this book. Use it as part of the learning process. The *ExamGear, Training Guide Edition* test simulation software included on the CD also provides you with an excellent opportunity to assess your knowledge.

You should set a goal for your pre-testing. A reasonable goal would be to score consistently in the 90-percent range.

See Appendix C, "Using the *ExamGear, Training Guide Edition* Software," for more explanation of the test simulation software.

EXAM PREP TIPS

Having mastered the subject matter, the final preparatory step is to understand how the exam will be presented. Make no mistake: A Microsoft Certified Professional (MCP) exam will challenge both your knowledge and your test-taking skills. This section starts with the basics of exam design, reviews a new type of exam format, and concludes with hints targeted to each of the exam formats.

The MCP Exam

Every MCP exam is released in one of three basic formats. What's being called exam format here is really little more than a combination of the overall exam structure and the presentation method for exam questions.

Understanding the exam formats is key to good preparation because the format determines the number of questions presented, the difficulty of those questions, and the amount of time allowed to complete the exam.

Each exam format uses many of the same types of questions. These types or styles of questions include several types of traditional multiple-choice questions, multiple-rating (or scenario-based) questions, and simulation-based questions. Some exams include other types of questions that ask you to drag and drop objects on the screen, reorder a list, or categorize things. Still other exams ask you to answer these types of questions in response to a case study you have read. It's important that you understand the types of questions you will be asked and the actions required to properly answer them.

The rest of this section addresses the exam formats and then tackles the question types. Understanding the formats and question types will help you feel much more comfortable when you take the exam.

Exam Format

As mentioned above, there are three basic formats for the MCP exams: the traditional fixed-form exam, the adaptive form, and the case study form. As its name implies, the fixed-form exam presents a fixed set of questions during the exam session. The adaptive form, however, uses only a subset of questions drawn from a larger pool during any given exam session. The case study form includes case studies that serve as the basis for answering the various types of questions.

Fixed-Form

A fixed-form computerized exam is based on a fixed set of exam questions. The individual questions are presented in random order during a test session. If you take the same exam more than once, you won't necessarily see the exact same questions. This is because two or three final forms are typically assembled for every fixed-form exam Microsoft releases. These are usually labeled Forms A, B, and C.

The final forms of a fixed-form exam are identical in terms of content coverage, number of questions, and allotted time, but the questions are different. You may notice, however, that some of the same questions appear on, or rather are shared among, different final forms. When questions are shared among multiple final forms of an exam, the percentage of sharing is generally small. Many final forms share no questions, but some older exams may have a 10–15 percent duplication of exam questions on the final exam forms.

Fixed-form exams also have a fixed time limit in which you must complete the exam. The *ExamGear, Training Guide Edition* software on the CD-ROM that accompanies this book provides fixed-form exams.

Finally, the score you achieve on a fixed-form exam, which is always reported for MCP exams on a scale of 0 to 1,000, is based on the number of questions you answer correctly. The passing score is the same for all final forms of a given fixed-form exam.

The typical format for the fixed-form exam is as follows:

- ◆ 50–60 questions.
- ◆ 75–90 minute testing time.
- ◆ Question review is allowed, including the opportunity to change your answers.

Adaptive Form

An adaptive-form exam has the same appearance as a fixed-form exam, but its questions differ in quantity and process of selection. Although the statistics of adaptive testing are fairly complex, the process is concerned with determining your level of skill or ability with the exam subject matter. This ability assessment begins with the presentation of questions of varying levels of difficulty and ascertaining at what difficulty level you can reliably answer them. Finally, the ability assessment determines whether that ability level is above or below the level required to pass that exam.

Examinees at different levels of ability will see quite different sets of questions. Examinees who demonstrate little expertise with the subject matter will continue to be presented with relatively easy questions. Examinees who demonstrate a high level of expertise will be presented progressively more difficult questions. Individuals of both levels of expertise may answer the same number of questions correctly, but because the higher-expertise examinee can correctly answer more difficult questions, he or she will receive a higher score and is more likely to pass the exam.

The typical design for the adaptive form exam is as follows:

◆ 20–25 questions.

◆ 90 minute testing time (although this is likely to be reduced to 45–60 minutes in the near future).

◆ Question review is not allowed, providing no opportunity for you to change your answers.

The Adaptive-Exam Process

Your first adaptive exam will be unlike any other testing experience you have had. In fact, many examinees have difficulty accepting the adaptive testing process because they feel that they were not provided the opportunity to adequately demonstrate their full expertise.

You can take consolation in the fact that adaptive exams are painstakingly put together after months of data gathering and analysis and that adaptive exams are just as valid as fixed-form exams. The rigor introduced through the adaptive testing methodology means that there is nothing arbitrary about the exam items you'll see. It is also a more efficient means of testing, requiring less time to conduct and complete than traditional fixed-form exams.

As you can see in Figure 1, a number of statistical measures drive the adaptive examination process. The measure most immediately relevant to you is the ability estimate. Accompanying this test statistic are the standard error of measurement, the item characteristic curve, and the test information curve.

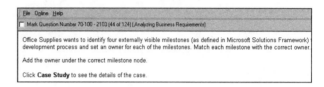

FIGURE 1
Microsoft's adaptive testing demonstration program.

The standard error, which is the key factor in determining when an adaptive exam will terminate, reflects the degree of error in the exam ability estimate. The item characteristic curve reflects the probability of a correct response relative to examinee ability. Finally, the test information statistic provides a measure of the information contained in the set of questions the examinee has answered, again relative to the ability level of the individual examinee.

When you begin an adaptive exam, the standard error has already been assigned a target value below which it must drop for the exam to conclude. This target value reflects a particular level of statistical confidence in the process. The examinee ability is initially set to the mean possible exam score (500 for MCP exams).

As the adaptive exam progresses, questions of varying difficulty are presented. Based on your pattern of responses to these questions, the ability estimate is recalculated. At the same time, the standard error estimate is refined from its first estimated value of one toward the target value. When the standard error reaches its target value, the exam is terminated. Thus, the more consistently you answer questions of the same degree of difficulty, the more quickly the standard error estimate drops, and the fewer questions you will end up seeing during the exam session. This situation is depicted in Figure 2.

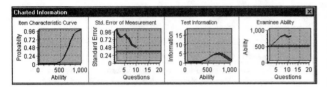

FIGURE 2
The changing statistics in an adaptive exam.

As you might suspect, one good piece of advice for taking an adaptive exam is to treat every exam question as if it were the most important. The adaptive scoring algorithm attempts to discover a pattern of responses that reflects some level of proficiency with the subject matter. Incorrect responses almost guarantee that additional questions must be answered (unless, of course, you get every question wrong). This is because the scoring algorithm must adjust to information that is not consistent with the emerging pattern.

Case Study Form

The case study-based format first appeared with the advent of the 70-100 exam (Solution Architectures). The questions in the case study format are not the independent entities that they are in the fixed and adaptive formats. Instead, questions are tied to a case study, a long scenario-like description of an information technology situation. As the test taker, your job is to extract from the case study the information that needs to be integrated with your understanding of Microsoft technology. The idea is that a case study will provide you with a situation that is more like a "real life" problem situation than the other formats provide.

The case studies are presented as "testlets." These are sections within the exam in which you read the case study, then answer 10 to 15 questions that apply to the case study. When you finish that section, you move onto another testlet with another case study and its associated questions. There may be as many as five of these testlets that compose the overall exam. You will be given more time to complete such an exam because it takes time to read through the cases and analyze them. You may have as much as three hours to complete the exam—and you may need all of it. The case studies are always available through a linking button while you are in a testlet. However, once you leave a testlet, you cannot come back to it.

Figure 3 provides an illustration of part of a case study.

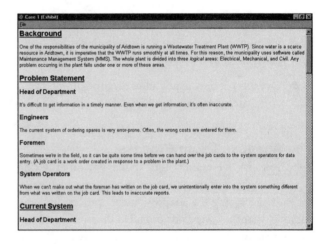

FIGURE 3
An example of a case study.

Question Types

A variety of question types can appear on MCP exams. Examples of many of the various types appear in this book and the *ExamGear, Training Guide Edition* software. We have attempted to cover all the types that were available at the time of this writing. Most of the question types discussed in the following sections can appear in each of the three exam formats.

The typical MCP exam question is based on the idea of measuring skills or the ability to complete tasks. Therefore, most of the questions are written so as to present you with a situation that includes a role (such as a system administrator or technician), a technology environment (100 computers running Windows 98 on a Windows 2000 Server network), and a problem to be solved (the user can connect to services on the LAN, but not the intranet). The answers indicate actions that you might take to solve the problem or create setups or environments that would function correctly from the start. Keep this in mind as you read the questions on the exam. You may encounter some questions that just call for you to regurgitate facts, but these will be relatively few and far between.

In the following sections we will look at the different question types.

Multiple-Choice Questions

Despite the variety of question types that now appear in various MCP exams, the multiple-choice question is still the basic building block of the exams. The multiple-choice question comes in three varieties:

◆ **Regular multiple-choice.** Also referred to as an alphabetic question, it asks you to choose one answer as correct.

◆ **Multiple-answer multiple-choice.** Also referred to as a multi-alphabetic question, this version of a multiple-choice question requires you to choose two or more answers as correct. Typically, you are told precisely the number of correct answers to choose.

◆ **Enhanced multiple-choice.** This is simply a regular or multiple-answer question that includes a graphic or table to which you must refer to answer the question correctly.

Examples of such questions appear at the end of each chapter.

Multiple-Rating Questions

These questions are often referred to as scenario questions. Similar to multiple-choice questions, they offer more extended descriptions of the computing environment and a problem that needs to be solved. Required and desired optional results of the problem-solving are specified, as well as a solution. You are then asked to judge whether the actions taken in the solution are likely to bring about all or part of the required and desired optional results. There is, typically, only one correct answer.

You may be asking yourself, "What is multiple about multiple-rating questions?" The answer is that rather than having multiple answers, the question itself may be repeated in the exam with only minor variations in the required results, optional results, or solution introduced to create "new" questions. Read these different versions very carefully; the differences can be subtle.

Examples of these types of questions appear at the end of the chapters.

Simulation Questions

Simulation-based questions reproduce the look and feel of key Microsoft product features for the purpose of testing. The simulation software used in MCP exams has been designed to look and act, as much as possible, just like the actual product. Consequently, answering simulation questions in an MCP exam entails completing one or more tasks just as if you were using the product itself.

The format of a typical Microsoft simulation question consists of a brief scenario or problem statement, along with one or more tasks that you must complete to solve the problem. An example of a simulation question for MCP exams is shown in the following section.

A Typical Simulation Question

It sounds obvious, but your first step when you encounter a simulation question is to carefully read the question (see Figure 4). Do not go straight to the simulation application! You must assess the problem that's presented and identify the conditions that make up the problem scenario. Note the tasks that must be performed or outcomes that must be achieved to answer the question, and then review any instructions you're given on how to proceed.

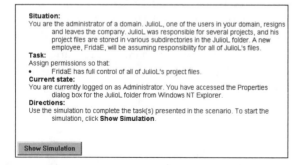

FIGURE 4
A typical MCP exam simulation question with directions.

The next step is to launch the simulator by using the button provided. After clicking the Show Simulation button, you will see a feature of the product, as shown in the dialog box in Figure 5. The simulation application will partially obscure the question text on many test center machines. Feel free to reposition the simulator and to move between the question text screen and

the simulator by using hotkeys or point-and-click navigation, or even by clicking the simulator's launch button again.

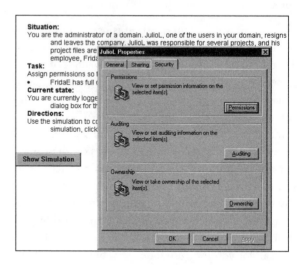

FIGURE 5
Launching the simulation application.

It is important for you to understand that your answer to the simulation question will not be recorded until you move on to the next exam question. This gives you the added capability of closing and reopening the simulation application (using the launch button) on the same question without losing any partial answer you may have made.

The third step is to use the simulator as you would the actual product to solve the problem or perform the defined tasks. Again, the simulation software is designed to function—within reason—just as the product does. But don't expect the simulator to reproduce product behavior perfectly. Most importantly, do not allow yourself to become flustered if the simulator does not look or act exactly like the product.

Figure 6 shows the solution to the example simulation problem.

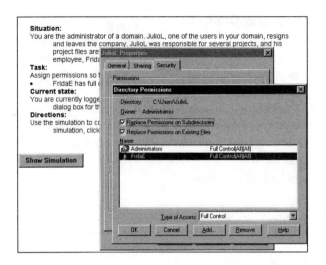

FIGURE 6
The solution to the simulation example.

Two final points will help you tackle simulation questions. First, respond only to what is being asked in the question; do not solve problems that you are not asked to solve. Second, accept what is being asked of you. You may not entirely agree with conditions in the problem statement, the quality of the desired solution, or the sufficiency of defined tasks to adequately solve the problem. Always remember that you are being tested on your ability to solve the problem as it is presented.

The solution to the simulation problem shown in Figure 6 perfectly illustrates both of those points. As you'll recall from the question scenario (refer to Figure 4), you were asked to assign appropriate permissions to a new user, Frida E. You were not instructed to make any other changes in permissions. Thus, if you were to modify or remove the administrator's permissions, this item would be scored wrong on an MCP exam.

Hot Area Question

Hot area questions call for you to click on a graphic or diagram in order to complete some task. You are asked a question that is similar to any other, but rather than clicking an option button or check box next to an answer, you click the relevant item in a screen shot or on a part of a diagram. An example of such an item is shown in Figure 7.

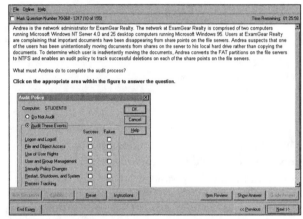

FIGURE 7
A typical hot area question.

Drag and Drop Style Questions

Microsoft has utilized two different types of drag and drop questions in exams. The first is a Select and Place question. The other is a Drop and Connect question. Both are covered in the following sections.

Select and Place

Select and Place questions typically require you to drag and drop labels on images in a diagram so as to correctly label or identify some portion of a network. Figure 8 shows you the actual question portion of a Select and Place item.

FIGURE 8
A Select and Place question.

Figure 9 shows the window you would see after you chose Select and Place. It contains the actual diagram in which you would select and drag the various server roles and match them with the appropriate computers.

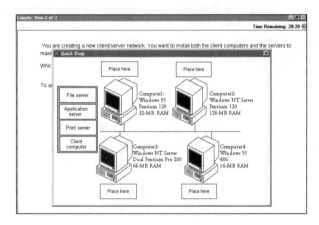

FIGURE 9
The window containing the diagram.

Drop and Connect

Drop and Connect questions provide a different spin on the drag and drop question. The question provides you with the opportunity to create boxes that you can label, as well as connectors of various types with which to link them. In essence, you are creating a model or diagram in order to answer the question. You might have to create a network diagram or a data model for a database system. Figure 10 illustrates the idea of a Drop and Connect question.

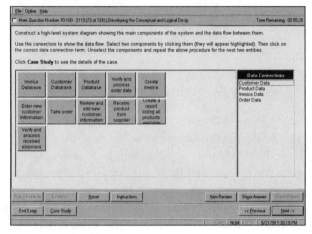

FIGURE 10
A Drop and Connect question.

Ordered List Questions

Ordered list questions simply require you to consider a list of items and place them in the proper order. You select items and then use a button to add them to a new list in the correct order. You have another button that you can use to remove the items in the new list in case you change your mind and want to reorder things. Figure 11 shows an ordered list item.

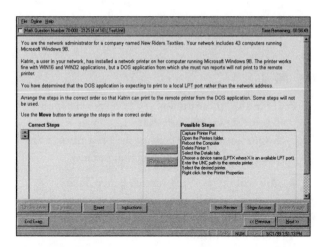

FIGURE 11
An ordered list question.

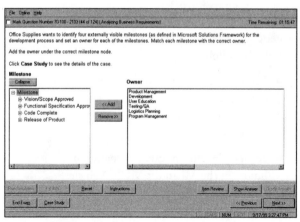

FIGURE 12
A tree question.

Tree Questions

Tree questions require you to think hierarchically and categorically. You are asked to place items from a list into categories that are displayed as nodes in a tree structure. Such questions might ask you to identify parent-child relationships in processes or the structure of keys in a database. You might also be required to show order within the categories, much as you would in an ordered list question. Figure 12 shows a typical tree question.

As you can see, Microsoft is making an effort to utilize question types that go beyond asking you to simply memorize facts. These question types force you to know how to accomplish tasks and understand concepts and relationships. Study so that you can answer these types of questions rather than those that simply ask you to recall facts.

Putting It All Together

Given all these different pieces of information, the task now is to assemble a set of tips that will help you successfully tackle the different types of MCP exams.

696   STUDY AND EXAM PREP TIPS

More Exam Preparation Tips

Generic exam-preparation advice is always useful. Tips include the following:

◆ Become familiar with the product. Hands-on experience is one of the keys to success on any MCP exam. Review the exercises and the Step by Steps in the book.

◆ Review the current exam-preparation guide on the Microsoft MCP Web site (www.microsoft.com/mcp/examinfo/exams.htm). The documentation Microsoft makes available over the Web identifies the skills every exam is intended to test.

◆ Memorize foundational technical details, but remember that MCP exams are generally heavier on problem solving and application of knowledge than on questions that require only rote memorization.

◆ Take any of the available practice tests. We recommend the one included in this book and the ones you can create using the *ExamGear* software on the CD-ROM. As a supplement to the material bound with this book, try the free practice tests available on the Microsoft MCP Web site.

◆ Look on the Microsoft MCP Web site for samples and demonstration items. These tend to be particularly valuable for one significant reason: They help you become familiar with new testing technologies before you encounter them on MCP exams.

During the Exam Session

The following generic exam-taking advice that you've heard for years also applies when you're taking an MCP exam:

◆ Take a deep breath and try to relax when you first sit down for your exam session. It is very important that you control the pressure you may (naturally) feel when taking exams.

◆ You will be provided scratch paper. Take a moment to write down any factual information and technical details that you committed to short-term memory.

◆ Carefully read all information and instruction screens. These displays have been put together to give you information relevant to the exam you are taking.

◆ Accept the non-disclosure agreement and preliminary survey as part of the examination process. Complete them accurately and quickly move on.

◆ Read the exam questions carefully. Reread each question to identify all relevant detail.

◆ Tackle the questions in the order in which they are presented. Skipping around won't build your confidence; the clock is always counting down (at least in the fixed form exams).

◆ Don't rush, but also don't linger on difficult questions. The questions vary in degree of difficulty. Don't let yourself be flustered by a particularly difficult or wordy question.

Fixed-Form Exams

Building from this basic preparation and test-taking advice, you also need to consider the challenges presented by the different exam designs. Because a fixed-form exam is composed of a fixed, finite set of questions, add these tips to your strategy for taking a fixed-form exam:

◆ Note the time allotted and the number of questions on the exam you are taking. Make a rough calculation of how many minutes you can spend on each question, and use this figure to pace yourself through the exam.

◆ Take advantage of the fact that you can return to and review skipped or previously answered questions. Record the questions you can't answer confidently on the scratch paper provided, noting the relative difficulty of each question. When you reach the end of the exam, return to the more difficult questions.

◆ If you have session time remaining after you complete all the questions (and if you aren't too fatigued!), review your answers. Pay particular attention to questions that seem to have a lot of detail or that require graphics.

◆ As for changing your answers, the general rule of thumb here is *don't*! If you read the question carefully and completely and you felt like you knew the right answer, you probably did. Don't second-guess yourself. If, as you check your answers, one clearly stands out as incorrect, however, of course you should change it. But if you are at all unsure, go with your first impression.

Adaptive Exams

If you are planning to take an adaptive exam, keep these additional tips in mind:

◆ Read and answer every question with great care. When you're reading a question, identify every relevant detail, requirement, or task you must perform and double-check your answer to be sure you have addressed every one of them.

◆ If you cannot answer a question, use the process of elimination to reduce the set of potential answers, and then take your best guess. Stupid mistakes invariably mean that additional questions will be presented.

◆ You cannot review questions and change answers. When you leave a question, whether you've answered it or not, you cannot return to it. Do not skip any question, either; if you do, it's counted as incorrect.

Case Study Exams

This new exam format calls for unique study and exam-taking strategies. When you take this type of exam, remember that you have more time than in a typical exam. Take your time and read the case study thoroughly. Use the scrap paper or whatever medium is provided to you to take notes, diagram processes, and actively seek out the important information. Work through each testlet as if each were an independent exam. Remember, you cannot go back after you have left a testlet. Refer to the case study as often as you need to, but do not use that as a substitute for reading it carefully initially and for taking notes.

FINAL CONSIDERATIONS

Finally, a number of changes in the MCP program will impact how frequently you can repeat an exam and what you will see when you do.

◆ Microsoft has instituted a new exam retake policy. The new rule is "two and two, then one and two." That is, you can attempt any exam twice with no restrictions on the time between attempts. But after the second attempt, you must wait two weeks before you can attempt that exam again. After that, you will be required to wait two weeks between subsequent attempts. Plan to pass the exam in two attempts or plan to increase your time horizon for receiving the MCP credential.

◆ New questions are being seeded into the MCP exams. After performance data is gathered on new questions, the examiners will replace older questions on all exam forms. This means that the questions appearing on exams will regularly change.

◆ Many of the current MCP exams will be republished in adaptive form. Prepare yourself for this significant change in testing; it is entirely likely that this will become the preferred MCP exam format for most exams. The exception to this may be the case study exams because the adaptive approach may not work with that format.

These changes mean that the brute-force strategies for passing MCP exams may soon completely lose their viability. So if you don't pass an exam on the first or second attempt, it is likely that the exam's form will change significantly by the next time you take it. It could be updated from fixed-form to adaptive, or it could have a different set of questions or question types.

Microsoft's intention is not to make the exams more difficult by introducing unwanted change, but to create and maintain valid measures of the technical skills and knowledge associated with the different MCP credentials. Preparing for an MCP exam has always involved not only studying the subject matter, but also planning for the testing experience itself. With the recent changes, this is now more true than ever.

This element consists of 65 questions that are meant to help you assess what you have learned from the Training Guide. It also includes questions that are representative of what you should expect on the actual exam. You will find that the questions here are mostly multiple choice. Some question forms, like those of simulations, are difficult or impossible to implement in book form because of the limitations of pencil and paper testing. Still, this exam should help you find out how well you understood the material presented in this Training Guide and give you some experience with Microsoft-style questions. When you take this exam, treat it as you would the real exam: Time yourself (about 90 minutes) and answer each question carefully, marking the ones you want to go back and double check. You will find the answers and their explanations at the end of the exam.

After you have taken this exam, follow up with New Riders' exclusive ExamGear test engine on the CD-ROM that came with this book. For more information, see Appendix B, "What's on the CD-ROM," and Appendix C, "Using the *ExamGear, Training Guide Edition* Software."

Practice Exam

EXAM QUESTIONS

1. You are an administrator of a group of Windows 2000 servers. These servers are configured with several different file systems. A user calls you to report that when she attempts to encrypt a file located on a share from one of the servers, she receives an error. What do you tell the user that the problem is?

   A. Only NTFS v5 and FAT32 support encryption. The share you are using has been formatted with the FAT file system.

   B. Only NTFS v5 and HPFS support encryption. The share you are using has been formatted with the NTFS V4 file system.

   C. Only NTFS v5 supports encryption. The share you are using has been formatted with the FAT32 file system.

   D. Only FAT32 supports encryption. The share you are using has been formatted with the HPFS file system.

2. You are a senior administrator of a Windows 2000 server. Your server will not boot. A junior administrator decided to change the boot disk from IDE to SCSI and modified the BOOT.INI file manually. His attempt was not successful, so he returned the original IDE drive to the server. Unfortunately, the server still will not boot. You believe one possible problem may be the configuration information in the BOOT.INI file. In the BOOT.INI file, what should the first ARC parameter be listed as for use with an IDE drive?

   A. MULTI

   B. EIDE

   C. SCSI

   D. IDE

3. You are an administrator of a Windows 2000 server. The users of one of these servers are complaining that it is very slow. You decide to use Performance Monitor to locate the problem. What should you do?

   A. Monitor the hard disk(s), the processor(s), the memory, and the network card(s).

   B. Monitor the controller, the processor(s), the memory, and the network card(s).

   C. Monitor the processor(s), the memory, the network card(s), and the application thread(s).

   D. Monitor the hard disk(s), the memory, the network card(s), and the application thread(s).

4. You are an administrator of a Windows 2000 network, and you have configured a Windows 2000 server as a domain controller. You want to add several domain-level users to local groups on the server to implement a local security model, but you can't find any local groups on the server itself. Why?

   A. On a domain controller, local groups are part of the Windows 2000 domain.

   B. On a domain controller, local groups are part of the Active Directory.

   C. On a domain controller, local groups are part of the domain group and, therefore, are not visible.

   D. On a domain controller, global groups are part of the Active Directory.

5. Your boss comes to you and says he wants to set up a Windows 2000 server at home. You decide to make the boot disks for him. What should you do to create the set of boot disks for Windows 2000? (Choose two answers.)

    A. Run MAKEBOOT.EXE.

    B. Run MAKEBT32.EXE.

    C. Run MKBOOT32.EXE.

    D. Run MAKE32.EXE.

6. As an administrator, you are responsible for creating a global management system to control all your company's print queues. You need to be able to pause and resume a printer; view, pause, resume, and cancel documents; and view the properties of your printers. What should you do to enable this functionality?

    A. Install Terminal Services on the server and then use the properties for the individual printer to pause, resume, and cancel documents and view the properties of your printers.

    B. Install a remote control package to the server and then use the properties for the individual printer to control that printer.

    C. Install Internet Information Server (IIS) on the server and use it to pause and resume a printer; view, pause, resume, and cancel documents; and view the properties of your printers.

    D. You can not enable this type of functionality with Windows 2000 Server.

7. You are an administrator of several Windows 2000 servers with a software development company. A software developer comes to you with questions about prioritizing his application on a Windows 2000 server. What are the available application priorities to support his needs?

    A. Idle, normal, high, and real-time.

    B. Idle, normal, fast, and real-time.

    C. Idle, slow, high, and real-time.

    D. Idle, normal, high, and near-time.

8. As an administrator of a Windows 2000 server, you notice the server is taking a long time to load results from a database query. This application was only recently added to this server. You need to identify the cause of the problem using the least possible amount of administrative effort. What should you do?

    A. Use the Memory\Transition Faults/sec performance counter from the Performance Monitor to display the ratio of transition fault positive hits to memory.

    B. Use the Memory\Pool Nonpaged Bytes performance counter from the Performance Monitor to display the ratio of positive hits to the memory pool of nonpaged bytes for data trying to be retrieved.

    C. Use the Cache\Data Map Hits performance counter from the Performance Monitor to display the ratio of positive hits to memory for data trying to be retrieved.

    D. Use the Memory\Cache Bytes performance counter from the Network Monitor to display the ratio of positive hits to memory for data trying to be retrieved.

9. You are an administrator of a Windows 2000 server. You receive a virus warning from your virus detection software that says your MBR now contains a virus. What does the term MBR mean?

   A. Master BIOS Record

   B. Master Boot Record

   C. Main Boot Record

   D. Multiple Boot Records

10. You are an administrator of a Windows 2000 server in a software development company. A developer comes to you with questions about what the User mode is for. What do you tell the developer?

    A. User mode is where all user-essential processes are run.

    B. User mode is the essential core of the Windows 2000 operating.

    C. User mode is where all user interaction happens; this includes logon and the Win32 subsystem where 32-bit programs are run.

    D. User mode is where all processes in the kernel are protected from direct user interaction, thus ensuring they have very limited ability to cause system crashes or to compromise security.

11. As an administrator of a Windows 2000 infrastructure, you are responsible for all upgrades to the server and desktop operating systems. Your office has Windows 95 running on Intel 486s and Pentium Pro PCs, Windows 98 running on AMD 586 processors, Windows NT 4.0 Workstation and Server running on Pentium 500MHz processors, and Windows 3.51

Workstation and Server running on older Pentium Pro processors. All PCs and servers have the minimum memory requirements for upgrading to Windows 2000. Which versions of Microsoft Windows can be upgraded to Windows 2000?

   A. Windows 98, Windows NT Workstation, and Windows NT Server

   B. Windows 95, Windows 98, Windows NT Workstation, and Windows NT Server

   C. Windows 95, Windows 98, Windows NT 3.51 Workstation, and Windows NT 3.51 Server, Windows NT Workstation, and Windows NT Server

   D. Windows NT Workstation and Windows NT Server

   E. DOS, Windows 95, Windows 98, Windows NT Workstation, and Windows NT Server

12. You are an administrator of a Windows 2000 Server domain. You are told by human resources that an employee is being terminated today. What is the first thing you should do to keep that user from logging into the network?

    A. Remove the check from the Account Is Disabled check box.

    B. Check the Account Is Disabled check box.

    C. Delete the user account.

    D. Rename the user account.

13. You are an administrator of a Windows 2000 infrastructure. You have been tasked to design a LAN/WAN environment for your corporate environment. You need to provide allow users to connect remotely through a secure connection.

Required Result:

All users must be able to securely connect to the corporate network with a minimum of effort.

Optional Desired Results:

All users must be able to be authenticated before they can gain access to the corporate network.

Both dial-up users and those who connect via the Internet must be supported.

Proposed Solution:

Configure Windows 2000 to support a VPN connection and a dial-up connection. Use the standard authentication used by Windows 2000 to authenticate the user.

Analysis:

Which result(s) does the proposed solution produce?

A. The proposed solution produces the required result, as well as both optional desired results.

B. The proposed solution produces the required result and one of the optional desired results.

C. The proposed solution produces the required result, but does not produce either of the optional desired results.

D. The proposed solution does not produce the required result.

14. You are an administrator of a Windows 2000 domain. You need to design a remote access solution for your company. Security is very important. What are the remote access authentication methods available in Windows 2000? Select five.

A. EAP

B. KERBEROS

C. MS-CHAP V2

D. CHAP

E. SLIP

F. SPAP

G. PAP

H. POP

15. You are an administrator for a large corporation using Windows 2000. You need to write a batch file that will automate the encryption process for any files in a particular directory. What should you do?

A. Use ENCRYPT.EXE.

B. Use CIKEY.EXE.

C. Use IPSEC.EXE.

D. Use CIPHER.EXE.

16. You have added a new hard drive to a Windows 2000 server and have made a variety of partition changes to the existing drives. Now the server will not boot. You know that changes were made in the BOOT.INI file to the third ARC parameter. What is the first acceptable value for this parameter?

A. 0

B. 1

C. 2

D. 3

17. You are an administrator of a Windows 2000 domain located in the XYZ Company. You are designing the login process for all the users at this company. You need all users to be able to log in to the Windows 2000 infrastructure from any Windows 2000-based computer. You also have several users who will never log in at any machine

other than their own. Management wants to understand what options are available. You need to be able to explain all the potential options and what they do. What different kinds of user profiles are available in Windows 2000?

A. Local, roaming, and mandatory.

B. Local, roaming, and required.

C. Local, mandatory, and secure.

D. Roaming, local, and directory-based.

18. You are an administrator of a Windows 2000 server. You have recently added several devices to the server. Now some of these devices will not work. How are devices with problems identified within the Device manager?

A. Highlighted in red

B. With a yellow circled exclamation mark

C. Highlighted in yellow

D. With a red circled exclamation mark

19. You are an administrator of a large number of Windows 2000 servers. You have been asked to set up a permission structure to protect resources available on a network. What is the recommended method for adding users to groups to protect resources?

A. Users → global groups → local groups → permission to access resources

B. Users → global groups → groups → permission to access resources

C. Users → local groups → global groups → permission to access resources

D. Users → groups → permission to access resources

20. You are the administrator for a small Windows 2000 network. You need to install Windows 2000 on one computer that doesn't support booting from CD and isn't currently connected to the network. You decide to create the setup disks. What should you do first?

A. Get three disks.

B. Get two disks.

C. Get five disks.

D. Get four disks.

21. You are responsible for the maintenance of a standalone Dfs root. What tasks can be completed via the Dfs Management console? (Select three.)

A. Adding Dfs links

B. Removing Dfs links

C. Disabling Dfs links

D. Deleting Dfs links

E. Moving Dfs links

F. Renaming Dfs links

G. Copying Dfs links

22. As a system administrator, you are having problems preventing users from installing shareware applications from the Internet. You decide to implement system policies that check for signatures on drivers. You want to restrict the installation of applications as much as you can. What should you do?

A. Choose to ignore signatures and allow the installation of drivers without checking for them.

B. Set the system to check signatures on drivers when they are installed and warn you if they are not signed; this gives you the chance to reconsider your decision to install an unverified driver.

C. Block the installation of unsigned drivers in order to ensure that your system is free of unverified and possibly corrupt drivers.

D. Disable the Signature Check feature completely via the Device manager.

23. You are the administrator of a large Windows 2000 server farm. You have just received a call that a server is down. A new application had been loaded, and now the server will not boot. What should you do?

    A. Rebuild the server.

    B. Use the Recovery console to repair the problem.

    C. Use a repair disk to overwrite the existing installation.

    D. Use the Recovery console to reinstall the existing operating system.

24. You are an administrator of a large corporation's Windows 2000 server infrastructure. You need to automate the compression of a set of single files on a Windows 2000 server. You decide to write a .CMD file and run it with the Scheduler service. What should you do to compress the files?

    A. Use a third-party compression utility and call it from the .CMD file.

    B. Use the ENCRYPT.EXE command with its command line options and call it from the .CMD file.

C. Use the COMPACT.EXE command with its command line options and call it from the .CMD file.

D. Running the compression utility from a command line is not possible.

25. You are an administrator of your company's Windows 2000 domain. Your corporate security office has decided that a RADIUS-based authentication process must be used to validate all dial-in users. What should you do?

    A. Install Dial-Up Networking and use the default settings.

    B. Install Internet Authentication Services (IAS) and configure it to use the corporate RADIUS server.

    C. Install Terminal Server and configure it to accept only remote logins to allow for access into the corporate network.

    D. Install Internet Information Server (IIS) and configure it for remote authentication.

26. You are an administrator on a Windows 2000 server that contains a limited number of disks and on which you need to install a new database application. You need to segment the data this application uses into different drives with unique drive letters.

Required Result:

You must improve the speed and response of an application that will be installed.

Optional Desired Results:

The application must be able to be split across multiple spindles to improve seek time.

The partitions must be of equal size.

Proposed Solution:

You create additional partitions on the existing drives by adding five partitions on each drive and then creating a RAID 0 configuration across those partitions.

Analysis:

Which result(s) does the proposed solution produce?

A. The proposed solution produces the required result, as well as both optional desired results.

B. The proposed solution produces the required result and one of the optional desired results.

C. The proposed solution produces the required result, but does not produce either of the optional desired results.

D. The proposed solution does not produce the required result.

27. You are an administrator of a large application server running on Windows 2000. You have a variety of applications running on the server. One of these must be given a higher priority on the processor. You must assign a specific numeric value to this application to enable it to access the processor more often. What is the numeric value assigned to a high application priority rating?

A. 9

B. 10

C. 13

D. 24

28. You are an administrator of a Windows 2000 server farm that will be used for intranet access within your company. You are building a secure intranet site. During testing, you find you are having problems connecting to the test site. It appears to be an authentication problem. Which authentication type does the system attempt to use first when connecting to the site?

A. Anonymous

B. Authenticated

C. Anonymous using port 8080

D. Authenticated using the port assigned to the Administrators Web site

29. You are an administrator of a Windows 2000 domain, and you are attempting to automate the deployment of several Windows 2000 servers. You have decided to use SYSPREP. What does SYSPREP do?

A. Prepares a disk for duplication

B. Prepares a disk differences file to be used later during duplication

C. Prepares a network drive to receive the duplicated disk image

D. Prepares an older version of Windows NT to be upgraded

30. Domain controllers and member servers play very important but unique roles in a Windows 2000 network. What is the most accurate definition of a Windows 2000 member server?

A. A Windows 2000 server that functions in a domain but does not hold a copy of the SAM

B. A Windows 2000 server that functions in a domain and holds a copy of the Active Directory

C. A Windows 2000 server that functions in a domain but does not hold a copy of the Active Directory

D. A Windows 2000 server that functions in a domain and holds a copy of the SAM

31. A member server is the working core of a Windows 2000 Server network. It has a wide variety of functional uses. What are the three main roles of a member server?

A. Applications server, domain controller, Web server

B. Print server, applications server, Web server

C. File server, print server, and applications server

D. Print server, domain controller, fax server

32. You are an administrator of a large mixed environment that contains Windows NT 4 servers, Windows 2000 servers, Windows 2000 workstations, and Macintosh workstations. The Macintosh users need to be able to access the Windows 2000 file servers. What would you implement to allow this?

A. File Services for Macintosh and Print Services for Macintosh

B. File Services for Macintosh and the AppleTalk protocol

C. File Services for Macintosh

D. Print Services for Macintosh and the AppleTalk protocol

33. You are an administrator of a large Windows 2000 network and you need to automate the backup of several directories at different times on all the Windows 2000 servers. To do this, you choose to create a .CMD file and use the Scheduler service. What is the most effective method for achieving this?

A. Copy the directories to a backup share on a Windows 2000 server.

B. Use the XCOPY.EXE command as part of the .CMD file to copy the files to a backup share on a Windows 2000 server.

C. Use NTBACKUP.EXE with the appropriate command line options to back up the files and directories to either tape or a central file server.

D. Use the NTBACKUP.EXE GUI to back up the files and directories to either tape or a central file server.

34. You are an administrator of a large number of Windows 2000 servers. All the servers are configured with the main system disk, which is on a mirrored drive to provide enhanced reliability. On one of the servers, one of the disks of the system mirrored disk fails. What is the first step you should take to repair the damaged drive and repair the mirror?

A. Re-establish the mirror to an alternate drive.

B. Remove the mirror.

C. Establish a duplicate mirror to an alternate drive.

D. Format the mirror.

35. You are the sole administrator for your site. You must use DNS to provide access for a large number of UNIX workstations that coexist on your network. For your Windows 2000 workstation, you want to automate the creation of DNS records.

    Required Result:

    You want to force the automatic update of DNS records.

    Optional Desired Results:

    Limit the amount of network bandwidth that is used by the automatic DNS update process.

    Use DNS on a UNIX server.

    Proposed Solution:

    Configure the Windows 2000 workstation to update DNS only if the DHCP client requests it and to use DNS bind version 8.1.3 on the UNIX server to provide DNS services.

    Analysis:

    Which result(s) does the proposed solution produce?

    A. The proposed solution produces the required result as well as both optional desired results.

    B. The proposed solution produces the required result and one of the optional desired results.

    C. The proposed solution produces the required result but does not produce either of the optional desired results.

    D. The proposed solution does not produce the required result.

36. You are attempting to secure, or "lock-down," a Windows 2000 server. What security options can be used to help secure a Windows 2000 server? (Select two.)

    A. Clear Virtual Memory Pagefile When System Shuts Down

    B. Display Last User Name in Logon Screen

    C. Message Text for Users Attempting to Log On

    D. Automatically Reboot on Power Cycle

    E. Disable the Ability to Boot off of a CD

37. You are an administrator of a Windows 2000 server, and you need to limit access to the resources on that server. What does the special local NTFS security permission Transverse Folder/Execute File do?

    A. The permission will allow or deny a user the ability to Read Extended Attributes on a folder to which he or she does not have access.

    B. The permission will allow or deny a user the ability to synchronize files on a folder to which he or she does not have access.

    C. The permission will allow or deny a user the ability to List Folder/Read Data on a folder to which he or she does not have access.

    D. The permission will allow or deny a user the ability to pass through a folder to which he or she does not have access.

38. You are an administrator of a large Windows NT 4.0 server farm. Management wants to determine the advantages and disadvantages of upgrading the existing server farm to a Windows 2000

environment. In particular, they are concerned about security for several of the applications that run on member servers. Management is asking for the definition of a local user on a Windows 2000 member server. What do you tell them?

A. A user that is logged onto the Windows 2000 member server

B. A user that exists only on the Windows 2000 member server and does not exist in the domain's Active Directory

C. A user account from an NT 4 domain that logs into a Windows 2000 member server

D. A user that exists on the Windows 2000 domain controller

39. You are an administrator of a large Windows NT 4.0 infrastructure. You are attempting to determine the factors that need to be taken into consideration when installing Windows 2000 Server (either from scratch or as an upgrade). From an overall perspective, what are the factors?

A. Software compatibility, disk speed, and current operating system upgradability

B. Hardware compatibility, disk size and partitions, and current operating system upgradability

C. Hardware compatibility, software compatibility, disk speed, and current operating system upgradability

D. Hardware compatibility, software compatibility, disk size and partitions, and current operating system upgradability

40. Windows 2000 allows for multiple processes to run at once through the use of multitasking. What type of multitasking does Windows 2000 use for 32 bit applications?

A. Preemptive multitasking

B. Cooperative multitasking

C. Distributive multitasking

D. Cross-process multitasking

41. Which of the items listed below are components of a profile? Select four.

A. Favorites

B. NTUSER.DB

C. My Documents

D. My Proxy

E. Recent Documents

F. Start Menu

G. Home drive location

42. The second ARC parameter is the number of hard drives. If the controller is *multi*, what is the associated disk parameter?

A. disk(x)

B. rdisk(y)

C. disk(z)

D. rdisk(v)

43. You are an administrator of a Windows 2000 environment, and you are attempting to implement quotas for a Windows 2000 server. Quotas are set for individuals and not for groups. You have yet to choose your file system. What should you do?

    A. Install HPFS.

    B. Install NTFS.

    C. Install FAT.

    D. Install FAT32.

44. An application developer has been attempting to create a share on a Windows 2000 member server but has been unable to complete the task. You check and determine that he is not in the Administrators group. What should you do to make sure the developer has the necessary permission to create shares on the member server?

    A. Add the developer to the Domain Admins and Power Users groups on the local machine.

    B. Add the developer to the Administrators or Power Users group on the local machine.

    C. Add the developer to the Power Users and Account Operators group on the local machine.

    D. Add the developer to the Administrators and Power Users group on the domain controller.

45. You are an administrator of a Windows 2000 server that is using Dfs. A client is complaining that the server is very slow to give him access to documents located on it. He is connecting through a Dfs share. What should you do to correct the problem?

    A. The problem is that the Dfs cache referral time has expired. The cache referral time is the length of time a Dfs client stores the location of the link to the remote machine. You must increase the timeout value for the Dfs cache referral time to allow for faster response.

    B. The problem is that the Dfs cache referral time has expired. The cache referral time is the length of time a Dfs client stores the location of the link to the remote machine. You must decrease the timeout value for the Dfs cache referral time to allow for faster reconnect time.

    C. The problem is that the Dfs cache referral time has timed out. The cache referral time is the length of time a Dfs server stores the location of the link to the client machine. You must increase the timeout value for the Dfs cache referral time to allow for faster response.

    D. The problem is that the Dfs cache referral time has timed out. The cache referral time is the length of time a Dfs server stores the location of the link to the client machine. You must decrease the timeout value for the Dfs cache referral time to allow for faster response.

46. You are an administrator for a Windows 2000 server, and you have received a new driver for a tape backup system. When you attempt to install the driver, Windows 2000 Server warns you that the driver is not signed. Which statement below correctly describes what Microsoft does to verify all drivers?

    A. Microsoft verifies and then digitally signs the drivers themselves.

B. Microsoft verifies each driver and then has each driver digitally signed by a third-party verification organization.

C. Microsoft has a third-party organization verify and then digitally sign each driver.

D. Microsoft has a third-party organization verify the driver, and then Microsoft digitally signs them.

47. You are creating a striped volume. You have attempted to stripe together 56 areas of free space but have failed. Why are you unable to create the striped volume?

A. The partition is FAT.

B. The maximum number of chunks of free space that can be joined is 16.

C. The maximum number of chunks of free space that can be joined is 32.

D. The partition is FAT32.

48. You are an administrator of a large Windows 2000 domain. You are attempting to use a DHCP server to issue IP addresses to the client computers. Unfortunately, the server will not give out addresses to any of the clients. What is the most likely cause of the problem?

A. The DHCP server must be authorized in the Active Directory before it can give out addresses.

B. The DHCP server requires that the DNS service be enabled in the Services portion of the Control Panel.

C. The DHCP server must have a WINS scope ID created for the Active Directory.

D. The default domain controller requires that Active Directory be enabled.

49. You are an administrator of a Windows 2000 server, and you need to convert the D: drive from FAT to NTFS. Which of the following commands should you use?

A. `CONVERT D:`

B. `CONVERT D: /FS:FAT:NTFS`

C. `CONVERT D: //FS:NTFS`

D. `CONVERT D: /FS:NTFS`

50. You are an administrator for a Windows 2000 server farm. You are attempting to install Windows 2000 Server to a computer that has a blank 1 gig hard drive, a Pentium 133MHz processor, and 24MB of RAM. This server will support approximately 100 users. The installation fails. Which of the following describes the least changes that are necessary to allow for a successful installation?

A. Increase the hard drive to a 2 gig drive minimum, increase the processor speed to a 200MHz minimum, and increase the RAM to at least 32MB.

B. Increase the hard drive to a 2 gig drive minimum, increase the processor speed to a 200MHz minimum, and increase the RAM to at least 64MB.

C. Increase the processor speed to a 166MHz minimum and increase the RAM to at least 128MB.

D. Increase the RAM to at least 256MB.

51. You are an administrator of a Windows 2000 server that is supporting NetWare clients. You are being told that no one is able to connect to any NetWare services from any client. You believe you

have the wrong version of NetWare software. What are the versions of File and Print Services for NetWare? (Select two.)

A. One for NetWare 3.x and 4.x clients

B. One for NetWare 5.x clients

C. One for Microsoft NT 4.0 clients

D. One for Microsoft NT 2000 clients

52. You are writing a justification document, and you need to explain why the Plug and Play manager is so important to the concept of reducing the cost of PC maintenance. What does the Plug and Play manager do? (Select two.)

A. Ensures that all Plug and Play compatible devices are automatically detected and that their drivers are installed.

B. Delivers the ability to configure printer queues automatically.

C. Increases the potential that Windows 2000 will locate devices that are not Plug and Play and have their drivers installed.

D. Automates the process of installing software updates to the operating systems.

53. Your customers have indicated that the time it takes to get data off the file server is getting worse. Which performance counters should you monitor for the disk object? (Select five.)

A. Physical Disk\Disk Reads/sec

B. Physical Disk\Disk Writes/sec

C. Logical Disk\% Free Space

D. Logical Disk\% Disk Time

E. Logical Disk\% Disk Free Time

F. Logical Disk\% Idle Time

54. You have been tasked with creating a secure remote access solution for your company. You are investigating what options Windows 2000 provides. What are the tunneling protocols available under Windows 2000 Remote Access Services? (Select two.)

A. Point to Point Tunneling Protocol

B. Layer Two Tunneling Protocol

C. Layer Four Tunneling Protocol

D. VPN Tunneling Protocol

55. You are an administrator for a Windows 2000 server farm for a small company. Your boss has come to you and expressed concern about people on the Internet being able to see the IP addresses of computers on your intranet. What feature of Windows 2000 would address his concerns?

A. Encryption

B. Network Address Translation

C. Packet filtering

D. Security authentication

56. You are an administrator for a Windows 2000 server that is configured for dual booting. You have NT 4.0 on one partition and Windows 2000 Server on another partition. You have enabled compression on the Windows 2000 partition. Now the Windows NT 4.0 partition can't read anything on the Windows 2000 partition. The file system versions do not appear to be compatible. What can you do to resolve the problem?

A. Don't dual boot. This problem can't be fixed.

B. Apply Service Pack 3 to the NT 4.0 partition to allow it to read from the Windows 2000 Server file system.

C. Apply Service Pack 4 to the NT 4.0 partition to allow it to read from the Windows 2000 Server file system.

D. Compatibility is problematic. Many features of the Windows 2000 file system are not supported in NT 4.0.

57. The CIO for your company has come to you and asked for your recommendation on the best methods for completing an unattended installation of Windows 2000 Server on all the new servers in the data center. What would you recommend? (Select three.)

A. Installation from scripts

B. Installation using disk images and third-party distribution software

C. Installation using Remote Installation Services

D. Installation from boot disks

E. Installation from an IIS server Web link

F. Installation from a disk image applied at a Remote Installation share point

58. You have been asked by your supervisor to document the steps necessary to create a roaming profile. This will be included in an upcoming deployment "how-to" document. What would be required?

A. Configure a shared folder on a server to hold the roaming profiles, create a folder within the shared folder for each user who is going to be roaming, copy an existing profile into the folder for each user, and configure the user's account to point to the roaming location.

B. Configure a folder on a server to hold the roaming profiles, create a folder within the server folder for each user who is going to be roaming, and configure the user's account to point to the roaming location.

C. Configure a shared folder on a server to hold the roaming profiles, create a folder within the shared folder for each user who is going to be roaming, and configure the user's account to point to the roaming location.

D. Configure a shared folder on a server to hold the roaming profiles, create a folder within the shared folder for each user who is going to be roaming, and copy an existing profile into the folder for each user.

59. You are an administrator of a large Windows 2000 server farm. You have just completed the installation of an additional Windows 2000 server. However, you discover that you did not configure the drives as required in the build document to support the Microsoft Exchange installation. Will you be able to change the existing drive letter assignments?

A. Yes, they can be changed at any time.

B. Yes, they can be changed at any time. The only exception is that you cannot change the drive letters of the System partition.

C. No, they cannot be changed anytime.

D. Yes, they can be changed at any time. The only exceptions are the System and Boot partitions; you cannot change the drive letters of either of those special partitions.

60. You have just completed the installation of a Windows 2000 server, and you discover that no one can access it from the network. Which tools are available to troubleshoot TCP/IP on a Windows 2000 server? (Select three.)

A. NETSTATE

B. IPCONFIG

C. PING

D. TRACERT

61. You are an administrator for a large company with several hundred Windows 2000 servers. Your manager has asked you how much trouble it would be to implement a password policy for the servers. You need to explain what is covered as part of the password policy. What do you say?

    A. Password history, minimum age, maximum age, minimum length, maximum length, and reverse encryption storage

    B. Password history, minimum age, maximum age, maximum length, complexity, and encryption storage

    C. Password history, minimum age, maximum age, minimum length, complexity, and reverse encryption storage

    D. Password history, minimum age, maximum age, minimum length, complexity, and encryption storage

62. You are an administrator of a Windows 2000 server for a software development company. An application developer comes to you and indicates that the Windows 2000 server he is using as a test box is slower than the Windows 2000 workstation he is using to develop his application on. He indicates that the application, when run in the foreground on the server, is slower than when its run on the workstation. The application is processor intensive. What's the likely cause of the problem?

    A. Windows 2000 Server runs foreground applications at the lowest possible priority, whereas Windows 2000 Professional does not.

    B. Windows 2000 Professional boosts foreground applications, whereas Windows 2000 Server does not.

    C. Windows 2000 Server and Windows 2000 Professional treat foreground applications the same. The server needs an additional processor.

    D. Windows 2000 Server boosts foreground applications but Windows 2000 Professional does not.

63. You are an administrator for a company that is rebuilding all their existing servers. All servers were Windows NT 3.51, and you are migrating to Windows 2000 server. As part of the installation, you are using the DELPART utility to delete the existing partitions, and then you are installing DOS onto the hard drive. From that point, you are attempting to install Windows 2000 Server from a DOS prompt. What should you do?

    A. Run WINSTALL.EXE.

    B. Run SETUP.EXE.

    C. Run WINNT.EXE.

    D. Run WINNT32.EXE.

64. You are attempting to Web share a folder, but the Web share function is not available. You determine this is because you do not have the correct access rights to complete the function. What level of access must you have to be able to Web share a folder?

    A. Administrator and Server Manager access

    B. Administrator and Power User access

    C. Power User, Server Manager, and Administrator access

    D. Power User, Backup Operator, and Administrator access

65. You are an administrator for several Windows 2000 servers. Purchasing has come to you and asked that you provide the hardware (memory, CPU, and disk size) requirements to support a client using Terminal Services for Windows 2000 Server. What are the minimum requirements for a client to use Terminal Services?

A. A Windows for Workgroups (Windows 3.11) client with 16MB of memory, a 386 processor, and a network card

B. A Windows 95/98 client with 32MB of memory, a 486 processor, and a network card

C. A Windows NT 3.51 client with 24MB of memory, a Pentium Pro processor, and a network card

D. A Windows for Workgroups (Windows 3.11) client with 32MB of memory, a 386 processor, and a network card

ANSWERS AND EXPLANATIONS

1. **C.** Although encryption is extremely useful for locally securing data, it comes with a price. Encrypted data cannot be used on file systems except NTFS version 5; this means that not only can it not be applied to FAT and FAT32 partition, it also cannot be accessed locally by NT 4.0 systems, regardless of the user account logged on with. In addition, encrypted files are secure only on the hard drive; if you access an encrypted file over the network, the network transmission of the data is not secure unless you also use network encryption like IPSec. Finally, encryption is not compatible with compression; if you encrypt a compressed file, the compression will be removed. As well, although encryption secures data from being accessed, that does not eliminate the need for NTFS security to be applied. Encryption keeps a file's contents from being viewed or modified; however, it does not prevent the file from being deleted. In order to ensure the best security, make sure that both Encryption and NTFS security are applied. For more information, see "Encrypting Data Using Encrypting File System" in Chapter 7, " Implementing, Monitoring, and Troubleshooting Security."

2. **A.** *Multi* indicates that the controller is either non-SCSI (IDE, EIDE, and so on) or SCSI with the BIOS enabled; most PC-based controllers fall into this category. *SCSI* indicates that the controller is SCSI with the BIOS disabled. This parameter's numbering scheme begins with 0, so the first controller is either *multi(0)* or *scsi(0)*. For more information, see "ARC Paths and Volumes/Partitions" in Chapter 5, "Managing, Configuring, and Troubleshooting Storage Use."

3. **A.** The components in a Windows 2000 server that are important to monitor are the hard disk(s), the processor(s), the memory, and the network card(s). Regardless of what kind of services the server is providing, these four areas interact to make your server efficient (thereby appearing fast) or inefficient. The actual speed or efficiency of each of the components will vary in importance depending on the application because in some applications, memory is more important than processor speed or availability, and in other applications, disk speed and availability are more important than fast network access. For more information, see "Monitoring and Optimizing System Resource Use" in Chapter 4, "Managing, Monitoring, and Optimizing System Performance, Reliability, and Availability."

4. **B.** Local groups are used to control access to resources on specific machines, whether those resources are data folders or printers. On a member server or a Windows 2000 Professional workstation, the local groups are a part of the local security model for the machine. On a domain controller, local groups are part of the Active Directory (something that is well beyond the scope of this book). For more information, see "Local Groups and Users" in Chapter 2, "Installing, Configuring, and Troubleshooting Access to Resources."

5. **A, B.** The disks are created using either MAKE-BOOT.exe or MAKEBT32.exe, both of which are found in the BOOTDISK folder on your Windows 2000 Server CD-ROM. Both programs do the same thing; however, the "32" version is designed to be run under 32-bit operating systems, whereas the other is designed to be run under 16-bit operating systems (like DOS and Windows 3.1). For more information, see "Install by Using Setup Diskettes and a CD-ROM" in Chapter 1, "Installing Windows 2000 Server."

6. **C.** If you have IIS installed on your Windows 2000 server, you can manage the print queue of any shared printer from a browser. You can pause and resume a printer; view, pause, resume, and cancel documents; and view the properties of your printers. For more information, see "Managing a Windows 2000 Printer from a Browser" in Chapter 2.

7. **A.** Application processes are divided into four categories: idle, normal, high, and real-time. Each of these categories is given a range of numbers in which to operate. In addition, each also has a base priority (the priority that a process running in that category is assigned by default). Idle ranges from 0 to 6, normal from 6 to 11, high from 11 to 15, and real-time from 16 to 31. For more information, see "Maintaining Windows 32-Bit Applications" in Chapter 4.

8. **C.** The Cache\Data Map Hits performance counter displays the ratio of positive hits to memory for data trying to be retrieved. You might have a memory bottleneck if this number is small because it indicates that a large percentage of the time, data has to be recovered from the disk instead of from memory. For more information, see the explanation of the counter Cache\Data Map Hits % in Table 4.3, "Explanation of Counters," in Chapter 4.

9. **B.** The Master Boot Record (MBR) tells the computer what to do to get an operating system loading. This MBR is always on the current active partition. The active partition can be set from within Windows 2000, but it is most often determined before Windows 2000 is even installed. Generally, a utility like FDISK will be used to specify the active partition. Windows 2000 refers to the location of the MBR as the System partition. When the BIOS of your computer determines which partition is the active partition, it looks to the MBR to tell it how to begin operating system boot. The MBR, in turn, looks to some special files that Windows 2000 uses to start the operating system. These files are BOOT.INI, NTDE-TECT.COM, and NTLDR. All three are located in the System partition. For more information, see "System and Boot Partitions" in Chapter 5.

10. **C.** The Windows 2000 operating system is divided into two primary operating environments called modes. User mode is where all user interaction happens; this includes logon and the Win32 subsystem, where 32-bit programs are run (more on that in Chapter 3). The other mode is called Kernel mode. The kernel is the essential core of the Windows 2000 operating system, and all essential processes run in this mode. Processes in the Kernel mode are protected from direct user interaction, to ensure that users have very limited ability to cause system crashes or to compromise security. For more information, see "Hardware and Drivers in Windows 2000," in Chapter 3, "Configuring and Troubleshooting Hardware Devices and Drivers."

11. **B.** Unlike NT 4.0, which could only be upgraded from Windows NT 3.x, Windows 2000 has upgrade paths for the following operating systems: Windows 95, Windows 98, Windows NT Workstation, and Windows NT Server. For more information, see "Current Operating System Upgradability" in Chapter 1.

12. **B.** Selecting/checking the Account Is Disabled check box makes the user account unusable. This feature is often used when a user is no longer with the company but you want to hold onto the account in case someone else ends up with the same job and, therefore, needs the same data access. If an account is deleted, the access that user had is removed from all ACLs. This is not a good solution to use if one person is to be replaced with another. Instead of deleting the account, you should disable the account; then, when a replacement is hired, you can rename the account with the new user's name. For more information, see "Managing Local Users" in Chapter 2.

13. **A.** The proposed solution provides for all the required and desired results. Five connection types are available via the Network Connection Wizard. These connections will automatically use the Windows 2000 authentication model by default. For more information, see Table 6.1 titled "Connection Types" in Chapter 6, "Configuring and Troubleshooting Windows 2000 Network Connections."

14. **A, C, D, F, G.** The available Remote Access Authentication methods are EAP, MS-CHAP v2, CHAP, SPAP, and PAP. The Extensible Authentication Method (EAP) is an authentication method that leaves open-ended the forms of authentication available. The Microsoft Challenge Handshake Authentication Protocol version 2 (MS-CHAP v2) allows for challenge-response authentication based on a two-way encryption algorithm and the user name/password combination provided. The Challenge Handshake Authentication Protocol (CHAP) method allows for encrypted authentication with non-Microsoft clients (or MS clients not capable of using MS-CHAP v2). The Shiva Password Authentication Protocol (SPAP) is an encryption mechanism employed by Shiva. This method is more secure than sending clear-text passwords (no encryption), but it's not as secure as MS-CHAP or CHAP. The Password Authentication Protocol (PAP) is the least secure method of authentication available in dial-up access. With this method, passwords are sent plain text without any sort of encryption. This method should be left available only if authentication is required and the client has no way of providing encryption. POP is not an authentication protocol. For more information, see Table 6.3, "Remote Access Authentication Methods," in Chapter 6.

15. **D.** This utility is called CIPHER.EXE. The utility encrypts files and folders with your encryption key. For more information, see "Encrypting Data Using Encrypting File System" in Chapter 7.

16. **B.** The third ARC parameter is *partition(z)*. This defines the physical partition number of the volume you want the path to point to. Unlike *controller* and *drive*, the numbering for *partition* begins at 1. For more information, see "ARC Paths and Volumes/Partitions" in Chapter 5.

17. **A.** Local profiles are stored on a specific computer and are available only from that computer. Roaming profiles are stored in a central location (like on a file server) and are accessed when a user logs into any machine. Mandatory profiles are roaming profiles that have been designated as read-only. For more information, see "Creating and Maintaining User Profiles" in Chapter 5.

18. **B.** Inside the Device manager, devices with problems are identified with a yellow-circled exclamation mark. For more information, see "Viewing Installed Devices" in Chapter 3.

19. **A.** This pattern (users → global groups → local groups → permission to access resources) is given the acronym "UGLP" and pronounced "uglip." For more information, see "Local Groups and Users" in Chapter 2.

20. **D.** The make boot disk process requires four blank formatted disks. For more information, see "Install by Using Setup Diskettes and a CD-ROM" in Chapter 1.

21. **A, B, C.** Maintenance of a standalone Dfs root consists of three tasks: adding Dfs links, removing Dfs links, and disabling Dfs links. You might add a new Dfs link when the Dfs tree needs to be expanded through the addition of a new link. You remove a link when you no longer need it and that need is deemed to be permanent. You will disable a Dfs link when you want to temporarily prevent a certain link from being accessed from within the Dfs tree. For more information, see "Standalone Dfs" in Chapter 2.

22. **C.** As a system administrator, you can implement system policies that check for signatures on your drivers. You have three choices of how to respond to the findings. You can choose to ignore signatures and allow the installation of drivers without checking for them. You can have the system check signatures on drivers when they are installed and warn you if the drivers are not signed; this gives you the chance to reconsider your decision to install an unverified driver. Finally, you can block the installation of unsigned drivers to ensure that your system is free of unverified and possibly corrupt drivers. For more information, see "Configuring Driver Signing Options" in Chapter 3.

23. **B.** The Recovery console is a powerful text-based boot alternative for Windows 2000 Server. If your system becomes so corrupt that it will not boot and no other repair process will help, you can boot to the Recovery console and copy files to or from your server. In addition, you can also stop and start services if a service that you have installed causes problems with booting. To boot to the Recovery console, either you can use the setup disks or boot from CD, or you can configure the Recovery console as a secondary boot in the boot menu and choose it at system startup. Because the Recovery console is so powerful, when it initiates, you must log in as the administrator. For more information, see "Recovering Systems with the Recovery Console" in Chapter 4.

24. **C.** COMPACT.EXE is the command line utility for compressing files. For most applications, you will find it most convenient to use the GUI to compress. However, there are some useful features that are available only in the command line version. For example, if you want to simply find out the compression status of a file, COMPACT will tell you that. In addition, if you want to compress only those files whose extension is .doc or .bmp you can do that with COMPACT. In addition, COMPACT will allow you to force compaction of files that Windows 2000 thinks are compacted but have not been because an error caused them not to compact completely. For example, if the power failed during compaction, a file's compacted attribute may have been set before the file was actually compacted. For more information, see "Compressing Files Using the Command Line Utility" in Chapter 5.

25. **B.** Remote Authentication Dial-In User Service (RADIUS) server. RADIUS is an industry standard for centralized authentication and accounting in a remote access environment. These servers are generally used in large-scale dial-up environments such as those of an Internet service provider (ISP). Windows 2000 Server has a RADIUS client that is capable of using the services of a RADIUS server. Windows 2000 also has the ability to function as a RADIUS server. This implementation is referred to as Internet Authentication Services (IAS) and allows for the centralization of many remote access management functions in an enterprise or multiple enterprise environment. For more information, see "Configuring the Server for Security and Network Access" in Chapter 6.

26. **D.** The proposed solution did not provide for the required result. On a single hard drive, you can have only one extended partition. That, coupled with the fact that you can have only four partitions in total on a hard drive, means you can combine partitions in the following ways: one primary; one primary and one extended; two primaries; two primaries and one extended; three primaries; three primaries and one extended; one extended. If you choose the last option, that hard drive does not have a bootable partition on it, and you can only use it in combination with another physical drive that has a primary partition. For more information, see "The Basic Disk" in Chapter 5.

27. **C.** The application priorities and their associated numeric values are Realtime(24), High (13), AboveNormal (Foreground – 10), Normal (Foreground – 9), BelowNormal (Foreground – 8), AboveNormal (Background – 8), Normal (Background – 7), BelowNormal (Background – 6), and Low (4). For more information, see "Assigning Priorities at Run Time" (and Table 4.1, "Priority Names and Their Values") in Chapter 4.

28. **A.** Web authentication happens at two levels: anonymous and authenticated. Anonymous access is the first method attempted when you connect to any Web site. If anonymous access is disabled, or if a Web user tries to perform a function that cannot be done by an anonymous user, authenticated access is attempted. Authenticated access always prompts you for a password. Whether one is required depends on whether a password has been configured for the account being used. For more information see "Controlling Web Site Access Through Authentication Methods" in Chapter 2.

29. **A.** When run from the Tools Management console or a command line, SYSPREP.EXE configures the disk image so that SIDS and other unique information are removed and re-created on the target machine. This ensures that no conflicts arise in interaction with other machines that have the same SID. For more information, see "Using SYSPREP.EXE" in Chapter 1.

30. **C.** A Windows 2000 server functions in a domain but does not hold a copy of the Active Directory. If a Windows 2000 server holds a copy of the Active Directory, it is known as a domain controller (DC). For more information, see "Windows 2000 Server and the 70-215 Exam" in Chapter 1.

31. **C.** The roles of a member server can be broken down into three main areas: file server, print server, and applications server. The primary function of each of these servers is self-explanatory. For more information, see "Giving and Controlling Data Access" in Chapter 2.

32. **B.** Although Apple Macintosh does not hold an overwhelming share of the PC market, it is not without its supporters and influence. Because of its strengths in desktop publishing and graphic manipulation, it has earned itself a place in a niche market of the computer industry. As a result, many companies with Windows 2000 servers also have one or more Apple Macintosh computers. For this reason, under Windows 2000, Microsoft continues to support three tools for Macintosh interoperability: File Services for Macintosh, Print Services for Macintosh, and the AppleTalk protocol. For more information, see "Interoperation with Apple Macintosh" in Chapter 2.

33. **C.** NTBACKUP.EXE is the command line tool used to back up a Windows 2000 machine. For more information, see Step by Step 4.17, "Scheduling Jobs for Backup using the Wizard," in Chapter 4.

34. **B.** To repair a damaged mirror, you must first remove the mirror (isolating the functioning volume) and then re-establish the mirror to an alternate drive (a new one that replaced the failed drive or the equivalent free space on an existing drive). For more information, see "Recovering from a Mirrored Data Volume Failure" in Chapter 5.

35. A. The proposed solution provides the required result and both of the desired results. Either Windows or UNIX may provide DNS. The requirement for dynamic DNS is that it must be version 8.1.3 or higher. Windows 2000 is bind version 8.1.3 compatible. Also, on the DNS property sheet, you can configure how DHCP interacts with DNS to make the DNS entries dynamic. If Automatically Update DHCP Client Information in DNS is selected, DNS records for Windows 2000 clients will be updated automatically when addresses are leased. Whether the client updates the DNS record or the DHCP server updates it depends on which option is selected: Update DNS Only If DHCP Client Requests or Always Update DNS. If the automatic update box is not selected, Windows 2000 clients never have DNS records created or updated when addresses are leased. Automatically update DNS does not exist. For more information, see "Installing and Configuring DHCP" in Chapter 6.

36. **A, C.** These items are security options that you might find helpful. 1) *Clear Virtual Memory Pagefile When System Shuts Down:* This ensures that when a server is shut down, the page file is deleted. So if someone shuts down the server, he will not be able to crack open the pagefile to examine data that has been paged to it. By default, this is not selected. 2) *Do Not Display Last User Name in Logon Screen:* This defines whether the user name of the last person to log onto a Windows 2000 machine is displayed for logon convenience. Although having the last user name displayed is convenient (especially if you were the last person to log on), it also provides one half of what is necessary to break into your server—a valid user name. If you enable this option, the User Name field always comes up blank. 3) *Message Text for Users Attempting to Log On:* This defines the text of a special security dialog box that appears just before the logon dialog box. This text box is used to make it clear to users who owns the system, who is welcome, and who is not. For example, you might configure a message such as "Network access is restricted to Company XYZ Inc. employees only!" If this option is not set, no dialog box appears before the logon dialog box. For more information, see "Implementing Security Options" in Chapter 7.

37. **D.** The Traverse Folder/Execute File permission allows or denies users the ability to pass through (traverse) a folder to which they do not have access in order to get to a folder or file to which they do have access. This property is applicable only if the user privilege Bypass Traverse Checking is not turned on in the system policy. By default, ByPass Traverse Checking is turned on for all users, so setting this permission has no effect. For more information, see Table 2.1, "Special Local (NTFS) Security Permissions," in Chapter 2.

38. **B.** A user that exists only on the Windows 2000 member server and does not exist in the domain's Active Directory is a local user. Local users are generally created only when you need to give access to resources to someone who does not log into your domain. For more information, see "Managing Local Users" in Chapter 2.

39. **D.** There are a number of factors you need to take into consideration when installing Windows 2000 Server (either from scratch or as an upgrade). These include hardware compatibility, software compatibility, disk size and partitions, and current operating system upgradability. You must consider and deal with each of these factors before you attempt an installation of Windows 2000 Server. For more information, see "Preparing for Installation" in Chapter 1.

40. **A.** Windows 2000 allows for multiple processes to run at once through the use of multitasking. This means that, regardless of the number of processors in a Windows 2000 server, more than one process can execute at one time. This is made possible through a specific kind of multitasking called preemptive multitasking. For more information, see "Introduction" in Chapter 4.

41. **A, C, E, F.** The components of a profile include Application, Cookies, Desktop, Favorites, Local Settings, My Documents, My Network Places, Printers, Recent Documents, SendTo, Start Menu, Templates, and NTUSER.DAT. For more information, see Table 5.1 "User Profile Components" in Chapter 5.

42. **B.** If the controller is *multi*, the disk parameter to watch is *rdisk*. Conversely, if the controller is *scsi*, the disk parameter to watch is *disk*. Regardless of the controller type, both elements of the parameter pair must be present. Like the controller number, disk numbers begin with 0; the first disk on a controller is numbered 0. For more information, see "ARC Paths and Volumes/Partitions" in Chapter 5.

43. **B.** Quotas are set at the volume (or partition) level. To implement them, the volume must be formatted using the NTFS file format because FAT does not support quotas. Quotas are set for individuals and not for groups (the Administrators group being the one exception to this rule). For more information, see "Monitoring and Configuring Disk Quotas" in Chapter 5.

44. **B.** Add the developer to either the Administrators group or the Power Users group on the local machine. These two are built-in groups (that is, they are created when the operating system is installed). Because they are built-in groups, their members have certain rights on the machine. One of the rights given to each of these groups is the ability to share files. It is important to note that whether in or out of a domain context, access to resources on a member server is completely controlled by the local security model. For more information, see "Setting Up and Maintaining Sharing" in Chapter 2.

45. **B.** The cache referral time is the length of time a Dfs client stores the location of the link to the remote machine. When this cache time expires, the client will have to consult with the Dfs server to reload the location. The default for this is 1800 seconds (30 minutes). For more information, see "Standalone Dfs" in Chapter 2.

46. **A.** Microsoft digitally signs each driver that Microsoft creates or verifies for other third-party companies. As a result, that driver is guaranteed to work with Windows 2000 and is verified to be free of corruption. Because that is the optimal state, you want all (or at least as many as possible) of your drivers to be signed. As hardware vendors create new drivers, they will be signed by Microsoft (or other trusted sources) and released. For more information, see "Configuring Driver Signing Options" in Chapter 3.

47. **C.** Striped volumes, like spanned volumes, consist of between 2 and 32 chunks of free space joined together. There are some differences between them, however. Whereas a spanned volume could consist of free space from a single hard drive, striped volumes must have free space from multiple hard drives. In addition, whereas the free space in spanned volumes does not have to be the same size, the pieces in a striped volume do. For more information, see "Creating Simple Volumes on Dynamic Disks" in Chapter 5.

48. **A.** If your DHCP server is a member server in a Windows 2000 domain, it must be authorized in the Active Directory before it can give out addresses. This is a safety precaution to ensure that DHCP servers cannot be accidentally enabled on the network, which would throw the configuration of TCP/IP addresses into chaos. For more information, see "Installing and Configuring DHCP" in Chapter 6.

49. **D.** CONVERT.EXE is a non-destructive conversion routine that does a one-time, one-way conversion from FAT or FAT32 to NTFS. It should be stressed at this time that this is one-way; you cannot convert back after your file system has been converted. For more information, see "The NTFS File System" in Chapter 2.

50. **C.** The minimum RAM required is 128MB for less than five clients. However, 256MB is recommended. For more information, see the section "Minimum Hardware Requirements" and Table 1.1, "Minimum Requirements for Windows 2000 Server Operating System Installation" in Chapter 1.

51. **A, B.** There are two versions for FPNW, one that allows NetWare 3.x and 4.x clients to access Windows resources, and another that allows 5.x clients to access resources. For more information, see "File and Print Services for NetWare" in Chapter 2.

52. **A, C.** The ability to configure Windows 2000 properly is essential to a smooth-running operating system. Windows 2000 makes the configuration of hardware devices very easy through the implementation of the Plug and Play manager. This manager ensures that all Plug and Play compatible devices are automatically detected and their drivers installed. Windows 2000 might locate devices that are not Plug and Play and have their drivers installed. This is especially true on hot-plug buses. As a result, the amount of time you will spend manually configuring hardware IRQs will be greatly reduced. For more information, see "Configuring Hardware Devices" in Chapter 3.

53. **A, B, C, D, F.** Under normal operation, only four system components will affect system performance: memory, processor, disk, and network card. That means you are looking to monitor the counters that will tell you the most about those four components so you can determine the answer to the two diagnostic questions. In preparation for logging to find bottlenecks, you must do two things: first, you have to enable some disk counters, and second, you have to enable network

segment counters. By default, there are counters available to monitor the physical disk object. This means that you can watch to see how much activity is happening on a physical disk. But to determine bottlenecks, you may need to see the disk in finer sections than that. For more information, see the section "Using Performance Monitor to Discover Bottlenecks and Optimize Resource Utilization," and also Table 4.3, "Counters to Monitor," in Chapter 4.

54. **A, B.** Two tunneling protocols are available under Windows 2000 Remote Access Services: Point to Point Tunneling Protocol (PPTP) and Layer Two Tunneling Protocol (L2TP). For more information, see "Installing, Configuring, and Troubleshooting VPNs" in Chapter 6.

55. **B.** NAT stands for Network Address Translation, the process of translating or hiding addresses on an internal network from the external network. This is very useful when a limited number of network addresses are available and you might need to use the Internet reserved address groups. NAT not only maps the internal address with a destination TCP/IP address but also assigns a port number to the transmission. When a user connects to a Web site, it uses the outgoing port 80 and the return port 1025. When this gets to the NAT server, it forwards the request to the appropriate public address, but then it changes the return port to something else (say 5000). When the information comes back, it is destined for port 5000. The NAT server checks its map and finds out that transmissions from this server on port 5000 are really destined for port 1025 on the appropriate private address. For more information, see "Configuring Shared Access Using NAT" in Chapter 6.

56. **C.** Windows NT supports NTFS version 4, and Windows 2000 is version 5; version 5 has been enhanced to provide file encryption (among other things) and is not 100% compatible with version 4. For more information, see "The NTFS File System" in Chapter 2.

57. **A, B, C.** An unattended installation is an installation in which the answers are provided by a script that has been created beforehand. There are four ways to perform an attended installation: 1) by booting to a CD-ROM and invoking the setup routing, 2) by booting to a current operating system with CD-ROM support and manually invoking the setup routine, 3) by booting to a set of four setup disks and then providing the CD-ROM when prompted, 4) by booting to a network-aware operating system and invoking setup over the network. For more information, see "Attended Installations of Windows 2000 Server" in Chapter 1.

58. **A** The creation of a roaming profile always follows the same basic steps: Configure a shared folder on a server to hold the roaming profiles; create a folder within the shared folder for each user who is going to be roaming (the name of the folder should be the user's login name); copy an existing profile into the folder for each user; configure the user's account to point to the roaming location. To get a profile to copy into the roaming location, it helps to create a user account with a local profile that can be configured the way you want each roaming user's desktop to begin. If the user is being converted from a local profile to a roaming profile, copy that local profile to the user's roaming location. For more information, see "Roaming User Profiles" in Chapter 5.

59. **D.** In Windows 2000, drive letters are not fixed to specific partitions. Rather, they can be changed at any time. The only exceptions are the System and Boot partitions. You cannot change the drive letters of either of those special partitions. The problem is that some programs record their positions in the Registry using the drive letter they were installed onto. If you change the drive letter of a partition, the references to it will not be updated, and many programs will no longer run. Therefore, you should exercise caution when changing drive letters and do it as soon after creating the partition as you can. For more information, see "Changing the Drive Letter of a Partition" in Chapter 5.

60. **B, C, D.** IPCONFIG is useful in troubleshooting because it not only allows you to see what your configuration is, it is helps you determine whether you have a TCP/IP address at all. PING tells you whether you can communicate with other computers using TCP/IP. TRACERT is used to determine what route is being taken from one host to another. NETSTATE does not exist. For more information, see "Troubleshooting TCP/IP" in Chapter 6.

61. **C.** A Windows 2000 password policy consists of six different settings: password history, minimum age, maximum age, minimum length, complexity, and reverse encryption storage. For more information, see "Implementing Local Password Policy" in Chapter 7.

62. **B.** By default, Windows 2000 Server does not boost foreground applications, whereas Windows 2000 Professional does. This reflects the typical uses of each operating system. Professional generally deals with interactive applications that are usually idle when running in the background. Server generally deals with applications that are left to run on their own, giving no priority to the running applications and keeping user input to a minimum. For more information, see "Controlling Normal Priority Applications" in Chapter 4.

63. **C.** WINNT.EXE is the only non-32 bit installation program for Windows NT and, therefore, is the only executable that will work with DOS. For more information, see "Script-Based Unattended Installation" in Chapter 1.

64. **B.** You must have Power User or Administrator access in order to Web share a folder. For more information, see "Web Sharing in Its Context" in Chapter 2.

65. **A.** A terminal service is a session hosting service that allows a Windows 2000 server to provide environment resources (memory, processor, hard drive), whereas a client provides only minimal memory and processor resources. The end result is that a client as "thin" as a Windows for Workgroups (Windows 3.11) client with 16MB of memory, a 386 processor, and a network card will be able to emulate a Windows 2000 environment with little loss of performance over a Pentium machine with 64MB of RAM running the same applications. For more information, see "Installing, Configuring, and Troubleshooting Terminal Services" in Chapter 6.

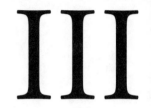

PART

III

APPENDIXES

Overview of the Certification Process

You must pass rigorous certification exams to become a Microsoft Certified Professional. These closed-book exams provide a valid and reliable measure of your technical proficiency and expertise. Developed in consultation with computer industry professionals who have experience with Microsoft products in the workplace, the exams are conducted by two independent organizations. Sylvan Prometric offers the exams at more than 2,000 authorized Prometric Testing Centers around the world. Virtual University Enterprises (VUE) testing centers offer exams at more than 1,400 locations as well.

To schedule an exam, call Sylvan Prometric Testing Centers at 800-755-EXAM (3926) (or register online at http://www.2test.com/register) or VUE at 888-837-8734 (or register online at http://www.vue.com/ms/msexam.html). At the time of this writing, Microsoft offered eight types of certification, each based on a specific area of expertise. Please check the Microsoft Certified Professional Web site for the most up-to-date information (www.microsoft.com/mcp/).

TYPES OF CERTIFICATION

◆ **Microsoft Certified Professional (MCP).** Persons with this credential are qualified to support at least one Microsoft product. Candidates can take elective exams to develop areas of specialization. MCP is the base level of expertise.

◆ **Microsoft Certified Professional+Internet (MCP+Internet).** Persons with this credential are qualified to plan security, install and configure server products, manage server resources, extend service to run CGI scripts or ISAPI scripts, monitor and analyze performance, and troubleshoot problems. Expertise is similar to that of an MCP but with a focus on the Internet.

◆ **Microsoft Certified Professional+Site Building (MCP+Site Building).** Persons with this credential are qualified to plan, build, maintain, and manage Web sites using Microsoft technologies and products. The credential is appropriate for people who manage sophisticated, interactive Web sites that include database connectivity, multimedia, and searchable content.

◆ **Microsoft Certified Database Administrator (MCDBA).** Qualified individuals can derive physical database designs, develop logical data models, create physical databases, create data services by using Transact-SQL, manage and maintain databases, configure and manage security, monitor and optimize databases, and install and configure Microsoft SQL Server.

◆ **Microsoft Certified Systems Engineer (MCSE).** These individuals are qualified to analyze the business requirements for a system architecture; design solutions; deploy, install, and configure architecture components; and troubleshoot system problems.

◆ **Microsoft Certified Systems Engineer+Internet (MCSE+Internet).** Persons with this credential are qualified in the core MCSE areas and also are qualified to enhance, deploy, and manage sophisticated intranet and Internet solutions that include a browser, proxy server, host servers, database, and messaging and commerce components. An MCSE+Internet-certified professional is able to manage and analyze Web sites.

◆ **Microsoft Certified Solution Developer (MCSD).** These individuals are qualified to design and develop custom business solutions by using Microsoft development tools, technologies, and platforms. The new track includes certification exams that test the user's ability to build Web-based, distributed, and commerce applications by using Microsoft products such as Microsoft SQL Server, Microsoft Visual Studio, and Microsoft Component Services.

◆ **Microsoft Certified Trainer (MCT).** Persons with this credential are instructionally and technically qualified by Microsoft to deliver Microsoft Education Courses at Microsoft-authorized sites. An MCT must be employed by a Microsoft Solution Provider Authorized Technical Education Center or a Microsoft Authorized Academic Training site.

NOTE For up-to-date information about each type of certification, visit the Microsoft Training and Certification Web site at http://www.microsoft.com/mcp. You can also contact Microsoft through the following sources:

- Microsoft Certified Professional Program: 800-636-7544
- mcp@msource.com
- Microsoft Online Institute (MOLI): 800-449-9333

CERTIFICATION REQUIREMENTS

The following sections describe the requirements for the various types of Microsoft certifications.

NOTE An asterisk following an exam in any of the following lists means that it is slated for retirement.

How to Become a Microsoft Certified Professional

To become certified as an MCP, you need only pass any Microsoft exam (with the exceptions of Networking Essentials, #70-058* and Microsoft Windows 2000 Accelerated Exam for MCPs Certified on Microsoft Windows NT 4.0, #70-240).

How to Become a Microsoft Certified Professional+Internet

To become an MCP specializing in Internet technology, you must pass the following exams:

◆ Internetworking with Microsoft TCP/IP on Microsoft Windows NT 4.0, #70-059*

◆ Implementing and Supporting Microsoft Windows NT Server 4.0, #70-067*

◆ Implementing and Supporting Microsoft Internet Information Server 3.0 and Microsoft Index Server 1.1, #70-077*

  OR Implementing and Supporting Microsoft Internet Information Server 4.0, #70-087*

How to Become a Microsoft Certified Professional+Site Building

To be certified as an MCP+Site Building, you need to pass two of the following exams:

◆ Designing and Implementing Web Sites with Microsoft FrontPage 98, #70-055

◆ Designing and Implementing Commerce Solutions with Microsoft Site Server 3.0, Commerce Edition, #70-057

◆ Designing and Implementing Web Solutions with Microsoft Visual InterDev 6.0, #70-152

How to Become a Microsoft Certified Database Administrator

There are two MCDBA tracks, one tied to Windows 2000, the other based on Windows NT 4.0.

Windows 2000 Track

To become an MCDBA in the Windows 2000 track, you must pass three core exams and one elective exam.

Core Exams

The core exams required to become an MCDBA in the Windows 2000 track are as follows:

◆ Installing, Configuring, and Administering Microsoft Windows 2000 Server, #70-215

  OR Microsoft Windows 2000 Accelerated Exam for MCPs Certified on Microsoft Windows NT 4.0, #70-240 (only for those who have passed exams #70-067*, #70-068*, and #70-073*)

◆ Administering Microsoft SQL Server 7.0, #70-028

◆ Designing and Implementing Databases with Microsoft SQL Server 7.0, #70-029

Elective Exams

You must also pass one elective exam from the following list:

◆ Implementing and Administering a Microsoft Windows 2000 Network Infrastructure, #70-216 (only for those who have *not* already passed #70-067*, #70-068*, and #70-073*)

OR Microsoft Windows 2000 Accelerated Exam for MCPs Certified on Microsoft Windows NT 4.0, #70-240 (only for those who have passed exams #70-067*, #70-068*, and #70-073*)

◆ Designing and Implementing Distributed Applications with Microsoft Visual C++ 6.0, #70-015

◆ Designing and Implementing Data Warehouses with Microsoft SQL Server 7.0 and Microsoft Decision Support Services 1.0, #70-019

◆ Implementing and Supporting Microsoft Internet Information Server 4.0, #70-087*

◆ Designing and Implementing Distributed Applications with Microsoft Visual FoxPro 6.0, #70-155

◆ Designing and Implementing Distributed Applications with Microsoft Visual Basic 6.0, #70-175

Windows NT 4.0 Track

To become an MCDBA in the Windows NT 4.0 track, you must pass four core exams and one elective exam.

Core Exams

The core exams required to become an MCDBA in the Windows NT 4.0 track are as follows:

◆ Administering Microsoft SQL Server 7.0, #70-028

◆ Designing and Implementing Databases with Microsoft SQL Server 7.0, #70-029

◆ Implementing and Supporting Microsoft Windows NT Server 4.0, #70-067*

◆ Implementing and Supporting Microsoft Windows NT Server 4.0 in the Enterprise, #70-068*

Elective Exams

You must also pass one elective exam from the following list:

◆ Designing and Implementing Distributed Applications with Microsoft Visual C++ 6.0, #70-015

◆ Designing and Implementing Data Warehouses with Microsoft SQL Server 7.0 and Microsoft Decision Support Services 1.0, #70-019

◆ Internetworking with Microsoft TCP/IP on Microsoft Windows NT 4.0, #70-059*

◆ Implementing and Supporting Microsoft Internet Information Server 4.0, #70-087*

◆ Designing and Implementing Distributed Applications with Microsoft Visual FoxPro 6.0, #70-155

◆ Designing and Implementing Distributed Applications with Microsoft Visual Basic 6.0, #70-175

How to Become a Microsoft Certified Systems Engineer

You must pass operating system exams and two elective exams to become an MCSE. The MCSE certification path is divided into two tracks: Windows 2000 and Windows NT 4.0.

The following lists show the core requirements for the Windows 2000 and Windows NT 4.0 tracks and the electives.

Windows 2000 Track

The Windows 2000 track requires you to pass five core exams (or an accelerated exam and another core exam). You must also pass two elective exams.

Core Exams

The Windows 2000 track core requirements for MCSE certification include the following for those who have *not* passed #70-067, #70-068, and #70-073:

◆ Installing, Configuring, and Administering Microsoft Windows 2000 Professional, #70-210

◆ Installing, Configuring, and Administering Microsoft Windows 2000 Server, #70-215

◆ Implementing and Administering a Microsoft Windows 2000 Network Infrastructure, #70-216

◆ Implementing and Administering a Microsoft Windows 2000 Directory Services Infrastructure, #70-217

The Windows 2000 Track core requirements for MCSE certification include the following for those who have passed #70-067*, #70-068*, and #70-073*:

◆ Microsoft Windows 2000 Accelerated Exam for MCPs Certified on Microsoft Windows NT 4.0, #70-240

All candidates must pass one of these three additional core exams:

◆ Designing a Microsoft Windows 2000 Directory Services Infrastructure, #70-219

   OR Designing Security for a Microsoft Windows 2000 Network, #70-220

   OR Designing a Microsoft Windows 2000 Infrastructure, #70-221

Elective Exams

Any MCSE elective exams that are current (not slated for retirement) when the Windows 2000 core exams are released can be used to fulfill the requirement of two elective exams. In addition, core exams #70-219,

#70-220, and #70-221 can be used as elective exams, as long as they are not already being used to fulfill the "additional core exams" requirement outlined previously. Exam #70-222 (Upgrading from Microsoft Windows NT 4.0 to Microsoft Windows 2000), can also be used to fulfill this requirement. Finally, selected third-party certifications that focus on interoperability may count for this requirement. Watch the Microsoft MCP Web site (www.microsoft.com/mcp) for more information on these third-party certifications.

Windows NT 4.0 Track

The Windows NT 4.0 track is also organized around core and elective exams.

Core Exams

The four Windows NT 4.0 track core requirements for MCSE certification are as follows:

◆ Implementing and Supporting Microsoft Windows NT Server 4.0, #70-067*

◆ Implementing and Supporting Microsoft Windows NT Server 4.0 in the Enterprise, #70-068*

◆ Microsoft Windows 3.1, #70-030*

   OR Microsoft Windows for Workgroups 3.11, #70-048*

   OR Implementing and Supporting Microsoft Windows 95, #70-064*

   OR Implementing and Supporting Microsoft Windows NT Workstation 4.0, #70-073*

   OR Implementing and Supporting Microsoft Windows 98, #70-098

◆ Networking Essentials, #70-058*

Elective Exams

For the Windows NT 4.0 track, you must pass two of the following elective exams for MCSE certification:

◆ Implementing and Supporting Microsoft SNA Server 3.0, #70-013

   OR Implementing and Supporting Microsoft SNA Server 4.0, #70-085

◆ Implementing and Supporting Microsoft Systems Management Server 1.2, #70-018

   OR Implementing and Supporting Microsoft Systems Management Server 2.0, #70-086

◆ Designing and Implementing Data Warehouse with Microsoft SQL Server 7.0, #70-019

◆ Microsoft SQL Server 4.2 Database Implementation, #70-021*

   OR Implementing a Database Design on Microsoft SQL Server 6.5, #70-027

   OR Implementing a Database Design on Microsoft SQL Server 7.0, #70-029

◆ Microsoft SQL Server 4.2 Database Administration for Microsoft Windows NT, #70-022*

   OR System Administration for Microsoft SQL Server 6.5 (or 6.0), #70-026

   OR System Administration for Microsoft SQL Server 7.0, #70-028

◆ Microsoft Mail for PC Networks 3.2-Enterprise, #70-037*

◆ Internetworking with Microsoft TCP/IP on Microsoft Windows NT (3.5–3.51), #70-053*

   OR Internetworking with Microsoft TCP/IP on Microsoft Windows NT 4.0, #70-059*

◆ Implementing and Supporting Web Sites Using Microsoft Site Server 3.0, #70-056

◆ Implementing and Supporting Microsoft Exchange Server 4.0, #70-075*

   OR Implementing and Supporting Microsoft Exchange Server 5.0, #70-076

   OR Implementing and Supporting Microsoft Exchange Server 5.5, #70-081

◆ Implementing and Supporting Microsoft Internet Information Server 3.0 and Microsoft Index Server 1.1, #70-077*

   OR Implementing and Supporting Microsoft Internet Information Server 4.0, #70-087*

◆ Implementing and Supporting Microsoft Proxy Server 1.0, #70-078

   OR Implementing and Supporting Microsoft Proxy Server 2.0, #70-088

◆ Implementing and Supporting Microsoft Internet Explorer 4.0 by Using the Internet Explorer Resource Kit, #70-079

   OR Implementing and Supporting Microsoft Internet Explorer 5.0 by Using the Internet Explorer Resource Kit, #70-080

◆ Designing a Microsoft Windows 2000 Directory Services Infrastructure, #70-219

◆ Designing Security for a Microsoft Windows 2000 Network, #70-220

◆ Designing a Microsoft Windows 2000 Infrastructure, #70-221

◆ Upgrading from Microsoft Windows NT 4.0 to Microsoft Windows 2000, #70-222

How to Become a Microsoft Certified Systems Engineer+Internet

You must pass seven operating system exams and two elective exams to become an MCSE specializing in Internet technology.

Core Exams

The following seven core exams are required for MCSE+Internet certification:

◆ Networking Essentials, #70-058*

◆ Internetworking with Microsoft TCP/IP on Microsoft Windows NT 4.0, #70-059*

◆ Implementing and Supporting Microsoft Windows 95, #70-064*

  OR Implementing and Supporting Microsoft Windows NT Workstation 4.0, #70-073*

  OR Implementing and Supporting Microsoft Windows 98, #70-098

◆ Implementing and Supporting Microsoft Windows NT Server 4.0, #70-067*

◆ Implementing and Supporting Microsoft Windows NT Server 4.0 in the Enterprise, #70-068*

◆ Implementing and Supporting Microsoft Internet Information Server 3.0 and Microsoft Index Server 1.1, #70-077*

  OR Implementing and Supporting Microsoft Internet Information Server 4.0, #70-087*

◆ Implementing and Supporting Microsoft Internet Explorer 4.0 by Using the Internet Explorer Resource Kit, #70-079

OR Implementing and Supporting Microsoft Internet Explorer 5.0 by Using the Internet Explorer Resource Kit, #70-080

Elective Exams

You must also pass two of the following elective exams for MCSE+Internet certification:

◆ System Administration for Microsoft SQL Server 6.5, #70-026

  OR Administering Microsoft SQL Server 7.0, #70-028

◆ Implementing a Database Design on Microsoft SQL Server 6.5, #70-027

  OR Designing and Implementing Databases with Microsoft SQL Server 7.0, #70-029

◆ Implementing and Supporting Web Sites Using Microsoft Site Server 3.0, # 70-056

◆ Implementing and Supporting Microsoft Exchange Server 5.0, #70-076

  OR Implementing and Supporting Microsoft Exchange Server 5.5, #70-081

◆ Implementing and Supporting Microsoft Proxy Server 1.0, #70-078

  OR Implementing and Supporting Microsoft Proxy Server 2.0, #70-088

◆ Implementing and Supporting Microsoft SNA Server 4.0, #70-085

How to Become a Microsoft Certified Solution Developer

The MCSD certification has undergone substantial revision. Listed below are the requirements for the new track (available fourth quarter 1998) as well as the old.

New Track

For the new track, you must pass three core exams and one elective exam.

Core Exams

The core exams are as follows. You must pass one exam in each of the following groups:

Desktop Applications Development (one required)

◆ Designing and Implementing Desktop Applications with Microsoft Visual C++ 6.0, #70-016

 OR Designing and Implementing Desktop Applications with Microsoft Visual FoxPro 6.0, #70-156

 OR Designing and Implementing Desktop Applications with Microsoft Visual Basic 6.0, #70-176

Distributed Applications Development (one required)

◆ Designing and Implementing Distributed Applications with Microsoft Visual C++ 6.0, #70-015

 OR Designing and Implementing Distributed Applications with Microsoft Visual FoxPro 6.0, #70-155

 OR Designing and Implementing Distributed Applications with Microsoft Visual Basic 6.0, #70-175

Solution Architecture (required)

◆ Analyzing Requirements and Defining Solution Architectures, #70-100

Elective Exam

You must pass one of the following elective exams:

◆ Designing and Implementing Distributed Applications with Microsoft Visual C++ 6.0, #70-015

◆ Designing and Implementing Desktop Applications with Microsoft Visual C++ 6.0, #70-016

◆ Designing and Implementing Data Warehouses with Microsoft SQL Server 7.0, #70-019

◆ Developing Applications with C++ Using the Microsoft Foundation Class Library, #70-024

◆ Implementing OLE in Microsoft Foundation Class Applications, #70-025

◆ Implementing a Database Design on Microsoft SQL Server 6.5, #70-027

◆ Implementing a Database Design on Microsoft SQL Server 7.0, #70-029

◆ Designing and Implementing Web Sites with Microsoft FrontPage 98, #70-055

◆ Designing and Implementing Commerce Solutions with Microsoft Site Server 3.0, Commerce Edition, #70-057

◆ Programming with Microsoft Visual Basic 4.0, #70-065*

◆ Application Development with Microsoft Access for Windows 95 and the Microsoft Access Developer's Toolkit, #70-069

◆ Designing and Implementing Solutions with Microsoft Office 2000 and Microsoft Visual Basic for Applications, #70-091

◆ Designing and Implementing Database Applications with Microsoft Access 2000, #70-097

◆ Designing and Implementing Collaborative Solutions with Microsoft Outlook 2000 and Microsoft Exchange Server 5.5, #70-105

◆ Designing and Implementing Web Solutions with Microsoft Visual InterDev 6.0, #70-152

◆ Designing and Implementing Distributed Applications with Microsoft Visual FoxPro 6.0, #70-155

◆ Designing and Implementing Desktop Applications with Microsoft Visual FoxPro 6.0, #70-156

◆ Developing Applications with Microsoft Visual Basic 5.0, #70-165

◆ Designing and Implementing Distributed Applications with Microsoft Visual Basic 6.0, #70-175

◆ Designing and Implementing Desktop Applications with Microsoft Visual Basic 6.0, #70-176

Old Track

For the old track, you must pass two core technology exams and two elective exams for MCSD certification. The following lists show the required technology exams and elective exams needed for MCSD certification.

Core Exams

You must pass the following two core technology exams to qualify for MCSD certification:

◆ Microsoft Windows Architecture I, #70-160*

◆ Microsoft Windows Architecture II, #70-161*

Elective Exams

You must also pass two of the following elective exams to become an MSCD:

◆ Designing and Implementing Distributed Applications with Microsoft Visual C++ 6.0, #70-015

◆ Designing and Implementing Desktop Applications with Microsoft Visual C++ 6.0, #70-016

◆ Designing and Implementing Data Warehouses with Microsoft SQL Server 7.0, #70-019

◆ Microsoft SQL Server 4.2 Database Implementation, #70-021*

   OR Implementing a Database Design on Microsoft SQL Server 6.5, #70-027

   OR Implementing a Database Design on Microsoft SQL Server 7.0, #70-029

◆ Developing Applications with C++ Using the Microsoft Foundation Class Library, #70-024

◆ Implementing OLE in Microsoft Foundation Class Applications, #70-025

◆ Programming with Microsoft Visual Basic 4.0, #70-065

   OR Developing Applications with Microsoft Visual Basic 5.0, #70-165

   OR Designing and Implementing Distributed Applications with Microsoft Visual Basic 6.0, #70-175

◆ Designing and Implementing Desktop Applications with Microsoft Visual Basic 6.0, #70-176

◆ Microsoft Access 2.0 for Windows-Application Development, #70-051*

 OR Microsoft Access for Windows 95 and the Microsoft Access Development Toolkit, #70-069

 OR Designing and Implementing Database Applications with Microsoft Access 2000, #70-097

◆ Developing Applications with Microsoft Excel 5.0 Using Visual Basic for Applications, #70-052*

◆ Programming in Microsoft Visual FoxPro 3.0 for Windows, #70-054*

 OR Designing and Implementing Distributed Applications with Microsoft Visual FoxPro 6.0, #70-155

 OR Designing and Implementing Desktop Applications with Microsoft Visual FoxPro 6.0, #70-156

◆ Designing and Implementing Web Sites with Microsoft FrontPage 98, #70-055

◆ Designing and Implementing Commerce Solutions with Microsoft Site Server 3.0, Commerce Edition, #70-057

◆ Designing and Implementing Solutions with Microsoft Office (code-named Office 9) and Microsoft Visual Basic for Applications, #70-091

◆ Designing and Implementing Collaborative Solutions with Microsoft Outlook 2000 and Microsoft Exchange Server 5.5, #70-105

◆ Designing and Implementing Web Solutions with Microsoft Visual InterDev 6.0, #70-152

Becoming a Microsoft Certified Trainer

To fully understand the requirements and process for becoming an MCT, you need to obtain the Microsoft Certified Trainer Guide document from the following WWW site:

```
http://www.microsoft.com/mcp/certstep/mct.htm
```

At this site, you can read the document as a Web page or display and download it as a Word file. The MCT Guide explains the process for becoming an MCT. The general steps for the MCT certification are as follows:

1. Complete and mail a Microsoft Certified Trainer application to Microsoft. You must include proof of your skills for presenting instructional material. The options for doing so are described in the MCT Guide.

2. Obtain and study the Microsoft Trainer Kit for the Microsoft Official Curricula (MOC) courses for which you want to be certified. Microsoft Trainer Kits can be ordered by calling 800-688-0496 in North America. Those of you in other regions should review the MCT Guide for information on how to order a Trainer Kit.

3. Take and pass any required prerequisite MCP exam(s) to measure your current technical knowledge.

4. Prepare to teach a MOC course. Begin by attending the MOC course for which you want to be certified. This is required so that you understand how the course is structured, how labs are completed, and how the course flows.

5. Pass any additional exam requirement(s) to measure any additional product knowledge that pertains to the course.

6. Submit your course preparation checklist to Microsoft so that your additional accreditation may be processed and reflect on your transcript.

> **WARNING**
>
> You should consider the preceding steps a general overview of the MCT certification process. The precise steps that you need to take are described in detail on the Web site mentioned earlier. Do not misinterpret the preceding steps as the exact process you must undergo.

If you are interested in becoming an MCT, you can obtain more information by visiting the Microsoft Certified Training WWW site at `http://www.microsoft.com/train_cert/mct/` or by calling 800-688-0496.

What's on the CD-ROM

This appendix is a brief rundown of what you'll find on the CD-ROM that comes with this book. For a more detailed description of the newly developed *ExamGear, Training Guide Edition* exam simulation software, see Appendix C, "Using the *ExamGear, Training Guide Edition* Software." All items on the CD-ROM are easily accessible from the simple interface. In addition to *ExamGear, Training Guide Edition*, the CD-ROM includes the electronic version of the book in Portable Document Format (PDF), several utility and application programs, and a complete listing of test objectives and where they are covered in the book.

EXAMGEAR, TRAINING GUIDE EDITION

ExamGear is an exam environment developed exclusively for New Riders Publishing. It is, we believe, the best exam software available. In addition to providing a means of evaluating your knowledge of the *Training Guide* material, *ExamGear, Training Guide Edition* features several innovations that help you to improve your mastery of the subject matter.

For example, the practice tests allow you to check your score by exam area or category to determine which topics you need to study more. In another mode, *ExamGear, Training Guide Edition* allows you to obtain immediate feedback on your responses in the form of explanations for the correct and incorrect answers.

Although *ExamGear, Training Guide Edition* exhibits most of the full functionality of the retail version of *ExamGear*, including the exam format and question types, this special version is written to the Training Guide content. It is designed to aid you in assessing how well you understand the Training Guide material and enable you to experience most of the question formats you will see on the actual exam. It is not as complete a simulation of the exam as the full *ExamGear* retail product. It also does not include some of the features of the full retail product, such as access to the mentored discussion groups. However, it serves as an excellent method for assessing your knowledge of the Training Guide content and gives you the experience of taking an electronic exam.

Again, for a more complete description of *ExamGear, Training Guide Edition* features, see Appendix C.

EXCLUSIVE ELECTRONIC VERSION OF TEXT

The CD-ROM also contains the electronic version of this book in Portable Document Format (PDF). The electronic version comes complete with all figures as they appear in the book. You will find that the search capabilities of the reader come in handy for study and review purposes.

Copyright Information and Disclaimer

New Riders Publishing's *ExamGear* **test simulator:**
Copyright ©2000 by New Riders Publishing. All rights reserved. Made in U.S.A.

Using the *ExamGear, Training Guide Edition* Software

This training guide includes a special version of *ExamGear*—a revolutionary new test engine that is designed to give you the best in certification exam preparation. *ExamGear* offers sample and practice exams for many of today's most in-demand technical certifications. This special Training Guide edition is included with this book as a tool to utilize in assessing your knowledge of the Training Guide material while also providing you with the experience of taking an electronic exam.

In the rest of this appendix, we describe in detail what *ExamGear, Training Guide Edition* is, how it works, and what it can do to help you prepare for the exam. Note that although the Training Guide edition includes nearly all the test simulation functions of the complete, retail version, the questions focus on the Training Guide content rather than on simulating the actual Microsoft exam. Also, this version does not offer the same degree of online support that the full product does.

EXAM SIMULATION

One of the main functions of *ExamGear, Training Guide Edition* is exam simulation. To prepare you to take the actual vendor certification exam, the Training Guide edition of this test engine is designed to offer the most effective exam simulation available.

Question Quality

The questions provided in the *ExamGear, Training Guide Edition* simulations are written to high standards of technical accuracy. The questions tap the content of the Training Guide chapters and help you review and assess your knowledge before you take the actual exam.

Interface Design

The *ExamGear, Training Guide Edition* exam simulation interface provides you with the experience of taking an electronic exam. This enables you to effectively prepare for taking the actual exam by making the test experience a familiar one. Using the this test simulation can help eliminate the sense of surprise or anxiety that you might experience in the testing center, because you will already be acquainted with computerized testing.

STUDY TOOLS

ExamGear provides you with several learning tools to help prepare you for the actual certification exam.

Effective Learning Environment

The *ExamGear, Training Guide Edition* interface provides a learning environment that not only tests you through the computer, but also teaches the material you need to know to pass the certification exam. Each question comes with a detailed explanation of the correct answer and provides reasons why the other options were incorrect. This information helps to reinforce the knowledge you have already and also provides practical information you can use on the job.

Automatic Progress Tracking

ExamGear, Training Guide Edition automatically tracks your progress as you work through the test questions. From the Item Review tab (discussed in detail later in this appendix), you can see at a glance how well you are scoring by objective, by unit, or on a question-by-question basis (see Figure C.1). You can also configure *ExamGear* to drill you on the skills you need to work on most.

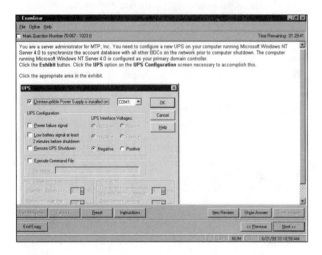

FIGURE C.1
Item review.

HOW *EXAMGEAR, TRAINING GUIDE EDITION* WORKS

ExamGear comprises two main elements: the interface and the database. The *interface* is the part of the program that you use to study and to run practice tests. The *database* stores all the question-and-answer data.

Interface

The *ExamGear, Training Guide Edition* interface is designed to be easy to use and provides the most effective study method available. The interface enables you to select from among the following modes:

◆ **Study Mode.** In this mode, you can select the number of questions you want to see and the time you want to allow for the test. You can select questions from all the chapters or from specific chapters. This enables you to reinforce your knowledge in a specific area or strengthen your knowledge in areas pertaining to a specific objective. During the exam, you can display the correct answer to each question along with an explanation of why it is correct.

◆ **Practice Exam.** In this mode, you take an exam that is designed to simulate the actual certification exam. Questions are selected from all test-objective groups. The number of questions selected and the time allowed are set to match those parameters of the actual certification exam.

◆ **Adaptive Exam.** In this mode, you take an exam simulation using the adaptive testing technique. Questions are taken from all test-objective groups. The questions are presented in a way that ensures your mastery of all the test objectives. After you have a passing score or if you reach a point where it is statistically impossible for you to pass, the exam is ended. This method provides a rapid assessment of your readiness for the actual exam.

Database

The *ExamGear, Training Guide Edition* database stores a group of test questions along with answers and explanations. At least three databases are included for each Training Guide edition product. One includes the questions from the ends of the chapters. Another includes the questions from the Assessment Exam. The third is a database of new questions that have not appeared in the book. Additional exam databases may also be available for purchase online and are simple to download. Look ahead to the section "Obtaining Updates" in this appendix to find out how to download and activate additional databases.

INSTALLING AND REGISTERING EXAMGEAR, TRAINING GUIDE EDITION

This section provides instructions for *ExamGear, Training Guide Edition* installation and describes the process and benefits of registering your Training Guide edition product.

Requirements

ExamGear requires a computer with the following:

◆ Microsoft Windows 95, Windows 98, Windows NT 4.0, or Windows 2000.

A Pentium or later processor is recommended.

◆ Microsoft's Internet Explorer 4.01 or later version.

Internet Explorer 4.01 (or a later version) must be installed. (Even if you use a different browser, you still need to have Internet Explorer 4.01 or later installed.)

◆ A minimum of 16MB of RAM.

As with any Windows application, the more memory, the better your performance.

◆ A connection to the Internet.

An Internet connection is not required for the software to work, but it is required for online registration, product updates, downloading bonus question sets, and for unlocking other exams. These processes are described in more detail later.

Installing *ExamGear, Training Guide Edition*

Install *ExamGear, Training Guide Edition* by running the setup program that you found on the *ExamGear, Training Guide Edition* CD. Follow these instructions to install the Training Guide edition on your computer:

1. Insert the CD in your CD-ROM drive. The Autorun feature of Windows should launch the software. If you have Autorun disabled, click Start, and choose Run. Go to the root directory of the CD and choose START.EXE. Click Open and OK.

2. Click the button in the circle, and you see the welcome screen. From here you can install *ExamGear*. Click the ExamGear button to begin installation.

3. The Installation Wizard appears onscreen and prompts you with instructions to complete the installation. Select a directory on which to install *ExamGear, Training Guide Edition* (the Installation Wizard defaults to C:\Program Files\ExamGear).

4. The Installation Wizard copies the *ExamGear, Training Guide Edition* files to your hard drive, adds ExamGear, Training Guide Edition to your Program menu, adds values to your Registry, and installs test engine's DLLs to the appropriate system folders. To ensure that the process was successful, the Setup program finishes by running *ExamGear, Training Guide Edition*.

5. The Installation Wizard logs the installation process and stores this information in a file named INSTALL.LOG. This log file is used by the uninstall process in the event that you choose to remove *ExamGear, Training Guide Edition* from your computer. Because the *ExamGear* installation adds Registry keys and DLL files to your computer, it is important to uninstall the program appropriately (see the section "Removing *ExamGear, Training Guide Edition* from your Computer").

Registering *ExamGear, Training Guide Edition*

The Product Registration Wizard appears when *ExamGear, Training Guide Edition* is started for the first time, and *ExamGear* checks at startup to see whether you are registered. If you are not registered, the main menu is hidden, and a Product Registration Wizard appears. Remember that your computer must have an Internet connection to complete the Product Registration Wizard.

The first page of the Product Registration Wizard details the benefits of registration; however, you can always elect not to register. The Show This Message at Startup Until I Register option enables you to decide whether the registration screen should appear every time *ExamGear, Training Guide Edition* is started. If you click the Cancel button, you return to the main menu. You can register at any time by selecting Online, Registration from the main menu.

The registration process is composed of a simple form for entering your personal information, including your name and address. You are asked for your level of experience with the product you are testing on and whether you purchased *ExamGear, Training Guide Edition* from a retail store or over the Internet. The information will be used by our software designers and marketing department to provide us with feedback about the usability and usefulness of this product. It takes only a few seconds to fill out and transmit the registration data. A confirmation dialog box appears when registration is complete.

After you have registered and transmitted this information to New Riders, the registration option is removed from the pull-down menus.

Registration Benefits

Remember that registration allows you access to download updates from our FTP site using *ExamGear, Training Guide Edition* (see the later section "Obtaining Updates").

Removing *ExamGear, Training Guide Edition* from Your Computer

In the event that you elect to remove the *ExamGear, Training Guide Edition* product from your computer, an uninstall process has been included to ensure that it is removed from your system safely and completely. Follow these instructions to remove *ExamGear* from your computer:

1. Click Start, Settings, Control Panel.

2. Double-click the Add/Remove Programs icon.

3. You are presented with a list of software that is installed on your computer. Select ExamGear, Training Guide Edition from the list and click the Add/Remove button. The *ExamGear, Training Guide Edition* software is then removed from your computer.

It is important that the INSTALL.LOG file be present in the directory where you have installed *ExamGear, Training Guide Edition* should you ever choose to uninstall the product. Do not delete this file. The INSTALL.LOG file is used by the uninstall process to safely remove the files and Registry settings that were added to your computer by the installation process.

USING *EXAMGEAR, TRAINING GUIDE EDITION*

ExamGear is designed to be user friendly and very intuitive, eliminating the need for you to learn some confusing piece of software just to practice answering questions. Because the software has a smooth learning curve, your time is maximized because you start practicing almost immediately.

General Description of How the Software Works

ExamGear has three modes of operation: Study Mode, Practice Exam, and Adaptive Exam (see Figure C.2).

All three sections have the same easy-to-use interface. Using Study Mode, you can hone your knowledge as well as your test-taking abilities through the use of the Show Answers option. While you are taking the test, you can expose the answers along with a brief description of why the given answers are right or wrong. This gives you the ability to better understand the material presented.

The Practice Exam section has many of the same options as Study Mode, but you cannot reveal the answers. This way, you have a more traditional testing environment with which to practice.

The Adaptive Exam questions continuously monitor your expertise in each tested topic area. If you reach a point at which you either pass or fail, the software ends the examination. As in the Practice Exam, you cannot reveal the answers.

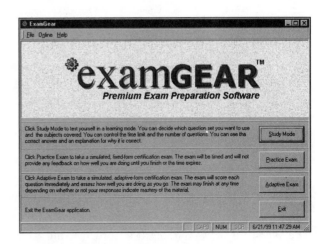

FIGURE C.2
The opening screen offers three testing modes.

Menu Options

The *ExamGear, Training Guide Edition* interface has an easy-to-use menu that provides the following options:

Menu	Command	Description
File	Print	Prints the current screen.
	Print Setup	Allows you to select the printer.
	Exit ExamGear	Exits the program.
Online	Registration	Starts the Registration Wizard and allows you to register online. This menu option is removed after you have successfully registered the product.
	Check for Product Updates	Downloads product catalog for Web-based updates.
	Web Browser	Opens the Web browser. It appears like this on the main menu, but more options appear after the browser is opened.
Help	Contents	Opens *ExamGear, Training Guide Edition's* help file.
	About	Displays information about *ExamGear, Training Guide Edition,* including serial number, registered owner, and so on.

File

The File menu allows you to exit the program and configure print options.

Online

In the Online menu, you can register *ExamGear, Training Guide Edition,* check for product updates (update the *ExamGear* executable as well as check for free, updated question sets), and surf Web pages. The Online menu is always available, except when you are taking a test.

Registration

Registration is free and allows you access updates. Registration is the first task that *ExamGear, Training Guide Edition* asks you to perform. You will not have access to the free product updates if you do not register.

Check for Product Updates

This option takes you to *ExamGear, Training Guide Edition's* Web site, where you can update the software. Registration is required for this option to be available. You must also be connected to the Internet to use this option. The *ExamGear* Web site lists the options that have been made available since your version of *ExamGear* was installed on your computer.

Web Browser

This option provides a convenient way to start your Web browser and connect to the New Riders Web site while you are working in *ExamGear, Training Guide Edition.* Click the Exit button to leave the Web browser and return to the *ExamGear* interface.

Help

As it suggests, this menu option gives you access to *ExamGear's* help system. It also provides important information like your serial number, software version, and so on.

Starting a Study Mode Session

Study Mode enables you to control the test in ways that actual certification exams do not allow:

◆ You can set your own time limits.

◆ You can concentrate on selected skill areas (units).

◆ You can reveal answers or have each response graded immediately with feedback.

◆ You can restrict the questions you see again to those missed or those answered correctly a given number of times.

◆ You can control the order in which questions are presented (random order or in order by skill area (unit).

To begin testing in Study Mode, click the Study Mode button from the main Interface screen. You are presented with the Study Mode configuration page (see Figure C.3).

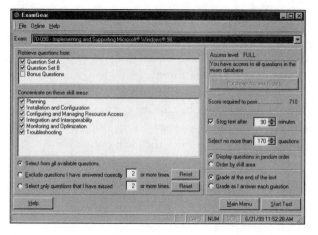

FIGURE C.3
The Study Mode configuration page.

At the top of the Study Mode configuration screen, you see the Exam drop-down list. This list shows the activated exam that you have purchased with your *ExamGear, Training Guide Edition* product, as well as any other exams you may have downloaded or any Preview exams that were shipped with your version of *ExamGear*. Select the exam with which you want to practice from the drop-down list.

Below the Exam drop-down list, you see the questions that are available for the selected exam. Each exam has at least one question set. You can select the individual

question set or any combination of the question sets if there is more than one available for the selected exam.

Below the Question Set list is a list of skill areas or chapters on which you can concentrate. These skill areas or chapters reflect the units of exam objectives defined by Microsoft for the exam. Within each skill area you will find several exam objectives. You can select a single skill area or chapter to focus on, or you can select any combination of the available skill areas/chapters to customize the exam to your individual needs.

In addition to specifying which question sets and skill areas you want to test yourself on, you can also define which questions are included in the test based on your previous progress working with the test. *ExamGear, Training Guide Edition* automatically tracks your progress with the available questions. When configuring the Study Mode options, you can opt to view all the questions available within the question sets and skill areas you have selected, or you can limit the questions presented. Choose from the following options:

◆ **Select from All Available Questions.** This option causes *ExamGear, Training Guide Edition* to present all available questions from the selected question sets and skill areas.

◆ **Exclude Questions I Have Answered Correctly** *X* **or More Times.** *ExamGear* offers you the option to exclude questions that you have previously answered correctly. You can specify how many times you want to answer a question correctly before *ExamGear* considers you to have mastered it (the default is two times).

◆ **Select Only Questions That I Have Missed** *X* **or More Times.** This option configures *ExamGear, Training Guide Edition* to drill you only on questions that you have missed repeatedly. You may specify how many times you must miss a question before *ExamGear* determines that you have not mastered it (the default is two times).

At any time, you can reset *ExamGear, Training Guide Edition*'s tracking information by clicking the Reset button for the feature you want to clear.

At the top-right side of the Study Mode configuration sheet, you can see your access level to the question sets for the selected exam. Access levels are either Full or Preview. For a detailed explanation of each of these access levels, see the section "Obtaining Updates" in this appendix.

Under your access level, you see the score required to pass the selected exam. Below the required score, you can select whether the test will be timed and how much time will be allowed to complete the exam. Select the Stop Test After 90 Minutes check box to set a time limit for the exam. Enter the number of minutes you want to allow for the test (the default is 90 minutes). Deselecting this check box allows you to take an exam with no time limit.

You can also configure the number of questions included in the exam. The default number of questions changes with the specific exam you have selected. Enter the number of questions you want to include in the exam in the Select No More than *X* Questions option.

You can configure the order in which *ExamGear, Training Guide Edition* presents the exam questions. Select from the following options:

◆ **Display Questions in Random Order.** This option is the default option. When selected, it causes *ExamGear, Training Guide Edition* to present the questions in random order throughout the exam.

◆ **Order by Skill Area.** This option causes *ExamGear* to group the questions presented in the exam by skill area. All questions for each selected skill area are presented in succession. The test progresses from one selected skill area to the next, until all the questions from each selected skill area have been presented.

ExamGear offers two options for scoring your exams. Select one of the following options:

◆ **Grade at the End of the Test.** This option configures *ExamGear, Training Guide Edition* to score your test after you have been presented with all the selected exam questions. You can reveal correct answers to a question, but if you do, that question is not scored.

◆ **Grade as I Answer Each Question.** This option configures *ExamGear* to grade each question as you answer it, providing you with instant feedback as you take the test. All questions are scored unless you click the Show Answer button before completing the question.

You can return to the *ExamGear, Training Guide Edition* main startup screen from the Study Mode configuration screen by clicking the Main Menu button. If you need assistance configuring the Study Mode exam options, click the Help button for configuration instructions.

When you have finished configuring all the exam options, click the Start Test button to begin the exam.

Starting Practice Exams and Adaptive Exams

This section describes practice exams and adaptive exams, defines the differences between these exam options and the Study Mode option, and provides instructions for starting them.

Differences Between the Practice and Adaptive Exams and Study Modes

Question screens in the practice and adaptive exams are identical to those found in Study Mode, except that the

Show Answer, Grade Answer, and Item Review buttons are not available while you are in the process of taking a practice or adaptive exam. The Practice Exam provides you with a report screen at the end of the exam. The Adaptive Exam gives you a brief message indicating whether you've passed or failed the exam.

When taking a practice exam, the Item Review screen is not available until you have answered all the questions. This is consistent with the behavior of most vendors' current certification exams. In Study Mode, Item Review is available at any time.

When the exam timer expires, or if you click the End Exam button, the Examination Score Report screen comes up.

Starting an Exam

From the *ExamGear, Training Guide Edition* main menu screen, select the type of exam you want to run. Click the Practice Exam or Adaptive Exam button to begin the corresponding exam type.

What Is an Adaptive Exam?

To make the certification testing process more efficient and valid and therefore make the certification itself more valuable, some vendors in the industry are using a testing technique called *adaptive testing*. In an adaptive exam, the exam "adapts" to your abilities by varying the difficulty level of the questions presented to you.

The first question in an adaptive exam is typically an easy one. If you answer it correctly, you are presented with a slightly more difficult question. If you answer that question correctly, the next question you see is even more difficult. If you answer the question incorrectly, however, the exam "adapts" to your skill level by presenting you with another question of equal or lesser difficulty on the same subject. If you answer that question correctly, the test begins to increase the difficulty level again. You must correctly answer several questions at a predetermined difficulty level to pass the exam. After you have done this successfully, the exam is ended and scored. If you do not reach the required level of difficulty within a predetermined time (typically 30 minutes), the exam is ended and scored.

Why Do Vendors Use Adaptive Exams?

Many vendors who offer technical certifications have adopted the adaptive testing technique. They have found that it is an effective way to measure a candidate's mastery of the test material in as little time as necessary. This reduces the scheduling demands on the test taker and allows the testing center to offer more tests per test station than they could with longer, more traditional exams. In addition, test security is greater, and this increases the validity of the exam process.

Studying for Adaptive Exams

Studying for adaptive exams is no different from studying for traditional exams. You should make sure that you have thoroughly covered all the material for each of the test objectives specified by the certification exam vendor. As with any other exam, when you take an adaptive exam, either you know the material or you don't. If you are well prepared, you will be able to pass the exam. *ExamGear, Training Guide Edition* allows you to familiarize yourself with the adaptive exam testing technique. This will help eliminate any anxiety you might experience from this testing technique and allow you to focus on learning the actual exam material.

ExamGear's Adaptive Exam

The method used to score the adaptive exam requires a large pool of questions. For this reason, you cannot use this exam in Preview mode. The adaptive exam is presented in much the same way as the practice exam. When you click the Start Test button, you begin answering questions. The adaptive exam does not allow item review, and it does not allow you to mark questions to skip and answer later. You must answer each question when it is presented.

Assumptions

This section describes the assumptions made when designing the behavior of the *ExamGear, Training Guide Edition* adaptive exam.

- ◆ You fail the test if you fail any chapter or unit, earn a failing overall score, or reach a threshold at which it is statistically impossible for you to pass the exam.

- ◆ You can fail or pass a test without cycling through all the questions.

- ◆ The overall score for the adaptive exam is Pass or Fail. However, to evaluate user responses dynamically, percentage scores are recorded for units and the overall score.

Algorithm Assumptions

This section describes the assumptions used in designing the *ExamGear, Training Guide Edition* Adaptive Exam scoring algorithm.

Unit Scores

You fail a unit (and the exam) if any unit score falls below 66%.

Overall Scores

To pass the exam, you must pass all units and achieve an overall score of 86% or higher.

You fail if the overall score percentage is less than or equal to 85% or if any unit score is less than 66%.

Inconclusive Scores

If your overall score is between 67 and 85%, it is considered to be *inconclusive*. Additional questions will be asked until you pass or fail or until it becomes statistically impossible to pass without asking more than the maximum number of questions allowed.

Question Types and How to Answer Them

Because certification exams from different vendors vary, you will face many types of questions on any given exam. *ExamGear, Training Guide Edition* presents you with different question types to allow you to become familiar with the various ways an actual exam may test your knowledge. The Solution Architectures exam, in particular, offers a unique exam format and utilizes question types other than multiple choice. This version of *ExamGear* includes cases—extensive problem descriptions running several pages in length, followed by a number of questions specific to that case. Microsoft refers to these case/question collections as *testlets*. This version of *ExamGear, Training Guide Edition* also includes regular questions that are not attached to a case study. We include these question types to make taking the actual exam easier because you will already be familiar with the steps required to answer each question type. This section describes each of the question types presented by *ExamGear* and provides instructions for answering each type.

Multiple Choice

Most of the questions you see on a certification exam are multiple choice (see Figure C.4). This question type asks you to select an answer from the list provided. Sometimes you must select only one answer, often indicated by answers preceded by option buttons (round selection buttons). At other times, multiple correct answers are possible, indicated by check boxes preceding the possible answer combinations.

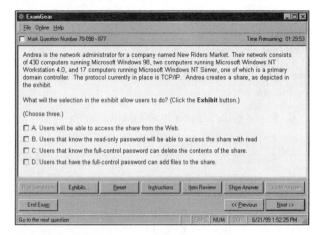

FIGURE C.4
A typical multiple-choice question.

You can use three methods to select an answer:

◆ Click the option button or check box next to the answer. If more than one correct answer to a question is possible, the answers will have check boxes next to them. If only one correct answer to a question is possible, each answer will have an option button next to it. *ExamGear, Training Guide Edition* prompts you with the number of answers you must select.

◆ Click the text of the answer.

◆ Press the alphabetic key that corresponds to the answer.

You can use any one of three methods to clear an option button:

◆ Click another option button.

◆ Click the text of another answer.

◆ Press the alphabetic key that corresponds to another answer.

You can use any one of three methods to clear a check box:

◆ Click the check box next to the selected answer.

◆ Click the text of the selected answer.

◆ Press the alphabetic key that corresponds to the selected answer.

To clear all answers, click the Reset button.

Remember that some of the questions have multiple answers that are correct. Do not let this throw you off. The *multiple correct* questions do not have one answer that is more correct than another. In the *single correct* format, only one answer is correct. *ExamGear, Training Guide Edition* prompts you with the number of answers you must select.

Drag and Drop

One form of drag and drop question is called a *drop and connect* question. These questions present you with a number of objects and connectors. The question prompts you to create relationships between the objects by using the connectors. The gray squares on the left side of the question window are the objects you can select. The connectors are listed on the right side of the question window in the Connectors box. An example is shown in Figure C.5.

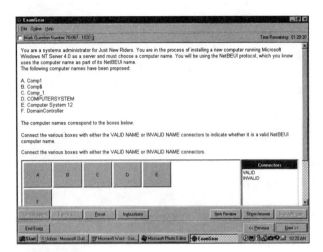

FIGURE C.5
A typical drop and connect question.

To select an object, click it with the mouse. When an object is selected, it changes color from a gray box to a white box. To drag an object, select it by clicking it with the left mouse button and holding the left mouse button down. You can move (or drag) the object to another area on the screen by moving the mouse while holding the left mouse button down.

To create a relationship between two objects, take the following actions:

1. Select an object and drag it to an available area on the screen.

2. Select another object and drag it to a location near where you dragged the first object.

3. Select the connector that you want to place between the two objects. The relationship should now appear complete. Note that to create a relationship, you must have two objects selected. If you try to select a connector without first selecting two objects, you are presented with an error message like that illustrated in Figure C.6.

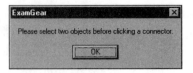

FIGURE C.6
The error message.

Initially, the direction of the relationship established by the connector is from the first object selected to the second object selected. To change the direction of the connector, right-click the connector and choose Reverse Connection.

You can use either of two methods to remove the connector:

◆ Right-click the text of the connector that you want to remove, and then choose Delete.

◆ Select the text of the connector that you want to remove, and then press the Delete key.

To remove from the screen all the relationships you have created, click the Reset button.

Keep in mind that connectors can be used multiple times. If you move connected objects, it will not change the relationship between the objects; to remove the relationship between objects, you must remove the connector that joins them. When *ExamGear, Training Guide Edition* scores a drag and drop question, only objects with connectors to other objects are scored.

Another form of drag and drop question is called the *select and place* question. Instead of creating a diagram as you do with the drop and connect question, you are asked a question about a diagram. You then drag and drop labels onto the diagram in order to correctly answer the question.

Ordered-Questions List

In the *ordered-list* question type (see Figure C.7), you are presented with a number of items and are asked to perform two tasks:

1. Build an answer list from items on the list of choices.

2. Put the items in a particular order.

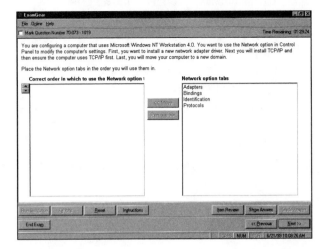

FIGURE C.7
A typical ordered-list question.

You can use any one of the following three methods to add an item to the answer list:

◆ Drag the item from the list of choices on the right side of the screen to the answer list on the left side of the screen.

◆ From the available items on the right side of the screen, double-click the item you want to add.

◆ From the available items on the right side of the screen, select the item you want to add; then click the Move button.

To remove an item from the answer list, you can use any one of the following four methods:

◆ Drag the item you want to remove from the answer list on the left side of the screen back to the list of choices on the right side of the screen.

◆ On the left side of the screen, double-click the item you want to remove from the answer list.

◆ On the left side of the screen, select the item you want to remove from the answer list, and then click the Remove button.

◆ On the left side of the screen, select the item you want to remove from the answer list, and then press the Delete key.

To remove all items from the answer list, click the Reset button.

If you need to change the order of the items in the answer list, you can do so using either of the following two methods:

◆ Drag each item to the appropriate location in the answer list.

◆ In the answer list, select the item that you want to move, and then click the up or down arrow button to move the item.

Keep in mind that items in the list can be selected twice. You may find that an ordered-list question will ask you to list in the correct order the steps required to perform a certain task. Certain steps may need to be performed more than once during the process. Don't think that after you have selected a list item, it is no longer available. If you need to select a list item more than once, you can simply select that item at each appropriate place as you construct your list.

Ordered Tree

The *ordered-tree* question type (see Figure C.8) presents you with a number of items and prompts you to create a tree structure from those items. The tree structure includes two or three levels of nodes.

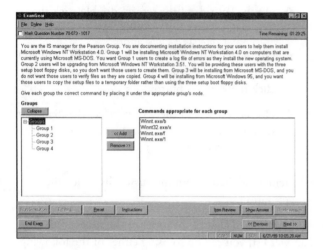

FIGURE C.8
A typical ordered-tree question.

An item in the list of choices can be added only to the appropriate node level. If you attempt to add one of the list choices to an inappropriate node level, you are presented with the error message shown in Figure C.9.

FIGURE C.9
The Invalid Destination Node error message.

Like the ordered-list question, realize that any item in the list can be selected twice. If you need to select a list item more than once, you can simply select that item for the appropriate node as you construct your tree.

Also realize that not every tree question actually requires order to the lists under each node. Think of them as simply tree questions rather than ordered-tree questions. Such questions are just asking you to categorize hierarchically. Order is not an issue.

You can use either of the following two methods to add an item to the tree:

◆ Drag the item from the list of choices on the right side of the screen to the appropriate node of the tree on the left side of the screen.

◆ Select the appropriate node of the tree on the left side of the screen. Select the appropriate item from the list of choices on the right side of the screen. Click the Add button.

You can use either of the following two methods to remove an item from the tree:

◆ Drag an item from the tree to the list of choices.

◆ Select the item and click the Remove button.

To remove from the tree structure all the items you have added, click the Reset button.

Simulations

Simulation questions (see Figure C.10) require you to actually perform a task.

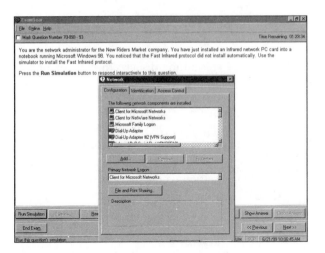

FIGURE C.10
A typical simulation question.

The main screen describes a situation and prompts you to provide a solution. When you are ready to proceed, you click the Run Simulation button in the lower-left corner. A screen or window appears on which you perform the solution. This window simulates the actual software that you would use to perform the required task in the real world. When a task requires several steps to complete, the simulator displays all the necessary screens to allow you to complete the task. When you have provided your answer by completing all the steps necessary to perform the required task, you can click the OK button to proceed to the next question.

You can return to any simulation to modify your answer. Your actions in the simulation are recorded, and the simulation appears exactly as you left it.

Simulation questions can be reset to their original state by clicking the Reset button.

Hot Spot Questions

Hot spot questions (see Figure C.11) ask you to correctly identify an item by clicking an area of the graphic or diagram displayed. To respond to the question, position the mouse cursor over a graphic. Then press the right mouse button to indicate your selection. To select another area on the graphic, you do not need to deselect the first one. Just click another region in the image.

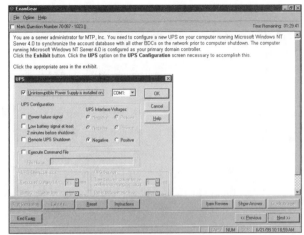

FIGURE C.11
A typical hot spot question.

Standard *ExamGear, Training Guide Edition* Options

Regardless of question type, a consistent set of clickable buttons enables you to navigate and interact with questions. The following list describes the function of each of the buttons you may see. Depending on the question type, some of the buttons will be grayed out and will be inaccessible. Buttons that are appropriate to the question type are active.

◆ **Run Simulation.** This button is enabled if the question supports a simulation. Clicking this button begins the simulation process.

◆ **Exhibits.** This button is enabled if exhibits are provided to support the question. An *exhibit* is an image, video, sound, or text file that provides supplemental information needed to answer the question. If a question has more than one exhibit, a dialog box appears, listing exhibits by name. If only one exhibit exists, the file is opened immediately when you click the Exhibits button.

◆ **Reset.** This button clears any selections you have made and returns the question window to the state in which it appeared when it was first displayed.

◆ **Instructions.** This button displays instructions for interacting with the current question type.

◆ **Item Review.** This button leaves the question window and opens the Item Review screen. For a detailed explanation of the Item Review screen, see the "Item Review" section later in this appendix.

◆ **Show Answer.** This option displays the correct answer with an explanation of why it is correct. If you choose this option, the current question will not be scored.

◆ **Grade Answer.** If Grade at the End of the Test is selected as a configuration option, this button is disabled. It is enabled when Grade as I Answer Each Question is selected as a configuration option. Clicking this button grades the current question immediately. An explanation of the correct answer is provided, just as if the Show Answer button were pressed. The question is graded, however.

◆ **End Exam.** This button ends the exam and displays the Examination Score Report screen.

◆ **<< Previous.** This button displays the previous question on the exam.

◆ **Next >>.** This button displays the next question on the exam.

◆ **<< Previous Marked.** This button is displayed if you have opted to review questions that you have marked using the Item Review screen. This button displays the previous marked question. Marking questions is discussed in more detail later in this appendix.

◆ **<< Previous Incomplete.** This button is displayed if you have opted to review questions that you have not answered using the Item Review screen. This button displays the previous unanswered question.

◆ **Next Marked >>.** This button is displayed if you have opted to review questions that you have marked using the Item Review screen. This button displays the next marked question. Marking questions is discussed in more detail later in this appendix.

◆ **Next Incomplete>>.** This button is displayed if you have opted to review questions, using the Item Review screen, that you have not answered. This button displays the next unanswered question.

Mark Question and Time Remaining

ExamGear provides you with two methods to aid in dealing with the time limit of the testing process. If you find that you need to skip a question or if you want to check the time remaining to complete the test, use one of the options discussed in the following sections.

Mark Question

Check this box to mark a question so that you can return to it later using the Item Review feature. The adaptive exam does not allow questions to be marked because it does not support item review.

Time Remaining

If the test is timed, the Time Remaining indicator is enabled. It counts down minutes remaining to complete the test. The adaptive exam does not offer this feature because it is not timed.

Item Review

The Item Review screen allows you to jump to any question. *ExamGear, Training Guide Edition* considers an *incomplete* question to be any unanswered question or any multiple-choice question for which the total number of required responses has not been selected. For example, if the question prompts for three answers and you selected only A and C, *ExamGear* considers the question to be incomplete.

The Item Review screen enables you to review the exam questions in different ways. You can enter one of two *browse sequences* (series of similar records): Browse Marked Questions or Browse Incomplete Questions. You can also create a custom grouping of the exam questions for review based on a number of criteria.

When using Item Review, if Show Answer was selected for a question while you were taking the exam, the question is grayed out in item review. The question can be answered again if you use the Reset button to reset the question status.

The Item Review screen contains two tabs. The Questions tab lists questions and question information in columns. The Current Score tab provides your exam score information, presented as a percentage for each unit and as a bar graph for your overall score.

The Item Review Questions Tab

The Questions tab on the Item Review screen (see Figure C.12) presents the exam questions and question information in a table. You can select any row you want by clicking in the grid. The Go To button is enabled whenever a row is selected. Clicking the Go To button displays the question on the selected row. You can also display a question by double-clicking that row.

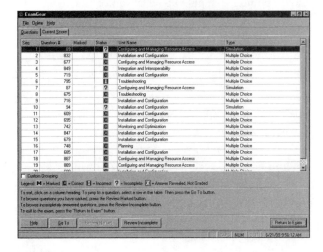

FIGURE C.12
The Questions tab on the Item Review screen.

Columns

The Questions tab contains the following six columns of information:

- ◆ **Seq.** Indicates the sequence number of the question as it was displayed in the exam.

- ◆ **Question Number.** Displays the question's identification number for easy reference.

- ◆ **Marked.** Indicates a question that you have marked using the Mark Question check box.

- ◆ **Status.** The status can be M for Marked, ? for Incomplete, C for Correct, I for Incorrect, or X for Answer Shown.

◆ **Unit Name.** The unit associated with each question.

◆ **Type.** The question type, which can be Multiple Choice, Drag and Drop, Simulation, Hot Spot, Ordered List, or Ordered Tree.

To resize a column, place the mouse pointer over the vertical line between column headings. When the mouse pointer changes to a set of right and left arrows, you can drag the column border to the left or right to make the column more or less wide. Simply click with the left mouse button and hold that button down while you move the column border in the desired direction.

The Item Review screen enables you to sort the questions on any of the column headings. Initially, the list of questions is sorted in descending order on the sequence number column. To sort on a different column heading, click that heading. You will see an arrow appear on the column heading indicating the direction of the sort (ascending or descending). To change the direction of the sort, click the column heading again.

The Item Review screen also allows you to create a *custom grouping*. This feature enables you to sort the questions based on any combination of criteria you prefer. For instance, you might want to review the question items sorted first by whether they were marked, then by the unit name, then by sequence number. The Custom Grouping feature allows you to do this. Start by checking the Custom Grouping check box (see Figure C.13). When you do so, the entire questions table shifts down a bit onscreen, and a message appears at the top of the table that reads `Drag a column header here to group by that column`.

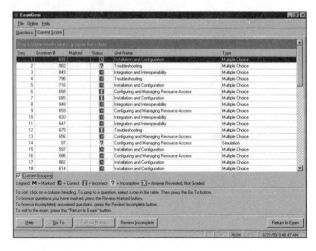

FIGURE C.13
The Custom Grouping check box allows you to create your own question sort order.

Simply click the column heading you want with the left mouse button, hold that button down, and move the mouse into the area directly above the questions table (the custom grouping area). Release the left mouse button to drop the column heading into the custom grouping area. To accomplish the custom grouping previously described, first check the Custom Grouping check box. Then, drag the Marked column heading into the custom grouping area above the question table. Next, drag the Unit Name column heading into the custom grouping area. You will see the two column headings joined together by a line that indicates the order of the custom grouping. Finally, drag the Seq column heading into the custom grouping area. This heading will be joined to the Unit Name heading by another line indicating the direction of the custom grouping.

Notice that each column heading in the custom grouping area has an arrow indicating the direction in which items are sorted under that column heading. You can reverse the direction of the sort on an individual column-heading basis using these arrows. Click the column heading in the custom grouping area to change the direction of the sort for that column heading only. For example, using the custom grouping created previously, you can display the question list sorted first in descending order by whether the question was marked, in descending order by unit name, and then in ascending order by sequence number.

The custom grouping feature of the Item Review screen gives you enormous flexibility in how you choose to review the exam questions. To remove a custom grouping and return the Item Review display to its default setting (sorted in descending order by sequence number), simply uncheck the Custom Grouping check box.

The Current Score Tab

The Current Score tab of the Item Review screen (see Figure C.14) provides a real-time snapshot of your score. The top half of the screen is an expandable grid. When the grid is collapsed, scores are displayed for each unit. Units can be expanded to show percentage scores for objectives and subobjectives. Information about your exam progress is presented in the following columns:

◆ **Unit Name.** This column shows the unit name for each objective group.

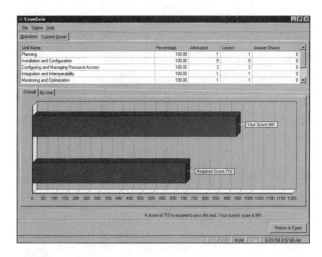

FIGURE C.14
The Current Score tab on the item review screen.

◆ **Percentage.** This column shows the percentage of questions for each objective group that you answered correctly.

◆ **Attempted.** This column lists the number of questions you answered either completely or partially for each objective group.

◆ **Correct.** This column lists the actual number of questions you answered correctly for each objective group.

◆ **Answer Shown.** This column lists the number of questions for each objective group that you chose to display the answer to using the Show Answer button.

The columns in the scoring table are resized and sorted in the same way as those in the questions table on the Item Review Questions tab. Refer to the earlier section "The Item Review Questions Tab" for more details.

A graphical overview of the score is presented below the grid. The graph depicts two red bars: The top bar represents your current exam score, and the bottom bar represents the required passing score. To the right of the bars in the graph is a legend that lists the required score and your score. Below the bar graph is a statement that describes the required passing score and your current score.

In addition, the information can be presented on an overall basis or by exam unit. The Overall tab shows the overall score. The By Unit tab shows the score by unit.

Clicking the End Exam button terminates the exam and passes control to the Examination Score Report screen.

The Return to Exam button returns to the exam at the question from which the Item Review button was clicked.

Review Marked Items

The Item Review screen allows you to enter a browse sequence for marked questions. When you click the Review Marked button, questions that you have previously marked using the Mark Question check box are presented for your review. While browsing the marked questions, you will see the following changes to the buttons available:

◆ The caption of the Next button becomes Next Marked.

◆ The caption of the Previous button becomes Previous Marked.

Review Incomplete

The Item Review screen allows you to enter a browse sequence for incomplete questions. When you click the Review Incomplete button, the questions you did not answer or did not completely answer are displayed for your review. While browsing the incomplete questions, you will see the following changes to the buttons:

◆ The caption of the Next button becomes Next Incomplete.

◆ The caption of the Previous button becomes Previous Incomplete.

Examination Score Report Screen

The Examination Score Report screen (see Figure C.15) appears when the Study Mode, Practice Exam, or Adaptive Exam ends—as the result of timer expiration, completion of all questions, or your decision to terminate early.

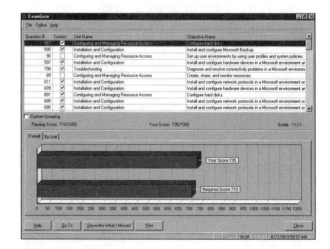

FIGURE C.15
The Examination Score Report screen.

This screen provides you with a graphical display of your test score, along with a tabular breakdown of scores by unit. The graphical display at the top of the screen compares your overall score with the score required to pass the exam. Buttons below the graphical display allow you to open the Show Me What I Missed browse sequence, print the screen, or return to the main menu.

Show Me What I Missed Browse Sequence

The Show Me What I Missed browse sequence is invoked by clicking the Show Me What I Missed button from the Examination Score Report or from the configuration screen of an adaptive exam.

Note that the window caption is modified to indicate that you are in the Show Me What I Missed browse sequence mode. Question IDs and position within the browse sequence appear at the top of the screen, in place of the Mark Question and Time Remaining indicators. Main window contents vary, depending on the question type. The following list describes the buttons available within the Show Me What I Missed browse sequence and the functions they perform:

◆ **Return to Score Report.** Returns control to the Examination Score Report screen. In the case of an adaptive exam, this button's caption is Exit, and control returns to the adaptive exam configuration screen.

◆ **Run Simulation.** Opens a simulation in Grade mode, causing the simulation to open displaying your response and the correct answer. If the current question does not offer a simulation, this button is disabled.

◆ **Exhibits.** Opens the Exhibits window. This button is enabled if one or more exhibits are available for the question.

◆ **Instructions.** Shows how to answer the current question type.

◆ **Print.** Prints the current screen.

◆ **Previous or Next.** Displays missed questions.

Checking the Web Site

To check the New Riders Home Page or the *ExamGear, Training Guide Edition* Home Page for updates or other product information, choose the desired Web site from the Web Sites option of the Online menu. You must be connected to the Internet to reach these Web sites. When you select a Web site, the Internet Explorer browser opens inside the *ExamGear, Training Guide Edition* window and displays the Web site.

OBTAINING UPDATES

The procedures for obtaining updates are outlined in this section.

The Catalog Web Site for Updates

Selecting the Check for Product Updates option from the Online menu shows you the full range of products you can either download for free or purchase. You can download additional items only if you have registered the software.

Product Updates Dialog Box

This dialog box appears when you select Check for Product Updates from the Online menu. *ExamGear, Training Guide Edition* checks for product updates from the New Riders Internet site and displays a list of products available for download. Some items, such as *ExamGear* program updates or bonus question sets for exam databases you have activated, are available for download free of charge.

Types of Updates

Several types of updates may be available for download, including various free updates and additional items available for purchase.

Free Program Updates

Free program updates include changes to the *ExamGear, Training Guide Edition* executables and runtime libraries (DLLs). When any of these items are downloaded, *ExamGear* automatically installs the upgrades. *ExamGear, Training Guide Edition* will be reopened after the installation is complete.

Free Database Updates

Free database updates include updates to the exam or exams that you have registered. Exam updates are contained in compressed, encrypted files and include exam databases, simulations, and exhibits. *ExamGear, Training Guide Edition* automatically decompresses these files to their proper location and updates the *ExamGear* software to record version changes and import new question sets.

CONTACTING NEW RIDERS PUBLISHING

At New Riders, we strive to meet and exceed the needs of our customers. We have developed *ExamGear, Training Guide Edition* to surpass the demands and expectations of network professionals seeking technical certifications, and we think it shows. What do you think?

If you need to contact New Riders regarding any aspect of the *ExamGear, Training Guide Edition* product line, feel free to do so. We look forward to hearing from you. Contact us at the following address or phone number:

New Riders Publishing
201 West 103 Street
Indianapolis, IN 46290
800-545-5914

You can also reach us on the World Wide Web:

    http://www.newriders.com

Technical Support

Technical support is available at the following phone number during the hours specified:

317-581-3833

Monday through Friday, 10:00 a.m.–3:00 p.m. Central Standard Time.

Customer Service

If you have a damaged product and need a replacement or refund, please call the following phone number:

800-858-7674

Product Updates

Product updates can be obtained by choosing *ExamGear, Training Guide Edition*'s Online pull-down menu and selecting Products Updates. You'll be taken to a private Web site with full details.

Product Suggestions and Comments

We value your input! Please email your suggestions and comments to the following address:

    certification@mcp.com

LICENSE AGREEMENT

YOU SHOULD CAREFULLY READ THE
FOLLOWING TERMS AND CONDITIONS
BEFORE BREAKING THE SEAL ON THE
PACKAGE. AMONG OTHER THINGS, THIS
AGREEMENT LICENSES THE ENCLOSED
SOFTWARE TO YOU AND CONTAINS
WARRANTY AND LIABILITY DISCLAIMERS.
BY BREAKING THE SEAL ON THE PACKAGE,
YOU ARE ACCEPTING AND AGREEING TO
THE TERMS AND CONDITIONS OF THIS
AGREEMENT. IF YOU DO NOT AGREE TO
THE TERMS OF THIS AGREEMENT, DO NOT
BREAK THE SEAL. YOU SHOULD PROMPTLY
RETURN THE PACKAGE UNOPENED.

LICENSE

Subject to the provisions contained herein, New Riders
Publishing (NRP) hereby grants to you a nonexclusive,
nontransferable license to use the object-code version of
the computer software product (Software) contained in
the package on a single computer of the type identified
on the package.

SOFTWARE AND DOCUMENTATION

NRP shall furnish the Software to you on media in
machine-readable object-code form and may also
provide the standard documentation (Documentation)
containing instructions for operation and use of the
Software.

LICENSE TERM AND CHARGES

The term of this license commences upon delivery
of the Software to you and is perpetual unless earlier
terminated upon default or as otherwise set forth
herein.

TITLE

Title, ownership right, and intellectual property
rights in and to the Software and Documentation
shall remain in NRP and/or in suppliers to NRP of
programs contained in the Software. The Software is
provided for your own internal use under this license.
This license does not include the right to sublicense
and is personal to you and therefore may not be
assigned (by operation of law or otherwise) or transferred without the prior written consent of NRP. You
acknowledge that the Software in source code form
remains a confidential trade secret of NRP and/or its
suppliers and therefore you agree not to attempt to
decipher or decompile, modify, disassemble, reverse
engineer, or prepare derivative works of the Software
or develop source code for the Software or knowingly
allow others to do so. Further, you may not copy the
Documentation or other written materials accompanying the Software.

UPDATES

This license does not grant you any right, license, or interest in and to any improvements, modifications, enhancements, or updates to the Software and Documentation. Updates, if available, may be obtained by you at NRP's then-current standard pricing, terms, and conditions.

LIMITED WARRANTY AND DISCLAIMER

NRP warrants that the media containing the Software, if provided by NRP, is free from defects in material and workmanship under normal use for a period of sixty (60) days from the date you purchased a license to it.

THIS IS A LIMITED WARRANTY AND IT IS THE ONLY WARRANTY MADE BY NRP. THE SOFTWARE IS PROVIDED "AS IS" AND NRP SPECIFICALLY DISCLAIMS ALL WARRANTIES OF ANY KIND, EITHER EXPRESS OR IMPLIED, INCLUDING, BUT NOT LIMITED TO, THE IMPLIED WARRANTY OF MERCHANTABILITY AND FITNESS FOR A PARTICULAR PURPOSE. FURTHER, COMPANY DOES NOT WARRANT, GUARANTEE, OR MAKE ANY REPRESENTATIONS REGARDING THE USE, OR THE RESULTS OF THE USE, OF THE SOFTWARE IN TERMS OR CORRECTNESS, ACCURACY, RELIABILITY, CURRENTNESS, OR OTHERWISE, AND DOES NOT WARRANT THAT THE OPERATION OF ANY SOFTWARE WILL BE UNINTERRUPTED OR ERROR FREE. NRP EXPRESSLY DISCLAIMS ANY WARRANTIES NOT STATED HEREIN. NO ORAL OR WRITTEN INFORMATION OR ADVICE GIVEN BY NRP, OR ANY NRP DEALER, AGENT, EMPLOYEE, OR OTHERS SHALL CREATE,

MODIFY, OR EXTEND A WARRANTY OR IN ANY WAY INCREASE THE SCOPE OF THE FOREGOING WARRANTY, AND NEITHER SUBLICENSEE OR PURCHASER MAY RELY ON ANY SUCH INFORMATION OR ADVICE. If the media is subjected to accident, abuse, or improper use, or if you violate the terms of this Agreement, then this warranty shall immediately be terminated. This warranty shall not apply if the Software is used on or in conjunction with hardware or programs other than the unmodified version of hardware and programs with which the Software was designed to be used as described in the Documentation.

LIMITATION OF LIABILITY

Your sole and exclusive remedies for any damage or loss in any way connected with the Software are set forth below.

UNDER NO CIRCUMSTANCES AND UNDER NO LEGAL THEORY, TORT, CONTRACT, OR OTHERWISE, SHALL NRP BE LIABLE TO YOU OR ANY OTHER PERSON FOR ANY INDIRECT, SPECIAL, INCIDENTAL, OR CONSEQUENTIAL DAMAGES OF ANY CHARACTER INCLUDING, WITHOUT LIMITATION, DAMAGES FOR LOSS OF GOODWILL, LOSS OF PROFIT, WORK STOPPAGE, COMPUTER FAILURE OR MALFUNCTION, OR ANY AND ALL OTHER COMMERCIAL DAMAGES OR LOSSES, OR FOR ANY OTHER DAMAGES EVEN IF NRP SHALL HAVE BEEN INFORMED OF THE POSSIBILITY OF SUCH DAMAGES, OR FOR ANY CLAIM BY ANOTHER PARTY. NRP'S THIRD-PARTY PROGRAM SUPPLIERS MAKE NO WARRANTY, AND HAVE NO LIABILITY WHATSOEVER, TO YOU. NRP's sole and exclusive obligation and liability and your exclusive remedy shall be: upon NRP's election, (i) the replacement of our defective media; or (ii) the repair or correction of your defective media if NRP is able, so that it will conform to the above warranty; or (iii) if NRP is unable to replace or repair, you may terminate this license by returning the Software. Only if you inform NRP of your problem during the applicable warranty period will NRP be obligated to honor this warranty. SOME STATES OR JURISDICTIONS DO NOT ALLOW THE EXCLUSION OF IMPLIED WARRANTIES OR LIMITATION OR EXCLUSION OF CONSE-QUENTIAL DAMAGES, SO THE ABOVE LIMITATIONS OR EXCLUSIONS MAY NOT APPLY TO YOU. THIS WARRANTY GIVES YOU SPECIFIC LEGAL RIGHTS AND YOU MAY ALSO HAVE OTHER RIGHTS WHICH VARY BY STATE OR JURISDICTION.

MISCELLANEOUS

If any provision of the Agreement is held to be ineffective, unenforceable, or illegal under certain circumstances for any reason, such decision shall not affect the validity or enforceability (i) of such provision under other circumstances or (ii) of the remaining provisions hereof under all circumstances, and such provision shall be reformed to and only to the extent necessary to make it effective, enforceable, and legal under such circumstances. All headings are solely for convenience and shall not be considered in interpreting this Agreement. This Agreement shall be governed by and construed under New York law as such law applies to agreements between New York residents entered into and to be performed entirely within New York, except as required by U.S. Government rules and regulations to be governed by Federal law.

YOU ACKNOWLEDGE THAT YOU HAVE READ THIS AGREEMENT, UNDERSTAND IT, AND AGREE TO BE BOUND BY ITS TERMS AND CONDITIONS. YOU FURTHER AGREE THAT IT IS THE COMPLETE AND EXCLUSIVE STATE-MENT OF THE AGREEMENT BETWEEN US THAT SUPERSEDES ANY PROPOSAL OR PRIOR AGREEMENT, ORAL OR WRITTEN, AND ANY OTHER COMMUNICATIONS BETWEEN US RELATING TO THE SUBJECT MATTER OF THIS AGREEMENT.

U.S. GOVERNMENT RESTRICTED RIGHTS

Use, duplication, or disclosure by the Government is subject to restrictions set forth in subparagraphs (a) through (d) of the Commercial Computer-Restricted Rights clause at FAR 52.227-19 when applicable, or in subparagraph (c) (1) (ii) of the Rights in Technical Data and Computer Software clause at DFARS 252.227-7013, and in similar clauses in the NASA FAR Supplement.

Index

SYMBOLS

32-bit applications, maintaining, 260-267

A

Above Normal priority level, 264, 673
access
  Dfs, 669
  files
    controlling, 98-134
    Web access, 126-134
  folders, controlling, 98-134
  local access, configuring/controlling, 107-116
  local printer management, 670-671
  network printer management, 668
  NTFS permissions, 669
  operating systems, interoperability, 180-197
  printers
    configuring/maintaining, 150-180
    sharing, 172-173
  remote access
    configuring, 512-529, 680
    installing, 512-529
    remote access policy, 523-526
    troubleshooting, 512-529
  share management, 669
  shared access
    configuring, 99-106, 498-511, 678
    controlling, 99-106
    installing, 498-511
    troubleshooting, 104-106, 498-511
  shared folders, controlling, 98-134
  Web services, 669-670
  Web sites
    authentication, 138-142
    certificates, 144-150
    controlling, 134-150
    domain name restrictions, 142-143
    Execute permissions, 137-138
    IP addresses, 142-143

    permissions, 135-137
    troubleshooting, 150
Access Control Settings dialog box, 114, 178
Access Control Settings for Object dialog box, 624
accessories, attended installation, 25
Account Logon audit policy area, 622
Account Management audit policy area, 622
accounts
  auditing, 622-624
    configuring, 621-627
    implementing, 621-627
    managing, 621-627
    troubleshooting, 621-627
  configuring, 682
  deleting, 598-599
  local password policies
    complexity requirements, 604-605
    history, 602
    implementing, 601-602
    maximum age, 602
    minimum age, 603
    minimum length, 604
    storage, 605-606
  passwords, resetting, 597-598
  policies
    configuring, 610-621, 682
    implementing, 610-621
    lockout, 606-609
    managing, 610-621
    system policies, 610-621
    troubleshooting, 609-621
  properties, changing, 595-597
  renaming, 594-595
  types, 592
active partitions, marking as, 389
active study strategies, 686
adapters, 444
adaptive exams
  described, 688-689
  process, 689-690
  tips for, 697
Add Counter dialog box, 270
Add IP Filter dialog box, 534

C

D

M

Q-R

Additional Tools for Certification Preparation

Taking the author-driven, no-nonsense approach that we pioneered with our *Landmark* books, New Riders proudly offers something unique for Windows 2000 administrators—an interesting and discriminating book on Windows 2000 Server, written by someone in the trenches who can anticipate your situation and provide answers you can trust.

INSIDE
Windows 2000 Server

William Boswell

ISBN: 1-56205-929-7

Windows 2000
ESSENTIAL REFERENCE

Includes coverage of Server, Workstation, and Professional

Steven Tate, et al.

ISBN: 0-7357-0869-X

Architected to be the most navigable, useful, and value-packed reference for Windows 2000, this book uses a creative "telescoping" design that you can adapt to your style of learning. It's a concise, focused, and quick reference for Windows 2000, providing the kind of practical advice, tips, procedures, and additional resources that every administrator will need.

Understanding the Network is just one of several new titles from New Riders' acclaimed *Landmark Series*. This book addresses the audience in practical terminology, and describes the most essential information and tools required to build high-availability networks in a step-by-step implementation format. Each chapter could be read as a stand-alone, but the book builds progressively toward a summary of the essential concepts needed to put together a wide area network.

Understanding the Network
A Practical Guide to Internetworking

Michael J. Martin

ISBN: 0-7357-0977-7

New Riders
Windows 2000 Resources

Advice and Experience for the Windows 2000 Networker

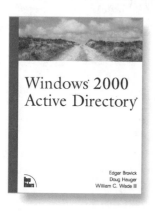

LANDMARK SERIES

We know how important it is to have access to detailed, solution-oriented information on core technologies. *Landmark* books contain the essential information you need to solve technical problems. Written by experts and subjected to rigorous peer and technical reviews, our *Landmark* books are hard-core resources for practitioners like you.

ESSENTIAL REFERENCE SERIES

The *Essential Reference* series from New Riders provides answers when you know what you want to do but need to know how to do it. Each title skips extraneous material and assumes a strong base of knowledge. These are indispensable books for the practitioner who wants to find specific features of a technology quickly and efficiently. Avoiding fluff and basic material, these books present solutions in an innovative, clean format—and at a great value.

CIRCLE SERIES

The *Circle Series* is a set of reference guides that meet the needs of the growing community of advanced, technical-level networkers who must architect, develop, and administer Windows NT/2000 systems. These books provide network designers and programmers with detailed, proved solutions to their problems.

The Road to MCSE Windows 2000

The new Microsoft Windows 2000 track is designed for information technology professionals working in a typically complex computing environment of medium to large organizations. A Windows 2000 MCSE candidate should have at least one year of experience implementing and administering a network operating system.

MCSEs in the Windows 2000 track are required to pass **five core exams and two elective exams** that provide a valid and reliable measure of technical proficiency and expertise.

See below for the exam information and the relevant New Riders title that covers that exam.

Core Exams

**w MCSE Candidates (Who Have Not Already Passed Windows NT 4.0 Exams)
ust Take All 4 of the Following Core Exams:**

am 70-210: Installing, Configuring
d Administering Microsoft®
ndows® 2000 Professional

am 70-215: Installing, Configuring
d Administering Microsoft
ndows 2000 Server

am 70-216: Implementing
d Administering a Microsoft
ndows 2000 Network
rastructure

am 70-217: Implementing
d Administering a Microsoft
ndows 2000 Directory
rvices Infrastructure

ISBN 0-7357-0965-3   ISBN 0-7357-0968-8

ISBN 0-7357-0966-1   ISBN 0-7357-0976-9

or

**MCPs Who Have Passed 3 Windows NT 4.0
Exams (Exams 70-067, 70-068, and 70-073)
Instead of the 4 Core Exams at Left, May Take:**

Exam 70-240: Microsoft Windows
2000 Accelerated Exam for MCPs
Certified on Microsoft Windows
NT 4.0.

(This accelerated, intensive exam, which
will be available until December 31, 2001,
covers the core competencies of exams
70-210, 70-215, 70-216, and 70-217.)

ISBN 0-7357-0979-3

**MCSE Training Guide:
Core Exams (Bundle)**

ISBN 0-7357-0976-9

PLUS - All Candidates - 1 of the Following Core Elective Exams Required:

xam 70-219: Designing a Microsoft Windows 2000 Directory
rvices Infrastructure

xam 70-220: Designing Security for a Microsoft Windows 2000 Network

xam 70-221: Designing a Microsoft Windows 2000
etwork Infrastructure

ISBN 0-7357-0983-1   ISBN 0-7357-0984-X   ISBN 0-7357-0982-3

PLUS - All Candidates - 2 of the Following Elective Exams Required:

ny current MCSE electives (visit www.microsoft.com for a list of current electives)

elected third-party certifications that focus on interoperability will be accepted as an alternative to one
ctive exam. Please watch for more information on the third-party certifications that will be acceptable.)

xam 70-219: Designing a Microsoft Windows 2000 Directory Services Infrastructure

xam 70-220: Designing Security for a Microsoft Windows 2000 Network

xam 70-221: Designing a Microsoft Windows 2000 Network Infrastructure

xam 70-222: Upgrading from Microsoft Windows NT 4.0 to Microsoft Windows 2000

ISBN 0-7357-0983-1   ISBN 0-7357-0984-X   ISBN 0-7357-0982-3

ore exams that can also be used as elective exams may only be counted once toward a certification; that is, if a candidate receives
edit for an exam as a core in one track, that candidate will not receive credit for that same exam as an elective in that same track.

WWW.NEWRIDERS.COM

Books for Networking Professionals

Windows NT/2000 Titles

Windows 2000 TCP/IP
By Karanjit Siyan, Ph.D.
2nd Edition
900 pages, $39.99
ISBN: 0-7357-0992-0

Windows 2000 TCP/IP cuts through the complexities and provides the most informative and complex reference book on Windows 2000–based TCP/IP topics. The book is a tutorial-reference hybrid, focusing on how Microsoft TCP/IP works, using hands-on tutorials and practical examples. Concepts essential to TCP/IP administration are explained thoroughly, and are then related to the practical use of Microsoft TCP/IP in a serious networking environment.

Windows 2000 DNS
By Roger Abell, Herman Knief, Andrew Daniels, and Jeffrey Graham
2nd Edition
450 pages, $39.99
ISBN: 0-7357-0973-4

The Domain Name System is a directory of registered computer names and IP addresses that can be instantly located. Without proper design and administration of DNS, computers wouldn't be able to locate each other on the network, and applications like email and Web browsing wouldn't be feasible. Administrators need this information to make their networks work. *Windows 2000 DNS* provides a technical overview of DNS and WINS, and how to design and administer them for optimal performance in a Windows 2000 environment.

Windows 2000 Registry
By Sandra Osborrne
2nd Edition
550 pages, $34.99
ISBN: 0-7357-0944-0
Available December 2000

Windows 2000 Registry is a powerful tool for accomplishing many important administration tasks, but little information is available on registry settings and how they can be edited to accomplish these tasks. This title offers unique insight into using registry settings to software or configure client systems in a Windows 2000 environment. The approach of the book is that of revealing the GUI through the registry, allowing system administrators to edit the registry settings to efficiently accomplish critical tasks such as configuration, installation, and management.

Windows 2000 Server Professional Reference
By Karanjit Siyan, Ph.D.
3rd Edition
1800 pages, $75.00
ISBN: 0-7357-0952-1

Windows 2000 Server Professional Reference is the benchmark of references available for Windows 2000. Although other titles take you through the setup and implementation phase of the product, no other book provides the user with detailed answers to day-to-day administration problems and tasks. Real-world implementations are key to help administrators discover the most viable solutions for their particular environments. Solid content shows administrators how to manage, troubleshoot, and fix problems that are specific to heterogeneous Windows networks, as well as Internet features and functionality.

Windows 2000 Professional

By Jerry Honeycutt
350 pages, $34.99 US
ISBN: 0-7357-0950-5

Windows 2000 Professional explores the power available to the Windows workstation user on the corporate network and Internet. The book is aimed directly at the power user who values the security, stability, and networking capabilities of NT alongside the ease and familiarity of the Windows 95/98 user interface. This book covers both user and administration topics, with a dose of networking content added for connectivity.

Windows NT Power Toolkit

By Stu Sjouwerman and Ed Tittel
1st Edition
800 pages, $49.99
ISBN: 0-7357-0922-X

This book covers the analysis, tuning, optimization, automation, enhancement, maintenance, and troubleshooting of Windows NT Server 4.0 and Windows NT Workstation 4.0. In most cases, the two operating systems overlap completely. Where the two systems diverge, each platform is covered separately. This advanced title comprises a task-oriented treatment of the Windows NT 4.0 environment. By concentrating on the use of operating system tools and utilities, resource kit elements, and selected third-party tuning, analysis, optimization, and productivity tools, this book will show you how to carry out everyday and advanced tasks.

Windows 2000 User Management

By Lori Sanders
300 pages, $34.99
ISBN: 1-56205-886-X

With the dawn of Windows 2000, it has become even more difficult to draw a clear line between managing the user and managing the user's environment and desktop. This book, written by a noted trainer and consultant, provides a comprehensive, practical advice to managing users and their desktop environments with Windows 2000.

Windows 2000 Deployment & Desktop Management

By Jeffrey A. Ferris, MCSE
1st Edition
400 pages, $34.99
ISBN: 0-7357-0975-0

More than a simple overview of new features and tools, *Windows 2000 Deployment & Desktop Management* is a thorough reference to deploying Windows 2000 Professional to corporate workstations. Incorporating real-world advice and detailed excercises, this book is a one-stop resource for any system administrator, integrator, engineer, or other IT professional.

Planning for Windows 2000

By Eric K. Cone, Jon Boggs, and Sergio Perez
1st Edition
400 pages, $29.99
ISBN: 0-7357-0048-6

Windows 2000 is poised to be one of the largest and most important software releases of the next decade, and you are charged with planning, testing, and deploying it in your enterprise. Are you ready? With this book, you will be. *Planning for Windows 2000* lets you know what the upgrade hurdles will be, informs you of how to clear them, guides you through effective Active Directory design, and presents you with detailed rollout procedures. Eric K. Cone, Jon Boggs, and Sergio Perez give you the benefit of their extensive experiences as Windows 2000 Rapid Deployment Program members by sharing problems and solutions they've encountered on the job.

Inside Windows 2000 Server

By William Boswell
2nd Edition
1533 pages, $49.99
ISBN: 1-56205-929-7

Finally, a totally new edition of New Riders' best-selling *Inside Windows NT Server 4.* Taking the author-driven, no-nonsense approach pioneered with the *Landmark* books, New Riders proudly offers something unique for Windows 2000 administrators—an interesting, discriminating book on Windows 2000 Server written by someone who can anticipate your situation and give you workarounds that won't leave a system unstable or sluggish.

SQL Server System Administration

By Sean Baird, Chris Miller, et al.
1st Edition
352 pages, $29.99
ISBN: 1-56205-955-6

How often does your SQL Server go down during the day when everyone wants to access the data? Do you spend most of your time being a "report monkey" for your coworkers and bosses? *SQL Server System Administration* helps you keep data consistently available to your users. This book omits introductory information. The authors don't spend time explaining queries and how they work. Instead, they focus on the information you can't get anywhere else, like how to choose the correct replication topology and achieve high availability of information.

Internet Information Services Administration
By Kelli Adam
1st Edition,
200 pages, $29.99
ISBN: 0-7357-0022-2

SMS 2 Administration
By Michael Lubanski
and Darshan Doshi
1st Edition
350 pages, $39.99
ISBN: 0-7357-0082-6

Are the new Internet technologies in Internet Information Services giving you headaches? Does protecting security on the Web take up all of your time? Then this is the book for you. With hands-on configuration training, advanced study of the new protocols, the most recent version of IIS, and detailed instructions on authenticating users with the new Certificate Server and implementing and managing the new e-commerce features, *Internet Information Services Administration* gives you the real-life solutions you need. This definitive resource prepares you for upgrading to Windows 2000 by giving you detailed advice on working with Microsoft Management Console, which was first used by IIS.

Microsoft's new version of its Systems Management Server (SMS) is starting to turn heads. Although complex, it allows administrators to lower their total cost of ownership and more efficiently manage clients, applications, and support operations. If your organization is using or implementing SMS, you'll need some expert advice. Michael Lubanski and Darshan Doshi can help you get the most bang for your buck with insight, expert tips, and real-world examples. Michael and Darshan are consultants specializing in SMS and have worked with Microsoft on one of the most complex SMS rollouts in the world, involving 32 countries, 15 languages, and thousands of clients.

SQL Server 7 Essential Reference
By Sharon Dooley
1st Edition
500 pages, $35.00 US
ISBN: 0-7357-0864-9

SQL Server 7 Essential Reference is a comprehensive reference of advanced how-tos and techniques for SQL Server 7 administrators. This book provides solid grounding in fundamental SQL Server 7 administrative tasks to help you tame your SQL Server environment. With coverage ranging from installation, monitoring, troubleshooting security and backup and recovery plans, this book breaks down SQL Server into its key conceptual areas and functions. This easy to use reference is a must-have for any SQL Server administrator.

UNIX/Linux Titles

Solaris Essential Reference
By John P. Mulligan
1st Edition
300 pages, $24.95
ISBN: 0-7357-0023-0

Looking for the fastest and easiest way to find the Solaris command you need? Need a few pointers on shell scripting? How about advanced administration tips and sound, practical expertise on security issues? Are you looking for trustworthy information about available third-party software packages that will enhance your operating system? Author John Mulligan—creator of the popular "Unofficial Guide to The Solaris™ Operating Environment" Web site (sun.icsnet.com)—delivers all that and more in one attractive, easy-to-use reference book. With clear and concise instructions on how to perform important administration and management tasks, and key information on powerful commands and advanced topics, *Solaris Essential Reference* is the book you need when you know what you want to do and only need to know how.

Linux System Administration
By M. Carling, Stephen Degler, and James Dennis
1st Edition
450 pages, $29.99
ISBN: 1-56205-934-3

As an administrator, you probably feel that most of your time and energy is spent in endless firefighting. If your network has become a fragile quilt of temporary patches and work-arounds, this book is for you. Have you had trouble sending or receiving email lately? Are you looking for a way to keep your network running smoothly with enhanced performance? Are your users always hankering for more storage, services, and speed? *Linux System Administration* advises you on the many intricacies of maintaining a secure, stable system. In this definitive work, the authors address all the issues related to system administration, from adding users and managing file permissions, to Internet services and Web hosting, to recovery planning and security. This book fulfills the need for expert advice that will ensure a trouble-free Linux environment.

GTK+/Gnome Application Development
By Havoc Pennington
1st Edition
492 pages, $39.99
ISBN: 0-7357-0078-8

This title is for the reader who is conversant with the C programming language and UNIX/Linux development. It provides detailed and solution-oriented information designed to meet the needs of programmers and application developers using the GTK+/Gnome libraries. Coverage complements existing GTK+/Gnome documentation, going into more depth on pivotal issues such as uncovering the GTK+ object system, working with the event loop, managing the Gdk substrate, writing custom widgets, and mastering GnomeCanvas.

Developing Linux Applications with GTK+ and GDK
By Eric Harlow
1st Edition
490 pages, $34.99
ISBN: 0-7357-0021-4

We all know that Linux is one of the most powerful and solid operating systems in existence. And as the success of Linux grows, there is an increasing interest in developing applications with graphical user interfaces that take advantage of the power of Linux. In this book, software developer Eric Harlow gives you an indispensable development handbook focusing on the GTK+ toolkit. More than an overview of the elements of application or GUI design, this is a hands-on book that delves into the technology. With in-depth material on the various GUI programming tools and loads of examples, this book's unique focus will give you the information you need to design and launch professional-quality applications.

Linux Essential Reference
By Ed Petron
1st Edition
350 pages, $24.95
ISBN: 0-7357-0852-5

This book is all about getting things done as quickly and efficiently as possible by providing a structured organization for the plethora of available Linux information. We can sum it up in one word—value. This book has it all: concise instructions on how to perform key administration tasks, advanced information on configuration, shell scripting, hardware management, systems management, data tasks, automation, and tons of other useful information. This book truly provides groundbreaking information for the growing community of advanced Linux professionals.

Lotus Notes and Domino Titles

Domino System Administration
By Rob Kirkland, CLP, CLI
1st Edition
850 pages, $49.99
ISBN: 1-56205-948-3

Your boss has just announced that you will be upgrading to the newest version of Notes and Domino when it ships. How are you supposed to get this new system installed, configured, and rolled out to all of your end users? You understand how Lotus Notes works—you've been administering it for years. What you need is a concise, practical explanation of the new features and how to make some of the advanced stuff work smoothly by someone like you, who has worked with the product for years and understands what you need to know. *Domino System Administration* is the answer—the first book on Domino that attacks the technology at the professional level with practical, hands-on assistance to get Domino running in your organization.

Lotus Notes & Domino Essential Reference

By Tim Bankes, CLP
and Dave Hatter, CLP, MCP
1st Edition
650 pages, $45.00
ISBN: 0-7357-0007-9

You're in a bind because you've been asked to design and program a new database in Notes for an important client who will keep track of and itemize a myriad of inventory and shipping data. The client wants a user-friendly interface that won't sacrifice speed or functionality. You are experienced (and could develop this application in your sleep), but feel you need something to facilitate your creative and technical abilities—something to perfect your programming skills. The answer is waiting for you: *Lotus Notes & Domino Essential Reference*. It's compact and simply designed. It's loaded with information. All of the objects, classes, functions, and methods are listed. It shows you the object hierarchy and the relationship between each one. It's perfect for you. Problem solved.

Networking Titles

Network Intrusion Detection: An Analyst's Handbook

By Stephen Northcutt
1st Edition
267 pages, $39.99
ISBN: 0-7357-0868-1

Get answers and solutions from someone who has been in the trenches. The author, Stephen Northcutt, original developer of the Shadow intrusion detection system and former director of the United States Navy's Information System Security Office at the Naval Security Warfare Center, gives his expertise to intrusion detection specialists, security analysts, and consultants responsible for setting up and maintaining an effective defense against network security attacks.

Understanding Data Communications, Sixth Edition

By Gilbert Held
Sixth Edition
600 pages, $39.99
ISBN: 0-7357-0036-2

Updated from the highly successful fifth edition, this book explains how data communications systems and their various hardware and software components work. More than an entry-level book, it approaches the material in textbook format, addressing the complex issues involved in internetworking today. A great reference book for the experienced networking professional that is written by the noted networking authority, Gilbert Held.

Other Books By New Riders

Microsoft Technologies

ADMINISTRATION

Inside Windows 2000 Server
1-56205-929-7 • $49.99 US / $74.95 CAN

Windows 2000 Essential Reference
0-7357-0869-X • $35.00 US / $52.95 CAN

Windows 2000 Active Directory
0-7357-0870-3 • $29.99 US / $44.95 CAN

Windows 2000 Routing and Remote Access Service
0-7357-0951-3 • $34.99 US / $52.95 CAN

Windows 2000 Deployment & Desktop Management
0-7357-0975-0 • $34.99 US / $52.95 CAN

Windows 2000 DNS
0-7357-0973-4 • $39.99 US / $59.95 CAN

Windows 2000 User Management
1-56205-886-X • $34.99 US / $52.95 CAN

Windows 2000 Professional
0-7357-0950-5 • $34.99 US / $52.95 CAN

Planning for Windows 2000
0-7357-0048-6 • $29.99 US / $44.95 CAN

Windows 2000 Server Professional Reference
0-7357-0952-1 • $75.00 US / $111.95 CAN

Windows 2000 Security
0-7357-0991-2 • $39.99 US / $59.95 CAN
Available September 2000

Windows 2000 TCP/IP
0-7357-0992-0 • $39.99 US / $59.95 CAN
Available August 2000

Windows 2000 Registry
0-7357-0944-0 • $34.99 US / $52.95 CAN
Available August 2000

Windows 2000 Terminal Services and Citrix MetaFrame
0-7357-1005-8 • $39.99 US / $59.95 CAN
Available October 2000

Windows NT/2000 Network Security
1-57870-253-4 • $45.00 US / $67.95 CAN
Available August 2000

Windows NT/2000 Thin Client Solutions
1-57870-239-9 • $45.00 US / $67.95 CAN

Windows 2000 Virtual Private Networking
1-57870-246-1 • $45.00 US / $67.95 CAN
Available September 2000

Windows 2000 Active Directory Design & Migration
1-57870-242-9 • $45.00 US / $67.95 CAN
Available September 2000

Windows 2000 and Mainframe Integration
1-57870-200-3 • $40.00 US / $59.95 CAN

Windows 2000 Server: Planning and Migration
1-57870-023-X • $40.00 US / $59.95 CAN

Windows 2000 Quality of Service
1-57870-115-5 • $45.00 US / $67.95 CAN

Windows NT Power Toolkit
0-7357-0922-X • $49.99 US / $74.95 CAN

Windows NT Terminal Server and Citrix MetaFrame
1-56205-944-0 • $29.99 US / $44.95 CAN

Windows NT Performance: Monitoring, Benchmarking, and Tuning
1-56205-942-4 • $29.99 US / $44.95 CAN

Windows NT Registry: A Settings Reference
1-56205-941-6 • $29.99 US / $44.95 CAN

Windows NT Domain Architecture
1-57870-112-0 • $38.00 US / $56.95 CAN

SYSTEMS PROGRAMMING

Windows NT/2000 Native API Reference
1-57870-199-6 • $50.00 US / $74.95 CAN

Windows NT Device Driver Development
1-57870-058-2 • $50.00 US / $74.95 CAN

DCE/RPC over SMB: Samba and Windows NT Domain Internals
1-57870-150-3 • $45.00 US / $67.95 CAN

APPLICATION PROGRAMMING

Delphi COM Programming
1-57870-221-6 • $45.00 US / $67.95 CAN

Windows NT Applications: Measuring and Optimizing Performance
1-57870-176-7 • $40.00 US / $59.95 CAN

Applying COM+
ISBN 0-7357-0978-5 • $49.99 US / $74.95 CAN
Available August 2000

WEB PROGRAMMING

Exchange & Outlook: Constructing Collaborative Solutions
ISBN 1-57870-252-6 • $40.00 US / $59.95 CAN

SCRIPTING

Windows Script Host
1-57870-139-2 • $35.00 US / $52.95 CAN

Windows NT Shell Scripting
1-57870-047-7 • $32.00 US / $45.95 CAN

Windows NT Win32 Perl Programming: The Standard Extensions
1-57870-067-1 • $40.00 US / $59.95 CAN

Windows NT/2000 ADSI Scripting for System Administration
1-57870-219-4 • $45.00 US / $67.95 CAN

Windows NT Automated Deployment and Customization
1-57870-045-0 • $32.00 US / $45.95 CAN

BACK OFFICE

SMS 2 Administration
0-7357-0082-6 • $39.99 US / $59.95 CAN

Internet Information Services Administration
0-7357-0022-2 • $29.99 US / $44.95 CAN

SQL Server System Administration
1-56205-955-6 • $29.99 US / $44.95 CAN

SQL Server Essential Reference
0-7357-0864-9 • $35.00 US / $52.95 CAN

Open Source

MySQL
0-7357-0921-1 • $49.99 US / $74.95 CAN

Web Application Development with PHP
0-7357-0997-1 • $45.00 US / $67.95 CAN

Available June 2000

PHP Functions Essential Reference
0-7357-0970-X • $35.00 US / $52.95 CAN
Available August 2000

Python Essential Reference
0-7357-0901-7 • $34.95 US / $52.95 CAN

Autoconf, Automake, and Libtool
1-57870-190-2 • $35.00 US / $52.95 CAN
Available August 2000

Linux/Unix

ADMINISTRATION

Linux System Administration
1-56205-934-3 • $29.99 US / $44.95 CAN

Linux Firewalls
0-7357-0900-9 • $39.99 US / $59.95 CAN

Linux Essential Reference
0-7357-0852-5 • $24.95 US / $37.95 CAN

UnixWare 7 System Administration
1-57870-080-9 • $40.00 US / $59.99 CAN

DEVELOPMENT

Developing Linux Applications with GTK+ and GDK
0-7357-0021-4 • $34.99 US / $52.95 CAN

GTK+/Gnome Application Development
0-7357-0078-8 • $39.99 US / $59.95 CAN

KDE Application Development
1-57870-201-1 • $39.99 US / $59.95 CAN

GIMP

Grokking the GIMP
0-7357-0924-6 • $39.99 US / $59.95 CAN

GIMP Essential Reference
0-7357-0911-4 • $24.95 US / $37.95 CAN

SOLARIS

Solaris Advanced System Administrator's Guide, Second Edition
1-57870-039-6 • $39.99 US / $59.95 CAN

Solaris System Administrator's Guide, Second Edition
1-57870-040-X • $34.99 US / $52.95 CAN

Solaris Essential Reference
0-7357-0023-0 • $24.95 US / $37.95 CAN

Networking

STANDARDS & PROTOCOLS

Cisco Router Configuration & Troubleshooting, Second Edition
0-7357-0999-8 • $34.99 US / $52.95 CAN

Understanding Directory Services
0-7357-0910-6 • $39.99 US / $59.95 CAN

Understanding the Network: A Practical Guide to Internetworking
0-7357-0977-7 • $39.99 US / $59.95 CAN

Understanding Data Communications, Sixth Edition
0-7357-0036-2 • $39.99 US / $59.95 CAN

LDAP: Programming Directory Enabled
Applications
1-57870-000-0 • $44.99 US / $67.95 CAN
Gigabit Ethernet Networking
1-57870-062-0 • $50.00 US / $74.95 CAN
Supporting Service Level Agreements
on IP Networks
1-57870-146-5 • $50.00 US / $74.95 CAN
Directory Enabled Networks
1-57870-140-6 • $50.00 US / $74.95 CAN
Differentiated Services for the Internet
1-57870-132-5 • $50.00 US / $74.95 CAN
Quality of Service on IP Networks
1-57870-189-9 • $50.00 US / $74.95 CAN
Designing Addressing Architectures for
Routing and Switching
1-57870-059-0 • $45.00 US / $69.95 CAN
Understanding & Deploying LDAP
Directory Services
1-57870-070-1 • $50.00 US / $74.95 CAN
Switched, Fast and Gigabit Ethernet, Third
Edition
1-57870-073-6 • $50.00 US / $74.95 CAN
Wireless LANs: Implementing
Interoperable Networks
1-57870-081-7 • $40.00 US / $59.95 CAN
Wide Area High Speed Networks
1-57870-114-7 • $50.00 US / $74.95 CAN
The DHCP Handbook
1-57870-137-6 • $55.00 US / $81.95 CAN
Designing Routing and Switching
Architectures for Enterprise Networks
1-57870-060-4 • $55.00 US / $81.95 CAN
Local Area High Speed Networks
1-57870-113-9 • $50.00 US / $74.95 CAN
Available June 2000
Network Performance Baselining
1-57870-240-2 • $50.00 US / $74.95 CAN
Economics of Electronic Commerce
1-57870-014-0 • $49.99 US / $74.95 CAN

SECURITY

Intrusion Detection
1-57870-185-6 • $50.00 US / $74.95 CAN
Understanding Public-Key Infrastructure
1-57870-166-X • $50.00 US / $74.95 CAN
Network Intrusion Detection: An Analyst's
Handbook
0-7357-0868-1 • $39.99 US / $59.95 CAN
Linux Firewalls
0-7357-0900-9 • $39.99 US / $59.95 CAN

LOTUS NOTES/DOMINO

Domino System Administration
1-56205-948-3 • $49.99 US / $74.95 CAN
Lotus Notes & Domino Essential Reference
0-7357-0007-9 • $45.00 US / $67.95 CAN

Software Architecture &
Engineering

Designing for the User with OVID
1-57870-101-5 • $40.00 US / $59.95 CAN

Designing Flexible Object-Oriented
Systems with UML
1-57870-098-1 • $40.00 US / $59.95 CAN
Constructing Superior Software
1-57870-147-3 • $40.00 US / $59.95 CAN
A UML Pattern Language
1-57870-118-X • $45.00 US / $67.95 CAN

Professional Certification

TRAINING GUIDES

MCSE Training Guide: Networking
Essentials, 2nd Ed.
156205919X • $49.99 US / $74.95 CAN
MCSE Training Guide: Windows NT Server
4, 2nd Ed.
1562059165 • $49.99 US / $74.95 CAN
MCSE Training Guide: Windows NT
Workstation 4, 2nd Ed.
1562059181 • $49.99 US / $74.95 CAN
MCSE Training Guide: Windows NT Server
4 Enterprise, 2nd Ed.
1562059173 • $49.99 US / $74.95 CAN
MCSE Training Guide: Core Exams
Bundle, 2nd Ed.
1562059262 • $149.99 US / $223.95 CAN
MCSE Training Guide: TCP/IP, 2nd Ed.
1562059203 • $49.99 US / $74.95 CAN
MCSE Training Guide: IIS 4, 2nd Ed.
0735708657 • $49.99 US / $74.95 CAN
MCSE Training Guide: SQL Server 7
Administration
0735700036 • $49.99 US / $74.95 CAN
MCSE Training Guide: SQL Server 7
Database Design
0735700044 • $49.99 US / $74.95 CAN
CLP Training Guide: Lotus Notes 4
0789715058 • $59.99 US / $84.95 CAN
MCSD Training Guide: Visual Basic 6
Exams
0735700028 • $69.99 US / $104.95 CAN
MCSD Training Guide: Solution
Architectures
0735700265 • $49.99 US / $74.95 CAN
MCSD Training Guide: 4-in-1 Bundle
0735709122 • $149.99 US / $223.95 CAN
CCNA Training Guide
0735700516 • $49.99 US / $74.95 CAN
A+ Certification Training Guide, 2nd Ed.
0735709076 • $49.99 US / $74.95 CAN
Network+ Certification Guide
073570077X • $49.99 US / $74.95 CAN
Solaris 2.6 Administrator Certification
Training Guide, Part I
157870085X • $40.00 US / $59.95 CAN
Solaris 2.6 Administrator Certification
Training Guide, Part II
1578700868 • $40.00 US / $59.95 CAN
MCSE Training Guide: Windows 2000
Professional
0735709653 • $49.99 US / $74.95 CAN •
MCSE Training Guide: Windows 2000
Server
0735709688 • $49.99 US / $74.95 CAN •

MCSE Training Guide: Windows 2000
Network Infrastructure
0735709661 • $49.99 US / $74.95 CAN
MCSE Training Guide: Windows 2000
Network Security Design
073570984X • $49.99 US / $74.95 CAN
MCSE Training Guide: Windows 2000
Network Infrastructure Design
0735709823 • $49.99 US / $74.95 CAN
MCSE Training Guide: Windows 2000
Directory Svcs. Infrastructure
0735709769 • $49.99 US / $74.95 CAN
MCSE Training Guide: Windows 2000
Directory Services Design
0735709831 • $49.99 US / $74.95 CAN
MCSE Training Guide: Windows 2000
Accelerated Exam
0735709793 • $59.99 US / $89.95 CAN
MCSE Training Guide: Windows 2000 Core
Exams Bundle
0735709882 • $149.99 US / $223.95 CAN

HOW TO CONTACT US

IF YOU NEED THE LATEST UPDATES ON A TITLE THAT YOU'VE PURCHASED:

1) Visit our Web site at www.newriders.com.

2) Enter the book ISBN number, which is located on the back cover in the bottom right-hand corner, in the site search box on the left navigation bar.

3) Select your book title from the list of search results. On the book page you'll find available updates and downlods for your title.

IF YOU ARE HAVING TECHNICAL PROBLEMS WITH THE BOOK OR THE CD THAT IS INCLUDED:

1) Check the book's information page on our Web site according to the instructions listed above, or

2) Email us at nrfeedback@newriders.com, or

3) Fax us at 317-581-4663 ATTN: Tech Support.

IF YOU HAVE COMMENTS ABOUT ANY OF OUR CERTIFICATION PRODUCTS THAT ARE NON-SUPPORT RELATED:

1) Email us at nrfeedback@newriders.com, or

2) Write to us at New Riders, 201 W. 103rd St., Indianapolis, IN 46290-1097, or

3) Fax us at 317-581-4663.

IF YOU ARE OUTSIDE THE UNITED STATES AND NEED TO FIND A DISTRIBUTOR IN YOUR AREA:

Please contact our international department at international@mcp.com.

IF YOU ARE INTERESTED IN BEING AN AUTHOR OR TECHNICAL REVIEWER:

Email us at opportunities@newriders.com. Include your name, email address, phone number, and area of technical expertise.

IF YOU WISH TO PREVIEW ANY OF OUR CERTIFICATION BOOKS FOR CLASSROOM USE:

Email us at nrmedia@newriders.com. Your message should include your name, title, training company or school, department, address, phone number, office days/hours, text in use, and enrollment. Send these details along with your request for desk/examination copies and/or additional information.

IF YOU ARE A MEMBER OF THE PRESS AND WOULD LIKE TO REVIEW ONE OF OUR BOOKS:

Email us at nrmedia@newriders.com. Your message should include your name, title, publication or website you work for, mailing address and email address.